Birds of MELANESIA

The Bismarcks, Solomons, Vanuatu and New Caledonia

HELM FIELD GUIDES

Birds of
MELANESIA

The Bismarcks, Solomons, Vanuatu and New Caledonia

Guy Dutson

Illustrated by
Richard Allen, Adam Bowley,
John Cox and Tony Disley

CHRISTOPHER HELM
LONDON

Published in 2011 by Christopher Helm, an imprint of Bloomsbury Publishing plc,
49–51 Bedford Square, London WC1B 3DP

ISBN (print) 978-0-7136-6540-6
ISBN (epdf) 978-1408I-5246-1
ISBN (epub) 978-14081-5245-4

A CIP catalogue record for this book is available from the British Library

This book is produced using paper that is made from wood grown in managed sustainable forests. It is natural, renewable and recyclable. The logging and manufacturing processes conform to the environmental regulations of the country of origin.

Commissioning editor: Nigel Redman
Project editor: Jim Martin
Designed by Marc Dando at Fluke Art

Printed in China by Lion Production Limited.

10 9 8 7 6 5 4 3 2 1

Illustration credits
Richard Allen: Plates 1–20
Adam Bowley: Plates 46–86
John Cox: Plates 31–45
Tony Disley: Plates 21–30

Cover illustrations
Front: Kagu (*John Cox*)
Back: Knob-billed Fruit Dove (*John Cox*), Superb Pitta (*Adam Bowley*), Moustached Kingfisher (*Adam Bowley*), Buff-bellied Monarch (*Adam Bowley*)

CONTENTS

ACKNOWLEDGEMENTS

My personal interest and love of the birds of Melanesia started on a student expedition in 1990 and has brought me on regular return visits. On these field visits, notably a year island-hopping in 1997–1998, I have had the fortune to observe almost all of the extant Melanesian birds. I am extremely grateful to those people who have assisted me through their time and effort.

Any visitor to Melanesia will soon realise that their greatest acknowledgements are owed to the local people whose generosity and kindness is a highlight of working in the region. This book must be dedicated to those Melanesians who have helped me, and to those who are willing to help similar visitors. I hope that this book is seen as a small gesture in return, and that it helps to cultivate interest in birds and bird conservation within the region.

On my 1990 visit, special thanks go to my fieldwork colleagues David Buckingham and Jonathan Newman, our main advisors notably Nigel Collar and Alison Stattersfield (BirdLife International, previously International Council for Bird Preservation) and Jared Diamond, and our financial sponsors (A. J. Burton 1956 Charitable Settlement, A. S. Butler Charitable Trust, Bartle-Frere Exhibition, British Ornithologists' Union, Cable and Wireless plc, Cambridge Expeditions Fund, Condor Conservation Trust, Cotton Trust, D. M. Charitable Trust, Ernest Kleinwort Charitable Trust, Godinton Trust, ICBP/FFPS, Interpet, King Edward's School Birmingham, L. A. Cadbury Charitable Trust, Mary Euphrasia Moseley Trust, New York Explorers' Club's Youth Activity Fund, People's Trust for Endangered Species, R. and M. Foreman Charitable Trust, Radley Charitable Trust, Rayne Foundation, Selwyn College, Spicers plc, Trinity Hall, Vincent Trust, The Wall Charitable Trust and Whitley Animal Protection Trust). Most of the fieldwork underpinning this book was undertaken in 1997–1998 with generous sponsorship from Bird Exploration Fund, A. J. Burton Charitable Trust, Harold Hyam Wingate Foundation, Keith Ewart Charitable Trust, Parrot Society, Percy Sladen Memorial Fund and the Peter Scott Trust for Education and Research in Conservation. Subsequent fieldwork and museum studies were sponsored by the American Museum of Natural History (Collection Studies Grant), Bird Exploration Fund and British Ornithologists' Union. I benefited from shared time in the field with Nicolas Barré, David Buckingham, Chris Eastwood, Phil Gregory, Yves Létocart, Jon Newman, John Pilgrim, Kester Wilson, and Birdquest and Sicklebill Safaris tour participants, and I am very grateful for logistic support and accommodation from Max Benjamin (Walindi Dive Resort), Ellen and Matthieu Degott-Rekowski, Eagon (Choiseul), Chris Eastwood, Mark Hafe, Ross Hepworth, Roy Hills, Seri Hite, KFPL, Solomon Islands Development Trust, William Manehage, Jérome Spaggiari, Tim Turner, Wild Dog mine, WWF-Solomon Islands and many village communities, especially those at which I stayed for several weeks, notably Rossun, Tirotonga, Kena, Hauta, Buma and Vatthe.

In Papua New Guinea, I was granted research permission by Michael Laki and staff of the National Research Institute and the Department of Environment and Conservation. In the Solomon Islands, I was granted research permission by Moses Biliki and Audrey Rusa and worked with the Solomon Island Development Trust and World Wide Fund for Nature–Solomons. In Vanuatu, I worked with the Environment Unit and Vatthe Conservation Area Project. In New Caledonia, I worked with the Société Calédonienne d'Ornithologie, with permission to visit the reserves from the DRN of Province Sud, and ASPO in Ouvéa.

In researching the text, I am extremely grateful to the following for their advice and access to data:
Mark Adams (Natural History Museum), Nicolas Barré (Société Calédonienne d'Ornithologie), Bruce Beehler, K. David Bishop, Vincent Bretagnolle (CNRS), Walter Boles (Australian Museum), Bill Bourne, Ian Burrows, Stuart Butchart, Brian Coates, Nigel Collar, Jared Diamond, Jonathan Ekstrom, Tom Evans, Chris Filardi, Clem Fisher (Liverpool Museum), James Fitzsimons, David Gibbs, Phil Gregory, Don Hadden, Jon Hornbuckle, Mary LeCroy, Yves Létocart, Ian McAllan, Tony Palliser, Robert Prys-Jones (Natural History Museum), Paul Sweet (American Museum of Natural History), Mike Tarburton, Joe Tobias, Stephen Totterman (VanBirds), Colin Trainor, Dick Watling (Environment Consultants Fiji) and H. Price Webb. In particular, I acknowledge the meticulous advice of Jared Diamond and Ian McAllan.

The artists, Richard Allen, Adam Bowley, John Cox and Tony Disley, have produced some exceptional artwork, often based on poor reference material, and have cheerfully updated their paintings as better references have appeared. The editors, Nigel Collar and Nigel Redman, have greatly improved the text, and the designer, Marc Dando, has expertly crafted the plates and text into a beautiful book.

Finally, it should be noted that all of this work is based on the efforts and results of previous visitors, as reviewed in Mayr & Diamond (2001). The pioneering efforts of the early collectors, especially those on the Whitney South Seas Expeditions, and the analysis of their specimens, notably by Ernst Mayr, remain the basis for our knowledge of Melanesian ornithology. This book is also dedicated to their work.

INTRODUCTION

AIMS OF THIS BOOK

Melanesia is one of the most fascinating regions in the world with an amazing range of endemic bird species and subspecies. However, these birds are poorly known as surprisingly few birdwatchers and scientists have visited the region, and there are few local ornithologists. This book aims to stimulate the study and conservation of these birds by providing a thorough yet practical identification guide.

The primary aim of this book is to allow accurate field identification of all the birds of Melanesia. It is the first book to give detailed identification notes and island distributions for all species, and brief notes for all subspecies. The level of detail in each species description reflects its plumage complexity and variation, how well it is known and how easily it can be identified. Species are compared with others on the same island, but not with closely related species on different islands. Vagrant species, especially seabirds, are treated in less detail, as information on these can be readily obtained from other field guides. Endemic species are given greater detail where information is available. The text aims to avoid jargon; however, some technical terms are essential for accuracy and brevity, and are illustrated on the topography drawings on pp 23–24.

GEOGRAPHICAL COVERAGE

Melanesia is a region of islands in the south-west Pacific. Melanesia often includes continental New Guinea but this book just covers the islands which could be referred to more precisely as Island Melanesia, using a biogeographical definition of the region (see map on pp 10–11): the archipelagos of the Admiralty, St Matthias and Bismarck islands off New Guinea, the Solomon Islands including Bougainville and Temotu (Santa Cruz), Vanuatu and New Caledonia, but excluding continental New Guinea, Polynesia to the east, and areas north of the equator. The western boundary includes Wuvulu in the north-west and all of the islands in the Vitiaz Strait between New Guinea and New Britain except for Karkar, the island closest to New Guinea. The eastern boundary follows the national boundaries of the Solomon Islands and Vanuatu, but excludes Fiji as belonging to Polynesia. The southern boundary follows that of New Caledonia, excluding Norfolk and Lord Howe Islands, which are administered by (and tend to be regarded by birdwatchers as part of) Australia, although they support some Melanesian bird species. Any species endemic to the region, but also occurring on Karkar or Norfolk I or Lord Howe I, is considered a Melanesian endemic. A fuller list of the islands is given on page 37 [before the checklist]. The distributions in the text refer to biogeographic rather than political areas, so the 'Solomons' includes Bougainville which is part of the biogeographic Solomons chain but not part of the Solomon Islands nation. The Bismarck Archipelago is treated as the islands around New Ireland and New Britain, and separate from the Admiralty Islands and St Matthias Islands. The total land area of Melanesia is 108,000 km^2.

ISLAND	NATION	LARGEST TOWNS	Area (km^2)	Max. altitude (m)
New Britain	Papua New Guinea	Rabaul, Kimbe	35742	2439
Grande Terre	New Caledonia (France)	Nouméa	16648	1618
Bougainville	Papua New Guinea	Kieta, Arawa	8591	2591
New Ireland	Papua New Guinea	Kavieng	7174	2399
Guadalcanal	Solomon Islands	Honiara	5281	2448
Malaita	Solomon Islands	Auki	4307	1280
(Santa) Isabel	Solomon Islands	Buala	4095	1250
(Espiritu) Santo	Vanuatu	Luganville	3955	1879
Makira	Solomon Islands	Kirakira	3090	1040
Choiseul	Solomon Islands	Taro	2966	970

Geographic features of the largest Melanesian islands

MAPS

NB: Throughout the book, islands are referred to by name alone, without the word 'Island'. 'Is' is used as an abbreviation for a group of islands e.g. Banks Is. 'I' is used as an abbreviation for Island where the name alone may refer to another area e.g. Norfolk I.

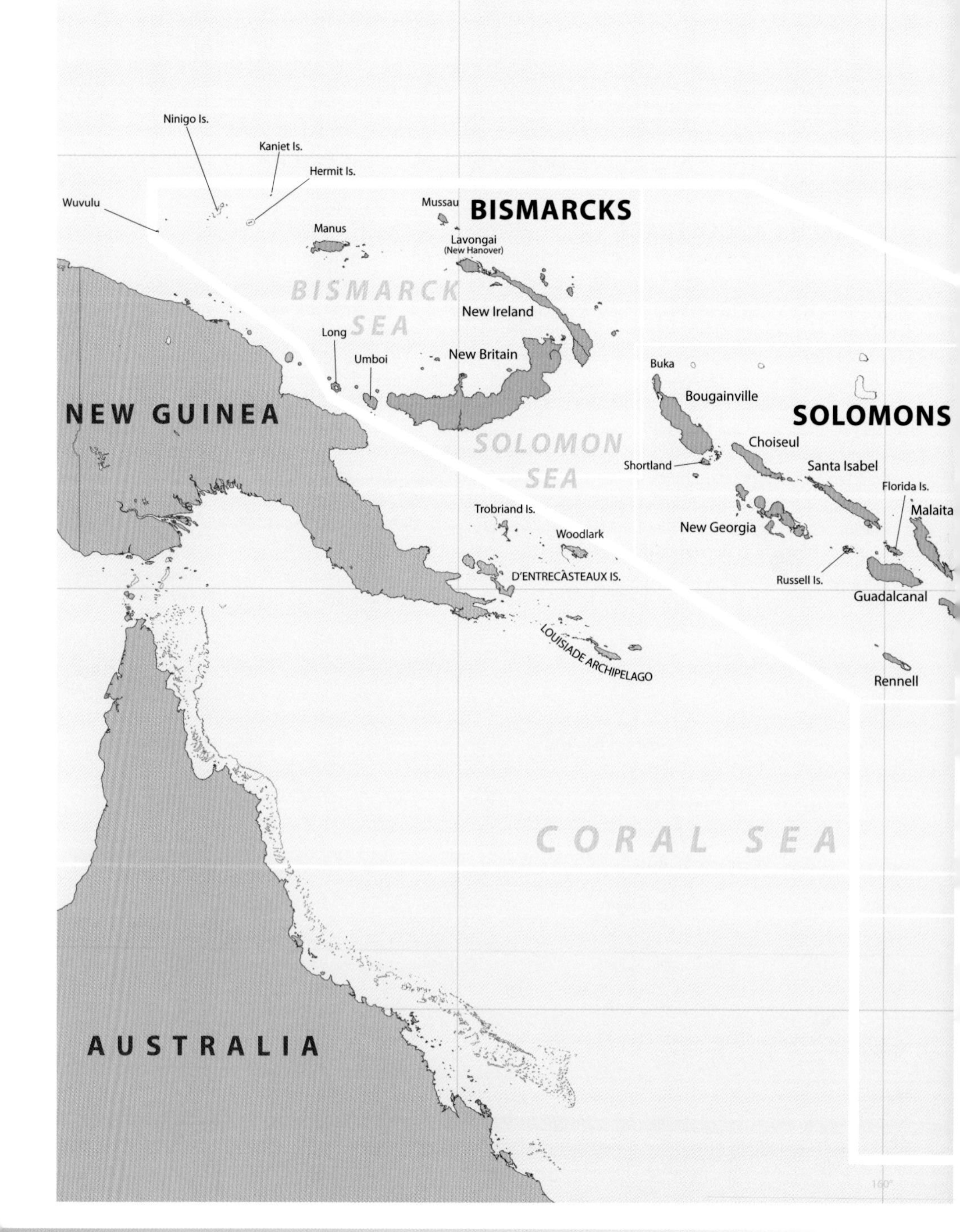

PACIFIC OCEAN
Ninigo Is.
Kaniet Is.
Hermit Is.
Wuvulu
Mussau
BISMARCKS
Manus
Lavongai
(New Hanover)
BISMARCK SEA
New Ireland
Long
Umboi
New Britain
Buka
Bougainville
NEW GUINEA
SOLOMONS
SOLOMON SEA
Choiseul
Shortland
Santa Isabel
Florida Is.
Trobriand Is.
Malaita
New Georgia
Woodlark
D'ENTRECASTEAUX IS.
Russell Is.
Guadalcanal
LOUISIADE ARCHIPELAGO
Rennell
CORAL SEA
AUSTRALIA
160°

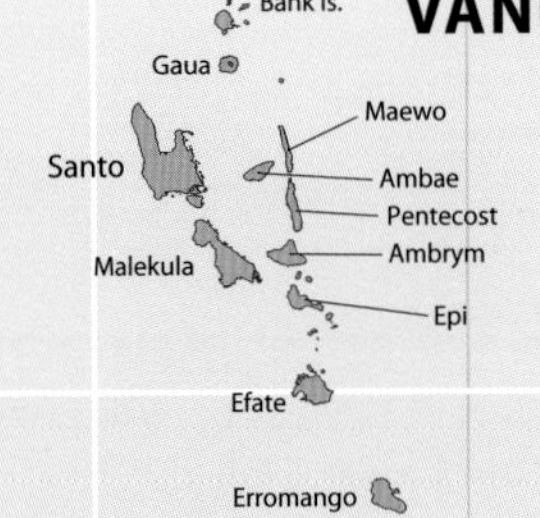
PACIFIC OCEAN
EQUATOR
NAURU
KIRIBATI
MELANESIA
TUVALU
Funafuti
Malaita
Makira
Nendo
TEMOTU
(Santa Cruz)
Utupua
Vanikoro
Torres Is.
Bank Is.
VANUATU
Gaua
Maewo
Santo
Ambae
Pentecost
Malekula
Ambrym
Epi
Efate
Erromango
Tanna
Aneityum
FIJI
Vanua Levu
Vitu Levu
Îles Belep
Ouvéa
Lifou
Grande Terre
Loyalty Is
Maré
Île des Pins
NEW CALEDONIA
(Nouvelle Calédonie)
170°
180°

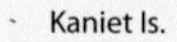

Ninigo Is.

Hermit Is.

Wuvulu

ADMIRALTY ISLANDS

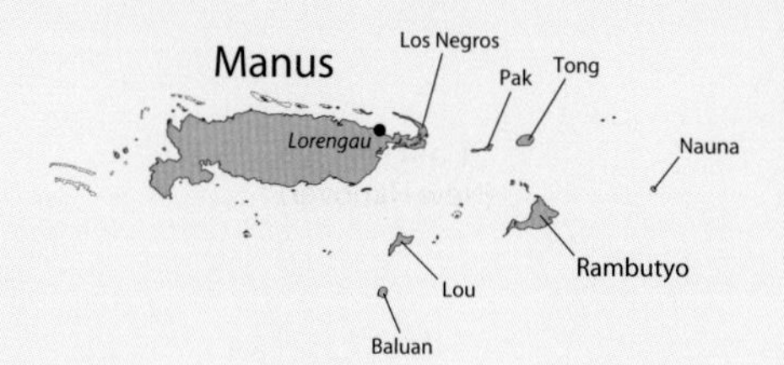

BISMARCK SEA

Karkar

Bagabag

Crown

Long

Tolokiwa

Sakar

Widom Lake

Umboi

NEW GUINEA

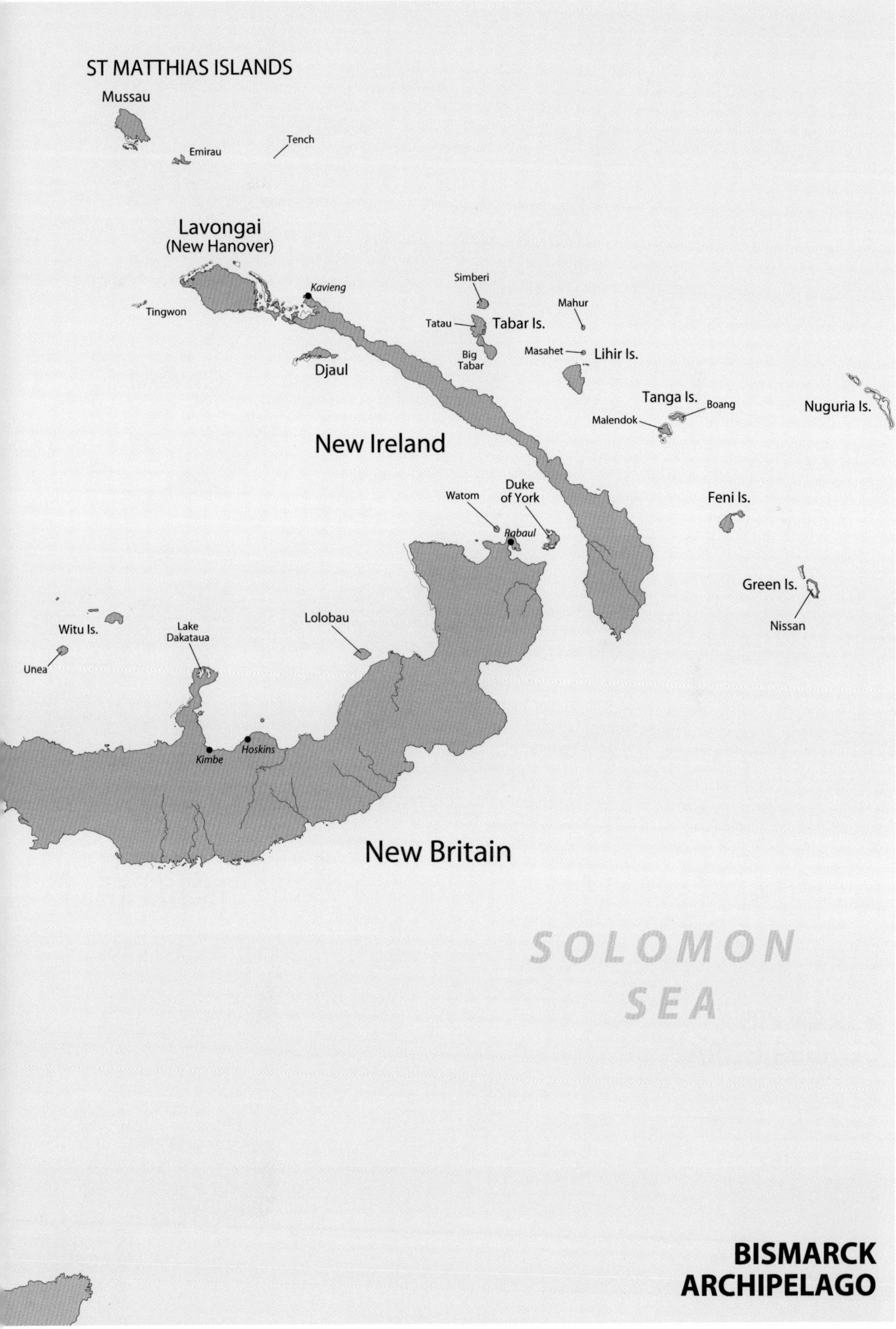

ST MATTHIAS ISLANDS

Mussau

Emirau

Tench

Lavongai
(New Hanover)

Tingwon

Kavieng

Simberi

Mahur

Tatau

Tabar Is.

Big
Tabar

Masahet

Lihir Is.

Djaul

Tanga Is.

Boang

Nuguria Is.

Malendok

New Ireland

Watom

Duke
of York

Feni Is.

Rabaul

Green Is.

Nissan

Witu Is.

Lake
Dakataua

Lolobau

Unea

Hoskins

Kimbe

New Britain

SOLOMON
SEA

BISMARCK ARCHIPELAGO

Nissan
Kilinailau
Takuu
Buka
Bougainville
Kieta
Arawa
Fauro
Choiseul
Shortland
Shortland Is
Wagina
Vella Lavella
Gizo
Mono
Bagga
Kolombangara
Ranongga
New Georgia
Simbo
Vonavona
SOLOMON SEA
Kohinggo
Rendova
Vangunu
Tetepare
Nggatokae

Duff Is
TEMOTU (Santa Cruz)
Nukapu
Pileni
Fenualoa
Nifiloli
Nupani
Taumako
Makalom
Reef Is
Tinakula
Lomlom
Matema
CORAL SEA

Nendo

Utupua
Vanikoro
Anuta
Tikopia

SOLOMONS

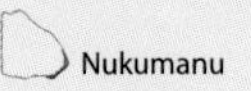
Nukumanu

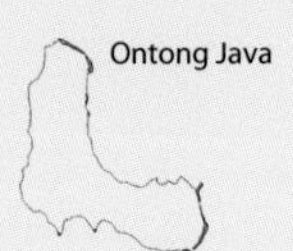
Ontong Java

PACIFIC
OCEAN
Ghaghe
Santa Isabel
Ndai
Sikaiana
Ramos
San Jorge
Florida Is
Nggela
Sule
Auki
Malaita
Mborokua
Savo
Pavuvu
Honiara
Russell Is
Mbanika
Guadalcanal
Ulawa
Ugi
Three
Sisters
Santa
Ana
Makira
(San Cristobal)
Santa
Catalina
Bellona
Rennell

Surprise I.

Îles Belep

Chesterfield Reefs

CORAL SEA

Koumac

Koné

Grande Terre

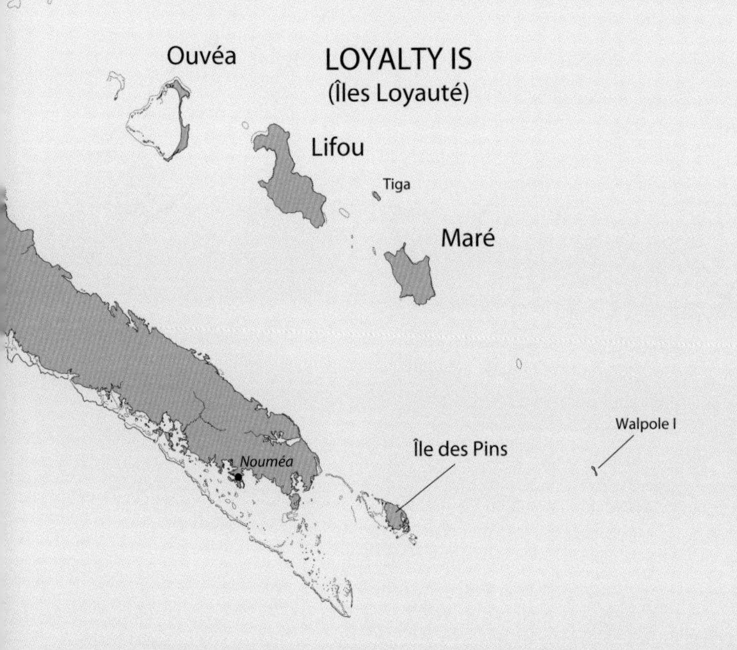

NEW CALEDONIA
(Nouvelle Calédonie)

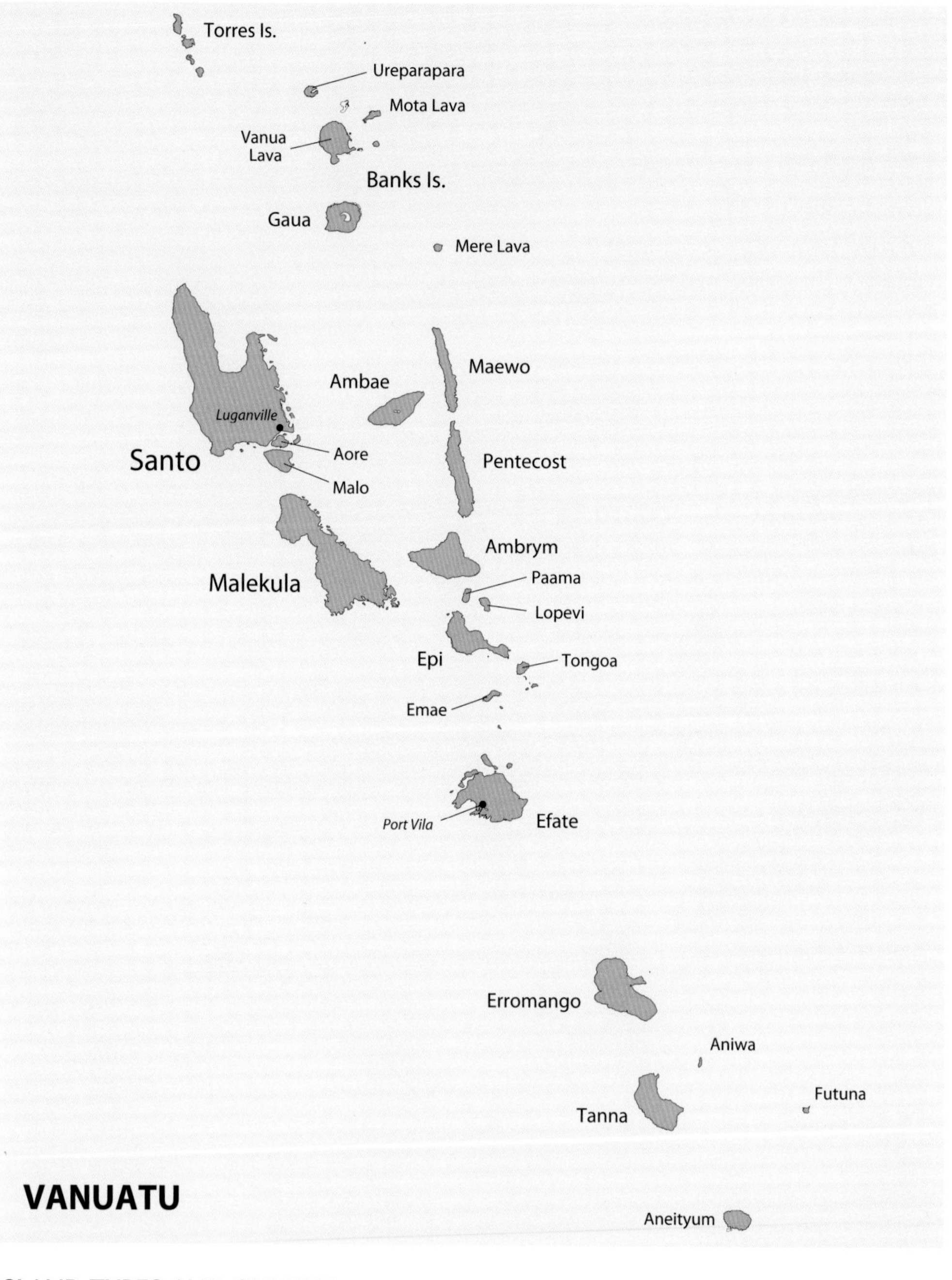

ISLAND TYPES AND CLIMATE

Most Melanesian islands arose from submarine volcanoes. However, some are coral atolls and others, such as Rennell and Lifou, are formed from raised coral ('makateas'), and New Caledonia is mostly derived from the ancient Gondwanaland continent. The volcanic islands are generally steep, mountainous and fertile; some have active volcanoes and new islands are still appearing. High volcanic islands support a high diversity of both widespread and endemic bird species. The atolls by contrast are small and low-lying, and generally lack endemic bird species or subspecies. The makateas are larger and rise higher above the sea, but are flat. Both atolls and makateas consist of coral or limestone, are infertile and lack streams and rivers. Grand Terre, the main island of New Caledonia, is an ancient weathered land, generally infertile but with many mineral deposits and mines.

Melanesia is a tropical region blessed by regular heavy rainfall. Indeed, the region was named Melanesia, meaning black islands, either because of the native peoples or rain clouds. Much of the region is in the path of south-easterly trade winds, which bring rain from November to April. Even the dry season from April to October is often fairly wet. On New Britain, there are opposite wet seasons to the north and the south of the mountain range. There is progressively lower rainfall south through Melanesia, with longer dry seasons in Vanuatu and especially New Caledonia. Rainfall increases with altitude on all islands. Annual rainfall varies from about 1200 mm in the west of New Caledonia to over 6000 mm in the wetter areas of New Britain. The temperatures are relatively constant and warm, but the south of the region has a distinctly cooler winter.

VEGETATION AND HABITATS

Vegetation is determined largely by the climate, geology and previous human use. Most of Melanesia has enough rain throughout the year to support tropical evergreen rainforest. Rainforest is usually quite a homogeneous habitat within any island but varies with altitude and rainfall. At higher altitudes, trees become smaller where lowland rainforest intergrades into montane rainforest. The altitude of this transition depends on the topography and the size of the island, but it usually lies at 500–1000 m. On exposed ridges and mountain-tops, the forest is often stunted and festooned with moss, and is sometimes called moss forest or cloud forest. Only the highest islands of New Britain, New Ireland, Bougainville, Kolombangara, Guadalcanal and Santo have distinct assemblages of montane birds. Other islands in the Solomons have a few montane species, including Makira which peaks at 1040 m; but New Caledonia, despite reaching 1618 m, has no montane species. On mountainous islands, each species has a typical altitudinal range, although individuals are often found at higher or lower altitudes. Where a lowland species is replaced by a closely related and ecologically similar species in the mountains, the two usually overlap for a few hundreds of metres altitude, such as the white-eyes on Bougainville: Yellow-throated White-eye ranges up to 900 m, occasionally to 1200 m, and Grey-throated White-eye down to 900 m, occasionally down to 750 m.

The trees and structure of rainforest also vary a little depending on geology and substrate, with distinct habitats on limestone and in swamps, but these are usually small in extent and support no characteristic birds. Some islands have a drier zone, usually the rain-shadow of large mountains, on the leeward slopes of the prevailing rain-bearing winds. These dry semi-deciduous forests have no additional bird species but may lack some species. True dry forest is only found on Grande Terre of New Caledonia, which also has extensive areas of savanna dominated by niaouli trees *Melaleuca quinquenervia* and maquis scrub. Maquis habitats on infertile, often ultrabasic or mineral-rich soils are very rich in endemic plants but not birds.

Limestone islands have distinctly drier forests with few large trees; the larger islands, such as Rennell and the Loyalties, have their own endemic bird species. Sandy coasts around many large islands support a distinct band of beach forest which is similar to the forests on very small islands and may support similar birds, as discussed below. Mangroves usually dominate intertidal areas with muddy substrates and support a characteristic subset of forest birds. Several birds such as Striated Heron and Little Kingfisher are more common in mangroves but no Melanesian bird is restricted to this habitat. Muddy beaches, sandy beaches and coral-reef flats support a range of migratory waders. Shallow seas support various terns and noddies, often roosting on exposed reefs and nesting on isolated islets, and the open seas support other seabirds, including shearwaters and petrels which nest on islets or in the hills of the larger mountains.

There are few freshwater wetlands in Melanesia, and therefore few waterbirds. The rivers of the larger islands in the Bismarck and Solomons have Little Pied Cormorants, herons and kingfishers. A few river estuaries are large enough to support swamps with herons, various migrant waterbirds and Australian Reed Warblers.

Grasslands on New Britain, New Ireland, Guadalcanal, Vanuatu and New Caledonia, and to a lesser extent on other islands, are probably largely caused and maintained by people lighting fires, but the occurrence of endemic subspecies of grassland quails, buttonquails and mannikins suggests that some grasslands are natural. Traditionally, the only other habitats created by people were areas of regenerating forest created by shifting cultivation and agro-forestry around settlements. Sites of old settlements and some tiny islands may be dominated by trees planted by people. Shifting cultivation is beneficial to some species and certainly creates easier birdwatching conditions, but the secondary forest regrowth is unsuitable for some forest-dependent species. After colonisation by western empires during the late 1800s, extensive areas of coastal plains were cleared for coconut plantations and cattle grazing. Coconut plantations support a few bird species, notably several nectarivores, and grasslands support even fewer. Much of lowland New Caledonia has been converted for European-style agriculture. In recent years, large areas of New Britain have been planted with oil-palm, which supports virtually no birds except for Bismarck Crows. The few towns support a handful of native species such as Willie Wagtail and Singing Starling in the Bismarcks and Solomons, and Grey-eared Honeyeater in Vanuatu and New Caledonia, alongside a few introduced species such as Common Myna.

MELANESIAN ORNITHOLOGY

NOMENCLATURE

Nomenclature is the assignment of names to birds. Each bird species has a scientific name, and one or more 'common' names in English, French and various local languages. The scientific name consists of a genus (capitalised) and species name, and where appropriate a subspecies name, all derived from Latin or Greek and written in italics. Scientific names only change following strict rules, but many have changed in recent years as genetic and other research has revised the genus or species to which birds belong. The scientific and English names often describe the bird or commemorate the name of the person it was described by or for. There is an ongoing debate about English names and some will continue to change. The book follows the nomenclature of the IOC (International Ornithological Congress) at the beginning of 2010, but alternative English names are given at the start of each species description. French names are given following CINFO (la Commission Internationale des Noms Français des Oiseaux) in 2010. Local language names are given in this book where only one language is spoken across a species's range, or where the species is virtually unknown except by local people. Producing lists of these local language names is important for communicating and promoting conservation with local people, and users of this book are encouraged to generate and use their own local-language name dictionaries. Dictionaries for the local languages around Bougainville are given by Hadden (2004) *Birds and Bird Lore of Bougainville and the North Solomons*. Scientific names and brief comparative descriptions are given for every subspecies found in Melanesia but very few of these subspecies have their own English names.

TAXONOMY

Taxonomy is the scientific identification and classification of birds and other life. Most birdwatchers and conservationists focus on the taxonomic level of species, but other taxonomic levels provide valuable information. These levels are illustrated here by the example of the Red-knobbed Imperial Pigeon:

Family: Columbidae or pigeons
Genus: *Ducula* or imperial pigeons
Species: *Ducula rubricera* (*D. rubricera*) or Red-knobbed Imperial Pigeon
Subspecies: *Ducula rubricera rubricera* (*D. r. rubricera*) or Bismarcks Red-knobbed Imperial Pigeon in the Bismarcks and *Ducula rubricera rubrigula* (*D. r. rubrigula*) or Solomons Red-knobbed Imperial Pigeon in the Solomons.

Identifying this bird as a pigeon requires an understanding of the basic features of its appearance, behaviour, calls and ecology. Identifying it as an imperial pigeon, Red-knobbed Imperial Pigeon or a specific subspecies, requires progressively more precise knowledge of these properties.

There is an ongoing debate about how to define a species and which subspecies could be treated as full species. Many resident forest bird species have a different subspecies on each large island or island group. A simple definition of a subspecies is a geographical population of birds which are different, usually in plumage or size, from other populations but would successfully interbreed and intergrade with them if given the chance. This definition creates problems when deciding whether to classify closely related forms on neighbouring islands (which are 'allopatric') as different subspecies within the same species or as separate species. These populations rarely cross the sea to each other's islands and so no-one can observe whether they are able to interbreed. One solution is to classify them as separate species when they differ from each other as much as other pairs of closely related species, but in some cases this requires a degree of subjective assessment. This book follows the IOC (International Ornithological Congress) taxonomy at the beginning of 2010, except for a few cases where I have published evidence for a different treatment. It is likely that further genetic research will support my view that many more subspecies should be treated as full species. The species texts indicate cases where authorities differ in their treatment of a taxon. This book describes all recognised subspecies and illustrates many of the more distinctive ones that may deserve full species status. Regardless of whether these birds are treated as species or subspecies, they are clearly different, and birdwatchers, conservationists and researchers should take an interest in them all.

BIOGEOGRAPHY AND ISLAND DISTRIBUTIONS

An understanding of biogeography is essential to explain and appreciate the distribution of birds in Melanesia. Fortunately there is an excellent and detailed explanation of the topic in Mayr & Diamond (2001). This only covers the Admiralties, Bismarcks and Solomons, but does include a number of references to similar analyses for Temotu and Vanuatu.

As most large Melanesian islands are volcanic and arose from the sea, all birds must have colonised from other islands. Most are believed to have spread from New Guinea through the Bismarcks to the Solomons, Temotu, Vanuatu and New Caledonia, with relatively small numbers colonising directly from Australia or Polynesia. Many species evolved in situ on the islands and some of these then colonised or recolonised other islands before evolving further. This history has given rise to many 'superspecies', groups of very closely related species that replace one another ecologically on adjacent islands, and has enabled a great variety of forms to evolve, notably across the Solomons. New Caledonia is a special case, believed to be an ancient piece of non-volcanic land. Species such as Kagu may already have existed on New Caledonia when it broke away from Gondwanaland, long before the other Melanesian islands were formed.

ENDEMISM

A high proportion of bird species and subspecies are endemic to Melanesia or a specific island or island group. At one extreme, Melanesian Megapode is highly dispersive, occurring on many tiny islets, and it shows little variation in plumage or calls from Manus to the eastern Solomons. At the other extreme, white-eyes on the neighbouring islands of Vella Lavella, Ranongga, Gizo and New Georgia are clearly closely related but differ in plumage, leg and bill colour, and voice, and are classified as four separate species. Melanesia supports one endemic family (Rhynochetidae), represented solely by the Kagu, about ten endemic genera and more endemic bird species for its area than any other biodiversity 'hotspot' except the vast expanse of Polynesia and Micronesia.

HOTSPOT	LAND AREA km^2	NO. ENDEMIC BIRD SPECIES
Polynesia–Micronesia	47,000	170
Melanesia	108,000	204
Caribbean	230,000	167
New Zealand	270,000	89
Philippines	297,000	185
Wallacea	338,000	265
Madagascar	600,000	183
New Guinea	829,000	334

Numbers from Conservation International's Hotspots Revisited (2004) except Melanesia which follows this book, and New Guinea which is treated as a High Biodiversity Wilderness, not a Hotspot.

Larger islands support more species but more isolated islands support fewer species. New Britain has the most species of any Melanesian island, and New Caledonia has relatively few for its size. At the other extreme, tiny islands support a range of 'tramp' species such as Island Monarch and Sclater's Myzomela. Tramps are highly dispersive but poorly competitive species, which colonise tiny and distant islands but not larger islands where they are presumably outcompeted by other closely related species. Some species such as Yellow-bibbed Fruit Dove are tramps in the Bismarcks, where the large islands support the closely related White-bibbed Fruit Dove, but are widespread on large islands in the Solomons, which lack closely related competing species.

Melanesia can be subdivided into islands or island groups that share more key bird species between themselves than with other neighbouring islands. The key factors determining whether birds are shared between islands are their geographical proximity, whether the islands were joined in prehistoric times, and the over-sea dispersal capabilities of each species. The captions opposite the plates indicate species' distributions across these island groups and the main text gives a detailed island-by-island distribution of each species and subspecies. Most accounts do not detail the range within any one island, as most Melanesian birds occur island-wide wherever suitable habitat exists within their altitudinal range. More detailed distributional ranges are given for the few known exceptions.

MIGRATION

Melanesia has relatively few migrant species, and is a significant destination for only a handful of these. Species are classified here as migrants if there is evidence of a significant annual movement to or from Melanesia, while species recorded irregularly are classified as vagrants. Most migrants breed in north Asia or in Australia and New Zealand. Most northern migrants migrate south from Russia and Alaska during September to March. These include 33 species of wader or shorebird, of which 15 are regular in Melanesia, although most occur in relatively small numbers. Some seabirds are regular migrants including Streaked Shearwater, Wedge-tailed Shearwater (pale phase), Bulwer's Petrel, Matsudaira's Storm Petrel and species of skuas and terns. Only two species of land bird are regular migrants from the north: Oriental Cuckoo and Red-rumped Swallow, and another seven are vagrants. Four northern species of duck are vagrants.

Australia and New Zealand have many fewer species of migrant, and only small numbers reach Melanesia. The Double-banded Plover is a regular migrant from New Zealand, and two other wader species are vagrants. Many petrels, shearwaters and storm petrels are regular migrants through Melanesian waters, but their migrations are poorly known. Three species of land bird, Long-tailed Cuckoo, Rainbow Bee-eater and Tree Martin, are regular migrants; four, Channel-billed Cuckoo, Shining Bronze Cuckoo, Sacred Kingfisher and Dollarbird, are regular migrants and also occur as resident populations; and seven are vagrants. There are also several species of irruptive vagrant, mostly waterbirds from Australia. Some of these, such as Little Black Cormorant, Great Cormorant, White-faced Heron, Cattle Egret and Masked Lapwing, have recently colonised or may be in the process of colonising Melanesia.

Migration within Melanesia is very limited as there is little latitudinal or habitat variation to stimulate movements. The migratory status of Fan-tailed Cuckoo is poorly known but it may move within Melanesia. A few species are reported to have fluctuating ranges, occurring on certain islands for a few or many years, and then disappearing, including Palm Lorikeet, Shining Bronze Cuckoo and Fan-tailed Cuckoo. Many species of Melanesian pigeon and parrot move across large areas and may be considered dispersive or nomadic, especially in times of food shortage. There is also some evidence for altitudinal movements, on a seasonal or daily basis, mostly involving pigeons and parrots that breed and/or roost at high altitudes but regularly fly to the lowlands to feed.

INTRODUCED SPECIES

Melanesia is fortunate in having few introduced or alien species, especially in comparison to other groups of tropical islands. A handful of species, notably Common Myna, were introduced in an attempt to control pests in coconut plantations. Others, such as Common (or Feral) Pigeon, have become established after escaping from captivity or deliberate release. However, New Caledonia has suffered from intentional introductions of many exotic birds in order to diversify the natural avifauna, which seemed inadequate to early European colonisers. New Caledonia also supports a range of gamebirds introduced for hunting. Elsewhere, Melanesia has very few introduced species, partly because colonials attempted to introduce fewer species, and partly because there are few artificial or anthropogenic habitats which provide niches unexploited by native species.

Most introduced bird species have no obvious impact on native species as they exploit under-utilised niches and habitats in artificial or anthropogenic environments. However, given the severe impacts from exotic species on islands elsewhere it is best to avoid new introductions, to eradicate any newly established populations, and to research the impact of established species. For instance, Common Myna is aggressive and may displace native species from nest sites, and the introduced Mallard hybridises with the native Pacific Black Duck.

HOW MANY BIRD SPECIES IN MELANESIA?

As noted in the sections above, it is difficult to be exact about the number of Melanesian bird species, as ongoing taxonomic research revises the number of species and subspecies, and additional seabird and vagrant species continue slowly to be discovered in Melanesia. The totals below are derived from this book's taxonomy, and include all records of seabirds and vagrants to the beginning of 2010 that have sufficient supporting details to be reasonably sure of their identification. Species known only from unconfirmed records are discussed [in brackets] in the text and excluded from this table.

NATION / REGION	BISMARCKS (including Admiralties & St Matthias)	SOLOMONS (including Bougainville & Temotu)	VANUATU	NEW CALEDONIA (including Loyalties)	MELANESIA (total)
Total number of species	281	293	127	197	501
No. species endemic to island group	57	85	11	20	173*
No. additional species endemic across Melanesia	13	21	12	8	24*
No. additional recently extinct endemic species**	0	2	1	4	7*
No. additional native breeding species	115	92	52	65	160
No. introduced species	3	2	8	13	16

* the total number of Melanesian endemics is made up of these three figures (= 204) ** discussed on page 21

BIRDWATCHING IN MELANESIA

IDENTIFYING BIRDS

As a guide for new birdwatchers, the key factors aiding accurate bird identification are knowledge of which species occur on which island, their calls and 'field marks'. One of the most important 'rules' is that resident forest bird species are virtually never seen on islands from which they have not previously been reported. This means that on each island there are relatively few forest bird species. Moreover, as most similar species are closely-related forms on different islands, their identification can be based on the island on which they were observed. However, many seabirds, coastal and wetland birds, and the few migrant land birds can potentially occur anywhere.

Birdwatching in Melanesia is challenging because most species of interest occur in dense forest. In most forest birdwatching, over 90% of bird identifications are based on the calls and songs of bird that are not seen. Calls are best learned by finding and identifying the individual bird calling, but this is a very lengthy process. Vocalisations can be learned from local guides but the accuracy of these identifications need to be checked. Few reference recordings are currently available. A CD of New Caledonian bird calls by Yves Létocart can be found in a few outlets in Nouméa, recordings of many Vanuatu species are posted on the VanBirds website (www.positiveearth.org/vanbirds), an increasing number of recordings of Bismarck and Solomons endemic species can be accessed on Xeno Canto (www.xeno-canto.org) and the Internet Bird Collection (http://ibc.lynxeds.com), and recordings of species also found in New Guinea or Australia are for sale from commercial retailers. Recording birds in the field and playing back their calls and songs can attract them closer for accurate identification. Anyone making accurately identified recordings is encouraged to submit these to the websites listed above.

When a bird is seen, it is important to assess the 'type' of bird as well as look for any notable markings. Recognising a bird as belonging to a certain family or genus will greatly aid identification. This takes practice and is based on a suite of factors including size, shape, colour and behaviour. Features visible in the field, or field marks, include size and shape of bill, leg length, colour of bill, eye and legs/feet, and any colour patterns in the plumage. Many species have pale patches or feather-tips on the head, wings or tail. The technical terms used to describe different parts of a bird and groups of feathers are illustrated here.

With experience, many birds can be identified on a very fleeting glimpse based on an overall impression of their appearance, often called their 'jizz'. Whilst identification based on jizz is usually very accurate, it is somewhat subjective and personal, and identification of any species poorly known to the observer, or unusual records, should be based on its markings.

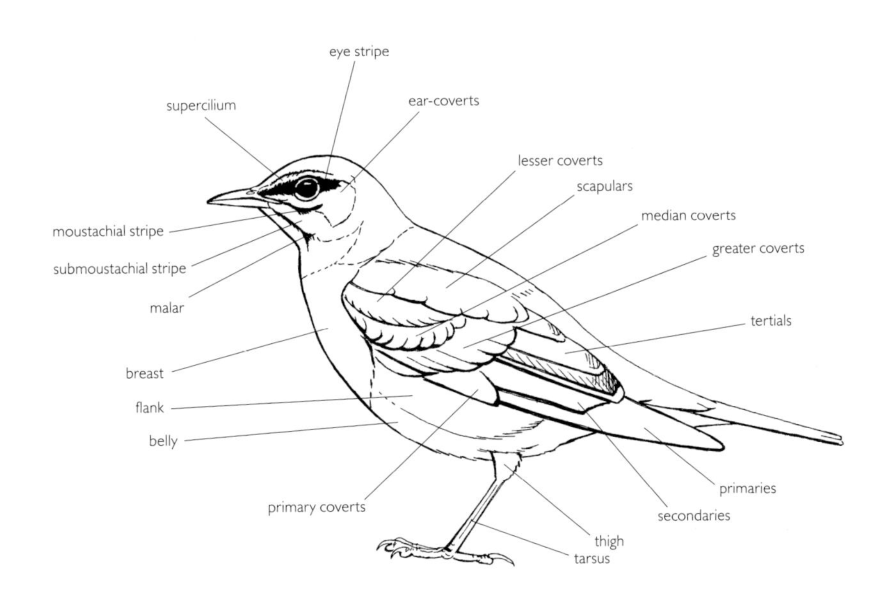

Topography of a passerine showing the main feather tracts of the body and wing

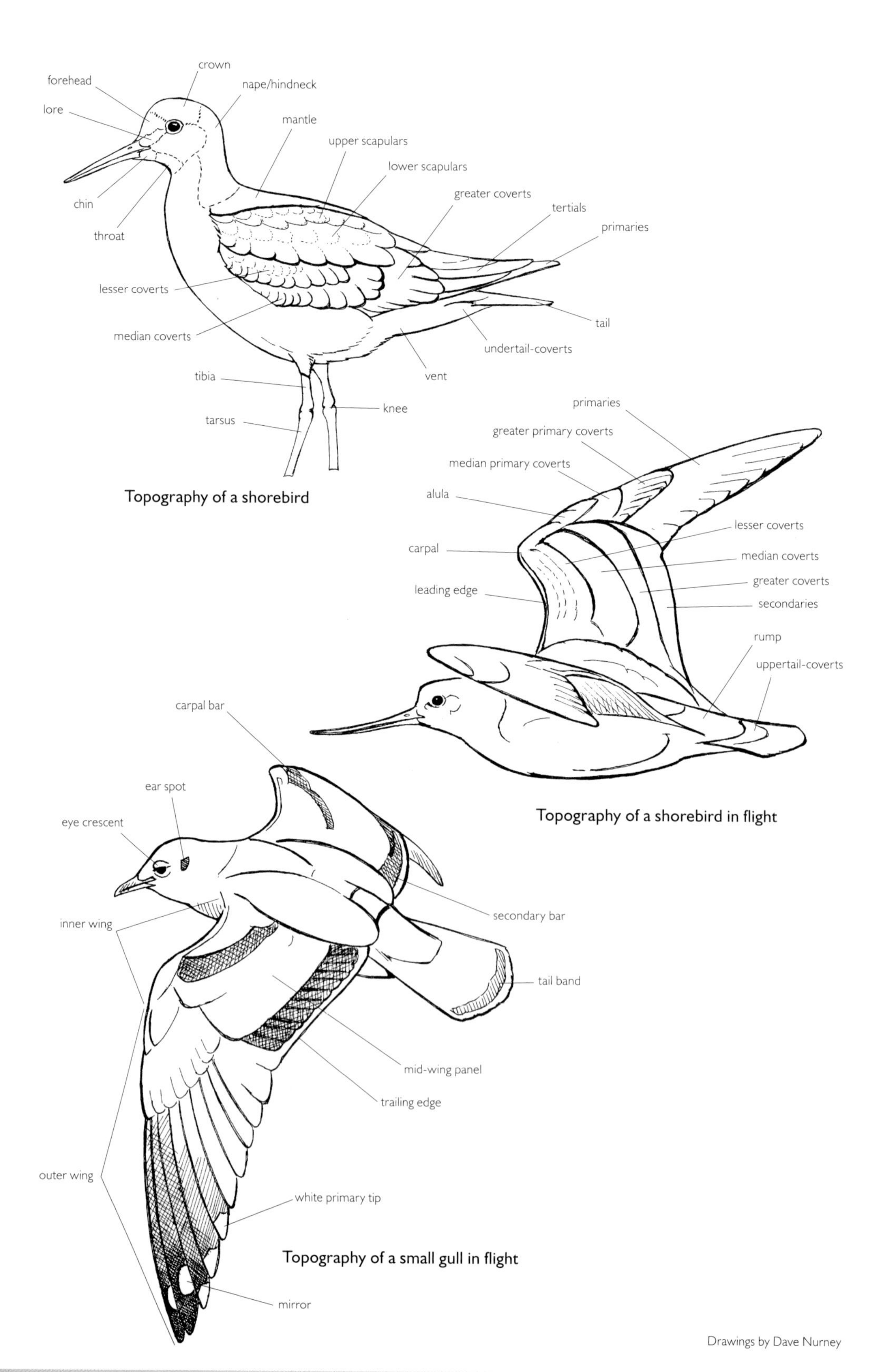

Topography of a shorebird

Topography of a shorebird in flight

Topography of a small gull in flight

Drawings by Dave Nurney

PLUMAGES AND MOULT

Birds moult their feathers once or twice a year. Newly grown feathers may often be distinguished as being darker and more colourful than older feathers. Birds in moult may show mixed patterns intermediate between the two plumages. The first set of feathers grown by a young bird is called the juvenile plumage. Many Melanesian species keep this juvenile plumage for a very short time and the plumage is not even described for some species. Most species then moult into an adult plumage but some species, especially those that are larger and slower to mature, have one or more immature plumages. Once attaining an adult plumage, some species moult annually into a breeding plumage before courtship and breeding, and then moult back into a non-breeding plumage after the chicks have been reared. In some species, males have a different plumage to females. Often the male has a bright plumage for display, whereas the female has a drab plumage designed for camouflage and avoidance of territorial conflicts. Juveniles and immatures often have a similar drab plumage to females and may be indistinguishable, although juveniles often have a yellow gape and base to the bill. Some species such as herons attain brighter colours on the bill or around the face during courtship and breeding. Most forest species breed at the end of the dry season, so that their brood can exploit the increase in insects at the beginning of the rains. Some species such as pigeons are less seasonal and may nest year-round, and the nesting seasons of inshore seabirds are not predictable on an annual cycle.

FINDING BIRDS

Many Melanesian birds are shy, perhaps because generations of local people, often hungry for protein, have hunted them. Observers are more likely to have good views of birds if they are dressed in drab or camouflaged clothes, standing still and partially hidden in vegetation. Making squeaking noises or 'pishing' will often bring smaller birds much closer to investigate the observer – observers should experiment with different tones and patterns of pishing. Pishing works best on fantails, monarchs and white-eyes, and the interest of these birds will also attract other nearby species. Playing recordings can also work well, especially for territorial species. The impact of playback, which is clearly intrusive to a territorial bird, is poorly known and is best avoided where possible. Use of playback is particularly discouraged for threatened birds and well frequented locations, and may be prohibited in some protected areas. Some ground birds are so shy that they are best seen by standing still for long periods, in the hope that they will return to an area where they are known or suspected to forage. Spending time with a local guide is usually the best way of seeing birds and improving birdwatching skills.

STUDYING BIRDS

As well as enjoying seeing birds, birdwatchers can gather useful data by:

Documenting new distributional records. Birds outside their known range must be adequately documented to gain acceptance – photographs, recordings or detailed notes are needed, and the record submitted for publication or collation.

Counting birds. Counting is a much more accurate method of determining a species's abundance than subjectively describing them as 'common' or 'rare'. However, counting forest birds is more difficult as many individual birds are overlooked, and observers must take great care in designing a counting method to generate meaningful results.

Comparing counts of birds in different habitats. For most of Melanesia, there is very limited data to assess the impact of habitat change such as logging and forest degradation. This is most important for assessing species' conservation status.

Documenting breeding records. Watching birds' behaviour can indicate whether they are nesting nearby. Breeding seasons, nest descriptions and even juvenile plumages are poorly known for many species.

Recording local language names. Recording local language names and local stories about specific species is of great help in building local conservation awareness.

BIRDWATCHING ETIQUETTE

All land in Melanesia is owned by local people. Their permission must be gained before walking on their land. Exceptions to this rule are public roads and areas of government and private land on New Caledonia. It is best to ask at the closest village for the head man or chief and to explain the purpose of the visit. A small gift must be given on any visit to a traditional New Caledonian village or *tribu*. Many Melanesian villages will ask for a *kastom* or access fee to visit their land. This should be paid but efforts should be made to ensure that it is paid to the correct person, perhaps with a receipt. Some villages have a poor understanding of monetary value or bad experiences with previous visitors, and may ask for excessively high payments. If this cannot be negotiated to a more reasonable fee, do not visit this land. Most villages will ask that a guide or two is employed. Usually the cost is nominal and the knowledge of the guides can be invaluable for finding trails, finding birds, and for safety. Melanesian people are generally very interested in anything related to their land and appreciate the opportunity to talk about visitors' experiences and interests. Although most Melanesian people know a little about their birds, it takes some perseverance and luck to find a good guide. Sadly, local knowledge of birds and their environment is being lost from many Melanesian communities as people have less need to spend time in the forest and are less reliant on hunting birds. The situation is different in New Caledonia, where many of the accessible birdwatching sites are on government land away from local Melanesian communities. Here, some park rangers and guides are skilled at birdwatching and guiding. Most guides will expect payment and this should be negotiated before engaging their services or entering private land. Many guides speak Pidgin English or French. Research requires permits from national governments.

BIRDWATCHING SITES

Few birdwatchers visit Melanesia and consequently few birding sites are known. Most visiting birders want to see the endemic species and restrict their visit to the sites closest to the main towns and airports. These sites are given below as an aid to the visitor with little time, but visitors are strongly encouraged to find and explore new sites. Most Melanesian birds occur wherever there is suitable habitat at a suitable altitude. Only a few are genuinely restricted to specific regions or sites. The main advantages of visiting one of the well-known sites, such as those listed below, is that these are relatively easy to visit and there may be knowledgeable guides. The disadvantage of these sites is that the birds are much better known than elsewhere, so the visitor does not have the fun of finding their own birds and is not adding to the knowledge of bird distributions. If the visitor has time to research and organise the travel and guides, it can be much more exciting and worthwhile to go to new sites. The organisations listed on page 32 would be very interested to receive observations from anywhere in Melanesia, especially new sites, and can suggest the undocumented areas most worthy of visits and surveys.

When visiting any of these sites, be aware of the need to obtain permission to walk on land, and try to support local guides and the local economy through fair payment for services such as access, guides, food, accommodation and transport.

Manus (Admiralty Is)

All of the Manus endemic birds are widespread except for the Manus Masked Owl, Superb Pitta and Manus Fantail. There have been no field records of the owl but visitors should ask their guides! Superb Pitta is reliably seen between Lorengau and Rossun village but is extremely difficult to see without a local guide. Manus Fantail is restricted to a few offshore islands, including Tong. This is an open-water journey and should be undertaken only in a suitable boat and taking proper precautions. Tong also supports various tramp species including Bismarck Black Myzomela.

Coastal birdwatching sites are usually easy to access, but most mountains lack roads and involve walking from close to sea-level as here on the south of New Ireland. *Guy Dutson.*

Mussau (St Matthias Is)

All of Mussau's endemic birds appear to be widespread except for Mussau Triller, which is restricted to high altitudes. The island has rarely been visited by birdwatchers, so there are no specific sites to visit.

New Ireland

New Ireland's lowland forest birds can be seen in any dense lowland forest including along roads south of Kavieng and at Limbin. The montane endemics can be seen on the Limbin road or in the mountains of the far south. The Limbin road is far easier logistically but the birds are not common. There are no roads up the southern mountains and this is a much more challenging place to visit. All airstrips and areas of rank grassland should be searched for the various mannikin species.

Many Melanesian islands are surrounded by a coral reef. The reef around the southern lagoon of New Caledonia is globally important for breeding seabirds. *Guy Dutson.*

New Britain

Birdwatching sites are in a state of flux as logging and oil-palm plantations have destroyed previous sites but created access to new ones. Around Hoskins/Kimbe in West New Britain, the Poikili/Lavege and Garu reserves and Kilu Ridge support most of the lowland species, but many occur at low densities and are rarely seen. A small entrance fee is payable at the village or in advance to the Walindi dive resort. The last gardens on the Lavege road are particularly good for pigeons and parrots in the early morning. Access into the hills is difficult. Buff-bellied Mannikins are usually found in the grasslands around Walindi and Hoskins airport. Around Rabaul in West New Britain, check whether the Wild Dog mine is open to visitors as this offers access to low mountains. Many smaller towns and airstrips on the south coast have forest close to roads but access into the hills is again difficult. There are no recommended montane birdwatching sites but all of the montane species, with the exception of New Britain Thicketbird, which is still only known from the type specimens, can be seen by organising a trek up the highest central mountain ranges. Treks into the mountains are serious multi-day expeditions requiring significant preparation and negotiation with local guides. The isolated volcanoes in the north support some of the lower montane species including the New Britain Thrush. Watom and the small islands in Kimbe Bay have a range of tramp species, notably Sclater's Myzomela, and offshore boat-trips have recorded Heinroth's Shearwater and Beck's Petrel. Visitors are encouraged to explore and document new birdwatching sites.

Bougainville

Bougainville has been politically unstable since 1990 and visitors should check protocol and safety for any visits, especially to the mountains. Birdwatching sites are described well in Hadden (2004) *Birds and Bird Lore of Bougainville*. Woodford's Rail can be seen in long grass around Arawa and the species endemic to Bougainville's lowlands can also be seen on Buka. Several species are endemic to the mountains.

High mountains are characterised by stunted montane forest on steep slopes, as seen here on Guadalcanal. Land-slips often create extensive areas of impenetrable thickets. *Guy Dutson.*

Unsustainable logging is the greatest threat to Melanesian birds. This lowland forest on Choiseul has been logged lightly, probably supports the full complement of bird species, and has the potential to regenerate. *Guy Dutson.*

Choiseul

Few birdwatchers have visited Choiseul and there are no specific areas to go birdwatching. A *Zoothera* thrush of poorly known taxonomic status is known from one specimen from the highest mountain but the Choiseul Pigeon is certainly extinct.

(Santa) Isabel

Many birdwatchers have visited the village of Tirotonga, a two-hour walk above Buala, to see some of the Solomons' rarest birds. Villagers know locations for all the Isabel species including Woodford's Rail, Fearful Owl, Solomons Frogmouth and Black-faced Pitta. Where possible, the village should be contacted in advance of any visit.

Gizo

In Gizo, birdwatchers can hire boats and contact local land-owners for visiting the New Georgia group of islands. Gizo White-eye is fairly common along roads a couple of kilometres out of town and Solomons Sea Eagles are often seen.

Vella Lavella, Ranongga, Rendova, Tetepare, Vangunu and New Georgia

These islands support endemic white-eyes but are rarely visited, and birdwatchers have to arrange transport, accommodation and access in advance. The white-eyes are generally widespread but the endemic monarch subspecies take much more time to find. The very rare Solomons Nightjar has been recorded from Tetepare, which has an ecotourism guest-house that can be booked through www.tetepare.org. Birdwatching can also be good around the ecotourism lodges on New Georgia and Vangunu, but all the species on these islands can be seen on Kolombangara.

Kolombangara

Kolombangara Leaf Warbler and Kolombangara Mountain White-eye, along with other montane Solomons species, can be seen by hiking for a long day and camping at about 1000 m altitude. Guides and porters are essential and can be organised from a number of villages or from Gizo. Lowland forest birds can be seen anywhere that retains old-growth forest, and Roviana Rail can be seen in areas with rank grass and overgrown gardens.

Guadalcanal

Most lowland species, including the occasional White-eyed Starling and Woodford's Rail, can be seen along the road up to Mount Austen and down to the Lungga River. Guides are not strictly necessary but can be useful. The Botanic Garden in Honiara supports several endemic species including Guadalcanal Boobook. The wetlands and grasslands around the airport and Betikamba support a range of more widespread species. Guadalcanal's montane birds are amongst the most difficult to see in Melanesia and very few birdwatchers have made this effort. A multi-day trek must be organised to the highest mountains with guides, porters and land-owners.

Malaita
Malaita's forests have been heavily cleared for cultivation, so it is best to hire a vehicle and head out of Auki. All of the endemic species and subspecies can be seen in roadside hill forest from the cross-island road, except for Malaita Fantail which is confined to the highest altitudes and requires a specific multi-day trek. A rail similar to Woodford's Rail, but of unknown taxonomic status, can be seen on the coastal road.

Makira (San Cristobal)
Anyone visiting Makira should arrange a trip with the land-holders from Hauta and East Bauro. These are best organised in advance through local guest-houses. With the birding knowledge of these trained guides, physically fit visitors can hope to see Yellow-legged Pigeon, Makira Thrush and a fantastic suite of endemics. The lowland forest around Kirakira supports many species but none of the montane specialities. A trip to Ugi or the Three Sisters is also worthwhile to see the endemic monarch and fantail subspecies, but good weather and a reliable boat are essential.

Rennell
Rennell offers amongst the easiest and most enjoyable birdwatching, as all the endemic species are fairly common across the island and can be seen by walking from the airport. Alternatively, accommodation and guides are available around Lake Tegano which supports nesting waterbirds as well as the forest endemics. Flights are often infrequent and visitors may wish to consider chartering a return flight.

Temotu
Visiting these islands is constrained by the infrequency and unreliability of flights to Nendo and the lack of any onward transport except for the open speed-boats ('canoes'), which should be avoided in all except the best weather. The commoner endemics can be seen around Lata town whereas Sanford's White-eye and especially Santa Cruz Shrikebill require travelling to old-growth forest. Polynesian Starling is widespread on the Reef Is and Duff Is but Palm Lorikeet is unpredictable in coastal coconuts. On Vanikoro, at least two days are needed to find local guides and Vanikoro Monarch and Vanikoro White-eye.

Santo
Vanuatu's lowland endemic species can all be seen at Loru Protected Area and Big Bay or Vatthe Conservation Area. Transport, accommodation and guides should be booked in advance from local agents. A camping expedition to Peak Santo or Mount Tabwemasana is necessary to see the montane species but Mountain Starling is very rare and several other species are scarce or difficult to see.

Melanesians traditionally lived in small villages of houses made from bamboo and palm leaves. Some traditional villages survive in remote areas such as the highlands of Santo. *Guy Dutson.*

New Caledonia supports large areas of unique scrubby *maquis* habitat. Although of limited interest to birdwatchers, this is a botanical hotspot but much has been degraded by mining activity. *Guy Dutson.*

Efate

Efate has several of Vanuatu's lowland endemic species and a range of open-country and coastal species including Blue-faced Parrotfinch at the golf course. There are no specific birdwatching sites but it is best to ask in town for access to old-growth forest where there is a chance of seeing Vanuatu Megapode and even Royal Parrotfinch.

Other Vanuatu islands

Few birdwatchers visit the outer islands but a perusal of www.positiveearth.org/vanbirds will indicate a range of interesting islands to explore. A trip to Emae or Tongoa gives the best opportunity to see Royal Parrotfinch. Boat trips, especially off the islands of Vanua Lava, Mere Lava and Tanna, give an opportunity to see shearwaters and petrels including Vanuatu Petrel.

Grande Terre, New Caledonia

A handful of popular birdwatching sites are well documented in many birdwatching reports available on the internet. The Rivière Bleue reserve, about two hours out of Nouméa, is the key location as Kagu are relatively common and confiding, Crow Honeyeaters occur and the rangers include some skilled birdwatching guides. Bookings must be made in advance for access, accommodation and guides. Mt Koaghis is on the outskirts of Nouméa and supports most of the commoner endemic species including New Caledonian Crow. New Caledonian Grassbird has been seen here but is much easier to see at Farino, about 100 km north of Nouméa, and other sites in the north. Other birdwatching sites are documented for the range of endemic species, including additional grassbird sites, and also sites for migratory shorebirds and nesting seabirds. Contact the SCO for details or check their book *Zones Importantes pour la Conservation des Oiseaux de Nouvelle-Calédonie*.

Lifou and Ouvéa (Loyalty Is.)

The endemic white-eyes of Lifou can be seen from the roads running inland from the airport or the ferry terminal. To see the Ouvéa Parakeet, visitors must arrange a guide in advance to arrange access to private land. The ferry from Nouméa to these islands can provide some great seabird-watching, including Tahiti and Gould's Petrels, but the ferry schedules are often unreliable.

ORGANISATIONS AND RECORDS

Unfortunately, there are few birdwatching organisations in Melanesia. In Papua New Guinea, there are no organisations but the journal *Muruk* (contact email: info@sicklebillsafaris.com) publishes birdwatchers' records. In the Solomon Islands, there are no birdwatching groups but the staff of various conservation organisations can help advise on places to visit and how to report interesting birds. In Vanuatu, the Wantok Environment Centre (www.positiveearth.org) welcomes help from visitors and can help with access to remote areas if visitors are helping the local community. The VanBirds bird atlas project is a simple way to research and help map Vanuatu's birds (www.positiveearth.org/vanbirds). In New Caledonia, the Société Calédonienne d'Ornithologie (www.sco.asso.nc) has regular birdwatching trips, research projects and publications, and is able to help visitors, particularly with information on lesser-known birdwatching areas. Fewer opportunities are available to visitors who do not speak French. All records of globally threatened birds should be checked against BirdLife International's species accounts on (www.birdlife.org/datazone/species) and any significant sightings should be reported to BirdLife's globally threatened bird forums. BirdLife International also offer good summaries of the endemic birds found in each of the main Melanesian regions (www.birdlife.org/datazone/eba). A much more detailed list of birds recorded from each island, including unsubstantiated records, is available on http://birdsofmelanesia.net.

Any records of species outside the island ranges given in this book should be substantiated by field notes, photographs and/or recordings. These should be published or shared with national organisations. The author would be pleased to receive records for future updates of this book (email: guydutson@hotmail.com).

FURTHER READING

Much of this book is based on the published work of others, and their contribution is readily acknowledged. The most useful material includes the following but note that guides to birds of adjacent regions may be based on different subspecies with different plumages and calls:

Barré, N. & Dutson, G. (2000) Liste commentée des oiseaux de Nouvelle-Calédonie. *Alauda* 68: 1-48 and subsequent updates in *Alauda*.

Beehler, B. M., Pratt, T. K. & Zimmerman, D. A. (1986) *Birds of New Guinea*. Princeton University Press, Princeton, USA.

Bregulla, H. L. (1992) *Birds of Vanuatu*. Anthony Nelson, Oswestry, UK.

Christidis, L. & Boles, W. E. (2007) *Systematics and Taxonomy of Australian Birds*. CSIRO Publishing, Melbourne.

Coates, B. J. (1985–1990) *The Birds of Papua New Guinea. Volumes I and II*. Dove Publications, Alderley, Australia.

Coates, B. J., Bishop, K. D. & Gardner, D. (1997) *A Guide to the Birds of Wallacea*. Dove Publications, Alderley, Australia.

Hadden, D. (2004) *Birds and Bird Lore of Bougainville and the North Solomons*. Dove Publications, Alderley, Australia.

del Hoyo, J. *et al.* (1992–2011) *Handbook of the Birds of the World*. Sixteen volumes. Lynx Edicions, Barcelona.

Marchant, S., Higgins, P. J. *et al.* (1990–2006) *Handbook of Australian, New Zealand and Antarctic Birds*. Seven volumes. Oxford University Press, Melbourne.

Mayr, E. (1945) *Birds of the Southwest Pacific*. Macmillan, New York.

Mayr, E. & Diamond, J. (2001) *The Birds of Northern Melanesia: Speciation, Ecology and Biogeography*. Oxford University Press, New York.

Pratt, H. D., Bruner, P. L. & Barrett, D. G. (1987) *The Birds of Hawaii and the Tropical Pacific*. Princeton University Press, Princeton, USA.

Steadman, D. W. (2006) *Extinction and Biogeography of Tropical Pacific Birds*. University of Chicago Press, London.

Watling, D. (2004) *A Guide to the Birds of Fiji and Western Polynesia*. Environmental Consultants (Fiji), Suva, Fiji.

Anyone studying Melanesian ornithology is also referred to journal papers. Many of the older papers are listed in *The Birds of Northern Melanesia* or are found in the journal *American Museum Novitates*, which is available on http://digitallibrary.amnh.org. Most of the newer papers can be found by searching the internet but some journals such as *Muruk*, the discontinued *Newsletter of the PNG Birdwatching Society* and *Le Cagou* are not currently indexed on the internet and have to be searched manually. Searching the internet will also reveal many birdwatching trip reports to the region with notes and tips on visiting the most popular sites.

CONSERVATION

THREATS AND SOLUTIONS

Melanesian forest birds are generally declining because of habitat loss and degradation. Until western colonisation, most islands were forested except for traditional shifting cultivation around villages. Colonists created coconut plantations on flat coastal land and cattle pastures on New Caledonia and small areas on Vanuatu and Guadalcanal. For many years, the complex local ownership and inaccessibility of most Melanesian forests saved them from large-scale destruction. However, in recent decades industrial timber operators have exploited weak governance systems to log much of the region. Logging is usually undertaken to a poor standard, often not meeting national laws and codes, and leaves highly degraded forest which is unsuitable for many bird species. In some cases, the forest may never recover to be suitable for these birds, nor indeed for future sustainable logging and other traditional uses by the land-owners. An additional threat, especially on New Britain, is clearance of lowland forests for oil-palm plantations. It is likely that most of the fertile flat lowlands of New Britain will be lost to oil-palm, which is of no value for native birds or biodiversity. The solutions to the damage caused by unsustainable logging are to enforce national laws and for the international community to avoid using illegal and unsustainable timber. Oil-palm is a more intractable threat as it generates ongoing income for land-owners, but forest reserves must be planned to conserve drinking water, other ecosystem services and biodiversity.

An additional threat to birds is the impact of rats, cats, dogs and other introduced species. More research is required to know the impact on birds across the region but it seems likely that the decline and extinction of terrestrial birds such as ground doves and rails have been caused by rats and cats. Cats are blamed for the extinction of Choiseul Pigeon and several native rodents in the Solomons, dogs are the greatest threat to Kagu on New Caledonia, and rats are a hazard everywhere to nesting seabirds. These alien species have the greatest impacts on isolated islands which lack native terrestrial mammals. It could be expected that birds on the larger islands of the Bismarcks and Solomons, which do have native rodents, would suffer less as they have evolved alongside these mammals. The impacts of mammals, especially rats, on the more isolated islands of Temotu, Vanuatu and New Caledonia, need more research but they are likely to have caused most of the historical extinctions from these islands.

Invasive alien mammals can be eradicated from small islands. Rats have been eradicated from small islets around New Caledonia, resulting in increases in the numbers and success of breeding seabirds. Australia and New Zealand are managing alien mammals by extensive poisoning and eradication from large islands and within large fenced areas on the mainland. These solutions need to be trialled in Melanesia.

The threat from hunting is relatively minor. Some large birds are traditionally hunted for meat and many birds are hunted recreationally by young people. Although logging roads create greater access into forest, hunting is generally in decline as more people want and can afford manufactured food such as farmed chickens and tinned fish.

GLOBALLY THREATENED SPECIES

Forty-nine or 13% of Melanesia's resident species are globally threatened, including 45 or 23% of the endemic species; this rate is slightly above the overall 12% of birds that are threatened around the world.

BirdLife International evaluates all bird species against the IUCN Red List criteria, which assign species to categories of extinction risk. This categorisation is less certain for poorly known species and those on islands where the rate of forest loss is poorly documented. For instance, a reassessment of forest loss on New Britain in 2007 concluded that 21 species endemic to Melanesia should be categorised as threatened or 'Near Threatened', compared to 12 species previously listed. The Red List category for each globally threatened species is given in the main species text following the abbreviation 'IUCN', and threatened breeding species are listed in table below. Fuller details for each species are available on the BirdLife International website (www.birdlife.org/datazone/species). Some additional species are threatened in Melanesia but not globally, and some endemic subspecies are threatened but not assessed by BirdLife/IUCN. The threat status of these species is given without the abbreviation 'IUCN'. Other species recognised by this book but not yet by BirdLife International may also be threatened. Birdwatchers can make a special effort to find and document threatened species: BirdLife International and the author would appreciate any information on threatened species to feed into conservation efforts and to update their threat assessments.

GLOBALLY THREATENED SPECIES BREEDING IN MELANESIA

SPECIES	IUCN THREAT STATUS (2010)	KEY THREATS
	ADMIRALTIES	
Heinroth's Shearwater	Vulnerable	Introduced predators?
Manus Masked Owl	Vulnerable	Forest loss
Superb Pitta	Vulnerable	Introduced predators?
Manus Fantail	Vulnerable	Introduced predators?
	BISMARCKS	
Beck's Petrel	Critically Endangered	Introduced predators?
Heinroth's Shearwater	Vulnerable	Introduced predators?
Black Honey Buzzard	Vulnerable	Forest loss
Slaty-mantled Goshawk	Vulnerable	Forest loss
New Britain Sparrowhawk	Vulnerable	Forest loss
New Britain Goshawk	Vulnerable	Forest loss
Yellow-legged Pigeon	Vulnerable	Forest loss; hunting
New Britain Bronzewing	Vulnerable	Forest loss
Blue-eyed Cockatoo	Vulnerable	Forest loss
Golden Masked Owl	Vulnerable	Forest loss
New Britain Boobook	Vulnerable	Forest loss
Bismarck Kingfisher	Vulnerable	Forest loss
New Britain Thicketbird	Vulnerable	Tiny range and population
	SOLOMONS (including Bougainville but not Temotu)	
Beck's Petrel	Critically Endangered	Introduced predators?
Heinroth's Shearwater	Vulnerable	Introduced predators?
Sanford's Sea Eagle	Vulnerable	Forest loss; hunting
Imitator Goshawk	Vulnerable	Forest loss
Makira Woodhen	Critically Endangered	Introduced predators?
Yellow-legged Pigeon	Vulnerable	Forest loss; hunting
Chestnut-bellied Imperial Pigeon	Vulnerable	Forest loss; hunting
Fearful Owl	Vulnerable	Forest loss
Moustached Kingfisher	Vulnerable	Introduced predators?
Black-faced Pitta	Vulnerable	Introduced predators?
Malaita Fantail	Vulnerable	Unknown
Kolombangara Leaf Warbler	Vulnerable	Tiny range and population
Ranongga White-eye	Vulnerable	Forest loss
Gizo White-eye	Endangered	Forest loss
White-eyed Starling	Endangered	Unknown (forest loss?)
Guadalcanal Thrush	Vulnerable	Tiny range and population
	TEMOTU	
Santa Cruz Ground Dove	Endangered	Introduced predators?
Palm Lorikeet	Vulnerable	Forest loss
Santa Cruz Shrikebill	Endangered	Unknown
	VANUATU	
Vanuatu Megapode	Vulnerable	Forest loss
Vanuatu Petrel	Endangered?	Introduced predators?
Polynesian Storm Petrel*	Endangered	Introduced predators?
Santa Cruz Ground Dove	Endangered	Introduced predators?
Vanuatu Imperial Pigeon	Vulnerable	Forest loss; hunting
Palm Lorikeet	Vulnerable	Forest loss
Mountain Starling	Vulnerable	Tiny range and population
Royal Parrotfinch	Vulnerable	Forest loss

NEW CALEDONIA		
Gould's Petrel*	Vulnerable	Introduced predators?
Polynesian Storm Petrel*	Endangered	Introduced predators?
Australasian Bittern*	Endangered	Loss of wetlands
Kagu	Endangered	Introduced predators
New Caledonian Rail	Critically Endangered	Introduced predators?
Fairy Tern*	Vulnerable	Introduced predators; disturbance
New Caledonian Lorikeet	Critically Endangered	Introduced predators?
Horned Parakeet	Vulnerable	Introduced predators?
Ouvéa Parakeet	Endangered	Habitat loss; trapping
New Caledonian Parakeet	Vulnerable	Introduced predators?
New Caledonian Owlet-nightjar	Critically Endangered	Introduced predators?
Crow Honeyeater	Critically Endangered	Introduced predators?

*Also breeds in Polynesia or Australia; all other species are endemic to Melanesia.

The following species are listed as 'Near Threatened', meaning that they are believed to be approaching the thresholds for qualifying as Vulnerable. However we have poor knowledge of the rates of forest loss and degradation in Melanesia and many of these species may prove to be threatened: Dwarf Cassowary, Collared Petrel, Tahiti Petrel, White-bellied Goshawk, Woodford's Rail, Pink-legged Rail, Roviana Rail, Beach Stone-curlew, Pied Cuckoo-Dove, Crested Cuckoo-Dove, Nicobar Pigeon, White-headed Fruit Dove, Cloven-feathered Dove, Red-knobbed Imperial Pigeon, Finsch's Imperial Pigeon, Goliath Imperial Pigeon, Yellowish Imperial Pigeon, Bismarck Hanging Parrot, White-naped Lory, Meek's Lorikeet, Duchess Lorikeet, Violaceous Coucal, White-mantled Kingfisher, Vanuatu Kingfisher, New Britain Honeyeater, Red-vested Myzomela, New Caledonian Cuckooshrike, Solomons Cuckooshrike, Cockerell's Fantail, Makira Fantail, Mussau Fantail, Vanikoro Monarch, Manus Monarch, Mussau Monarch, Solomons Monarch, Kolombangara Monarch, Makira Flycatcher, Bougainville Bush Warbler, Guadalcanal Thicketbird, Bougainville Thicketbird, Vella Lavella White-eye, Sanford's White-eye, Atoll Starling, Rusty-winged Starling, New Britain Thrush and Makira Thrush. Finally, Mayr's Swiftlet is listed as Data Deficient which means that it may be threatened but there is insufficient information to know either way.

EXTINCT SPECIES

Three endemic species are generally accepted to have become extinct since being collected by western explorers in the late 1800s or early 1900s: Choiseul Pigeon, Thick-billed Ground Dove and Tanna Ground Dove. These lived on the ground and were probably exterminated by cats or dogs. Other species such as New Caledonian Rail, New Caledonian Lorikeet, New Caledonian Nightjar and New Caledonian Owlet-nightjar are likely to have become extinct, but there is some hope that they survive and they are still formally listed as threatened. However, many other species appear to have become extinct before they were documented by western people. These species are known from subfossil remains and were probably exterminated by Melanesian and Polynesian people or by the rats, dogs and pigs which they brought with them. Few suitable sites have been investigated for subfossil remains and it is likely that many more species have disappeared, as in Polynesia where thousands of species are estimated to have become extinct. On New Ireland, subfossils have been found of at least eight undescribed, probably endemic, birds including a hawk, cockatoo and two owls. On New Caledonia, subfossils from extinct endemic birds include hawks, pigeons, an owl, an additional species of Kagu and a giant 30 kg megapode. Some species have been extirpated from some islands but survive on others. For instance, Santa Cruz Ground Dove has not been seen in recent years in Temotu (Santa Cruz) but it survives on Santo in Vanuatu, and Island Thrush has become extirpated from Grande Terre and Lifou in New Caledonia. It is hoped that an increased understanding and interest in Melanesian birds will encourage activities to ensure that no more species become extinct.

USING THE PLATES AND SPECIES TEXTS

This book aims to enable the accurate identification of any bird seen in Melanesia. Users are encouraged to identify the type of bird and to use the contents listing to see which plates to check. Then look at all of the relevant illustrations. Check the illustration, short text and distribution of the closest species. Turn to the main text for a full description of the bird, the likely confusion species, and its exact geographical, altitudinal and habitat range. The key features of each subspecies are given at the end of the species text, with subspecies listed in geographical order from west to east and comparisons are made with the preceding subspecies.

Not all subspecies and plumages are illustrated. If the bird differs from the closest illustration, check the full text for a description of other plumages and subspecies. Note that birds moulting between plumages may have intermediate, often scruffy or patchy, plumage. The subspecies is indicated for each illustration where multiple subspecies occur across Melanesia.

Each distinct song or call is described, and any obvious territorial song is described first. Songs and calls sometimes vary between islands or between individuals and an individual may show great variation itself. All descriptions of breeding species are from Melanesian birds unless noted otherwise. Songs and calls are described in words where possible and often transliterated into a similar-sounding English phrase given in *italics*. Particularly loud or stressed syllables are given in CAPITALS. Syllables given without pause are written without gaps e.g. *cheechee*, a short pause is indicated by a dash e.g. *chee-chee*, a longer pause by a long dash or em-rule e.g. *chee—chee*, a longer gap between notes by a comma e.g. *chee, chee*, a long gap by a series of dots e.g. *chee… chee*, and an ongoing series by a final hanging dash or series of dots e.g. *chee-chee-* or *chee, chee…*

All species texts are ordered taxonomically. The non-passerine plates are ordered taxonomically, except for a few species that have been moved to appear next to unrelated but easily confused species. **The passerine plates, however, are divided into groups of plates for each of the main island groups: Bismarcks, Solomons, Makira, Rennell, Temotu, Vanuatu and New Caledonia**. These groupings reflect broad biogeographical divisions, rather political boundaries. Thus, the Solomons includes Bougainville (administered by Papua New Guinea), whilst the outlying islands of Makira, Rennell and Temotu (all belonging to the Solomons) have separate passerine plate sections due to their distinct avifaunas. These plate groupings are colour-coded in their headers for ease of use. This arrangement has inevitably resulted in a few images being repeated on two or more plates, although in many cases the forms on different island groups are represented by separate subspecies.

With such a large region of widely separated islands, the inclusion of species distribution maps is not particularly helpful. Instead, we have provided a distribution bar for all species except extreme vagrants. For this purpose, the region has been divided into 14 territories as detailed below, representing the seven main biogeographic island groups (and belonging to four different nations). A full listing of these island groups and their principal component islands is given on page 37. Species' occurrence in these areas is indicated by colour shading (see below). For species with very limited ranges (for example, those that occur only on one or two small islands within a group), more specific information is given in the caption text.

Papua New Guinea					Solomon Islands						Vanuatu	New Caledonia	
Mn	Mu	NI	NB	Bv	Gu	MI	NG	Mk	RI	Te	VU	Lo	GT
Bismarcks				Solomons				Makira	Rennell	Temotu	Vanuatu	New Caledonia	

Status codes

Distribution bars are colour-coded with a species' status as follows:

LILAC	e	endemic to Melanesia (the region covered by the book)
GREEN	r	resident (but some seabirds may be considered 'resident' at sea without breeding)
YELLOW	m	migrant or non-breeding visitor, usually regular in small or large numbers
BLUE	v	vagrant or rare non-breeding visitor, rarely and unpredictably recorded; but more observations may indicate that many of these species are actually regular migrants
ORANGE	i	introduced
GREY	x	extinct or extirpated in historic times within Melanesia
HATCHED	?	uncertain status (colour-coded as appropriate)

ISLAND GROUPS OF MELANESIA

The 14 island groups as used in the distribution bars and in the Checklist are listed below. Many islands have changed their names since independence and many have alternative spellings for their names. In this book, names of islands (and the English names of birds named after islands) have been updated to follow current local usage, with some older names listed in brackets after the current name.

- **Mn** **Admiralty Is** or **Manus group** Wuvulu, Ninigo, Hermit, Kaniet, Manus, Baluan, Lou, Los Negros, Pak, Tong, Rambutyo and Nauna (see map on pp 12–13).
- **Mu** **St Matthias Is** Mussau, Emirau and Tench (see map on pp 12–13).
- **NI** **New Ireland group** Tingwon, Lavongai (New Hanover), New Ireland, Djaul (Dyaul), Tabar, Lihir, Tanga, Feni and Nissan (see map on pp 12–13).
- **NB** **New Britain group** Crown, Long, Tolokiwa, Umboi, Sakar, New Britain, Unea, Witu, Lolobau, Watom and Duke of York (see map on pp 12–13).
- **Bv** **Bougainville** including Buka and Shortland Is, Choiseul and (Santa) Isabel (see map on pp 14–15).
- **Gu** **Guadalcanal** including Russell Is, Savo and Florida Is (see map on pp 14–15).
- **Ml** **Malaita** and Ulawa (see map on pp 14–15).
- **NG** **New Georgia group** Vella Lavella, Bagga, Ranongga, Simbo, Gizo, Kolombangara, New Georgia, Vonavona, Kohinggo, Rendova, Tetepare, Vangunu and Nggatokae (see map on pp 14–15).
- **Mk** **Makira (San Cristobal) group** Makira, Ugi, Three Sisters, Santa Ana and Santa Catalina (see map on pp 14–15).
- **Rl** **Rennell** and Bellona (see map on pp 14–15).
- **Te** **Temotu** Tinakula, Nendo (Santa Cruz), Reef Is, Duff Is, Utupua, Vanikoro, Tikopia and Anuta (see map on p 14).
- **Vu** **Vanuatu** (formerly New Hebrides) All islands within the political state of Vanuatu from the Torres Is and Banks Is in the north through (Espiritu) Santo and Efate to Aneityum in the south (see map on p 18).
- **Lo** **Loyalty Is** (or Îles Loyauté) Ouvéa (Uvea), Lifou (Lifu) and Maré (see map on pp 16–17).
- **GT** **Grande Terre (New Caledonia** or Nouvelle Calédonie) Grande Terre (mainland), Île des Pins (Isle of Pines) and offshore atolls and reefs (Chesterfield, Surprise, Hunter, Matthew, Walpole) (see map on pp 16–17).

Note 1: **The Bismarcks** are usually defined to include the Admiralty, St Matthias, New Ireland and New Britain island groups. For clarity, the text distributions specifically note whether a bird occurs in the Admiralty and St Matthias groups as well as the core Bismarcks of the New Ireland and New Britain island groups.

Note 2: **Bougainville** (and Buka) is a semi-autonomous region of Papua New Guinea but biogeographically part of the Solomons archipelago.

Note 3: **Gazetteer** A full list of all the islands mentioned in this book is presented in the Gazetteer on pp 427–431, giving old and alternative names, and the various archipelagos and nations that they belong to.

CHECKLIST OF THE BIRDS OF MELANESIA

This list tabulates the status of all birds recorded in each of the main island groups to 2010, incorporating all published and specimen records, and some unpublished records by the author or supplied to the author. Some records have been omitted if they seem unlikely and lack substantiating details. The list excludes unconfirmed species, but these are described in the main text in brackets. Taxonomy and nomenclature largely follow that of the IOC (International Ornithological Congress) – see page 20. The table uses the same island groups as those used in the distribution bars opposite the plates (see page 37), with the addition of a column for the species' conservation status.

Globally Threatened Species (GTS) Species considered to be globally threatened by BirdLife International are assigned one of the following codes, based on IUCN Red List criteria:

EX (Extinct), **CR** (Critically Endangered), **EN** (Endangered), **VU** (Vulnerable), **NT** (Near Threatened) or **DD** (Data Deficient)

		GTS	✔	Manus	Mussau	New Ireland	New Britain	Bougainville	Guadalcanal	Malaita	New Georgia	Makira	Rennell	Temotu	Vanuatu	Loyalties	Grande Terre
Dwarf Cassowary	*Casuarius bennetti*	NT					r										
Melanesian Megapode	*Megapodius eremita*			e	e	e	e	e	e	e	e	e					
Vanuatu Megapode	*Megapodius layardi*	VU													e		
Wild Turkey	*Meleagris gallopavo*																i
King Quail	*Excalfactoria chinensis*					r	r										
Red Junglefowl	*Gallus gallus*			i										i	i		i
Common Pheasant	*Phasianus colchicus*																i
Indian Peafowl	*Pavo cristatus*																i
Spotted Whistling Duck	*Dendrocygna guttata*					v	r	v									
Plumed Whistling Duck	*Dendrocygna eytoni*											v	v				v
Wandering Whistling Duck	*Dendrocygna arcuata*						r										v
Mallard	*Anas platyrhynchos*														i		i
Pacific Black Duck	*Anas superciliosa*			r	r	r	r	r	r	r	r	r	x	r	r	r	r
Australasian Shoveler	*Anas rhynchotis*																v
Northern Shoveler	*Anas clypeata*						v										
Grey Teal	*Anas gracilis*						v						x		r		r
Northern Pintail	*Anas acuta*						v	v									
Garganey	*Anas querquedula*					v	v										
Hardhead	*Aythya australis*														r		r
Tufted Duck	*Aythya fuligula*						v										
Laysan Albatross	*Phoebastria immutabilis*	NT		v								v					
Wandering Albatross	*Diomedea exulans*	VU															v
Northern Royal Albatross	*Diomedea sanfordi*	EN															v
Light-mantled Albatross	*Phoebetria palpebrata*	NT														v	
Campbell Albatross	*Thalassarche impavida*	VU													v		v?
Buller's Albatross	*Thalassarche bulleri*	NT															v
Southern Giant Petrel	*Macronectes giganteus*														v		v
Northern Giant Petrel	*Macronectes halli*																v

		GTS	✔	Manus	Mussau	New Ireland	New Britain	Bougainville	Guadalcanal	Malaita	New Georgia	Makira	Rennell	Temotu	Vanuatu	Loyalties	Grande Terre
Cape Petrel	*Daption capense*														v	v	v
Antarctic Prion	*Pachyptila desolata*														v		
Providence Petrel	*Pterodroma solandri*	VU						v									v
Kermadec Petrel	*Pterodroma neglecta*						v										v
Herald Petrel	*Pterodroma heraldica*								v								r
Mottled Petrel	*Pterodroma inexpectata*	NT															v
Vanuatu Petrel	*Pterodroma occulta*	EN?										m?		m?	e	m?	m?
Black-winged Petrel	*Pterodroma nigripennis*																r
Gould's Petrel	*Pterodroma leucoptera*	VU					v					v			v	m	r
Collared Petrel	*Pterodroma brevipes*	NT							v			v		m	r	v	m
Cook's Petrel	*Pterodroma cookii*	VU													v		v
Tahiti Petrel	*Pseudobulweria rostrata*	NT			m	m	m	m	m			m	m	m	r	r	r
Beck's Petrel	*Pseudobulweria becki*	CR				e	e	e			v			v	v		
Grey Petrel	*Procellaria cinerea*	NT															v
Streaked Shearwater	*Calonectris leucomelas*			m	m	m	m	m	v								v
Christmas Shearwater	*Puffinus nativitatis*				v	v											
Wedge-tailed Shearwater	*Puffinus pacificus*			m	m	m	m	m	m	m	m	m	m	m	r	r	r
Buller's Shearwater	*Puffinus bulleri*															v	v
Fluttering Shearwater	*Puffinus gavia*														v		v
Tropical Shearwater	*Puffinus bailloni*					v	v	v	v		v		v	m	r		v
Heinroth's Shearwater	*Puffinus heinrothi*	VU		v		e	e	e	v	v	e						
Sooty Shearwater	*Puffinus griseus*	NT					v										v
Short-tailed Shearwater	*Puffinus tenuirostris*					v	v		v		v		v	v	v	m	m
Flesh-footed Shearwater	*Puffinus carneipes*					v	v					v		v	v		v
Bulwer's Petrel	*Bulweria bulwerii*			v	v	v			v					v			
Wilson's Storm Petrel	*Oceanites oceanicus*					v	v	v	v				v	v	v		v
White-faced Storm Petrel	*Pelagodroma marina*															v	v
Black-bellied Storm Petrel	*Fregetta tropica*								v			v		v		v	v
Polynesian Storm Petrel	*Nesofregetta fuliginosa*	EN													r	v	r
Leach's Storm Petrel	*Oceanodroma leucorhoa*				v										v		
Matsudaira's Storm Petrel	*Oceanodroma matsudairae*			v	v	v	v	v									
Little Grebe	*Tachybaptus ruficollis*					r	r?	r									
Australasian Grebe	*Tachybaptus novaehollandiae*			v			r?		r				r		r		r
Red-tailed Tropicbird	*Phaethon rubricauda*					v	v	v							r	m	r
White-tailed Tropicbird	*Phaethon lepturus*				r	r	m	r	m		m	m	m	r	r	m	r
Australian White Ibis	*Threskiornis molucca*							v					r				
Straw-necked Ibis	*Threskiornis spinicollis*					v											
Glossy Ibis	*Plegadis falcinellus*			v				v			v						v
Royal Spoonbill	*Platalea regia*												v				v

		GTS	✔	Manus	Mussau	New Ireland	New Britain	Bougainville	Guadalcanal	Malaita	New Georgia	Makira	Rennell	Temotu	Vanuatu	Loyalties	Grande Terre
Australasian Bittern	*Botaurus poiciloptilus*	EN														r?	r?
Black-backed Bittern	*Ixobrychus dubius*	NT?															r
Yellow Bittern	*Ixobrychus sinensis*			v			v	r									
Black Bittern	*Dupetor flavicollis*			r	r	r	r	r	r	r	r		r				
Nankeen Night Heron	*Nycticorax caledonicus*			r		r	r	r	r	r	r	r			v		r
Striated Heron	*Butorides striata*			v	v	r	v	r	r	r	r	r		r	r	v	v
Eastern Cattle Egret	*Bubulcus coromandus*			v		v	v		v							v	v
Eastern Great Egret	*Ardea modesta*			v			r	m	m		m		m		v	v	m
Intermediate Egret	*Egretta intermedia*			v			v	v				v					
Pied Heron	*Egretta picata*																v
White-faced Heron	*Egretta novaehollandiae*							v	v					v	v	v	r
Little Egret	*Egretta garzetta*						v	v			v						
Pacific Reef Heron	*Egretta sacra*			r	r	r	r	r	r	r	r	r	r	r	r	r	r
Great Frigatebird	*Fregata minor*			r	r	r	r	r	r	r	r	r	r	r	r	r	r
Lesser Frigatebird	*Fregata ariel*			r	r	r	r	r	r	r	r	r	r	r	r	r	r
Australian Pelican	*Pelecanus conspicillatus*					v	v	v	v	v	v	v	v	v	v		v
Australasian Gannet	*Morus serrator*																v
Masked Booby	*Sula dactylatra*			v		v	v	v	v		v		v	v	v	v	r
Red-footed Booby	*Sula sula*			r	r	r	r	r	r	r	r	r	r	r	r	r	r
Brown Booby	*Sula leucogaster*			r	r	r	r	r	r	r	r	r	r	r	r	r	r
Little Pied Cormorant	*Microcarbo melanoleucos*						r	r	r		m	r	r	r	m		r
Little Black Cormorant	*Phalacrocorax sulcirostris*			v			v	v									r
Great Cormorant	*Phalacrocorax carbo*										v		r				r
Australasian Darter	*Anhinga novaehollandiae*						v										
Eastern Osprey	*Pandion cristatus*			r	r	r	r	r	r	r	r	r	r				r
Pacific Baza	*Aviceda subcristata*			r		r	r	r	r	r	r	r					
Black Honey Buzzard	*Henicopernis infuscatus*	VU					e										
Black Kite	*Milvus migrans*						v										v
Whistling Kite	*Haliastur sphenurus*																r
Brahminy Kite	*Haliastur indus*			r	r	r	r	r	r	r	r	r					
White-bellied Sea Eagle	*Haliaeetus leucogaster*			r	r	r	r										
Solomons Sea Eagle	*Haliaeetus sanfordi*	VU						e	e	e	e	e					
Swamp Harrier	*Circus approximans*								v			v			r	r	r
Variable Goshawk	*Accipiter hiogaster*			r	r	r	r	r	r	r	r						
Brown Goshawk	*Accipiter fasciatus*												r		r	r	r
Pied Goshawk	*Accipiter albogularis*					e		e	e	e	e	e		e			
White-bellied Goshawk	*Accipiter haplochrous*	NT															e
Slaty-mantled Goshawk	*Accipiter luteoschistaceus*	VU					e										
Imitator Goshawk	*Accipiter imitator*	VU						e									

		GTS	✔	Manus	Mussau	New Ireland	New Britain	Bougainville	Guadalcanal	Malaita	New Georgia	Makira	Rennell	Temotu	Vanuatu	Loyalties	Grande Terre
New Britain Goshawk	*Accipiter princeps*	VU					e										
New Britain Sparrowhawk	*Accipiter brachyurus*	VU				e	e										
Meyer's Goshawk	*Accipiter meyerianus*			r		r	r		r		r						
Nankeen Kestrel	*Falco cenchroides*															v	v
Oriental Hobby	*Falco severus*			r	r	r	r	r	r	r	r	r					
Australian Hobby	*Falco longipennis*						v										v?
Brown Falcon	*Falco berigora*						Long										
Peregrine Falcon	*Falco peregrinus*					r	r	r	r		r	r			r	r	r
Kagu	*Rhynochetos jubatus*	EN															e
Red-necked Crake	*Rallina tricolor*				r	r											
Woodford's Rail	*Nesoclopeus woodfordi*	NT						e	e	e?							
New Caledonian Rail	*Gallirallus lafresnayanus*	CR															ex
Pink-legged Rail	*Gallirallus insignis*	NT					e										
Buff-banded Rail	*Gallirallus philippensis*			r		r	r		r	r	r	r		r	r	r	r
Roviana Rail	*Gallirallus rovianae*	NT									e						
Bare-eyed Rail	*Gymnocrex plumbeiventris*					v?											
Pale-vented Bush-hen	*Amaurornis moluccana*					r	r	r	r	r	r	r					
Baillon's Crake	*Porzana pusilla*																v
Spotless Crake	*Porzana tabuensis*								r		r	r	r	r	r	r	r
White-browed Crake	*Porzana cinerea*				r	r	r	r	r			r		r	r	r	r
Purple Swamphen	*Porphyrio porphyrio*			r		r	r	r	r	r	r	r	r	r	r	r	r
Makira Woodhen	*Gallinula silvestris*	CR										e					
Dusky Moorhen	*Gallinula tenebrosa*						r		v								r
Red-backed Buttonquail	*Turnix maculosus*						r		r								
Painted Buttonquail	*Turnix varius*																x
Beach Stone-curlew	*Esacus magnirostris*	NT		r	r	r	r	r	r	r	r	r		r	r	r	r
South Island Oystercatcher	*Haematopus finschi*														v		v
White-headed Stilt	*Himantopus leucocephalus*						r							v			
Masked Lapwing	*Vanellus miles*										v				v		r
Pacific Golden Plover	*Pluvialis fulva*			m	m	m	m	m	m	m	m	m	m	m	m	m	m
Grey Plover	*Pluvialis squatarola*			m		m	m	m	m					m	m		m
Common Ringed Plover	*Charadrius hiaticula*					v											
Semipalmated Plover	*Charadrius semipalmatus*																v
Little Ringed Plover	*Charadrius dubius*					r	r										
Double-banded Plover	*Charadrius bicinctus*														v		m
Lesser Sand Plover	*Charadrius mongolus*			m	m	m	m	m				m		m	m		v
Greater Sand Plover	*Charadrius leschenaultii*					m	m	m					v	m	m		v
Oriental Plover	*Charadrius veredus*					v		v			v		v				v
Comb-crested Jacana	*Irediparra gallinacea*						r										

		GTS	✔	Manus	Mussau	New Ireland	New Britain	Bougainville	Guadalcanal	Malaita	New Georgia	Makira	Rennell	Temotu	Vanuatu	Loyalties	Grande Terre
Swinhoe's Snipe	*Gallinago megala*			m	m	m	m	m	m								
Asian Dowitcher	*Limnodromus semipalmatus*	NT						v									
Black-tailed Godwit	*Limosa limosa*	NT					v	m							v		v
Bar-tailed Godwit	*Limosa lapponica*			m	m	m	m	m	m		m	m	m	m	m	m	m
Little Curlew	*Numenius minutus*			v			v	v	v								v
Whimbrel	*Numenius phaeopus*			m	m	m	m	m	m	m	m	m	m	m	m		m
Bristle-thighed Curlew	*Numenius tahitiensis*	VU		v						v		v		v			
Eastern Curlew	*Numenius madagascariensis*	VU		v		v	v	v							v		v
Marsh Sandpiper	*Tringa stagnatilis*					v	v	v					v				v
Common Greenshank	*Tringa nebularia*						v	v									v
Wood Sandpiper	*Tringa glareola*						v	v									
Grey-tailed Tattler	*Tringa brevipes*			m	m	m	m	m	m	m	m	m		m	m		m
Wandering Tattler	*Tringa incana*			m	m	m	m	m	m		m	m	m	m	m	m	m
Terek Sandpiper	*Xenus cinereus*					v	v	v									v
Common Sandpiper	*Actitis hypoleucos*			m	m	m	m	m	m	m	m	m	m	m	m		v
Ruddy Turnstone	*Arenaria interpres*			m	m	m	m	m	m		m	m		m	m	m	m
Great Knot	*Calidris tenuirostris*	VU															v
Red Knot	*Calidris canutus*																v
Sanderling	*Calidris alba*						v	m			v			v			m
Red-necked Stint	*Calidris ruficollis*			m		m	m	m	m			m	m			v	m
Long-toed Stint	*Calidris subminuta*					v	v						v				
Pectoral Sandpiper	*Calidris melanotos*					v	v	v					v				
Sharp-tailed Sandpiper	*Calidris acuminata*			m	m	m	m	m	m		m	m	m	m	m		m
Curlew Sandpiper	*Calidris ferruginea*					v	v	v									v
Ruff	*Philomachus pugnax*			v		v	v	v									
Red-necked Phalarope	*Phalaropus lobatus*			v	v	v	v										
Australian Pratincole	*Stiltia isabella*					v	v	v									v
Oriental Pratincole	*Glareola maldivarum*					v	v	v									
Brown Noddy	*Anous stolidus*			r	r	r	r	r	r	r	r	r	r	r	r	r	r
Black Noddy	*Anous minutus*			r	r	r	r	r	r	r	r	r	r	r	r	r	r
Grey Noddy	*Procelsterna albivitta*														v		r
White Tern	*Gygis alba*			r	r	r	m	r	m				m	r	v		r
Silver Gull	*Chroicocephalus novaehollandiae*														v	v	r
Black-headed Gull	*Chroicocephalus ribibundus*							v									
Black-tailed Gull	*Larus crassirostris*							v									
Great Crested Tern	*Thalasseus bergii*			r	r	r	r	r	r	r	r	r	r	r	r	r	r
Lesser Crested Tern	*Thalasseus bengalensis*			v?				v									
Little Tern	*Sternula albifrons*			m	m	m	r	r			m				m		m
Fairy Tern	*Sternula nereis*	VU															r

		GTS	✔	Manus	Mussau	New Ireland	New Britain	Bougainville	Guadalcanal	Malaita	New Georgia	Makira	Rennell	Temotu	Vanuatu	Loyalties	Grande Terre
Spectacled Tern	*Onychoprion lunatus*			v	v	v	v	v	v		v			v?			
Bridled Tern	*Onychoprion anaethetus*			r	r	r	r	r	r	r	r	r	r	r	r	r	r
Sooty Tern	*Onychoprion fuscatus*			r		r	r	r	r		r	r	r	r	r	r	r
Roseate Tern	*Sterna dougallii*						r	r	r		r		r			v	r
Black-naped Tern	*Sterna sumatrana*			r	r	r	r	r	r	r	r	r	r	r	r	r	r
Common Tern	*Sterna hirundo*			m	m	m	m	m	m	m	m	m		m			
Whiskered Tern	*Chlidonias hybrida*						m	m									v
White-winged Tern	*Chlidonias leucopterus*						m	m					v				v
South Polar Skua	*Stercorarius maccormicki*								v							v	v
Brown Skua	*Stercorarius antarcticus*															v	
Pomarine Skua	*Stercorarius pomarinus*			m	m	m	m	m	m		m			m	m	m	m
Arctic Skua	*Stercorarius parasiticus*					m	m	m	m				m	m	m	m	m
Long-tailed Skua	*Stercorarius longicaudus*			m		m	m	m	m			m				v	
Rock Dove	*Columba livia*			i											i		i
Metallic Pigeon	*Columba vitiensis*					r	r	r	r	r	r	r			r	r	r
Yellow-legged Pigeon	*Columba pallidiceps*	VU				e	e	e	e		e	e					
Spotted Dove	*Spilopelia chinensis*																i
Slender-billed Cuckoo-Dove	*Macropygia amboinensis*			r	r	r	r										
Bar-tailed Cuckoo-Dove	*Macropygia nigrirostris*					r	r										
Mackinlay's Cuckoo-Dove	*Macropygia mackinlayi*			e	e	e	e	e	e	e	e	e	e	e	e		
Pied Cuckoo-Dove	*Reinwardtoena browni*	NT		e		e	e										
Crested Cuckoo-Dove	*Reinwardtoena crassirostris*	NT						e	e	e	e	e					
Pacific Emerald Dove	*Chalcophaps longirostris*													r	r	r	r
Stephan's Emerald Dove	*Chalcophaps stephani*			r	r	r	r	r	r	r	r	r					
New Britain Bronzewing	*Henicophaps foersteri*	VU					e										
Zebra Dove	*Geopelia striata*																i
Nicobar Pigeon	*Caloenas nicobarica*	NT		r	r	r	r	r	r	r	r	r					
White-breasted Ground Dove	*Gallicolumba jobiensis*			r		r	r		r		r	r					
Santa Cruz Ground Dove	*Gallicolumba sanctaecrucis*	EN												e	e		
Tanna Ground Dove	*Gallicolumba ferruginea*	EX													ex		
Thick-billed Ground Dove	*Gallicolumba salamonis*	EX										ex					
Bronze Ground Dove	*Gallicolumba beccarii*			r	r	r	r	r	r		r	r	r				
Choiseul Pigeon	*Microgoura meeki*	EX						ex									
Tanna Fruit Dove	*Ptilinopus tannensis*														e		
Superb Fruit Dove	*Ptilinopus superbus*			r	r	r	r	r	r	r	r						
Silver-capped Fruit Dove	*Ptilinopus richardsii*											e	e				
Red-bellied Fruit Dove	*Ptilinopus greyii*													e	e	e	e
White-bibbed Fruit Dove	*Ptilinopus rivoli*					r	r										
Yellow-bibbed Fruit Dove	*Ptilinopus solomonensis*			r	r	r	r	r	r	r	r	r					

		GTS	✔	Manus	Mussau	New Ireland	New Britain	Bougainville	Guadalcanal	Malaita	New Georgia	Makira	Rennell	Temotu	Vanuatu	Loyalties	Grande Terre
Claret-breasted Fruit Dove	*Ptilinopus viridis*			r		r		r	r	r	r						
White-headed Fruit Dove	*Ptilinopus eugeniae*	NT										e					
Knob-billed Fruit Dove	*Ptilinopus insolitus*				e	e	e										
Cloven-feathered Dove	*Drepanoptila holosericea*	NT															e
Pacific Imperial Pigeon	*Ducula pacifica*			r	r								r	r	r	r	v
Red-knobbed Imperial Pigeon	*Ducula rubricera*	NT				e	e	e	e	e	e	e					
Finsch's Imperial Pigeon	*Ducula finschii*	NT				e	e										
Island Imperial Pigeon	*Ducula pistrinaria*			r	r	r	r	r	r	r	r	r					
Chestnut-bellied Imperial Pigeon	*Ducula brenchleyi*	VU							e	e		e					
Vanuatu Imperial Pigeon	*Ducula bakeri*	VU													e		
Goliath Imperial Pigeon	*Ducula goliath*	NT															e
Black Imperial Pigeon	*Ducula melanochroa*					e	e										
Torresian Imperial Pigeon	*Ducula spilorrhoa*						v										
Yellowish Imperial Pigeon	*Ducula subflavescens*	NT		e		e	e										
Papuan Mountain Pigeon	*Gymnophaps albertisii*					r	r										
Pale Mountain Pigeon	*Gymnophaps solomonensis*							e	e	e	e						
Solomons Cockatoo	*Cacatua ducorpsii*							e	e	e	e						
Blue-eyed Cockatoo	*Cacatua ophthalmica*	VU					e										
Bismarck Hanging Parrot	*Loriculus tener*	NT				e	e										
Buff-faced Pygmy Parrot	*Micropsitta pusio*						r										
Meek's Pygmy Parrot	*Micropsitta meeki*			e	e												
Finsch's Pygmy Parrot	*Micropsitta finschii*					e		e	e	e	e	e	e				
Red-breasted Pygmy Parrot	*Micropsitta bruijnii*					r	r	r	r		r						
Cardinal Lory	*Chalcopsitta cardinalis*					e		e	e	e	e	e					
Coconut Lorikeet	*Trichoglossus haematodus*			r	r	r	r	r	r	r	r	r		r	r	i	r
Purple-bellied Lory	*Lorius hypoinochrous*					r	r										
White-naped Lory	*Lorius albidinucha*	NT				e											
Yellow-bibbed Lory	*Lorius chlorocercus*								e	e		e	e				
Palm Lorikeet	*Charmosyna palmarum*	VU												e	e		
Red-chinned Lorikeet	*Charmosyna rubrigularis*					e	e										
Meek's Lorikeet	*Charmosyna meeki*	NT						e	e	e	e						
Red-flanked Lorikeet	*Charmosyna placentis*					r	r	r									
New Caledonian Lorikeet	*Charmosyna diadema*	CR															ex
Duchess Lorikeet	*Charmosyna margarethae*	NT						e	e	e	e	e					
Horned Parakeet	*Eunymphicus cornutus*	VU															e
Ouvéa Parakeet	*Eunymphicus uvaeensis*	EN														e	
New Caledonian Parakeet	*Cyanoramphus saisseti*	VU															e
Song Parrot	*Geoffroyus heteroclitus*					e	e	e	e	e	e	e	e				
Eclectus Parrot	*Eclectus roratus*			r		r	r	r	r	r	r	r					

		GTS	✔	Manus	Mussau	New Ireland	New Britain	Bougainville	Guadalcanal	Malaita	New Georgia	Makira	Rennell	Temotu	Vanuatu	Loyalties	Grande Terre
Buff-headed Coucal	*Centropus milo*								e		e						
White-necked Coucal	*Centropus ateralbus*					e	e										
Violaceous Coucal	*Centropus violaceus*	NT				e	e										
Pacific Koel	*Eudynamys orientalis*					r	r	r	r	r	r	r					
Long-tailed Cuckoo	*Urodynamis taitensis*			m			m	m	m	m	m	m		m	m		v
Channel-billed Cuckoo	*Scythrops novaehollandiae*			v	v	r	r				v		v				v
Shining Bronze Cuckoo	*Chrysococcyx lucidus*			m	m	m	m	m	m	m	m	v	r	v	r	r	r
Fan-tailed Cuckoo	*Cacomantis flabelliformis*							v?	v?		v?		v?		r	r	r
Brush Cuckoo	*Cacomantis variolosus*			r		r	r	r	r	r	r	r					
Oriental Cuckoo	*Cuculus optatus*			v			v	v	v	v	v	v					
Manus Masked Owl	*Tyto manusi*	VU		e													
Golden Masked Owl	*Tyto aurantia*	VU					e										
Eastern Barn Owl	*Tyto javanica*					r?	r?	r	r	r	r	r	r	r	r	r	r
Eastern Grass Owl	*Tyto longimembris*																v
Manus Boobook	*Ninox meeki*			e													
New Ireland Boobook	*Ninox variegata*					e											
New Britain Boobook	*Ninox odiosa*	VU					e										
West Solomons Boobook	*Ninox jacquinoti*							e									
Guadalcanal Boobook	*Ninox granti*								e								
Malaita Boobook	*Ninox malaitae*	VU?								e							
Makira Boobook	*Ninox roseoaxillaris*	VU?										e					
Fearful Owl	*Nesasio solomonensis*	VU						e									
Solomons Frogmouth	*Rigidipenna inexpectata*	NT?						e									
Solomons Nightjar	*Eurostopodus nigripennis*	EN?						e			e						
New Caledonian Nightjar	*Eurostopodus exul*	EX															ex
Large-tailed Nightjar	*Caprimulgus macrurus*					r	r										
New Caledonian Owlet-nightjar	*Aegotheles savesi*	CR															ex
Moustached Treeswift	*Hemiprocne mystacea*			r	r	r	r	r	r	r	r	r	r				
Glossy Swiftlet	*Collocalia esculenta*			r		r	r	r	r	r	r	r	r	r	r	r	r
White-rumped Swiftlet	*Aerodramus spodiopygius*			r	r	r	r	r	r	r	r	r	r	r	r	r	r
Mayr's Swiftlet	*Aerodramus orientalis*	DD				e		e	e								
Uniform Swiftlet	*Aerodramus vanikorensis*			r	r	r	r	r	r	r	r	r	r	r	r		
White-throated Needletail	*Hirundapus caudacutus*					v	v										v
Fork-tailed Swift	*Apus pacificus*										v						
Dollarbird	*Eurystomus orientalis*			r	v	r	r	r	r	r	r	r					
Moustached Kingfisher	*Actenoides bougainvillea*	VU						e	e								
Black-capped Paradise Kingfisher	*Tanysiptera nigriceps*						e										
Forest Kingfisher	*Todiramphus macleayii*					v	v				v						
White-mantled Kingfisher	*Todiramphus albonotatus*	NT					e										

		GTS	✔	Manus	Mussau	New Ireland	New Britain	Bougainville	Guadalcanal	Malaita	New Georgia	Makira	Rennell	Temotu	Vanuatu	Loyalties	Grande Terre
Ultramarine Kingfisher	*Todiramphus leucopygius*							e	e								
Vanuatu Kingfisher	*Todiramphus farquhari*	NT													e		
Collared Kingfisher	*Todiramphus chloris*				r	r	r	r	r	r	r	r	r	r	r		
Beach Kingfisher	*Todiramphus saurophagus*			r	r	r	r	r	r	r	r	r					
Sacred Kingfisher	*Todiramphus sanctus*			m	m	m	m	m	m	m	m	m				r	r
Variable Dwarf Kingfisher	*Ceyx lepidus*			r		r	r	r	r	r	r	r					
Bismarck Kingfisher	*Alcedo websteri*	VU				e	e										
Little Kingfisher	*Ceyx pusillus*					r	r	r	r	r	r						
Common Kingfisher	*Alcedo atthis*			r	r	r	r	r	r	r	r	r					
Blue-tailed Bee-eater	*Merops philippinus*						r										
Rainbow Bee-eater	*Merops ornatus*			m	m	m	m										
Blyth's Hornbill	*Aceros plicatus*					r	r	r	r	r	r						
Red-bellied Pitta	*Pitta erythrogaster*					r	r										
Hooded Pitta	*Pitta sordida*						Long etc										
Superb Pitta	*Pitta superba*	VU		e													
Black-faced Pitta	*Pitta anerythra*	VU						e									
Guadalcanal Honeyeater	*Guadalcanaria inexpectata*								e								
Crow Honeyeater	*Gymnomyza aubryana*	CR															e
New Britain Friarbird	*Philemon cockerelli*						e										
New Ireland Friarbird	*Philemon eichhorni*					e											
Manus Friarbird	*Philemon albitorques*			e													
New Caledonian Friarbird	*Philemon diemenensis*															e	e
New Britain Honeyeater	*Melidectes whitemanensis*	NT					e										
Makira Honeyeater	*Meliarchus sclateri*											e					
Bougainville Honeyeater	*Stresemannia bougainvillei*							e									
Barred Honeyeater	*Glycifohia undulata*																e
Vanuatu Honeyeater	*Glycifohia notabilis*														e		
Grey-eared Honeyeater	*Lichmera incana*														e	e	e
Ashy Myzomela	*Myzomela cineracea*						e										
Red Myzomela	*Myzomela cruentata*					r	r										
New Ireland Myzomela	*Myzomela pulchella*					e											
New Caledonian Myzomela	*Myzomela caledonica*																e
Cardinal Myzomela	*Myzomela cardinalis*											r	r	r	r	r	
Sclater's Myzomela	*Myzomela sclateri*						e										
Bismarck Black Myzomela	*Myzomela pammelaena*			e	e	e	e										
Red-capped Myzomela	*Myzomela lafargei*							e									
Crimson-rumped Myzomela	*Myzomela eichhorni*										e						
Red-vested Myzomela	*Myzomela malaitae*	NT								e							
Black-headed Myzomela	*Myzomela melanocephala*								e								

		GTS	✔	Manus	Mussau	New Ireland	New Britain	Bougainville	Guadalcanal	Malaita	New Georgia	Makira	Rennell	Temotu	Vanuatu	Loyalties	Grande Terre
Sooty Myzomela	*Myzomela tristrami*											e					
Black-bellied Myzomela	*Myzomela erythromelas*						e										
Fan-tailed Gerygone	*Gerygone flavolateralis*												e		e	e	e
White-breasted Woodswallow	*Artamus leucorynchus*														r	r	r
White-backed Woodswallow	*Artamus insignis*					e	e										
Dusky Woodswallow	*Artamus cyanopterus*																v
Black-faced Cuckooshrike	*Coracina novaehollandiae*					v	v	v			v		v				v
South Melanesian Cuckooshrike	*Coracina caledonica*														e	e	e
North Melanesian Cuckooshrike	*Coracina welchmani*							e	e		e						
Barred Cuckooshrike	*Coracina lineata*					r	r	r	r	r	r	r	r				
White-bellied Cuckooshrike	*Coracina papuensis*			r		r	r	r	r	r	r						
New Caledonian Cuckooshrike	*Coracina analis*	NT															e
Common Cicadabird	*Coracina tenuirostris*			r	r	r	r	r	r	r	r						
Makira Cicadabird	*Coracina salomonis*											e					
Solomons Cuckooshrike	*Coracina holopolia*	NT						e	e	e	e						
Varied Triller	*Lalage leucomela*					r	r										
Mussau Triller	*Lalage conjuncta*	VU?			e												
Polynesian Triller	*Lalage maculosa*													r	r		
Long-tailed Triller	*Lalage leucopyga*											e			e	e	e
Bismarck Whistler	*Pachycephala citreogaster*			r	r	r	r										
Oriole Whistler	*Pachycephala orioloides*							e	e	e	e	e					
Melanesian Whistler	*Pachycephala caledonica*													e	e	e	e
White-throated Whistler	*Pachycephala vitiensis*													r			
Mangrove Golden Whistler	*Pachycephala melanura*					r	r	r									
Rennell Whistler	*Pachycephala feminina*												e				
Guadalcanal Hooded Whistler	*Pachycephala implicata*								e								
Bougainville Hooded Whistler	*Pachycephala richardsi*							e									
Rufous Whistler	*Pachycephala rufiventris*																r
Olive-backed Oriole	*Oriolus sagittatus*						v										
Spangled Drongo	*Dicrurus bracteatus*						r		r			r					
Paradise Drongo	*Dicrurus megarhynchus*					e											
Willie Wagtail	*Rhipidura leucophrys*				r	r	r	r	r	r	r	r					
Northern Fantail	*Rhipidura rufiventris*			r	r	r	r										
Cockerell's Fantail	*Rhipidura cockerelli*	NT						e	e	e	e						
Grey Fantail	*Rhipidura albiscapa*											r			r		r
Brown Fantail	*Rhipidura drownei*							e	e								
Makira Fantail	*Rhipidura tenebrosa*	NT										e					
Rennell Fantail	*Rhipidura rennelliana*												e				
Streaked Fantail	*Rhipidura verreauxi*														r	r	r

		GTS	✔	Manus	Mussau	New Ireland	New Britain	Bougainville	Guadalcanal	Malaita	New Georgia	Makira	Rennell	Temotu	Vanuatu	Loyalties	Grande Terre
Bismarck Fantail	*Rhipidura dahli*					e	e										
Mussau Fantail	*Rhipidura matthiae*	NT			e												
Malaita Fantail	*Rhipidura malaitae*	VU								e							
Manus Fantail	*Rhipidura semirubra*	VU		e													
Rufous Fantail	*Rhipidura rufifrons*							r	r	r	r	r		r			
Vanikoro Monarch	*Mayrornis schistaceus*	NT												e			
Buff-bellied Monarch	*Neolalage banksiana*														e		
Southern Shrikebill	*Clytorhynchus pachycephaloides*														e		e
Santa Cruz Shrikebill	*Clytorhynchus sanctaecrucis*	EN												e			
Rennell Shrikebill	*Clytorhynchus hamlini*												e				
Manus Monarch	*Symposiachrus infelix*	NT		e													
Mussau Monarch	*Symposiachrus menckei*	NT			e												
Black-tailed Monarch	*Symposiachrus verticalis*					e	e										
Solomons Monarch	*Symposiachrus barbatus*	NT						e	e	e							
Kolombangara Monarch	*Symposiachrus browni*	NT									e						
White-collared Monarch	*Symposiachrus vidua*											e					
Island Monarch	*Monarcha cinerascens*			r	r	r	r	r									
Bougainville Monarch	*Monarcha erythrostictus*							e									
Chestnut-bellied Monarch	*Monarcha castaneiventris*							e	e	e		e					
White-capped Monarch	*Monarcha richardsii*										e						
Golden Monarch	*Carterornis chrysomela*					r	v										
Leaden Flycatcher	*Myiagra rubecula*					v	v										
Steel-blue Flycatcher	*Myiagra ferrocyanea*							e	e	e	e						
Makira Flycatcher	*Myiagra cervinicauda*	NT										e					
Melanesian Flycatcher	*Myiagra caledonica*												e		e	e	e
Vanikoro Flycatcher	*Myiagra vanikorensis*													r			
Satin Flycatcher	*Myiagra cyanoleuca*					v	v										
Shining Flycatcher	*Myiagra alecto*			r		r	r										
Mussau Flycatcher	*Myiagra hebetior*	VU?			e												
Velvet Flycatcher	*Myiagra eichhorni*					e	e										
New Caledonian Crow	*Corvus moneduloides*															i	e
White-billed Crow	*Corvus woodfordi*							e	e								
Bougainville Crow	*Corvus meeki*							e									
Bismarck Crow	*Corvus insularis*					e	e										
Torrent Flyrobin	*Monachella muelleriana*						r										
Yellow-bellied Flyrobin	*Microeca flaviventris*																e
Bismarck Flyrobin	*Microeca sp.*					e	e										
Pacific Robin	*Petroica multicolor*							r	r		r	r			r		
Red-vented Bulbul	*Pycnonotus cafer*																i

		GTS	✔	Manus	Mussau	New Ireland	New Britain	Bougainville	Guadalcanal	Malaita	New Georgia	Makira	Rennell	Temotu	Vanuatu	Loyalties	Grande Terre
Barn Swallow	*Hirundo rustica*			v													
Pacific Swallow	*Hirundo tahitica*			r		r	r	r	r	r	r	r		r	r	r	v
Welcome Swallow	*Hirundo neoxena*															m	m
Red-rumped Swallow	*Cecropis daurica*					m	m	v									
Tree Martin	*Petrochelidon nigricans*					v	m	v	v	v							v
Shade Bush Warbler	*Cettia parens*											e					
Bougainville Bush Warbler	*Cettia haddeni*	NT						e									
Arctic Warbler	*Phylloscopus borealis*			v													
Island Leaf Warbler	*Phylloscopus poliocephalus*				r	r	r	r	r	r	r	r					
Kolombangara Leaf Warbler	*Phylloscopus amoenus*	VU									e						
Australian Reed Warbler	*Acrocephalus australis*					r	r	r	r								
Papuan Grassbird	*Megalurus macrurus*					r	r										
New Caledonian Thicketbird	*Megalurulus mariei*																e
New Britain Thicketbird	*Megalurulus grosvenori*	VU					e										
Bougainville Thicketbird	*Megalurulus llaneae*	NT						e									
Guadalcanal Thicketbird	*Megalurulus turipavae*	NT							e								
Santo Thicketbird	*Megalurulus whitneyi*														e		
Rusty Thicketbird	*Megalurulus rubiginosus*						e										
Gray's Grasshopper Warbler	*Locustella fasciolata*					v											
Golden-headed Cisticola	*Cisticola exilis*					r	r										
Bismarck White-eye	*Zosterops hypoxanthus*			e		e	e										
Louisiade White-eye	*Zosterops griseotinctus*			Nauna		Nissan	Long etc										
Yellow-throated White-eye	*Zosterops metcalfii*							e									
Rennell White-eye	*Zosterops rennellianus*												e				
Vella Lavella White-eye	*Zosterops vellalavella*	NT									e						
Gizo White-eye	*Zosterops luteirostris*	EN									e						
Ranongga White-eye	*Zosterops splendidus*	VU									e						
Solomons White-eye	*Zosterops kulambangrae*										e						
Kolombangara White-eye	*Zosterops murphyi*										e						
Grey-throated White-eye	*Zosterops ugiensis*							e	e			e					
Malaita White-eye	*Zosterops stresemanni*									e							
Santa Cruz White-eye	*Zosterops sanctaecrucis*													e			
Vanikoro White-eye	*Zosterops gibbsi*													e			
Vanuatu White-eye	*Zosterops flavifrons*														e		
Small Lifou White-eye	*Zosterops minutus*															e	
Green-backed White-eye	*Zosterops xanthochroa*															e	e
Silvereye	*Zosterops lateralis*														r	r	r
Large Lifou White-eye	*Zosterops inornatus*															e	
Bare-eyed White-eye	*Woodfordia superciliosa*												e				

		GTS	✔	Manus	Mussau	New Ireland	New Britain	Bougainville	Guadalcanal	Malaita	New Georgia	Makira	Rennell	Temotu	Vanuatu	Loyalties	Grande Terre
Sanford's White-eye	*Woodfordia lacertosa*	NT												e			
Metallic Starling	*Aplonis metallica*			r	r	r	r	r	r	r	r	r					
Singing Starling	*Aplonis cantoroides*			r	r	r	r	r	r	r	r	r	r				
Atoll Starling	*Aplonis feadensis*	NT		atolls	atolls	atolls		atolls									
Rennell Starling	*Aplonis insularis*												e				
White-eyed Starling	*Aplonis brunneicapillus*	EN						e	e		e						
Brown-winged Starling	*Aplonis grandis*							e	e	e	e						
Makira Starling	*Aplonis dichroa*											e					
Rusty-winged Starling	*Aplonis zelandica*	NT												e	e		
Striated Starling	*Aplonis striata*															e	e
Mountain Starling	*Aplonis santovestris*	VU													e		
Polynesian Starling	*Aplonis tabuensis*													r			
Long-tailed Myna	*Mino kreffti*					e	e	e	e	e	e						
Common Myna	*Acridotheres tristis*							x	i			i			i		i
Common Starling	*Sturnus vulgaris*															v	
Russet-tailed Thrush	*Zoothera heinei*				r			r									
New Britain Thrush	*Zoothera talaseae*	NT					e										
Bougainville Thrush	*Zoothera atrigena*	NT?						e									
Makira Thrush	*Zoothera margaretae*	NT										e					
Guadalcanal Thrush	*Zoothera turipavae*	VU							e								
Island Thrush	*Turdus poliocephalus*				r	r	r	r	r		r		r	r	r	x	r
Song Thrush	*Turdus philomelos*														v		
Pied Bush Chat	*Saxicola caprata*					r	r										
Red-banded Flowerpecker	*Dicaeum eximium*					e	e										
Midget Flowerpecker	*Dicaeum aeneum*							e	e	e							
Mottled Flowerpecker	*Dicaeum tristrami*											e					
Black Sunbird	*Leptocoma sericea*					r	r										
Olive-backed Sunbird	*Cinnyris jugularis*			r	r	r	r	r	r	r	r	r					
House Sparrow	*Passer domesticus*														i		i
Eurasian Tree Sparrow	*Passer montanus*						i		v	v							
Common Waxbill	*Estrilda astrild*														i		i
Blue-faced Parrotfinch	*Erythrura trichroa*				r	r	r	r	r		r				r	r	
Red-throated Parrotfinch	*Erythrura psittacea*																e
Royal Parrotfinch	*Erythrura regia*	VU													e		
Streak-headed Mannikin	*Lonchura tristissima*						Umboi										
Chestnut Munia	*Lonchura atricapilla*														i		
Hooded Mannikin	*Lonchura spectabilis*						r										
Forbes's Mannikin	*Lonchura forbesi*					e											
Hunstein's Mannikin	*Lonchura hunsteini*					e											

		GTS	✔	Manus	Mussau	New Ireland	New Britain	Bougainville	Guadalcanal	Malaita	New Georgia	Makira	Rennell	Temotu	Vanuatu	Loyalties	Grande Terre
Chestnut-breasted Mannikin	*Lonchura castaneothorax*														i?		i
Buff-bellied Mannikin	*Lonchura melaena*					e	e	ex									
Eastern Yellow Wagtail	*Motacilla tschutschensis*					v	v	v									
Grey Wagtail	*Motacilla cinerea*					v											
Common Redpoll	*Carduelis flammea*														v		

Melanesia supports many seabird colonies. Larger numbers and more species are generally found on the more isolated atolls and islets. Sooty Terns are commonly seen at sea but nest on only a handful of islets. *Guy Dutson.*

Little Grebe *Tachybaptus ruficollis* Page 247

25 cm. Small dumpy waterbird. Adult is dark with yellow spot at bill-base and chestnut face and neck. Immature and non-breeding adult have pale face and throat. Dark red eye. In flight, white wing-bar on secondaries only. Lakes, ponds and other fresh water. Sits high or low on water and dives. Rare.

Mn	Mu	Nl	NB	Bv	Gu	Ml	NG	Mk	Rl	Te	Vu	Lo	GT

Australasian Grebe *Tachybaptus novaehollandiae leucosternos* Page 248

25 cm. Small dumpy waterbird. Adult is dark with yellow spot at bill-base and chestnut on ear-coverts and sides of upper neck. Immature and non-breeding adult have pale face and throat. Yellow or orange eye. In flight, white wing-bar across onto most primaries. Lakes, ponds and other fresh water. Sits high or low on water and dives. Uncommon.

Mn	Mu	Nl	NB	Bv	Gu	Ml	NG	Mk	Rl	Te	Vu	Lo	GT

Spotted Whistling Duck *Dendrocygna guttata* Page 228

43 cm. Brown duck with greyer face, dark cap, white round spots on neck, breast and flanks, and dark red-brown legs. In flight, broad plain wings, relatively short neck and plain dark brown rump. Freshwater marshes and lakes. Swims, dabbles, grazes short grass and often perches in trees. Fairly common.

Mn	Mu	Nl	NB	Bv	Gu	Ml	NG	Mk	Rl	Te	Vu	Lo	GT

Plumed Whistling Duck *Dendrocygna eytoni* Page 228

51 cm. Pale brown duck with long buff flank-plumes which extend over wings, pink legs, pink on bill and pale eye. In flight, broad plain wings, narrow white rump-band and pale underwing. Waterside grass, freshwater lakes and marshes. Swims, dabbles and grazes. Vagrant.

Mn	Mu	Nl	NB	Bv	Gu	Ml	NG	Mk	Rl	Te	Vu	Lo	GT

Wandering Whistling Duck *Dendrocygna arcuata australis* Page 228

48 cm. Reddish-brown duck with dark cap, paler neck, short white flank-plumes and black legs. In flight, broad dark wings with chestnut upperwing-coverts, white rump and dark underwing. Lakes and swamps. Swims, dives, grazes and perches in trees. Rare.

Mn	Mu	Nl	NB	Bv	Gu	Ml	NG	Mk	Rl	Te	Vu	Lo	GT

Hardhead *Aythya australis* Page 231

52 cm. Diving duck. Plain chestnut or chocolate-brown with white undertail-coverts. Male has white eye and blue on bill. Female has dark eye and duller bill. In flight, broad white upperwing-bar, white underwings and white belly. Large lakes. Rests on water and dives. Uncommon.

Mn	Mu	Nl	NB	Bv	Gu	Ml	NG	Mk	Rl	Te	Vu	Lo	GT

Tufted Duck *Aythya fuligula* Page 232

44 cm. Diving duck. Male is black and white with crest which is variable and sometimes absent. Female is dark brown with paler brown flanks and shorter crest. In flight, broad white upperwing-bar and white underwings. Large lakes. Vagrant.

Mn	Mu	Nl	NB	Bv	Gu	Ml	NG	Mk	Rl	Te	Vu	Lo	GT

breeding
Little Grebe
breeding
non-breeding
breeding
non-breeding
Australian Grebe
breeding
Wandering Whistling Duck
Plumed Whistling Duck
Spotted Whistling Duck
♂
Hardhead
♀
♀
Tufted Duck
♂

Grey Teal *Anas gracilis* Page 230

39 cm. Small duck. Grey-brown with paler fringes, darker cap and paler face and throat. In flight, broad white bar, dark green speculum, narrow white trailing edge and short white wedge on underwing. Small flocks dabble in shallow lakes. Common to rare.

Mn	Mu	Nl	NB	Bv	Gu	Ml	NG	Mk	Rl	Te	Vu	Lo	GT

Mallard *Anas platyrhynchos* Page 229

58 cm. Male has yellow bill, green head, brown breast and grey body. In flight, shows blue speculum. Female is warm brown with dark streaks, pale supercilium, dark eye-stripe and dull orange bill and legs. Breeds with domestic ducks to produce hybrids of variety of shapes and plumages. Dabbles in fresh water and grazes grass, often in artificial habitats. Locally fairly common.

Mn	Mu	Nl	NB	Bv	Gu	Ml	NG	Mk	Rl	Te	Vu	Lo	GT

Pacific Black Duck *Anas superciliosa* Page 229

53 cm. Large blackish duck. Mottled dark brown with distinct dark brown and buff stripes on face. In flight, green speculum and white underwing. Grey bill and dirty yellow legs and feet. Dabbles in fresh water, including tiny patches of water, water in forest and sometimes mangroves and coasts. Usually the commonest duck.

Mn	Mu	Nl	NB	Bv	Gu	Ml	NG	Mk	Rl	Te	Vu	Lo	GT

Northern Pintail *Anas acuta* Page 231

54 cm. Long-necked duck with pointed tail. Male has dark head, white neck and breast, grey body and long pointed tail. Female is grey-brown with fine dark markings and slightly elongated tail. In flight, green speculum. Dabbles in shallow fresh water. Vagrant.

Garganey *Anas querquedula* Page 231

40 cm. Small duck. Male has brown head and breast with long white supercilium and grey body with long grey plumes. Female is warm brown with dark eye-stripe and cheek-stripe. In flight, blue upperwing-coverts, white wing-bar and green speculum. Dabbles in swamps and shallow lakes. Vagrant.

Australasian Shoveler *Anas rhynchotis* Page 230

50 cm. Large duck with long heavy dark grey bill. Male has mottled grey-blue head and rich rufous breast and belly. Female is dull brown, mottled darker. In flight, blue upperwing-coverts and green speculum. Feeds by sweeping bill from side to side in shallow lakes. Vagrant.

Northern Shoveler *Anas clypeata* Page 230

50cm. Large duck with long heavy dark grey bill. Male has greenish head, dark upperparts, white underparts and rich rufous flanks. Female is dull mottled brown with orange on bill and white on outer tail. Wing pattern and habits like Australasian Shoveler. Vagrant.

Grey Teal
Mallard
♂
♀
♂
Pacific Black Duck
♀
Northern Pintail
♂
Garganey
♀
♂
Australasian Shoveler
♀
♂
Northern Shoveler
♀
♂

Laysan Albatross *Phoebastria immutabilis* (not illustrated) Page 232

80 cm (wingspan 220 cm). Dark upperwing, mantle, upper rump, tail, eye-patch and some mottling on underwing. Vagrant.

Wandering Albatross *Diomedea e. exulans* Page 232

125 cm (wingspan 300 cm). Huge seabird. Very large plain pink bill. Adult has white body and underwings, and some white on black upperwings. Immature has brown cap, body and upperwings. Many intermediate plumages. Vagrant.

Northern Royal Albatross *Diomedea sanfordi* Page 233

115 cm (wingspan 320 cm). Huge seabird. Very large pink bill with black cutting edges. Adult has white body and underwings, and all-black upperwings. Adult Southern Royal Albatross *D. epomophora* has white extending along leading edge of upperwing. Vagrant.

Light-mantled Albatross *Phoebastria palpebrata* (not illustrated) Page 233

84 cm (wingspan 205 cm). Slender with long pointed tail. Dark brown with greyer mantle and underparts. Vagrant.

Campbell Albatross *Thalassarche impavida* Page 233

80 cm (wingspan 220 cm). Small albatross. White with black wings, mantle and tail, wide black underwing margins and small black eyebrow. Adult has yellow bill and pale eye. Juvenile has dull bill. Vagrant.

Buller's Albatross *Thalassarche bulleri* (not illustrated) Page 234

78 cm (wingspan 207 cm). Similar to Campbell Albatross but grey head and yellow stripes on black bill. Vagrant.

Southern Giant Petrel *Macronectes giganteus* Page 234

90 cm (wingspan 195 cm). Huge bulky petrel. Adult is brown with white head and pale underwing or all white with dark speckles. Heavy pink or horn bill with greenish tip. Immature is blackish or brown. Vagrant.

Northern Giant Petrel *Macronectes halli* (not illustrated) Page 234

90 cm (wingspan 195 cm). Like Southern Giant Petrel but darker reddish bill-tip, and adult has white only on face. Vagrant.

Great-winged Petrel *Pterodroma macroptera* Page 235

41 cm (wingspan 102 cm). Large bulky petrel. Dark grey-brown. Underwing may reflect pale. Variable pale grey face-patch in Grey-faced Petrel *P. (m.) gouldii*. Solitary. Vagrant. See smaller petrels (Plates 5 and 6).

Providence Petrel *Pterodroma solandri* Page 235

40 cm (wingspan 100 cm). Large bulky petrel. Dark grey-brown with double white patch on outer underwing. Some white around forehead and bill-base. Solitary. Vagrant. See smaller petrels (Plates 5 and 6).

Grey Petrel *Procellaria cinerea* Page 240

49 cm (wingspan 122 cm). Thickset grey-brown petrel with white underbody and pale bill. Solitary. Strong, flies on straight stiff wings, often high above sea. Vagrant.

Streaked Shearwater *Calonectris leucomelas* Page 240

48 cm (wingspan 122 cm). Large heavy shearwater. Mid-brown upperparts, often with pale bars, and white underparts and underwings. Mottled white on face and pale bill. Gregarious. Fairly common October–March.

Mn	Mu	NI	NB	Bv	Gu	MI	NG	Mk	RI	Te	Vu	Lo	GT

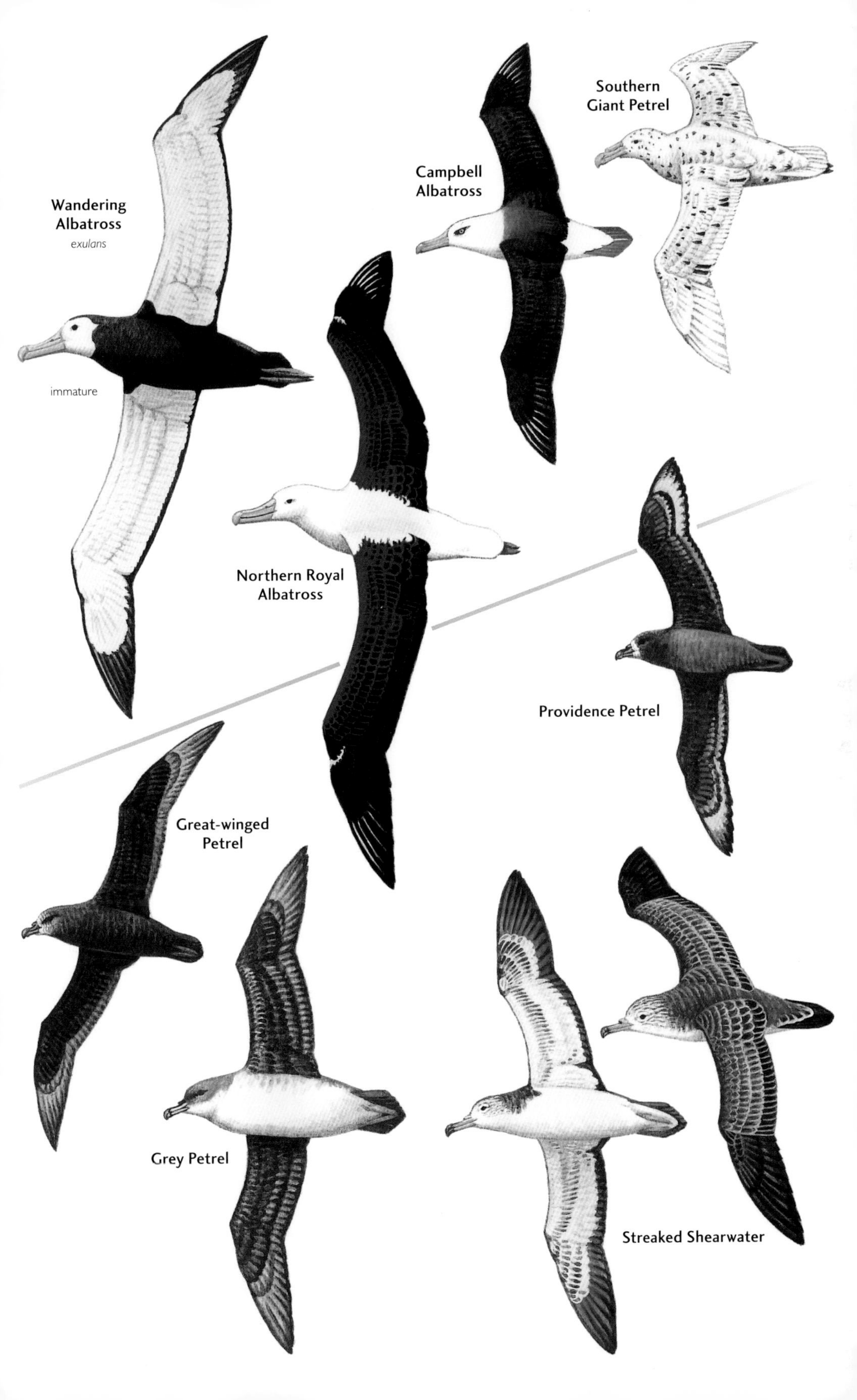
Wandering
Albatross
exulans
immature
Campbell
Albatross
Southern
Giant Petrel
Northern Royal
Albatross
Providence Petrel
Great-winged
Petrel
Grey Petrel
Streaked Shearwater

PLATE 4: LARGER SHEARWATERS AND SMALLER ALL-DARK PETRELS

Flesh-footed Shearwater *Puffinus carneipes* — Page 243

47 cm (wingspan 115 cm). Large bulky shearwater. All dark brown but underwing often reflects pale. Pale pink feet and stout pale pink bill with black tip. Uncommon.

Mn	Mu	NI	NB	Bv	Gu	MI	NG	Mk	RI	Te	Vu	Lo	GT

Wedge-tailed Shearwater *Puffinus pacificus* — Page 241

46 cm (wingspan 98 cm). Large slender shearwater. Long pointed tail. Chocolate-brown, with paler bars on wing-coverts, or white underbody and underwing. Slow flight low over sea, with carpals held forward and outer wings bowed. Gregarious. Nests on beaches and small islands. Locally common. See small shearwaters (Plate 6).

Mn	Mu	NI	NB	Bv	Gu	MI	NG	Mk	RI	Te	Vu	Lo	GT

Buller's Shearwater *Puffinus bulleri* — (not illustrated) Page 241

44 cm (wingspan 98 cm). Relatively long wings, neck and wedge-shaped tail. Ashy-grey upperparts with sooty crown, tail and M across upperwings. White underparts with narrow dark underwing margins and blackish tail. Vagrant.

Sooty Shearwater *Puffinus griseus* — Page 243

43 cm (wingspan 100 cm). Large dark shearwater. Long narrow wings with silvery underwing-bar. Vagrant.

Short-tailed Shearwater *Puffinus tenuirostris* — Page 243

42 cm (wingspan 97 cm). Large dark shearwater. Similar to Sooty Shearwater but shorter neck and tail, slimmer, less mottled silver on underwing and faster wing-beats. Gregarious, often in large dense flocks. Migrant in March–May and October–November. See small shearwaters (Plate 6).

Mn	Mu	NI	NB	Bv	Gu	MI	NG	Mk	RI	Te	Vu	Lo	GT

Cape Petrel *Daption capense* — Page 235

38 cm (wingspan 85 cm). Stocky petrel. Chequered black and white upperparts. White underparts with black throat, wing margins and tail-tip. Vagrant.

Bulwer's Petrel *Bulweria bulwerii* — Page 244

27 cm (wingspan 68 cm). Long-winged petrel with long tail. Plain sooty-brown with indistinct paler greater covert bar, not visible at long range. Underwing may reflect paler off sea. Flies low over water, carpals held forward and wings slightly bowed like Wedge-tailed Shearwater. Uncommon. See storm petrels (Plate 7).

Mn	Mu	NI	NB	Bv	Gu	MI	NG	Mk	RI	Te	Vu	Lo	GT

Jouanin's Petrel *Bulweria fallax* — Page 244

31 cm (wingspan 79 cm). Like Bulwer's Petrel but less pale on upperwing, heavier bill, shorter tail and flight more languid. Vagrant?

Fiji Petrel *Pseudobulweria macgillivrayi* — Page 240

29 cm (wingspan 73 cm). Like small dark Tahiti Petrel. Plain sooty with medium-length tail and stout bill. Similar length and wingspan as Black Noddy. Vagrant?

Wedge-tailed Shearwater

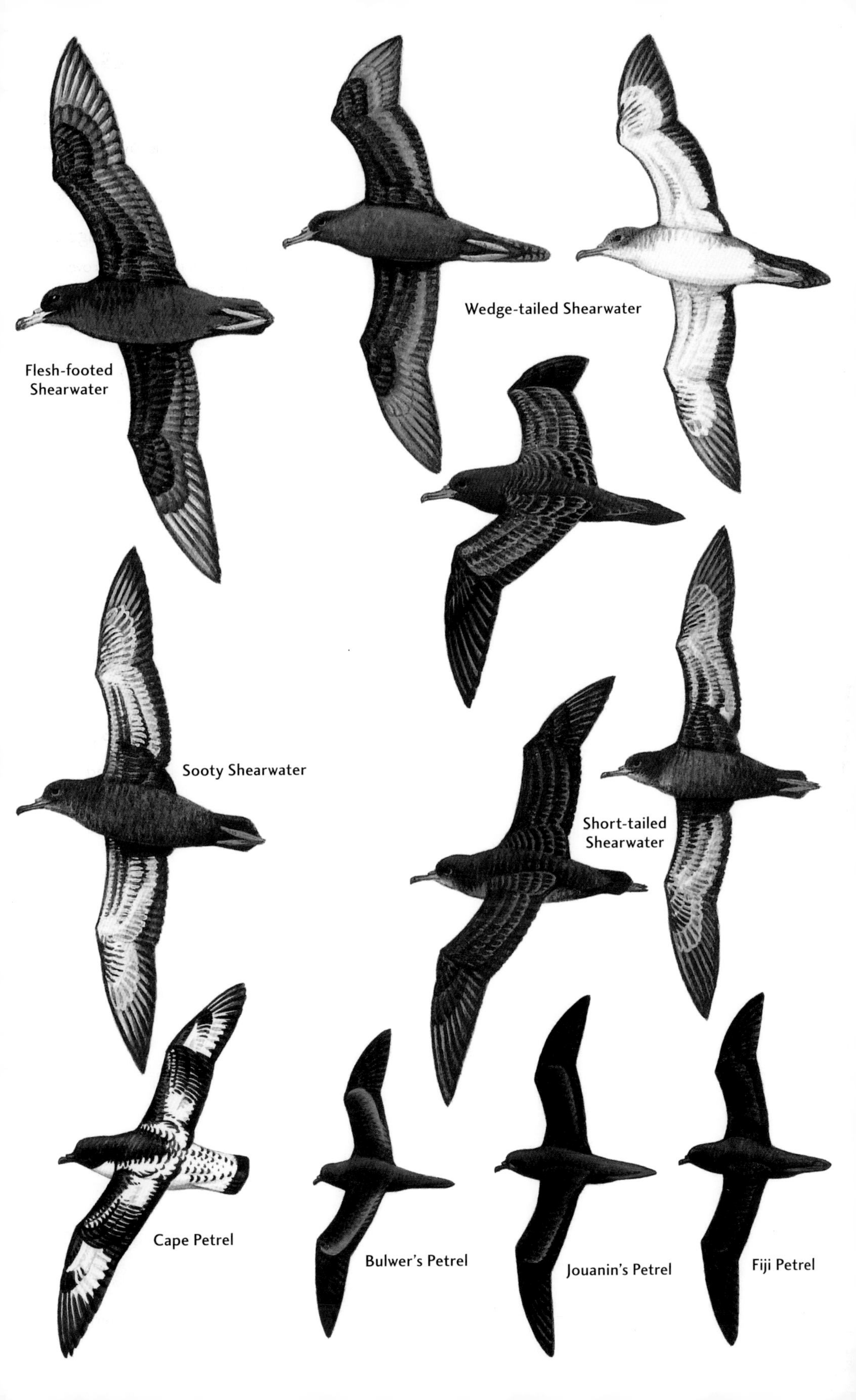
Flesh-footed Shearwater
Wedge-tailed Shearwater
Sooty Shearwater
Short-tailed Shearwater
Cape Petrel
Bulwer's Petrel
Jouanin's Petrel
Fiji Petrel

PLATE 5: SMALLER *PTERODROMA* PETRELS AND PRIONS

Mottled Petrel *Pterodroma inexpectata* — Page 236

35 cm (wingspan 85 cm). Large bulky *Pterodroma*. Dark grey breast, flanks and belly. White underparts with broad black bar from carpals to greater coverts. Pale grey upperparts with dark M. Uncommon migrant or vagrant.

Mn Mu NI NB Bv Gu MI NG Mk RI Te Vu Lo GT

Vanuatu Petrel *Pterodroma occulta* — Page 237

40 cm (wingspan about 94 cm). Large slender *Pterodroma* petrel with white collar and dark cap. Grey upperparts with black M. White underparts with short black bar. From White-necked Petrel by smaller size, grey underneath primaries, slightly longer tail, heavier bill and sometimes dark leading edge to underwing. Breeds in mountains. Local and uncommon.

Mn Mu NI NB Bv Gu MI NG Mk RI Te Vu Lo GT

White-necked Petrel *Pterodroma cervicalis* — Page 237

43 cm (wingspan 100 cm). Large slender *Pterodroma* petrel. See Vanuatu Petrel. Vagrant?

Cook's Petrel *Pterodroma cookii* — Page 239

30 cm (wingspan 65 cm). Small *Pterodroma*. Pale grey upperparts with black M, grey crown and small eye-patch. White underwing with short narrow black bar and very narrow black margins. Vagrant.

Gould's Petrel *Pterodroma leucoptera* — Page 238

30 cm (wingspan 70 cm). Small round-winged *Pterodroma*. Black crown and nape extends onto neck-sides. Paler mantle and upperwings with dark M. White underwing with short black bar and narrow black margins.

P. l. caledonica (breeds in mountains of New Caledonia) is uncommon at sea.

P. l. leucoptera (breeds in Australia and a likely migrant) has darker grey mantle, darker neck-sides with more extension as partial collar, more prominent underwing-bar and grey not white inner webs of outer tail feathers.

Mn Mu NI NB Bv Gu MI NG Mk RI Te Vu Lo GT

Collared Petrel *Pterodroma brevipes* — Page 238

30 cm (wingspan 70 cm). Small round-winged *Pterodroma*. Black crown and nape extends as partial or complete black breast-band. Paler mantle and upperwings with dark M. White underwing with short bar and narrow margins. Many have dark grey breast to vent. Breeds in mountains. Uncommon.

P. b. brevipes (breeds on Tanna and possibly elsewhere in Vanuatu) has variable plumage.

P. b. magnificens (breeds on Vanua Lava) is always dark with slightly shorter wings and longer tail.

Mn Mu NI NB Bv Gu MI NG Mk RI Te Vu Lo GT

Black-winged Petrel *Pterodroma nigripennis* — Page 237

29 cm (wingspan 67 cm). Small round-winged *Pterodroma*. White underwing with broad black band from greater coverts along leading edge of outer wing, broad black wing-tip and black trailing edge. Grey upperparts, extending onto neck-sides, with darker M. Uncommon.

Mn Mu NI NB Bv Gu MI NG Mk RI Te Vu Lo GT

Antarctic Prion *Pachyptila desolata* — Page 235

26 cm (wingspan 63 cm). Like small short-winged *Pterodroma* petrel. Flies like storm petrel. Other species of prion differ in head pattern and bill structure. Vagrant.

Gould's Petrel

Mottled Petrel
White-necked Petrel
Vanuatu Petrel
Cook's Petrel
leucoptera
caledonica
Gould's Petrel
brevipes
Collared Petrel
magnificens
Antarctic Prion
Black-winged Petrel

PLATE 6: SMALLER SHEARWATERS AND PETRELS

Christmas Shearwater *Puffinus nativitatis* Page 241

35 cm (wingspan 76 cm). Small all sooty-brown shearwater. Underwing sometimes reflects pale. Short round wings. Relatively small dark bill and dark feet. Flies close to sea with fast flapping flight. Vagrant. See large shearwaters (Plates 3 and 4).

Fluttering Shearwater *Puffinus gavia* Page 242

35 cm (wingspan 76 cm). Small shearwater with plain brown upperparts and white underparts. Some brown mottling on neck-sides and axillaries. White extends onto undertail and sometimes sides of rump. Fairly long neck, short wings and fluttering flight. Vagrant.

Tropical Shearwater *Puffinus bailloni* Page 242

31 cm (wingspan 69 cm). Small black and white shearwater. Blackish upperparts, extending to level of eye and onto neck-sides. White underparts with black wing-tips, broad borders and black undertail-coverts. White flanks often extend onto sides of rump. Legs blue with pinkish webs. Fluttering flight. Breeds in mountains. Uncommon but fairly common off Temotu and north Vanuatu.

Mn	Mu	NI	NB	Bv	Gu	MI	NG	Mk	RI	Te	Vu	Lo	GT

Little Shearwater *Puffinus assimilis* Page 243

27 cm (wingspan 61 cm). Very small black and white shearwater. Blue-black upperparts. White underparts with narrow black tips and trailing edge. White extends above eye. Short rounded wings. Light blue feet. Fluttering or whirring flight. Vagrant?

Heinroth's Shearwater *Puffinus heinrothi* Page 242

27 cm (wingspan 59 cm). Very small sooty-brown shearwater. Size similar to Black Noddy. Variable silvery underwing bar. Sometimes pale on chin and central belly. Long slender dark bill, pale blue eye and pale pink feet. Short wings and fluttering flight. Breeds on mountainous islands. Local and uncommon. See large shearwaters (Plates 3 and 4).

Mn	Mu	NI	NB	Bv	Gu	MI	NG	Mk	RI	Te	Vu	Lo	GT

Tahiti Petrel *Pseudobulweria rostrata* Page 239

39 cm (wingspan 84 cm). Medium-sized long-winged petrel. Blackish-brown with white belly and variable narrow white underwing bar. Distinctive long narrow stiff straight wings. Flight intermediate between shearwaters and *Pterodroma* petrels. Breeds in mountains and small islets. Fairly common off New Caledonia, rare elsewhere.

Mn	Mu	NI	NB	Bv	Gu	MI	NG	Mk	RI	Te	Vu	Lo	GT

Beck's Petrel *Pseudobulweria becki* Page 239

29 cm (wingspan 70 cm). Like Tahiti Petrel but 10–20% smaller, narrower wings, shorter wingspan, slighter and slimmer body, 25% shorter bill on small head, and sometimes flies more like *Pterodroma*. Local and uncommon.

Mn	Mu	NI	NB	Bv	Gu	MI	NG	Mk	RI	Te	Vu	Lo	GT

Herald Petrel *Pterodroma heraldica* Page 236

37 cm (wingspan 95 cm). Medium-sized polymorphic petrel. Plain brown upperparts with faint darker M. Dark underwing with extensive white at base of primaries and primary coverts, extending variably onto inner wing. Most have white underparts with variable dusky collar. Some have all-dark head and body. Breeds on isolated reefs. Rare. See large petrels (Plate 3).

Mn	Mu	NI	NB	Bv	Gu	MI	NG	Mk	RI	Te	Vu	Lo	GT

Kermadec Petrel *Pterodroma neglecta* Page 236

38 cm (wingspan 100 cm). Medium-sized polymorphic petrel. Plain dark brown upperwing with pale primary shafts. Dark underwing with white on primary bases and primary coverts. Dark brown or white head and body or intermediates. Vagrant. See large petrels and skuas (Plates 3 and 30).

Heinroth's Shearwater

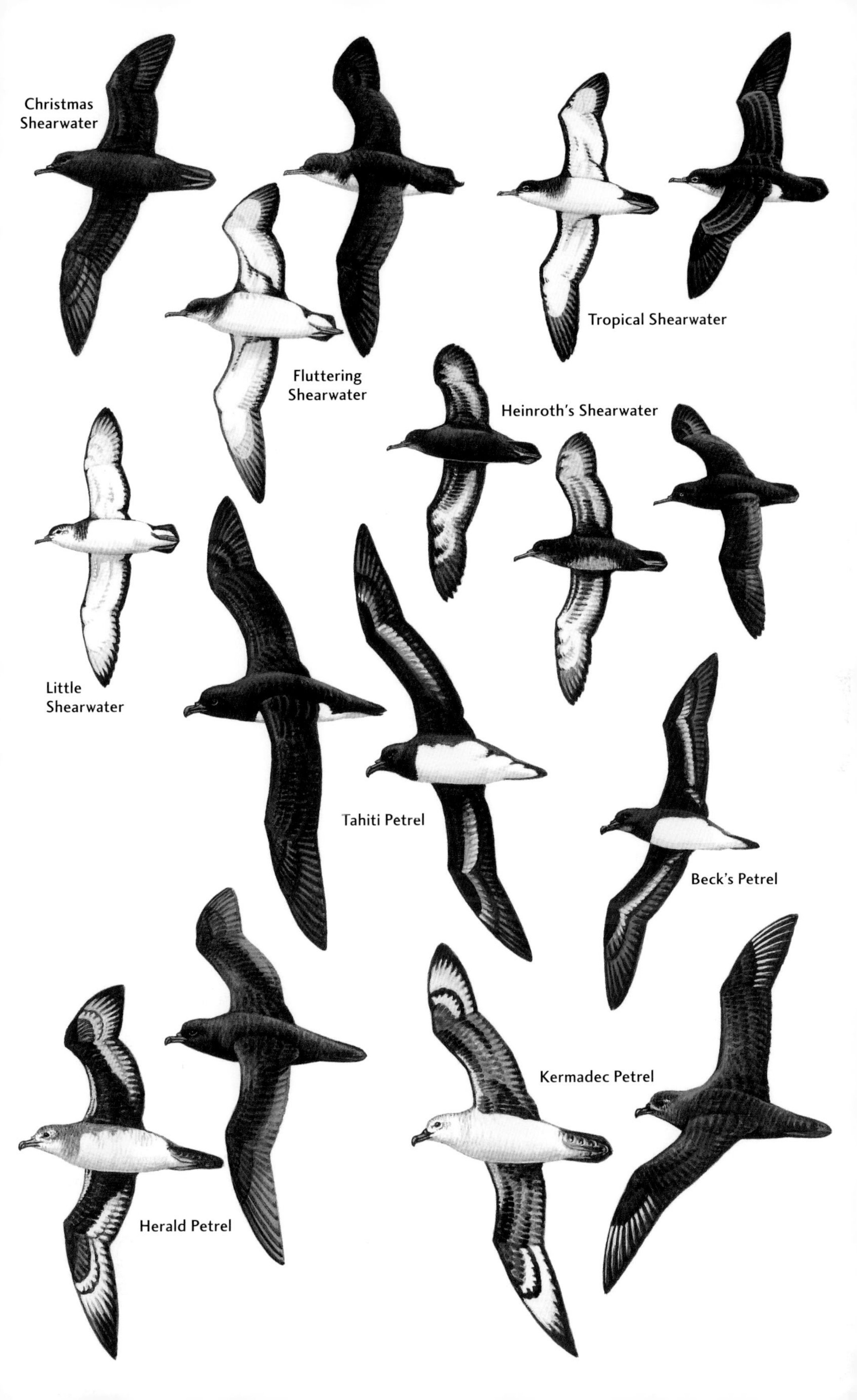
Christmas Shearwater
Tropical Shearwater
Fluttering Shearwater
Heinroth's Shearwater
Little Shearwater
Tahiti Petrel
Beck's Petrel
Kermadec Petrel
Herald Petrel

Wilson's Storm Petrel *Oceanites oceanicus* Page 244

17 cm (wingspan 40 cm). Blackish with pale wing-bar and white rump extending around sides onto undertail-coverts. Yellow webs on feet which protrude beyond tail. Short round wings and short square tail. Patters on sea and follows ships. Uncommon.

Mn	Mu	NI	NB	Bv	Gu	MI	NG	Mk	RI	Te	Vu	Lo	GT

White-faced Storm Petrel *Pelagodroma marina* Page 245

19 cm (wingspan 42 cm). Blackish wings and tail, grey wing-coverts and back, and pale grey rump. Grey head with white supercilium and throat. White underparts with dark grey flight feathers. Long legs with yellowish webs. Vagrant.

Black-bellied Storm Petrel *Fregetta tropica* Page 245

20 cm (wingspan 46 cm). Black with slight pale wing-bar, white rump, belly and central underwing. Variable black midline stripe, sometimes absent. Short broad wings and square tail. Bounces off sea on long legs and glides on flat wings. Uncommon.

Mn	Mu	NI	NB	Bv	Gu	MI	NG	Mk	RI	Te	Vu	Lo	GT

White-bellied Storm Petrel *Fregetta grallaria* Page 245

20 cm (wingspan 46 cm). Like Black-bellied Storm Petrel but has shorter legs not projecting beyond tail, straight or concave black border across breast, pale grey scales on mantle and upperwing-coverts, no black stripe or smudges on belly midline and all-black throat. Vagrant?

Polynesian Storm Petrel *Nesofregetta fuliginosa* Page 246

24 cm (wingspan 52 cm). Brown upperparts with pale wing-bar. Most have narrow white rump, white underparts with dark breast-band and white underwing with dark margins. Some have less white. Broad rounded straight wings. Feet project beyond long forked tail. Kicks off sea and glides on horizontal wings. Breeds on mountains or tiny islets. Rare.

Mn	Mu	NI	NB	Bv	Gu	MI	NG	Mk	RI	Te	Vu	Lo	GT

Band-rumped Storm Petrel *Oceanodroma castro* Page 246

20 cm (wingspan 46 cm). All sooty-brown except for white rump which extends slightly onto undertail-coverts, and faint pale wing-bar. Medium-length wings angled at carpals and slightly forked tail. Vagrant?

Leach's Storm Petrel *Oceanodroma leucorhoa* Page 246

20 cm (wingspan 46 cm). Sooty-brown with variable pale wing-bar. Narrow white rump may have dark on midline. Long pointed wings, often angled at carpals, and deeply forked tail, often held closed. Vagrant.

New Zealand Storm Petrel *Oceanites maorianus* Page 245

18 cm (wingspan 39 cm). Blackish with broad white rump, white central underwing and white belly. Variable amounts of dark streaking on underparts. Shape and behaviour like Wilson's Storm Petrel but narrower wings. Vagrant?

Tristram's Storm Petrel *Oceanodroma tristrami* Page 247

25 cm (wingspan 56 cm). Sooty-brown with long broad pale wing-bar and long forked tail. Behaves like Wilson's Storm Petrel. Vagrant? See Bulwer's Petrel (Plate 4).

Matsudaira's Storm Petrel *Oceanodroma matsudairae* Page 247

24 cm (wingspan 56 cm). Sooty-brown with white bases to shafts of outer primaries and narrow pale wing-bar on inner wing. Long wings angled at carpals and long forked tail which is often closed. Uncommon. See Bulwer's Petrel (Plate 4).

Mn	Mu	NI	NB	Bv	Gu	MI	NG	Mk	RI	Te	Vu	Lo	GT

Polynesian Storm Petrel

Wilson's Storm Petrel
White-faced Storm Petrel
Black-bellied Storm Petrel
White-bellied Storm Petrel
Polynesian Storm Petrel
Band-rumped Storm Petrel
Leach's Storm Petrel
Tristram's Storm Petrel
Matsudaira's Storm Petrel
New Zealand Storm Petrel

Australasian Gannet *Morus serrator* — Page 256

88 cm. Adult is white with black primaries and secondaries except white inner secondaries, black central tail feathers, yellowish head and grey bill. Juvenile has grey-brown upperparts with white spots, and off-white breast, belly and underwing with broad dark margins. Vagrant.

Abbott's Booby *Papasula abbotti* — Page 257

79 cm. White head, body and underwing, black upperwing and tail, white spots on wing-coverts, a few black spots on flanks and rump, and narrow black margins to underwing. Pale grey or pink bill with black tip. Narrower head, neck and wings than other boobies. Extinct in region.

Masked Booby *Sula dactylatra* — Page 257

80 cm. Adult is white with black tail and flight feathers extending to tertials, black mask at base of yellowish bill and dark grey or green legs. Tiny black spot on underwing-coverts. Juvenile has brown hood separated from mottled brown upperparts by whitish collar and upper mantle. Often solitary, flying fairly high over sea far offshore.

S. d. personata (rare at sea and breeding on remote atolls) has pale eye.

S. d. fullagari (rare at sea) has dark eye.

Mn	Mu	NI	NB	Bv	Gu	MI	NG	Mk	RI	Te	Vu	Lo	GT

Red-footed Booby *Sula sula* — Page 257

75 cm. Adult has blue bill, pink around bill-base and bright red feet. Most are white with black primaries, secondaries and underwing primary coverts. Some have black tail. Some have brown head and body, variably paler than wings, with white tail, rump and vent. Some are all chocolate-brown. Juvenile is dark brown with variably pale belly and central underwing, grey-brown bill and facial skin and grey feet. Often gregarious, flying fairly low over sea offshore. Breeds on tree-tops or cliffs. Fairly common.

Mn	Mu	NI	NB	Bv	Gu	MI	NG	Mk	RI	Te	Vu	Lo	GT

Brown Booby *Sula leucogaster* — Page 258

69 cm. Adult is dark chocolate-brown with sharply marked white belly and underwings. Greenish-yellow feet and yellowish-grey bill, with blue or yellow bill-base and blue facial skin. Juvenile is slightly paler, with brown mottling on poorly defined white belly and underwing. Often solitary, flying fairly low over sea close inshore. Breeds on tree-tops or on ground. Fairly common.

Mn	Mu	NI	NB	Bv	Gu	MI	NG	Mk	RI	Te	Vu	Lo	GT

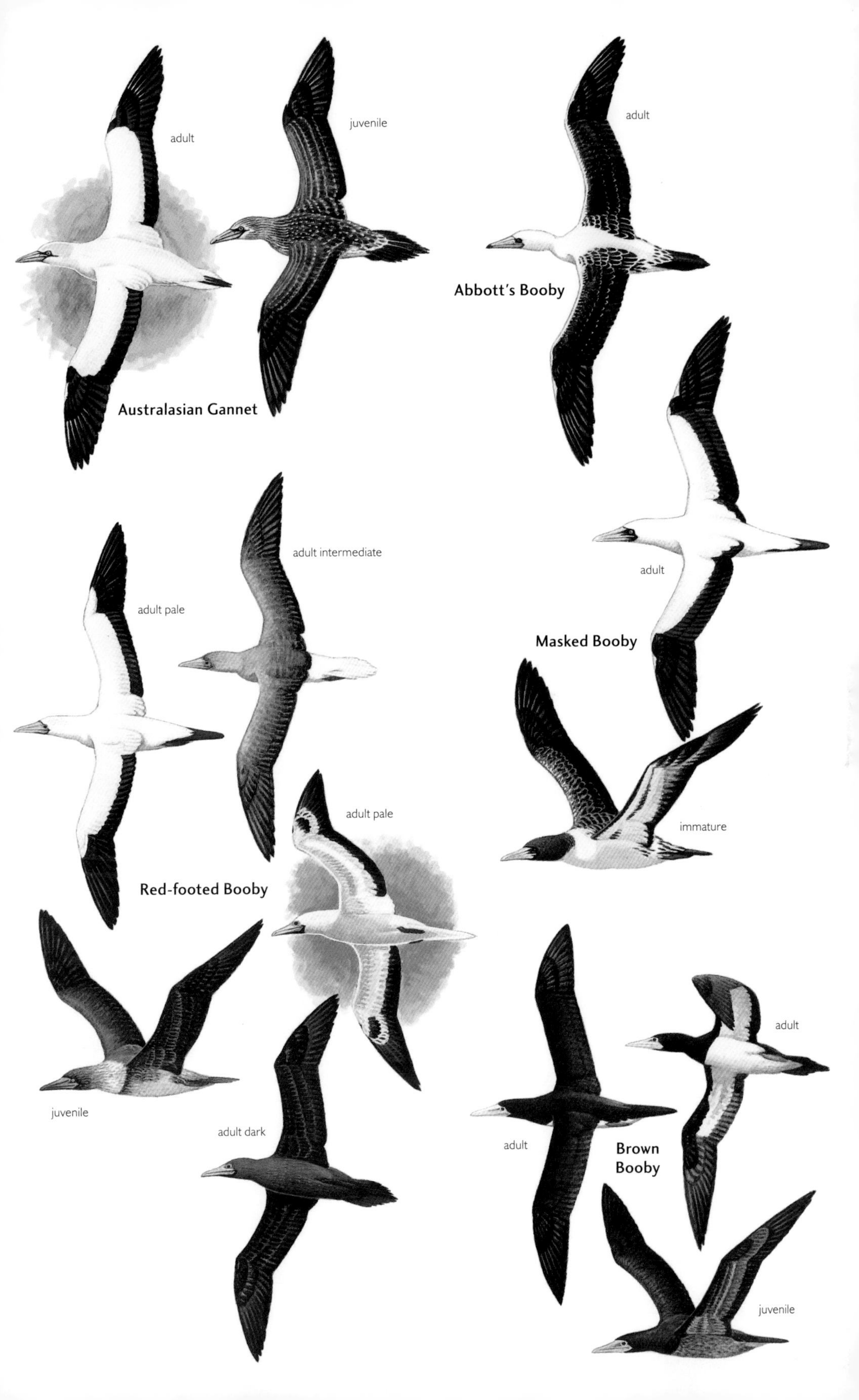
adult
juvenile
Australasian Gannet
adult
Abbott's Booby
adult intermediate
adult pale
adult
Masked Booby
immature
adult pale
Red-footed Booby
juvenile
adult dark
adult
Brown Booby
adult
juvenile

Red-tailed Tropicbird *Phaethon rubricauda* — Page 248

46 cm + tail-streamers. Stocky white seabird. Adult all white, sometimes tinted pink, with red tail-streamers, black tertial centres and red bill. Juvenile has grey-black bill and black bars and streaks including primary coverts and streaks widening towards primary tips. Solitary, flying steadily high over sea or sat on sea, often far offshore. Nests on cliffs or small atolls. Rare. See gulls and terns (Plate 27).

Mn	Mu	NI	NB	Bv	Gu	MI	NG	Mk	RI	Te	Vu	Lo	GT

White-tailed Tropicbird *Phaethon lepturus* — Page 249

38 cm + tail-streamers. Adult is white with white tail-streamers, large black inner wing-bar, black on outer primaries and yellow bill. Juvenile has dark grey bill and black bars and streaks, but white primary coverts and streaks narrowing towards primary tips. Habits like Red-tailed Tropicbird but also nests in tree-holes. Uncommon. See gulls and terns (Plate 27).

Mn	Mu	NI	NB	Bv	Gu	MI	NG	Mk	RI	Te	Vu	Lo	GT

Christmas Frigatebird *Fregata andrewsi* — Page 255

95 cm. Male is black with white lower breast and belly, sometimes extending onto axillaries. Female has black hood and spur on breast, and white collar to belly and spur on underwing. Immature usually has spurs like female. Habits like Great Frigatebird. Vagrant?

Great Frigatebird *Fregata minor* — Page 255

89 cm. Male is all black. Female is black with white from chin to upper belly. Juvenile has buff or white head, black breast-band, white lower breast and belly, and some have white from central breast onto axillaries. Soars on long flexed wings and long narrow forked tail, snatching food from sea or chasing other seabirds. Gregarious. Breeds colonially in trees. Fairly common but rarer than Lesser Frigatebird.

Mn	Mu	NI	NB	Bv	Gu	MI	NG	Mk	RI	Te	Vu	Lo	GT

Lesser Frigatebird *Fregata ariel* — Page 256

76 cm. Male is black with narrow white bar from flanks onto underwing-coverts. Female has black hood and white breast with triangular spurs onto axillaries. Juvenile has buff or white head, black breast-band, triangular white breast-patch and white spurs. Habits like Great Frigatebird. Common.

Mn	Mu	NI	NB	Bv	Gu	MI	NG	Mk	RI	Te	Vu	Lo	GT

Australian Pelican *Pelecanus conspicillatus* — Page 256

170 cm. Huge white waterbird with very long pink bill and black on wing and tail. In flight, black and white upperparts, and white underwing with black primaries and secondaries. Usually seen settled on water, shoreline or trees beside lakes or estuaries. Flies slowly and soars with retracted neck. Vagrant.

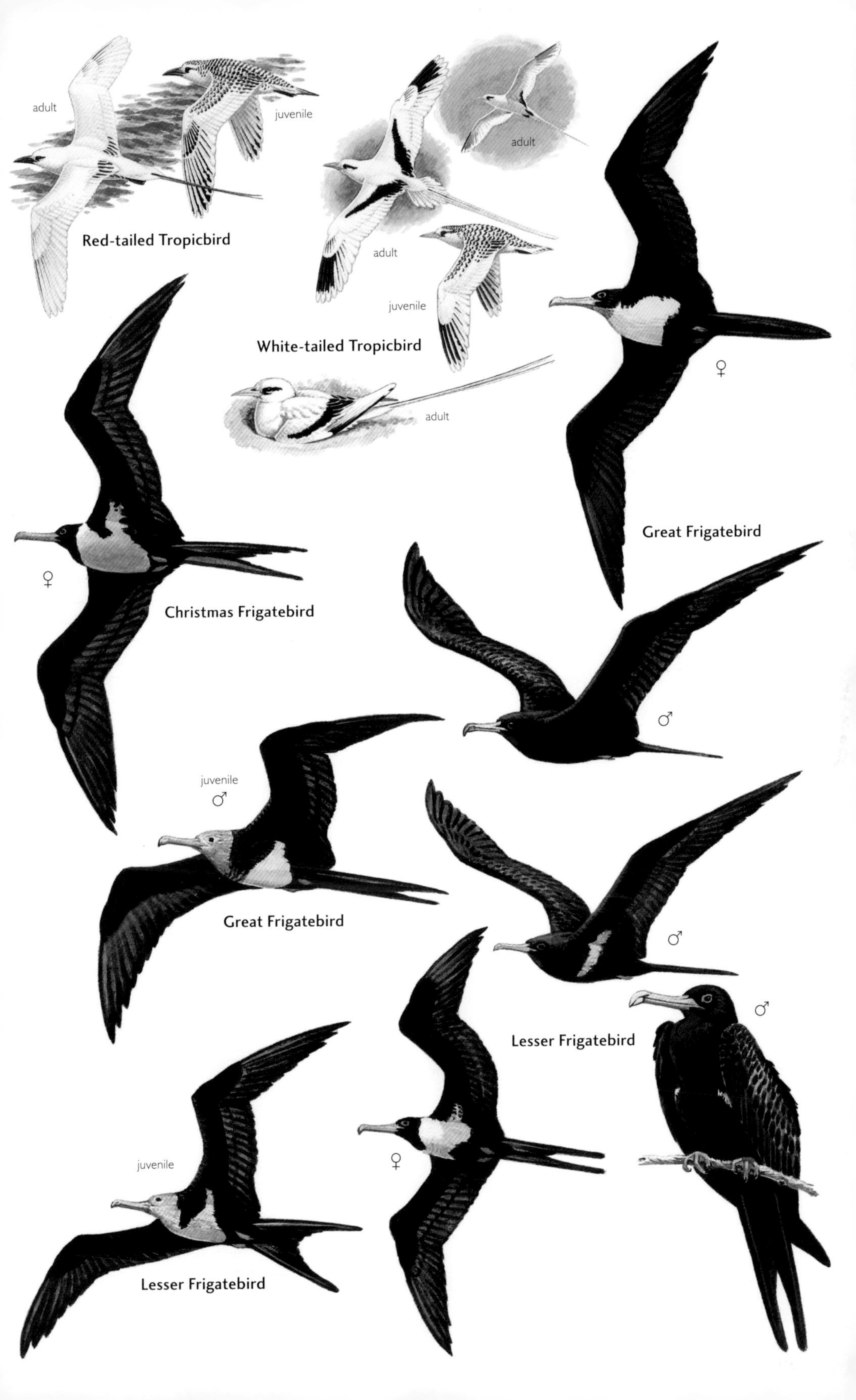
adult
juvenile
Red-tailed Tropicbird
adult
adult
juvenile
White-tailed Tropicbird
adult
♀
Great Frigatebird
♀
Christmas Frigatebird
♂
juvenile
♂
Great Frigatebird
♂
♂
Lesser Frigatebird
juvenile
♀
Lesser Frigatebird

PLATE 10: CASSOWARY, CORMORANTS, MEGAPODES AND JUNGLEFOWL

Dwarf Cassowary *Casuarius bennetti* — Page 225

105 cm. Huge flightless bird. Adult is glossy black with bright blue and red neck. Juvenile is pale brown with dark brown stripes, then plain. Leaves large three-toed footprints and faecal mounds full of fruit stones. Forest, especially in hills. Rare.

Mn Mu Nl NB Bv Gu Ml NG Mk Rl Te Vu Lo GT

Little Black Cormorant *Phalacrocorax sulcirostris* — Page 259

60 cm. Small all-black cormorant with grey bill and face. Breeding adult has white streaks on head. Lakes, sometimes large rivers and coasts. Swims low on water, perches upright on branches, often with wings held open, and flies with stretched neck. Gregarious. Nests colonially in tops of large trees beside water. Rare.

Mn Mu Nl NB Bv Gu Ml NG Mk Rl Te Vu Lo GT

Great Cormorant *Phalacrocorax carbo* — Page 259

83 cm. Large all-black cormorant. Adult has yellow and white patch on face. Breeding adult has white flank-spot and white on neck-sides. Immature is browner, with small yellow bill-base and dirty-white or pale brown underparts. Rare.

Mn Mu Nl NB Bv Gu Ml NG Mk Rl Te Vu Lo GT

Little Pied Cormorant *Microcarbo melanoleucos* — Page 258

61 cm. Small cormorant with white face and underparts and short yellow bill. White underparts may be stained orange. Habits like Little Black Cormorant but also on small rivers and often in singles, pairs or small flocks. Locally common.

Mn Mu Nl NB Bv Gu Ml NG Mk Rl Te Vu Lo GT

Australasian Darter *Anhinga novaehollandiae* — Page 259

90 cm. Very slender bill, head and neck, often held kinked, and long tail. Dark brown upperparts with silvery plumes and fringes on wings. Male is glossy brown with fine white stripe on face. Female has greyer upperparts, narrow white and black stripes on face, and buffy-white underparts. Habits like Little Black Cormorant but also soars, often with fanned tail. Vagrant.

Melanesian Megapode *Megapodius eremita* — Page 225

34 cm. Fat grey-brown ground-bird with big feet, thin neck and slight crest. Variable red, blue and yellow on face and bill, and grey legs. Chick is dark brown, with fine barring on upperparts. Immature is darker and plainer. Forest. Singles, pairs and small groups scratch in leaf-litter. Nests singly in forest or in colonies in volcanic areas. Fairly common.

Mn Mu Nl NB Bv Gu Ml NG Mk Rl Te Vu Lo GT

Vanuatu Megapode *Megapodius layardi* — Page 226

32 cm. Fat sooty-brown ground-bird with bright red naked facial skin and bright yellow legs. Chick and immature like Melanesian Megapode. Forest, usually primary lowland forest. Habits like Melanesian Megapode. Uncommon.

Mn Mu Nl NB Bv Gu Ml NG Mk Rl Te Vu Lo GT

Red Junglefowl *Gallus gallus* — Page 227

44–70 cm. Like domestic chicken. Male has long drooping tail, red comb and wattle, and golden, maroon and green plumage. Female is dark brown with buff and black streaks, medium-long blackish tail, red face and greyish legs. Chick is buff with dark and pale stripes on crown and mantle. Lowland forest. Singles and pairs scratch in leaf-litter. Fairly common.

Mn Mu Nl NB Bv Gu Ml NG Mk Rl Te Vu Lo GT

Wild Turkey *Meleagris gallopavo* — (not illustrated) Page 226

85-110 cm. Huge dark ground bird with long drooping tail. Introduced to open habitats on Grande Terre, New Caledonia.

Common Pheasant *Phasianus colchicus* — (not illustrated) Page 227

58- 84 cm. Similar to a long-tailed junglefowl. Introduced to thickets and open habitats on Grande Terre, New Caledonia.

Indian Peafowl *Pavo cristatus* — (not illustrated) Page 227

95-200 cm. Male is blue and green, female brown and white, with long tail. Introduced to forest edge habitats on Grande Terre, New Caledonia.

Little Pied Cormorant
Little Black Cormorant
Little Black Cormorant
Great Cormorant
Dwarf Cassowary
chick
Australasian Darter
♀
Little Pied Cormorant
chick
Melanesian Megapode
♂
♀
Vanuatu Megapode
chick
Red Junglefowl

PLATE 11: HERONS, EGRETS, IBIS AND SPOONBILL

Intermediate Egret *Egretta intermedia* Page 253

64 cm. White egret with long neck and slight jowl under bill-base. Medium-length yellow bill has variable dusky or black tip. Legs are usually black but may be yellow, dusky or red. Breeding adult has plumes on breast and back, red bill, red upper legs and black lower legs. Singles or small flocks beside fresh water and damp grassland. Vagrant.

Eastern Great Egret *Ardea modesta* Page 253

84 cm. Tall white egret with long neck, often kinked; neck longer than body when outstretched. Gape-line extends onto cheeks beyond eye. Non-breeding adult and immature have yellow bill with variable dusky tip and dark yellowish legs. Breeding adult has plumes on mantle, black bill and black or reddish legs. Wetlands, sometimes grasslands. Uncommon.

Mn Mu Nl **NB** **Bv** **Gu** Ml **NG** Mk **Rl** Te **Vu** **Lo** **GT**

Pied Heron *Egretta picata* (not illustrated) Page 254

47 cm. All dark grey with white throat, neck and upper breast, yellow bill and medium-long legs. Vagrant.

White-faced Heron *Egretta novaehollandiae* Page 254

66 cm. Elegant blue-grey heron with white face-patch and reddish-pink on breast. In flight, upperwing has darker flight feathers than wing-coverts. Solitary or loose groups by lakes, rivers, mangroves, coasts, reefs and grasslands including airfields. Fairly common.

Mn Mu Nl NB **Bv** **Gu** Ml NG Mk Rl **Te** **Vu** **Lo** **GT**

Little Egret *Egretta garzetta* Page 254

56 cm. Elegant white egret. White with slim black bill, yellow facial skin, black legs and greenish-yellow soles to feet. Immature has duller bare parts. Shallow fresh water, estuaries and creeks, often actively chasing and darting after prey. Vagrant.

Pacific Reef Heron *Egretta sacra* Page 254

64 cm. Thick-set stout-billed egret with relatively short stout legs. All white, all dark grey or rarely patchy intermediates. Breeding adult has plumes on nape and short plumes on mantle and breast. Bill varies from yellow, often dusky on tip, to dark. Legs are usually greenish. Solitary or pairs along all coasts, especially reefs, rocky coasts and mangroves, and sometimes inland up rivers. Common.

Mn **Mu** **Nl** **NB** **Bv** **Gu** **Ml** **NG** **Mk** **Rl** **Te** **Vu** **Lo** **GT**

Eastern Cattle Egret *Bubulcus coromandus* Page 253

50 cm. Dumpy white egret with bulging chin and short yellow bill. Legs are relatively short and greenish or blackish. Breeding adult has orange on head, neck and mantle and has red bill and legs. Gregarious. Walks on short grassland and airfields, often with cattle. Vagrant.

Australian White Ibis *Threskiornis molucca pygmaeus* Page 249

64 cm. White but often stained dirty, with long curved black bill, and black legs, head, neck, tertials and tips to primaries. Flocks walk around dry open habitats and forest clearings. Common.

Mn Mu Nl NB **Bv** Gu Ml NG Mk **Rl** Te Vu Lo GT

Straw-necked Ibis *Threskiornis spinicollis* Page 249

68 cm. Glossy black upperparts and breast, white upper neck, lower breast to vent and tail, and dark grey head and long decurved bill. In flight, white on belly extends as wedge onto black underwing-coverts. Flocks inhabit short grassland and wetland margins. Vagrant.

Royal Spoonbill *Platalea regia* Page 250

77 cm. White with long black bill with spoon-shaped tip, black facial skin and long black legs. Immature has duller bare parts and black primary tips. Freshwater lakes and swamps, occasionally sheltered muddy seas. Wades in shallow water, sweeping bill from side to side. Vagrant.

Glossy Ibis *Plegadis falcinellus* Page 249

60 cm. Dark ibis with long decurved bill. Breeding adult has bronze and green iridescence. Immature is duller with some pale mottling on head. Gregarious in freshwater wetlands, occasionally coastal or dry habitats. Vagrant.

non-breeding
Intermediate Egret
breeding
breeding
Eastern Great Egret
non-breeding
White-faced Heron
non-breeding
Little Egret
breeding
Eastern Cattle Egret
non-breeding
dark
white
Pacific Reef Heron
patchy
Australian White Ibis
Royal Spoonbill
Straw-necked Ibis
Glossy Ibis

Striated Heron *Butorides striata solomonensis* Page 252

45 cm. Dumpy heron, often with hunched neck. In flight, conspicuous yellowish legs, and wing-coverts slightly paler than flight feathers. Adult has black cap, slim dark grey bill, dark grey back and wings and plain grey underparts with black spots on white throat. Juvenile has grey-brown upperparts with pale tips on wing-coverts and heavily streaked buffy underparts. Coasts, mangroves, rivers, swamps and sometimes dry thickets. Solitary. Usually hidden in undergrowth but sometimes on open reefs. Common to rare. See other herons (Plate 11).

Mn	Mu	Nl	NB	Bv	Gu	Ml	NG	Mk	Rl	Te	Vu	Lo	GT

Nankeen Night Heron *Nycticorax caledonicus mandibularis* Page 252

58 cm. Stocky heron with short stout bill. Adult has brown upperparts, paler orange on neck and throat, black crown, grey bill and white belly. Juvenile is warm brown with large buffy-white spots on upperparts, brown streaks on white underparts and yellowish on bill. Broad rounded wings in flight. Beside water, usually forested lakes and rivers, but also open marshes and coasts. Crepuscular and nocturnal, small flocks roosting in trees, flying high and slow at dusk like flying-foxes. Fairly common.

Mn	Mu	Nl	NB	Bv	Gu	Ml	NG	Mk	Rl	Te	Vu	Lo	GT

Yellow Bittern *Ixobrychus sinensis* Page 251

35 cm. Warm buffy-brown with faintly streaked throat and darker mantle. Adult male has blackish crown. Adult female is duller with more prominent streaks on throat, breast and mantle. Juvenile has dark streaks on upperparts, pale fringes on darker wing-coverts and many fine streaks on buffy-white underparts. In flight, pale wing-coverts contrast with blackish flight feathers. Dense marshes, usually in reeds, but also rice, mangroves and scrub. Hides in cover during day. Rare.

Mn	Mu	Nl	NB	Bv	Gu	Ml	NG	Mk	Rl	Te	Vu	Lo	GT

Black-backed Bittern *Ixobrychus dubius* Page 250

30 cm. Adult male has black crown, back and tail, chestnut head and neck, pale buff wing-coverts and buffy and dark streaks along midline underparts. Adult female has dark brown crown, rufous-brown back and paler underparts. Juvenile has blotchy dark streaks across orange-rufous upperparts and dark and pale streaks on underparts. In flight, pale wing-coverts contrast with blackish flight feathers. Dense marshes, usually in reeds or rushes beside small lakes. Singles or pairs skulk in cover. Very rare.

Mn	Mu	Nl	NB	Bv	Gu	Ml	NG	Mk	Rl	Te	Vu	Lo	GT

Black Bittern *Dupetor flavicollis australis* Page 251

58 cm. Black to rufous with buffy stripe or patch on throat-sides, fine white and buffy streaking on throat midline, and dull green-grey legs. Juvenile has pale fringes and heavily streaked underparts. In flight, appears all dark or rufous. Some New Britain birds creamy, with buffy and dark patches. Silent when flushed. Lowland swamps or small streams in thick vegetation, sometimes dry forest and mangroves. Solitary and crepuscular. Often roosts high in dense foliage. Uncommon to fairly common.

D. f. woodfordi (Solomons) female has tawny-rufous upperparts.

Mn	Mu	Nl	NB	Bv	Gu	Ml	NG	Mk	Rl	Te	Vu	Lo	GT

Australasian Bittern *Botaurus poiciloptilus* Page 250

70 cm. Stout heron with cryptic plumage. All warm brown with blackish and buffy mottles and streaks, stout pale bill, dark moustachial stripe, paler underparts and short greenish legs. In flight, wing-coverts are slightly paler than flight feathers. Solitary; skulks deep within reeds and other tall marshes. Very rare.

Mn	Mu	Nl	NB	Bv	Gu	Ml	NG	Mk	Rl	Te	Vu	Lo	GT

Kagu *Rhynochetos jubatus* Page 270

55 cm. Ash-grey with slightly darker mantle, wings and tail, and strong dark-and-white barring on spread wings. Long wispy crest usually droops over nape but erected fan-like in display. Medium-long orange-red bill, legs and eye. Juvenile is faintly barred and browner with orange bill and legs. Wet forests. Flightless. Rare.

Mn	Mu	Nl	NB	Bv	Gu	Ml	NG	Mk	Rl	Te	Vu	Lo	GT

adult
Australasian Bittern
adult
Striated Heron
juvenile
adult
Striated Heron
mandibularis
adult
Nankeen Night Heron
juvenile
Nankeen Night Heron
Black-backed Bittern
♂
adult
Yellow Bittern
♂
juvenile
♀
Black Bittern
Australasian Bittern
juvenile
adult
adult
adult displaying
juvenile
Kagu
adult

PLATE 13: KITES, HARRIER AND HONEY BUZZARD

Black Kite *Milvus migrans affinis* — Page 261

55 cm. Dark brown with paler window on base of outer primaries. Droops and flexes long tail, which has shallow fork but appears square when fully spread. Long wings usually angled at carpals, primary tips spread. Open, wetland and urban habitats. Vagrant.

Brahminy Kite *Haliastur indus girrenera* — Page 262

48 cm. Adult is rich chestnut with white head, neck and breast and black primary tips. Juvenile is untidy brown, paler on head and belly. Juvenile in flight has patchy plumage, with black tips to outer primaries and pale on primary bases extending to body. Fairly short tail and long broad wings. All lowland habitats, particularly coasts, wetlands and plantations. Gregarious. Soars with carpals angled forward, wings bowed and tail often twisted, or flaps buoyantly. Usually the commonest large raptor. ***H. i. flavirostris*** (Solomons) has yellower bill.

Mn	Mu	Nl	NB	Bv	Gu	Ml	NG	Mk	Rl	Te	Vu	Lo	GT

Whistling Kite *Haliastur sphenurus* — Page 261

56 cm. Plain sandy-brown. In flight, long wings have blackish secondaries and outer primaries, contrasting with pale brown inner primaries and remainder of underparts. Long, slightly rounded pale tail. Juvenile is more streaked and spotted. Lakes and swamps, open habitats including farmland, and less often coasts. Singles, pairs or small flocks. Glides, flaps or soars on drooped and often angled wings. Common. See Swamp Harrier.

Mn	Mu	Nl	NB	Bv	Gu	Ml	NG	Mk	Rl	Te	Vu	Lo	GT

Swamp Harrier *Circus approximans* — Page 263

55 cm. Slim, with long wings and tail. Dark brown, streaked paler on head and underparts, with white rump. Wings and tail become greyer with age, especially males. Juvenile is uniform dark brown, with pale grey bases to underwing primaries and narrow pale rump. Open habitats and forest. Flies slowly and buoyantly low over ground or canopy, wings in shallow V. Fairly common.

Mn	Mu	Nl	NB	Bv	Gu	Ml	NG	Mk	Rl	Te	Vu	Lo	GT

Black Honey Buzzard *Henicopernis infuscatus* — Page 261

50 cm. Sooty-brown with paler bars on wings and tail. In flight, has three pale bars across wings and tail but sometimes only one bar visible. In flight, long tail, broad wings held forward, pinched in at base and bulging outer primaries. Primary hill forest. Perches within canopy or glides but rarely soars. Uncommon. See Meyer's Goshawk (Plate 15).

Mn	Mu	Nl	NB	Bv	Gu	Ml	NG	Mk	Rl	Te	Vu	Lo	GT

Black Kite
atinis
Brahminy Kite
flavirostris
adult
juvenile
girrenera
adult
juvenile
Whistling Kite
adult
adult
Black Honey Buzzard
adult
♂
Swamp Harrier
juvenile
adult
♀

PLATE 14: OSPREY AND SEA EAGLES

Eastern Osprey *Pandion cristatus* — Page 260

57cm. Striped head and largely white underparts. Brown upperparts, hindneck and broad eye-stripe, white crown and underparts, and faint streaking on breast. White underwing with dark carpal patch and barred wing feathers and short tail. Long thin wings usually angled at carpal joints and held flat or bowed. Coasts, small islets and some large lakes. Singles, pairs and families, often perching conspicuously in dead trees. Loose flaps, glides, soars and hovers. Dives for and carries large fish. Fairly common.

Mn	Mu	NI	NB	Bv	Gu	MI	NG	Mk	RI	Te	Vu	Lo	GT

White-bellied Sea Eagle *Haliaeetus leucogaster* — Page 262

75 cm. Massive eagle with heavy bill. Distinctive flight shape of thin head and neck, bulging secondaries, slightly pointed wings and very short wedge-shaped tail. Adult is white with grey upperparts and black flight feathers. Juvenile is untidy buff and mid-brown, with strong contrast on underwing between white primary bases and black primary tips and secondaries. Brownest juvenile always has white on axillaries and base of tail and paler lower breast and belly. Coasts, large lakes, rivers and forest, into low mountains. Singles or pairs perch in dead trees and soar high with wings swept up into V. Fairly common.

Mn	Mu	NI	NB	Bv	Gu	MI	NG	Mk	RI	Te	Vu	Lo	GT

Solomons Sea Eagle *Haliaeetus sanfordi* — Page 262

73 cm. Massive brown eagle with heavy bill. Warm brown plumage with black tail, paler head and sometimes paler buff patches on wings. Juvenile is darker. Flight action and shape like White-bellied Sea Eagle but slightly broader wings. Coasts, especially coastal forest and reefs, and inland to at least 1500 m. Singles and pairs cruise high in sky. Fairly common to rare.

Mn	Mu	NI	NB	Bv	Gu	MI	NG	Mk	RI	Te	Vu	Lo	GT

Eastern Osprey
juvenile
adult
White-bellied Sea Eagle
juvenile
Solomons Sea Eagle
adult
adult
juvenile

PLATE 15: VARIABLE GOSHAWK AND BISMARCKS HAWKS

Variable Goshawk *Accipiter hiogaster* Page 263

40 cm. Variable hawk with short wings. Adult has grey head, throat and upperparts, rufous underparts, red eye and orange or yellow cere, loral skin and legs. Juvenile has dark brown upperparts with fine rufous fringes and barred tail, streaked throat, spots or bars on breast, bars on belly, plain orange-buff thighs and white vent. Immature has grey wash to head and upperparts and rufous wash to underparts. Immature may have rufous half-collar and subadult may retain barred tail and duller upperparts. Solitary or pairs in forest, usually forest edge in lowlands. Commonest hawk. See Pied Goshawk (Plate 16).

A. n. pulchellus (Guadalcanal) is deep plain grey and reddish.
A. n. lavongai (New Ireland) is larger and darker; all subspecies have rufous underwing-coverts.
A. n. dampieri (New Britain) is paler, with faint barring on belly.

Mn	**Mu**	**NI**	**NB**	**Bv**	**Gu**	**MI**	**NG**	Mk	RI	Te	Vu	Lo	GT

Slaty-mantled Goshawk *Accipiter luteoschistaceus* Page 266

34 cm. Medium-small hawk with short wings. Adult has slaty-black upperparts and undertail, white to pale cinnamon underparts and sometimes faint grey barring on upper breast. Orange eye, cere, loral skin, eye-ring and legs. Juvenile has black crown, heavy black bars on rufous upperparts, prominent bars on uppertail, broad brown bars on off-white underparts, extending to vent and thighs, and yellow bare parts. Lowland forest. Rare.

Mn	Mu	NI	**NB**	Bv	Gu	MI	NG	Mk	RI	Te	Vu	Lo	GT

New Britain Sparrowhawk *Accipiter brachyurus* Page 267

30 cm. Small hawk with relatively short tail, fairly pointed wings and long legs and toes. Adult has slaty-grey upperparts, orange-rufous collar and very pale grey underparts, sometimes with rufous tint on breast. Red-brown eye and yellow cere, loral skin and legs. Pale grey underwing with black primary tips. Juvenile has rufous upperparts with black blotches, plainer black crown and pale buff underparts with dark streaks. Uppertail has indistinct darker bars but undertail has equal-width heavy dark and pale bars. Forest, possibly montane. Rare.

Mn	Mu	**NI**	**NB**	Bv	Gu	MI	NG	Mk	RI	Te	Vu	Lo	GT

New Britain Goshawk *Accipiter princeps* Page 266

40 cm. Medium-large hawk, appearing bulky with short rounded wings. Adult is pale blue-grey with paler underparts and darker primary tips. Faint barring on breast. Red-orange eye, lores, cere and legs. Hill and montane forest. Uncommon to rare.

Mn	Mu	NI	**NB**	Bv	Gu	MI	NG	Mk	RI	Te	Vu	Lo	GT

Meyer's Goshawk *Accipiter meyerianus* Page 267

52 cm. Large bulky hawk, with bulging chest in flight. Adult is black and white with fine black streaking or barring, broad grey bars on tail and black-and-white bars on outer underwing. Dark morph is glossy black with grey bars on tail and underwing. Red-brown eye and yellow cere and legs. Juvenile has brown upperparts with buff fringes, barred tail and rich buff underparts with dark streaks. Forest. Rare. See Black Honey Buzzard and other hawks (Plates 13 and 16).

Mn	Mu	**NI**	**NB**	Bv	**Gu**	MI	**NG**	Mk	RI	Te	Vu	Lo	GT

Variable Goshawk
dampieri
immature
immature
juvenile
pulchellus
adult
lavongai
adult
dampieri
adult
juvenile
adult
adult
Slaty-mantled
Goshawk
juvenile
adult
adult
adult
New Britain Sparrowhawk
New Britain
Goshawk
adult
dark morph
adult
adult
Meyer's Goshawk
juvenile

Pied Goshawk *Accipiter albogularis* — Page 264

36 cm. Variable pied hawk with fairly long tail and wings. Pale morph has mid-grey upperparts with rufous hindcollar and white underparts, white underwings with grey tips to primaries and secondaries, and grey undertail. Pied morph is similar but has black upperparts, and rufous collar is variable or absent. Black morph is all black with silvery bases on underwing primaries. Legs yellow, eye yellow, orange or orange-red. Juvenile has rufous-brown upperparts with darker crown and black barring and mottling, and white or dark rufous underparts with dark brown streaks on lower throat, becoming bars on breast and belly. Forest. Fairly common. See Meyer's Goshawk (Plate 15).

A. a. eichhorni (Feni) is mid-grey with broad pink-rufous collar and faint grey barring on breast.

A. a. albogularis (Makira) never has rufous collar.

Mn	Mu	**Nl**	NB	**Bv**	**Gu**	**Ml**	**NG**	**Mk**	Rl	**Te**	Vu	Lo	GT

Imitator Goshawk *Accipiter imitator* — Page 266

30 cm. Very like Pied Goshawk but smaller, with shorter wings and dark eye. All adults have jet-black upperparts, black undertail, black undersides to outer primaries and no rufous on collar. Pied adult has black or streaked or white throat, and white, pale buff or pale grey underparts. Juvenile has finely barred underparts, dark crown contrasting with indistinctly barred rufous upperparts, faint barring on uppertail and yellow eye. Lowland and hill forest. Rare.

Mn	Mu	Nl	NB	**Bv**	Gu	Ml	NG	Mk	Rl	Te	Vu	Lo	GT

White-bellied Goshawk *Accipiter haplochrous* — Page 265

34 cm. Stocky pied hawk with short broad wings. Adult has slate-grey upperparts and head, slightly paler on throat and upper breast, white lower breast to vent, white underwing with black wing-tip, yellow legs and cere, and orange-red eye. Juvenile has dark brown upperparts with fine rufous barring and paler collar, creamy underparts with blackish-brown streaks on throat and upper breast, becoming spots and bars on lower underparts, and yellow eye. Forest and scrub. Fairly common.

Mn	Mu	Nl	NB	Bv	Gu	Ml	NG	Mk	Rl	Te	Vu	Lo	**GT**

Brown Goshawk *Accipiter fasciatus vigilax* — Page 264

45 cm. Large hawk with long wings and tail. In flight, has slightly bulging secondaries and more pointed wings than other *Accipiter* hawks. Adult has grey-brown upperparts with rufous collar, and rufous underparts with fine white bars. Juvenile has dark brown upperparts and off-white underparts with dark brown streaks on throat, becoming heavy spots on upper breast, bars on lower breast and belly, and fine rufous bars on thighs. Open habitats with scattered trees, forest edge and degraded forest at all altitudes, sometimes primary forest. Common. See Swamp Harrier (Plate 13).

Mn	Mu	Nl	NB	Bv	Gu	Ml	NG	Mk	**Rl**	Te	**Vu**	**Lo**	**GT**

albogularis
adult
adult
dark morph
eichhorni
adult
Pied Goshawk
dark juvenile
adult
pied morph
pale juvenile
adult
juvenile
pied
morph
imitator
imitator
Imitator Goshawk
dark
morph
juvenile
adult
adult
White-bellied Goshawk
juvenile
adult
adult
Brown Goshawk

PLATE 17: PACIFIC BAZA AND FALCONS

Pacific Baza *Aviceda subcristata bismarckii* — Page 260

39 cm. Grey head and neck with short crest and yellow eye, black-and-white barred breast and belly, and rufous vent. In flight, broad wings pinched in at base, deep fingered hands and short tail. Rufous underwing-coverts, fine black bars on silvery underwing and tail, and broad black tail-band. Lowland forest. Hunts within forest canopy or soars on flat wings. Fairly common. See kites (Plate 13).

Mn	Mu	NI	NB	Bv	Gu	MI	NG	Mk	RI	Te	Vu	Lo	GT

Nankeen Kestrel *Falco cenchroides* — Page 268

32 cm. Small falcon. Dark moustachial stripe across pale throat and cheeks, brown upperparts with black spots, black primaries and tail-band, white underparts with black streaks and white underwing with black barring. Male has grey crown and tail. Female has brown crown and barred tail. Open habitats, usually grasslands. Hovers, soars, and perches on exposed perches. Vagrant.

Australian Hobby *Falco longipennis* — Page 269

33 cm. Adult has grey upperparts with black bars on tail, blackish head with short moustachial stripe, white cheeks and throat, blue bill and eye-ring, and pale orange underparts with fine black streaks. Juvenile browner. Open lowlands, especially grasslands. Shape, flight and habits like Oriental Hobby. Vagrant.

Oriental Hobby *Falco severus* — Page 268

28 cm. Small slender falcon with long narrow pointed wings which project beyond tail when perched. Yellow bare parts. Adult has blackish upperparts with pointed mask on white cheeks and throat, and rufous underparts and underwing-coverts. Juvenile has black streaks on buff underparts. Forest edge and gardens, sometimes closed forest. Perches in dead trees and chases flying insects or birds. Uncommon.

Mn	Mu	NI	NB	Bv	Gu	MI	NG	Mk	RI	Te	Vu	Lo	GT

Brown Falcon *Falco berigora* — Page 269

45 cm. Sluggish, scruffy and rather round-winged falcon. Variable plumage with dark moustachial and cheek-stripes contrasting with paler throat, mid-cheek and hind-cheek. Grasslands. Only on Long I.

Mn	Mu	NI	NB	Bv	Gu	MI	NG	Mk	RI	Te	Vu	Lo	GT

Peregrine Falcon *Falco peregrinus ernesti* — Page 269

44 cm. Stocky falcon with bulging chest, broad-based pointed wings and medium-length tail. Adult has blue-grey upperparts, darker head and cheeks, white throat and half-collar and dense black bars on white underparts. Juvenile is dark brown above and pale buff with brown streaks below. Soars high over coasts and open country. Rare. See hawks (Plates 15 and 16).
F. p. nesiotes (Vanuatu and New Caledonia) has buff or rufous wash on underparts.

Mn	Mu	NI	NB	Bv	Gu	MI	NG	Mk	RI	Te	Vu	Lo	GT

immature
adult
adult
Pacific Baza
♂
Nankeen
Kestrel
♀
Oriental Hobby
Australian Hobby
nesiotes
adult
ernesti
juvenile
Peregrine Falcon
ernesti
adult
Brown Falcon

King Quail *Excalfactoria chinensis lepida*

Page 226

13 cm. Male has black and white throat, blue-grey head, breast and flanks, chestnut belly and vent, mottled brown upperparts and yellow feet. Female is warm brown, mottled and barred grey and black. In flight, uniform brown upperwing. Dry or damp grassland. Chatters when flushed. Rare.

Mn	Mu	**Nl**	**NB**	Bv	Gu	Ml	NG	Mk	Rl	Te	Vu	Lo	GT

Red-backed Buttonquail *Turnix maculosus salomonis*

Page 276

14 cm. Rufous or buff head and underparts with black stripes and spots, barred and mottled upperparts, and yellow legs and bill. Male has less rufous. Juvenile is more extensively mottled black. In flight, buff wing-coverts contrast with darker flight feathers. Silent when flushed. Dry grassland. Uncommon.

T. m. ***saturata*** (New Britain) has less rufous on collar and upperparts.

Mn	Mu	Nl	**NB**	Bv	**Gu**	Ml	NG	Mk	Rl	Te	Vu	Lo	GT

Painted Buttonquail *Turnix varius novaecaledoniae*

Page 277

16 cm. Upperparts mottled rufous, grey, black and white, greyer head with pale supercilium and throat, rufous shoulders and greyer underparts with white belly. Female has more rufous. Very rare or extinct.

Mn	Mu	Nl	NB	Bv	Gu	Ml	NG	Mk	Rl	Te	Vu	Lo	**GT**

Spotless Crake *Porzana tabuensis*

Page 274

17 cm. Sooty with brown mantle and wings, and white bars on undertail-coverts. Red eye and legs, and dark grey bill. Juvenile has paler underparts, duller eye and legs. Quiet motorcycle-like purrs. Dense waterside vegetation, and dry scrub on small islands. Rare.

Mn	Mu	Nl	NB	Bv	**Gu**	Ml	**NG**	**Mk**	**Rl**	**Te**	**Vu**	**Lo**	**GT**

Baillon's Crake *Porzana pusilla*

Page 274

16 cm. Grey face, throat and breast, black-and-white barred belly and undertail, and spotted brown upperparts. Green bill and legs. Juvenile has buff face, throat and breast. Swamps. Vagrant.

White-browed Crake *Porzana cinerea*

Page 275

17 cm. Pale grey head to belly with two white stripes on face, buff vent and undertail-coverts, and brown upperparts with dark mottling. Juvenile has less contrasting head pattern and pale buff neck and underparts. Rapid nasal chattering *chika-chika-chika-*. Beside lakes, ponds and swamps. Uncommon.

Mn	**Mu**	**Nl**	**NB**	**Bv**	**Gu**	Ml	NG	**Mk**	Rl	**Te**	**Vu**	**Lo**	**GT**

Red-necked Crake *Rallina tricolor*

Page 270

28 cm. Dark olive-brown with chestnut head and neck, and pale barring on belly to undertail-coverts. Red eye, green bill and olive legs. Juvenile is all dark with buffy face. In flight, shows white bars on wing. Harsh *neek-neak-neek-*. Rainforest with wet ground. Rare.

Mn	**Mu**	**Nl**	NB	Bv	Gu	Ml	NG	Mk	Rl	Te	Vu	Lo	GT

♂
♀
King Quail
saturata
salamonis
Red-backed Buttonquail
♀
Painted Buttonquail
Baillon's Crake
adult
juvenile
Spotless Crake
immature
adult
Red-necked Crake
White-browed Crake

Pale-vented Bush-hen *Amaurornis moluccana ultima* Page 274

26 cm. Olive-brown upperparts, grey underparts, pale buffy-rufous vent and undertail-coverts, and greenish-yellow legs and stout bill. Cat-like wailing. Dense grassland and overgrown gardens, sometimes in forest. Fairly common.

Mn	Mu	NI	NB	Bv	Gu	MI	NG	Mk	RI	Te	Vu	Lo	GT

Buff-banded Rail *Gallirallus philippensis meyeri* Page 272

28 cm. Rufous head with pale supercilium, and brown upperparts with white spots. Grey throat and upper breast, black-and-white barred underparts and often orange breast-band. Dull pink bill and legs. Varied calls. Lowland grassland, thickets and gardens. Fairly common.

G. p. swindellsi (New Caledonia) lacks breast-band.

Mn	Mu	NI	NB	Bv	Gu	MI	NG	Mk	RI	Te	Vu	Lo	GT

Roviana Rail *Gallirallus rovianae* Page 273

30 cm. Dark brown upperparts with pale grey supercilium. Pale grey throat and breast, buff breast-band and black-and-white barred underparts. Some have finer bars and indistinct breast-band. Dark grey bill and legs. Staccato chattering. Lowland grassy vegetation, plantations and gardens. Flightless. Uncommon.

Mn	Mu	NI	NB	Bv	Gu	MI	NG	Mk	RI	Te	Vu	Lo	GT

Pink-legged Rail *Gallirallus insignis* Page 272

33 cm. Plain rufous-brown head and upperparts and strongly barred black-and-silver underparts including underwing. Stout dark bill and pink legs. Forest, especially thickets and damp areas in hills and mountains. Varied calls include squeals and yaps. Flightless. Uncommon.

Mn	Mu	NI	NB	Bv	Gu	MI	NG	Mk	RI	Te	Vu	Lo	GT

New Caledonian Rail *Gallirallus lafresnayanus* Page 271

47 cm. Plain brown upperparts and greyer underparts with some faint barring. Long dark horn bill and dark horn or brown legs. Rainforest. Flightless. Probably extinct.

Mn	Mu	NI	NB	Bv	Gu	MI	NG	Mk	RI	Te	Vu	Lo	GT

Bare-eyed Rail *Gymnocrex plumbeiventris intactus* Page 273

32 cm. Bright chestnut head, neck, upper mantle and breast, brown wings and lower mantle, ashy-grey lower breast and belly, and erect black tail. Green, yellowish or brownish bill, and pink legs and bare skin around eye. Forest and sometimes wet grasslands and swamps. Deep gulping and grunting. Vagrant?

Pale-vented Bush-hen
meyeri
Buff-banded Rail
swindellsi
Roviana Rail
Pink-legged Rail
variant
New Caledonian Rail
Bare-eyed Rail

Woodford's Rail *Nesoclopeus woodfordi* — Page 271

30 cm. Very dark brown upperparts and slightly greyer underparts, often appearing all black. May have tawny or brown patches, especially on head, and faint buff or white barring on underparts and underwings. Damp lowland grassland and grassy thickets within forest. Single and series of staccato yelps. Flightless. Uncommon.

N. w. ? (Malaita) has white barring and dark bill.

N. w. tertius (Bougainville) has faint white barring and yellow-horn bill.

N. w. immaculatus (Isabel) has no barring and ivory bill.

N. w. woodfordi (Guadalcanal) has dark grey bill and pale grey head.

Mn	Mu	NI	NB	**Bv**	**Gu**	Ml	NG	Mk	RI	Te	Vu	Lo	GT

Purple Swamphen *Porphyrio porphyrio* — Page 275

41 cm. Adult has red massive bill, frontal shield and legs. Blue-purple head and body, dark brown mantle, wings and uppertail, and white undertail-coverts. Juvenile is all black including bare parts. Immature is duller than adult with smaller bill. Lowland wet freshwater habitats and dry forest thickets, gardens and grassland. Varied calls include wheezing yelps. Usually on ground but climbs up dense vegetation and often flies. Flushes with heavy flight. Common.

Mn	Mu	**NI**	**NB**	**Bv**	**Gu**	**Ml**	**NG**	**Mk**	**RI**	**Te**	**Vu**	**Lo**	**GT**

Makira Woodhen *Gallinula silvestris* — Page 275

26 cm. Black with blue gloss on neck, browner on underparts and especially wings. Bright scarlet legs and bill, grey frontal shield and yellow facial skin. Hill forest. Tail-less and flightless. Probably extinct.

Mn	Mu	NI	NB	Bv	Gu	Ml	NG	**Mk**	RI	Te	Vu	Lo	GT

Dusky Moorhen *Gallinula tenebrosa* — Page 276

31 cm. Adult is blue-grey with browner mantle and wings, and white on undertail-coverts. Breeding adult has red legs, bill and frontal shield, and yellow bill-tip. Juvenile is duller and browner, with dull, often olive-brown bill and legs. Well-vegetated lakes and swamps. Varied short sharp calls. Swims in ponds and lakes, and grazes waterside vegetation, usually flicking tail. Very rare.

Mn	Mu	NI	**NB**	Bv	**Gu**	Ml	NG	Mk	RI	Te	Vu	Lo	**GT**

Comb-crested Jacana *Irediparra gallinacea* — Page 282

23 cm. Adult has red comb and frontal shield, buff-washed white head and neck, black breast-band, white belly and brown upperparts. Exceptionally long grey legs and toes. Juvenile lacks shield, comb, buff wash and breast-band. Shrill trilling. Walks on floating vegetation on lowland swamps and lakes. Rare.

Mn	Mu	NI	**NB**	Bv	Gu	Ml	NG	Mk	RI	Te	Vu	Lo	GT

tertius
immaculatus
Malaita
Woodford's Rail
woodfordi
adult
Purple Swamphen
immature
chick
Makira Woodhen
adult
juvenile
Dusky Moorhen
adult
Comb-crested Jacana
juvenile

South Island Oystercatcher *Haematopus finschi* Page 277

46 cm. Black and white with long straight orange-red bill and fairly short pink-red legs. In flight, mainly black above with white lower back, rump and wing-bar on secondaries. Coasts. Vagrant.

Beach Stone-curlew *Esacus magnirostris* Page 277

56 cm. Stout with massive yellow and black bill, and dull yellow legs. Brown with dark brown and white stripes on face, paler underparts, and dark bar and grey panel on wing. In flight, white patches on black outer primaries, white inner primaries and pale grey secondaries. White underwing with black tips. Shrill wailing *keer-lee*. Beaches, reefs and mangroves, especially on small islands. Uncommon or rare.

Mn	Mu	NI	NB	Bv	Gu	MI	NG	Mk	RI	Te	Vu	Lo	GT

White-headed Stilt *Himantopus leucocephalus* Page 278

37 cm. Elegant pied wader with exceptionally long pink legs and long fine black bill. Adult is white with black wings, mantle and hindneck. Immature has blackish smudging on head and browner upperparts. In flight, extremely long pink legs, black wings, and head, body and underwing-coverts. Repeated loud yapping *kyap, kyap…* . Shallow muddy waters. Rare.

Mn	Mu	NI	NB	Bv	Gu	MI	NG	Mk	RI	Te	Vu	Lo	GT

Masked Lapwing *Vanellus miles novaehollandiae* Page 278

37 cm. Yellow bill and facial wattle, black cap, nape and breast-sides, brown mantle and wings, and white underparts. In flight, broad wings, brown and black upperparts, white rump and black tail-band. White underwing-coverts. Loud grating staccato *kree-kree-kree-*. Open short grasslands. Noisy and aggressive. Rare.

Mn	Mu	NI	NB	Bv	Gu	MI	NG	Mk	RI	Te	Vu	Lo	GT

Australian Pratincole *Stiltia isabella* Page 292

23 cm. Slim with very long wings which extend far past short tail. Non-breeding adult and immature are sandy-brown with paler throat and dusky flank-patches on white belly. Breeding adult is brighter with black and chestnut band across flanks. In flight, long pointed wings, sandy upperwing with black primaries, black underwing with paler trailing edge, and legs projecting beyond short black-centred white tail. Liquid *weetweet* and tern-like trilling. Grassland or bare habitats. Runs or flies high in sky. Vagrant.

Oriental Pratincole *Glareola maldivarum* Page 293

23 cm. Small and slender with short legs, long wings and graceful flight. Brown upperparts, paler underparts, shading into white belly and buff throat-patch. In flight, long pointed dark wings with chestnut underwing-coverts, white rump and belly, and black fork on white tail. Harsh tern-like chattering. Habits like Australian Pratincole. Vagrant.

South Island Oystercatcher
Beach Stone-curlew
adult
White-headed Stilt
immature
Masked Lapwing
breeding
breeding
Oriental Pratincole
Australian Pratincole
immature
immature

PLATE 22: PLOVERS

Pacific Golden Plover *Pluvialis fulva* — Page 279

25 cm. Short-billed with golden spangling on crown and upperparts, fading to creamy-buff. Non-breeding adult and immature have buffy mottled head, neck and underparts, indistinct broad supercilium and dark spot on ear-coverts. Breeding adult has black face and underparts bordered by broad white band. In flight, plain buffy-brown with indistinct narrow white wing-bar and dusky underwings. Clear hurried *chew-it*. Short grassland and coasts, especially airfields and playing fields. Usually in small flocks. Commonest wader, especially inland.

Mn	Mu	NI	NB	Bv	Gu	MI	NG	Mk	RI	Te	Vu	Lo	GT

Grey Plover *Pluvialis squatarola* — Page 279

29 cm. Like Pacific Golden Plover but plumage cold grey, rarely with slight buffy wash, bill stouter, shape dumpier and armpits black. In flight, white wing-bar, rump and underwing with black armpits. Loud plaintive drawn-out *klee-oo-wee*. Coasts. Usually solitary. Uncommon.

Mn	Mu	NI	NB	Bv	Gu	MI	NG	Mk	RI	Te	Vu	Lo	GT

Little Ringed Plover *Charadrius d. dubius* — Page 280

15 cm. Adult has black breast-band and mask from forehead to ear-coverts, white underparts and collar, short pinkish legs, blackish bill with yellow or pink base and broad yellow eye-ring. Immature has indistinct brown bands and narrower eye-ring. In flight, very fine white wing-bar and rump-sides. Harsh *chit, chit, chit*. Breeds on gravel beds in rivers. Rare.

Mn	Mu	NI	NB	Bv	Gu	MI	NG	Mk	RI	Te	Vu	Lo	GT

Common Ringed Plover *Charadrius hiaticula* — Page 279

19 cm. Dark breast-band and eye-mask, white underparts and collar, brown crown, mantle and wings, very short orange and black bill and short orange legs. Breeding adult has black head and breast markings. In flight, broad white wing-bar and rump-sides. Soft mellow rising *too-lee*. Coasts. Vagrant.

Semipalmated Plover *Charadrius semipalmatus* — Page 280

17 cm. Like Common Ringed Plover but tiny webs between toes, shorter thicker bill, narrower breast-band and very thin pale eye-ring. Immature has white above gape at bill-base. Clear sharp rising *chewee*. Coasts. Vagrant.

Greater Sand Plover *Charadrius leschenaultii* — Page 281

23 cm. Long yellowish-green legs. Heavy bill. Non-breeding adult and immature have brown breast-patches and white supercilium. Breeding adult has black mask, and rufous on head, neck and breast. In flight, white wing-bar and rump-sides, and toes project distinctly beyond tail. Trilled *prrit*, *trri*, etc. Coasts. Uncommon.

Mn	Mu	NI	NB	Bv	Gu	MI	NG	Mk	RI	Te	Vu	Lo	GT

Lesser Sand Plover *Charadrius mongolus* — Page 281

20 cm. Like Greater Sand Plover but smaller size, shorter and finer bill, rounder head, shorter, greyer legs and, on breeding male, black border to throat. In flight, white wing-bar and rump-sides, and toes only project slightly beyond tail. Sharp *drrit*, *chi-chi-chi*, etc. Coasts. Uncommon.

Mn	Mu	NI	NB	Bv	Gu	MI	NG	Mk	RI	Te	Vu	Lo	GT

Oriental Plover *Charadrius veredus* — Page 281

24 cm. Slender with long yellowish legs and long wings. Non-breeding adult and immature have brown breast and white supercilium. Breeding adult has buffy or white head and neck, and rufous and dark breast. In flight, long plain brown wings and dusky underwings. Sharp whistled *tink, tink, tink*. Short dry grassland. Vagrant.

Double-banded Plover *Charadrius bicinctus* — Page 280

19 cm. Short yellow-green legs and small black bill. Non-breeding adult and immature have two buffy patches or washes on breast-sides. Breeding adult has black upper and chestnut lower breast-band. In flight, narrow white wing-bar, rump-sides and outer tail feathers. Clear incisive *chip*. Coasts and short grassland. Uncommon.

Mn	Mu	NI	NB	Bv	Gu	MI	NG	Mk	RI	Te	Vu	Lo	GT

breeding
non-breeding
Pacific Golden Plover
non-breeding
non-breeding
Grey Plover
breeding
non-breeding
immature
adult
Little Ringed Plover
immature
non-breeding
breeding
Semipalmated Plover
non-breeding
breeding
Common Ringed Plover
non-breeding
♂ breeding
Greater Sand Plover
non-breeding
non-breeding
♂ breeding
non-breeding
Lesser Sand Plover
Oriental Plover
♂ breeding
non-breeding
non-breeding
Double-banded Plover
breeding

Little Curlew *Numenius minutus* Page 284

30 cm. Fine decurved bill. Buff with fine dark streaks, heavy dark mottling on upperparts and striped head, but eye-stripe not reaching bill. In flight, dark brown upperwing with paler inner coverts, body and tail, brown underwing and white belly. Call shorter, higher-pitched and more metallic than Whimbrel. Short grassland. Uncommon.

Mn Mu Nl NB Bv Gu Ml NG Mk Rl Te Vu Lo GT

Bristle-thighed Curlew *Numenius tahitiensis* Page 285

42 cm. Inconspicuous bristles on thighs. Long decurved bill. Buff to creamy with dark streaks on neck and breast, dark wings with large buff spots and striped head. In flight, finely barred buffy with cinnamon underwing and buffy rump and tail. Whistled *chi-u-wit*. Coasts, especially small isolated islands. Rare.

Mn Mu Nl NB Bv Gu Ml NG Mk Rl Te Vu Lo GT

Whimbrel *Numenius phaeopus* Page 285

43 cm. Long decurved bill. Buff, creamy or greyish-white with dark streaks on neck, breast and flanks, darker wings with buffy-white spots and striped head. In flight, finely barred brown with white rump, upper back and belly to vent. Rapid rippling *quiquiquiquiqui*. Coasts and mangroves. Common.

Mn Mu Nl NB Bv Gu Ml NG Mk Rl Te Vu Lo GT

Eastern Curlew *Numenius madagascariensis* Page 285

63 cm. Extremely long decurved bill. Buffy-brown head, neck and breast with dark streaks, and dark mottling on mantle and wings. In flight, finely patterned brown upperparts, darker primaries and finely barred underwings. Loud, slow *ker-leee*. Coasts. Rare.

Mn Mu Nl NB Bv Gu Ml NG Mk Rl Te Vu Lo GT

Black-tailed Godwit *Limosa limosa* Page 284

40 cm. Long black legs and very long straight bill. Non-breeding adult and immature have grey-brown head, neck and upperparts. Breeding adult has orange-rufous head and neck, and black bars on white breast and belly. In flight, black wings and tail with white rump, broad wing-bar and underwing-coverts. Chattering repeated *rita*. Coasts, usually muddy. Rare.

Mn Mu Nl NB Bv Gu Ml NG Mk Rl Te Vu Lo GT

Bar-tailed Godwit *Limosa lapponica* Page 284

40 cm. Long black legs and very long slightly upcurved bill. Non-breeding adult and immature have slightly streaked buffy-brown head, neck and upperparts. Breeding adult has chestnut head, neck and underparts. In flight, brown wings and tail with fine white barring. Repeated *kit*, *kew-kew*, etc. Coasts, usually sandy. Fairly common.

Mn Mu Nl NB Bv Gu Ml NG Mk Rl Te Vu Lo GT

Asian Dowitcher *Limnodromus semipalmatus* (not illustrated) Page 283

34 cm. Medium-long black legs and long straight black bill. Non-breeding adult and immature have grey upperparts with barring on throat, breast, flanks and undertail. Breeding adult has orange face, neck and underparts. In flight, rather plain upperparts with fine white wing-bar and pale grey rump. Coasts, usually muddy. Vagrant.

Ruddy Turnstone *Arenaria interpres* Page 288

23 cm. Dumpy with white and dark patches on head and breast, short straight black bill and short orange legs. Non-breeding adult and immature have sooty bands on neck and breast and paler brown head and upperparts. Breeding adult has black bands on white head and on rufous mantle and wings. In flight, black tail-band, white lower mantle and rump, white shoulder-stripe, white wing-bar, and white underwing with black margins. Low-pitched grating rattle, combinations of *tuk*, *tuk* and *tuk-i-tuk*. Coasts. Fairly common.

Mn Mu Nl NB Bv Gu Ml NG Mk Rl Te Vu Lo GT

Whimbrel
Bristle-thighed Curlew
Eastern Curlew
Little Curlew
Whimbrel
Bristle-thighed Curlew
Little Curlew
♂ breeding
Black-tailed Godwit
non-breeding
♂ breeding
non-breeding
breeding
non-breeding
Bar-tailed Godwit
non-breeding
Ruddy Turnstone

Wood Sandpiper *Tringa glareola* Page 286

21 cm. Slim with medium-long dark bill, greenish-yellow legs, dark eye-stripe and pale supercilium. Non-breeding adult and immature have brown upperparts with small buff spots. Breeding adult has larger white spots. In flight, plain upperwing, white rump and uppertail-coverts, and finely barred tail. Toes extend beyond tail. Rushed *chiff-iff-iff*. Fresh water. Vagrant.

Common Greenshank *Tringa nebularia* Page 286

32 cm. Fairly long neck, long greenish legs and slightly upturned long greenish-based black bill. Grey upperparts, darker wing-coverts, faint eye-stripe, white supercilium, and streaked neck and breast. In flight, plain upperwing with white from lower mantle onto finely barred tail. Toes extend slightly beyond tail. Loud rushed series of ringing *tew-tew-tew*. Fresh water and coasts. Rare.

Mn	Mu	Nl	NB	Bv	Gu	Ml	NG	Mk	Rl	Te	Vu	Lo	GT

Marsh Sandpiper *Tringa stagnatilis* Page 286

23 cm. Slender with long fine yellowish legs and long fine bill. Pale grey upperparts with darker wing-coverts, indistinct white supercilium and streaked neck. Breeding adult has warm brown upperparts and dark spots on breast. In flight, plain upperwing with white from lower mantle onto finely barred tail. Legs extend beyond tail. Short plaintive *plew*. Fresh water. Rare.

Mn	Mu	Nl	NB	Bv	Gu	Ml	NG	Mk	Rl	Te	Vu	Lo	GT

Common Sandpiper *Actitis hypoleucos* Page 288

20 cm. Medium straight bill, short greenish legs and long tail beyond wing-tips. Brown upperparts and breast-sides, sharply cut off from white shoulder-spur and underparts. In flight, long narrow white wing-bar, white sides to tail, and characteristic flicking shallow wing-beats and gliding on downswept wings. Plaintive piping *tswee-wee-wee-*. Coastal and inland wetlands and rivers. Often bobs head and tail. Common.

Mn	Mu	Nl	NB	Bv	Gu	Ml	NG	Mk	Rl	Te	Vu	Lo	GT

Terek Sandpiper *Xenus cinereus* Page 287

23 cm. Orange-yellow long upcurved bill and fairly short legs. Grey-brown upperparts and breast with darker wing-coverts and white supercilium. Breeding adult has black stripe on scapulars. In flight, plain upperparts including rump and tail with broad white trailing edge to secondaries. Rippling trilled *du-du-du-*. Sharper *tee-te-tee-* or *twit-wit-wit-*. Coasts. Often bobs and rushes with head held low. Uncommon.

Mn	Mu	Nl	NB	Bv	Gu	Ml	NG	Mk	Rl	Te	Vu	Lo	GT

Wandering Tattler *Tringa incana* Page 287

27 cm. Stocky with medium-short yellowish legs and medium yellow-based bill. Grey upperparts with indistinct eye-stripe and short white supercilium. Non-breeding adult and immature have grey face to breast and flanks. Breeding adult has broad bars across all underparts. In flight, plain grey upperparts and underwing. Fast rippling trill of *c.*10 notes, similar to Whimbrel. Often fewer notes, sometimes as few as two, but always staccato unlike slurred notes of Grey-tailed Tattler. Coasts. Fairly common.

Mn	Mu	Nl	NB	Bv	Gu	Ml	NG	Mk	Rl	Te	Vu	Lo	GT

Grey-tailed Tattler *Tringa brevipes* Page 287

25 cm. Like Wandering Tattler but paler greyer plumage, longer supercilium meeting above bill and extending beyond eye, contrasting eye-stripe, and wing-tips hardly extending beyond tail. Breeding adult has paler, finer barring on breast and flanks. In flight, plain grey upperparts and underwing. Soft liquid rising *tloo-eep*, scratchy *tu-wi* or *twiwiwi* or strident *klee*. Notes variable but always slurred and often like Pacific Golden Plover. Coasts. Common.

Mn	Mu	Nl	NB	Bv	Gu	Ml	NG	Mk	Rl	Te	Vu	Lo	GT

breeding
Marsh Sandpiper
breeding
Common Greenshank
breeding
Wood Sandpiper
Common Sandpiper
breeding
Terek Sandpiper
immature
immature
Marsh Sandpiper
non-breeding
Common Greenshank
Wood Sandpiper
breeding
Common Sandpiper
breeding
non-breeding
Terek Sandpiper
breeding
non-breeding
breeding
Grey-tailed Tattler
Wandering Tattler
non-breeding
immature
non-breeding

Red Knot *Calidris canutus* Page 289

24 cm. Compact with short greenish legs and medium-length straight black bill. Non-breeding adult and immature have grey upperparts with fine streaking on breast, darker eye-stripe and white supercilium. Breeding adult has chestnut face and underparts, and chestnut and black spots on upperparts. In flight, grey upperparts with narrow white wing-bar and finely barred uppertail which appears plain at distance. Throaty *knut*. Coasts. Rare.

Mn	Mu	NI	NB	Bv	Gu	Ml	NG	Mk	Rl	Te	Vu	Lo	GT

Great Knot *Calidris tenuirostris* Page 288

27 cm. Compact with medium-short dark legs and medium-long, very slightly decurved black bill. Non-breeding adult and immature like Red Knot. Breeding adult has black streaks on crown, neck and mantle, spots on breast, and chestnut and black on wing-coverts. In flight, grey upperparts with narrow white wing-bar and white uppertail-coverts. Throaty *nhut* or *nyut-nyut*. Coasts. Vagrant.

Ruff *Philomachus pugnax* Page 291

23–29 cm. Elegant with long neck, small head, plain head pattern, pale lores, and variably pale-coloured medium slightly decurved bill and medium-long legs. Non-breeding adult and immature have scaly brown upperparts and streaked brown breast. Breeding adult has variably coloured patches or ruff on head and neck. In flight, brown with broad white oval on rump-sides and narrow white wing-bar. Toes project beyond tail. Usually silent. Fresh water. Vagrant.

Swinhoe's Snipe *Gallinago megala* Page 283

28 cm. Stocky with very long straight bill, short legs and mottled brown plumage. Distinct dark lateral crown-stripe, dark eye-stripe, pale yellow stripes on mantle and barred flanks. In flight, dumpy with short dark wings. Toes project slightly beyond short tail which has rufous centre and white tips. Harsh *raaap*. Damp grassland and wetland edges. Uncommon.

Mn	Mu	NI	NB	Bv	Gu	Ml	NG	Mk	Rl	Te	Vu	Lo	GT

Pintail Snipe *Gallinago stenura* Page 283

26 cm. Like Swinhoe's and Latham's Snipe but shorter bill, tail projects very little beyond wings and primaries very little beyond tertials. In flight, dumpy with short dark wings. Almost full length of toes project beyond tail and less white on tail-tips. Louder and slightly harsher call. Vagrant?

Latham's Snipe *Gallinago hardwickii* Page 282

29 cm. Like Swinhoe's and Pintail Snipe but tail projects well beyond wings, and primaries very little beyond tertials. In flight, dumpy with short dark wings. Toes do not project beyond tail. Shorter lower-pitched *rak*. Vagrant?

Red-necked Phalarope *Phalaropus lobatus* Page 292

18 cm. Dark mask through eye and ear-coverts. Fine short black bill. Non-breeding adult and immature have dark crown and pale grey hindneck and upperparts with paler fringes. Immature is browner with buff mantle-stripes. Breeding adult has dark grey upperparts with chestnut neck, white throat and buff mantle-stripes. Swims on sea or coastal lakes. In flight, pale grey mantle, prominent white wing-bar on dark wings, and white rump-sides. Soft *chuk* or sharp *twit*. Rare.

Mn	Mu	NI	NB	Bv	Gu	Ml	NG	Mk	Rl	Te	Vu	Lo	GT

non-breeding
Red Knot
breeding
breeding
Red Knot
breeding
Great Knot
non-breeding
non-breeding
Ruff
non-breeding
Ruff
breeding
♂
Swinhoe's
Snipe
Latham's Snipe
Pintail Snipe
non-breeding
Red-necked
Phalarope
breeding
♀
non-breeding

Sanderling *Calidris alba* Page 289

20 cm. Stocky wader with medium-short straight black bill and short black legs. Non-breeding adult and immature have pale grey head, upperparts and breast-sides with blackish shoulders, indistinct white supercilium and plain white underparts. Breeding adult has rufous on head, neck and upperparts, with black mottling. In flight, very prominent white wing-bar and white rump-sides. Quiet liquid *kwik* or *ket*, sometimes repeated as trill. Sandy beaches. Uncommon.

Mn	Mu	NI	NB	Bv	Gu	MI	NG	Mk	RI	Te	Vu	Lo	GT

Red-necked Stint *Calidris ruficollis* Page 289

15 cm. Short straight black bill and short black legs. Non-breeding adult and immature have pale grey head and upperparts, white supercilium, some grey streaks on breast and plain white underparts. Breeding adult has plain rufous neck and breast, mottled black and rufous on mantle, and dark spots on breast. In flight, grey upperparts with white wing-bar and white rump-sides. Thin *kreep* or *chit*, sometimes trilled. Coasts. Uncommon.

Mn	Mu	NI	NB	Bv	Gu	MI	NG	Mk	RI	Te	Vu	Lo	GT

Sharp-tailed Sandpiper *Calidris acuminata* Page 290

20 cm. Brown upperparts with rufous crown, white supercilium, scaly mantle and wing-coverts, and brown streaks on buffy neck and breast merging into white lower breast and belly. Medium greenish legs and medium slightly decurved bill with indistinct pale base. Breeding adult is darker with black arrowheads on flanks. In flight, brown with faint white wing-bar and white rump-sides. Dry *trit-trit-* or twittering, e.g. *prtt-wheet-eet-*. Fresh water, grassland and coasts. Fairly common.

Mn	Mu	NI	NB	Bv	Gu	MI	NG	Mk	RI	Te	Vu	Lo	GT

Pectoral Sandpiper *Calidris melanotos* Page 290

21 cm. Like Sharp-tailed Sandpiper but more heavily streaked breast with sharp lower border, less rufous cap, longer bill with distinct pale base, yellower legs, more upright posture and, on breeding adult, no arrowheads. In flight, brown with faint white wing-bar and white rump-sides. Dry croaky trilling *prrt*. Fresh water, sometimes grassland and coasts. Vagrant.

Long-toed Stint *Calidris subminuta* Page 290

15 cm. Resembles tiny elongate Sharp-tailed Sandpiper. Short, slightly decurved black bill with pale base, and yellowish-brown to greenish legs and long toes. Brown upperparts with darker crown, pale supercilium, streaks on neck and breast, and mottled wings. Breeding adult and immature has rufous crown, and rufous fringes and white lines on mantle. In flight, brownish-grey upperparts with narrow white wing-bar and white rump-sides. Toes extend beyond tail. Trilling *chee*, soft rolling *kurrip* or short *prit*. Fresh water. Vagrant.

Curlew Sandpiper *Calidris ferruginea* Page 291

21 cm. Elegant with long fine decurved black bill and medium-long black legs. Non-breeding adult and immature have grey upperparts, smudged breast-sides and prominent pale supercilium. Immature has buff scales on upperparts and buff wash on breast-sides. Breeding adult is all chestnut with black, chestnut and white on mantle and scapulars. In flight, plain white rump and white wing-bar. Liquid *chirup*. Musical *tirri-tirri-tirri*. Coasts. Uncommon.

Mn	Mu	NI	NB	Bv	Gu	MI	NG	Mk	RI	Te	Vu	Lo	GT

Broad-billed Sandpiper *Limicola falcinellus* Page 291

17 cm. Long black bill slightly drooping at tip and striped head with white lateral crown-stripe and white supercilium. Grey upperparts and white underparts with streaks on neck and breast, and short greenish legs. Immature and breeding adult have black and rufous mottling on upperparts. In flight, narrow white wing-bar, white rump-sides and darker bar on lesser wing-coverts. Dry buzzing trilled *triit*. Coasts. Vagrant?

breeding
Sanderling
non-breeding
breeding
breeding
non-breeding
Red-necked Stint
breeding
breeding
immature
breeding
breeding
Sharp-tailed Sandpiper
breeding
Pectoral
Sandpiper
immature
breeding
non-breeding
Long-toed
Stint
breeding
breeding
Curlew Sandpiper
breeding
non-breeding
breeding
non-breeding
Broad-billed
Sandpiper

PLATE 27: GULLS AND LARGE TERNS

Black-tailed Gull *Larus crassirostris* — Page 295

46 cm. Large gull with broad black subterminal tail-band. Adult has white head, underparts and tail, dark grey mantle and wings, black wing-tips, heavy dark-tipped yellow bill and yellow-green legs. Non-breeding adult has grey streaks on head and nape. First-year is greyish-brown with whitish forehead, throat, rump and vent, blackish tail with narrow white terminal band and pinkish legs and bill with dark tip. Second-year is like adult but mottled brown. Vagrant? Note that other large gull species may occur as vagrants. See skuas (Plate 27).

Silver Gull *Chroicocephalus novaehollandiae* — Page 295

42 cm. Small gull with red bill and legs. Adult is white with pale grey mantle and wings, and black wing-tips enclosing white spot. Immature has duller bare parts, brown mottling on mantle and wings, brown terminal tail-band and trailing edge to wing. Coasts. Common.

Mn	Mu	Nl	NB	Bv	Gu	Ml	NG	Mk	Rl	Te	Vu	Lo	GT

Black-headed Gull *Chroicocephalus ridibundus* — Page 295

40 cm. Small gull with red bill and legs. Adult is white with pale grey mantle and wings, white wedge along outer primaries, narrow black trailing edge to primaries, and dusky underside to primaries. Breeding adult has brown hood with white eye-lids. Non-breeding adult has white head with dark smudges. Immature is mottled brown on wing-coverts, has blackish trailing band across wings and tail, and duller bill and legs. Coasts. Vagrant. Note that other smaller gull species may occur as vagrants.

Gull-billed Tern *Gelochelidon nilotica* — Page 296

39 cm. Stocky tern with stout gull-like black bill. White with short shallowly forked tail, pale grey mantle and wings and ill-defined dusky trailing edge to primaries. Breeding adult has black cap from forehead to nape. Non-breeding adult has black ear-covert patch, often mottled. Immature has darker upperwings, faintly mottled brown, and dusky tail-tip. Sheltered coasts and inland waters. Usually picks prey from surface, rarely diving. Vagrant?

Great Crested Tern *Thalasseus bergii* — Page 296

46 cm. Large tern with long cold yellow bill, grey mantle and wings. Breeding adult has narrow white forehead, shaggy black cap and indistinct dark trailing edge to outer primaries. Non-breeding adult has white forehead, black mask and streaky black hindcrown. Juvenile has heavy brown mottling on upperparts including tail, dark grey primaries, four dark bars across inner wing and duller bill. Immature similar, but has grey mantle and faded wing-bars. Coasts and seas. Colonies breed on small islets. Common.

Mn	Mu	Nl	NB	Bv	Gu	Ml	NG	Mk	Rl	Te	Vu	Lo	GT

Lesser Crested Tern *Thalasseus bengalensis* — Page 296

39 cm. Large tern with long slender yellow-orange bill and medium-grey mantle, wings and tail. Breeding adult has shaggy black cap from bill to nape. Non-breeding adult has white forehead, black mask, streaky black hindcrown and paler bill. Upperwing has darker outer primaries or dusky trailing edge to outer primaries. Immature has darker grey primaries, dusky subterminal secondary bar, faint dusky lesser-covert and secondary-covert bars, some mottling on upperparts including tail, and duller bill. Inshore seas. Vagrant.

1st-year
non-breeding
1st-year
Black-tailed Gull
non-breeding
1st-year
immature
adult
adult
immature
Silver Gull
immature
non-breeding
Black-headed Gull
immature
breeding
breeding
non-breeding
Gull-billed Tern
immature
non-breeding
immature
non-breeding
non-breeding
Great Crested Tern
breeding
breeding
Lesser
Crested Tern

PLATE 28: SMALLER TERNS

Roseate Tern *Sterna dougallii* — Page 299

38 cm. Breeding adult has reddish bill and legs, long tail-streamers and sometimes pink on underparts. Non-breeding adult has white forehead and black bill. In flight, adult breeding has plain upperwing with white trailing edge, faintly darker outer primaries and faint trailing edge to underwing primaries. Non-breeding adult has darker outer primaries and faint lesser-covert bar. Juvenile has dark fringes on mantle, wing-coverts and especially tertials, mid-grey upperwings with darker secondary bar and outer primaries. Coasts. Uncommon.

Mn	Mu	Nl	NB	Bv	Gu	Ml	NG	Mk	Rl	Te	Vu	Lo	GT

Black-naped Tern *Sterna sumatrana* — Page 299

31 cm. Breeding adult has black mask from eye to nape, black bill and legs, pale upperparts and sometimes pink on underparts. Non-breeding adult has streaky hindcrown. In flight, very pale grey mantle and upperwing. Juvenile has dark fringes on mantle, wing-coverts and tertials, and darker secondaries and primaries. First-year like adult but darker lesser-covert bar and slightly darker primaries. Coasts. Common.

Mn	Mu	Nl	NB	Bv	Gu	Ml	NG	Mk	Rl	Te	Vu	Lo	GT

Common Tern *Sterna hirundo* — Page 299

34 cm. Non-breeding adult has black bill, dark red legs, black hindcrown and darker lesser coverts and primaries. In flight, adult upperwing has dark trailing edges to primaries, darker outer primaries, and white trailing edge to secondaries. Underwing has translucent secondaries contrasting with darker primaries which have smudged dark trailing edge. Non-breeding adult has dark lesser-covert bar. First-year has darker lesser-covert bar, secondary bar and outer primaries. Coasts. Fairly common.

Mn	Mu	Nl	NB	Bv	Gu	Ml	NG	Mk	Rl	Te	Vu	Lo	GT

Arctic Tern *Sterna paradisaea* — Page 300

34 cm. Like Common Tern but shorter bill and legs, and paler primaries. At sea. Vagrant?

Fairy Tern *Sternula nereis* — Page 297

23 cm. Breeding adult has yellow bill and white forehead from lores to just over eye. Non-breeding adult has duller bill, white streaks on crown and dark lesser coverts. In flight, adult has plain grey mantle and wings and short forked white tail. Non-breeding adult has faint lesser-covert bar. Juvenile has dark fringes on mantle, wing-coverts and tertials, and darker lesser-covert bar and outer primaries. First-year lacks barring on upperparts. Coasts. Rare.

Mn	Mu	Nl	NB	Bv	Gu	Ml	NG	Mk	Rl	Te	Vu	Lo	GT

Little Tern *Sternula albifrons* — Page 297

23 cm. Like Fairy Tern but dark outer primaries and breeding adult has black bill-tip and white forehead extending sharply over black lores. In flight, non-breeding birds have more prominent dark lesser-covert bar. Coasts. Fairly common.

Mn	Mu	Nl	NB	Bv	Gu	Ml	NG	Mk	Rl	Te	Vu	Lo	GT

Whiskered Tern *Chlidonias hybrida* — Page 300

26 cm. Breeding adult is all grey except white cheeks, and red bill and legs. Non-breeding adult has dark bill and black mask from eye to nape, streaked on hindcrown. In flight, broad plain grey wings and short grey tail. Breeding adult has darker grey body and wing-coverts. Non-breeding adult has black mask from eye to nape with dark streaks on hindcrown or just an ear-covert patch. Juvenile has buff and black fringes on mantle. Fresh water. Uncommon.

Mn	Mu	Nl	NB	Bv	Gu	Ml	NG	Mk	Rl	Te	Vu	Lo	GT

White-winged Tern *Chlidonias leucopterus* — Page 301

23 cm. Breeding adult has black head and body, pale upperwing, red legs and small blackish bill. Non-breeding adult has white body and black rounded ear-covert patch. In flight, broad grey wings, white rump and short grey tail. Non-breeding adult has darker lesser-covert and secondary bars. First-year has even darker lesser-covert and secondary bars. Fresh water. Uncommon.

Mn	Mu	Nl	NB	Bv	Gu	Ml	NG	Mk	Rl	Te	Vu	Lo	GT

juvenile
non-breeding
Roseate Tern
breeding
juvenile
breeding
Black-naped Tern
breeding
non-breeding
Common Tern
non-breeding
Arctic Tern
non-breeding
juvenile
Fairy Tern
breeding
non-breeding
non-breeding
Whiskered Tern
breeding
Little Tern
non-breeding
breeding
White-winged Tern
breeding

Sooty Tern *Onychoprion fuscatus* Page 298

43 cm. Adult has black upperparts including tail and white forehead extending to eye. Juvenile is sooty with white lower belly. In flight, adult has dark underside of primaries and secondaries contrasting with white underwing-coverts. Juvenile is all sooty-brown with white underwing-coverts and white belly. Immature has patchy brown underparts. Far out to sea. Fairly common.

Mn	Mu	NI	NB	Bv	Gu	MI	NG	Mk	RI	Te	Vu	Lo	GT

Bridled Tern *Onychoprion anaethetus* Page 298

38 cm. Adult has black cap, white forehead to behind eye, pale collar and brown upperparts including tail. In flight, underwing has white-centred black primaries and secondaries contrasting slightly with white underwing-coverts. Juvenile has scruffier head pattern and buff fringes on upperparts. At sea. Common.

Mn	Mu	NI	NB	Bv	Gu	MI	NG	Mk	RI	Te	Vu	Lo	GT

Spectacled Tern *Onychoprion lunatus* Page 297

38 cm. Adult as Bridled Tern but grey upperparts; underwing primaries are white with black tips. At sea. Vagrant.

Black Noddy *Anous minutus* Page 294

34 cm. Sooty-brown with white cap. Slender bill is longer than cap. In flight, has uniform upperwings. Underwing-coverts are slightly darker than primaries and secondaries. Long wedge-shaped tail is forked when spread, and often paler or greyer than rest of upperparts. Juvenile has smaller cap and buffy fringes on upperparts. Seas. Common.

Mn	Mu	NI	NB	Bv	Gu	MI	NG	Mk	RI	Te	Vu	Lo	GT

Brown Noddy *Anous stolidus* Page 293

42 cm. Chocolate-brown with silvery crown, whiter on forehead. Stout bill is shorter than cap. In flight, shows paler central upperwing-bar and slightly darker long wedge-shaped tail, forked when spread. Underwings are paler with dark margins. Juvenile has browner cap and buffy fringes on upperparts. Seas. Common.

Mn	Mu	NI	NB	Bv	Gu	MI	NG	Mk	RI	Te	Vu	Lo	GT

Grey Noddy *Procelsterna albivitta* Page 294

29 cm. Whitish head and underparts and grey mantle and wings. Seas close to Matthew, Hunter and Walpole Is only.

Mn	Mu	NI	NB	Bv	Gu	MI	NG	Mk	RI	Te	Vu	Lo	GT

Blue Noddy *Procelsterna cerulea* Page 294

29 cm. Blue-grey, slightly darker on mantle and wings. Seas. Vagrant?

White Tern *Gygis alba* Page 294

31 cm. All white with large black eye and black-tipped blue bill. Juvenile has buffy wash. In flight, has relatively short wings, short forked tail and fine dark primary shafts. Primaries, secondaries and tail appear translucent from below. Juvenile has buffy wash on body, wing-coverts and tail and broader black primary shafts. Seas close to breeding atolls. Uncommon.

Mn	Mu	NI	NB	Bv	Gu	MI	NG	Mk	RI	Te	Vu	Lo	GT

juvenile
Sooty Tern
breeding
breeding
juvenile
Bridled Tern
breeding
breeding
Spectacled Tern
breeding
adult
juvenile
adult
juvenile
Brown Noddy
Black Noddy
adult
adult
adult
adult
Grey Noddy
White Tern
adult
Blue Noddy
adult

PLATE 30: SKUAS AND JAEGERS

South Polar Skua *Stercorarius maccormicki* Page 301

53 cm. Stocky. Dark cold brown or grey-brown with very large white primary-base patch on dark upperwing and underwing. Some have pale greyish or milk-coffee-coloured collar or nape or head and breast. Dark birds have pale at bill-base. Immature usually lacks pale on head and neck, has fine pale fringes on upperparts and black-tipped blue bill. Seas. Vagrant.

Brown Skua *Stercorarius antarcticus* Page 301

63 cm. Stocky. All chocolate-brown with very large white primary-base patch on upperwing and underwing and some indistinct yellow streaking on hindneck, or across upperparts and breast. Immature lacks streaking, has less white on wing and may have mottled orange on upperparts. Seas. Vagrant.

Pomarine Skua *Stercorarius pomarinus* Page 302

45 cm + tail-streamers. Fairly stocky, often with prominent chest. Dark brown upperparts and wings with white streaky flash on upperwing and broad flash on underwing, and narrow silvery crescent on underwing primary coverts. Pale breeding adult has yellow cheeks, white face and underparts, and variable brown on breast-band, flanks and vent. Long central tail feathers twisted to appear spoon-shaped, but often broken or absent. Non-breeding adult often has barred tail-coverts, shorter tail-streamers and more brown on underparts. Pale immature is cold brown with pale barring, prominent on uppertail-coverts and underwing-coverts, and short blunt projection of central tail feathers. Dark immature is sooty-brown with pale barring restricted to tail-coverts. Seas. Uncommon.

Mn	Mu	NI	NB	Bv	Gu	MI	NG	Mk	RI	Te	Vu	Lo	GT

Arctic Skua/Parasitic Jaeger *Stercorarius parasiticus* Page 302

41 cm + tail-streamers. Like Pomarine Skua but slighter build and bill, narrower wings, more buoyant flight and no white bases to underwing primary coverts. Pale breeding adult is greyer, has pointed central tail-streamers, less dark on breast, flanks and vent, and paler yellow on face. Immature has less prominent barring on underwing, flanks, vent and tail-coverts. Seas. Uncommon.

Mn	Mu	NI	NB	Bv	Gu	MI	NG	Mk	RI	Te	Vu	Lo	GT

Long-tailed Skua/Long-tailed Jaeger *Stercorarius longicaudus* Page 302

38 cm + tail-streamers. Like Arctic and Pomarine Skuas but slighter build, shorter bill and more elongated body and tail behind narrower wings. Breeding adult has very long pointed tail-streamers, paler greyer mantle and upperwing-coverts, white shafts of outer two upperwing primaries and outermost underwing primary, and grey lower belly. Immature lacks rusty or cinnamon tones, and has heavily barred underwing-coverts and tail-coverts. Immatures with pale grey or white head and belly are distinctive. Uncommon.

Mn	Mu	NI	NB	Bv	Gu	MI	NG	Mk	RI	Te	Vu	Lo	GT

immature
South Polar Skua
pale adult
adult
Brown Skua
pale immature
non-breeding
pale breeding
dark immature
Pomarine Skua
pale immature
non-breeding
pale breeding
dark immature
Arctic Skua
pale immature
non-breeding
breeding
dark immature
Long-tailed Skua

Slender-billed Cuckoo-Dove *Macropygia amboinensis carteretia* Page 305

36 cm. Plain brown with fine black barring on neck and breast. Male has pale buffy underparts with green or purple-pink gloss on neck-sides, and some fine black barring on neck and breast. Female lacks iridescence, has darker underparts and stronger barring on neck and breast. Forest. Fairly common.

Mn	Mu	NI	NB	Bv	Gu	MI	NG	Mk	RI	Te	Vu	Lo	GT

Mackinlay's Cuckoo-Dove *Macropygia m. mackinlayi* Page 306

32 cm. Rufous-brown to grey-brown with distinct black spots on breast. Slightly paler head and underparts, and darker wings. Grey morph is dark ash-grey with paler grey underparts. Some females are intermediate between normal and grey morphs. Juvenile has finely barred underparts. Forest, especially secondary regrowth, mangroves and mountains. Common.

Mn	Mu	NI	NB	Bv	Gu	MI	NG	Mk	RI	Te	Vu	Lo	GT

Bar-tailed Cuckoo-Dove *Macropygia nigrirostris* Page 305

29 cm. Uniform ruddy-brown plumage with darker wings and narrow black bars on uppertail. Female has black spots on head and black bars on neck, upperparts and breast. Forest and forest edge. Uncommon.

Mn	Mu	NI	NB	Bv	Gu	MI	NG	Mk	RI	Te	Vu	Lo	GT

Pied Cuckoo-Dove *Reinwardtoena b. browni* Page 306

45 cm. Dark slate-grey upperparts with blue gloss, and off-white head and underparts. Juvenile is sooty-grey, slightly paler on underparts. In flight, appears robust, larger and shorter-tailed than *Macropygia* cuckoo-doves. Primary or old-growth forest, especially in hills. Uncommon.

Mn	Mu	NI	NB	Bv	Gu	MI	NG	Mk	RI	Te	Vu	Lo	GT

Crested Cuckoo-Dove *Reinwardtoena crassirostris* Page 307

42 cm. Wispy up-swept crest along nape, thick bill, mid-grey head, neck and underparts, and dark blue-black wings, back and tail with slight gloss. Juvenile has slight crest and darker head and underparts. In flight, appears robust, larger and shorter-tailed than Mackinlay's Cuckoo-Dove but crest not visible. Primary and secondary forest, especially hills. Fairly common to rare.

Mn	Mu	NI	NB	Bv	Gu	MI	NG	Mk	RI	Te	Vu	Lo	GT

Slender-billed
Cuckoo-Dove
♂
♀
♀
♂
♂
♀
♀
♂
♂
Mackinlay's
Cuckoo-Dove
Bar-tailed
Cuckoo-Dove
grey morph
adult
adult
Crested
Cuckoo-Dove
Pied Cuckoo-Dove
juvenile
juvenile
adult
adult

Pacific Emerald Dove *Chalcophaps longirostris sandwichensis* Page 307

26 cm. Shiny green wings and mantle, bright pale blue shoulder, muddy purple-rufous head and underparts, and bright orange-red bill. Juvenile has less green, broad rufous wing-bars, dull bill, and dark fringes on underparts. In flight, green can be inconspicuous, and pale bars on back. Forest, especially secondary, and coconuts and gardens. Common.

Mn Mu NI NB Bv Gu MI NG Mk RI **Te** **Vu** **Lo** **GT**

Stephan's Emerald Dove *Chalcophaps s. stephani* Page 308

23 cm. Rich rufous-brown with shiny green wings and orange-red bill. Male has clear white forehead and purple wash to crown and nape. Female has grey, less defined forehead and lacks purple. Juvenile has green initially only on median wing-coverts, paler around eye, dull bill and some black barring. In flight, green can be inconspicuous, and pale bars on back. Forest, especially degraded forest including coconuts. Common.

Mn **Mu** **NI** **NB** **Bv** **Gu** **MI** **NG** **Mk** RI Te Vu Lo GT

White-breasted Ground Dove *Gallicolumba j. jobiensis* Page 309

25 cm. Blackish with white supercilium, throat and breast, and purple gloss on mantle and wing-coverts. Female is variable, often with greyish wash and less purple gloss. Juvenile is dark olive-brown, with rufous edgings, paler greyish throat, and purple feathers soon appearing on wing-coverts and grey or white feathers on breast. Forest, especially secondary growth. Uncommon.

G. j. ***chalconota*** (Solomons) female is dark grey-brown with green gloss on upperparts and cinnamon on throat and breast.

Mn Mu **NI** **NB** Bv **Gu** MI **NG** **Mk** RI Te Vu Lo GT

Santa Cruz Ground Dove *Gallicolumba sanctaecrucis* Page 310

23 cm. Male has ashy-grey head and nape, brown upperparts with purple gloss especially on shoulder, pale pinkish-buff throat and breast, and dark brown belly. Female is duller, with rufous-brown head, neck and underparts, dark olive upperparts with greenish gloss, and grey belly. Juvenile is uniform brown, sometimes with a glossy purple shoulder-patch. Old-growth forest at 300–1000 m. Rare on Santo and possibly extinct in Temotu.

Mn Mu NI NB Bv Gu MI NG Mk RI **Te** **Vu** Lo GT

Tanna Ground Dove *Gallicolumba ferruginea* Page 310

27 cm. Male has white head, throat and breast, and reddish-black upperparts and belly. Female has rusty-brown head and breast, reddish-purple back, dark green wings and grey belly. Extinct. Tanna only.

Mn Mu NI NB Bv Gu MI NG Mk RI Te **Vu** Lo GT

Thick-billed Ground Dove *Gallicolumba salamonis* Page 311

26 cm. Chestnut upperparts with purple iridescence on shoulder, paler head, throat and breast, chocolate-brown belly and heavy bill. Extinct. Ramos and Makira only.

Mn Mu NI NB Bv Gu MI NG **Mk** RI Te Vu Lo GT

Bronze Ground Dove *Gallicolumba beccarii johannae* Page 311

19 cm. Ashy-grey head and breast, often broad white eye-ring, rufous-brown mantle and wings with bronze-green gloss and maroon shoulder. Female is duller, without iridescence, and grey breast merges into rufous belly. Juvenile is uniform warm brown with rusty fringes on wings, and grey feathers soon appear on head and breast. Forest, usually old-growth forest in hills. Uncommon.

G. b. ***masculina*** (Nissan) male lacks white eye-ring and has paler lower breast.

G. b. ***solomonensis*** (east Solomons) has slightly bronzier upperparts.

Mn **Mu** **NI** **NB** **Bv** **Gu** MI **NG** **Mk** **RI** Te Vu Lo GT

♂
♀
juvenile
Pacific Emerald Dove
♀
♂
♂ jobiensis
juvenile
Stephan's Emerald Dove
juvenile
♀
♀ chalconota
White-breasted Ground Dove
juvenile
♀
♂
Santa Cruz
Ground Dove
Tanna Ground Dove
♂
masculina
♂
johannae
♂
Bronze Ground Dove
solomonensis
♀
juvenile
Thick-billed Ground Dove

Tanna Fruit Dove *Ptilinopus tannensis* — Page 312

Length 26 cm. Green with variable yellowish on crown, yellow tips to tertials and greater-coverts, grey shoulder-spots and yellow vent. Juvenile has yellow fringes, greener crown and no shoulder-spots. Forest and large trees. Fairly common.

Mn	Mu	NI	NB	Bv	Gu	MI	NG	Mk	RI	Te	**Vu**	Lo	GT

Superb Fruit Dove *Ptilinopus superbus* — Page 312

23 cm. Male has purple crown, rusty-orange nape and shoulders, silvery throat and breast, black lower breast-band and white belly with two green flank-bars. Female is green with green bars on white belly, dark spots on scapulars and small dark nape-patch. Juvenile as female but has yellow fringes on wings and lacks nape-patch and scapular spots. Forest. Common.

Mn	**Mu**	**NI**	**NB**	**Bv**	**Gu**	**MI**	**NG**	Mk	RI	Te	Vu	Lo	GT

Silver-capped Fruit Dove *Ptilinopus richardsii cyanopterus* — Page 313

21 cm. Grey-green head and breast, bright orange belly to undertail-coverts, silvery-grey crown and dark green upperparts. Juvenile is green with grey-washed head, yellow fringes on upperparts, yellow vent to undertail-coverts, and a few orange feathers. Forest and scattered large trees. Common.

Mn	Mu	NI	NB	Bv	Gu	MI	NG	**Mk**	**RI**	Te	Vu	Lo	GT

Red-bellied Fruit Dove *Ptilinopus greyii* — Page 313

23 cm. Green with greyer wash on head, neck and breast, fine black streaks on breast, purple forecrown, purple belly-patch and orange-pink on vent to undertail-coverts. Juvenile is green with little or no purple, yellower vent to undertail-coverts, and yellow fringes to most feathers. Forest and scattered large trees. Common.

Mn	Mu	NI	NB	Bv	Gu	MI	NG	Mk	RI	**Te**	**Vu**	**Lo**	**GT**

White-bibbed Fruit Dove *Ptilinopus rivoli* — Page 313

23 cm. Male has purple forehead, broad white breast-bib, purple central belly, yellow vent, and yellowish bill and lores. Female is dark green with yellow bill, lores and vent to undertail-coverts. Forest, especially in mountains. Common.

Mn	Mu	**NI**	**NB**	Bv	Gu	MI	NG	Mk	RI	Te	Vu	Lo	GT

Yellow-bibbed Fruit Dove *Ptilinopus solomonensis ocularis* — Page 314

21 cm. Male is green with variable purple forehead-spot, broad yellow breast-bib, large purple belly-patch and yellow vent to undertail-coverts. Female is all-green with yellow vent to undertail-coverts and greenish bill and eye-ring. Juvenile as female with yellow fringes. Forest, often restricted to mountains. Common.

Mn	**Mu**	**NI**	**NB**	**Bv**	**Gu**	**MI**	**NG**	**Mk**	RI	Te	Vu	Lo	GT

Claret-breasted Fruit Dove *Ptilinopus viridis lewisii* — Page 315

21 cm. Green with variably grey head, red-based yellow bill, pale grey shoulder-patch and tertial spots, red breast and yellow vent to undertail-coverts. Juvenile has smaller mottled red breast, indistinct grey shoulder-patch and yellow wing-covert fringes. Lowland forest. Common.

Mn	Mu	**NI**	NB	**Bv**	**Gu**	**MI**	**NG**	Mk	RI	Te	Vu	Lo	GT

White-headed Fruit Dove *Ptilinopus eugeniae* — Page 315

20 cm. Green, greyer on lower breast and belly, with white head, red breast, grey spots on shoulder and tertials, and yellowish vent to undertail-coverts. Juvenile has greener head, little red on breast, indistinct grey shoulder-patch and yellow wing-covert fringes. Lowland forest. Fairly common.

Mn	Mu	NI	NB	Bv	Gu	MI	NG	**Mk**	RI	Te	Vu	Lo	GT

Knob-billed Fruit Dove *Ptilinopus i. insolitus* — Page 315

23 cm. Green with red knob on bill, orange belly-patch, grey shoulder-patch and spots, and yellow vent to undertail-coverts. Juvenile probably has small knob and all-green plumage with yellow fringes, especially on underparts. Lowland forest, especially secondary habitats. Gregarious. Common.

P. i. inferior (Mussau) has smaller knob and rusty-brown beside grey shoulder-patch.

Mn	**Mu**	**NI**	**NB**	Bv	Gu	MI	NG	Mk	RI	Te	Vu	Lo	GT

juvenile
♂
Tanna Fruit Dove
♀
♂
Superb Fruit Dove
adult
juvenile
Red-bellied Fruit Dove
adult
Silver-capped
Fruit Dove
juvenile
♀
♂
White-bibbed Fruit Dove
juvenile
♂
Yellow-bibbed Fruit Dove
♂
juvenile
Claret-breasted Fruit Dove
White-headed
Fruit Dove
insolitus
inferior
Knob-billed
Fruit Dove

PLATE 34: IMPERIAL PIGEONS I

Pacific Imperial Pigeon *Ducula p. pacifica* Page 316

39 cm. Large black knob on bill, grey head and neck, pink wash on breast and belly, chestnut vent to undertail-coverts, and green-glossed dark mantle, wings and tail. Juvenile lacks enlarged cere and pink wash. In flight, dark grey underwing-coverts are only slightly paler than flight feathers. Glossy dark upperwings and tail. Small islands; also larger islands in Vanuatu. Forest and scattered trees. Common.

Mn	Mu	NI	NB	Bv	Gu	MI	NG	Mk	RI	Te	Vu	Lo	GT

Finsch's Imperial Pigeon *Ducula finschii* Page 317

36 cm. Pale grey crown to nape, pinkish-grey face to breast, paler spectacles and orange-rufous belly to undertail-coverts. Dark metallic green upperparts and well-defined pale grey tail-band. In flight, relatively short-tailed with pale grey tail-band; glossy green upperwings and tail. Old-growth forest and forest edge. Solitary in forest mid-storey or canopy. Never flies above forest canopy. Fairly common.

Mn	Mu	NI	NB	Bv	Gu	MI	NG	Mk	RI	Te	Vu	Lo	GT

Red-knobbed Imperial Pigeon *Ducula r. rubricera* Page 317

41 cm. Large red knob on bill, grey head, neck and breast with pink wash, dark rufous belly to undertail-coverts and metallic green upperparts. Juvenile has smaller duller cere. In flight, pale grey underwing-coverts contrast with darker flight feathers. Glossy dark green upperwings and tail. Forest. Common.

*D. r. **rufigula*** (Solomons) is darker grey with pink restricted to throat and ear-coverts.

Mn	Mu	NI	NB	Bv	Gu	MI	NG	Mk	RI	Te	Vu	Lo	GT

Island Imperial Pigeon *Ducula p. pistrinaria* Page 318

43 cm. Pale grey head, neck and underparts with white around bill-base and eye, pink wash to face and breast, chestnut undertail-coverts and dark greenish-grey upperparts. Juvenile is duller without pink wash or gloss. In flight, pale pink-grey underparts and pale grey underwing-coverts contrast with dark wing feathers, undertail-coverts and tail. Small islands and coasts of larger islands. Fairly common.

*D. p. **rhodinolaema*** (Admiralties) has darker glossy green upperparts and grey underparts with pink restricted to face.

*D. p. **vanwyckii*** (Bismarcks) has darker, glossier, greener upperparts and pink restricted to throat and ear-coverts.

Mn	Mu	NI	NB	Bv	Gu	MI	NG	Mk	RI	Te	Vu	Lo	GT

Chestnut-bellied Imperial Pigeon *Ducula brenchleyi* Page 318

38 cm. Sooty-grey upperparts, paler grey head and upper neck, deep purple-grey throat and breast, and chestnut belly to undertail-coverts and undertail. Juvenile has sooty-grey head and breast lacking any purple tones. In flight, relatively slender with paler grey head and dark chestnut on belly extending onto underwing-coverts and undertail, contrasting with dark grey underwing. Old-growth forest, commonest in hills. Uncommon or rare.

Mn	Mu	NI	NB	Bv	Gu	MI	NG	Mk	RI	Te	Vu	Lo	GT

juvenile
adult
Pacific Imperial Pigeon
rufigula
rufigula
juvenile
Red-knobbed Imperial Pigeon
Finsch's Imperial Pigeon
rubricera
vanwyckii
pistrinaria
rhodinolaena
Island Imperial Pigeon
juvenile
adult
Chestnut-bellied Imperial Pigeon

Vanuatu Imperial Pigeon *Ducula bakeri* — Page 319

40 cm. Blue-grey head contrasts with sooty-grey upperparts and dark purple-chestnut collar, neck and breast, which merges into deep chestnut belly and undertail-coverts. Juvenile is much duller, without gloss. In flight, relatively slender with dark head and upperparts; chestnut on underparts extends onto underwing-coverts and flight feathers slightly paler rufous. Forest, especially in hills and mountains. Fairly common from Banks Is to Ambrym.

Mn	Mu	NI	NB	Bv	Gu	MI	NG	Mk	RI	Te	**Vu**	Lo	GT

Goliath Imperial Pigeon *Ducula goliath* — Page 319

51 cm. Very large with long tail. Streaky blue-grey head, neck and breast, sooty-grey upperparts with paler primary bases, chestnut tail-band, chestnut belly and buffy undertail-coverts. Juvenile is duller and browner. Forest. Fairly common.

Mn	Mu	NI	NB	Bv	Gu	MI	NG	Mk	RI	Te	Vu	Lo	**GT**

Black Imperial Pigeon *Ducula melanochroa* — Page 319

43 cm. All glossy black with pale grey scalloping on wings, dark chestnut undertail-coverts, silver-grey undertail and red eye. In flight, heavy with slow wing-beats and deep chest; all glossy black with silver-grey undertail. Forest, especially old-growth hill forest. Fairly common.

Mn	Mu	**NI**	**NB**	Bv	Gu	MI	NG	Mk	RI	Te	Vu	Lo	GT

Torresian Imperial Pigeon *Ducula spilorrhoa* — Page 320

38 cm. Creamy-white with black primaries and secondaries, greater primary coverts and alula (but white lesser primary coverts) and tail-tip (but hardly any black on outer feathers), and narrow bars on undertail-coverts. Small forested islands and coastal forest. Vagrant.

Mn	Mu	NI	**NB**	Bv	Gu	MI	NG	Mk	RI	Te	Vu	Lo	GT

Yellowish Imperial Pigeon *Ducula subflavescens* — Page 320

38 cm. Creamy-yellow with black primaries, secondaries, all primary coverts, and tail-tip (but narrower on outer feathers), and broad black bars on undertail-coverts. Forest, usually close to the coast. Fairly common.

Mn	Mu	**NI**	**NB**	Bv	Gu	MI	NG	Mk	RI	Te	Vu	Lo	GT

juvenile
adult
Vanuatu Imperial Pigeon
Goliath Imperial Pigeon
Black Imperial Pigeon
Torresian
Imperial Pigeon
Yellowish
Imperial Pigeon

PLATE 36: OTHER PIGEONS I

Rock Dove *Columba livia* Page 303

33 cm. Variable plumage, typically grey with black wing-bars, white rump, and green and purple gloss on neck. May be darker, blackish, paler or all-white. Fast flight with deep wing-beats. On ground and around buildings. Rare non-native.

Mn	Mu	NI	NB	Bv	Gu	MI	NG	Mk	RI	Te	**Vu**	Lo	**GT**

Metallic Pigeon *Columba vitiensis halmaheira* Page 304

37 cm. Blackish pigeon with white throat-patch and green and purple gloss. Juvenile has browner underparts and less gloss. Rather heavy flight with deeper wing-beats and longer more pointed wings than imperial pigeons. Forest, also open forest and savanna. Canopy to ground. Fairly common to rare. See imperial pigeons (Plates 34-35).

C. v. leopoldi (Vanuatu) has variably brown underparts.

C. v. hypoenochroa (New Caledonia) has chestnut underparts and purple gloss on breast.

Mn	Mu	**NI**	**NB**	**Bv**	**Gu**	**MI**	**NG**	**Mk**	RI	Te	**Vu**	**Lo**	**GT**

Yellow-legged Pigeon *Columba pallidiceps* Page 304

37 cm. Black with broad green, purple and pink iridescent fringes, grey head and yellow legs. Juvenile has brownish head and less iridescence. In flight, iridescent black with silvery-grey head. Note that many imperial pigeons may appear to be dark with pale heads when seen from above in flight. Flight as Metallic Pigeon. Forest. Rare. See imperial pigeons (Plates 34-35).

Mn	Mu	**NI**	**NB**	**Bv**	**Gu**	MI	**NG**	**Mk**	RI	Te	Vu	Lo	GT

Spotted Dove *Spilopelia chinensis* Page 304

30 cm. Slim and long-tailed with white-spotted black neck-patch, pinkish neck and underparts and dull brown upperparts. Juvenile is dull greyish-brown with indistinct neck marks. Fields and open habitats. On ground. Locally common non-native.

Mn	Mu	NI	NB	Bv	Gu	MI	NG	Mk	RI	Te	Vu	Lo	**GT**

Zebra Dove *Geopelia striata* Page 308

21 cm. Slim and long-tailed with grey head, grey-brown upperparts and pink to white underparts, with black barring across most of plumage. Juvenile is duller with less distinct bars. Open grassy habitats. On ground. Very local non-native.

Mn	Mu	NI	NB	Bv	Gu	MI	NG	Mk	RI	Te	Vu	Lo	**GT**

New Britain Bronzewing *Henicophaps foersteri* Page 308

39 cm. Iridescent blackish mantle, wings and tail with strong gloss on wing-coverts, orange-brown head and neck, and buffy-white face and underparts. Male has white face to belly, and female has white ear-coverts, and darker breast to belly. Old-growth forest. On ground. Rare. See ground doves (Plate 32).

Mn	Mu	NI	**NB**	Bv	Gu	MI	NG	Mk	RI	Te	Vu	Lo	GT

halmaheira
juvenile
hypoenochroa
adult
Rock Dove
Metallic Pigeon
leopoldi
adult
juvenile
Yellow-legged Pigeon
adult
juvenile
Spotted Dove
Zebra Dove
♂
♀
New Britain Bronzewing

Cloven-feathered Dove *Drepanoptila holosericea* — Page 316

28 cm. Bright green with silvery bars on wings and tail, white and black breast-band, yellow belly to undertail-coverts and fluffy white legs. Female is duller with ill-defined silver-grey bars. Juvenile lacks silvery bars but has broad yellow fringes on wings. Forest. Common.

Mn	Mu	NI	NB	Bv	Gu	MI	NG	Mk	RI	Te	Vu	Lo	GT

Choiseul Pigeon *Microgoura meeki* — Page 312

31 cm. Pale blue crest, red and blue bill, black and pink face, blue-grey neck, mantle and breast, orange belly, brown wings and short purple tail. Lowland forest. On ground. Extinct. Choiseul only.

Mn	Mu	NI	NB	Bv	Gu	MI	NG	Mk	RI	Te	Vu	Lo	GT

Nicobar Pigeon *Caloenas nicobarica* — Page 309

34 cm. Glossy black with long neck-hackles and very short white tail. Juvenile has black tail and lacks neck hackles and gloss. Distinctive flight shape of very short tail, deep chest, long broad wings and rather long neck with head held up. Adult has white tail, dark in immature. Flushes up from ground or flies high, often to offshore islets. Lowland forest, especially on small islets. On ground but flies high. Rare.

Mn	Mu	NI	NB	Bv	Gu	MI	NG	Mk	RI	Te	Vu	Lo	GT

Papuan Mountain Pigeon *Gymnophaps albertisii* — Page 320

34 cm. Relatively slender and long-tailed. Dark grey head, neck and upperparts with black scalloping, red eye-patch, off-white breast and chestnut belly. Male has purple-chestnut throat and ear-coverts. Female is greyer all over. In flight, dark wings and tail with whitish lower throat to breast and pale terminal tail-band.
Forest. Uncommon. See imperial pigeons (Plates 34-35).

Mn	Mu	NI	NB	Bv	Gu	MI	NG	Mk	RI	Te	Vu	Lo	GT

Pale Mountain Pigeon *Gymnophaps solomonensis* — Page 321

38 cm. Relatively slender and long-tailed. Pale grey head, neck, underparts and tail, dark grey mantle and wings with black scalloping. Forest. Fairly common to uncommon. See imperial pigeons (Plates 34-35).

Mn	Mu	NI	NB	Bv	Gu	MI	NG	Mk	RI	Te	Vu	Lo	GT

juvenile
Choiseul Pigeon
♂
Cloven-feathered
Dove
juvenile
Nicobar Pigeon
adult
Papuan Mountain Pigeon
Pale Mountain Pigeon
♀
♂

PLATE 38: COCKATOOS AND LORIES

Solomons Cockatoo *Cacatua ducorpsii* Page 321

34 cm. White with yellow wash on underwing and undertail, and pale blue eye-ring. Buoyant but erratic flight, including shallow fluttering and deep high wing-beats, short glides on down-swept wings and banking from side to side. Lowland forest. Common.

Mn	Mu	Nl	NB	**Bv**	**Gu**	**Ml**	**NG**	Mk	Rl	Te	Vu	Lo	GT

Blue-eyed Cockatoo *Cacatua ophthalmica* Page 321

50 cm. White with yellow wash on underwing and undertail, yellow on crest and pale blue eye-ring. In flight, as Solomons Cockatoo but larger and yellow on crest. Lowland forest. Fairly common.

Mn	Mu	Nl	**NB**	Bv	Gu	Ml	NG	Mk	Rl	Te	Vu	Lo	GT

Cardinal Lory *Chalcopsitta cardinalis* Page 324

31 cm. Dull crimson, darker on wings and mantle, with orange-red bill and long rounded tail. In flight, all dull red. Tail appears long and rounded or diamond-shaped. Broader tail, rounder wings and stouter shape than Coconut Lorikeet. Lowland forests and open habitats. Pairs or flocks, often mixing with Coconut Lorikeets. Common.

Mn	Mu	**Nl**	NB	**Bv**	**Gu**	**Ml**	**NG**	**Mk**	Rl	Te	Vu	Lo	GT

White-naped Lory *Lorius albidinucha* Page 325

26 cm. Red with black cap and green wings and tail. At close range, white triangle on nape, black cere above orange bill and some yellow on breast. Forest at 500–2000 m. Usually in pairs. Fairly common.

Mn	Mu	**Nl**	NB	Bv	Gu	Ml	NG	Mk	Rl	Te	Vu	Lo	GT

Yellow-bibbed Lory *Lorius chlorocercus* Page 326

28 cm. Red with green wings and tail, black cap and yellow bib with black extensions. In flight, purple-blue underwing-coverts, broad red underwing-bar and yellow tail-tip. Flies low with rapid shallow beats of short wings. From Song Parrot by broader wings and more whirring wing-beats. Forest. Usually in pairs. Common.

Mn	Mu	Nl	NB	Bv	**Gu**	**Ml**	NG	**Mk**	**Rl**	Te	Vu	Lo	GT

Purple-bellied Lory *Lorius hypoinochrous* Page 325

26 cm. Red with green wings and tail, purple belly, black cap and white cere above orange bill. In flight, red underwing-coverts, broad yellow underwing-bar, and yellowish tail-tip. Flight as Yellow-bibbed Lory. Lowland forest. Usually in pairs. Fairly common.

Mn	Mu	**Nl**	**NB**	Bv	Gu	Ml	NG	Mk	Rl	Te	Vu	Lo	GT

Solomons
Cockatoo
Solomons
Cockatoo
Blue-eyed
Cockatoo
Blue-eyed
Cockatoo
Cardinal Lory
Yellow-bibbed Lory
White-naped Lory
Purple-bellied Lory

Coconut Lorikeet *Trichoglossus haematodus massena* Page 324

27 cm. Bright green with red breast, dark violet head, orange-red bill and yellowish hind-collar. In flight, green with red breast and underwing-coverts, broad yellow underwing-bar and yellow underside to long pointed tail. From *Charmosyna* lorikeets by larger, bulkier shape and red plumage. Forest and open habitats. Pairs or flocks, often mixing with other lorikeets. Common

T. h. flavicans (Admiralties) has bronze-yellow upperparts

Mn Mu NI NB Bv Gu MI NG Mk RI Te Vu Lo GT

Duchess Lorikeet *Charmosyna margarethae* Page 328

20 cm. Red body and long tail, green wings and back, and yellow breast-band with black borders. Male has red rump-sides; female yellow. In flight, red underwing-coverts, and red upperside and yellow underside to long pointed tail. Forest, especially primary hill forest. Small flocks. Uncommon.

Mn Mu NI NB Bv Gu MI NG Mk RI Te Vu Lo GT

Ouvéa Parakeet *Eunymphicus uvaeensis* Page 329

32 cm. Green with blackish mask, small red forehead-patch, crest of up to six fine dark green feathers and blue on primaries and tail. Forest and adjacent gardens. Pairs or small flocks. Uncommon on Ouvéa.

Mn Mu NI NB Bv Gu MI NG Mk RI Te Vu Lo GT

Horned Parakeet *Eunymphicus cornutus* Page 328

32 cm. Green with yellowish head, black mask, red forehead, crest of two fine black feathers with red tips, and blue on primaries and tail. In flight, green with blue on upper primaries and long broad tail. From Coconut Lorikeet by all-green underparts, slower deeper wing-beats, more rounded tail and wings, and low flight. Humid forest. Pairs or small flocks. Uncommon on Grande Terre.

Mn Mu NI NB Bv Gu MI NG Mk RI Te Vu Lo GT

New Caledonian Parakeet *Cyanoramphus saisseti* Page 329

26 cm. Green and long-tailed with blue on primaries, and red forehead and eye-stripe. Smaller and slimmer than Horned Parakeet with more pointed, greener tail. From Coconut Lorikeet by all-green underparts, slower deeper wing-beats and low flight. Forest, savanna and scrub. Uncommon.

Mn Mu NI NB Bv Gu MI NG Mk RI Te Vu Lo GT

Song Parrot *Geoffroyus h. heteroclitus* Page 329

24 cm. Green; male with dull yellow head and bill and grey collar, female with brownish-grey head and bill. In flight, green with dark grey underwing, blue underwing-coverts and dull yellow undertail. Flies fast, banking low over forest, usually calling. From Eclectus Parrot by shorter, more pointed wings, longer tail and faster wing-beats. From lories by slower wing-beats and longer tail. Forest. Pairs or small flocks. Fairly common.

Mn Mu NI NB Bv Gu MI NG Mk RI Te Vu Lo GT

Eclectus Parrot *Eclectus roratus* Page 330

31 cm. Male is green with orange-red bill, red underwing-coverts and flanks, and blue primaries. Female is red, darker on mantle and wings, with blue upper mantle, lower breast, belly and primaries, and black bill. In flight, male is green with red underwing-coverts; female is red with blue on body and underwing-coverts. Long rounded wings and short tail. Often flies high with head stretched out, rapid shallow beats with wings not raised above body; glides on down-swept wings. Lowland forest including open forest. Fairly common.

Mn Mu NI NB Bv Gu MI NG Mk RI Te Vu Lo GT

flavicans
massena
Coconut Lorikeet
♀
Duchess
Lorikeet
♂
New Caledonian
Parakeet
♂
♀
Horned Parakeet
♂
Ouvéa Parakeet
Song Parrot
♀
♂
♂
♀
Eclectus Parrot

Palm Lorikeet *Charmosyna palmarum* — Page 326

16 cm. Green with orange-red bill and legs, red chin, darker wings with bronze wash on mantle and yellow tip to long tail. Female has less red on chin and lacks bronze on mantle. Forests; on Santo, only in mountains. Small flocks. Locally common.

Mn | Mu | NI | NB | Bv | Gu | MI | NG | Mk | RI | **Te** | **Vu** | Lo | GT

Red-chinned Lorikeet *Charmosyna rubrigularis* — Page 327

17 cm. Green with orange-red bill and legs, small red throat-patch, darker wings and yellow tip to long tail. Forest, especially in mountains. Flocks. Common.

Mn | Mu | **NI** | **NB** | Bv | Gu | MI | NG | Mk | RI | Te | Vu | Lo | GT

Meek's Lorikeet *Charmosyna meeki* — Page 327

16 cm. Green with orange-red bill and legs, small red throat-patch, darker wings with bronze wash on mantle, slight grey wash on crown and yellow tip to long tail. Forest, especially in mountains. Flocks. Fairly common.

Mn | Mu | NI | NB | **Bv** | **Gu** | **MI** | **NG** | Mk | RI | Te | Vu | Lo | GT

Red-flanked Lorikeet *Charmosyna placentis* — Page 327

17 cm. Green with orange-red bill and legs and red-tipped yellow undertail. Male has blue ear-coverts and red throat and flanks. Female has yellow-streaked cheeks. Lowland forest. Pairs or small flocks. Common.

Mn | Mu | **NI** | **NB** | **Bv** | Gu | MI | NG | Mk | RI | Te | Vu | Lo | GT

New Caledonian Lorikeet *Charmosyna diadema* — Page 328

19 cm. Green with blue crown, orange-red bill and legs, yellow cheeks and throat, darker wings, red on vent and red-based yellow undertail. Extinct.

Mn | Mu | NI | NB | Bv | Gu | MI | NG | Mk | RI | Te | Vu | Lo | **GT**

Buff-faced Pygmy Parrot *Micropsitta p. pusio* — Page 322

8 cm. Green with buff face, dark blue crown, black and blue uppertail and yellow undertail-coverts. Female has paler face and crown. Immature has greener crown. Lowland and hill forest. Creeps on trunks and branches. Fairly common.

Mn | Mu | NI | **NB** | Bv | Gu | MI | NG | Mk | RI | Te | Vu | Lo | GT

Meek's Pygmy Parrot *Micropsitta m. meeki* — Page 323

10 cm. Green with grey-brown crown, face and throat, yellow supercilium, neck, breast, central belly and undertail-coverts, and dark scaly fringes. Forest and scrub. Creeps on trunks and branches. Fairly common to uncommon.
M. m. proxima (St Matthias Is) has larger yellow supercilium.

Mn | **Mu** | NI | NB | Bv | Gu | MI | NG | Mk | RI | Te | Vu | Lo | GT

Finsch's Pygmy Parrot *Micropsitta f. finschii* — Page 323

9 cm. Green with blue-washed cap, black and blue uppertail and yellow undertail-coverts. Male has blue-washed chin and sometimes orange-red on breast. Female has buff-pink wash on chin. Forest. Creeps on trunks and branches. Fairly common.
M. f. viridifrons (New Ireland) male has extensive blue on crown and cheeks.

Mn | Mu | **NI** | NB | **Bv** | **Gu** | **MI** | **NG** | **Mk** | **RI** | Te | Vu | Lo | GT

Red-breasted Pygmy Parrot *Micropsitta bruijnii rosea* — Page 324

9 cm. Male is green with orange face and crown, orange-red breast to undertail, broad dark blue eye-stripe and breast-band joining on nape, and black and blue uppertail. Female is green with orange-buff face and forehead, dark blue crown extending near to eye and yellow undertail-coverts. Montane forest. Creeps on trunks and branches. Fairly common.

Mn | Mu | **NI** | **NB** | **Bv** | **Gu** | MI | **NG** | Mk | RI | Te | Vu | Lo | GT

Bismarck Hanging Parrot *Loriculus tener* — Page 322

10 cm. Green with orange-red throat-patch, yellowish rump and uppertail-coverts, pale blue undertail and black bill. Female has blue wash on face. Immature lacks red throat-spot. In flight, appears longer-tailed and less dumpy than pygmy-parrots, more like a short-tailed lorikeet with blue underwing. Lowland forest. Unobtrusive in canopy. Uncommon.

Mn | Mu | **NI** | **NB** | Bv | Gu | MI | NG | Mk | RI | Te | Vu | Lo | GT

Red-chinned Lorikeet
Palm Lorikeet
Meek's Lorikeet
♂
New Caledonian
Lorikeet
♀
immature
♂
adult
Red-flanked Lorikeet
Buff-faced
Pygmy Parrot
proxima
♂
meeki
Meek's Pygmy
Parrot
viridifrons
♂
♀
♂
♂
finschii
♀
Red-breasted
Pygmy Parrot
immature
♀
Finsch's Pygmy Parrot
finschii
♂
Bismarck Hanging Parrot

PLATE 41: CUCKOOS

Oriental Cuckoo *Cuculus optatus* — Page 335

31 cm. Blue-grey head, upper breast and upperparts, black bars on white lower breast to vent, long graduated blackish tail with white spots, and yellow eye-ring, legs and bill-base. Rare hepatic phase is rufous-brown with black barring. Immature has dark brown-grey upperparts with white fringes and bars. Lowland forest and forest edge. Uncommon.

Mn Mu Nl NB Bv Gu Ml NG Mk Rl Te Vu Lo GT

Brush Cuckoo *Cacomantis variolosus addendus* — Page 334

22 cm. Grey-brown upperparts, head and upper breast, warm buff lower breast and belly, white tips and spots on edges of uppertail and bold white bars on undertail. In flight, long pointed wings with pale underwing-bar. Juvenile is warm brown with narrow dark and white bars across underparts and bold rufous bars across all upperparts. Forest. Common.

C. v. macrocercus (Bismarcks) sometimes has all-grey underparts.

Mn Mu Nl NB Bv Gu Ml NG Mk Rl Te Vu Lo GT

Fan-tailed Cuckoo *Cacomantis flabelliformis pyrrhophanus* — Page 333

25 cm. Sooty-grey, with few white bars and white tips on black uppertail, white bars on black undertail and rich orange-rufous underparts. In flight, long pointed wings with pale underwing-bar. Juvenile has dark brown upperparts with fine rufous fringes, unmarked primaries, heavy brown barring on white underparts and larger buff bars on undertail. Forest. Fairly common to rare.

C. f. schistaceigularis (Vanuatu) has grey throat and upper breast.

Mn Mu Nl NB Bv Gu Ml NG Mk Rl Te Vu Lo GT

Shining Bronze Cuckoo *Chrysococcyx l. lucidus* — Page 333

17 cm. Glossy green crown and upperparts, white face and underparts with black bars, finer or absent on face and throat, and white bars on outer undertail. In flight, long pointed wings with pale underwing-bar. Juvenile has duller upperparts with obscure markings on face, throat and underparts. Forest and scrub. Common resident or uncommon migrant.

C. l. harterti (Rennell) female has light brown wash on throat and breast.

C. l. layardi (Vanuatu and New Caledonia) has white throat and grey wash on head and nape.

Mn Mu Nl NB Bv Gu Ml NG Mk Rl Te Vu Lo GT

Long-tailed Cuckoo *Urodynamis taitensis* — Page 332

41 cm. Tail slightly longer than body. Warm brown upperparts with blackish barring, barred tail with white tips, creamy supercilium and moustachial stripe, dark submoustachial stripe and buffy-white underparts with brown streaking. Juvenile has warm buffy supercilium and underparts, and white spots on mantle and wings. Forest and scrub, especially on small islands. Rare. See Koels (Plate 42).

Mn Mu Nl NB Bv Gu Ml NG Mk Rl Te Vu Lo GT

♀ hepatic
Oriental Cuckoo
immature
adult
macrocercus
addendus
Brush Cuckoo
juvenile
pyrrhophanus
juvenile
juvenile
Long-tailed Cuckoo
schistaceigularis
Fan-tailed Cuckoo
adult
lucidus
lucidus immature
Shining Bronze Cuckoo
harterti ♀
layardi

PLATE 42: COUCALS AND KOEL

Channel-billed Cuckoo *Scythrops novaehollandiae* Page 332

63 cm. Massive grey-black and cream bill, grey head and neck, dark mantle and wings with obscure black barring, and black band and white tips on long tail. In flight, long head, long pointed wings with black trailing edge and long tail. Juvenile has pale buff head, neck and underparts, buff spots on mantle and wing and smaller pinkish bill. Lowland forest. Canopy. Flies high, often calling. Uncommon.

Mn	Mu	Nl	NB	Bv	Gu	Ml	NG	Mk	Rl	Te	Vu	Lo	GT

Buff-headed Coucal *Centropus m. milo* Page 330

64 cm. Buffy-yellow head and body with glossy black wings, mantle and tail, and stout decurved black bill. Juvenile is rufous-brown with blackish bars on upperparts, streaky darker head and neck, and irregular blackish bars on rufous-brown underparts. Forest and scrub. Fairly common.

C. m. albidiventris (New Georgia group) has buffy-yellow also on belly.

Mn	Mu	Nl	NB	Bv	Gu	Ml	NG	Mk	Rl	Te	Vu	Lo	GT

Violaceous Coucal *Centropus violaceus* Page 331

67 cm. All black with a violet gloss, blue-white skin around dark red eye and pale legs. Juvenile is duller, with duller eye-patch. Forest, usually old growth. Fairly common.

Mn	Mu	Nl	NB	Bv	Gu	Ml	NG	Mk	Rl	Te	Vu	Lo	GT

White-necked Coucal *Centropus ateralbus* Page 331

46 cm. Typical morph is glossy black with pale buff head, neck and breast, white patch on wing-coverts, and usually a black mask or cap. All-black morph usually has white wing-covert patch. Rare leucistic morph is all creamy-white. Juvenile is dark sooty-brown, with fine buffy streaks on head, neck and breast. Lowland forest and scrub. Fairly common.

Mn	Mu	Nl	NB	Bv	Gu	Ml	NG	Mk	Rl	Te	Vu	Lo	GT

Pacific Koel *Eudynamys orientalis alberti* Page 331

41 cm. Male is glossy black with greenish-white bill and red eye. Female has rufous-brown upperparts, fine whitish moustachial stripe, darker barring on wings and tail, and fine black bars on paler brown underparts. Juvenile as female but paler, with black eye-stripe and submoustachial stripe. Forest and large trees. Rarely seen but commonly heard. Fairly common.

Mn	Mu	Nl	NB	Bv	Gu	Ml	NG	Mk	Rl	Te	Vu	Lo	GT

juvenile
adult
adult
Channel-billed Cuckoo
albidiventris
milo
adult
juvenile
Buff-headed Coucal
Violaceous Coucal
adult
juvenile
White-necked
Coucal
juvenile
♂
white adult
♀
Pacific Koel

New Caledonian Nightjar *Eurostopodus exul* Page 340

26 cm. Pale grey upperparts with sooty crown, sooty streaks on mantle, mottling on wing-coverts, indistinct tail bars and grey-brown underparts with small white throat-bar. In flight, dark brown wings with orange spots and narrow white subterminal spots on three outer wing feathers. Coastal savanna. Probably extinct.

Mn	Mu	Nl	NB	Bv	Gu	Ml	NG	Mk	Rl	Te	Vu	Lo	**GT**

Solomons Nightjar *Eurostopodus nigripennis* Page 340

27 cm. Dark brown with grey mottling, orange spots especially on wing-coverts, indistinct orange-rufous nape and narrow white throat-bar. In flight, white subterminal spots on 2–4 outer wing feathers. Female and immature have buffy-white wing-spots, other markings duller buffy-orange and smaller throat-patch. Forest, often on sandy beaches. Rare and localised.

Mn	Mu	Nl	NB	**Bv**	Gu	Ml	**NG**	Mk	Rl	Te	Vu	Lo	GT

Large-tailed Nightjar *Caprimulgus macrurus* Page 341

27 cm. Dark brown, mottled grey, buff and black, with buffy tips on wing-coverts and narrow white throat-bar. In flight, large white tail corners and large white subterminal bar across wing-tip. Female has buff wash on white patches. Forest and open habitats close to forest. Fairly common.

Mn	Mu	**Nl**	**NB**	Bv	Gu	Ml	NG	Mk	Rl	Te	Vu	Lo	GT

New Caledonian Owlet-nightjar *Aegotheles savesi* Page 341

29 cm. Blackish-brown with very fine greyish bars and yellow eyes. Probably extinct.

Mn	Mu	Nl	NB	Bv	Gu	Ml	NG	Mk	Rl	Te	Vu	Lo	**GT**

Solomons Frogmouth *Rigidipenna inexpectata* Page 339

37 cm. Rufous- or grey-brown with white spots on wing-coverts, throat and breast, white stripe down breast, yellowish eyes and pale bars on wings and long tail. Uncommon.

Mn	Mu	Nl	NB	**Bv**	Gu	Ml	NG	Mk	Rl	Te	Vu	Lo	GT

Eastern Grass Owl *Tyto longimembris* Page 336

35 cm. Similar to Eastern Barn Owl but darker upperparts, longer legs project beyond barred tail, longer broader wings and dark wing-tips and primary coverts. Grasslands. Vagrant.

Eastern Barn Owl *Tyto javanica delicatula* Page 336

33 cm. Grey-buff upperparts with fine mottling, white underparts with few sooty speckles and white facial disc with black eyes. In flight, white underwings and indistinct barring. Open habitats. Fairly common to rare.

Mn	Mu	**Nl**	**NB**	**Bv**	**Gu**	**Ml**	**NG**	**Mk**	**Rl**	**Te**	**Vu**	**Lo**	**GT**

Manus Masked Owl *Tyto manusi* Page 335

33 cm. Blackish crown and upperparts with buffy-orange spots and bars, buffy facial disc with black eyes, and sooty spots on rich buff underparts and sides of head. Very rare.

Mn	Mu	Nl	NB	Bv	Gu	Ml	NG	Mk	Rl	Te	Vu	Lo	GT

Golden Masked Owl *Tyto aurantia* Page 335

30 cm. Golden-buff with sooty spots, heavier sooty mottling or barring on upperparts and unmarked pale buff facial disc with black eyes. Very rare.

Mn	Mu	Nl	**NB**	Bv	Gu	Ml	NG	Mk	Rl	Te	Vu	Lo	GT

New Caledonian Nightjar
Large-tailed Nightjar
Solomons Nightjar
New Caledonian
Owlet-nightjar
Solomons
Frogmouth
Manus Masked Owl
Eastern Grass Owl
Eastern Barn Owl
Golden Masked Owl

Manus Boobook *Ninox meeki* Page 337

30 cm. Rufous-brown head and upperparts with white and buffy-brown barring, yellow eyes, and brown streaks on rufous throat and white underparts. Fairly common.

Mn Mu NI NB Bv Gu MI NG Mk RI Te Vu Lo GT

New Ireland Boobook *Ninox variegata* Page 337

27 cm. Grey-brown head and upperparts with white spots and bars, yellow eyes, and brown bars on rufous-brown throat and white underparts. Fairly common.

Mn Mu **NI** NB Bv Gu MI NG Mk RI Te Vu Lo GT

New Britain Boobook *Ninox odiosa* Page 337

25 cm. Brown head, breast and upperparts with white spots, orange eyes, white eyebrows and throat, and brown crescents or streaks on white lower breast to vent. Fairly common.

Mn Mu NI **NB** Bv Gu MI NG Mk RI Te Vu Lo GT

West Solomons Boobook *Ninox j. jacquinoti* Page 338

26 cm. Brown head, upper breast and upperparts with buffy speckles and bars, orange-yellow eyes, white eye-brows and throat, and creamy lower breast to vent. Fairly common.

Mn Mu NI NB **Bv** Gu MI NG Mk RI Te Vu Lo GT

Guadalcanal Boobook *Ninox granti* Page 338

25 cm. Brown head, upper breast and upperparts with white spots and bars, orange-yellow eyes, white eyebrows and throat, and white underparts with brown bars. Fairly common.

Mn Mu NI NB Bv **Gu** MI NG Mk RI Te Vu Lo GT

Malaita Boobook *Ninox malaitae* Page 338

22 cm. Brown with buff spots and bars, black eyes, fine white eyebrows and throat, and buffy bars on underparts, especially belly and flanks. Rare.

Mn Mu NI NB Bv Gu **MI** NG Mk RI Te Vu Lo GT

Makira Boobook *Ninox roseoaxillaris* Page 339

21 cm. Warm brown with black eyes, indistinct eyebrows, white throat, indistinct white spots on upperparts and faint buffy bars on orangey underparts. Rare.

Mn Mu NI NB Bv Gu MI NG **Mk** RI Te Vu Lo GT

Fearful Owl *Nesasio solomonensis* Page 339

37 cm. Orange-rufous with dark brown streaking on body and barring on wings and tail, and orange-yellow eyes on black and white face. Uncommon.

Mn Mu NI NB **Bv** Gu MI NG Mk RI Te Vu Lo GT

Manus Boobook
New Ireland Boobook
New Britain Boobook
West Solomons Boobook
Guadalcanal Boobook
Fearful Owl
Malaita Boobook
Makira Boobook

PLATE 45: SWIFTS

Glossy Swiftlet *Collocalia esculenta* Page 342

9 cm. Relatively short rounded wings, glossy blue upperparts, variable white or dark rump, dark throat and upper breast, and white lower breast and belly. Often has narrow white underwing-bar and shows white spots on undertail when tail fanned. Flies low. Common.

C. e. ***stresemanni*** (Admiralties) has variable black mottling on narrow white rump.

C. e. ***uropygialis*** (Temotu and Vanuatu) has narrow white rump.

C. e. ***becki*** (Solomons) has plain dark upperparts and grey, sometimes scaly, belly.

Mn	Mu	NI	NB	Bv	Gu	MI	NG	Mk	RI	Te	Vu	Lo	GT

White-rumped Swiftlet *Aerodramus spodiopygius* Page 343

10 cm. Plumage, size, wing shape and flight action are intermediate between Glossy and Uniform Swiftlets. White or pale grey rump-band on sooty-brown upperparts, pale grey lower breast and darker or paler throat. Locally common but often absent.

A. s. ***reichenowi*** (Solomons) has darker underparts but paler throat.

A. s. ***leucopygius*** (New Caledonia) has slight gloss, white rump and pale face and underparts.

Mn	Mu	NI	NB	Bv	Gu	MI	NG	Mk	RI	Te	Vu	Lo	GT

Mayr's Swiftlet *Aerodramus orientalis* Page 343

14 cm. Similar to Uniform Swiftlet but greyish rump-band and blue-glossed blackish upperparts. Known only from three specimens at 900–1200 m.

A. o. ***leletensis*** (New Ireland) has very dark upperparts with blue gloss and indistinct grey rump.

A. o. ***orientalis*** (Guadalcanal) has less glossy upperparts and broader paler rump.

A. o. ? (Bougainville) has browner upperparts, hardly paler rump and darker underparts.

Mn	Mu	NI	NB	Bv	Gu	MI	NG	Mk	RI	Te	Vu	Lo	GT

Uniform Swiftlet *Aerodramus v. vanikorensis* Page 344

13 cm. Relatively long pointed wings, grey-brown upperparts, often with darker cap and upperwings, and pale grey-brown throat shading into dusky underparts. Flocks fly high. Common.

A. v. ***coultasi*** (Admiralties) has paler mantle and paler greyer rump.

Mn	Mu	NI	NB	Bv	Gu	MI	NG	Mk	RI	Te	Vu	Lo	GT

Fork-tailed Swift *Apus pacificus* Page 345

18 cm. Slender with long pointed wings and long, deeply forked tail often held closed, uniformly sooty with broad white rump, less obvious white throat and obscure white scaling on underbody. Vagrant.

White-throated Needletail *Hirundapus caudacutus* Page 344

20 cm. Thickset with long body, short tail and relatively broad wings. Dark brown underparts with white throat and white on vent extending onto flanks, darker glossy upperparts with paler mantle and white spots on forehead and tertials. Vagrant.

Moustached Treeswift *Hemiprocne mystacea aeroplanes* Page 341

29 cm. Very long wings which cross when perched, and very long tail-streamers often held closed. Grey with blackish wings and tail, two white facial plumes and pale underwing-bar in flight. Juvenile has orange-buff fringes on upperparts and facial stripes, and dark and orange-buff mottling and barring on underparts. Pairs perch, swoop and hawk. Fairly common.

H. m. ***woodfordiana*** (Solomons) is darker with hardly paler belly.

Mn	Mu	NI	NB	Bv	Gu	MI	NG	Mk	RI	Te	Vu	Lo	GT

stresemanni
Glossy Swiftlet
uropygialis
becki
reichenowi
leucopygius
White-rumped Swiftlet
coultasi
Uniform Swiftlet
leletensis
Mayr's Swiftlet
orientalis
Bougainville
vanikorensis
Uniform Swiftlet
vanikorensis
Fork-tailed Swift
juvenile
Moustached Treeswift
White-throated
Needletail
woodfordiana
adult
aeroplanes

PLATE 46: SMALL KINGFISHERS

Common Kingfisher *Alcedo atthis* — Page 351

16 cm. Blue upperparts, white throat and ear-coverts, orange underparts, black bill and orange legs. Large rivers, lakes and sheltered coasts. Uncommon.

A. a. hispidoides (Bismarcks) has bluer upperparts and a little orange behind eye.

A. a. salomonensis (Solomons) has greener upperparts and almost no orange behind eye.

Mn	**Mu**	**NI**	**NB**	**Bv**	**Gu**	**MI**	**NG**	**Mk**	RI	Te	Vu	Lo	GT

Bismarck Kingfisher *Alcedo websteri* — Page 350

22 cm. Greenish-blue upperparts and half-collar, white ear-coverts, creamy underparts, black legs and heavy black bill. Female has buffy-orange underparts and less blue on breast. Slow rivers in lowland forest. Uncommon.

Mn	Mu	**NI**	**NB**	Bv	Gu	MI	NG	Mk	RI	Te	Vu	Lo	GT

Little Kingfisher *Ceyx pusillus* — Page 351

11 cm. Blue upperparts and breast-band, white loral spot, ear-coverts and underparts, black bill and legs. Juvenile has greener upperparts and buff wash. Forested coasts. Uncommon.

C. p. masauji (Bismarcks) has complete blue breast-band and white undertail-coverts.

C. p. bougainvillei (Bougainville, Choiseul and Isabel) has partial blue breast-band.

C. p. richardsi (New Georgia group) has complete blue breast-band and blue undertail-coverts.

Mn	Mu	**NI**	**NB**	**Bv**	**Gu**	**MI**	**NG**	Mk	RI	Te	Vu	Lo	GT

Variable Dwarf Kingfisher *Ceyx lepidus* — Page 350

14 cm. Purple-blue upperparts, white throat and ear-coverts, orange underparts, black or red bill and orange legs. Forest understorey. Fairly common.

C. l. dispar (Manus) has red bill, male has blue head, and female has orange head with blue on crown.

C. l. mulcatus (New Ireland) has black bill and yellowish throat.

C. l. meeki (Bougainville, Choiseul and Isabel) has black bill, greenish-blue upperparts, and buffy ear-coverts and underparts.

C. l. nigromaxilla (Guadalcanal) has purple-blue upperparts, orange underparts and black bill with red base.

C. l. gentianus (Makira) has white loral spot, ear-coverts and underparts, and black bill.

Mn	Mu	**NI**	**NB**	**Bv**	**Gu**	**MI**	**NG**	**Mk**	RI	Te	Vu	Lo	GT

hispidoides
salomonensis
Common Kingfisher
♂
♀
Bismarck Kingfisher
masauji
richardsi
Little Kingfisher
bougainvillei
juvenile
mulcatus
dispar
♀
dispar
♂
Variable Dwarf Kingfisher
meeki
nigromaxilla
gentianus

PLATE 47: LARGE BISMARCK KINGFISHERS

Forest Kingfisher *Todiramphus macleayii incinctus* Page 346

20 cm. White wing-patch in flight. Dark blue upperparts, greener on back, white loral spot, collar and underparts, sometimes with buff flanks. Female has blue hindneck. Immature has buffy underparts. Open habitats. Rare.

Mn	Mu	**Nl**	**NB**	Bv	Gu	Ml	**NG**	Mk	Rl	Te	Vu	Lo	GT

White-mantled Kingfisher *Todiramphus albonotatus* Page 347

17 cm. Pale blue crown, black mask, blue wings and tail, white loral spot, mantle and underparts. Back and rump are white in male and blue in female. Slender black bill. Juvenile has buffy wash and fringes. Lowland forest. Canopy. Uncommon.

Mn	Mu	Nl	**NB**	Bv	Gu	Ml	NG	Mk	Rl	Te	Vu	Lo	GT

Collared Kingfisher *Todiramphus chloris* Page 348

23 cm. Greenish-blue upperparts, buff loral spot or supercilium, darker mask, white or buff collar and underparts and heavy pale-based black bill. Open forest or open country. Canopy. Common.

T. c. ***tristrami*** (New Britain) has greenish-blue upperparts and buff or white underparts, collar and loral stripe.

T. c. ***bennetti*** (Nissan) has sooty-green head, mantle and wings.

T. c. ***matthiae*** (St Matthias Is) has green, white or buff crown, black mask and dark blue mantle and wings.

Mn	**Mu**	**Nl**	**NB**	**Bv**	**Gu**	**Ml**	**NG**	**Mk**	**Rl**	**Te**	**Vu**	Lo	GT

Beach Kingfisher *Todiramphus saurophagus admiralitatis* Page 349

30 cm. Pale blue mantle, wings and tail, white head and underparts with white or green-blue crown, black eye-stripe and large pale-based black bill. Coasts. Fairly common. See Plate 48.

Mn	**Mu**	**Nl**	**NB**	**Bv**	**Gu**	**Ml**	**NG**	**Mk**	Rl	Te	Vu	Lo	GT

Sacred Kingfisher *Todiramphus s. sanctus* Page 349

21 cm. Like Collared Kingfisher but smaller, with shorter finer less angular bill, greenish-blue upperparts, always buff underparts, and sometimes black fringes on flanks. Open habitats and coasts. Uncommon.

Mn	**Mu**	**Nl**	**NB**	**Bv**	**Gu**	**Ml**	**NG**	**Mk**	Rl	Te	Vu	**Lo**	**GT**

Black-capped Paradise Kingfisher *Tanysiptera n. nigriceps* Page 346

23 cm + tail-streamers. Red bill, black head and scapulars, orange-buff underparts, blue wings and outer tail, white mantle, rump and long central tail. Juvenile is duller with short blue tail. Dense forest understorey. Fairly common.

Mn	Mu	Nl	**NB**	Bv	Gu	Ml	NG	Mk	Rl	Te	Vu	Lo	GT

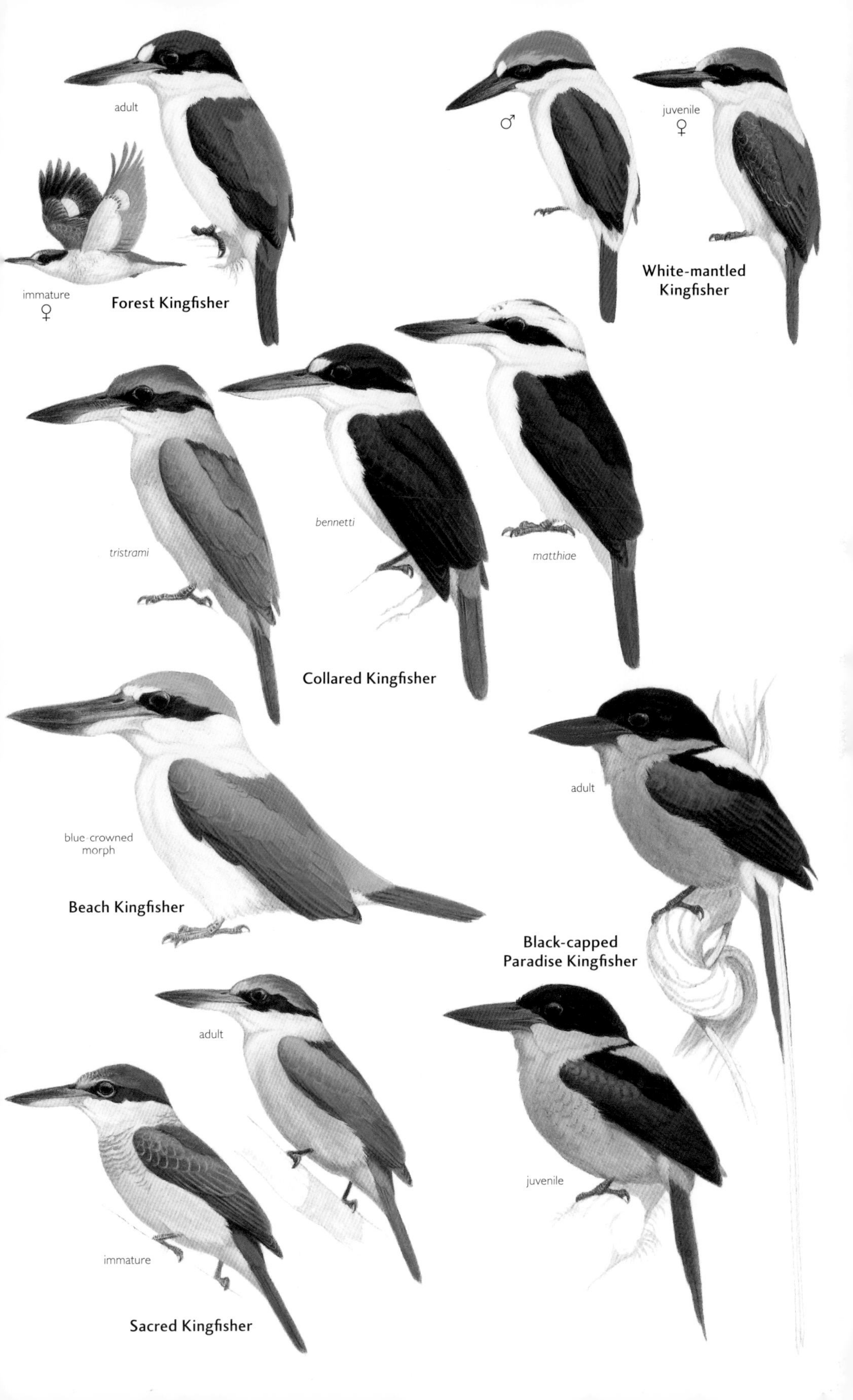
adult
immature
♀
Forest Kingfisher
♂
juvenile
♀
White-mantled
Kingfisher
tristrami
bennetti
matthiae
Collared Kingfisher
blue crowned
morph
Beach Kingfisher
adult
Black-capped
Paradise Kingfisher
adult
immature
Sacred Kingfisher
juvenile

PLATE 48: LARGE SOLOMONS, VANUATU & NEW CALEDONIA KINGFISHERS

Ultramarine Kingfisher *Todiramphus leucopygius* — Page 347

21 cm. Purple-blue crown, mantle, wings and tail, white collar and underparts, and black bill and mask. Chestnut-purple undertail-coverts. Male has white back, and female has blue back. Juvenile has fine black bars on buffy underparts. Lowland secondary forest. Fairly common.

Mn | Mu | NI | NB | **Bv** | **Gu** | MI | NG | Mk | RI | Te | Vu | Lo | GT

Vanuatu Kingfisher *Todiramphus farquhari* — Page 347

19 cm. Purple-blue crown, mantle, wings and tail, black bill and mask, white collar and chestnut underparts. Female has white belly. Juvenile duller, with rufous wash on collar and lores. Closed-canopy lowland and hill forest. Fairly common.

Mn | Mu | NI | NB | Bv | Gu | MI | NG | Mk | RI | Te | **Vu** | Lo | GT

Collared Kingfisher *Todiramphus chloris* — Page 348

23 cm. Greenish-blue upperparts, buff loral spot or supercilium, darker mask, white or buff collar and underparts and heavy pale-based black bill. Open forest or open country. Canopy. Common.

T. c. alberti (Bougainville to Guadalcanal) has buffy loral spot, collar and underparts, paler on throat and belly.

T. c. amoenus (Rennell) has variable supercilium and buff collar and breast.

T. c. melanoderus (Vanikoro) has black fringes on breast and small orange loral spot.

T. c. juliae (central Vanuatu) has long rufous supercilium.

Mn | **Mu** | **NI** | **NB** | **Bv** | **Gu** | **MI** | **NG** | **Mk** | **RI** | **Te** | **Vu** | Lo | GT

Sacred Kingfisher *Todiramphus sanctus sanctus* — Page 349

21 cm. Like Collared Kingfisher but smaller, with shorter finer less angular bill, greenish-blue upperparts, always buff underparts, and sometimes black fringes on flanks. All habitats. Common resident or uncommon migrant.

Mn | **Mu** | **NI** | **NB** | **Bv** | **Gu** | **MI** | **NG** | **Mk** | RI | Te | Vu | **Lo** | **GT**

Beach Kingfisher *Todiramphus saurophagus admiralitatis* — Page 349

30 cm. Pale blue mantle, wings and tail, white head and underparts with white or green-blue crown, black eye-stripe and large pale-based black bill. Coasts. Fairly common.

Mn | **Mu** | **NI** | **NB** | **Bv** | **Gu** | **MI** | **NG** | **Mk** | RI | Te | Vu | Lo | GT

Moustached Kingfisher *Actenoides bougainvillei* — Page 346

32 cm. Long red bill, orange head, neck and underparts, two blue stripes on head, and blue wings and tail. Male has blue mantle and scapulars. Montane forest. Probably crepuscular. Rare.

A. b. bougainvillei (Bougainville): female has orange upper back.

A. b. excelsus (Guadalcanal): female has green back and pale orange underparts.

Mn | Mu | NI | NB | **Bv** | **Gu** | MI | NG | Mk | RI | Te | Vu | Lo | GT

♂
juvenile
♀
Ultramarine
Kingfisher
♂
immature/♀
Vanuatu
Kingfisher
alberti
Collared Kingfisher
amoenus
melanoderus
adult
Sacred
Kingfisher
immature
Collared Kingfisher
juliae
excelsus
♀
bougainvillei
♂
Moustached Kingfisher
Beach Kingfisher

PLATE 49: BEE-EATERS, DOLLARBIRD, HORNBILL AND PITTAS

Blue-tailed Bee-eater *Merops philippinus* — Page 352

23 cm + tail-streamers. Greenish with blue rump, tail and long streamers, black eye-mask and orange-rufous throat. In flight, plain green upperwing and rufous underwing. Juvenile is duller with pale chestnut wash on throat and short or no tail-streamers. Dry open lowland habitats. Rare.

Mn	Mu	NI	**NB**	Bv	Gu	MI	NG	Mk	RI	Te	Vu	Lo	GT

Rainbow Bee-eater *Merops ornatus* — Page 352

20 cm + tail-streamers. Greenish with blue rump, blackish tail and narrow streamers. Orange-yellow throat and black eye-mask and bar on lower throat. Upperwing has rufous flight feathers, green wing-coverts, blue-green mantle and rump, and plain rufous underwing. Juvenile is duller and lacks throat-band and tail-streamers. Forest edge and open habitats. Uncommon.

Mn	**Mu**	**NI**	**NB**	Bv	Gu	MI	NG	Mk	RI	Te	Vu	Lo	GT

Dollarbird *Eurystomus orientalis crassirostris* — Page 345

27 cm. Stocky with short tail, stout red bill, dusky brown head and turquoise body, with purple on throat and wings. Long broad wings have silvery patch on outer wing. Juvenile is browner with dusky-yellow bill. Forest edge, especially gardens and clearings. Singles and pairs perch on exposed branches and sally or hawk with deep wing-beats. Fairly common.

Mn	**Mu**	**NI**	**NB**	**Bv**	**Gu**	**MI**	**NG**	**Mk**	RI	Te	Vu	Lo	GT

Blyth's Hornbill *Aceros plicatus* — Page 352

75 cm. Huge, black with massive pale bill, long broad wings and long white tail. Pale blue skin around eye and throat. Male has pale orange head and neck, black in female. Very loud deep honks and grunts. Wings 'whoosh' in flight. Old-growth forest. Often flies high over land and sea. Fairly common.

Mn	Mu	**NI**	**NB**	**Bv**	**Gu**	**MI**	**NG**	Mk	RI	Te	Vu	Lo	GT

Hooded Pitta *Pitta sordida* — Page 353

17 cm. Green with black hood, silvery-blue wing-coverts and red central belly to undertail-coverts. In flight, blue wing-coverts and white spot on dark primaries. Juvenile is dull grey-brown with black head, buffy throat and reddish undertail-coverts. Double whistle *kuhwee-kuwee*? Forest. Only on Crown, Long and Tolokiwa.

Mn	Mu	NI	**NB**	Bv	Gu	MI	NG	Mk	RI	Te	Vu	Lo	GT

Superb Pitta *Pitta superba* — Page 354

21 cm. Glossy black with silvery-blue wing-coverts and bright red belly to undertail-coverts. Immature is duller with no gloss and duller pinker belly and undertail-coverts. Double quavering whistle *hwoow-whoow*. Thickets in primary forest. Rare.

Mn	Mu	NI	NB	Bv	Gu	MI	NG	Mk	RI	Te	Vu	Lo	GT

Red-bellied Pitta *Pitta erythrogaster* — Page 353

17 cm. Bright blue breast and red belly, brownish head and throat with rufous cap and nape, greenish-blue mantle and blue wings. In flight, small white spot on primaries, and blue rump and uppertail. Juvenile is buffy-brown with paler underparts, creamy lower throat, and soon showing some green, blue and red. Low tremulous double whistle. Forest, especially secondary growth. Uncommon.

P. e. splendida (Tabar) has blackish head and throat with deep blue upperparts.

P. e. gazellae (New Britain) has some blue in crown, and grey-brown throat.

Mn	Mu	**NI**	**NB**	Bv	Gu	MI	NG	Mk	RI	Te	Vu	Lo	GT

Black-faced Pitta *Pitta anerythra* — Page 354

16 cm. Dark head, green mantle and wings, silvery-blue wing-coverts and buff underparts. In flight, green with blue wing-covert patch and small white spot on primaries. Double quavering whistle *tooi, toiii*. Patchworks of forest and secondary growth. Rare.

P. a. pallida (Bougainville) has paler underparts and black head sometimes with chestnut nape-band.

P. a. anerythra (Isabel) has chestnut-brown crown and deeper buff underparts.

Mn	Mu	NI	NB	**Bv**	Gu	MI	NG	Mk	RI	Te	Vu	Lo	GT

adult
juvenile
Rainbow Bee-eater
adult
juvenile
Dollarbird
adult
Blue-tailed Bee-eater
adult
♂
Blyth's Hornbill
♀
♀
Hooded Pitta
Superb Pitta
splendida
gazellae
immature
Red-bellied Pitta
pallida
anerythra
Black-faced Pitta

PLATE 50: BISMARCKS SWALLOWS, WAGTAILS AND TRILLERS

Sand Martin *Riparia riparia* — Page 394

12 cm. Dumpy swallow with chocolate-brown upperparts, underwings and shallowly forked tail, and white underparts with distinct brown breast-band. Open habitats, usually by fresh water. Vagrant?

Barn Swallow *Hirundo rustica* — Page 395

18 cm. Glossy blue-black upperparts, chestnut forehead and throat, dark breast-band and white underparts and underwing-coverts. Forked tail has white spots near tip and long streamers. Immature is duller, often incomplete breast-band and no streamers. Open habitats. Vagrant.

Pacific Swallow *Hirundo tahitica subfusca* — Page 395

13 cm. Glossy blue-black upperparts, rufous forehead to upper breast, pale dusky underparts and underwing-coverts, and dark undertail-coverts with pale fringes. Forked tail has pointed corners and, on New Britain, small white spots. Immature duller. Open habitats, especially beaches and towns. Uncommon. See swiftlets (Plate 40).

Mn	Mu	**NI**	**NB**	**Bv**	**Gu**	**MI**	**NG**	**Mk**	RI	**Te**	**Vu**	**Lo**	**GT**

Red-rumped Swallow *Cecropis daurica* — Page 396

19 cm. Glossy blue-black upperparts, chestnut rump and behind eye, white face and underparts with black streaks, and black tail-coverts and forked tail with long streamers. Immature is duller. Open habitats, especially grasslands and towns. Rare.

Mn	Mu	**NI**	**NB**	**Bv**	Gu	MI	NG	Mk	RI	Te	Vu	Lo	GT

Tree Martin *Petrochelidon nigricans* — Page 396

13 cm. Blue-black upperparts with off-white rump, rufous forehead, buffy-white underparts and notched tail. Immature is duller. Open habitats, especially forest edge. Rare.

Mn	Mu	**NI**	**NB**	**Bv**	**Gu**	**MI**	NG	Mk	RI	Te	Vu	Lo	**GT**

Eastern Yellow Wagtail *Motacilla tschutschensis simillima* — Page 424

17 cm. Slender with dark legs and long black tail with white outer feathers. Non-breeding adult and immature have olive upperparts, pale yellow or white supercilium and underparts, and white fringes on dark wing. Breeding adult has green upperparts and bright yellow underparts. Short grassland. Walks, pumping tail. Vagrant.

Grey Wagtail *Motacilla cinerea* — Page 425

18 cm. Slender with pink legs and long black tail with white outer feathers. Grey upperparts with white supercilium, blackish wings, buffy-white underparts and bright yellow vent and rump. In flight, white wing-bar. Breeding adult has bright yellow underparts, male with black throat. By rivers and streams. Walks and stands on rocks, pumping tail. Vagrant.

Varied Triller *Lalage leucomela falsa* — Page 369

18 cm. Male has glossy black upperparts and white supercilium, wing-bars, wing-panels and rump-bars. White underparts with black barring and plain buff vent. Female has dark grey upperparts, and more barred underparts. Juvenile has pale scaling on upperparts and short dusky streaks, becoming broken bars, on underparts. Forest. Fairly common.
L. l. ottomeyeri (Lihir): male has plain white underparts.

Mn	Mu	**NI**	**NB**	Bv	Gu	MI	NG	Mk	RI	Te	Vu	Lo	GT

Mussau Triller *Lalage conjuncta* — Page 370

16 cm. Glossy black upperparts with large white wing-covert patch and rump-patch, and white fringes on tertials and secondaries. White face, throat and upper breast, and chestnut lower breast to vent. Forest. Fairly common.

Mn	**Mu**	NI	NB	Bv	Gu	MI	NG	Mk	RI	Te	Vu	Lo	GT

Sand Martin
Barn Swallow
Pacific Swallow
Tree Martin
Red-rumped Swallow
Eastern Yellow Wagtail
falsa
♂
Grey Wagtail
falsa
♀
Varied Triller
ottomeyeri
♂
Mussau Triller

Black-faced Cuckooshrike *Coracina novaehollandiae* Page 366

33 cm. Pale grey upperparts and breast, darker wings and tail with white tail-tips, black forehead, face and throat, and paler belly. Immature has less defined black patch on ear-coverts only, and finely barred throat and breast. Open habitats with trees. Rare.

Mn	Mu	NI	NB	Bv	Gu	MI	NG	Mk	RI	Te	Vu	Lo	GT

Barred Cuckooshrike *Coracina lineata sublineata* Page 367

23 cm. Yellow eye. Male is plain blue-grey with black lores and darker wings and tail. Female is plain blue-grey with fine black-and-white barring on lower breast to undertail-coverts. Juvenile has creamy scaling on upperparts and barred underparts. Forest. Fairly common. See Oriental Cuckoo (Plate 41).

Mn	Mu	NI	NB	Bv	Gu	MI	NG	Mk	RI	Te	Vu	Lo	GT

White-bellied Cuckooshrike *Coracina papuensis sclateri* Page 367

25 cm. Pale grey head with black bill and mask from lores to just behind eye, mid-grey upperparts and greyish-white underparts. Juvenile has buffy fringes on upperparts and breast, and indistinct mask. Forest edge and trees in open habitats. Common.

C. p. ingens (Manus) is larger with a deeper bill. Sometimes split as a separate species: Manus Cuckooshrike.

Mn	Mu	NI	NB	Bv	Gu	MI	NG	Mk	RI	Te	Vu	Lo	GT

Common Cicadabird *Coracina tenuirostris heinrothi* Page 368

25 cm. Male is dark blue-grey with indistinct blackish face-mask, grey fringes on black wings and black outer tail. Female has blue-grey crown, dark eye-stripe, rufous-brown upperparts, black centres and rufous fringes on wings, and paler rufous underparts, often with fine black barring. Juvenile like female but has brown cap and buffy fringes on upperparts. Forest. Fairly common.

C. t. remota (New Ireland): female has unbarred rich rufous underparts.

Mn	Mu	NI	NB	Bv	Gu	MI	NG	Mk	RI	Te	Vu	Lo	GT

adult
immature
Black-faced Cuckooshrike
♂
Barred Cuckooshrike
♀
sclateri
adult
juvenile
White-bellied
Cuckooshrike
heinrothi
♂
Common Cicadabird
heinrothi
♀
remota
♀

Black Sunbird *Leptocoma sericea caeruleogula* — Page 418

11 cm. Male is glossy black with iridescent green crown, wing-coverts and mantle, blue throat and purple tail, and long decurved bill. Female has grey head, olive upperparts, black tail with white corners, pale grey throat and dull yellow underparts. Juvenile like female but plainer underparts. Forest edge and sometimes closed forest. Common. See myzomelas (Plate 53).

Mn Mu **NI** **NB** Bv Gu MI NG Mk RI Te Vu Lo GT

Olive-backed Sunbird *Cinnyris jugularis flavigaster* — Page 419

11 cm. Dull olive upperparts, dark tail with white corners, bright yellow underparts and fine supercilium, and long decurved bill. Male has metallic blue throat. Female has yellow throat. Open forest habitats, including towns. Common. See myzomelas (Plate 53).

Mn **Mu** **NI** **NB** **Bv** **Gu** **MI** **NG** **Mk** RI Te Vu Lo GT

Red-banded Flowerpecker *Dicaeum eximium layardorum* — Page 417

8 cm. Dumpy with stubby bill. Plain brown upperparts with red rump and black tail, grey-brown neck extending onto upper breast, buffy-olive flanks and white central underparts. Male has red breast-spot and dark stripe on lower breast and belly. Female has white stripe along underparts and short white supercilium. Forest. Fairly common.

D. e. eximium (New Ireland) has browner head.

Mn Mu **NI** **NB** Bv Gu MI NG Mk RI Te Vu Lo GT

Manus Friarbird *Philemon albitorques* — Page 356

35 cm. Lanky with fairly long stout blackish bill, dark brown naked head, dark brown mantle, wings and tail, narrow white terminal tail-bar, downy white collar and creamy-white underparts. Open forest. Loud, noisy and conspicuous. Flies with heavy flaps and glides, with long broad wings and long neck and tail. Common.

Mn Mu NI NB Bv Gu MI NG Mk RI Te Vu Lo GT

New Britain Friarbird *Philemon cockerelli* — Page 356

34 cm. Lanky with blackish bill, dark brown head, grey hindneck, dark brown upperparts, narrow pale terminal tail-bar, pale grey-buff throat and upper breast, sometimes slight brown breast-band, and warmer buffy on belly. Juvenile has paler grey hindneck, olive on wings and tail, and yellow on breast. Forest and forest edge. Loud, noisy and conspicuous. Common.

Mn Mu NI **NB** Bv Gu MI NG Mk RI Te Vu Lo GT

New Ireland Friarbird *Philemon eichhorni* — Page 356

32 cm. Lanky with stout blackish bill, dark brown head, mantle, wings and tail, broad white terminal tail-bar, white throat and hindneck with dark mottling, pale brown neck and breast with white spots or scales, and plain buff lower belly. Juvenile has white fringes on upperparts and yellowish throat. Montane forest above 750 m. Fairly common.

Mn Mu **NI** NB Bv Gu MI NG Mk RI Te Vu Lo GT

New Britain Honeyeater *Melidectes whitemanensis* — Page 357

22 cm. Plain olive-brown with brighter yellow-green fringes on wings and tail, small yellow-grey naked patch below and behind eye, and long decurved black bill. Montane forest above 850 m. Uncommon. See myzomelas (Plate 53).

Mn Mu NI **NB** Bv Gu MI NG Mk RI Te Vu Lo GT

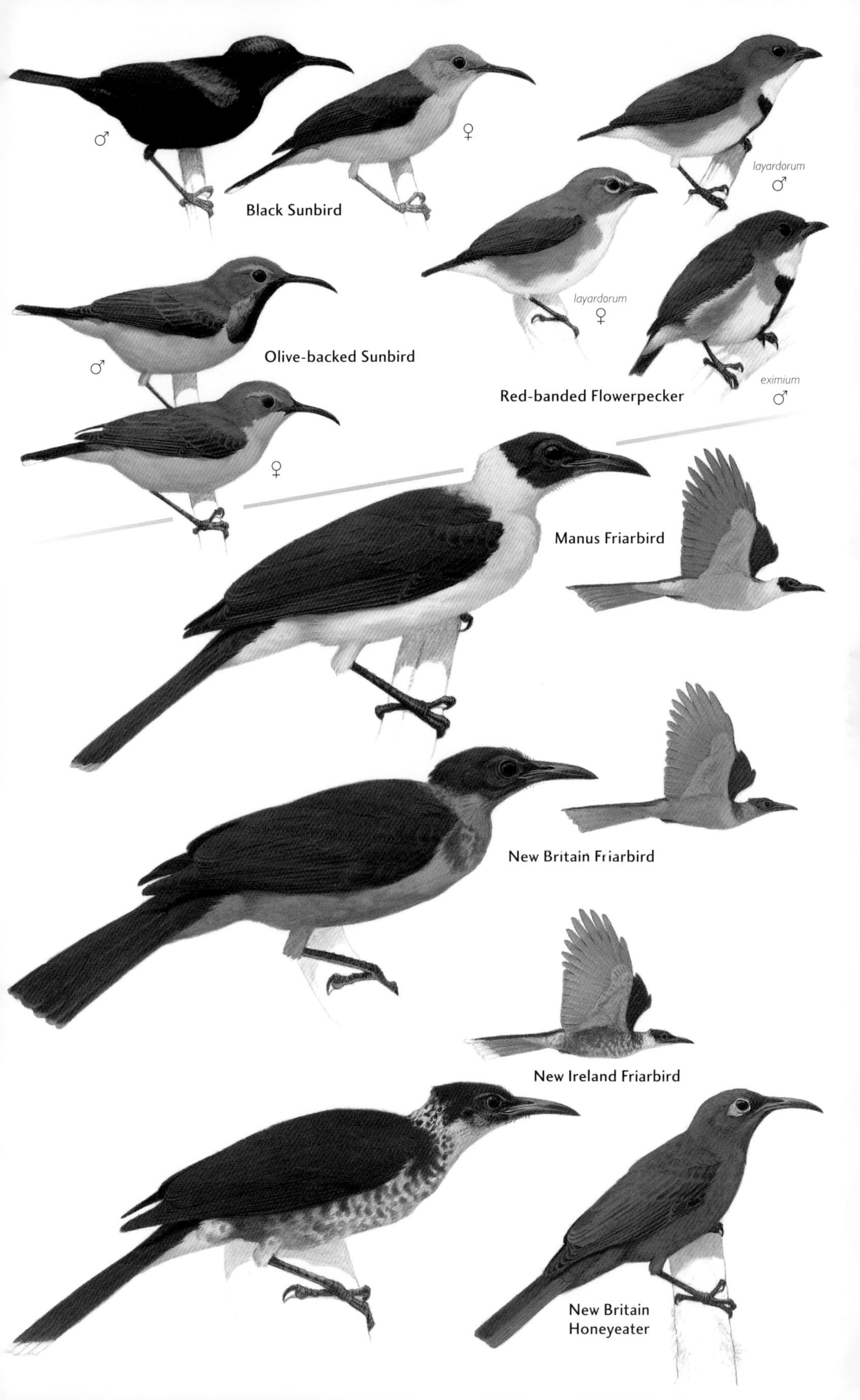
♂
♀
Black Sunbird
layardorum
♂
layardorum
♀
♂
Olive-backed Sunbird
♀
Red-banded Flowerpecker
eximium
♂
Manus Friarbird
New Britain Friarbird
New Ireland Friarbird
New Britain
Honeyeater

Ashy Myzomela *Myzomela cineracea* — Page 359

15 cm. Large, long-billed and relatively long-tailed myzomela. Plain dark dull grey, slightly darker on head and throat, paler on underparts and sometimes green fringes on wings. White underwing in flight. Red chin-patch is tiny on male and very small on female. Juvenile has yellowish bill-base. Forest, especially degraded forest. Unobtrusive in understorey. Common.

Mn	Mu	NI	**NB**	Bv	Gu	MI	NG	Mk	RI	Te	Vu	Lo	GT

Red Myzomela *Myzomela cruentata* — Page 359

11 cm. Male is plain dull pink-red, darker and browner on wings and tail. Female is grey-brown with red on forehead, chin and tail, or like male but duller, paler and browner-red. Juvenile is browner, especially on underparts. Forest. Fairly common.

M. c. coccinea (New Britain): male is pink-red, female and juvenile grey-brown with red on forehead, chin and tail.

M. c. erythrina (New Ireland): male is duller, darker and less pink, female duller and slightly paler, and juvenile dull rosy, browner on breast and belly.

Mn	Mu	**NI**	**NB**	Bv	Gu	MI	NG	Mk	RI	Te	Vu	Lo	GT

New Ireland Myzomela *Myzomela pulchella* — Page 360

11 cm. Bright red head and throat, black lores, brown nape and upperparts, dark mottling on breast, and pale yellowish-buff underparts. Juvenile is dull olive, with scattered red feathers on face and throat. Forest above 350 m, occasionally to 150 m. Fairly common.

Mn	Mu	**NI**	NB	Bv	Gu	MI	NG	Mk	RI	Te	Vu	Lo	GT

Sclater's Myzomela *Myzomela sclateri* — Page 361

11 cm. Male has bright red throat, sooty head and upper mantle, dark brown upperparts with olive fringes on wings, and dusky upper breast fading to yellowish belly with faint streaks. Female lacks red throat or has small faint chin-patch, and darker brown upperparts. Forest and coconuts. Common. Only on small islands.

Mn	Mu	NI	**NB**	Bv	Gu	MI	NG	Mk	RI	Te	Vu	Lo	GT

Bismarck Black Myzomela *Myzomela p. pammelaena* — Page 361

12 cm. All black except grey or whitish underwing. Male is shiny but not iridescent, female duller, and juvenile dusky with browner underparts. Forest and secondary growth. Common on small islands.

Mn	**Mu**	**NI**	**NB**	Bv	Gu	MI	NG	Mk	RI	Te	Vu	Lo	GT

Black-bellied Myzomela *Myzomela erythromelas* — Page 363

10 cm. Male is glossy black with bright red head and throat. Female is olive-brown, with smaller, duller, orange-red head and throat, faint streaks on paler underparts and olive fringes on wings. Forest, especially secondary forest. Fairly common.

Mn	Mu	NI	**NB**	Bv	Gu	MI	NG	Mk	RI	Te	Vu	Lo	GT

juvenile
coccinea
♀
coccinea
♂
Red Myzomela
adult
Ashy Myzomela
erythrina
♀
erythrina
♂
juvenile
Red Myzomela
New Ireland Myzomela
juvenile
adult
juvenile
juvenile
Sclater's
Myzomela
Bismarck
Black Myzomela
adult
adult
adult
juvenile
Black-bellied Myzomela

Bismarck Fantail *Rhipidura dahli antonii* Page 380

14 cm. Dull grey head with short white supercilium and moustachial stripe, dull orange-rufous upperparts, darker centres to wing feathers, broad dark subterminal tail-band, dull grey breast and rich buff underparts. Juvenile has indistinct head pattern with creamy supercilium and moustachial stripe. Forest, usually 800–1800 m but sometimes lowlands. Understorey. Fairly common.

Mn	Mu	**NI**	**NB**	Bv	Gu	MI	NG	Mk	RI	Te	Vu	Lo	GT

Mussau Fantail *Rhipidura matthiae* Page 381

15 cm. Glossy black head and breast with white forecrown and broad moustachial stripe. Rufous-orange upperparts, brighter on tail and darker on wings, silver belly, and buff flanks and vent. Juvenile is duller and messier. Forest and secondary regrowth. Understorey. Common.

Mn	**Mu**	NI	NB	Bv	Gu	MI	NG	Mk	RI	Te	Vu	Lo	GT

Manus Fantail *Rhipidura semirubra* Page 381

14 cm. Bright rufous crown, mantle and rump, darker browner wings and dark brown tail with bold white tips. White throat, narrow white eye-ring, black face, broad black upper breast-band, black spots on lower breast, white belly, buffy flanks and rufous undertail-coverts. Forest, scrub and coconuts. Common on small islands but extinct on Manus.

Mn	Mu	NI	NB	Bv	Gu	MI	NG	Mk	RI	Te	Vu	Lo	GT

Willie Wagtail *Rhipidura leucophrys melaleuca* Page 377

20 cm. Black head, throat and upperparts with white lower breast to vent and indistinct white supercilium. Juvenile is duller with broader dull eyebrow and buffy tips to wing-coverts. Open habitat including coasts, towns and sometimes forest clearings. Runs on ground and sallies from low perches, drooping wings and waving tail. Common.

Mn	**Mu**	**NI**	**NB**	**Bv**	**Gu**	**MI**	**NG**	**Mk**	RI	Te	Vu	Lo	GT

Northern Fantail *Rhipidura rufiventris finschii* Page 378

17 cm. Dark grey with white throat, creamy belly and vent, white tertial fringes and white tail-corners. Indistinct short white supercilium and sometimes white streaks on breast. Juvenile has browner upperparts and breast-band with buffy tips. Forest. Perches upright, less active than other fantails and never fans tail. Common.

Mn	**Mu**	**NI**	**NB**	Bv	Gu	MI	NG	Mk	RI	Te	Vu	Lo	GT

Mangrove Golden Whistler *Pachycephala melanura dahli* Page 374

16 cm. Male has black head and breast-band, white throat, bright yellow underparts and collar, green mantle, black wings and uppertail, and pale grey fringes on secondaries and primaries. Female has mottled white throat, buffy-grey upper breast, yellow underparts, olive-grey upperparts, grey fringes on wings and black uppertail. Juvenile like female but has pale bill, rufous on wings, and rufous underparts when just fledged. Coastal vegetation. Understorey. Common on small islands.

Mn	Mu	**NI**	**NB**	**Bv**	Gu	MI	NG	Mk	RI	Te	Vu	Lo	GT

Bismarck Whistler *Pachycephala c. citreogaster* Page 371

16 cm. Male has black head and breast-band, white throat, yellow underparts and collar, and olive upperparts with black centres to wing feathers and tail. Female has olive-brown upperparts, mottled greyish-white throat, and buffy breast becoming dull yellow on belly. Juvenile like female but has pale bill, rufous on wings and rufous underparts when just fledged. Forest. Common.

Mn	**Mu**	**NI**	**NB**	Bv	Gu	MI	NG	Mk	RI	Te	Vu	Lo	GT

Bismarck Fantail
adult
juvenile
Mussau Fantail
Manus Fantail
Willie Wagtail
Northern Fantail
adult
juvenile
♂
Mangrove Golden Whistler
♂
Bismarck Whistler
♀
♀
juvenile

Island Monarch *Monarcha cinerascens perpallidus* — Page 386

18 cm. Dull ash-grey upperparts, head and upper breast, and orange-chestnut lower breast and belly. Prominent black eye on plain face and heavy steel-blue bill. Juvenile is duller and browner. Forest and scrub. Understorey. Common on small islands.

Mn	Mu	NI	NB	Bv	Gu	MI	NG	Mk	RI	Te	Vu	Lo	GT

Golden Monarch *Carterornis c. chrysomela* — Page 387

13 cm. Male has bright golden-yellow head, underparts, wing-panel and rump, and glossy black face, throat, mantle, wings and tail. Female has yellow-olive upperparts and dull yellow underparts with pale spot before eye. Juvenile like female but darker bill and sometimes no eye-spot. Forest. Mid- and upper storeys. Common.
C. c. pulcherrimus (Djaul): male has yellow mantle, female more yellow on face and rump.

Mn	Mu	NI	NB	Bv	Gu	MI	NG	Mk	RI	Te	Vu	Lo	GT

Manus Monarch *Symposiachrus i. infelix* — Page 384

15 cm. Glossy black upperparts, throat and breast, white ear-covert patch, white wing-covert patch, and black and white tail. Juvenile has pale grey or grey-buff upperparts, variable white wing-covert spots, pale grey throat and upper breast, and buffy lower breast and belly. Closed-canopy forest. Uncommon.
S. i. coultasi (Rambutyo and Tong) has white rump and tail except black central tail-tip, and more white on ear-coverts and wing.

Mn	Mu	NI	NB	Bv	Gu	MI	NG	Mk	RI	Te	Vu	Lo	GT

Mussau Monarch *Symposiachrus menckei* — Page 384

15 cm. Mostly white with black forehead, face and throat with variable black on ear-coverts and spots on crown, mantle, breast and belly, black flight feathers, some wing-coverts and central tail. Juvenile has variable blackish mask, black or grey crown and upperparts, and buffy-pink wash on underparts. Forest. Common.

Mn	Mu	NI	NB	Bv	Gu	MI	NG	Mk	RI	Te	Vu	Lo	GT

Black-tailed Monarch *Symposiachrus v. verticalis* — Page 384

16 cm. Glossy black bib, forehead, crown and upperparts with white face, neck-sides, underparts, wing-covert patch and rump. Juvenile has grey crown, nape and mantle, brown wings with variable buff or white wing-covert patch, white rump, and orange-pink face and underparts, darkest on upper breast and fading across belly. Closed-canopy forest. Fairly common.
S. v. ateralbus (Djaul) is larger and has white tips to outer three pairs of tail feathers, with more white on rump; juvenile has more orange on face.

Mn	Mu	NI	NB	Bv	Gu	MI	NG	Mk	RI	Te	Vu	Lo	GT

Island Monarch
chrysomela
♂
pulcherrimus
♂
chrysomela
♀
Golden Monarch
pulcherrimus
♀
juvenile
infelix
adult
Manus Monarch
juvenile
adult
coultasi
adult
Mussau Monarch
juvenile
ateralbus
juvenile
adult
Black-tailed Monarch
ateralbus
adult

Leaden Flycatcher *Myiagra rubecula* (not illustrated) Page 388

15 cm. Very similar to Satin Flycatcher. Male has greyer upperparts with convex bulging border onto white lower breast. Female has paler upperparts without gloss and sometimes paler throat. Open forest. Vagrant.

Satin Flycatcher *Myiagra cyanoleuca* Page 390

16 cm. Male is glossy blue-black with white lower breast and belly. Female has blue-grey upperparts, browner wings and tail, narrow white eye-ring, orange throat and breast, and white belly. Open forested habitats. Canopy. Shivers tail. Rare.

Mn	Mu	**Nl**	**NB**	Bv	Gu	Ml	NG	Mk	Rl	Te	Vu	Lo	GT

Shining Flycatcher *Myiagra alecto* Page 390

17 cm. Large and lanky with angular crown. Male is glossy blue-black with flat cap and medium-long bill. Female has blue-black head, rufous upperparts and tail, and white underparts. Forest and scrub thickets, especially beside water, including mangroves. Close to ground. Male often calls with extended neck, wagging fanned tail and exposing red mouth. Common.

Mn	Mu	**Nl**	**NB**	Bv	Gu	Ml	NG	Mk	Rl	Te	Vu	Lo	GT

Velvet Flycatcher *Myiagra eichhorni* Page 391

16 cm. Male is glossy blue-black with rounded crown and medium-short bill. Female has grey head and underparts, and rufous upperparts. Closed-canopy forest, especially thickets in mid-montane forest. Understorey. Never wags or fans tail. Uncommon.

M. e. eichhorni (New Ireland and New Britain): female has mid-grey head and underparts.

M. e. cervinicolor (Djaul): female has pale grey head and very pale grey underparts.

Mn	Mu	**Nl**	**NB**	Bv	Gu	Ml	NG	Mk	Rl	Te	Vu	Lo	GT

Mussau Flycatcher *Myiagra hebetior* Page 390

15 cm. Male (not illustrated) like Velvet Flycatcher but greener gloss. Female has blue-black head, rufous upperparts, darker tail and creamy underparts. Juvenile like female but has dark brown crown. Forest. Fairly common.

Mn	**Mu**	Nl	NB	Bv	Gu	Ml	NG	Mk	Rl	Te	Vu	Lo	GT

Torrent Flyrobin *Monarchella muelleriana coultasi* Page 392

14 cm. Sooty-black cap, white forehead-spots, black wings and tail, grey back, white throat and pale grey underparts. Juvenile lacks forehead-spots, has brown mottling on upper breast, and pale tips on crown and wing-coverts. Fast-flowing rocky rivers. Perches on riverside boulders, bare ground and branches. Rare.

Mn	Mu	Nl	**NB**	Bv	Gu	Ml	NG	Mk	Rl	Te	Vu	Lo	GT

Bismarck Flyrobin *Microeca* sp Page 393

12cm. Dark olive-brown upperparts with darker wings, pale buffy-grey underparts, paler and yellower on flanks, and paler on vent. Dark eye and indistinct dusky cap, pale supercilium and dark eye-stripe. Short dark bill with pale lower mandible and short dark legs. Forest and forest clearings. Canopy. Lowlands on New Britain and at 700–1400 m on New Ireland. Rare.

Mn	Mu	**Nl**	**NB**	Bv	Gu	Ml	NG	Mk	Rl	Te	Vu	Lo	GT

Satin Flycatcher
♂
♀
Shining Flycatcher
♂
♀
Velvet Flycatcher
♂
Velvet Flycatcher
eichorni
♀
cervinicolor
♀
Mussau Flycatcher
♀
adult
juvenile
Torrent Flyrobin
Bismarck Flyrobin

PLATE 57: BISMARCKS THRUSHES, WARBLERS AND WHITE-EYES

Russet-tailed Thrush *Zoothera heinei eichhorni* — Page 414

19 cm. Brown upperparts with black crescents, buffy wing-bars, blotchy primary bases and crescents on buffy-white underparts. White tail-corners, and black and white underwing. Forest. On ground. Fairly common on Mussau.

Mn	Mu	NI	NB	Bv	Gu	MI	NG	Mk	RI	Te	Vu	Lo	GT

New Britain Thrush *Zoothera talaseae* — Page 414

23 cm. Slate-grey upperparts with black fringes, two white wing-bars, white on face, and black scales on white underparts. White tail-corners, and black and white underwing. Forest above 600 m. On ground. Uncommon.

Mn	Mu	NI	NB	Bv	Gu	MI	NG	Mk	RI	Te	Vu	Lo	GT

Island Thrush *Turdus poliocephalus* — Page 415

20 cm. Blackish-brown with yellow bill, legs and eye-ring. Juvenile has rufous spots and streaks. Montane forest. On ground and low bushes. Locally common.

T. p. beehleri (above 1500 m on New Ireland) is blackish with grey-brown face, female with paler fringes on belly.

T. p. heinrothi (all altitudes on Mussau) is dark brown with slightly paler underparts.

Mn	Mu	NI	NB	Bv	Gu	MI	NG	Mk	RI	Te	Vu	Lo	GT

Island Leaf Warbler *Phylloscopus poliocephalus* — Page 397

10 cm. Olive-green upperparts, long supercilium, dark eye-stripe, fine pale wing-bar, whitish throat, and yellow breast and belly. Montane forest. Canopy. Fairly common.

P. p. leletensis (above 850 m on New Ireland) has darker crown.

P. p. moorhousei (above 1100 m on New Britain) has duller yellow underparts.

P. p. matthiae (all altitudes on Mussau) has brighter yellow underparts and white tail-corners.

Mn	Mu	NI	NB	Bv	Gu	MI	NG	Mk	RI	Te	Vu	Lo	GT

Arctic Warbler *Phylloscopus borealis* — Page 397

12 cm. Olive-green upperparts with long broad supercilium, 1–2 pale wing-bars, off-white underparts and pale legs. Forest including mangroves. Canopy. Vagrant.

Bismarck White-eye *Zosterops hypoxanthus* — Page 402

11 cm. Blackish-brown hood, broad white eye-ring, blue-grey bill and legs, dull olive upperparts and dirty yellow underparts. Forest, especially secondary forest. Lowlands on Manus, and hills and mountains on New Ireland and New Britain. Fairly common.

Z. h. admiralitatis (Manus) has larger browner hood.

Z. h. hypoxanthus (New Britain) has smaller blacker hood.

Mn	Mu	NI	NB	Bv	Gu	MI	NG	Mk	RI	Te	Vu	Lo	GT

Louisiade White-eye *Zosterops griseotinctus* — Page 402

12 cm. Plain olive with broad white eye-ring, dull orange-yellow bill, brown legs and slightly paler yellower underparts. All forest and scrub. Restricted to a few small islands. Common.

Z. g. eichhorni (Nissan, Crown, Long and Tolokiwa) has olive lores and dull underparts.

Z. g. ottomeyeri (Nauna) has yellower lores, throat and underparts.

Mn	Mu	NI	NB	Bv	Gu	MI	NG	Mk	RI	Te	Vu	Lo	GT

Russet-tailed Thrush
New Britain Thrush
heinrothi
immature
beehleri
Island Thrush
moorhousei
Island Leaf Warbler
matthiae
Arctic Warbler
admiralitatis
Bismarck White-eye
eichhorni
hypoxanthus
Louisiade White-eye
ottomeyeri

PLATE 58: BISMARCKS THICKETBIRDS, WARBLERS AND BUSH CHAT

Papuan Grassbird *Megalurus macrurus* — Page 399

20 cm. Buffy-brown upperparts with rufous cap, pale supercilium, black streaks on back, wings and long ragged tail, and buffy-white underparts. Tall grassland and grassy scrub. Rare.

Mn	Mu	**NI**	**NB**	Bv	Gu	MI	NG	Mk	RI	Te	Vu	Lo	GT

New Britain Thicketbird *Megalurulus grosvenori* — Page 400

18 cm. Rusty-brown upperparts, crown and long tail with pointed tips, broad rufous-buff supercilium, sooty mask and rufous-buff underparts. Montane forest at 1580 m. On or near ground. Rare.

Mn	Mu	NI	**NB**	Bv	Gu	MI	NG	Mk	RI	Te	Vu	Lo	GT

Rusty Thicketbird *Megalurulus rubiginosus* — Page 401

19 cm. Rusty-brown upperparts, crown and long tail with rounded tips, orange-rufous underparts and dark supercilium behind eye. Hill forest with dense ground vegetation to 1400 m. On or near ground. Cocks tail. Uncommon.

Mn	Mu	NI	**NB**	Bv	Gu	MI	NG	Mk	RI	Te	Vu	Lo	GT

Oriental Reed Warbler *Acrocephalus orientalis* — Page 398

19 cm. Olive-brown upperparts, dark eye-stripe, relatively large bill and relatively long supercilium, buffy-white underparts and usually indistinct streaks on upper breast. Reeds, grass and scrub by water. Vagrant?

Australian Reed Warbler *Acrocephalus australis* — Page 399

16 cm. Olive-brown upperparts, short supercilium, dark eye-stripe and buff-white underparts. Orange-yellow mouth visible when singing. Reeds, grass and scrub by water. Common.

Mn	Mu	**NI**	**NB**	**Bv**	**Gu**	MI	NG	Mk	RI	Te	Vu	Lo	GT

Gray's Grasshopper Warbler *Locustella fasciolata* — Page 401

18 cm. Brownish-grey with silvery supercilium, dark eye-stripe and buff undertail-coverts. Rounded tail, curved short wing and long undertail-coverts. Dense thickets and grassland. Close to ground. Vagrant.

Golden-headed Cisticola *Cisticola exilis* — Page 401

10 cm. Buffy-brown with black streaks on back and wings, blackish tail and long orange legs. Male has yellow-rufous head and short tail. Female has streaked crown and longer tail. Grassland and savanna. Has high song-flight. Common.

Mn	Mu	**NI**	**NB**	Bv	Gu	MI	NG	Mk	RI	Te	Vu	Lo	GT

Pied Bush Chat *Saxicola caprata* — Page 417

14 cm. Male is glossy black with white wing-streak, rump and vent. Female is dark grey-brown with indistinct streaking, paler underparts, white rump and vent and blackish tail. Juvenile like female but has pale buff spots on head, breast and upperparts, and male has white wing-streak and rump. Open habitats, especially grasslands. Sits conspicuously on low perches. Rare.

Mn	Mu	**NI**	**NB**	Bv	Gu	MI	NG	Mk	RI	Te	Vu	Lo	GT

Papuan Grassbird
New Britain
Thicketbird
Rusty Thicketbird
Oriental Reed
Warbler
Australian
Reed Warbler
♂
Golden-headed
Cisticola
♀
Gray's Grasshopper
Warbler
♂
♀
juvenile
Pied Bush Chat

Paradise Drongo *Dicrurus megarhynchus* — Page 377

40 cm & tail-streamers. Long forked tail and very long twisted outer tail feathers, often broken or absent. All black with blue gloss and small blue spots on neck and breast, and red eye. Closed forest. Noisy, obtrusive and active. Fairly common.

Mn	Mu	**NI**	NB	Bv	Gu	MI	NG	Mk	RI	Te	Vu	Lo	GT

Spangled Drongo *Dicrurus bracteatus laemostictus* — Page 376

30 cm. Long tail is forked and splayed outwards. All black with purple-blue gloss, small blue spots on crown, neck and breast, and red eye. Juvenile is dull sooty-black with dark brown eye. Forest. Noisy, obtrusive and active, swooping flight, often in small groups. Common.

Mn	Mu	NI	**NB**	Bv	**Gu**	MI	NG	**Mk**	RI	Te	Vu	Lo	GT

White-backed Woodswallow *Artamus insignis* — Page 365

19 cm. White with sooty-black hood, wings and tail, stout blue-grey bill and blue-grey eye-ring. Juvenile has brown wash on head, and white tips on wings and tail. Forest and forest clearings. Perches on exposed branches and glides high over forest. Uncommon.

Mn	Mu	**NI**	**NB**	Bv	Gu	MI	NG	Mk	RI	Te	Vu	Lo	GT

Bismarck Crow *Corvus insularis* — Page 392

41 cm. Glossy black with heavy black bill and pale blue eye. Juvenile duller with pale blue or brown eye.
Open habitats, including plantations and towns. Feeds on ground. Flies high with deep wing-beats and short glides. Noisy. Fairly common.

Mn	Mu	**NI**	**NB**	Bv	Gu	MI	NG	Mk	RI	Te	Vu	Lo	GT

Atoll Starling *Aplonis feadensis heureka* — Page 409

20 cm. All glossy black with lemon-yellow eye, broad round wings and short square tail. Juvenile is dull sooty-brown with buff scales on underparts, striped on vent, and eye first blue, then green, then yellow. Forest and scrub. Solitary nests in tree-holes. Common. Nissan and remote atolls only. See flying bird on Plate 69.

Mn	**Mu**	**NI**	NB	**Bv**	Gu	MI	NG	Mk	RI	Te	Vu	Lo	GT

Metallic Starling *Aplonis metallica nitida* — Page 408

24 cm. All glossy black with long pointed tail, fairly long neck feathers and red eye. Juvenile has shorter tail, dark brown upperparts, creamy-white underparts with blackish streaks and eye first dark brown, then greenish, then orange-red. Immature has glossy black upperparts and heavily or sparsely streaked underparts. Forest and gardens. Gregarious. Hanging nests in large colonies. Common. See flying bird on Plate 69.

Mn	**Mu**	**NI**	**NB**	**Bv**	**Gu**	**MI**	**NG**	**Mk**	RI	Te	Vu	Lo	GT

Singing Starling *Aplonis cantoroides* — Page 409

19 cm. All glossy black with medium-short square tail, fairly long neck feathers and red eye. Juvenile has grey-brown upperparts, off-white underparts with heavy dark streaks and eye first dark brown, then yellowish, then orange-red. Immature has glossy black upperparts and heavily or sparsely streaked underparts. Trees and bushes in open habitats including towns. Small colonies nest in holes. Common. See flying bird on Plate 69.

Mn	**Mu**	**NI**	**NB**	**Bv**	**Gu**	**MI**	**NG**	**Mk**	**RI**	Te	Vu	Lo	GT

Long-tailed Myna *Mino kreffti* — Page 413

28 cm. Glossy black with yellow-orange bill, legs and large eye-patch, yellow lower belly, and white wing-patch, upper- and undertail-coverts. Forest. Noisy calls and whirring wings. Common. See flying bird on Plate 69.

Mn	Mu	**NI**	**NB**	**Bv**	**Gu**	**MI**	**NG**	Mk	RI	Te	Vu	Lo	GT

Olive-backed Oriole *Oriolus sagittatus* — Page 376

26 cm. Greyish-green head and upperparts, black streaks on white underparts, red bill and iris and white tail-corners and fringes on wings. Immature has grey-brown upperparts and grey-brown bill and iris. Forest. Canopy. Vagrant.

adult
White-backed Woodswallow
juvenile
Spangled Drongo
Paradise Drongo
Bismarck Crow
adult
Metallic Starling
immature
adult
Atoll Starling
juvenile
adult
Singing Starling
immature
Long-tailed Myna
Olive-backed Oriole

PLATE 60: BISMARCKS PARROTFINCH AND MANNIKINS

Blue-faced Parrotfinch *Erythrura trichroa sigillifera* Page 420

12 cm. Bright grass-green with blue face, rusty-red rump and uppertail, and blackish bill. Juvenile duller with yellower underparts, pale bill and no blue on face. Forest, especially with thickets, bamboo and *Casuarina* trees. Uncommon.

Mn	Mu	NI	NB	Bv	Gu	MI	NG	Mk	RI	Te	Vu	Lo	GT

Streak-headed Mannikin *Lonchura tristissima* Page 422

10 cm. Heavy blue-grey bill, dark rufous-brown upperparts with variable buffy or grey spots and streaks on head, back and wings, sooty-brown underparts, bright buffy-yellow rump and black tail. Juvenile has dull rump and less distinct streaks on head. Clearings, cultivation and grassland in forest. Rare; on Umboi only.

Mn	Mu	NI	NB	Bv	Gu	MI	NG	Mk	RI	Te	Vu	Lo	GT

Hooded Mannikin *Lonchura spectabilis* Page 422

10 cm. Heavy blue-grey bill, black hood, brown upperparts with orange rump and tail, creamy-white underparts with black belly to undertail-coverts, and sometimes brownish breast and flanks. Juvenile is pale buffy-brown, with faint streaks on face and throat, pale buff underparts and brighter rump, head soon becoming darker. Grassland and grassy cultivation. Gregarious. Common.

Mn	Mu	NI	NB	Bv	Gu	MI	NG	Mk	RI	Te	Vu	Lo	GT

Forbes's Mannikin *Lonchura forbesi* Page 423

11 cm. Massive blue-grey bill, black hood, chestnut mantle and wings, orange rump and uppertail, orange-brown underparts and sooty belly to undertail-coverts. Juvenile is pale buffy-brown, faintly streaked black on face and throat, paler underparts and brighter rump, head soon becoming darker. Grassland, including forest clearings. Uncommon.

Mn	Mu	NI	NB	Bv	Gu	MI	NG	Mk	RI	Te	Vu	Lo	GT

Hunstein's Mannikin *Lonchura hunsteini* Page 423

10 cm. Sooty-black with heavy blue-grey bill, bright chestnut rump and uppertail and variable silvery spots on head and neck. Juvenile has dull brown upperparts with warm brown rump, darker head and throat, and pale tawny lower breast and belly, soon developing pale speckling. Grassland, including forest clearings. Gregarious. Common.

L. h. hunsteini (New Ireland) has silvery spots on head.

L. h. nigerrima (Lavongai or New Hanover) lacks spots on black head and has paler orange rump and uppertail.

Mn	Mu	NI	NB	Bv	Gu	MI	NG	Mk	RI	Te	Vu	Lo	GT

Buff-bellied Mannikin *Lonchura m. melaena* Page 424

11 cm. Massive blue-grey bill, black head to lower breast, dark mantle and wings, orange rump and uppertail, orange-buff belly with black spots or bars on flanks, and black central belly to vent. Juvenile is pale buffy-brown, faintly streaked darker on face and throat, paler buff on underparts, and rufous rump, head soon becoming darker. Grasslands, including forest clearings. Gregarious. Common.

Mn	Mu	NI	NB	Bv	Gu	MI	NG	Mk	RI	Te	Vu	Lo	GT

Eurasian Tree Sparrow *Passer montanus* (not illustrated) Page 420

13 cm. Stocky with heavy bill. Rusty-brown with white cheeks and nape, chestnut cap, black ear-covert spot and chin, white wing-bar and plain buffy underparts. Towns. Possibly colonising Kimbe.

Mn	Mu	NI	NB	Bv	Gu	MI	NG	Mk	RI	Te	Vu	Lo	GT

Blue-faced Parrotfinch
adult
juvenile
Streak-headed Mannikin
adult
juvenile
immature
adult
Hooded Mannikin
immature
Forbes's Mannikin
adult
hunsteini
immature
hunsteini
adult
immature
nigerrima
juvenile
Hunstein's Mannikin
nigerrima
adult
Buff-bellied Mannikin
adult

PLATE 61: SOLOMONS CUCKOOSHRIKES

North Melanesian Cuckooshrike *Coracina welchmani bougainvillei* Page 366

32 cm. Plain blackish-grey with slightly paler underparts. Male has glossy black face and throat. Female has black ear-coverts. Immature has indistinct black face and faint pale grey fringes. Forest, and also mangroves and coastal forest in New Georgia group. Uncommon.

Mn	Mu	NI	NB	**Bv**	**Gu**	MI	**NG**	Mk	RI	Te	Vu	Lo	GT

Solomons Cuckooshrike *Coracina h. holopolia* Page 369

21 cm. Male has pale grey crown, mantle, wings and rump, black tail, tertial centres and primaries, and glossy black face and underparts. Female is plain pale grey with black on wings and tail, and indistinct eye-stripe. Juvenile has brown fringes on upperparts, and black and pale grey bars on underparts. Fairly common.

C. h. ***tricolor*** (Malaita) is paler grey on wings, male with black forehead and collar.

Mn	Mu	NI	NB	**Bv**	**Gu**	**MI**	**NG**	Mk	RI	Te	Vu	Lo	GT

Black-faced Cuckooshrike *Coracina novaehollandiae* Page 366

33 cm. Pale grey upperparts and breast, darker wings and tail with white tail-tips, black forehead, face and throat, and paler belly. Immature has less defined black patch on ear-coverts only, and finely barred throat and breast. Open habitats with trees. Rare.

Mn	Mu	**NI**	**NB**	**Bv**	Gu	MI	**NG**	Mk	**RI**	Te	Vu	Lo	**GT**

Barred Cuckooshrike *Coracina lineata pusilla* Page 367

23 cm. Yellow eye. Male is plain blue-grey with black lores and darker wings and tail. Female is plain blue-grey with fine black-and-white barring on lower breast to undertail-coverts. Juvenile has creamy scaling on upperparts and barred underparts. Forest. Fairly common. See Oriental Cuckoo (Plate 41).

Mn	Mu	**NI**	**NB**	**Bv**	**Gu**	**MI**	**NG**	**Mk**	**RI**	Te	Vu	Lo	GT

White-bellied Cuckooshrike *Coracina papuensis perpallida* Page 367

25 cm. Pale grey head with black bill and mask from lores to just behind eye, mid-grey upperparts and white underparts. Juvenile has buffy fringes on upperparts and breast, and indistinct mask. Forest edge and trees in open habitats. Common. See Plate 51.

Mn	Mu	**NI**	**NB**	**Bv**	**Gu**	**MI**	**NG**	Mk	RI	Te	Vu	Lo	GT

Common Cicadabird *Coracina tenuirostris erythropygia* Page 368

25 cm. Male is dark blue-grey with indistinct blackish face-mask, grey fringes on black wings and black outer tail. Female has blue-grey crown, dark eye-stripe, rufous-brown upperparts, black centres and rufous fringes on wings, and unbarred rufous underparts. Juvenile like female but has brown cap and buffy fringes on upperparts. Forest. Fairly common.

Mn	**Mu**	**NI**	**NB**	**Bv**	**Gu**	**MI**	**NG**	Mk	RI	Te	Vu	Lo	GT

♀
♂
North Melanesian Cuckooshrike
holopolia
♀
holopolia
♂
juvenile
tricolor
♂
Solomons Cuckooshrike
adult
Black-faced Cuckooshrike
immature
♂
♀
Barred Cuckooshrike
♂
♀
White-bellied Cuckooshrike
Common Cicadabird

PLATE 62: SOLOMONS SUNBIRD, FLOWERPECKER AND HONEYEATERS

For Makira, Rennell and Temotu, see Plates 70–77.

Olive-backed Sunbird *Cinnyris jugularis flavigaster* — Page 419

11 cm. Dull olive upperparts, dark tail with white corners, bright yellow underparts and fine supercilium, and long decurved bill. Male has metallic blue throat. Female has yellow throat. Open forest habitats, including towns. Common.

Mn **Mu** **NI** **NB** **Bv** **Gu** **MI** **NG** **Mk** RI Te Vu Lo GT

Midget Flowerpecker *Dicaeum a. aeneum* — Page 418

8 cm. Dumpy with tiny bill, glossy dark grey upperparts, grey face and breast-sides, white throat and buffy flanks, belly and vent. Male has red central breast and dark grey lower breast. Female is creamy-white from chin to belly, has white eyelids and sometimes a short white loral stripe or supercilium. Forest, including isolated trees. Canopy. Common.

Mn Mu NI NB **Bv** **Gu** **MI** NG Mk RI Te Vu Lo GT

Red-capped Myzomela *Myzomela lafargei* — Page 362

12 cm. Male has black hood and upperparts with variable red central crown, green fringes on wings and greenish-yellow breast and belly. Female and juvenile are duller, lack red on crown and some have red wash on face. Forest, sometimes coconuts and gardens. Uncommon.

Mn Mu NI NB **Bv** Gu MI NG Mk RI Te Vu Lo GT

Crimson-rumped Myzomela *Myzomela e. eichhorni* — Page 362

12 cm. Male is olive-brown with darker head, scarlet throat and rump, and yellower breast and belly. Pale underwing in flight. Female is duller, with rusty wash to rump and smaller duller red throat. Forest and scrub, sometimes coconuts and gardens. Fairly common.

M. e. atrata (Vella Lavella) is darker with blackish hood and upperparts merging into dark olive belly.

Mn Mu NI NB Bv Gu MI **NG** Mk RI Te Vu Lo GT

Red-vested Myzomela *Myzomela malaitae* — Page 363

13 m. Male has crimson throat, breast, flanks and rump, and blackish upperparts, neck-sides, central belly and vent. Female has grey-brown upperparts and tawny-olive underparts and is often washed red on throat. Juvenile male like female but has red forehead and central throat, and often reddish rump. Forest, especially primary forest above 1000 m. Uncommon.

Mn Mu NI NB Bv Gu **MI** NG Mk RI Te Vu Lo GT

Black-headed Myzomela *Myzomela melanocephala* — Page 363

12 cm. Olive-green with glossy black forehead, face and throat, darker wings and tail, and paler flanks and belly. Pale underwing in flight. Female is duller and has less black on head and throat. Juvenile is rufous-brown with an indistinctly darker head. Forest, especially forest edge. Fairly common.

Mn Mu NI NB Bv **Gu** MI NG Mk RI Te Vu Lo GT

Bougainville Honeyeater *Stresemannia bougainvillei* — Page 357

17 cm. Olive-grey upperparts with slightly brighter olive fringes on wings and tail, slightly paler greyer underparts, long decurved blackish-grey bill and blue-grey legs. Montane forest above 700 m. Uncommon.

Mn Mu NI NB **Bv** Gu MI NG Mk RI Te Vu Lo GT

Guadalcanal Honeyeater *Guadalcanaria inexpectata* — Page 355

20 cm. Slate-grey upperparts with olive wings and tail, yellow stripe or patch between ear-coverts and neck, fairly long decurved black bill, white throat and pale grey underparts with heavy dark streaks. Sometimes shows plain white flanks. Montane forest above 950 m. Canopy. Fairly common.

Mn Mu NI NB Bv **Gu** MI NG Mk RI Te Vu Lo GT

♂
Olive-backed Sunbird
♀
♂
Midget Flowerpecker
♀
♂
Red-capped Myzomela
♀
eichhorni
♂
atrata
♂
eichhorni
♀
Crimson-rumped Myzomela
♂
Black-headed Myzomela
♂
juvenile
Red-vested Myzomela
juvenile
Bougainville Honeyeater
Guadalcanal Honeyeater

PLATE 63: SOLOMONS WHISTLERS

Oriole Whistler *Pachycephala orioloides* Page 372

17 cm. Many varied subspecies. Male has glossy black head and usually breast-band, with yellow throat and underparts and often collar, and olive and black upperparts. Female has dull olive or brown upperparts, sometimes rufous on wings, and dull yellow or buff underparts, sometimes streaked. Fledgling is all rufous. Juvenile usually similar to female but has pale bill and extensive rufous on wings. Forest, less common in lowlands. Males often forage alone in canopy, females and juveniles in mid-storey or undergrowth. Common.

P. o. bougainvillei*, *P. o. orioloides and ***P. o. centralis*** (Bougainville, Choiseul, Isabel and New Georgia group) have typical male, and female has brownish-olive upperparts, sometimes darker head, rufous wings, and grey-washed yellow underparts.

P. o. cinnamomea (Guadalcanal) has typical male, female with rufous-brown upperparts, rufous wings, cinnamon underparts and pale yellow vent.

P. o. melanonota (Vella Lavella and Ranongga): male has black upperparts and broad breast-band.

P. o. sanfordi (Malaita): male lacks black breast-band and yellow collar, and female has rufous-olive upperparts, dark streaks on dull buffy underparts, and yellow vent.

Mn	Mu	Nl	NB	Bv	Gu	Ml	NG	Mk	Rl	Te	Vu	Lo	GT

Guadalcanal Hooded Whistler *Pachycephala implicata* Page 375

16 cm. Male has dark grey hood and upper breast, olive upperparts, darker wings and tail and brighter olive underparts. Female has mid-grey cap, olive upperparts, white throat, narrow buffy breast-band and dull yellow lower breast and belly. Fledgling has dull rufous and olive upperparts and dull orange-rufous underparts. Forest above 1100 m. Common.

Mn	Mu	Nl	NB	Bv	Gu	Ml	NG	Mk	Rl	Te	Vu	Lo	GT

Mangrove Golden Whistler *Pachycephala melanura whitneyi* Page 374

16 cm. Male like typical male Oriole Whistler but has some yellow on white throat, grey fringes on primaries and secondaries, black uppertail sometimes with greenish fringes, and paler grey-brown legs. Female has white throat, greyish upper breast, dull yellow underparts, olive-brown upperparts, slightly greyer fringes on primaries and secondaries, and olive and black uppertail. Fledgling is all rufous. Juvenile like female but pale bill and rufous on wings. Coastal vegetation. Common on small islands off Bougainville only.

Mn	Mu	Nl	NB	Bv	Gu	Ml	NG	Mk	Rl	Te	Vu	Lo	GT

Bougainville Hooded Whistler *Pachycephala richardsi* Page 375

16 cm. Male has glossy black hood and upper breast, green upperparts, black on wings and tail, and yellow underparts. Female has mid-grey cap, olive upperparts, white throat, broad grey breast-band and greenish-yellow lower breast and belly. Fledgling has rufous upperparts with olive fringes and tawny underparts. Forest above 1200 m. Fairly common.

Mn	Mu	Nl	NB	Bv	Gu	Ml	NG	Mk	Rl	Te	Vu	Lo	GT

cinnamomea
♀
fledgling
orioloides
♀
orioloides
♂
Oriole Whistler
sanfordi
♀
sanfordi
♂
melanonota
♂
♂
♀
♂
Guadalcanal Hooded
Whistler
Mangrove Golden
Whistler
♀
♀
fledgling
Bougainville Hooded
Whistler
♂

PLATE 64: SOLOMONS FANTAILS AND FLYCATCHERS

Willie Wagtail *Rhipidura leucophrys* Page 377

20 cm. Black head, throat and upperparts with white lower breast to vent and indistinct white supercilium. Juvenile is duller with broader dull eyebrow and buffy tips to wing-coverts. Open habitat including coasts, towns and sometimes forest clearings. Runs on ground and sallies from low perches, drooping wings and waving tail. Common.

Mn	Mu	NI	NB	Bv	Gu	MI	NG	Mk	RI	Te	Vu	Lo	GT

Brown Fantail *Rhipidura drownei* Page 379

16 cm. Grey-brown upperparts with greyer head, browner wings and paler brown tail with pale outer fringes. Very fine short white supercilium and ear-covert streak, pale throat and buffy-grey underparts with indistinct white streaks. Juvenile is duller, often lacking head markings, and has broader wing-bars. Forest above 900 m. Active, often with fanned tail. Common.

R. d. drownei (Bougainville) has indistinct head-stripes, two buffy wing-bars, buffy undertail-coverts and mottled throat.

R. d. ocularis (Guadalcanal) has clear white head-stripes, white undertail-coverts and throat.

Mn	Mu	NI	NB	Bv	Gu	MI	NG	Mk	RI	Te	Vu	Lo	GT

Cockerell's Fantail *Rhipidura cockerelli* Page 378

17 cm. Glossy black upperparts with indistinct fine white supercilium and variable white on tertials. Black throat and breast, variable white spots on breast, and white belly to vent. Closed forest. Perches upright, waving but rarely fanning tail. Fairly common.

R. c. septentrionalis, ***R. c. interposita*** and ***R. c. cockerelli*** (Bougainville, Choiseul, Isabel and Guadalcanal) have large white spots on breast and extensive white on tertials.

R. c. lavellae (Vella Lavella and Ranongga) has small white spots on breast and narrow white fringes on tertials.

R. c. albina (New Georgia group) has little or no white on breast.

R. c. coultasi (Malaita) has white throat, large white spots on breast and very fine fringes on tertials.

Mn	Mu	NI	NB	Bv	Gu	MI	NG	Mk	RI	Te	Vu	Lo	GT

Malaita Fantail *Rhipidura malaitae* Page 381

16 cm. Plain dull rusty-orange with darker wings, paler buffier underparts and prominent dark eye. Forest above 600 m, usually above 1000 m. Active, drooping wings, cocking and fanning tail, often in mixed-species flocks. Rare.

Mn	Mu	NI	NB	Bv	Gu	MI	NG	Mk	RI	Te	Vu	Lo	GT

Rufous Fantail *Rhipidura rufifrons commoda* Page 381

15 cm. Brown head, mantle and wings, bright orange-rufous rump, tail-base and forehead, and remainder of tail black with broad white tips. White throat, black breast-band, black spots on lower breast, and buffy underparts. Forest, especially open forest. Understorey. Hyperactive, with drooped wings and waving fanned tail. Common.

Mn	Mu	NI	NB	Bv	Gu	MI	NG	Mk	RI	Te	Vu	Lo	GT

Steel-blue Flycatcher *Myiagra ferrocyanea* Page 388

14 cm. Male is plain glossy purple-black with white lower breast and belly. Female has ash-grey crown, ash-grey or brown upperparts with broad rufous fringes on wings and tail, and white underparts. Forest and scattered large trees. Actively sallies and flycatches in canopy. Shivers tail and often raises crown feathers. Common.

M. f. cinerea and ***M. f. ferrocyanea*** (Bougainville, Choiseul, Isabel and Guadalcanal): female has rufous mantle, wings and tail, and grey wash on throat.

M. f. feminina (New Georgia group): female has grey mantle and scapulars, and dull grey-brown wings and tail.

M. f. malaitae (Malaita): female has grey mantle, dull brown wings and tail, and rusty fringes on secondaries.

Mn	Mu	NI	NB	Bv	Gu	MI	NG	Mk	RI	Te	Vu	Lo	GT

Willie Wagtail
cockerelli
lavellae
drownei
Brown Fantail
albina
coultasi
ocularis
Cockerell's
Fantail
Malaita Fantail
Rufous Fantail
♂
feminina
♀
ferrocyanea
♀
malaitae
♀
Steel-blue Flycatcher

Island Monarch *Monarcha cinerascens impediens* Page 386

18 cm. Dull mid-grey upperparts, throat and upper breast, and orange-chestnut lower breast and belly. Prominent black eye on plain face and heavy steel-blue bill. Juvenile duller and browner. Forest and scrub. Understorey. Common on small islands.

Mn Mu NI NB Bv Gu MI NG Mk RI Te Vu Lo GT

Bougainville Monarch *Monarcha erythrostictus* Page 386

17 cm. Glossy black head, upperparts and throat, deep chestnut lower breast and belly, and pale blue-grey bill. Male has pale yellow crescent in front of eye. Female has rufous spot in front of eye. Juvenile is duller with browner wings. Closed forest. Fairly common.

Mn Mu NI NB Bv Gu MI NG Mk RI Te Vu Lo GT

Chestnut-bellied Monarch *Monarcha castaneiventris* Page 387

17 cm. Glossy black head, upperparts and breast, deep chestnut lower breast and belly, and pale blue-grey bill. Juvenile is duller with browner wings. Forest, less often regrowth and scrub. Common.

Mn Mu NI NB Bv Gu MI NG Mk RI Te Vu Lo GT

White-capped Monarch *Monarcha richardsii* Page 387

17 cm. Glossy blue-black head, upperparts and breast, deep chestnut lower breast and belly, and variable extent of white on crown and hindneck. Juvenile has mid-grey upperparts, head and breast, with dull chestnut underparts; white is initially restricted to eyelids, then eyebrow, then subadults have many intermediate and mottled patterns. Forest and scrub. Common.

Mn Mu NI NB Bv Gu MI NG Mk RI Te Vu Lo GT

Kolombangara Monarch *Symposiachrus browni* Page 385

15 cm. Black head and large bib, with white lower breast to vent and large white patches on ear-coverts, wing-coverts and tail-tips. Juvenile has dark rufous-grey upperparts and ear-coverts, developing orange-rufous to white patch on wing-coverts, orange-buff underparts from chin to belly, and white vent. Primary forest. Uncommon.

S. b. browni (New Georgia group) has black bib extending to upper breast and connecting to black wings.

S. b. ganongae (Ranongga) has small black bib not connecting to wings and more white on tail.

S. b. nigrotectus (Vella Lavella) lacks white on wing-coverts and has small black bib not connecting to wings.

Mn Mu NI NB Bv Gu MI NG Mk RI Te Vu Lo GT

Solomons Monarch *Symposiachrus barbatus* Page 385

15 cm. Glossy black head, throat and upperparts with white ear-covert patch, wing-covert patch and tips to outer tail feathers. Juvenile has grey-brown upperparts, darker ear-coverts, orange-buff lores and throat fading paler to vent, and variably sized buffy to white wing-covert patch. Closed-canopy forest. Uncommon.

S. b. barbatus (Bougainville, Choiseul, Isabel and Guadalcanal) has black bib not connected to black wings.

S. b. malaitae (Malaita) has black bib connected to wings and tail white except black central feathers.

Mn Mu NI NB Bv Gu MI NG Mk RI Te Vu Lo GT

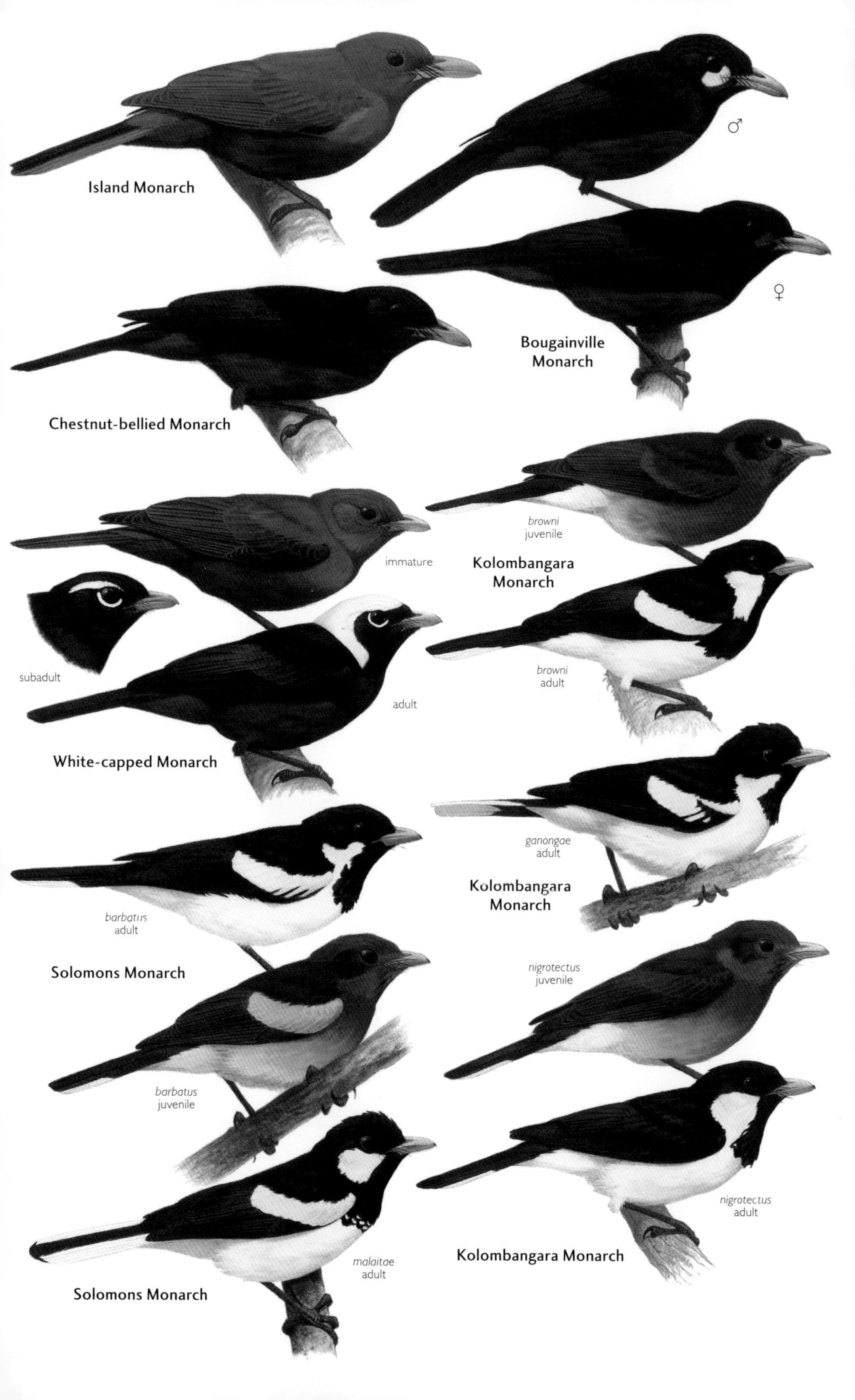
Island Monarch
♂
♀
Bougainville
Monarch
Chestnut-bellied Monarch
browni
juvenile
immature
Kolombangara
Monarch
subadult
browni
adult
adult
White-capped Monarch
ganongae
adult
barbatus
adult
Kolombangara
Monarch
Solomons Monarch
nigrotectus
juvenile
barbatus
juvenile
nigrotectus
adult
malaitae
adult
Kolombangara Monarch
Solomons Monarch

Pacific Swallow *Hirundo tahitica subfusca* Page 395

13 cm. Glossy blue-black upperparts, rufous forehead to upper breast, pale dusky underparts and underwing-coverts, and dark undertail-coverts with pale fringes. Forked tail has pointed corners. Immature duller. Open habitats, especially beaches and towns. Uncommon.

Mn	Mu	NI	NB	Bv	Gu	MI	NG	Mk	RI	Te	Vu	Lo	GT

Tree Martin *Petrochelidon nigricans* Page 396

13 cm. Blue-black upperparts with off-white rump, rufous forehead, buffy-white underparts and notched tail. Immature is duller. Open habitats, especially forest edge. Rare.

Mn	Mu	NI	NB	Bv	Gu	MI	NG	Mk	RI	Te	Vu	Lo	GT

Russet-tailed Thrush *Zoothera heinei choiseuli* Page 414

20 cm. Brown upperparts with black crescents, creamy wing-bars and primary bases, and dark crescents on buffy-white underparts. White tail-corners, and black and white underwing. On ground in mountains. Very rare on Choiseul.

Mn	Mu	NI	NB	Bv	Gu	MI	NG	Mk	RI	Te	Vu	Lo	GT

Bougainville Thrush *Zoothera atrigena* Page 414

20 cm. Slaty-black upperparts with two broken white wing-bars, and white underparts with black scales on flanks. Black underwing with white stripe. On ground above 1500 m. Rare on Bougainville.

Mn	Mu	NI	NB	Bv	Gu	MI	NG	Mk	RI	Te	Vu	Lo	GT

Guadalcanal Thrush *Zoothera turipavae* Page 415

20 cm. Plain dark upperparts with indistinct buffy eye-ring and moustachial stripe, creamy-buff underparts with dusky-brown scales, and whiter belly and vent. Dark underwing with white stripe. On ground above 1400m. Rare on Guadalcanal.

Mn	Mu	NI	NB	Bv	Gu	MI	NG	Mk	RI	Te	Vu	Lo	GT

Island Thrush *Turdus poliocephalus kulambangrae* Page 415

20 cm. Blackish-brown with yellow bill, legs and eye-ring. Juvenile has rufous fringes on underparts. On ground and low bushes above 1000 m. Common on Bougainville, Kolombangara and Guadalcanal.

Mn	Mu	NI	NB	Bv	Gu	MI	NG	Mk	RI	Te	Vu	Lo	GT

Bougainville Crow *Corvus meeki* Page 392

41 cm. Bulky black crow with massive, slightly downcurved black bill. Immature has pale blue-grey eye. Forest, gardens and coconuts. Flicks wings when perched. Front-heavy and short-tailed in fluttering flight with shallow wing-beats. Fairly common on Bougainville.

Mn	Mu	NI	NB	Bv	Gu	MI	NG	Mk	RI	Te	Vu	Lo	GT

White-billed Crow *Corvus woodfordi* Page 391

41 cm. Bulky black crow with massive, slightly downcurved white bill, with black tip and often pink wash. Closed forest and nearby trees. Canopy. Flicks or shuffles wings when perched. Front-heavy and short-tailed in fluttering flight with shallow wing-beats. Fairly common on Choiseul, Isabel and Guadalcanal.

Mn	Mu	NI	NB	Bv	Gu	MI	NG	Mk	RI	Te	Vu	Lo	GT

Eurasian Tree Sparrow *Passer montanus* (not illustrated) Page 420

13 cm. Stocky with heavy bill. Rusty-brown with white cheeks and nape, chestnut cap, black ear-covert spot and chin, white wing-bar and plain buffy underparts. Towns. Vagrant, possibly colonising.

Mn	Mu	NI	NB	Bv	Gu	MI	NG	Mk	RI	Te	Vu	Lo	GT

Pacific Swallow
Tree Martin
Bougainville Thrush
Russet-tailed Thrush
Guadalcanal Thrush
Island Thrush
Bougainville Crow
White-billed Crow

PLATE 67: SOLOMONS WARBLERS, ROBIN, PARROTFINCH AND MANNIKIN

Australian Reed Warbler *Acrocephalus australis* Page 399

16 cm. Olive-brown upperparts, short supercilium, dark eye-stripe and buff-white underparts. Orange-yellow mouth visible when singing. Reeds, grass and scrub by water. Common.

Mn	Mu	NI	NB	Bv	Gu	MI	NG	Mk	RI	Te	Vu	Lo	GT

Kolombangara Leaf Warbler *Phylloscopus amoenus* Page 398

11 cm. Dark olive with heavy brownish bill, mottled ear-coverts, darker crown, indistinct wing-bar, supercilium and eye-stripe, yellower underparts with slight streaking, and pinkish-brown legs. Short-tailed and dumpy. Understorey above 1200 m. Uncommon on Kolombangara.

Mn	Mu	NI	NB	Bv	Gu	MI	NG	Mk	RI	Te	Vu	Lo	GT

Island Leaf Warbler *Phylloscopus poliocephalus* Page 397

10 cm. Olive upperparts, long supercilium, dark eye-stripe, pale wing-bar, whitish throat, and usually yellow breast and belly. Forest above 700 m. Canopy. Fairly common.

P. t. bougainvillei (Bougainville) has greyish-yellow underparts.

P. p. becki (Isabel, Guadalcanal and Malaita) has brighter yellow underparts.

P. p. pallescens (Kolombangara) has greyish-white underparts.

Mn	Mu	NI	NB	Bv	Gu	MI	NG	Mk	RI	Te	Vu	Lo	GT

Guadalcanal Thicketbird *Megalurulus turipavae* Page 400

18 cm. Dark olive-brown upperparts, darker on crown, and long graduated tail. Broad black eye-stripe and rich buff broad supercilium and underparts. Juvenile unknown. On or near ground above 1200 m. Cocks tail. Uncommon.

Mn	Mu	NI	NB	Bv	Gu	MI	NG	Mk	RI	Te	Vu	Lo	GT

Bougainville Thicketbird *Megalurulus llaneae* Page 400

17 cm. Dark brown upperparts, crown and long graduated tail. Broad black eye-stripe and orange-rufous broad supercilium and underparts, browner on flanks and belly. Juvenile has rich chestnut breast with dark streaks and no head markings. On or near ground above 1200 m. Cocks tail. Uncommon on Bougainville.

Mn	Mu	NI	NB	Bv	Gu	MI	NG	Mk	RI	Te	Vu	Lo	GT

Bougainville Bush Warbler *Cettia haddeni* Page 397

13 cm. Dark rufous-brown upperparts, brighter orange on head, with prominent black eye, off-white throat and dark grey underparts with white mottling. Forest undergrowth above 700 m. Fairly common on Bougainville.

Mn	Mu	NI	NB	Bv	Gu	MI	NG	Mk	RI	Te	Vu	Lo	GT

Pacific Robin *Petroica multicolor septentrionalis* Page 393

10 cm. Male has black hood and upperparts with white on forehead, wings, outer tail, flanks and vent, and scarlet breast and belly. Female has browner upperparts, no white on forehead, white or brown throat and pale scarlet wash on underparts. Juvenile is uniformly brown with buffy mottling. Fairly common above 1000 m on Bougainville, Kolombangara and Guadalcanal.

Mn	Mu	NI	NB	Bv	Gu	MI	NG	Mk	RI	Te	Vu	Lo	GT

Blue-faced Parrotfinch *Erythrura trichroa woodfordi* Page 420

12 cm. Bright grass-green with blue face, rusty-red rump and uppertail, and blackish bill. Juvenile is duller with yellower underparts, pale bill and no blue on face. Forest, especially with thickets, bamboo and *Casuarina* trees. Rare. See juvenile on Plate 60.

Mn	Mu	NI	NB	Bv	Gu	MI	NG	Mk	RI	Te	Vu	Lo	GT

Buff-bellied Mannikin *Lonchura melaena bukaensis* Page 424

11 cm. Massive blue-grey bill, blackish upperparts, throat and breast, dark rufous rump and uppertail, orange-buff belly with black spots or bars on flanks, and black central belly to vent. Juvenile is pale buffy-brown, paler buff on underparts, head soon becoming darker. Grasslands. Rare or extinct on Buka. See immature on Plate 60.

Mn	Mu	NI	NB	Bv	Gu	MI	NG	Mk	RI	Te	Vu	Lo	GT

becki
Island Leaf Warbler
Australian
Reed
Warbler
Kolombangara
Leaf Warbler
pallescens
Bougainville
Thicketbird
Guadalcanal Thicketbird
♀
♂
Bougainville
Bush Warbler
Pacific Robin
juvenile
Blue-faced
Parrotfinch
Buff-bellied
Mannikin

Vella Lavella White-eye *Zosterops vellalavella* — Page 403

12 cm. Olive upperparts, blackish lores, broad white eye-ring, dull orange-yellow bill and legs, yellow throat, broad olive breast-band, silvery lower breast and belly, and greenish-yellow vent. Forest, including coconuts and scattered old trees. Fairly common on Vella Lavella.

Mn	Mu	Nl	NB	Bv	Gu	Ml	**NG**	Mk	Rl	Te	Vu	Lo	GT

Ranongga White-eye *Zosterops splendidus* — Page 404

12 cm. Olive upperparts, blackish around lores, black bill, broad white eye-ring, lemon-yellow underparts with green wash on breast and flanks, and orange-yellow legs. Forest and regrowth. Fairly common on Ranongga.

Mn	Mu	Nl	NB	Bv	Gu	Ml	**NG**	Mk	Rl	Te	Vu	Lo	GT

Gizo White-eye *Zosterops luteirostris* — Page 403

12 cm. Olive upperparts, blackish lores and forehead, narrow white eye-ring, bright orange-yellow bill and legs, and lemon-yellow underparts with green wash on breast and flanks. Forest and regrowth. Fairly common on Gizo.

Mn	Mu	Nl	NB	Bv	Gu	Ml	**NG**	Mk	Rl	Te	Vu	Lo	GT

Solomons White-eye *Zosterops kulambangrae* — Page 404

12 cm. Olive with slightly yellower underparts, especially throat and vent, black lores and fine bill, and yellowish legs. Forest and gardens in lowlands and hills. Fairly common.

Z. k. kulambangrae (New Georgia group) has narrow white eye-ring and plain olive underparts.

Z. k. tetiparius (Tetepare) has dark skin around eye, silvery belly and flanks, and pale yellow vent.

Z. k. paradoxus (Rendova) has dark skin around eye and yellow from belly to vent.

Mn	Mu	Nl	NB	Bv	Gu	Ml	**NG**	Mk	Rl	Te	Vu	Lo	GT

Kolombangara White-eye *Zosterops murphyi* — Page 404

12 cm. Plain dull olive, only slightly paler on underparts, with very broad white eye-ring, dark bill and legs. Gregarious. Very common above 1000 m, uncommon in lower hills, on Kolombangara.

Mn	Mu	Nl	NB	Bv	Gu	Ml	**NG**	Mk	Rl	Te	Vu	Lo	GT

Yellow-throated White-eye *Zosterops metcalfii* — Page 403

11 cm. Olive upperparts, dark lores, bill and legs, and lemon-yellow throat, upper breast, vent and undertail-coverts contrasting with silvery lower breast and belly. Forest and gardens to 1200 m. Common.

Z. m. exiguus and ***Z. m. metcalfii*** (Bougainville, Choiseul and Isabel) have narrow white eye-ring.

Z. m. floridanus (Florida Is) has no white eye-ring.

Mn	Mu	Nl	NB	**Bv**	Gu	Ml	NG	Mk	Rl	Te	Vu	Lo	GT

Grey-throated White-eye *Zosterops ugiensis* — Page 405

12 cm. Warbler-like white-eye with olive upperparts, greener wings, silvery-grey underparts, yellow undertail-coverts, black bill and dark legs. Hill and montane forest. Common.

Z. u. oblitus (above 500 m on Guadalcanal) has narrow dark grey eye-ring and silvery-grey from chin to belly.

Z. u. hamlini (above 900 m on Bougainville) has narrow white eye-ring, dark brown forehead, greenish throat and darker grey breast.

Mn	Mu	Nl	NB	**Bv**	**Gu**	Ml	NG	**Mk**	Rl	Te	Vu	Lo	GT

Malaita White-eye *Zosterops stresemanni* — Page 405

13 cm. Stout. Olive-green, with yellowish wash on rump, throat, belly and vent. Indistinct dark grey bare skin around eye, stout pale bill and greyish legs. Hill and montane forest and regrowth. Fairly common on Malaita.

Mn	Mu	Nl	NB	Bv	Gu	**Ml**	NG	Mk	Rl	Te	Vu	Lo	GT

Vella Lavella White-eye
Ranongga White-eye
Gizo White-eye
kulambangrae
paradoxus
tetiparius
Solomons White-eye
exiguus
floridanus
Yellow-throated White-eye
Kolombangara White-eye
oblitus
Grey-throated White-eye
hamlini
Malaita White-eye

Spangled Drongo *Dicrurus bracteatus meeki* Page 376

30 cm. Long tail is forked and splayed outwards. All black with purple-blue gloss, small blue spots on crown, neck and breast, and red eye. Juvenile is dull sooty-black with dark brown iris. Forest. Uncommon.

Mn	Mu	NI	NB	Bv	Gu	MI	NG	Mk	RI	Te	Vu	Lo	GT

Brown-winged Starling *Aplonis g. grandis* Page 410

25 cm. Large bulky starling. All glossy black with dark to pale brown primaries and secondaries, long feathers on neck and upper breast, and red-brown eye. In flight, fairly round wings and square medium-long tail. Juvenile is duller, with short neck feathers and orange-red eye. Forest edge, including scattered trees. Usually in pairs. Solitary bulky domed nest in subcanopy. Fairly common.
A. g. malaitae (Malaita) has white eye, slightly longer tail and slimmer shape.

Mn	Mu	NI	NB	Bv	Gu	MI	NG	Mk	RI	Te	Vu	Lo	GT

White-eyed Starling *Aplonis brunneicapillus* Page 410

21 cm + tail-streamers. All glossy black with white eye, heavy black bill, browner crown, lower breast and belly, fairly long neck feathers and fairly long rounded tail with very long central feathers often broken or missing. Juvenile has dull eye, finer bill, browner underparts with some white streaks, and no tail-streamers. Forest, including clearings. Gregarious, mixing with Metallic and Singing Starlings. Colonial, nests tunnelled into epiphytes in exposed tree. Rare.

Mn	Mu	NI	NB	Bv	Gu	MI	NG	Mk	RI	Te	Vu	Lo	GT

Metallic Starling *Aplonis metallica nitida* Page 408

24 cm. All glossy black with long pointed tail, fairly long neck feathers and red eye. Juvenile has shorter tail, dark brown upperparts, creamy-white underparts with blackish streaks and eye first dark brown, then greenish, then orange-red. Immature has glossy black upperparts and heavily or sparsely streaked underparts. Forest and gardens. Gregarious. Hanging nests in large colonies. Common.

Mn	Mu	NI	NB	Bv	Gu	MI	NG	Mk	RI	Te	Vu	Lo	GT

Atoll Starling *Aplonis f. feadensis* Page 409

20 cm. All glossy black with lemon-yellow eye, broad round wings and short square tail. Juvenile is dull sooty-brown with buff scales on underparts, striped on vent, and eye first blue, then green, then yellow. Solitary nests in tree-holes. Common. Remote atolls only.

Mn	Mu	NI	NB	Bv	Gu	MI	NG	Mk	RI	Te	Vu	Lo	GT

Singing Starling *Aplonis cantoroides* Page 409

19 cm. All glossy black with medium-short square tail, fairly long neck feathers and red eye. Juvenile has grey-brown upperparts, off-white underparts with heavy dark streaks and eye first dark brown, then yellowish, then orange-red. Immature has glossy black upperparts and heavily or sparsely streaked underparts. Trees and bushes in open habitats including towns. Small colonies nest in holes. Common.

Mn	Mu	NI	NB	Bv	Gu	MI	NG	Mk	RI	Te	Vu	Lo	GT

Common Myna *Acridotheres tristis* Page 413

25 cm. Blackish-brown with yellow bill and eye-patch, white vent, wing-patches and tail-tip, and long yellow legs. In flight, dark brown with large white wing-patch, white vent and undertail-coverts, white tail-tips and yellow face-patch. Open habitats, especially grassland and towns. Gregarious. Locally common.

Mn	Mu	NI	NB	Bv	Gu	MI	NG	Mk	RI	Te	Vu	Lo	GT

Long-tailed Myna *Mino kreffti* Page 413

28 cm. Glossy black with yellow-orange bill, legs and large eye-patch, yellow lower belly, and white wing-patch, upper- and undertail-coverts. In flight, black with white wing patch, upper- and undertail-coverts, and yellow eye-patch and lower belly. Noisy calls and whirring wings. Forest. Common.

Mn	Mu	NI	NB	Bv	Gu	MI	NG	Mk	RI	Te	Vu	Lo	GT

Spangled Drongo
grandis
Brown-winged Starling
malaitae
adult
juvenile
White-eyed Starling
adult
Metallic Starling
immature
adult
Atoll Starling
juvenile
adult
Singing Starling
immature
Common Myna
Long-tailed Myna

Pacific Robin *Petroica multicolor polymorpha* Page 393

10 cm. Male has black hood and upperparts with white forehead-spot, or rusty-brown head with paler forehead-spot, white on wings, outer tail, flanks and vent, and scarlet breast and belly. Female has browner upperparts especially head and forehead, less white on wing, white or brown throat and pale scarlet wash on underparts. Immature like female but buffy-white wing markings and less red. Juvenile is all brown with buffy streaks and mottling. Fairly common above 800 m.

Mn	Mu	NI	NB	Bv	Gu	MI	NG	Mk	RI	Te	Vu	Lo	GT

Mottled Flowerpecker *Dicaeum tristrami* Page 418

9 cm. Dumpy with tiny bill, chocolate-brown crown and upperparts, black chin and variable bib, variable whitish supercilium extending behind ear-coverts, white scaling on crown, face and bib, and pale brownish-white underparts. Male has blackish from chin and lower ear-coverts onto upper breast. Female has smaller brown bib and more white around eye and ear-coverts. Forest. Common.

Mn	Mu	NI	NB	Bv	Gu	MI	NG	Mk	RI	Te	Vu	Lo	GT

Olive-backed Sunbird *Cinnyris jugularis flavigaster* Page 419

11 cm. Dull olive upperparts, dark tail with white corners, bright yellow underparts and fine supercilium, and long decurved bill. Male has metallic blue throat. Female has yellow throat. Open forest habitats, including villages. Common. Ugi and Three Sisters only.

Mn	Mu	NI	NB	Bv	Gu	MI	NG	Mk	RI	Te	Vu	Lo	GT

Cardinal Myzomela *Myzomela cardinalis pulcherrima* Page 360

12 cm. Male has crimson head and body, and black wings, tail, belly and vent, with variable amount of black on underparts and back. Female has red head, mantle and rump, olive fringes on wings and red-washed dark underparts. Immature is duller with variable amounts of red. Coastal scrub and coconuts. Fairly common.

Mn	Mu	NI	NB	Bv	Gu	MI	NG	Mk	RI	Te	Vu	Lo	GT

Sooty Myzomela *Myzomela tristrami* Page 363

12 cm. Black with slight gloss and long decurved bill. In flight, shows some white on underwing primary bases. Juvenile has sooty upperparts, grey-olive underparts and black-tipped orange-yellow bill. Immature has scruffy black and grey mottling on underparts. Forest and scrub, sometimes in coconuts. Common.

Mn	Mu	NI	NB	Bv	Gu	MI	NG	Mk	RI	Te	Vu	Lo	GT

Grey-throated White-eye *Zosterops ugiensis ugiensis* Page 405

12 cm. Warbler-like white-eye with olive upperparts, sooty-brown forehead, greener wings, silvery-grey underparts, black bill, dark legs and sometimes very narrow white eye ring. Hill and montane forest. Common.

Mn	Mu	NI	NB	Bv	Gu	MI	NG	Mk	RI	Te	Vu	Lo	GT

♂
Mottled
Flowerpecker
♂
juvenile
♀
♀
Pacific Robin
♂
♂
Olive-backed Sunbird
♀
♀
Cardinal Myzomela
immature
adult
Sooty Myzomela
immature
Grey-throated
White-eye

Shade Bush Warbler *Cettia parens* — Page 396

12 cm. Plain rufous-brown upperparts, paler supercilium, dark eye-stripe, paler orange-brown underparts, paler throat and fairly long pale legs. Juvenile is darker olive-brown with olive-yellow throat and no supercilium. Forest with dense undergrowth above 500 m. Understorey. Tail often half-cocked. Fairly common.

Mn	Mu	Nl	NB	Bv	Gu	Ml	NG	Mk	Rl	Te	Vu	Lo	GT

Island Leaf Warbler *Phylloscopus poliocephalus makirensis* — Page 397

10 cm. Olive upperparts, long silvery supercilium, dark eye-stripe, pale yellow wing-bar, dirty white throat and lemon-yellow underparts. Forest above 500 m. Canopy. Fairly common. Often split as a separate species: Makira (San Cristobal) Leaf Warbler.

Mn	Mu	Nl	NB	Bv	Gu	Ml	NG	Mk	Rl	Te	Vu	Lo	GT

Pacific Swallow *Hirundo tahitica subfusca* — Page 395

13 cm. Glossy blue-black upperparts, rufous forehead to upper breast, pale dusky underparts and underwing-coverts, and dark undertail-coverts with pale fringes. Forked tail has pointed corners. Immature duller. Open habitats, especially beaches and towns. Fairly common.

Mn	Mu	Nl	NB	Bv	Gu	Ml	NG	Mk	Rl	Te	Vu	Lo	GT

Makira Fantail *Rhipidura tenebrosa* — Page 379

17 cm. Dark brown, paler and greyer on underparts, narrow white throat-bar sometimes dark in centre, two golden wing-bars and large white tail-tips. Juvenile has buff fringes on wings and underparts. Closed forest, especially on hills. Droops wings and half-fans tail in understorey. Uncommon.

Mn	Mu	Nl	NB	Bv	Gu	Ml	NG	Mk	Rl	Te	Vu	Lo	GT

Grey Fantail *Rhipidura albiscapa brenchleyi* — Page 379

15 cm. Grey-brown upperparts, narrow black breast-band, white throat, short supercilium, short ear-covert streak, double wing-bar, tertial fringes and tail-tips, and pale buff underparts. Juvenile is duller with buff wash. Forest above 500 m. Active and restless, often with drooped wings and fanned tail. Uncommon.

Mn	Mu	Nl	NB	Bv	Gu	Ml	NG	Mk	Rl	Te	Vu	Lo	GT

Rufous Fantail *Rhipidura rufifrons russata* — Page 381

15 cm. Brown head and wings, bright orange-rufous forehead and mantle to tail-base, and remainder of tail black with broad white tips. Usually has white throat. Black breast-band, black spots on lower breast, and buffy underparts. Forest, especially open forest. Understorey. Hyperactive, with drooped wings and waving fanned tail. Common.
R. r. ugiensis (Ugi) has little or no white on throat.

Mn	Mu	Nl	NB	Bv	Gu	Ml	NG	Mk	Rl	Te	Vu	Lo	GT

Willie Wagtail *Rhipidura leucophrys* — Page 377

20 cm. Black head, throat and upperparts with white lower breast to vent and white supercilium. Juvenile is duller with broader dull eyebrow and buffy tips to wing-coverts. Open habitat including coasts, towns and forest clearings. Runs on ground and sallies from low perches, drooping wings and waving tail. Common.

Mn	Mu	Nl	NB	Bv	Gu	Ml	NG	Mk	Rl	Te	Vu	Lo	GT

Long-tailed Triller *Lalage leucopyga affinis* — Page 371

17 cm. Male has glossy black upperparts with white wing-coverts, rump, tertial fringes and underparts. Female has browner upperparts. Juvenile is browner and buffier, with pale tips on upperparts. Forest, including regrowth and villages. Fairly common.

Mn	Mu	Nl	NB	Bv	Gu	Ml	NG	Mk	Rl	Te	Vu	Lo	GT

Shade
Bush Warbler
Island
Leaf Warbler
Pacific Swallow
Makira Fantail
ugiensis
Grey Fantail
Rufous Fantail
ugiensis
russata
Willie Wagtail
juvenile
♀
♂
Long-tailed Triller

Makira Flycatcher *Myiagra cervinicauda* Page 389

14 cm. Male is glossy black, greyer on mantle, with white lower breast and belly. Female has ash-grey head, pale eye-ring, brown mantle, darker wings, rufous fringes to wing and tail, buff outer tail feathers, deep orange throat and breast, and buff belly. Closed forest. Flycatches and gleans in canopy. Wags or shakes tail. Fairly common.

Mn	Mu	NI	NB	Bv	Gu	MI	NG	**Mk**	RI	Te	Vu	Lo	GT

Chestnut-bellied Monarch *Monarcha castaneiventris megarhynchus* Page 387

17 cm. Glossy black head, upperparts and breast, deep chestnut lower breast and belly, and pale blue bill. Juvenile is duller with browner wings. Forest and scrub on small islands. Common.

M. c. ugiensis (Ugi, Three Sisters, Santa Ana and Santa Catalina) is all glossy blue-black, and juvenile may have tawny fringes on lower belly.

Mn	Mu	NI	NB	**Bv**	**Gu**	**MI**	NG	**Mk**	RI	Te	Vu	Lo	GT

White-collared Monarch *Symposiachrus vidua vidua* Page 386

15 cm. Black head and throat, separated by broad white collar from black mantle, wings and tail, with white rump, tail-tips and scaly white wing-patch of variable extent. Juvenile is slightly browner with dark bill. Forest. Fairly common.

S. v. squamulatus (Ugi) has solid or scaly black on breast below black throat and variably less white on collar and wing-coverts.

Mn	Mu	NI	NB	Bv	Gu	MI	NG	**Mk**	RI	Te	Vu	Lo	GT

Oriole Whistler *Pachycephala orioloides christophori* Page 372

15 cm. Male has black, yellow or olive crown and ear-coverts, black breast-band, yellow throat, underparts and neck-sides, and olive upperparts. Female has dull olive upperparts, browner head and duller yellow underparts with greenish breast-band. Juvenile is similar to female but has pale bill and extensive rufous on wings. Forest. Common.

Mn	Mu	NI	NB	**Bv**	**Gu**	**MI**	**NG**	**Mk**	RI	Te	Vu	Lo	GT

♀
♂
Makira Flycatcher
megarhynchus
ugiensis
Chestnut-bellied Monarch
ugiensis
immature
♂
Oriole
Whistler
vidua
White-collared Monarch
♀
squamulatus
squamulatus
juvenile

Barred Cuckooshrike *Coracina lineata makirae* Page 367

23 cm. Yellow eye. Male is blue-grey with black lores, darker wings and tail, and indistinct white bars on breast becoming clear black-and-white bars on belly. Female has clear black-and-white bars from lower breast to vent. Juvenile has creamy scaling on upperparts and barred underparts. Forest. Fairly common.

Mn Mu NI NB Bv Gu MI NG Mk RI Te Vu Lo GT

Makira Cicadabird *Coracina salomonis* Page 369

23 cm. Male is mid-grey with black lores, tail and wing feathers. Female upperparts as male, with rufous-orange underparts and orange on outer tail. Juvenile like female, with pale and black scaling and paler underparts. Forest. Fairly common.

Mn Mu NI NB Bv Gu MI NG Mk RI Te Vu Lo GT

Makira Honeyeater *Meliarchus sclateri* Page 357

25 cm. Large and scrawny with long pale creamy, greenish or grey bill and eye-patch. Olive-brown upperparts with pale streaks on crown, warm brown tail, long dark moustachial stripe, and buffy underparts with short stripes on breast and belly. Juvenile has darker bill, less contrasting head pattern and less streaked yellower underparts. Forest, including gardens and coconuts. Noisy and quarrelsome. Ungainly bounding flight. Common.

Mn Mu NI NB Bv Gu MI NG Mk RI Te Vu Lo GT

Makira Thrush *Zoothera margaretae* Page 415

23 cm. Olive-brown upperparts with two irregular white wing-bars, pale mottling on head, white underparts with dark mottling on throat, large dark scales on breast and belly, and long pink legs. In flight, dark underwing with white stripe. Forest at 200–700 m, especially steep gullies. On ground. Fairly common.

Mn Mu NI NB Bv Gu MI NG Mk RI Te Vu Lo GT

Spangled Drongo *Dicrurus bracteatus longirostris* Page 376

30 cm. Long tail has shallow fork. All black with purple-blue gloss, small blue spots on crown, neck and breast, long black bill, and red eye. Juvenile is dull sooty-black with dark brown iris. Forest. Tail is often fanned and flicked. Fairly common.

Mn Mu NI NB Bv Gu MI NG Mk RI Te Vu Lo GT

Metallic Starling *Aplonis metallica nitida* Page 408

24 cm. All glossy black with long pointed tail, fairly long neck feathers and red eye. Juvenile has shorter tail, dark brown upperparts, creamy-white underparts with blackish streaks and eye first dark brown, then greenish, then orange-red. Forest and gardens. Gregarious. Hanging nests in large colonies. Common. See flying and immature birds on Plate 69.

Mn Mu NI NB Bv Gu MI NG Mk RI Te Vu Lo GT

Makira Starling *Aplonis dichroa* Page 411

20 cm. Glossy black head, body and wing-coverts, fairly long neck and throat feathers, pale brown wings and red eye. Juvenile is duller, with pale yellow-brown eye. Forest, especially secondary forest in hills to at least 800 m. Solitary bulky domed nest in subcanopy. Common.

Mn Mu NI NB Bv Gu MI NG Mk RI Te Vu Lo GT

Singing Starling *Aplonis cantoroides* Page 409

19 cm. All glossy black with medium-short square tail, fairly long neck feathers and red eye. Juvenile has grey-brown upperparts, off-white underparts with heavy dark streaks and eye first dark brown, then yellowish, then orange-red. Trees and bushes by coast and towns. Small colonies nest in holes. Uncommon. See flying and immature birds on Plate 69.

Mn Mu NI NB Bv Gu MI NG Mk RI Te Vu Lo GT

Common Myna *Acridotheres tristis* Page 413

25 cm. Blackish-brown with yellow bill and eye-patch, white vent, wing-patches and tail-tip, and long yellow legs. In flight, dark brown with large white wing-patch, white vent and undertail-coverts, white tail-tips and yellow face-patch. Open habitats, especially grassland and towns. Gregarious. Locally common on Three Sisters. See flying bird on Plate 69.

Mn Mu NI NB Bv Gu MI NG Mk RI Te Vu Lo GT

♂
♀
♂
Barred Cuckooshrike
Makira Cicadabird
Makira Honeyeater
Makira Thrush
Spangled Drongo
Metallic Starling
adult
Singing
Starling
Makira Starling
juvenile
adult
Common Myna

Barred Cuckooshrike *Coracina lineata gracilis* — Page 367

23 cm. Male and female are blue-grey with yellow eye, black lores and clear black-and-white bars from lower breast to vent. Juvenile has creamy scaling on upperparts and barred underparts. Fairly common. See Shining Bronze Cuckoo (Plate 41).

Mn Mu NI NB Bv Gu MI NG Mk RI Te Vu Lo GT

Black-faced Cuckooshrike *Coracina novaehollandiae* — Page 366

33 cm. Pale grey upperparts and breast, darker wings and tail with white tail-tips, black forehead, face and throat, and paler belly. Immature has less defined black patch on ear-coverts only, and finely barred throat and breast. Open habitats with trees. Rare.

Mn Mu NI NB Bv Gu MI NG Mk RI Te Vu Lo GT

Rennell Shrikebill *Clytorhynchus hamlini* — Page 384

19 cm. Orange-brown, darker wings and tail, white under wing, very long blue-grey bill and glossy black mask and upper throat. Female duller. Juvenile even duller. Singles and pairs in understorey. Fairly common.

Mn Mu NI NB Bv Gu MI NG Mk RI Te Vu Lo GT

Rennell Starling *Aplonis insularis* — Page 410

17 cm. All glossy black with yellow eye. Short tail and short heavy bill. In flight, has broad round wings and bulging belly. Juvenile is dull grey-brown with pale buff scales on underparts, more striped on vent, and blue, green, yellow or orange-yellow eye. Pairs call from dead tree-tops. Uncommon.

Mn Mu NI NB Bv Gu MI NG Mk RI Te Vu Lo GT

Singing Starling *Aplonis cantoroides* — Page 409

19 cm. All glossy black with medium-short square tail, fairly long neck feathers and red eye. Juvenile has grey-brown upperparts, off-white underparts with heavy dark streaks and eye first dark brown, then yellowish, then orange-red. Immature has glossy black upperparts and heavily or sparsely streaked underparts. Trees and bushes in open habitats including towns. Small colonies nest in holes. Common.

Mn Mu NI NB Bv Gu MI NG Mk RI Te Vu Lo GT

Island Thrush *Turdus poliocephalus rennellianus* — Page 415

20 cm. Sooty-brown with bright orange-yellow bill, legs and eye-ring, and rufous or white fringes on flanks to undertail-coverts. Female and juvenile are paler and browner. Common.

Mn Mu NI NB Bv Gu MI NG Mk RI Te Vu Lo GT

Barred
Cuckooshrike
Black-faced Cuckooshrike
adult
immature
Rennell
Shrikebill
♂
juvenile
adult
Rennell Starling
juvenile
adult
immature
Singing Starling
Island Thrush

PLATE 75: RENNELL PASSERINES II

Rennell Fantail *Rhipidura rennelliana* — Page 380

16 cm. Grey-brown with white on outer tail feathers, tiny white supercilium, buff double wing-bar and fringes to wings, and paler underparts especially throat and undertail-coverts. Juvenile has cinnamon on underparts and rusty fringes on wings. Active with drooped wings and cocked fanned tail. Common.

Mn	Mu	NI	NB	Bv	Gu	MI	NG	Mk	**RI**	Te	Vu	Lo	GT

Melanesian Flycatcher *Myiagra caledonica occidentalis* — Page 389

14 cm. Male is glossy black with white lower breast and belly. Female has mid-grey head and mantle, silvery eye-ring, dull brown wings and tail with white on outer tail, orange throat and breast, and white belly. Juvenile like female but duller with buff fringes on upperparts. Often pumps tail and sometimes raises crown feathers. Uncommon.

Mn	Mu	NI	NB	Bv	Gu	MI	NG	Mk	**RI**	Te	**Vu**	**Lo**	**GT**

Rennell Whistler *Pachycephala feminina* — Page 375

15 cm. Dull rufous head, wings and tail, more olive on mantle, and dull yellow throat, vent and undertail-coverts. Pale buff eye-ring, horn or dull pink bill and dark grey legs. Juvenile is duller and more rusty on crown and underparts. Singles are unobtrusive, usually close to ground. Fairly common.

Mn	Mu	NI	NB	Bv	Gu	MI	NG	Mk	**RI**	Te	Vu	Lo	GT

Fan-tailed Gerygone *Gerygone flavolateralis citrina* — Page 364

10 cm. Grey head with white supercilium and eyelids, olive upperparts, white spots on tail, white throat and upper breast and yellow lower breast and belly. Juvenile lacks supercilium, has browner upperparts and uniformly yellow underparts. Restless and vocal. Abundant.

Mn	Mu	NI	NB	Bv	Gu	MI	NG	Mk	**RI**	Te	**Vu**	**Lo**	**GT**

Rennell White-eye *Zosterops rennellianus* — Page 403

12 cm. Plain dull olive with slightly paler underparts, yellow wash on throat and vent, creamy axillaries, dull orange bill and legs, and narrow blue-grey eye-ring. Pairs and small flocks. Fairly common.

Mn	Mu	NI	NB	Bv	Gu	MI	NG	Mk	**RI**	Te	Vu	Lo	GT

Bare-eyed White-eye *Woodfordia superciliosa* — Page 408

14 cm. Greyish-brown with long horn-coloured bill, dark grey eye-mask with silvery margin, paler underparts and grey legs. Dumpy, front-heavy and short-tailed; broad-winged in fluttering flight. Small groups move slowly. Abundant.

Mn	Mu	NI	NB	Bv	Gu	MI	NG	Mk	**RI**	Te	Vu	Lo	GT

Cardinal Myzomela *Myzomela cardinalis sanfordi* — Page 360

12 cm. Long fine decurved black bill. Male has crimson head and body, black wings, tail and central belly, and variable black on underparts and back. Female is olive-brown with red head, throat, mantle and rump. Immature is duller with variable amounts of red. Common.

Mn	Mu	NI	NB	Bv	Gu	MI	NG	**Mk**	**RI**	**Te**	**Vu**	**Lo**	GT

Rennell
Fantail
Melanesian Flycatcher
♂
♀
adult
Rennell Whistler
juvenile
adult
juvenile
Fan-tailed Gerygone
Rennell
White-eye
♀
Cardinal Myzomela
♂
Bare-eyed
White-eye

Rufous Fantail *Rhipidura rufifrons* Page 381

15 cm. Brown upperparts, becoming black on tail with broad white tips. Black ear-coverts, throat and upper breast, white moustachial stripe, black spots on lower breast and off-white underparts. Hyperactive, with drooped wings and waving fanned tail. Common.

R. r. melanolaema (Vanikoro) has short white supercilium and olive-grey upperparts.

R. r. agilis (Nendo) has dull brown forehead and no supercilium.

R. r. utupuae (Utupua) has white forehead and supercilium, and rusty-brown crown and mantle.

Mn Mu NI NB Bv Gu MI NG Mk RI Te Vu Lo GT

Polynesian Triller *Lalage maculosa melanopygia* Page 370

15 cm. Dumpy. Male has black upperparts, grey on rump, white on wing, tail-tips, supercilium, face and underparts, with faint barring on neck and flanks and sometimes crown. Female is browner with more bars on underparts. Juvenile is browner with creamy tips, fringes and wash. Forest, including gardens. Fairly common on Nendo, Utupua and Vanikoro. See plate 80.

Mn Mu NI NB Bv Gu MI NG Mk RI Te Vu Lo GT

Vanikoro Monarch *Mayrornis schistaceus* Page 382

14 cm. Slaty-grey with black tail, broad white tips to outer tail feathers, and whitish undertail-coverts. Juvenile has less contrasting tail. Cocks and fans tail. Common Vanikoro endemic.

Mn Mu NI NB Bv Gu MI NG Mk RI Te Vu Lo GT

Santa Cruz Shrikebill *Clytorhynchus sanctaecrucis* Page 383

19 cm. Male has long blue-grey bill, black head, neck and upperparts, and white ear-coverts, fine supercilium and lower breast to vent. Female is plain rufous-brown, slightly paler around face and underparts. Immature like female, and male develops grey, then black on face. Rare Nendo (Santa Cruz) endemic.

Mn Mu NI NB Bv Gu MI NG Mk RI Te Vu Lo GT

Vanikoro Flycatcher *Myiagra vanikorensis* Page 389

13 cm. Male is glossy blue-black with orange lower breast and belly, fading to vent. Female has blue-grey head and mantle, browner wings, brown tail with buffy outer fringes, and buffy-orange underparts, paler on throat and vent. Sometimes shimmers tail. Fairly common on Vanikoro.

Mn Mu NI NB Bv Gu MI NG Mk RI Te Vu Lo GT

Pacific Swallow *Hirundo tahitica subfusca* Page 395

13 cm. Glossy blue-black upperparts, rufous forehead to upper breast, pale dusky underparts and underwing-coverts, and dark undertail-coverts with pale fringes. Forked tail has pointed corners. Immature duller. Open habitats, especially beaches and towns. Fairly common on larger islands.

Mn Mu NI NB Bv Gu MI NG Mk RI Te Vu Lo GT

Polynesian Triller
♂
juvenile
melanolaema
Rufous Fantail
agilis
utupuae
adult
Vanikoro Monarch
juvenile
♂
Santa Cruz Shrikebill
♀
♂
♀
Vanikoro
Flycatcher
Pacific Swallow

White-throated Whistler *Pachycephala vitiensis ornata* Page 374

15 cm. Male has black upperparts and breast-band, with olive fringes on wings, white throat and yellow underparts. Female has grey-brown upperparts, dirty white throat, cinnamon breast-band and yellow underparts. Juvenile has rufous fringes on wings and buffier underparts. Common on Nendo, Reef Is, Duff Is and Utupua.

Mn	Mu	NI	NB	Bv	Gu	MI	NG	Mk	RI	Te	Vu	Lo	GT

Melanesian Whistler *Pachycephala caledonica vanikorensis* Page 373

17 cm. Male has black hood and breast-band, olive mantle and fringes on wings and tail, white throat and yellow underparts. Female has grey hood, brownish-olive upperparts, dirty white throat, brownish breast-band and pale yellow underparts. Juvenile has rufous on wings and head, and yellow on throat. Common on Vanikoro.

Mn	Mu	NI	NB	Bv	Gu	MI	NG	Mk	RI	Te	Vu	Lo	GT

Island Thrush *Turdus poliocephalus vanikorensis* Page 415

20 cm. Blackish-brown with yellow bill, legs and eye-ring. Juvenile has rufous fringes on underparts. On ground and low bushes above 1000 m. Rare or extinct on Utupua and Vanikoro.

Mn	Mu	NI	NB	Bv	Gu	MI	NG	Mk	RI	Te	Vu	Lo	GT

Rusty-winged Starling *Aplonis z. zelandica* Page 411

19 cm. Grey-brown upperparts with chestnut flight feathers and rump, and paler underparts with tawny flanks and undertail-coverts. Forest, including gardens, to over 1000 m. Uncommon on Vanikoro.

Mn	Mu	NI	NB	Bv	Gu	MI	NG	Mk	RI	Te	Vu	Lo	GT

Polynesian Starling *Aplonis tabuensis* Page 412

19 cm. Grey-brown upperparts with pale buff wing-panel, pale streaks on dark buff underparts, yellow-buff undertail-coverts, and yellow-brown eye. Juvenile has dull rufous-brown eye. Common.

A. t. pachyrampha (Tinakula and Reef Is) has slightly green glossed dark cap.

A. t. tucopiae (Tikopia) has less streaking on darker underparts and slight purple gloss on cap.

Mn	Mu	NI	NB	Bv	Gu	MI	NG	Mk	RI	Te	Vu	Lo	GT

Vanikoro White-eye *Zosterops gibbsi* Page 406

12 cm. Plain olive with long slightly decurved black bill, pale grey eye-ring, pale orange legs and slightly paler underparts with yellowish throat. Forest, especially secondary and montane forest. Fairly common Vanikoro endemic.

Mn	Mu	NI	NB	Bv	Gu	MI	NG	Mk	RI	Te	Vu	Lo	GT

Santa Cruz White-eye *Zosterops sanctaecrucis* Page 405

12 cm. Plain olive with dark grey bill, lores and eye-ring creating slight mask, dark blue-grey legs and slightly paler underparts, especially chin, vent and undertail-coverts. Fairly common Nendo (Santa Cruz) endemic.

Mn	Mu	NI	NB	Bv	Gu	MI	NG	Mk	RI	Te	Vu	Lo	GT

Sanford's White-eye *Woodfordia lacertosa* Page 408

15 cm. Rufous-buff crown and upperparts, paler face and underparts, broad silvery eye-ring, dull yellow bill and dull yellow-horn legs. Dumpy, with short tail. Fairly common Nendo (Santa Cruz) endemic.

Mn	Mu	NI	NB	Bv	Gu	MI	NG	Mk	RI	Te	Vu	Lo	GT

Cardinal Myzomela *Myzomela cardinalis sanctaecrucis* Page 360

12 cm. Long fine decurved black bill. Male has crimson head and body, and black wings, tail and belly to vent. Female is olive-brown with red rump and red wash on mantle and breast. Immature is duller with variable red. Common on all islands.

Mn	Mu	NI	NB	Bv	Gu	MI	NG	Mk	RI	Te	Vu	Lo	GT

♂
White-throated Whistler
♀
♂
Melanesian Whistler
♀
Island Thrush
immature
Rusty-winged
Starling
pachyrampha
lucopiae
Polynesian Starling
Vanikoro
White-eye
Santa Cruz
White-eye
♀
♂
Sanford's White-eye
Cardinal Myzomela

Santo Thicketbird *Megalurulus whitneyi* Page 400

17 cm. Dark brown upperparts, with darker crown, broad eye-stripe and long graduated tail with pointed tips, and rich rufous supercilium and underparts. Forest with dense undergrowth above 700 m, rarely down to 160 m. On or near ground. Cocks tail. Fairly common on Santo.

Mn	Mu	NI	NB	Bv	Gu	Ml	NG	Mk	Rl	Te	**Vu**	Lo	GT

Silvereye *Zosterops lateralis tropicus* Page 407

12 cm. Olive upperparts with blackish lores, broad white eye-ring, dark grey mantle and scapulars, yellowish-green throat, silvery underparts and stout horn-coloured bill. Secondary forest and gardens. Fairly common.
Z. l. valuensis (Mota Lava) has plain olive upperparts and yellower throat and vent.

Mn	Mu	NI	NB	Bv	Gu	Ml	NG	Mk	Rl	Te	**Vu**	**Lo**	**GT**

Vanuatu White-eye *Zosterops flavifrons efatensis* Page 406

12 cm. Yellowish-olive upperparts with darker wings and tail, broad white eye-ring, fine dark bill, dark lores and yellower forehead and underparts. Forest, scrub and bushes. Gregarious. Very common.
Z. f. majuscula (Aneityum) has darker upperparts, greener underparts, and only slightly paler forehead.

Mn	Mu	NI	NB	Bv	Gu	Ml	NG	Mk	Rl	Te	**Vu**	Lo	GT

Grey-eared Honeyeater *Lichmera incana griseoviridis* Page 358

16 cm. Plain grey-brown with long decurved black bill, dark grey head with dark skin around eye, slight silver wash on ear-coverts, olive-brown upperparts with brighter green wing-panel, and paler underparts. Juvenile is paler and lacks silver on ear-coverts. Loud and noisy. Open forest and bushes. Common north to Malo.

Mn	Mu	NI	NB	Bv	Gu	Ml	NG	Mk	Rl	Te	**Vu**	**Lo**	**GT**

Vanuatu Honeyeater *Glycifohia n. notabilis* Page 358

19 cm. Black crown, face and ear-coverts with white speckles, long decurved black bill, rufous-brown upperparts, and white underparts with dark brown streaks on breast-sides and flanks. Juvenile has plain underparts or faint streaks, and pale streaks and fringes on upperparts. Forest and clearings. Common, but sometimes rare in lowlands from Banks Is to Epi.
G. n. superciliaris (Maewo, Pentecost, Malekula, Ambrym and Epi) has more white on supercilium but less on crown.

Mn	Mu	NI	NB	Bv	Gu	Ml	NG	Mk	Rl	Te	**Vu**	Lo	GT

Cardinal Myzomela *Myzomela c. cardinalis* Page 360

12 cm. Long fine decurved black bill. Male has crimson head and body, and black wings, tail and lower breast to vent. Female is olive-brown with dull red on chin, forecrown and rump. Immature male has red hood and some red on mantle and rump. Forest and bushes. Common.

Mn	Mu	NI	NB	Bv	Gu	Ml	NG	**Mk**	**Rl**	**Te**	**Vu**	**Lo**	GT

Fan-tailed Gerygone *Gerygone flavolateralis correiae* Page 364

10 cm. Grey head with white supercilium and eyelids, olive upperparts, white spots on tail, white throat and upper breast, and yellow lower breast and belly. Juvenile lacks supercilium, has browner upperparts and uniformly yellow underparts. Forest and bushes. Restless and vocal. Common between Banks Is and Epi.

Mn	Mu	NI	NB	Bv	Gu	Ml	NG	Mk	**Rl**	Te	**Vu**	**Lo**	**GT**

Silvereye
tropicus
valuensis
Santo Thicketbird
Vanuatu White-eye
efatensis
majuscula
adult
Grey-eared
Honeyeater
Vanuatu Honeyeater
juvenile
♀
♂
Cardinal Myzomela
immature
adult
Fan-tailed Gerygone
juvenile

Buff-bellied Monarch *Neolalage banksiana* Page 383

15 cm. Black crown, mantle, breast-band, flight feathers and central tail. White face, throat, neck and outer tail. Orange-buff to creamy wing-coverts, tertials, rump, lower breast and belly. Juvenile has brownish-black upperparts, with dark mottling on face and wings, and yellowish bill. Forest. Often cocks tail. Common from Banks Is to Efate.

Mn Mu NI NB Bv Gu MI NG Mk RI Te Vu Lo GT

Grey Fantail *Rhipidura albiscapa brenchleyi* Page 379

15 cm. Grey-brown upperparts, narrow black breast-band, white throat, short supercilium, short ear-covert streak, double wing-bar, tertial fringes and tail-tips, and pale buff underparts. Juvenile is duller with buff wash. Forest edge, bushes and isolated trees. Active and restless, often with drooped wings and fanned tail. Common.

Mn Mu NI NB Bv Gu MI NG Mk RI Te Vu Lo GT

Streaked Fantail *Rhipidura verreauxi spilodera* Page 380

17 cm. Grey-brown upperparts with short white supercilium and ear-covert stripe, pale bill-base, pale fringes to wing-coverts, tertials and tail, pale tail-tips, white throat, and pale grey lower breast and belly with heavy black spots. Closed forest. Active with drooped wings and fanned tail. Common from Banks Is to Efate.

Mn Mu NI NB Bv Gu MI NG Mk RI Te Vu Lo GT

Melanesian Flycatcher *Myiagra caledonica marinae* Page 389

14 cm. Male is glossy black with white lower breast and belly. Female has mid-grey head and mantle, silvery eye-ring, dull brown wings and tail with white on outer tail, orange throat and breast, and white belly to vent. Juvenile like female but duller with buff fringes on upperparts. Open forest and isolated trees. Often pumps tail and sometimes raises crown feathers. Common.

Mn Mu NI NB Bv Gu MI NG Mk RI Te Vu Lo GT

Southern Shrikebill *Clytorhynchus pachycephaloides grisescens* Page 383

19 cm. Plain brown upperparts, paler greyer underparts, long darker tail with broad white tips, and heavy blue-grey bill. Juvenile has dark brown bill. Closed forest. Noisy but unobtrusive. Fairly common.

Mn Mu NI NB Bv Gu MI NG Mk RI Te Vu Lo GT

Melanesian Whistler *Pachycephala caledonica* Page 373

17 cm. Male has black hood and breast-band, olive mantle and fringes on wings and tail, white throat and yellow underparts. Female has brownish-olive crown and upperparts, dirty white throat, narrow brown breast-band, pale yellow or buff underparts and yellow vent. Juvenile like female but has rufous fringes on wings. Forest. Common.

P. c. cucullata (Aneityum): male has blackish upperparts with olive fringes on wings and tail.

P. c. chlorura (Erromango): male has more olive mantle.

Mn Mu NI NB Bv Gu MI NG Mk RI Te Vu Lo GT

Pacific Robin *Petroica multicolor ambrynensis* Page 393

10 cm. Male has black hood and upperparts with white forehead-spot, white on wings, outer tail, flanks and vent, and scarlet breast and belly. Female has browner upperparts especially crown, pale buff forehead-spot, less white on wing and pale orange-red wash on underparts. Juvenile is all brown with buff streaks and mottling. Forest. Fairly common.

P. m. feminina (Efate): male has brown upperparts with red wash on crown, white upper throat and small buffy wing-patch.

Mn Mu NI NB Bv Gu MI NG Mk RI Te Vu Lo GT

juvenile
Buff-bellied Monarch
adult
Grey Fantail
Streaked Fantail
♀
♂
Melanesian Flycatcher
Southern Shrikebill
chlorura
♀
cucullata
♂
ambrynensis
♂
feminina
♂
Melanesian Whistler
chlorura
♂
Pacific Robin
♀
juvenile
juvenile

South Melanesian Cuckooshrike *Coracina caledonica thilenii* Page 366

35 cm. Uniformly slaty-grey, blacker around lores and eye, with pale yellow eye and short heavy black bill. Immature has dull eye. Forest and scattered trees. Fairly common on Santo, Malo, Malekula and Erromango.

Mn Mu NI NB Bv Gu MI NG Mk RI Te Vu Lo GT

Polynesian Triller *Lalage maculosa modesta* Page 370

15 cm. Dumpy. Male has black upperparts, grey on rump, white on wing, tail-tips, supercilium, face and underparts, with faint barring on neck and flanks and sometimes crown. Female is browner with more bars on underparts. Juvenile is browner with creamy tips, fringes and wash. Forest, including gardens. Uncommon between Santo and Efate.

Mn Mu NI NB Bv Gu MI NG Mk RI Te Vu Lo GT

Long-tailed Triller *Lalage leucopyga albiloris* Page 371

17 cm. Slender. Male has glossy black upperparts with white on wing, rump and short supercilium, and white or pale buff underparts. Female has browner upperparts. Juvenile is browner and buffier, with pale tips on upperparts and sometimes bars on underparts. Forest, including scattered trees. Fairly common.

Mn Mu NI NB Bv Gu MI NG Mk RI Te Vu Lo GT

Island Thrush *Turdus poliocephalus* Page 415

20 cm. Dark warm brown or greyish-brown with yellow bill, legs and eye-ring, and sometimes white on underparts, especially undertail-coverts. Juvenile is variable, often warm brown with pale spots or streaks on upperparts, and orange or brown spots or bars on dark or buff underparts. Forest. On ground and in understorey. Common to rare.

T. p. albifrons and ***T. p. pritzbueri*** (Erromango and Tanna) are sooty with white or brownish-grey hood and sometimes pale fringes or rufous on breast and white on undertail-coverts.

T. p. efatensis (Efate) male is sooty-brown with white on vent and undertail-coverts, female more rufous-brown.

T. p. vanikorensis, ***T. p. placens*** and ***T. p. whitneyi*** (Utupua, Vanikoro, Banks Is, Santo, Malo) are plain sooty but female has paler greyer or rufous underparts with some white on undertail-coverts.

T. p. malekulae and ***T. p. becki*** (Pentecost and Malekula to Emae) have sooty upperparts, greyer underparts, white vent, and sometimes orange-rufous flanks and belly or buff breast.

Mn Mu NI NB Bv Gu MI NG Mk RI Te Vu Lo GT

Song Thrush *Turdus philomelos* (not illustrated) Page 417

22 cm. Plain olive-brown upperparts, and creamy underparts with small round black spots. Dark bill and pink legs. Usually on ground. Vagrant.

Rusty-winged Starling *Aplonis zelandica rufipennis* Page 411

19 cm. Grey-brown upperparts with chestnut flight feathers and rump, and paler underparts with tawny flanks and undertail-coverts. Forest, including gardens, to over 1000 m. Uncommon from Banks Is to Ambrym.

Mn Mu NI NB Bv Gu MI NG Mk RI Te Vu Lo GT

Mountain Starling *Aplonis santovestris* Page 412

17 cm. Plain rufous-brown with white eye, darker crown, wings and tail, and slightly paler underparts. Forest at 1200–1700 m. Rare on Mt Watiamasan, Mt Tabwemasana and Peak Santo on Santo.

Mn Mu NI NB Bv Gu MI NG Mk RI Te Vu Lo GT

South Melanesian Cuckooshrike
♀
Polynesian Triller
♂
Long-tailed Triller
♂
♀
juvenile
juvenile
vanikorensis immature
Island Thrush
albifrons
efatensis ♂
malekulae
Rusty-winged Starling
Mountain Starling

PLATE 81 : VANUATU PASSERINES IV

White-breasted Woodswallow *Artamus leucorynchus tenuis* Page 365

18 cm. Dark grey with white rump and underparts, and blue-grey bill. Juvenile has brownish bill. Open habitats with scattered trees, including forest gaps. Perches on dead branches or wires and has gliding flight. Fairly common.

Mn Mu NI NB Bv Gu MI NG Mk RI Te Vu Lo GT

Pacific Swallow *Hirundo tahitica subfusca* Page 395

13 cm. Glossy blue-black upperparts, rufous forehead to upper breast, pale dusky underparts and underwing-coverts, and dark undertail-coverts with pale fringes. Forked tail has pointed corners. Immature duller. Open habitats, especially beaches and towns. Fairly common.

Mn Mu NI NB Bv Gu MI NG Mk RI Te Vu Lo GT

Common Myna *Acridotheres tristis* Page 413

25 cm. Blackish-brown with yellow bill and eye-patch, white vent, wing-patches and tail-tip, and long yellow legs. In flight, shows white on primaries and tail. Open habitats, especially grassland and towns. Gregarious. On ground. Common on scattered islands. See flying bird on Plate 69.

Mn Mu NI NB Bv Gu MI NG Mk RI Te Vu Lo GT

House Sparrow *Passer domesticus* Page 419

15 cm. Stocky with heavy bill. Male has grey cap, cheeks and underparts, black bib and brown upperparts with dark stripes and white wing-bar. Female is buffy-brown with paler supercilium, dark stripes on mantle and wings, and white wing-bar. Towns. Gregarious. Common in Port Vila only.

Mn Mu NI NB Bv Gu MI NG Mk RI Te Vu Lo GT

Common Waxbill *Estrilda astrild* Page 420

12 cm. Red bill and eye-mask, greyish upperparts and long pointed tail, paler underparts with fine barring, red belly and black undertail-coverts. Juvenile has black bill, duller eye-mask and less distinct barring. Grassland. Gregarious. Common on Efate.

Mn Mu NI NB Bv Gu MI NG Mk RI Te Vu Lo GT

Blue-faced Parrotfinch *Erythrura trichroa cyanofrons* Page 420

12 cm. Bright grass-green with blue face and rusty-red rump and tail. Juvenile is duller with pale bill and no blue on face. Forest, clearings, gardens and grass lawns. Uncommon. See juvenile on Plate 60.

Mn Mu NI NB Bv Gu MI NG Mk RI Te Vu Lo GT

Royal Parrotfinch *Erythrura regia* Page 421

12 cm. Red hood, rump and tail, blue neck and underparts, and blue-green wings, belly and vent. Female greener. Juvenile duller with grey-blue face. Closed forest, forest edge and large fig trees. Feeds in canopy of fig trees. Uncommon or rare.

Mn Mu NI NB Bv Gu MI NG Mk RI Te Vu Lo GT

Chestnut-breasted Mannikin *Lonchura castaneothorax* Page 423

11 cm. Black face, grey crown, chestnut mantle and wings, golden rump and uppertail, orange breast, black breast-band, white belly and black vent. Juvenile is plain grey-brown with paler underparts and orange wash on breast. Gregarious. Grassland, cultivation and savanna. Rare and local on Santo.

Mn Mu NI NB Bv Gu MI NG Mk RI Te Vu Lo GT

Chestnut Munia *Lonchura atricapilla* Page 422

11 cm. Black hood, chestnut body and wings, and brighter rump and tail. Juvenile is plain buffy-brown, soon becoming darker on head. Grassland, especially long wet grass. Gregarious. Common on Santo, Aore, Malo and Malekula.

Mn Mu NI NB Bv Gu MI NG Mk RI Te Vu Lo GT

Common Redpoll *Carduelis flammea* (not illustrated) Page 425

12 cm. Brown upperparts with dark streaks, two pale wing-bars, black chin, and buffy-white underparts with heavy dark brown streaks. Very short bill, variable red on head and breast, and forked tail. Vagrant.

White-breasted
Woodswallow
Pacific Swallow
Common Myna
♀
adult
House Sparrow
♂
Common Waxbill
juvenile
adult
Royal Parrotfinch
Blue-faced Parrotfinch
juvenile
juvenile
adult
Chestnut Munia
Chestnut-breasted Mannikin

Silvereye *Zosterops lateralis* Page 407

12 cm. Olive upperparts with pale bill, blackish lores, broad white eye-ring, dark grey mantle and scapulars, yellowish-green throat and silvery underparts. Secondary forest and gardens. Fairly common.
Z. l. griseonota (Grande Terre) is mid-grey on upperparts with black lores.
Z. l. melanops (Lifou) is dark grey on upperparts with black head.
Z. l. nigrescens (Maré and Ouvéa) is mid-grey on upperparts with black face.

Mn	Mu	NI	NB	Bv	Gu	MI	NG	Mk	RI	Te	Vu	Lo	GT

Green-backed White-eye *Zosterops xanthochroa* Page 407

11 cm. Dull olive upperparts with broad white eye-ring, greenish-yellow throat, pale grey flanks, yellowish vent, short dark bill and blue-grey legs. Forest, less common in scrub, gardens and parks. Very common on Grand Terre and Maré.

Mn	Mu	NI	NB	Bv	Gu	MI	NG	Mk	RI	Te	Vu	Lo	GT

Large Lifou White-eye *Zosterops inornatus* Page 407

14 cm. Dull olive upperparts and throat with grey mantle, pale grey underparts, large pale pink legs and fairly long heavy dark bill with pink base. Appears dumpy and front-heavy. Forest, especially forest edge. Fairly common on Lifou.

Mn	Mu	NI	NB	Bv	Gu	MI	NG	Mk	RI	Te	Vu	Lo	GT

Small Lifou White-eye *Zosterops minutus* Page 406

10 cm. Olive-green upperparts with yellowish forehead, dark lores, broad white eye-ring, yellow underparts contrasting with silvery flanks, and dark grey legs and short bill. Forest, especially forest edge. Gregarious. Very common on Lifou.

Mn	Mu	NI	NB	Bv	Gu	MI	NG	Mk	RI	Te	Vu	Lo	GT

New Caledonian Myzomela *Myzomela caledonica* Page 360

11 cm. Long fine decurved black bill. Male has scarlet head, back, rump and breast, black wings and tail, and white flanks and belly. Female is grey-brown, with paler underparts, indistinct red wash on forehead and slight red on throat and rump. Forest, savanna and scrub with large trees. Fairly common.

Mn	Mu	NI	NB	Bv	Gu	MI	NG	Mk	RI	Te	Vu	Lo	GT

Cardinal Myzomela *Myzomela cardinalis lifuensis* Page 360

12 cm. Long fine decurved black bill. Male is glossy black with crimson hood. Female is olive-brown with paler underparts and dull red on chin, fore-crown and rump. Immature male has more red. Forest and bushes. Common on Loyalties.

Mn	Mu	NI	NB	Bv	Gu	MI	NG	Mk	RI	Te	Vu	Lo	GT

Fan-tailed Gerygone *Gerygone f. flavolateralis* Page 364

10 cm. Grey head with white supercilium and eyelids, olive upperparts, white spots on tail, white throat and upper breast, and yellow lower breast and belly. Juvenile has browner upperparts, uniformly yellow underparts and no supercilium. Forest and bushes. Restless and vocal. Common.

Mn	Mu	NI	NB	Bv	Gu	MI	NG	Mk	RI	Te	Vu	Lo	GT

griseonota
melanops
nigrescens
Silvereye
Large Lifou
White-eye
Green-backed White-eye
juvenile
Small Lifou
White-eye
♂
♀
Cardinal Myzomela
New Caledonian
Myzomela
♂
adult
Fan-tailed Gerygone
juvenile

PLATE 83: NEW CALEDONIA PASSERINES II

Grey Fantail *Rhipidura albiscapa bulgeri* Page 379

15 cm. Grey upperparts, black breast-band, white throat, short supercilium and ear-covert streak, pale tail-fringes and pale buff underparts. Juvenile is duller and with buff wash. Forest, scrub and savanna. Active with drooped wings and fanned tail. Common.

Mn Mu NI NB Bv Gu MI NG Mk RI Te Vu Lo GT

Streaked Fantail *Rhipidura v. verreauxi* Page 380

17 cm. Grey upperparts, rusty on mantle, with white throat, short supercilium and ear-covert stripe, pale tail-fringes and black spots on pale breast and belly. Forest. Active with drooped wings and fanned tail. Common.

Mn Mu NI NB Bv Gu MI NG Mk RI Te Vu Lo GT

Southern Shrikebill *Clytorhynchus p. pachycephaloides* Page 383

19 cm. Warm brown upperparts, paler underparts, long darker tail with broad white tips, and heavy blue-grey bill. Juvenile has dark brown bill. Forest. Fairly common.

Mn Mu NI NB Bv Gu MI NG Mk RI Te Vu Lo GT

New Caledonian Thicketbird *Megalurulus mariei* Page 399

18 cm. Dark brown upperparts and long tail, with large white supercilium, dark mask, white throat, warm buff breast and long pink legs. Scrub and savanna, especially maquis. Singles and pairs secretive on or near ground. Locally common.

Mn Mu NI NB Bv Gu MI NG Mk RI Te Vu Lo GT

Melanesian Flycatcher *Myiagra c. caledonica* Page 389

14 cm. Male is glossy black with white breast and belly and outer tail-tips. Female has grey head and mantle, silvery eye-ring, browner wings and tail, white tail-corners and orange and white underparts. Juvenile like female but duller with buff fringes on upperparts. Forest and scattered trees. Often pumps tail and sometimes raises crown feathers. Common.

Mn Mu NI NB Bv Gu MI NG Mk RI Te Vu Lo GT

Rufous Whistler *Pachycephala rufiventris* Page 376

15 cm. Male has grey upperparts, black border around white throat, and pale rufous underparts. Female has grey upperparts and fine black streaks on white throat and buff breast and belly. Open forest, savanna and scrub. Common.

Mn Mu NI NB Bv Gu MI NG Mk RI Te Vu Lo GT

Melanesian Whistler *Pachycephala caledonica* Page 373

17 cm. Male has dark hood and breast-band, olive upperparts, white throat and yellow underparts. Female has brownish crown and upperparts, white throat, buffy-yellow underparts and yellow vent. Forest. Common.

P. c. caledonica (Grande Terre): male has grey hood, female buffy underparts.

P. c. littayei (Lifou and Ouvéa): male has black hood, female yellow underparts.

Mn Mu NI NB Bv Gu MI NG Mk RI Te Vu Lo GT

Grey Fantail
Streaked Fantail
Southern Shrikebill
New Caledonian Thicketbird
♀
♂
Melanesian Flycatcher
♀
Rufous Whistler
♂
caledonica
♀
caledonica
♂
littayei
♂
littayei
♀
Melanesian Whistler

South Melanesian Cuckooshrike *Coracina c. caledonica* Page 366

35 cm. Uniformly slaty-grey, blacker around lores and eye, with pale yellow eye and short heavy black bill. Immature has dull eye. Forest and scattered trees. Fairly common on Grande Terre and Lifou.

Mn Mu NI NB Bv Gu MI NG Mk RI Te Vu Lo GT

Black-faced Cuckooshrike *Coracina novaehollandiae* Page 366

33 cm. Pale grey upperparts and breast, darker wings and tail with white tail-tips, black forehead, face and throat, and paler belly. Immature has less defined black patch on ear-coverts only, and finely barred throat and breast. Open habitats with trees. Rare.

Mn Mu NI NB Bv Gu MI NG Mk RI Te Vu Lo GT

New Caledonian Cuckooshrike *Coracina analis* Page 368

28 cm. Dark grey with rufous vent, rufous underwing-coverts often visible at shoulder, heavy dark bill and dark eye. Juvenile is paler with buff wash and black mottling on head and underparts, and buff fringes on wings. Forest, including nearby scrub, in hills and mountains. Fairly common.

Mn Mu NI NB Bv Gu MI NG Mk RI Te Vu Lo GT

Grey-eared Honeyeater *Lichmera i. incana* Page 358

16 cm. Plain grey-brown with long decurved bill, dark grey head with dark skin around eye, silver wash on ear-coverts, olive-brown upperparts with brighter green wing-panel and paler underparts. Juvenile is paler and lacks silver on ear-coverts. Loud and noisy. Open forest and bushes. Common.

Mn Mu NI NB Bv Gu MI NG Mk RI Te Vu Lo GT

Barred Honeyeater *Glycifohia undulata* Page 358

19 cm. Dark brown upperparts with white scales on crown and nape, plainer greener wings, darker ear-coverts, silvery malar stripe, long fine decurved bill and heavy black barring on whitish underparts. Juvenile is duller with only faint barring. Forest and maquis. Fairly common.

Mn Mu NI NB Bv Gu MI NG Mk RI Te Vu Lo GT

Crow Honeyeater *Gymnomyza aubryana* Page 355

39 cm. Glossy black with red naked skin around eye, yellow on bill-base and pinkish-yellow legs. Immature lacks facial skin but has yellow patch on ear-coverts. Loose floppy flight, with long rounded wings, long tail and fairly long neck. Humid forest. Rare and very localised.

Mn Mu NI NB Bv Gu MI NG Mk RI Te Vu Lo GT

New Caledonian Friarbird *Philemon diemenensis* Page 356

28 cm. Dark brown upperparts with long stout bill, pale stripe on ear-coverts, blue-grey fringes on wings and tail, and streaky silvery breast extending over buffy-brown belly. Juvenile lacks streaks on breast and has plainer head. Forest, open habitats with trees and maquis. Fairly common.

Mn Mu NI NB Bv Gu MI NG Mk RI Te Vu Lo GT

Long-tailed Triller *Lalage leucopyga montrosieri* Page 371

17 cm. Male has black upperparts, and white underparts, wing-patch and rump. Female browner. Juvenile browner with pale tips and sometimes bars on underparts. Forest and scattered trees. Fairly common. See Plate 80.

Mn Mu NI NB Bv Gu MI NG Mk RI Te Vu Lo GT

Red-vented Bulbul *Pycnonotus cafer* Page 394

22 cm. Black head and breast, short shaggy crest, brown upperparts with pale scales, dusky spots on lower breast, white belly and red vent. In flight, shows white rump and white tail-tips. Bushes in towns, farms and open forest. Uncommon around Nouméa only.

Mn Mu NI NB Bv Gu MI NG Mk RI Te Vu Lo GT

South Melanesian Cuckooshrike
adult
immature
Black-faced Cuckooshrike
adult
Grey-eared Honeyeater
immature
juvenile
adult
New Caledonian Cuckooshrike
Barred Honeyeater
New Caledonian Friarbird
Crow Honeyeater
Long-tailed Triller
Red-vented Bulbul

PLATE 85: NEW CALEDONIA PASSERINES IV

White-breasted Woodswallow *Artamus leucorynchus melaleucus* Page 365

18 cm. Dark grey with white rump and underparts, and blue-grey bill. Juvenile has brownish bill. Open habitats with scattered trees, including forest gaps. Perches on dead branches or wires and has gliding flight. Fairly common.

Mn	Mu	Nl	NB	Bv	Gu	Ml	NG	Mk	Rl	Te	Vu	Lo	GT

Dusky Woodswallow *Artamus cyanopterus* (not illustrated) Page 365

18 cm. Plain dark smoky-brown with darker mask, blue-grey bill and white streak on grey-blue wings. In flight, shows white underwings and tail-corners. Vagrant.

Yellow-bellied Flyrobin *Microeca flaviventris* Page 393

15 cm. Olive-grey upperparts, grey face, neck and breast, white throat, indistinct dark breast-band, and yellow lower breast and belly. Juvenile is brown with pale buff streaks on upperparts, and soon develops yellow. Wet forest. Often perches on side of tree-trunk. Common.

Mn	Mu	Nl	NB	Bv	Gu	Ml	NG	Mk	Rl	Te	Vu	Lo	GT

Island Thrush *Turdus poliocephalus xanthopus* Page 415

20 cm. Dark warm brown, mottled paler on underparts and white around vent, with yellow bill, legs and eye-ring. Juvenile has pale spots on upperparts and dark spots on paler underparts. Forest. Very rare, perhaps only on Yandé. See other subspecies on Plate 80.

Mn	Mu	Nl	NB	Bv	Gu	Ml	NG	Mk	Rl	Te	Vu	Lo	GT

New Caledonian Crow *Corvus moneduloides* Page 391

41 cm. Glossy black with heavy, slightly upturned black bill and dark eye and legs. Relatively bulky, with broad wings and medium-length tail. Forest and savanna. Flicks wings when perching, like cuckooshrike. Fairly common.

Mn	Mu	Nl	NB	Bv	Gu	Ml	NG	Mk	Rl	Te	Vu	Lo	GT

Striated Starling *Aplonis s. striata* Page 412

18 cm. Male is glossy black with dark brown wings and tail, heavy black bill, and eye varying from red to orange-yellow. Female is pale grey, darker on lores, wings and tail, slightly streaked on throat, and paler on lower breast to vent. Juvenile like female but eye browner. In flight, round-winged and short-tailed. Forest, savanna and gardens. Common.
A. s. atronitens (Loyalties): female is darker, sometimes much darker grey with greenish gloss.

Mn	Mu	Nl	NB	Bv	Gu	Ml	NG	Mk	Rl	Te	Vu	Lo	GT

Common Myna *Acridotheres tristis* Page 365

25 cm. Blackish-brown with yellow bill and eye-patch, white vent, wing-patches and tail-tip, and long yellow legs. In flight, shows white on primaries and tail. Open habitats, especially grassland and towns. Gregarious. On ground. Common. See flying bird on Plate 69

Mn	Mu	Nl	NB	Bv	Gu	Ml	NG	Mk	Rl	Te	Vu	Lo	GT

Common Starling *Sturnus vulgaris* (not illustrated) Page 413

21 cm. Dumpy glossy black bird with variable creamy spotting and fringes, dark eye, short tail and medium-long fine pointed bill. Feeds on short grassland, in bushes and in trees, often in towns. Vagrant.

White-breasted Woodswallow
juvenile
adult
Yellow-bellied Flyrobin
Island Thrush
New Caledonian Crow
striata
♂
striata
♀
Striated Starling
atronitens
♀
Common Myna

Pacific Swallow *Hirundo tahitica subfusca*

Page 395

13 cm. Glossy blue-black upperparts, rufous forehead to upper breast, pale dusky underparts and underwing-coverts, and dark undertail-coverts with pale fringes. Forked tail has pointed corners. Immature duller. Open habitats, especially beaches and towns. Fairly common on Ouvéa (Loyalties).

Mn	Mu	NI	NB	Bv	Gu	MI	NG	Mk	RI	Te	Vu	Lo	GT

Welcome Swallow *Hirundo neoxena*

Page 395

15 cm. Glossy blue-black upperparts, chestnut forehead to upper breast, pale dusky underparts and underwing-coverts, and dark undertail-coverts with pale fringes. Forked tail has small white spots near tip and long streamers. Immature is duller with no streamers. Open habitats, especially grassland and fresh water. Uncommon on New Caledonia.

Mn	Mu	NI	NB	Bv	Gu	MI	NG	Mk	RI	Te	Vu	Lo	GT

Tree Martin *Petrochelidon nigricans*

Page 396

13 cm. Blue-black upperparts with off-white rump, rufous forehead, buffy-white underparts and notched tail. Immature is duller. Open habitats, especially forest edge. Rare.

Mn	Mu	NI	NB	Bv	Gu	MI	NG	Mk	RI	Te	Vu	Lo	GT

House Sparrow *Passer domesticus*

Page 419

15 cm. Stocky with heavy bill. Male has grey cap, cheeks and underparts, black bib and brown upperparts with dark stripes and white wing-bar. Female is buffy-brown with paler supercilium, dark stripes on mantle and wings, and white wing-bar. Towns and farms. Gregarious. Common.

Mn	Mu	NI	NB	Bv	Gu	MI	NG	Mk	RI	Te	Vu	Lo	GT

Common Waxbill *Estrilda astrild*

Page 420

12 cm. Red bill and eye-mask, greyish upperparts and long pointed tail, paler underparts with fine barring, red belly-patch and black undertail-coverts. Juvenile has black bill, duller eye-mask and less distinct barring. Grassland, especially tall wet grassland. Gregarious. Common.

Mn	Mu	NI	NB	Bv	Gu	MI	NG	Mk	RI	Te	Vu	Lo	GT

Red-throated Parrotfinch *Erythrura psittacea*

Page 421

12 cm. Plain grass-green with red face-patch, rump and long tail. Juvenile is duller with green head and pale bill. Forest edge, scrub and grassy habitats. Feed on ground, in bushes and forest canopy. Common.

Mn	Mu	NI	NB	Bv	Gu	MI	NG	Mk	RI	Te	Vu	Lo	GT

Blue-faced Parrotfinch *Erythrura trichroa cyanofrons*

Page 420

12 cm. Bright grass-green with blue face and rusty-red rump and tail. Juvenile is duller with pale bill and no blue on face. Forest, clearings, gardens and grass lawns. Uncommon on Loyalties. See juvenile on Plate 60.

Mn	Mu	NI	NB	Bv	Gu	MI	NG	Mk	RI	Te	Vu	Lo	GT

Chestnut-breasted Mannikin *Lonchura castaneothorax*

Page 423

11 cm. Black face, grey crown, chestnut mantle and wings, golden rump and uppertail, orange breast, black breast-band, white belly and black vent. Juvenile is plain grey-brown with paler underparts and orange wash on breast. Gregarious. Grassland, cultivation and savanna. Fairly common.

Mn	Mu	NI	NB	Bv	Gu	MI	NG	Mk	RI	Te	Vu	Lo	GT

Pacific Swallow
Welcome Swallow
Tree Martin
House Sparrow
♀
♂
Common Waxbill
juvenile
adult
Red-throated
Parrotfinch
adult
juvenile
Blue-faced
Parrotfinch
adult
immature
Chestnut-breasted Mannikin

CASSOWARIES Casuariidae

Cassowaries are huge thickset flightless birds which are often hunted and sometimes kept as pets or reared for meat. Often detected by their large footprints and faecal mounds full of fruit stones.

DWARF CASSOWARY *Casuarius bennetti* — Plate 10

(Casoar de Bennett)

Description 105 cm. Huge dark flightless bird. Adult is glossy black with a low rounded helmet, bright blue neck and bright red on hindneck. Female is larger and more brightly coloured. Juvenile is small and pale brown, initially with about four broad dark brown stripes on back, then becoming plain warm or dark brown, and attaining adult colours after about two years. Three large toes leave distinctive footprints.

Similar species Adult is much larger than any other terrestrial bird. When seen or heard running away, may be confused with pigs. Chick differs from Melanesian Megapode by larger size, striped when small, then paler and plainer plumage, and usually seen with an adult.

Voice Very deep booms and grunts; much deeper than other birds.

Habits Forest from coast to mountaintops, especially in hills and lower mountains, but rarer and shy where hunted. Usually solitary but small juveniles are tended by the adult male. Booming display given with bill pointing between legs.

Conservation status Rare. Locally threatened by hunting. IUCN: Near Threatened.

Range New Britain, where probably introduced prehistorically and now widely distributed. Elsewhere, occurs across New Guinea and Yapen I.

MEGAPODES (SCRUBFOWL) Megapodiidae

Megapodes or scrubfowl are dumpy ground birds which forage by scratching the leaf-litter with strong feet. Nest sites range from single birds laying in rotting vegetation to thousands of birds congregating at communal nest grounds in volcanically heated soil or sand. Highly dispersive, flying long distances with slow strong wing-beats interspersed with glides, usually at night, and colonising tiny isolated islands. Chicks are independent and able to fly at hatching but often nocturnal and rarely seen.

MELANESIAN MEGAPODE *Megapodius eremita* — Plate 10

(Melanesian Scrubfowl; Mégapode mélanésien)

Description 34 cm. Fat grey-brown ground bird with large feet, thin neck and slight crest. Dark warm brown mantle and wings and dark grey head, neck and underparts. Naked skin on face and bill has variable extent and amounts of blue-grey, orange, red and pink, and yellow bill-tip. Legs are dull grey, brown or olive. Female is slightly brighter and browner. Chick is dark brown, paler on cheeks and underparts, with fine barring on upperparts. Immature is darker and plainer.

Similar species Distinctive dumpy shape, scratching habits, short stout legs, red facial skin and crest. Differs from immature Purple Swamphen by facial colours, crest, dark undertail and dumpier shape. Differs from ground pigeons by shorter tail and upright posture, especially when alarmed. From rails by stockier shape with shorter neck and legs. When flushed, differs from Purple Swamphen by faster flight, climbing more steeply upwards, and from immature Nicobar Pigeon by crest and longer, trailing legs. Chicks differ from small crakes by plain brown plumage.

Voice Varied, most commonly a repeated wailing upslurred *kee-oow?*, or upslurred then downslurred *keee-ah* or *kee-ee-ah*. Chicken-like chuckles *poo-er, poo-er....* Low grunting *ko—ko—ko—*.

Habits Forest, often heavily degraded forest and thickets, from sea-level to at least 1500 m. Especially common around nesting grounds in volcanically heated soils or decomposing vegetation. Singles, pairs and small groups forage on forest floor. When flushed, flies heavily and noisily with broad rounded wings and trailing legs, steeply upwards, often perching high to look back at observer.

Conservation status Fairly common. Largest nesting grounds on New Britain may host tens of thousands of birds. Often common on smallest islands but uncommon on large non-volcanic islands. Often hunted, eggs over-collected, and locally declining. Not threatened.

Range Endemic across Admiralties, St Matthias Is, Bismarcks and Solomons, from Ninigo to Santa Ana including smallest islands but not Rennell or Temotu, where subfossil bones may relate to this or another species. Eastern birds are paler and more rufous and have been separated as subspecies *M. e. brenchleyi*. Birds of Long and Umboi show some characters of New Guinea Scrubfowl *M. decollatus*, which is paler, browner, longer-crested, with different bare-part colours and calls, and intergrades occur on Karkar.

VANUATU MEGAPODE *Megapodius layardi* Plate 10

(New Hebrides Scrubfowl; Skrab Dak: Namalau; Mégapode de Layard)

Description 32 cm. Dark chicken-like ground bird with large feet and thin neck. Sooty brown with bright red naked facial skin and bright yellow legs. Female is duller, especially legs. Chick is dark brown, paler on cheeks and underparts, with fine barring on upperparts. Immature is darker and plainer.
Similar species Adult has distinctive yellow legs and red facial skin contrasting with blackish plumage. Also differs from Red Junglefowl by dumpier shape, shorter tail and darker, more uniform plumage. From immature Purple Swamphen by dark undertail and dumpier shape. From ground pigeons by shorter tail and stands alert rather than crouching when alarmed. When flushed, differs from Purple Swamphen by stronger flight, usually steeply upwards. Chick differs from crakes and Red Junglefowl chick by plainer brown plumage, and is independent of adults unlike junglefowl.
Voice Loud wailing upslurred *ko-wah* followed by a descending series of *wo-wo-wo-* quacks. Repeated *took-tooorrrr*, trailing off in volume.
Habits Forest, rarely logged forest, and absent from other habitats except coastal vegetation adjacent to coastal nesting grounds. Singles, pairs and small groups forage on forest floor, sometimes alongside Red Junglefowl, from sea-level to c.800 m, at higher altitudes more often in valleys. Often shy, running away when disturbed or flushing with rounded wings and trailing legs.
Conservation status Varies in abundance, usually uncommon and localised but may be abundant close to communal nesting grounds. Threatened by habitat loss and over-collection of eggs. IUCN: Vulnerable.
Range Endemic to Vanuatu. Breeds on most islands from Torres Is to Efate. Appears to be extinct on Tanna.

PHEASANTS Phasianidae

Fat ground birds with a short bill, head and neck, foraging by scratching on the ground. Similar to megapodes but pairs nest singly and rear their chicks. Fly heavily with noisy whirring wing-beats interspersed with glides. Forest species fly up to roost in trees. Turkeys are very large species introduced from America. Quail are tiny short-tailed grassland birds. Junglefowl, pheasant and peafowl are familiar introduced species, males often with ornate plumage and long tails.

WILD TURKEY *Meleagris gallopavo* (not illustrated)

(Dindon sauvage)

Description Male 110 cm; female 85 cm. Huge ground bird with long drooping tail. Plumage is dark brown with green, bronze and chestnut gloss, and fine black and white barring. Legs and throat are pink, rest of naked head is blue-grey. Male has larger red wattle on throat and hanging tuft on breast. Juvenile is dark brown, including head, with buff tips but lacks the metallic gloss.
Similar species Larger than any other ground bird except Indian Peafowl, from which it differs by glossy black plumage and lack of crest.
Voice Male territorial call is a loud liquid gobbling, given when strutting with drooped wings and fanned tail. Sharp yelping *keow, keow*. Liquid *cluk-cluk*. Various other yelps, barks, purrs, croaks, hisses and trills.
Habits Open forest, savanna, and nearby fields and farmland in lowlands. Small groups, often with one male, forage on the ground.
Range Introduced to Grande Terre, New Caledonia, in 1966, where fairly common along the west coast. Elsewhere, native in North America and established in a few countries including Hawaii and New Zealand.

KING QUAIL *Excalfactoria chinensis* Plate 18

(Blue-breasted/Painted/Chinese/Asian Blue Quail; *Coturnix chinensis*; Caille peinte)

Description 13 cm. Very small fat ground bird. Male is dark with black-and-white-striped throat, blue-grey head, breast and flanks, chestnut belly and vent, mottled brown upperparts and yellow feet. Female is warm brown, mottled grey and black on upperparts, paler unmarked throat and fine black bars on underparts. Juvenile as female but underparts are more spotted. In flight, shows uniform brown upperwing and sometimes trails yellow feet.
Similar species Differs from Red-backed Buttonquail by shorter, uniformly brown wings and distinctive male plumage and calls. Differs from crakes and rails by dumpy shape, short neck, short legs and whirring flight.
Voice Quiet hoarse rasping descending *khrooooo* similar to first half of Red-bellied Pitta call. Mewing *keeow*. Quiet hoarse chattering *chu-chu-chu-* when flushed.

Habits Dense dry or damp but not wet grassland, including weedy gardens. Pairs and small groups skulk and are usually only seen when crossing roads or paths, or when flushed, flying fast and low with rapid wing-beats and gliding back to ground.
Conservation status Inexplicably rare with only a few recent records, from New Britain and New Ireland, and may be threatened. Not globally threatened.
Range *C. c. lepida* is endemic to Bismarcks, including Lavongai, New Ireland, Tabar, Lihir, Tanga, New Britain, Watom and Duke of York; has a smaller area of chestnut on belly than New Guinea and Australian subspecies. Elsewhere, other subspecies breed from India to New Guinea and Australia.

RED JUNGLEFOWL *Gallus gallus* — Plate 10

(Coq bankiva)

Description Male 70 cm; female 44 cm. Ancestor of familiar domestic chickens. Melanesian birds are rather variable, perhaps indicating ongoing interbreeding with domestic chickens. Adult male is brightly coloured with long drooping tail, red comb and wattle, and iridescent golden, maroon and green plumage. Female and immature are variable but usually dark brown with buff and black streaks and bars on upperparts, paler plainer underparts, medium-long blackish tail, red or pinkish naked face and greyish legs. Chick is buff with prominent dark and pale stripes on crown and mantle.
Similar species Told from domestic chicken by shy behaviour, forest use, different call and male plumage. Female differs from Vanuatu Megapode by paler plumage, longer tail and bare-part colours; from female Common Pheasant by shorter blackish tail and pink facial skin.
Voice Crowing of male similar to domestic chicken but higher-pitched and with quieter final notes *kokaah-rah-hooo*. Variable clucks, often with terminal flourish: *cluk-cluk-cluk-cluk, clu-eerk!* Alarm call a sharp *gwark!*
Habits Lowland forest, especially secondary forest and thickets, to 500 m. Pairs and small groups turn over leaf-litter. Shy, especially where hunted, but emerges into open habitats in early morning. When flushed, flies off heavily, not trailing legs and usually landing distantly on ground.
Conservation status Fairly common, but usually rare where hunted. All Melanesian populations are feral from historical introductions and probably interbreed with domestic chickens. Not threatened.
Range Introduced across Temotu and Vanuatu, where established on Nendo, Utupua and across Vanuatu and Ile des Pins but probably extinct elsewhere on New Caledonia. Free-ranging, escaped and temporarily established chickens may occur on any inhabited island. Recently recorded on Ninigo and Hermit Is, where of unknown origin. Elsewhere, native birds breed patchily in India and South-East Asia, and feral birds are established in many scattered countries including Polynesia.

COMMON PHEASANT *Phasianus colchicus* — (not illustrated)

(Ring-necked Pheasant; Faisan de Colchide)

Description Male 84 cm; female 58 cm. Large long-tailed chicken-like bird. Rich buff with fine black mottling on body and black bars on very long tail. Male is brighter with large red wattles, dark green head and neck and usually a white neck-ring. Juvenile as female but duller and initially shorter-tailed and smaller.
Similar species Long straight tail is distinctive. Young juveniles differ from female Red Junglefowl by barred brown tail and lack of pink facial skin.
Voice Male territorial call is a loud explosive crowing *korkk korkk, KO, OK korkk-kok*, often followed by wing-whirring. Alarm call a loud *gog-OK, gog-OK…*
Habits Dense understorey or thickets, often in drier forest and scrub, foraging in nearby fields and grassland. Singles and small groups forage on ground and flush with explosive whirring of wings and rapid flight.
Conservation status Fairly common non-native. Not threatened.
Range Introduced to New Caledonia, where widespread on the west coast of Grande Terre. Elsewhere, native across central Eurasia and introduced patchily to North America, Europe and Pacific.

INDIAN PEAFOWL *Pavo cristatus* — (not illustrated)

(Common Peacock; Blue Peacock; Paon bleu)

Description Male 200 cm; female 95 cm. Very large long-tailed ground bird with white facial markings and fan-shaped crest. Male has bright green tail of long uppertail-coverts with large eye patterns, blue head, neck and breast, and black-and-white barring and rufous on wings. Female has green wash on neck, finely barred breast, white belly and uniform grey-brown upperparts with rufous on wings. Immature and non-breeding males have a shorter tail but retain bright neck and breast.

Similar species Male tail is unmistakable. Moulting and immature male have shorter tail but distinctive plumage and crest. Female is larger than any other ground bird except Wild Turkey from which it differs by its white belly and crest.
Voice Loud mournful trumpeting *kee-ow!*, repeated several times. Faster *ka-an* repeated 6–8 times. Alarm call *kok-kok*.
Habits Forest, forest edge and adjacent grassland. Singles and small groups, often flocks of males, forage on ground. Rarely flies, except to roost high in trees.
Conservation status Uncommon and local non-native. Not threatened.
Range Introduced to New Caledonia where small scattered populations appear to be established in the west of Grande Terre. Elsewhere, native in Indian subcontinent and established patchily elsewhere in world.

DUCKS Anatidae

Familiar gregarious waterbirds occurring on or beside fresh water, usually lakes. Whistling ducks *Dendrocygna* often perch in trees or graze waterside grass and call frequently in their distinctive hunch-backed, drooped-neck flight. Dabbling ducks *Anas* usually dabble, up-end or graze in shallows and many show 'speculum' of brightly coloured secondaries in flight. Males often have bright breeding plumage, and a brief female-like 'eclipse' post-breeding plumage. Diving ducks *Aythya* dive in deeper water. Other migratory species may be expected as vagrants.

SPOTTED WHISTLING DUCK *Dendrocygna guttata* Plate 1

(Spotted Tree-Duck; Dendrocygne tacheté)

Description 43 cm. Brown duck with greyer face, darker cap and upperparts, small white spots on neck and breast, large white spots on flanks and dark red-brown legs. Spots are sometimes obscured on swimming birds and are less distinct, more streaked, on juveniles. In flight, has typical broad plain dark wings, drooped neck and hunched back of whistling ducks. Rump is usually plain dark brown but sometimes has narrow white bar.
Similar species Differs from other whistling ducks by large rounded spots on flanks and, in flight, plainer rump, shorter straighter neck and shorter foot-projection.
Voice Nasal whistled *zheou*, often repeated as a series of three notes, the last higher-pitched. Sometimes given as a long series of whistles.
Habits Freshwater marshes and lakes, usually around vegetated margins. Occurs in pairs or small flocks, often mixed with other ducks. Grazes short grass, swims, dabbles and often perches in trees, even inside open canopy.
Conservation status Locally fairly common and probably not threatened.
Range New Britain and Umboi where widespread in suitable habitat. A few records from Bougainville and a report from New Ireland. Elsewhere, breeds in Philippines, east Indonesia and New Guinea.

PLUMED WHISTLING DUCK *Dendrocygna eytoni* Plate 1

(Plumed/Grass Tree-Duck; Dendrocygne d'Eyton)

Description 51 cm. Pale brown duck with long buff flank-plumes which project over the wings, pink legs, pink on bill and pale eye. In flight, shape as other whistling ducks and shows narrow white rump-band, pale underwings and white on lower belly and undertail-coverts. Immature is duller with less distinct breast-bars.
Similar species Pale bare parts are distinctive. Differs from other whistling ducks by having few large flank-plumes and greyer, paler plumage.
Voice Single whistles, and twittering series of whistles.
Habits Grazes waterside grass, and dabbles and up-ends in freshwater lakes and marshes.
Range Single records from Makira, Rennell and Grande Terre, New Caledonia. Breeds in Australia and a rare vagrant elsewhere.

WANDERING WHISTLING DUCK *Dendrocygna arcuata* Plate 1

(Wandering/Water Tree-Duck; Dendrocygne à lunules)

Description 48 cm (*D. a. pygmaea* = 41 cm). Reddish-brown duck with dark cap, paler neck, short creamy-white flank-plumes and black legs. In flight, has typical broad plain dark wings, drooped neck and hunched back of whistling ducks and shows white rump, chestnut upperwing-coverts and dark underwing. Immature is duller.
Similar species Differs from other whistling ducks by redder plumage with short flank-plumes. In flight, has chestnut upperwing-coverts and dark underwing.
Voice A single whistle or a rapid series of high-pitched twitters.

Habits Lakes and swamps. Gregarious. Grazes, swims, dabbles, up-ends and dives. Sometimes perches in open or dead trees.
Conservation status *D. a. pygmaea* is rare and threatened, possibly close to extinction. The species is not globally threatened.
Range Umboi, New Britain and New Caledonia.
D. a. pygmaea breeds on New Britain and probably Umboi (subspecific identity unknown). Elsewhere, occurred in Fiji where extinct. Differs from other subspecies by small size.
D. a. australis, recorded several times as a vagrant on Grande Terre, New Caledonia, breeds in Australia and New Guinea, and elsewhere *D. a. arcuata* breeds in Philippines and Indonesia.

[CANADA GOOSE *Branta canadensis*]

(Bernache du Canada)

Description 110 cm. A large brown waterbird with black head and neck contrasting with broad white chin-stripe.
Similar species The only goose known from Melanesia but beware other species escaped from captivity and domestic geese.
Habits Flocks graze on short grassland, usually close to lakes, often in artificial habitats and tolerant of humans.
Range Occasional records on Grande Terre, New Caledonia, are probably escaped birds but possibly vagrants from the feral New Zealand population of mixed subspecies. Elsewhere, breeds in North America and introduced to north-west Europe and New Zealand.

MALLARD *Anas platyrhynchos* — Plate 2

(Canard colvert)

Description 58 cm. Large duck with brightly coloured male. Breeding male has yellow bill, bottle-green head, purple-brown breast, grey back and belly and black around the tail. In flight, shows blue speculum on upperwing secondaries. Female is warm brown, finely streaked darker, with pale supercilium, fine dark eye-stripe, and dull orange bill and legs. Eclipse male usually retains yellow bill and hints of breeding plumage. Juvenile as female but has darker bill and is more streaked. Often interbreeds with domestic ducks to produce ducks of a variety of shapes and plumages, often with white feathering.
Similar species Breeding male is distinctive. Female is similar to many female vagrant ducks and Grey Teal but blue speculum is distinctive. Differs from Pacific Black Duck by paler, warmer plumage, orange bare parts, blue speculum, less contrasting head pattern and no dark chin-stripe. However, hybridises with Pacific Black Duck, the offspring usually showing less contrasting facial pattern than Pacific Black Duck, and duller speculum and bare-part colours than Mallard.
Voice Quacking similar to Pacific Black Duck.
Habits On or near fresh water, often in artificial habitats such as urban parks, and tolerant of human disturbance. Pairs or small flocks dabble and up-end in water and graze on grass.
Conservation status Locally fairly common and increasing introduced species. An estimated population of 150 plus 500 hybrids in New Caledonia in 2002. Not threatened.
Range Introduced to New Caledonia where localised around Nouméa, Moindou and Koumac, and on Tanna, Vanuatu. Has also occurred as a vagrant from feral population on Norfolk I. Introduced and escaped birds are possible close to any urban area. Elsewhere, breeds across the temperate Eurasia and Americas, and introduced to Australia and New Zealand.

PACIFIC BLACK DUCK *Anas superciliosa* — Plate 2

(Canard à sourcils)

Description 53 cm. The common large duck of Melanesia. Mottled dark brown plumage with very dark brown and pale buff stripes on face. Has grey bill and dirty yellow legs and feet. In flight, shows green speculum on the inner upperwing, which sometimes appears dark blue, and white underwing. Female has slightly more contrasting pale fringes on body and wing-coverts. Juvenile has more streaked underparts.
Similar species Distinctive head pattern and white underwing. See Mallard, with which it hybridises in New Caledonia. See female vagrant ducks.
Voice Single *quack* or series of quacks. Often calls when flushed.
Habits Rivers, ponds, swamps, estuaries and mangroves, including very small areas of water and within forest, but less common on large lakes. Pairs or small flocks dabble in shallow water and are often seen flying between small wetlands.

Conservation status Fairly common but locally threatened by hunting and by hybridisation with Mallard on New Caledonia.
Range Across Melanesia. Extinct on Rennell and absent from many small and remote islands lacking suitable habitat, such as Nissan, Ulawa, many islands in Temotu and Vanuatu, Lifou and Maré. Elsewhere, *A. s. pelewensis* breeds in north New Guinea and Polynesia, and other subspecies breed in Indonesia, Australia and New Zealand.

AUSTRALASIAN SHOVELER *Anas rhynchotis* Plate 2

(Canard bride)

Description 50 cm. Large duck with long heavy dark grey bill and yellow-orange legs. Male has white crescent on grey-blue head, rich rufous breast and belly mottled black, and white patch on rear flanks. In flight, shows pale blue upperwing-coverts and green speculum. Female is dull brown, mottled darker, with duller feet than similar eclipse-plumage male.
Similar species Breeding male is distinctive. Upperwing pattern is similar only to Garganey and Northern Shoveler. Massive bill is shared only by Northern Shoveler. Female differs from Northern Shoveler by darker plumage, uniformly dark grey bill and lacks white on outer tail feathers. Female differs from Garganey by plain head pattern.
Habits Often swims with hunched neck; feeds by sweeping bill from side to side. Usually mixed with other ducks on larger, well-vegetated lakes.
Range Rare vagrant to New Caledonia. Elsewhere, resident in Australia and New Zealand.

NORTHERN SHOVELER *Anas clypeata* Plate 2

(Canard souchet)

Description 50cm. Large duck with long heavy bill and yellow-orange legs. Breeding male has greenish-black head, dark upperparts, white underparts and rich rufous flanks. In flight, shows pale blue upperwing-coverts and green speculum. Female is dull mottled brown, with duller feet than similar eclipse male.
Similar species Breeding male is distinctive. Upperwing pattern is similar only to Garganey and Australasian Shoveler. Massive bill is shared only by Australasian Shoveler. Female differs from Australasian Shoveler by paler plumage, duller greyer legs and feet, and some white on outer tail feathers; dark grey bill often has dull orange at base of cutting edges.
Habits As Australasian Shoveler.
Range One record from New Britain. Breeds in northern Eurasia and disperses south to tropical Asia in September–April with occasional vagrants to Australia.

GREY TEAL *Anas gracilis* Plate 2

(Also treated as a subspecies of Sunda Teal *Anas gibberifrons*; Sarcelle australasienne)

Description 39 cm. Small grey-brown duck. Grey-brown plumage, with paler mottling and fringes, slightly darker cap and paler face and throat. In flight, inner upperwing has broad white bar, dark green speculum and narrow white trailing edge, and the underwing has short white wedge. Female is paler with duller eye. Juvenile is paler still.
Similar species Differs from all other ducks by smaller size, wing pattern and plainer face. From whistling ducks, which also have plain face, by shorter neck and greyer plumage. See grebes.
Voice Female gives a rapid laughing series of quacks. Male gives soft clear *peep* and grunting whistle *gdeeoo*.
Habits Flocks dabble in shallow lakes, sometimes mixed with Pacific Black Ducks.
Conservation status Common on New Caledonia, rare in Vanuatu and extinct on Rennell. Threatened locally by hunting but not globally threatened.
Range Vanuatu and New Caledonia.
A. g. gracilis breeds in Vanuatu, where recorded from Aore, Epi, Efate and Tanna, and New Caledonia, where recorded from Grande Terre, and is a rare vagrant to New Britain. Elsewhere, breeds in Australia and New Zealand, and rarely in New Guinea.
A. g. remissa, endemic to Rennell but extinct, was much smaller with darker buff underparts.

[BROWN TEAL *Anas chlorotis*]

(Sarcelle de Nouvelle-Zélande)

Description 42 cm. Small duck with narrow white eye-ring. Breeding male has dark glossy green head, red-brown breast and belly and grey bare parts. Female is uniformly dark brown with paler fringes. In flight, the inner upperwing

has dark green speculum bordered by white, and the underwing has short white wedge.
Similar species Female differs from Grey Teal by eye-ring, darker, warmer brown plumage without paler throat, and less white on upperwing. Both sexes differ from Chestnut Teal *A. castanea*, an Australian species not recorded in Melanesia, by the white eye-ring.
Range Two records from New Caledonia in 1961–2 were possibly escaped or introduced. Breeds in New Zealand where rare and sedentary, and wild birds are unlikely to reach Melanesia.

NORTHERN PINTAIL *Anas acuta* Plate 2

(Canard pilet)

Description 54 cm (plus up to 12 cm tail). Elegant long-necked duck with pointed tail. In flight, shows green speculum and narrow white trailing edge on upperwing and dusky striped underwing. Breeding male has dark head, white neck and breast, greyish upperparts and flanks, long pointed tail and dark grey bare parts. Female is pale grey-brown, finely scalloped and finely barred darker, with whiter belly and much shorter pointed tail.
Similar species Breeding male is distinctive. Female differs from other ducks by long neck, shared only with whistling ducks, from which told by greyer plumage, wing pattern and white belly. From Grey Teal by larger size and lack of white on upperwing-coverts. From Pacific Black Duck by paler plumage, plain face and brownish underwings. See other female vagrant ducks.
Habits Up-ends and grazes in shallow fresh water.
Range Single records from Umboi and Bougainville. Breeds in temperate Northern Hemisphere and disperses south to tropical Asia in September–April.

GARGANEY *Anas querquedula* Plate 2

(Sarcelle d'été)

Description 40 cm. Small duck. In flight, shows pale blue lesser upperwing-coverts, white wing-bar, green speculum and white trailing edge. Breeding male has reddish-brown head and breast with long curved white supercilium and grey-striped flanks. Female is warm brown, mottled and fringed paler, with dark cap and nape, pale spot at bill-base, dark eye-stripe and dark cheek-stripe.
Similar species Breeding male is distinctive. Differs from Grey Teal by striped face and wing pattern; from other ducks by small size. Female face pattern is more contrasting than other ducks except Pacific Black Duck; smaller and paler than latter with less contrasting facial stripes and pale blue wing-coverts. Blue wing-coverts shared only with shovelers, from which differs by smaller size and bill and different head pattern.
Habits Usually hides in emergent waterside vegetation in swamps and shallow lakes.
Range Single records from New Ireland and New Britain. Breeds in northern Eurasia and disperses south in August–May, occasionally to New Guinea and Australia.

HARDHEAD *Aythya australis* Plate 1

(White-eyed Duck; Fuligule austral)

Description 52 cm. Rich chestnut or chocolate-coloured diving duck with white undertail-coverts. In flight, shows broad white upperwing-bar, white underwings with narrow black margins and white belly and undertail patches. Male has white eye and blue-grey bill with paler subterminal band. Female is duller, paler brown with dark eye and less contrasting bill pattern. Immature is slightly paler than female.
Similar species Distinctive plain warm brown plumage, peaked head shape and frequent diving. See Tufted Duck and grebes.
Voice Usually silent. Male has soft whistle. Female has harsh rattle.
Habits Large lakes. Small flocks usually rest during day or dive; keeps further out on deeper lakes than other ducks. Flies low over water on take-off and rarely seen out of water.
Conservation status Localised and uncommon resident breeder, locally threatened by hunting and habitat loss. Locally threatened in Melanesia but not globally threatened.
Range Vanuatu and New Caledonia, from Banks Is to Tanna, where sometimes separated as smaller endemic subspecies *A. a. extima*, and on Grande Terre. Elsewhere, breeds in Australia and sometimes disperses to east Indonesia, New Guinea and New Zealand, where has bred.

TUFTED DUCK *Aythya fuligula* — Plate 1

(Fuligule morillon)

Description 44 cm. Black and white or brown diving duck with distinctive crest which is variable and sometimes apparently absent. In flight, shows broad white upperwing-bar, white underwings with narrow grey margins and white belly. Male is glossy purple-black with long drooping crest, pure white flanks and belly, yellow eye and pale grey bill with black tip. Immature and eclipse male duller, with shorter crest and grey wash on flanks. Female is blackish-brown with paler brown flanks and short tufted crest, sometimes with white around bill-base and on undertail-coverts.
Similar species Distinctive crest and white or pale flanks. Female and immature differ from Hardhead, the only other Melanesian diving duck, by darker, duller plumage, usually a suggestion of crest on nape, and less white on upperwing.
Habits As Hardhead.
Range One record from New Britain. Breeds in northern Eurasia, and disperses in September–April south to tropical Asia.

ALBATROSSES Diomedeidae

These largest seabirds are usually seen gliding effortlessly on long narrow wings or sat on the sea, often behind fishing boats. Three species breed in the north Pacific and many more in southern oceans. Six species have been recorded as vagrants to Melanesia, often as banding recoveries from dead birds, but other species are to be expected. There are unconfirmed recent records of Black-footed Albatross from north of the Bismarcks. Identification is often difficult, especially the immature plumages.

LAYSAN ALBATROSS *Phoebastria immutabilis* — (not illustrated)

(Albatros de Laysan)

Description 80 cm (wingspan 220 cm). Small albatross, but still much larger than other common Melanesian seabirds. Dark upperwing and mantle, extending onto upper rump, and dark terminal tail-band. White head, underparts and rump, with dark eye-patch, some faint grey below eye and heavy pink bill with darker bluish tip. Underwing has narrow dark margins with variable amount of dark extending onto white central panel. Immature is similar but has duller bill and more dark on rump.
Similar species Differs from Campbell Albatross and other small albatross species, not yet recorded from Melanesia, by dark back extending beyond wings, blue-tipped pink bill and often dark markings on central underwing.
Habits All Melanesian records have been recoveries of banded birds.
Conservation status IUCN: Near Threatened.
Range Rare vagrant, with single records from Manus and Makira. Breeds in Hawaii and off Japan and Mexico, and disperses across the north Pacific.

WANDERING ALBATROSS *Diomedea exulans* — Plate 3

(Snowy Albatross; Albatros hurleur)

Description 125 cm (wingspan 300 cm). Huge seabird with very long black and white wings. Underwings are always white with black flight feathers showing as black tips and narrow trailing edge, and a very large plain pink bill. Adult has white upper body with variable amount of white extending along wing-coverts onto otherwise black wings. Juvenile has dark brown head, body and upperwings, with white face and underwings. In transition immature plumages to adult, body becomes white, then white spreads onto upperwing-coverts from centre of upperwing.
Similar species Very like (Southern) Royal Albatross, especially in some immature plumages but, at very close range, unmarked pink bill is distinctive as Royal Albatross has dark cutting edges. Some adults differ by having some fine black scaling or barring on head and body or retaining some dark feathers on crown and tail. Immature differs by dark on body, which is all white in Royal except some mottling on upperparts, and white developing first on central upperwing, whereas white first develops on leading edge of Royal. Immature differs from smaller albatrosses by larger size and longer wings; young immature has dark underparts, and always lacks black leading margin to underwing. Immature differs from giant petrels by much longer wings, smaller body and largely white underwing and face. Very similar to Antipodean Albatross *D. antipodensis*, not yet recorded from Melanesia but breeds off New Zealand and disperses to south-east Australia and north of New Zealand.
Habits Usually solitary at sea, often following ships.

Conservation status IUCN: Vulnerable.
Range Rare vagrant, with records from New Caledonia and a report at sea off Vanuatu. One specimen reported as *D. (e.) exulans*. Breeds on sub-Antarctic islands and wanders across seas south of the tropics.

NORTHERN ROYAL ALBATROSS *Diomedea sanfordi* — Plate 3

(Albatros royal)

Description 115 cm (wingspan 320 cm). Huge seabird with white body and mantle, and very long black upperwings. Adult is white with black upperwings, black tips and very narrow trailing edge on underwings, and very large pink bill with black cutting edges. Juvenile has some dark mottling on upperparts and narrow terminal tail-band.
Similar species Differs from very similar Wandering Albatross by black cutting edges to bill and adult always has pure white head and body. Juvenile differs by unmarked black upperwings and dark on body restricted to mantle and narrow tail-band. All differ from Black-browed Albatross by larger size, longer wings, mottled or white mantle, and no black leading margin to underwing. Adult told from Southern Royal Albatross *D. epomophora*, not yet recorded from Melanesia but breeds off New Zealand, by no white on leading edge of inner wings, but immatures are very similar.
Habits Usually solitary at sea. One banded bird found dead in Melanesia.
Conservation status IUCN: Endangered.
Range Rare vagrant, with one recent record from New Caledonia.
Breeds on Campbell Is off New Zealand and ranges rarely to the tropics.

LIGHT-MANTLED ALBATROSS *Phoebetria palpebrata* — (not illustrated)

(Light-mantled Sooty Albatross; Albatros fuligineux)

Description 84 cm (wingspan 205 cm). Dark small albatross with slender body, long narrow wings and long pointed wedge-shaped tail. Brownish-grey mantle and underparts contrasts with dark brown hood, wings and tail. Narrow white eye-ring and primary shafts. Immature has dark scaling on pale upper body.
Similar species Distinctive all-dark underwings. From immature giant petrels by contrastingly pale body.
Habits Usually solitary at sea. When windy, glides effortlessly and rarely flaps wings.
Conservation status IUCN: Near Threatened.
Range Rare vagrant, with one recent record off Lifou. Breeds on sub-Antarctic islands and wanders across sub-Antarctic seas, uncommonly to southern Australia.

[BLACK-BROWED ALBATROSS *Thalassarche melanophris*] — (not illustrated)

(*Diomedea melanophris*; à sourcils noirs)

Description 88 cm (wingspan 225 cm). As Campbell Albatross but adult has dark eye.
Similar species Adult differs from Campbell Albatross by dark eye, slightly smaller dark eye patch and more black on underwing, especially leading edge of inner-wing, where black is patchy and extends close to black trailing edge. Immatures are indistinguishable. See Campbell Albatross for differences from other albatross species.
Conservation status IUCN: Endangered.
Range Records off New Caledonia may refer to this species or Campbell Albatross. May occur anywhere at sea in southern Melanesia. Breeds on sub-Antarctic islands and disperses across sub-Antarctic and subtropical seas.

CAMPBELL ALBATROSS *Thalassarche impavida* — Plate 3

(*Diomedea impavida*; also treated as a subspecies of Black-browed Albatross *T. melanophris*; Albatros des Campbell)

Description 80 cm (wingspan 220 cm). Stocky small albatross, but still larger than other common Melanesian seabirds, with relatively short neck and broad wings. White with black wings, mantle and tail, wide black margins to underwing, especially leading edge, and small black eyebrow. Adult has yellow eye and yellow-orange bill with red tip. Juvenile has dusky underwings with ill-defined white central stripe, grey mottling on head and neck, dull bill and dark eye.
Similar species See Black-browed Albatross. Differs from much larger Wandering and Royal Albatrosses by black mantle, tail and underwing margins, and orange bill. Differs from Buller's Albatross and other small albatross species, not yet recorded from Melanesia, by head patterning, bare-part colour and exact underwing patterns.
Habits Often mixed with other seabirds and follows ships. A dead banded bird was found in Vanuatu.

Conservation status IUCN: Vulnerable.
Range Rare vagrant, with records from Vanuatu and probably New Caledonia. May occur anywhere at sea in southern Melanesia. Breeds on Campbell Island off New Zealand and wanders at sea including up east coast of Australia.

BULLER'S ALBATROSS *Thalassarche bulleri* (not illustrated)

(*Diomedea bulleri*; Albatros de Buller)

Description 78 cm (wingspan 207 cm). Lightly built small albatross, but still larger than other common Melanesian seabirds. Grey head and neck with paler crown, dark around eye and bright yellow stripes along top and underside of black bill. Grey mantle, sooty upperwing, white rump, black tail, white underparts and black margins to white underwing, broadest on wing-tips and leading edge. Immature has dark-tipped brown bill and brownish-grey head and neck.
Similar species Differs from much larger Wandering and Royal Albatrosses by dark mantle, tail and leading edge of underwing, and yellow on bill. Differs from Campbell Albatross and other small albatross species, not yet recorded from Melanesia, by grey head, underwing pattern and adult's yellow-striped bill.
Habits Often mixed with other seabirds and follows ships.
Conservation status IUCN: Near Threatened.
Range Rare vagrant, with one recent record off New Caledonia. Breeds on islands off New Zealand and wanders across southern Pacific.

PETRELS AND SHEARWATERS Procellariidae

Pelagic seabirds with a few species breeding in Melanesia, others recorded as scarce migrants and many other species likely to occur as vagrants from southern oceans. All have long narrow wings and black, brown, grey and white plumage. Most species feed in deep offshore waters, some following ships. Petrels may have more distinct patterning, and generally feed singly by picking from the surface. In windy conditions, petrels glide in high banking arcs, interspersed with a few flaps, whereas shearwaters generally keep lower to the sea and small shearwaters flap much more frequently and rapidly. Shearwaters are generally uniformly dark above, with longer wings and slighter bodies than petrels. Shearwaters generally feed in small flocks by shallow dives from the air or plunges from the surface. Flight action is an important identification feature but varies greatly with wind. Birds return to land only after dark to nest in burrows or in rock screes and crevices; sometimes found shuffling on the ground around their burrows. Call loudly in flight over breeding sites and at burrow entrances. Occasionally 'crash' into bright lights at night.

SOUTHERN GIANT PETREL *Macronectes giganteus* Plate 3

(Antarctic Giant Petrel; Pétrel géant)

Description 90 cm (wingspan 195 cm). Huge bulky albatross-sized petrel. Juvenile is uniform blackish with heavy pale bill. Immature is faded scruffy sooty-brown, becoming whiter on head and underwing. Adult is pale greyish-brown with white head and pale underwing and white leading edge to upper- and underwing. Uncommon white-phase adults are all white with scattered dark feathers. Heavy pink or horn-coloured bill has greenish tip.
Similar species Differs from albatrosses by heavier flight, larger body and relatively shorter wings. Dark birds differ from very similar Northern Giant Petrel by greenish bill-tip, adult with white head and dark eye and adult and immature with white leading edge to wing.
Habits All Melanesian records have been of immatures, following ships or scavenging in harbours.
Range Rare vagrant, with records from Efate and New Caledonia but may occur throughout the region. Breeds across the southern oceans, rarely ranging to the tropics, especially May to November.

NORTHERN GIANT PETREL *Macronectes halli* (not illustrated)

(Pétrel de Hall)

Description 90 cm (wingspan 190 cm). Huge bulky albatross-sized petrel. Juvenile is uniform blackish with heavy pale bill. Immature plumage is a faded scruffy sooty-brown, becoming whiter on head. Adult is pale greyish-brown with off-white face and underparts. Heavy pink or horn-coloured bill has reddish tip. Eye becomes pale in adult.
Similar species Differs from albatrosses by heavier flight, larger body and shorter wings. Differs from very similar Southern Giant Petrel by darker dull red or orange bill-tip and adult has white face contrasting with darker cap and neck-sides, and pale eye.

Habits Immatures often follow ships or scavenge in harbours.
Range Rare vagrant, with two recent records from New Caledonia in June and July. Breeds across the southern oceans, rarely ranging to the tropics, especially May to November.

CAPE PETREL *Daption capense* — Plate 4

(Cape Pigeon; Damier du Cap)

Description 38 cm (wingspan 85 cm). Medium-sized stocky petrel with black head and chequered black and white upperparts. Underparts are largely white with black throat, wing margins and tail-tip.
Similar species Distinctive black and white patches on upperparts.
Habits Glides on stiff wings between bursts of shallow mechanical wing-beats, low over sea. Often follows ships but also associates with terns and noddies.
Range Rare vagrant, with four records at sea around Vanuatu and New Caledonia in August to January, but may occur more widely. Two subspecies breed around the Antarctic, ranging to subtropical seas.

ANTARCTIC PRION *Pachyptila desolata* — Plate 5

(Prion de la desolation)

Description 26 cm (wingspan 63 cm). Small pale petrel with short wings and flight action similar to Storm Petrels. Upperparts pale grey with black M-band across wings and tail-tips similar to some *Pterodroma* petrels. Underparts plain white except for grey neck-sides and dark tail-tip.
Similar species Differs from small pale *Pterodroma* petrels by flight action, plain underwing and short rounded wings. Several other very similar species of prion may occur in Melanesia, differing mostly in head pattern and bill structure.
Habits Fast buoyant flight with glides and shallow wing-beats, often feeding by pattering and zigzagging low over the water, behaving like a storm petrel.
Range One historical specimen from Vanuatu. Three subspecies breed across the southern oceans, ranging very rarely to tropics, especially April to September. Other species of prion are perhaps more likely to occur in Melanesia.

[GREAT-WINGED PETREL *Pterodroma macroptera*] — Plate 3

(Also treated as a separate species, Grey-faced Petrel *P. gouldii*; Pétrel noir)

Description 41 cm (wingspan 102 cm). Large bulky petrel with big head and neck, long broad wings (dark on undersides) and long wedge-shaped tail. Plumage dark grey-brown, becoming chocolate-brown when worn, with variable pale grey face-patch in Grey-faced Petrel.
Similar species Uniform dark underwings are distinctive, but underwing may sometimes reflect pale off bright seas.
Habits Solitary, flying relatively high and fast, rarely flapping.
Range No definite records from Melanesia but Grey-faced Petrel recently recorded in seas just south of New Caledonia. Grey-faced Petrel *P. (macroptera) gouldii* breeds off north-east New Zealand and disperses to nearby seas. Great-winged Petrel *P. m. macroptera* breeds off southern Australia and across southern oceans.

PROVIDENCE PETREL *Pterodroma solandri* — Plate 3

(Solander's Petrel; Pétrel de Solander)

Description 40 cm (wingspan 100 cm). Large heavy dark brown petrel with double white patch on outer underwing. Upperparts uniformly dark grey-brown, with very obscure dark M across wings. Underparts grey-brown with large white patch on base of primaries, darker tips to primary coverts and less conspicuous smaller white patch on primary coverts. Relatively long wedge-shaped tail. At close range, note inconspicuous frosting around forehead and bill-base. At long range, underside of whole outer wing may look silvery.
Similar species See similar Kermadec and Herald Petrels. Differs from skuas by flight action and lack of white on upperwing.
Habits Usually solitary at sea. Typical *Pterodroma* flight.
Conservation status IUCN: Vulnerable.
Range Several recent records at sea off New Caledonia, one off Buka and likely to occur in small numbers across south Melanesian seas. Breeds on Lord Howe and Phillip Is, between New Caledonia and New Zealand, from March to November, and ranges to Australia and north Pacific.

KERMADEC PETREL *Pterodroma neglecta* Plate 6

(Pétrel des Kermadec)

Description 38 cm (wingspan 100 cm). Large polymorphic petrel with pale primary shafts on otherwise plain dark brown upperwing. Dark underwing has extensive white on primary bases and primary coverts, and narrow white leading edge. Dark morph has dark brown head, body and inner wings. Pale morph has white head and underparts with variably pale crown and darker collar. Intermediate morph has dark head with white around bill-base and white breast to undertail-coverts. Rather short square tail.
Similar species White wing-flashes on upperwings are distinctive, shared only by skuas from which differs by longer wings and flight action. Otherwise, very like Providence and Herald Petrels but pale morph has all-pale head, and slightly broader wings and squarer tail than Herald.
Habits Similar to Herald Petrel but wings slightly less flexed at carpals. Sometimes chases other seabirds.
Range Rare vagrant with one record from near New Britain and occasional records from seas off New Caledonia, but probably disperses throughout southern Melanesia. *P. n. neglecta* breeds across the south Pacific, including Phillip and Lord Howe Is, dispersing north, and *P. n. juana* breeds off Chile.

HERALD PETREL *Pterodroma heraldica* Plate 6

(Also treated as a subspecies of Trindade Petrel *P. arminjoniana*; Pétrel hérault)

Description 37 cm (wingspan 95 cm). Large polymorphic petrel. Plain grey-brown upperparts with faint darker M-pattern. Dark underwing with extensive white at base of primaries and primary coverts, narrow white leading edge to forewing and inconspicuous pale mottled bars on secondaries and secondary coverts. Most birds are white from chin to vent except for a variable, sometimes indistinct dark collar and sometimes mottled underparts. Dark morph, which may not occur in Melanesia, has uniformly dark body, some with white throat, and less white on underwings.
Similar species Differs from very similar Kermadec Petrel by plain upperwing pattern and slightly narrower wings and longer, more pointed tail. From Providence Petrel by white on underwing secondaries and leading edge of underwing. From shearwaters and skuas by flight and structure.
Voice High-pitched chattering *ti-ti-ti-* repeated rapidly for up to ten seconds in aerial display over breeding islands, occasionally from ground. A draw-out low-pitched nasal mew. (Call descriptions from Australia.)
Habits A typical *Pterodroma* petrel, wheeling and banking in long arcing flights between deep slow wing-beats. Nests on Raine under coastal scrub and grass from July to September, returning as early as February; sometimes flies over nesting island before dark.
Conservation status Breeds on Hunter and possibly on Chesterfield Reefs, but in very small numbers. Probably threatened in Melanesia, but common on some central Pacific islands.
Range Recent breeding records from Hunter and historical records from Chesterfield, west of New Caledonia, and recent reports at sea off Guadalcanal. Probably occurs in small numbers at sea throughout Melanesia. Breeds on Raine between Australia and New Guinea, where numbers very small, and southern Polynesia from Tonga to Easter Island, dispersing locally.

MOTTLED PETREL *Pterodroma inexpectata* Plate 5

(Pétrel maculé)

Description 35 cm (wingspan 85 cm). Typical *Pterodroma* petrel with distinctive dark grey breast, flanks and belly. Dark M across pale grey upperparts, and white underwing with broad black bar from carpals to greater coverts, not axillaries. Fresh adult has frosted forehead, short white supercilium to above eye and darker eye-patch. Juvenile is scaled above. Larger, bulkier and shorter-winged than other grey *Pterodroma* species.
Similar species Dark underparts is distinctive, shared only by dark-morph Collared Petrel, from which it differs by crown same colour as mantle, inconspicuous and incomplete half-collar, grey belly contrasting with white vent, undertail-coverts and underwings, and heavier flight.
Habits Singles and small flocks migrate far offshore. Vigorous high arcing flight with rapid shallow wing-beats, heavier and smoother than small *Pterodroma* species.
Conservation status IUCN: Near Threatened.
Range Uncommon migrant off New Caledonia. Breeds in south New Zealand and migrates to north Pacific in April and May, returning in October.

[WHITE-NECKED PETREL *Pterodroma cervicalis*] Plate 5

(Pétrel à col blanc)

Description 43 cm (wingspan 100 cm). A large attenuated *Pterodroma* petrel with clear white collar. Upper body and wings grey with black M and clear black cap from eye across hindneck. Underwing largely white with patchy black bar from outer secondary coverts through carpal to outer primaries and narrow grey extension onto neck-sides.
Similar species Very like Vanuatu Petrel, which see for differences from this and other petrels.
Habits Solitary at sea, with slower, less frenzied flight with fewer wing-beats than small *Pterodroma* petrels.
Conservation status IUCN: Vulnerable.
Range Rare at sea, mostly off New Caledonia but as far north as Makira, but not definitely distinguished from Vanuatu Petrel. Breeds on Kermadec and Phillip Is north and west of New Zealand, and disperses into the central Pacific, probably reaching but not definitely identified from southern Melanesia.

VANUATU PETREL *Pterodroma occulta* Plate 5

(Also treated as a subspecies of White-necked Petrel *P. cervicalis*; name on Vanua Lava is Qolav; Pétrel des Vanuatu)

Description 40 cm (wingspan c.94 cm). A large attenuated *Pterodroma* petrel with clear white collar and contrasting dark cap. Upper body and wings grey with black M and black tail-tip. Underwing largely white with black bar from carpals onto outer secondary coverts, possibly a dark leading edge to outer upperwing and narrow grey extension onto neck-sides.
Similar species Differs from White-necked Petrel by smaller size, dark grey undersides of primaries contrasting with white underwing primary coverts (although only 90% of White-necked have white undersides of primaries), dark leading edge to outer underwing from outer secondary coverts through carpals to outer primaries, slightly longer narrower tail and heavier shorter bill. Wing is about 6% smaller (male White-necked = 309 mm; Vanuatu = 289 mm), bill about 8% shorter (male White-necked = 36 mm; Vanuatu = 33 mm) and tarsus about 12% shorter (male White-necked = 41 mm; Vanuatu = 36 mm). From Gould's Petrel by white collar demarcating black cap, and larger size. From Black-winged Petrel by little black on underwing-coverts, prominent black cap and white collar, and larger size. From Juan Fernandez Petrel *P. externa*, not recorded from Melanesia but has reached Australia and New Zealand, by white collar and longer dark underwing-bar.
Voice Recorded calling at breeding sites in February. Rapid decelerating *kek-kek-kek-kek-kek-kek-kek*. Drawn-out *tooooo-wit*.
Habits Small loose groups at sea, with slower, less frenzied flight with fewer wing-beats than small *Pterodroma* petrels. Breeds at c.600 m on Mount Suretamata in February–April, probably coming ashore from October.
Conservation status Known from a handful of records including breeding on Vanua Lava, a few seen at sea in central Vanuatu, one off New Caledonia, and six birds collected off Mere Lava in 1927. Threatened by predation by introduced mammals and possibly Peregrine Falcons; has a very small population and is probably Endangered.
Range Breeds on Vanua Lava, Vanuatu and probably occurs at sea across southern Melanesia. Elsewhere known from one record in Australia.

BLACK-WINGED PETREL *Pterodroma nigripennis* Plate 5

(Pétrel à ailes noires)

Description 29 cm (wingspan 67 cm). Medium-small round-winged petrel with much black on underwing. Underwing white with broad black band from central greater coverts to carpal and along leading edge of outer wing, broad black wing-tip and narrower black trailing edge. Upperparts grey with darker M across wings and terminal tail-bar. Head and extensions onto neck-sides are grey, uniform with mantle, but some white mottling above bill and darker around eye. Occasional birds show a white collar.
Similar species Underwing pattern and grey extensions onto neck-sides are distinctive, similar only to Gould's and Collared Petrels, from which also differs by lacking contrast between head and mantle. From larger White-necked and Vanuatu Petrels also by plainer head pattern, which rarely also has white collar. From Mottled Petrel by all-white belly. See also Antarctic Prion.
Voice Calls over breeding grounds. Loud shrill whistle, averaging four syllables, higher-pitched than Gould's Petrel, sometimes prefixed by disyllabic lower *ahh-oo*. Laughing series of *ha-haa* notes. Mews. (Call descriptions from Chatham Is.)
Habits At sea, glides in high arcs or low over surface, often rather jerky and erratic flight. Breeds on small rat-free islets, usually flying over nesting grounds in late afternoon during breeding season.

Conservation status Uncommon and localised. Not globally threatened.
Range Breeds on small islets and atolls around Grande Terre, New Caledonia, including lagoon islets, Matthew and Walpole, from October to May, but rarely seen at sea during these months. Elsewhere, breeds on several islands off Australia, New Zealand and south Polynesia, migrating north in July–November.

GOULD'S PETREL *Pterodroma leucoptera* — Plate 5

(Pétrel de Gould)

Description 30 cm (wingspan 70 cm). Small round-winged petrel with black crown and nape extending onto neck-sides and contrasting with paler grey mantle. Contrast of dark M-band across upperwings and dark tail-tips varies with wear. Underparts white except slight extension of black hood onto neck-sides, narrow black margins to underwing, and short greater-covert bar from carpals.
Similar species Distinctive black hood shared only with Collared Petrel. Differs from very similar pale-morph Collared Petrel by narrower black underwing margins and neck-sides extending less as a partial collar, but these are difficult to see at sea. Also differs from Black-winged Petrel by much narrower black margins on underwing. From Cook's Petrel by broader dark margins and bar on underwing. See also Antarctic Prion.
Voice Calls in flight high over breeding sites. Most commonly, a series of staccato, rapidly pulsed whistles. Also a squeaky whistle and tremulous growl.
Habits Solitary or in small scattered groups at sea. In windy conditions, banks and arcs over sea, interspersed with glides, usually slower than other petrels. Rather rounded wings flexed at carpals. Returns after dark to breeding sites in forests at 400–650 m in scattered colonies in rocks and scrub on steep mountains between November and April, calling in November–December.
Conservation status Numbers poorly known but several thousand pairs breeding in at least five colonies on New Caledonia. Potentially threatened by rat, cat and pig predation. IUCN: Vulnerable.
Range Breeds on New Caledonia and possibly Vanuatu, and probably occurs at sea across southern Melanesia.
P. l. leucoptera breeds on Cabbage Tree and Boondelbah Is east of Australia, and likely to occur on passage through Melanesia; slightly smaller than *P. l. caledonica* and has darker grey mantle, darker neck-sides with more extension as partial collar, more prominent underwing-bar and grey rather than white inner webs of outer tail feathers.
P. l. caledonica is endemic to Grande Terre, New Caledonia, and nearby seas, and disperses to New Zealand and probably also to the north-east Pacific. Taxonomic status of birds possibly breeding on Vanuatu, breeding in small numbers in Cook Islands and French Polynesia, and involved in two old records from near New Britain and Makira, uncertain; may be intermediate between *P. l. caledonica* and Collared Petrel.

COLLARED PETREL *Pterodroma brevipes* — Plate 5

(Also treated as a subspecies of Gould's Petrel *P. leucoptera*; name on Tanna is Tekerkark; Pétrel à collier)

Description 30 cm (wingspan 70 cm). Medium-small round-winged petrel with black hood shading onto grey mantle. Contrast of dark M-band across grey upperwings varies with wear. All have white throat contrasting with black hood, most have partial or complete black breast-band and many have dark grey breast and belly. Darkest birds have uniformly very dark grey underparts, contrasting with white throat and inner underwing-coverts and paler median-covert bar on largely dark underwing.
Similar species Dark birds are distinctive but see Mottled Petrel which has dark belly but grey head, and white vent and undertail-coverts. Dark crown and partial collar differs from other *Pterodroma* petrels, notably Black-winged Petrel, and also Antarctic Prion. Palest birds differ only very slightly from Gould's Petrel by more extension of neck-sides as partial collar, wider black underwing margins and, at close range, wholly dark outer tail feathers and sometimes a slight white crescent over eye, but these features are difficult to see at sea.
Voice Various calls over breeding grounds at night: a series of about six staccato *kek-kek-kek-* whistles, longer *cher-cher* or *cher-chewee*, low moaning *guorr* and thick purring call. (Call descriptions from Fiji.)
Habits Usually solitary at sea, where it has an erratic banking, flicking and flapping flight, often low over the water. Race *magnificens* noted feeding with large mixed seabird flocks. Breeds in hill and mountain forests, with nesting records from above 300 m on Tanna, coming into land only well after dark and probably only calls at beginning of breeding season which is about February to July for *brevipes* and earlier for *magnificens* on Vanua Lava. Probably remains at sea around breeding islands all year round, keeping well offshore.
Conservation status Uncommon. Known to breed on Vanua Lava and Tanna but breeding status elsewhere in Melanesia unknown. May be threatened by introduced mammals. IUCN: Near Threatened.

Range Current status is poorly known, with regular records of small numbers at sea across Solomons, Temotu, Vanuatu and New Caledonia, especially around breeding islands.
P. b. brevipes breeds on Tanna and historically known from Aneityum, and possibly Efate and Makira. Elsewhere, breeds Fiji and possibly Cook Is and elsewhere in Polynesia.
P. b. magnificens, endemic to Vanua Lava and perhaps other Banks Is in Vanuatu, is always dark or very dark, and has slightly shorter wings and longer tail.

COOK'S PETREL *Pterodroma cookii* — Plate 5

(Pétrel de Cook)

Description 30 cm (wingspan 65 cm). Small typical *Pterodroma* petrel. Upperparts pale grey crossed with black M, pale grey crown and nape with white on bill-base, fine white supercilium and small dark eye-patch, tail with narrow white sides and darker tips. Underwing largely white with short narrow black bar from carpals onto outer secondary coverts and fine black margins and tips.
Similar species Differs from Black-winged and Gould's Petrels by much smaller black bar and finer black margins on underwing, paler upperparts and smaller paler eye-patch. [Differs from very similar Pycroft's Petrel *P. pycrofti*, reported west and south of Melanesia, by shorter tail, uniform bluish head to mantle, heavier bill, less white on forehead and less contrasting eye-patch.]
Habits Rapid erratic flight weaving, banking and arcing on fast jerky wing-beats. Usually solitary.
Conservation status IUCN: Vulnerable.
Range Rare vagrant, with single records at sea off Vanuatu and New Caledonia. Breeds off New Zealand and disperses to north-east Pacific, most leaving in March and returning in August.

TAHITI PETREL *Pseudobulweria rostrata* — Plate 6

(*Pterodroma rostrata*; Pétrel de Tahiti)

Description 39 cm (wingspan 84 cm). Long-winged medium-sized petrel. Blackish-brown with sharply demarcated white belly and sometimes narrow white underwing-bar. Underwing-bar is obscure and faint but may appear conspicuous from reflection of light off sea. Distinctive long narrow straight wings and relatively long narrow head, neck and tail.
Similar species See Beck's Petrel. Differs from Herald and Kermadec Petrels by proportionately longer wings, underwing-bar, lack of white bases to outer primaries and all-dark head. From juvenile Sooty Tern by flight action and jizz. From Phoenix Petrel *Pterodroma alba*, unrecorded from Melanesia but breeding as close as Tonga, by straight wings, flight action, dark throat, and no white on leading edge of underwing.
Voice Noisy at breeding grounds. Varied calls, the commonest noted here. Long elaborate series of upslurred whistles, usually given in flight. A drawn-out braying whistle comprised of five main parts, a hiccup, pause, harmonics, whistle and moan, usually given from the ground.
Habits Usually solitary at sea, banking and towering more than shearwaters, but not high above the water like *Pterodroma* petrels. Distinctive flight action, banking on long stiff straight wings in strong winds or gliding slow over the sea with deep languid flaps in light winds. Returns after dark to breeding sites and calls in flight and at the nest. Breeds in small scattered colonies in mountain rainforest in very steep slopes at c.500 m altitude, or on small rat-free islets, January–May.
Conservation status Fairly common off New Caledonia but uncommon in Solomons and Bismarcks. Hundreds or thousands of pairs breed on Grande Terre. Potentially threatened by rat and cat predation. IUCN: Near Threatened.
Range Breeds in New Caledonia, and occurs at sea across Melanesia.
P. r. trouessarti, endemic to New Caledonia where it breeds on Grande Terre, occurs at sea north to the Bismarcks. Elsewhere, *P. r. rostrata* breeds in Fiji and Polynesia, and has a smaller bill.

BECK'S PETREL *Pseudobulweria becki* — Plate 6

(*Pterodroma becki*; also treated as a subspecies of Tahiti Petrel *P. rostrata*; Pétrel de Beck)

Description 29 cm (wingspan 70 cm). Very like Tahiti Petrel. A long-winged medium-sized blackish-brown petrel with sharply demarcated white belly. A pale central underwing is a variable feature, as the all-dark underwing of juveniles becomes paler with age and wear.
Similar species Differs from Tahiti Petrel by smaller size (10–20% smaller), narrower wings, shorter wingspan (Tahiti Petrel has a similar wingspan to Wedge-tailed Shearwater), slighter and slimmer body, shorter bill (about 25% shorter)

on small head, so bill appears proportionally more massive, and may show whiter undertail and smudgier border between black throat and white breast. In flight, sometimes has more rapid wing-beats, shorter, more swooping glides, and shorter and steeper arcing/banking, almost like a *Pterodroma* petrel, in comparison to Tahiti Petrel's stronger flight with more gliding and long arcs, more like a miniature albatross. However, field identification is extremely difficult. In hand, wing 240–245 mm (Tahiti Petrel 278–308), tail 98–99 mm (Tahiti Petrel 109–121), tarsus 36–37 mm (Tahiti Petrel 45–50), exposed culmen 25–27 mm (Tahiti Petrel 34–39), depth of bill 8–8.4 mm (Tahiti Petrel 10–14). Differs from Phoenix Petrel by whitish leading edge to underwing.

Voice Unknown.

Habits Similar to Tahiti Petrel but may gather in loose groups of several birds.

Conservation status Locally fairly common, with up to 50 birds seen in 2006–2008, but previously known from just two specimens in 1928 and 1929. A handful of other unconfirmed sightings in this area. Potentially threatened by predation by introduced mammals at its unknown breeding grounds. IUCN: Critically Endangered.

Range Endemic, only recorded from seas between New Britain, New Ireland and the central Solomons, with sightings between southern New Ireland, New Britain, Feni and Bougainville, reports off Temotu and Vanuatu, and previous specimens off Buka and off Rendova. Most common off Cape St George on southern New Ireland and may breed in Hans Meyer mountains.

[FIJI PETREL *Pseudobulweria macgillivrayi*] Plate 4

(Pétrel des Fidji)

Description 29 cm (wingspan 73 cm). A small, uniformly dark brown petrel with long narrow wings and relatively long head and neck and thin tapered tail. Stout bulbous bill and bluish-pink legs and webs. Length and wingspan as Black Noddy.

Similar species Differs from Bulwer's Petrel by larger size, shorter square-ended tail, lack of pale upperwing-bars, and flight action. From Christmas Shearwater by longer tail, robust bulbous bill, lack of upperwing-bar and feet not extending beyond tail.

Habits Known at sea from only one series of records, where its behaviour was similar to Tahiti and Beck's Petrels.

Conservation status Two unconfirmed records in Melanesia. IUCN: Critically Endangered.

Range Two records of unidentified petrels off Bougainville and north New Britain may have been this species or an undescribed taxon. Fiji Petrel breeds on Gau in Fiji where only known from a handful of records of birds coming to lights and seen offshore.

GREY PETREL *Procellaria cinerea* Plate 3

(Puffin gris)

Description 49 cm (wingspan 122 cm). Thickset plain grey-brown petrel with plain white underside of body. White from chin to undertail-coverts, with dark undertail; merges below eye onto grey-brown head. Underwing uniform grey-brown with silver sheen. Slender horn-coloured to greenish-yellow bill.

Similar species Differs from Streaked Shearwater and pale-morph Wedge-tailed Shearwater by uniformly dark underwings and heavier body.

Habits Solitary. Strong flight on straight stiff wings, often high above sea. Appears similar to a shearwater.

Conservation status IUCN: Near Threatened.

Range Rare vagrant, with one record from seas between New Caledonia and Australia. Breeds across southern oceans, dispersing locally.

STREAKED SHEARWATER *Calonectris leucomelas* Plate 3

(Puffin leucomèle)

Description 48 cm (wingspan 122 cm). Large gregarious broad-winged shearwater with white underparts. White from chin to vent and underwing except dark primaries and secondaries and some dark mottling on primary coverts. Variable amount of white on forehead and around eye, with white streaks on head and pale bill. Upperparts uniform mid-brown often with pale bars on upperwing-coverts and white bands on rump.

Similar species Differs from pale-morph Wedge-tailed Shearwater by pale vent, white on cap and face, more dark on underwing primary coverts, paler bill, shorter tail, stouter build and straighter wings. See Grey Petrel.

Habits Steady flaps between glides on bowed wings, sometimes bent at carpals. In calm weather, flaps heavily like large gull. In wind, may soar. Often close inshore. Gregarious, sometimes in flocks of thousands.

Range Locally common off the Bismarcks and Bougainville from October to April, especially December to March. Single records from Guadalcanal and New Caledonia. Breeds around Japan, dispersing south.

CHRISTMAS SHEARWATER *Puffinus nativitatis* Plate 6

(Christmas Island Shearwater; Kiritimati Shearwater; Puffin de la Nativité)

Description 35 cm (wingspan 76 cm). Small sooty-brown shearwater, sometimes showing a white underwing flash. Rather short round wings and short round tail. Relatively small dark bill and dark feet.
Similar species Differs from Heinroth's Shearwater by dark underwing and belly, larger size and shorter bill. From Sooty and Short-tailed Shearwaters by smaller size. From Wedge-tailed Shearwater by smaller size, darker plumage, narrower wings, shorter tail and faster flight. From Bulwer's Petrel by flight action, longer straighter wings, shorter tail and uniform upperwing.
Habits Flies close to sea with fast flapping flight and long glides on stiff wings. Often mixes with other seabirds.
Range Vagrant recorded north of Bismarcks, with singles off Mussau and Feni and unconfirmed off New Ireland, but could occur anywhere at sea. Breeds in central Pacific between Hawaii and Pitcairn, and probably disperses locally.

WEDGE-TAILED SHEARWATER *Puffinus pacificus* Plate 4

(Puffin fouquet)

Description 46 cm (wingspan 98 cm). Large slender shearwater with a relatively long pointed tail, wedge-shaped when fanned. Dark morph is uniformly chocolate-brown, with variably paler bars on greater and median upperwing-coverts, and slightly paler central underwing. Pale morph has slightly greyer upperparts, off-white underparts and underwing-coverts, with some mottling along leading edge and axillaries. Long bill is dark grey, sometimes appearing paler with dark tip. Wings are broad-based; flies with carpals held forward and outer wings bowed. Tail extends beyond wing-tips when settled on sea. Juvenile has grey wash to upperparts and paler greater-covert bar.
Similar species Long pointed tail, broader wing-bases and angled, bowed wings are distinctive, except from Bulwer's Petrel, which is smaller with more distinct pale upperwing-bar. Dark morph differs from Flesh-footed Shearwater by paler plumage, slimmer body and duller thinner bill. From Short-tailed and Sooty Shearwaters by no silver on underwings, broader wings, slower flight and paler feet. See smaller Christmas Shearwater. Pale morph differs from Streaked Shearwater by dark vent, unmarked dark cap extending over forehead and cheeks and onto neck-sides, less dark on underwing primary coverts, slimmer build and narrower wings.
Voice Usually calls from the ground but also in flight. Loud multisyllabic crooning wails and moans at breeding colonies, e.g. *ka-whoooo-ahhh*. Higher-pitched strained mewing.
Habits Usually the commonest inshore shearwater, flapping leisurely between glides, keeping close to the sea. Often gregarious and mixes with other seabirds. Breeds in dense colonies, usually in sandy ground or between rocks by the coast or on small offshore islands.
Conservation status Locally common but some colonies threatened by hunting and introduced mammals. Not globally threatened.
Range At sea across Melanesia. Dark morph breeds on small and usually uninhabited islands across Vanuatu and New Caledonia, where locally abundant, and probably Temotu. Dark morph is widespread at sea, commoner further south, usually seen on migration in north, and probably includes migrants from central Pacific especially in May to November. Pale morph is a fairly common migrant to the Bismarcks and rare elsewhere. Elsewhere, breeds in tropical Indian and Pacific Oceans, usually considered monotypic but Melanesian birds sometimes included in subspecies *P. p. chlororhynchus*.

BULLER'S SHEARWATER *Puffinus bulleri* (not illustrated)

(Puffin de Buller)

Description 44 cm (wingspan 98 cm). Large shearwater with ashy-grey upperparts and sooty crown, tail and M-stripe across wing-coverts and primaries. White underparts with extremely narrow dark underwing margins and blackish tail, and sometimes shows grey neck-sides. Wings, neck and wedge-shaped tail relatively long.
Similar species Distinctive grey and black upperparts. From pale Wedge-tailed and Streaked Shearwater by more distinctly grey on upperparts and cleaner white underwing.
Habits Usually with other shearwaters and often follows boats. Flight is slow and leisurely, often with bowed wings.
Range Rare vagrant, with one record from New Caledonia. Breeds off north New Zealand, dispersing to north Pacific in May to September.

FLUTTERING SHEARWATER *Puffinus gavia* — Plate 6

(Puffin volage)

Description 35 cm (wingspan 76 cm). Small shearwater with plain brown upperparts and white underparts. Upperparts vary from blackish-brown to pale brown. Underbody and underwing-coverts white, smeared brown on neck-sides and axillaries. White may extend from flanks to sides of rump, both in flight and when settled on sea. Fairly long slender neck and short wings.
Similar species Differs from Tropical Shearwater by white undertail, more white on underwing, browner upperparts smudging onto neck and axillaries, less often white on rump-sides and pinkish-brown feet. From pale Wedge-tailed and Streaked Shearwater by small size and flight action. Very similar Hutton's Shearwater *P. huttoni*, not recorded from Melanesia, has less defined cap, with more brown on neck-sides, throat and axillaries.
Habits Usually inshore seas. Gregarious. Flight is low, fast and more fluttering with shorter glides than large shearwaters.
Range One or two historical records from New Caledonia and possibly Vanuatu. Breeds around New Zealand, dispersing to south and east Australian coast, especially April to September.

TROPICAL SHEARWATER *Puffinus bailloni* — Plate 6

(Also treated as a subspecies of Audubon's Shearwater *P. lherminieri*; Puffin d'Audubon)

Description 31 cm (wingspan 69 cm). Small black and white shearwater. Upperparts sooty-black, browner when worn, with clear-cut border from bill-base to below eye to rear ear-coverts, then extending lower on neck-sides. Underparts white with black wing-tips and broad borders, variable amounts of black on leading edge and sometimes a dark primary-covert bar. Most Melanesian birds have black undertail-coverts but this needs further study. White flanks often extend onto sides of rump. Legs blue with pinkish webs.
Similar species Differs from Heinroth's Shearwater by white underbody, broad white central underwing, blacker upperparts and shorter bill. From Fluttering Shearwater by blacker upperparts, dark undertail, more clear-cut black and white on face, more clear-cut broad black margins on underwing and clearer white extensions onto rump. See Little Shearwater.
Voice Calls after dark at breeding sites. Disyllabic *shoo-kree*, the first note a rasping inhalation, the second a screeching exhalation. (Call description from Polynesia.)
Habits Usually in small flocks, often with mixed feeding flocks, not far offshore. Flies with short fluttering bursts of wing-beats followed by long glides. May sit on sea off breeding islands. Comes ashore after dark to nesting sites, nesting in burrows or gaps in rocks, screes and cliffs in mountains. Breeding reported between November and February above 700 m on Mere Lava, and may nest on other islands.
Conservation status Generally uncommon in Melanesia but fairly common around Temotu and Banks Is. Likely to be locally threatened by introduced mammals and possibly over-harvesting at breeding colonies. Globally not threatened.
Range Across Melanesia. *P. b. gunax* may be endemic to Vanuatu, where breeds on Mere Lava at least, and historical specimens from Tongoa, Efate, Tanna and Aneityum, and may also breed around Temotu and New Caledonia. Occasional records at sea from Bismarcks, Solomons, Temotu and Vanuatu, not identified to subspecies. Elsewhere, other subspecies, with variably white or dark undertail-coverts, are scattered in tropical Indian and Pacific Oceans, as close as Micronesia and Fiji but generally sedentary.

HEINROTH'S SHEARWATER *Puffinus heinrothi* — Plate 6

Description 27 cm (wingspan 59 cm). Small sooty-brown shearwater with a variable silvery underwing-bar. Size similar to Black Noddy. Underwing-bar varies in extent and brightness, but is always conspicuous. Underparts dark sooty-brown, sometimes with pale on chin and central belly. Distinctive long slender dark bill, pale blue eye and pale pink feet.
Similar species Differs from Tropical Shearwater by browner plumage, largely dark underparts, less white on underwing and long bill. From Short-tailed Shearwater by small size, short stubby wings, weak flight and longer bill. From Christmas Shearwater by paler underwing, smaller size, rounder wings and longer bill.
Voice Unknown.
Habits Flight more fluttering and lower over sea than larger shearwaters. Usually seen in singles or small groups with other feeding seabirds. Breeds on mountainous forested islands, probably at high altitudes.
Conservation status Uncommon and localised. Maximum count of 250 off Bougainville, but no more than 20 off Bismarcks and 10 elsewhere in Solomons. Possibly threatened by introduced mammals. IUCN: Vulnerable.

Range Endemic to Admiralties, Bismarcks and Solomons. Recorded from Manus to Guadalcanal and Malaita, with most records from around Bougainville, Kolombangara and Rendova, where it probably breeds, and perhaps New Ireland and New Britain. Outside Melanesia, non-breeding birds are occasionally seen off adjacent coasts of north New Guinea.

[LITTLE SHEARWATER *Puffinus assimilis*] Plate 6

(Petit Puffin)

Description 27 cm (wingspan 61 cm). Small black and white shearwater. Upperparts blue-black. Underparts white with narrow black tips and trailing edge, white extending up above eye. Relatively short rounded wings.
Similar species Distinctive extension of white above eye. From Tropical and Fluttering Shearwaters by blacker upperparts, white undertail, less black on underwing, light blue feet and smaller size.
Habits Usually singles or small groups. Flight is more fluttering, almost whirring, than other shearwaters, usually flying shorter distances, low over sea, and often sits on sea.
Range One series of records reported from seas off Temotu, between Solomons and Vanuatu. May occur more widely as breeds as close as Norfolk and Lord Howe Is. Elsewhere, breeds in temperate southern oceans and north-east Atlantic; usually fairly sedentary.

SOOTY SHEARWATER *Puffinus griseus* Plate 4

(Puffin fuligineux)

Description 43 cm (wingspan 100 cm). Large dark shearwater with long narrow wings and a silvery underwing-bar. All sooty-brown except silvery underwing primary coverts and brown-barred silvery outer underwing secondary coverts. Toes just project beyond tip of short tail.
Similar species Differs from Short-tailed Shearwater by longer bill and flatter forehead, longer neck and tail, bulkier size and broader wings, more extensive but more mottled silver on underwings, slower wing-beats and longer arcs in flight; many in wing moult in January to March. Also see Flesh-footed, Wedge-tailed, Christmas and Heinroth's Shearwaters.
Habits Gregarious, but vagrants often alone or mixed with other species. Flies fast and straight, with straight wings, usually flapping fast 2–8 times then a long glide, and banking with conspicuous flashes of white on underwing.
Conservation status IUCN: Near Threatened.
Range Vagrant, with single records from New Britain, south of Vanuatu and New Caledonia. Probably overlooked and may occur anywhere in Melanesia. Breeds on small islands off Australia, New Zealand, Falklands and Chile, dispersing to northern oceans in April and May and returning September and October.

SHORT-TAILED SHEARWATER *Puffinus tenuirostris* Plate 4

(Puffin à bec grêle)

Description 42 cm (wingspan 97 cm). Large dark shearwater with long narrow wings and a variable silvery underwing-bar. Feet project just beyond the short tail, but may be difficult to see.
Similar species Differs from Wedge-tailed and Flesh-footed Shearwaters by variable silvery underwing-bar, narrower straighter wings, shorter tail, dark bare parts and different flight action. From Sooty Shearwater by shorter bill and steeper forehead, shorter neck and tail, slighter size and narrower wings, silver on underwings more variable and less mottled, faster wing-beats and shorter arcs in flight; in wing moult in May–July, when absent from Melanesia. From Heinroth's Shearwater by much larger size, longer wings and faster, more towering flight. See Christmas Shearwater.
Habits Gregarious, often in large dense flocks. Flies faster than other shearwaters with bursts of rapid flapping on stiff wings between banking glides. Many Melanesian records are of migrating flocks, flying fast and direct.
Range Migrates through Melanesian seas but mostly to east of Melanesia. Scattered individuals and flocks recorded throughout north Melanesia and large numbers on passage off New Caledonia and once off Solomons and Vanuatu, mostly March–May and October–November. Breeds south of Australia, dispersing to north Pacific April–October.

FLESH-FOOTED SHEARWATER *Puffinus carneipes* Plate 4

(Puffin à pieds pales)

Description 47 cm (wingspan 115 cm). Large bulky sooty-brown shearwater. Plumage all dark brown but underwing often reflects pale off bright sea. Pale pink feet and stout pink or whitish bill with black tip. Long broad wings and broad tail.

Similar species Stout pale bill is distinctive. Also differs from Wedge-tailed Shearwater by stout build, shorter square tail and straight wings. From Short-tailed and Sooty Shearwaters by pale feet, less silver on underwings, broad wings and slower flight. From White-chinned *Procellaria aequinoctialis*, Westland *P. westlandica* and Black (Parkinson's) *P. parkinsoni* Petrels, recorded just to the south of Melanesia, by pink, not yellowish, bill and less massive bill, head and neck.
Habits Usually singles or small groups. Flies steadily and slowly with easy shallow flaps and glides on rather stiff straight wings.
Range Uncommon migrant throughout Melanesia. A handful of records, including New Ireland, New Britain, Makira, Temotu, Vanuatu and New Caledonia. Breeds on islands south of Australia and around New Zealand, dispersing to north Pacific in April–May, returning in September–October.

BULWER'S PETREL *Bulweria bulwerii* — Plate 4

(Pétrel de Bulwer)

Description 27 cm (wingspan 68 cm). A uniform sooty-brown petrel with paler bar on greater coverts, not visible at long range. Rather long pointed wings and long wedge-shaped tail, usually held closed and appearing pointed. Underwing may reflect paler off bright sea.
Similar species Flight action and proportions are distinctive. Differs from Matsudaira's Storm Petrel by larger size, long wedge-shaped tail, no pale primary bases, larger size and more direct flight. From Wedge-tailed Shearwater by smaller size, longer tail and more distinct upperwing-bar. From noddies by upperwing-bar and more rounded wings. From Fiji Petrel by upperwing-bar, longer pointed tail, shorter wings usually flexed at carpals.
Habits Solitary at sea. Flaps and glides low over water, carpals often held forward and wings slightly bowed like Wedge-tailed Shearwater. Rapid changes in direction and height like a storm petrel. May glide between flaps in strong winds.
Range Uncommon migrant to Bismarcks, Solomons and Temotu. Recorded July to November but perhaps occurs all year. Breeds in northern tropical oceans, including Polynesia, dispersing across tropical seas.

[JOUANIN'S PETREL *Bulweria fallax*] — Plate 4

(Pétrel de Jouanin)

Description 31 cm (wingspan 79 cm). Uniform sooty-brown petrel with faint fine paler bar along greater coverts, which may be more distinct along inner coverts when worn. Underwing may reflect paler off bright sea. Rather long pointed wings and long wedge-shaped tail, usually held closed and appearing pointed.
Similar species Differs from Bulwer's Petrel by less pale on upperwing, heavier bill and shorter tail. From Wedge-tailed Shearwater by smaller size, narrower wings, heavier bill and more uniformly silvery underwing.
Habits Similar to Bulwer's Petrel but flight more languid and less often zigzagging like a storm petrel.
Range No records from Melanesia but has occurred as a vagrant to Australia and Hawaii. Breeds in Indian Ocean.

STORM PETRELS Hydrobatidae

Small, seemingly fragile seabirds which flutter and glide very low over the sea, often pattering the surface on long legs with wings raised high. Occurring far offshore, they sometimes follow ships and may congregate around a feeding area. Return after dark to breeding islands.

WILSON'S STORM PETREL *Oceanites oceanicus* — Plate 7

(Océanite de Wilson)

Description 17 cm (wingspan 40 cm). Small short-winged storm petrel with large white rump. Plumage sooty-brown with pale upperwing-bar and large white rump extending around sides of rump. At close range, yellow webs visible when feet are trailing. Short round wings, short square tail and long legs protrude beyond the tail.
Similar species Differs from Band-rumped and Leach's Storm Petrels by short square tail, shorter rounder wings, broader pure white rump extending onto underside and longer legs extending beyond tail. From other storm petrels by large white rump extending slightly onto otherwise completely black underparts.
Habits Usually far offshore. Strong swallow-like fluttering flight above waves, or slow feeding flight with wings held up high and feet dragged or pattering on sea, rarely gliding. Singles or small loose groups, often following ships.
Range Scarce migrant throughout Melanesia, with records from New Ireland, New Britain, Solomons, Vanuatu and New Caledonia, most in April–November. Two subspecies breed throughout sub-Antarctic oceans, dispersing north to tropics.

[NEW ZEALAND STORM PETREL *Oceanites maorianus*] Plate 7

(*Pealeornis maoriana*)

Description 18 cm (wingspan 39 cm). Small storm petrel with long legs and square tail. Blackish-brown with broad white rump, white central underwing and white belly. Indistinct pale upperwing-bar. Variable amounts of dark streaking on white lower breast and flanks. Relatively narrow-winged like Wilson's Storm Petrel.
Similar species Differs from White-bellied and Black-bellied Storm Petrels by jizz and behaviour, which is closer to Wilson's Storm Petrel, longer narrower wings and longer feet. Streaked underparts differ from all except some White-bellied Storm Petrels, from which also differs in its longer legs and feet, solid black on breast extending further down towards belly, and no pale fringes on back.
Habits Solitary at sea, pattering along surface with wings held horizontally or shallowly upwards.
Conservation status IUCN: Critically Endangered.
Range Single storm petrels seen off New Caledonia in 2008 and 2010 were similar to this species but larger and may be an undescribed taxon. The species is otherwise known only from small numbers off Auckland, New Zealand, where presumed to breed, and vagrants off the east coast of Australia.

WHITE-FACED STORM PETREL *Pelagodroma marina* Plate 7

(Océanite frégate)

Description 19 cm (wingspan 42 cm). Medium-sized storm petrel with white underparts and contrasting head pattern. Wings and tail blackish, contrasting with brownish-grey wing-coverts and back, and pale grey rump. Grey crown, mask through eye, and sides of neck contrast with white lores and supercilium. Underparts and underwing white with dark grey primaries and secondaries. Relatively long rounded wings and very long legs with yellowish webs between toes.
Similar species From other storm petrels by distinctive white underparts from chin to vent, and head-pattern. From Antarctic Prion by upperwing pattern, shorter wings, and flight action. From Red-necked Phalarope by habits and shape.
Habits Singles or scattered groups have swift erratic flight, or pattering feeding flight.
Range Vagrant off New Caledonia in May to July and one unconfirmed report north of the Bismarcks. Six subspecies breed around Australia, New Zealand and east Atlantic, dispersing to tropical oceans, including east Pacific.

[WHITE-BELLIED STORM PETREL *Fregetta grallaria*] Plate 7

(Océanite à ventre blanc)

Description 20 cm (wingspan 46 cm). Medium-sized storm petrel with white rump, flanks and central underwing. Polymorphic but most birds are pale morph. Pale morph has sharp demarcation between black breast and all-white belly, intermediate usually has black mottling on rump, axillaries and underwing, and dark morph is all dark with slight white mottling on belly and rump.
Similar species Differs from Black-bellied Storm Petrel by shorter legs not projecting beyond tail in level flight, straight or even concave division of black from white on breast, pale grey scales on mantle and upperwing-coverts, no black stripe or smudges on belly midline (not on all Black-bellieds) and all-black throat. Intermediate morph also differs by dusky black on flanks and axillaries, white on underwing restricted to inner wing, and sometimes more extensive black on belly-sides and rump. Dark morph differs from Wilson's Storm Petrel by small ill-defined white rump-patch, feet not projecting beyond tail, white mottling on mid-belly and larger size and broader wings. See Leach's and New Zealand Storm Petrels.
Habits As Black-bellied Storm Petrel.
Range Two reports from seas off New Caledonia, but may have been confused with Black-bellied Storm Petrel. Breeds in subtropical islands as far north as Lord Howe I, and disperses to subtropical oceans.

BLACK-BELLIED STORM PETREL *Fregetta tropica* Plate 7

(Océanite à ventre noir)

Description 20 cm (wingspan 46 cm). Medium-sized storm petrel with white rump, flanks and central underwing. Upperparts black with slightly paler wing-covert bar. Appears white-bellied at a distance but most have narrow black midline belly-stripe; other uncommon morphs include black belly with white mottles, broad black midline-stripe or all-white belly. Some have pale mottled throat and often some dark mottling on underwing-bar. Short broad wings and square tail.
Similar species Differs from Wilson's Storm Petrel by white on flanks and underwings, and larger size. From

Polynesian Storm Petrel by black head to upper breast, square tail and usually black on midline underparts. See White-bellied and New Zealand Storm Petrels.
Habits Zigzags over the sea, bouncing off surface on long legs and gliding on flat wings. Often in small loose flocks, sometimes following ships.
Range Scarce migrant to southern Melanesia, with records from Solomons, Temotu and New Caledonia plus historical reports from Vanuatu. *F. t. tropica* breeds throughout sub-Antarctic oceans, dispersing north to the tropics from June to November, and *F. t. melanoleuca* breeds in the South Atlantic.

POLYNESIAN STORM PETREL *Nesofregetta fuliginosa* Plate 7

(White-throated Storm Petrel; Océanite à gorge blanche)

Description 24 cm (wingspan 52 cm). Large polymorphic storm petrel, usually with white underparts broken by brown breast-band. All have brown upperparts with pale upperwing-bar. Pale morph has narrow white rump, white underparts with dark breast-band, and white underwing with dark margins. Intermediate morph has broader breast-band, some dark streaking and mottling on underparts and rump, and more dark on underwing. Dark morph, known only from Samoa, has uniformly dark plumage. Broad rounded straight wings. Feet project beyond long forked tail.
Similar species Distinctive wing shape and flight action. Pale morph differs from Black-bellied Storm Petrel by clear white throat, narrow white rump, long forked tail and larger size. From Wilson's Storm Petrel by white on underparts, smaller white rump and larger size. Dark morph from Matsudaira's Storm Petrel by shorter straight wings without pale primary patch.
Voice Soft whistling and monotonous piping at nest sites. (Call descriptions from Polynesia.)
Habits Solitary at sea, often close inshore to nesting islands. Bounces along surface with strong kick, then gliding for 20–30 seconds, then kicking off in another direction, wings held rigidly horizontal. In level flight, loose rapid wing-beats giving a butterfly-like flight. Returns after dark to nests in burrows in montane rainforest on large islands, or on tiny islets.
Conservation status Rare. Threatened by predation by rats and cats. IUCN: Endangered.
Range Has bred in very small numbers on Vanuatu and New Caledonia, with occasional records at sea. Historical breeding records from Aneityum and Tanna and recent records from islets in southern lagoon of Grande Terre. Rarely seen at sea. Elsewhere breeds in Fiji and Polynesia.

[BAND-RUMPED STORM PETREL *Oceanodroma castro*] Plate 7

(Madeiran Storm Petrel; Océanite de Castro)

Description 20 cm (wingspan 46 cm). Medium-sized storm petrel with broad white rump-patch. All sooty-brown except for white rump which extends slightly onto undertail-coverts, and faint paler upperwing-bar. Medium-length wings angled at carpals, and slightly forked tail.
Similar species Differs from Wilson's Storm Petrel by narrower rump-patch (less than tail-length) extending less onto undersides, less distinct wing-bar, wings more angled at carpals, tail more forked, legs not projecting beyond tail-tip and stronger flight. From Leach's Storm Petrel by clean white rump-patch extending onto sides, tail less forked, pale upperwing-bar not reaching leading edge of wing, wings more rounded and less angled at carpals, and slower flight.
Habits Flies with steady banking zigzag, rapid wing-beats and low glides. Feeds by hopping on sea, not pattering, with wings held horizontally.
Range Unconfirmed records off New Ireland and New Caledonia. Breeds scattered across tropical and temperate Pacific and Atlantic, but no closer than Hawaii, and disperses more widely.

LEACH'S STORM PETREL *Oceanodroma leucorhoa* Plate 7

(Océanite cul-blanc)

Description 20 cm (wingspan 46 cm). Medium-sized storm petrel with prominent white rump. Sooty-brown with variably broad and contrasting pale upperwing-bar. Narrow white rump has variable dark line on midline, rarely all dark in east Pacific. Wings are relatively long and pointed. Tail is deeply forked but often held closed.
Similar species Differs from Wilson's and dark-phase White-bellied Storm Petrels by longer forked tail, longer angled wings and narrow white rump with some dark on midline and extending slightly onto underside. See Band-rumped Storm Petrel. Dark-rumped morph differs from Matsudaira's Storm Petrel by shorter, less forked tail and lack of white basal primary shafts.
Habits Direct flight is strong and fast with deep wing-beats and glides. Feeding flight is erratic and bounding, wings often held slightly raised. Wings are usually angled at carpals.

Range Vagrant, with a handful of recent records north of the Bismarcks and west of Vanuatu. *O. l. leucorhoa* breeds in the north Atlantic and north Pacific, dispersing south to subtropical oceans especially September–May, and very small number breed off South Africa, possibly New Zealand, and other subspecies off Mexico.

[TRISTRAM'S STORM PETREL *Oceanodroma tristrami*] Plate 7

(Océanite de Tristram)

Description 25 cm (wingspan 56 cm). Large all-dark storm petrel with broad pale upperwing-bar on greater secondary coverts from carpal to scapulars. May appear to have darker hood, greyish back and paler rump. Long, deeply forked tail.
Similar species Differs from Matsudaira's Storm Petrel by paler rump, plain dark primaries and broader upperwing-bar reaching the forewing. From Leach's Storm Petrel by white rump and larger size. From dark phase Polynesian Storm Petrel by narrower pointed wings and flight action. From Swinhoe's Storm Petrel *O. monorhis*, recorded off north-west Australia but not yet in Melanesia, by more forked tail and broader upperwing-bar reaching the forewing.
Habits Flutters and patters like a Wilson's Storm Petrel, with steep banking turn and glides.
Range No records from Melanesia but has been recorded between Melanesia and Australia.

MATSUDAIRA'S STORM PETREL *Oceanodroma matsudairae* Plate 7

(Océanite de Matsudaira)

Description 24 cm (wingspan 56 cm). Large all-dark storm petrel with distinctive silvery flash halfway between carpal joint and wing-tip. All dark brown except for whitish bases to shafts of outer primaries, which can be difficult to see, and narrow pale upperwing-bar along greater secondary coverts but not reaching the carpal joint. Long wings are angled at carpals and long deeply forked tail is often held closed.
Similar species Differs from Bulwer's Petrel by pale bases to primaries, wing-shape, forked tail, flight action and smaller size. From dark-morph Polynesian Storm Petrel by longer angled wings with pale primary patch. From Leach's Storm Petrel by pale primary patch and narrower upperwing-bar. See Tristram's Storm Petrel.
Habits Slow flight with a few flaps and long glides, often banking. Feeds with wings held high and occasional flaps.
Range Regular migrant around New Ireland and to the north of the Bismarcks and Buka, in small numbers July–August. Breeds Volcano Is, Japan, and disperses to Indonesian seas and tropical Indian Ocean, June–January.

GREBES Podicepedidae

Small dumpy, tail-less diving birds of ponds and lakes. Sit high on water with a rounded and squat shape, or sit very low on water when diving, with a long narrow neck. Often gregarious. Weak fluttering flight pattering low over water surface, but usually dive when disturbed.

LITTLE GREBE *Tachybaptus ruficollis* Plate 1

(Red-throated Little Grebe; Dabchick; Grèbe castagneux)

Description 25 cm. Small dumpy waterbird with darker crown and back. In flight, white wing-bar on secondaries. Adult breeding plumage, sometimes retained through year, has blackish crown, hindneck and breast with chestnut face and neck and large yellow spot at bill-base. Immature and non-breeding adult have off-white face and throat contrasting with dark cap and hindneck, and smaller yellow patch at base of pale bill. Juvenile as immature but with one or more facial stripes.
Similar species Differs from Australasian Grebe by dark or red eye, often paler gape patch, wing-bar not extending beyond secondaries, and chestnut on face of breeding birds extending onto throat and foreneck; but chestnut often poorly discernible on dark neck.
Voice Trill similar to Australasian Grebe but stronger and longer phrases with more marked rise and then fall in tone.
Habits As Australasian Grebe but also in mountains, breeding at 1400 m on Bougainville.
Conservation status Rare and very localised in Melanesia. Not globally threatened.
Range *T. r. collaris* occurs in Bismarcks and Bougainville, with breeding records on New Ireland and at Lake Loloru on Bougainville, and other records from Long, Umboi, New Britain, Witu and Lolobau, and possibly on Nuguria. Elsewhere, *T. r. collaris* occurs in northern New Guinea, and other subspecies occur across Eurasia and Africa.

AUSTRALASIAN GREBE *Tachybaptus novaehollandiae* Plate 1

(Australian [Little] Grebe; Grèbe Australasien)

Description 25 cm. Small dumpy waterbird with yellow or orange eye, large yellow spot at bill-base, and white wing-bar from inner secondaries onto most primaries. Adult breeding plumage, sometimes retained through year, has black head and neck with chestnut on ear-coverts and sides of upper neck. Immature and non-breeding adult have off-white face and throat contrasting with dark cap and hindneck, and smaller yellow patch at base of pale bill. Juvenile as immature but retains one or more facial stripes.
Similar species Smaller and dumpier than ducks. From Little Grebe by yellow eye, longer wing-bar and face pattern of breeding birds, but these may be difficult to discern.
Voice Explosive tittering trill lasting *c.*1.5 seconds and repeated irregularly.
Habits Lakes, including small ponds, usually with waterside and or floating vegetation. Swims high or low on water, dives for food and when disturbed. Often gregarious.
Conservation status Uncommon and localised, usually one or a few pairs on each suitable lake. Not globally threatened.
Range Scattered across Melanesia.
T. n. incola recorded from Manus where possibly a vagrant and on New Britain where a localised breeding resident, but status confused with Little Grebe, and elsewhere occurs in northern New Guinea.
T. n. rennellianus, endemic to Rennell where common on the lake, has slightly larger bill and more white on wings than *T. n. incola*.
T. n. leucosternos, endemic to Vanuatu and New Caledonia, where recorded from Gaua, Santo, Malo, Ambae, Maewo, Malekula, Ambrym, Epi, Efate and Grande Terre, mostly in west, has pure white lower breast.
Birds of an unknown subspecies have been reported on Guadalcanal at Lake Lauvi. Other subspecies occur from Indonesia to New Zealand.

TROPICBIRDS Phaethontidae

Medium-sized gull-like seabirds. Pelagic, usually solitary, sitting on sea or flapping slowly high over the sea and diving down to the surface. Pairs and small groups perform fast manoeuvres high over breeding islands, often calling loudly.

RED-TAILED TROPICBIRD *Phaethon rubricauda* Plate 9

(Phaéton à brins rouges)

Description 46 cm plus up to 55 cm tail-streamers. Stocky white tropicbird. Adult appears all white at distance, sometimes tinted pink, but has red tail-streamers, fine black streaks on outer primaries and bold black tertial centres. The bill is usually red but rarely orange or yellow. Juvenile lacks streamers and has grey-black bill, soon becoming red, fine black barring on neck, mantle and wing-coverts, and black streaks on outer primaries and sometimes primary coverts and uppertail.
Similar species Adult differs from White-tailed Tropicbird by bill and streamer colour, little black on wing, and bulkier build. Juvenile differs by bill grey becoming red, dark shaft-streaks on primary coverts, and dark shaft-streaks on the outer primaries broadening subterminally to show black primary tips when perched. Differs from gulls and large terns by stocky build and all-white plumage, which is shared by Black-naped and White Terns.
Voice Loud screams and croaks around breeding islands, and other loud calls at nest.
Habits Pelagic, rarely following ships, and coming close inshore only around breeding islands. Heavier flight than White-tailed Tropicbird. Nests on cliffs, or under bushes and rocks on flat atolls.
Conservation status Rare and localised in Melanesia. At risk locally from rats and cats but not globally threatened.
Range Breeds in Vanuatu and New Caledonia, and is rare at sea. Two unconfirmed records from Bismarcks and two from Solomons. Breeds on Tongoa, probably Laika and perhaps elsewhere in Vanuatu, and on the distant New Caledonian islands of Surprise, Walpole, Matthew, Hunter and perhaps Île de Pins. Rarely recorded at sea. Sometimes considered monotypic; otherwise *P. r. roseotincta* also breeds on islets off Australia and other subspecies breed in tropical Pacific and Indian Oceans.

WHITE-TAILED TROPICBIRD *Phaethon lepturus* Plate 9

(Phaéton à bec jaune)

Description 38 cm plus up to 45 cm tail-streamers. Slender white tropicbird with bold black upperwing-bars. Adult is white with white tail-streamers, large solid black inner wing-bar, black on outer primaries and rich yellow bill. Juvenile lacks streamers and has barred neck, mantle, rump and inner wing-coverts, black streaks on outer primaries and dark grey bill soon becoming yellow.
Similar species Adult differs from Red-tailed Tropicbird by bill and streamer colour, solid black on wing, and slender build. Juvenile differs by greyer bill becoming yellow, white primary coverts and dark streaks on outer primaries narrowing towards tips which appear all-white when perched.
Voice Loud *kek-kek-kek* and screams over breeding islands. Other guttural calls on nest.
Habits Pelagic, often following ships, coming close inshore only around breeding islands. Nests in tree-holes, or under bushes on tree-less atolls.
Conservation status Uncommon and localised in Melanesia. At risk locally from rats and cats but not globally threatened.
Range Breeds on remote islands across Melanesia and is scarce at sea across the region. Breeds in small numbers on Tench, Nuguria, Kilinailau, Nukumanu, Tikopia, Anuta, Malo, Walpole, Matthew and Hunter. Sometimes considered monotypic; otherwise *P. l. dorotheae* also breeds across the tropical Pacific and other subspecies breed in the Caribbean, tropical Atlantic and Indian Oceans.

IBISES AND SPOONBILLS Threskiornithidae (Plataleidae)

Large wading birds with long legs, necks and bills, similar to herons but stockier. Ibises have decurved bills and spoonbills have flattened spoon-shaped bills. Fly with outstretched necks, often gliding between steady wing-beats.

AUSTRALIAN WHITE IBIS *Threskiornis molucca* Plate 11

(Australian Ibis; Ibis à cou noir)

Description 64 cm (*T. m. pygmaeus*). White but often stained dirty, with greyish-black long curved bill, legs, naked head and neck, tertials and tips to primaries. Breeding adult has black tertial plumes and pink-red skin visible on underwing, nape and sometimes legs. Juvenile has short black feathers on head and shorter bill. In flight, all white with black bill, head, legs and primary tips.
Similar species Black head and curved bill is distinctive. Differs from immature Royal Spoonbill by bill-shape and black tertials. From Straw-necked Ibis by white wings and body.
Voice Deep honking *ghar-ghar-ghar-*.
Habits Flocks wander around dry open habitats and forest clearings. Perch in tree-tops. Often tame.
Conservation status Common and not threatened.
Range *T. m. pygmaeus* is endemic to Rennell and Bellona. Two vagrants reported from Mono were probably *T. m. molucca*, which is larger and longer-billed than *T. m. pygmaeus*, and breeds in east Indonesia, New Guinea and Australia.

STRAW-NECKED IBIS *Threskiornis spinicollis* Plate 11

(Ibis d'Australie)

Description 68 cm. Pied ibis with iridescent black upperparts and breast and dark grey head and bill. White upper neck, breast to vent and tail. Adult has straw-coloured neck-plumes and breeding adult has red legs. Juvenile has dull matt-black upperparts, blackish legs and shorter bill. In flight, white on belly extends as wedge onto black underwing-coverts.
Similar species Differs from Australian White Ibis and Glossy Ibis by black upperparts and white underparts.
Voice Usually silent but sometimes grunts.
Habits Flocks walk on short grassland and beside wetlands. Often perches in dead trees.
Range One record from New Ireland. Elsewhere, breeds in Australia and erratic visitor to New Guinea.

GLOSSY IBIS *Plegadis falcinellus* Plate 11

(Ibis falcinelle)

Description 60 cm. Uniformly dark ibis with very fine white line around facial skin and long decurved bill. Breeding adult has bronze and green iridescence; non-breeding is duller and sometimes has some white on head. Immature is duller with some pale mottling on head and shorter bill.

Similar species Dark plumage and decurved bill distinctive. Differs from curlews and whimbrels by plain blackish plumage.
Voice Usually silent but sometimes grunts.
Habits Gregarious in freshwater wetlands, usually in wet short herbaceous vegetation, occasionally coastal or dry habitats. Flies with drooping bill, neck and legs.
Range Vagrant to Manus, Buka, Bougainville, Kolombangara and Grande Terre, New Caledonia. Elsewhere, patchily cosmopolitan distribution, including Australia, and migrates erratically to New Guinea.

ROYAL SPOONBILL *Platalea regia* Plate 11

(Spatule royale)

Description 77 cm. Tall white waterbird possessing long black bill with spoon-shaped tip, black facial skin and long black legs. Adult has yellow patch above eye and red patch on crown. Breeding adult has shaggy crest and buff wash on breast. Immature has duller bare-parts and black primary tips.
Similar species Bill shape is distinctive. Differs from immature Australian White Ibis by larger size and straight bill. From egrets by stouter shape and long rounded bill.
Voice Usually silent.
Habits Freshwater lakes and swamps, occasionally sheltered muddy seas. Singles and small groups wade in shallow water, sweeping bill from side to side. Flies on flat wings with neck outstretched and soars high.
Range Vagrant to Three Sisters, Bellona and Rennell, where it may have bred, and uncommon migrant to Grande Terre and Ile des Pins, New Caledonia. Elsewhere, breeds in east Indonesia, Australia and New Zealand with migrants reaching New Guinea.

HERONS Ardeidae

Tall birds with long legs and necks, which stalk fish from the edge of water. Fly short distances with neck outstretched and longer distances with neck coiled in S-bend, legs trailing. Bitterns are solitary hunched skulkers with cryptic plumage. Egrets are usually white, and develop plumes and brighter bare parts during the breeding season.

AUSTRALASIAN BITTERN *Botaurus poiciloptilus* Plate 12

(Australian Bittern; Butor d'Australie)

Description 70 cm. Stout heron with cryptic mottled brown plumage. Upperparts are warm brown, mottled and streaked with buff and black, underparts paler with dark streaks, and throat paler or white with broad dark moustachial stripe. Stout dull yellow bill and short greenish legs. In flight, wing-coverts are slightly paler than flight feathers, and feet project behind tail.
Similar species Differs from immature Nankeen Night Heron by larger size, dark mottled plumage, and no pale spots on upperparts.
Voice Territorial call is a very deep resonant boom like a distant foghorn *woomph!*, most often at dusk and through night. Hoarse *kra-ak* when flushed.
Habits Solitary and skulking deep within reeds and other tall herbaceous marshes. When disturbed, creeps off into cover or freezes pointing bill upwards or flies slowly and heavily for a short distance before landing back in cover. Does not perch in trees. Often more active at dawn and dusk, and perhaps at night.
Conservation status Status in Melanesia unknown but no recent confirmed records, so presumed to be very rare and threatened. IUCN: Endangered.
Range New Caledonia, on Grande Terre and Ouvéa, where current status is unknown. Elsewhere, breeds in Australia and New Zealand.

BLACK-BACKED BITTERN *Ixobrychus dubius* Plate 12

(Australian Little Bittern; also treated as a subspecies of Little Bittern *I. minutus*; Blongios nain)

Description 35 cm. Very small bittern with darker back and wings. In flight, pale wing-coverts contrast with blackish primaries and secondaries and black or dark brown back. Adult male has black crown, back and tail, chestnut head and neck, pale buff wing-covert patch, and dark brown double-stripe from throat to mid-belly, flanked by some indistinct broad buff streaks. Adult female is duller, with dark brown crown, rufous-brown back and paler underparts. Juvenile

has blotchy dark streaks across orange-rufous upperparts, many long dark and pale streaks along underparts and no dark cap. In flight, juvenile shows little contrast between wing-coverts and flight feathers, which have rufous tips.
Similar species Differs from juvenile Striated Heron by smaller size and contrasting pale wing-coverts. From juvenile Nankeen Night Heron by smaller slimmer size and plain upperparts. From very similar Yellow Bittern by greener legs; slightly blunter bill is shorter than head. Black back of male is distinctive. Female from Yellow Bittern by dark brown mantle and dark double line down centre of throat and breast. Juvenile is very like Yellow Bittern but has rufous tips to wing feathers.
Voice Territorial call a series of deep croaking *kowh* notes repeated regularly at half-second intervals for up to ten seconds. Single or repeated sharp *koh!* when flushed. (Call descriptions from Australia.)
Habits Dense marshes, usually in reeds or rushes, often beside small lakes including in city parks. Singles or pairs skulk, hiding in cover during day, occasionally flying over water, and freeze in outstretched position or fly when disturbed.
Conservation status Rare and local in Melanesia, and may be Near Threatened.
Range One breeding record from New Caledonia, where a pair nested in Nouméa from 2001. Elsewhere, breeds in Australia, where only a few thousand pairs, and possibly New Guinea.

YELLOW BITTERN *Ixobrychus sinensis* — Plate 12

(Blongios de Chine)

Description 35 cm. Very small bittern with brown back and blackish wings. Warm buffy-brown with narrow dark crown, faintly streaked throat and darker mantle. In flight, pale wing-coverts contrast with blackish primaries and secondaries. Adult male has blackish crown. Adult female is variably duller with more prominent streaks on throat, breast and mantle. Juvenile has dark streaks on upperparts, pale fringes to darker wing-coverts and many fine streaks on off-white underparts.
Similar species Wing pattern is distinctive. Differs from juvenile Striated Heron by smaller size and paler warmer brown plumage. From juvenile Nankeen Night Heron by smaller slimmer size and no spots on upperparts. From Black-backed Bittern on New Caledonia, see above.
Voice Territorial call a series of low *wHOa* hoots, evenly spaced every two seconds. Occasional harsh *kak-kak-kak* when flushed.
Habits Dense marshes, usually in reeds, but also rice-paddies, mangroves and scrub beside swamps. Skulks, hiding in cover during day, and freezes in upright position or flushes when disturbed.
Conservation status Rare and local in Melanesia, but not globally threatened.
Range Very localised breeder on Bougainville. Records from New Britain, Watom and Ninigo Is may be breeding, wintering or vagrant birds. Elsewhere, breeds from Asia to Micronesia and possibly New Guinea, and winters south to New Guinea.

BLACK BITTERN *Dupetor flavicollis* — Plate 12

(*Ixobrychus flavicollis*; Blongios à cou jaune)

Description 58 cm. Medium-small heron with broad buffy lateral throat-stripe, appearing as patch when neck hunched. Otherwise, all dark with buffy and white streaking along middle of throat and breast, and dull green-grey legs. Adult male is almost black except for throat markings. Adult female and immature male upperparts vary from grey-rufous to bright rufous with black cap, buffy throat-stripe and sometimes buffy streaking on orange-buff underparts, and in flight show darker, often blackish primaries and secondaries contrasting with rufous mantle and wing-coverts. Juvenile is dull brown with pale fringes on upperparts and heavily spotted or barred underparts. A rare albino form, usually with black cap, buffy neck and variable amounts of dark plumage on upperparts, occurs on New Britain.
Similar species Throat pattern is distinctive. From juvenile Striated Heron by larger size, plainer underparts except for streaks on throat, and dull-coloured legs. White birds from egrets by stockier shape and usually creamier plumage.
Voice Territorial call is a loud booming *GHou*, repeated at irregular intervals and often given at dawn or dusk. Silent when flushed.
Habits Usually beside swamps or small streams in densely vegetated habitats but also in dry dense forest and mangroves. Only in extreme lowlands. Solitary and crepuscular or nocturnal, creeping along edge of water or very low branch over water. Often roosts high in dense foliage. When disturbed, flushes to perch in canopy or freezes with bill pointed upwards.
Conservation status Uncommon to fairly common, and not threatened.

Range Admiralties, St Matthias Is, Bismarcks and Solomons.
D. f. australis breeds across Bismarcks, including Hermit, Ninigo, Admiralty and St Matthias Is, and elsewhere breeds in Indonesia, New Guinea and Australia.
D. f. woodfordi is endemic to Solomons, where probably widespread, with records from Bougainville, Shortland, Choiseul, Isabel, New Georgia group, Guadalcanal, Ulawa and Rennell but not Makira; male is black with white throat-streaks and female has tawny-rufous upperparts and buffy-ochre underparts with a few black spots on midline upper throat.
Elsewhere, *D. f. flavicollis* breeds from Pakistan to Indonesia.

NANKEEN NIGHT HERON *Nycticorax caledonicus* — Plate 12

(Rufous Night-Heron; Bihoreau cannelle)

Description 58 cm. Medium-sized orange-brown heron with stocky shape and short stout bill. Adult has orange-brown upperparts, paler on neck and throat, white belly, black crown and grey bill. Breeding adult has two long white plumes from crown. Juvenile is warm brown with large off-white spots on upperparts, narrow white streaks on crown, broad brown streaks on buffy-white underparts and greenish-yellow and grey bill. Immature first develops black crown and plain mantle. In flight, shows broad rounded wings and stubby bill.
Similar species Adult's orange-brown plumage, plain wing pattern and stout black bill is distinctive. Juvenile and immature differ from juvenile bitterns by stockier shape, stouter bill and heavier pale spots; also larger and paler than Striated Heron and Black Bittern, and lack buffy throat-stripe.
Voice Loud *kyok* often given in flight.
Habits Close to water, usually along forested lakes and rivers but also open marshes and coasts, up to 700 m. Crepuscular and nocturnal, often roosting communally in tree-tops. Singles and small flocks leave roost at dusk, flying high and slow like flying-foxes.
Conservation status Fairly common and not threatened.
Range Across Melanesia except St Matthias, Rennell, Temotu, Vanuatu where a rare vagrant, and Loyalties.
N. c. hilli breeds on Admiralties, Ninigo Is, Kaniet and Long; elsewhere breeds in Indonesia, New Guinea, Australia and New Zealand.
N. c. mandibularis, endemic to Bismarcks and Solomons, occurring on many tiny islands but not St Matthias or Temotu, has richer chestnut upperparts with black tips to occipital plumes and no white above eye, but birds on some islands off New Britain are intermediates with *N. c. hilli*.
N. c. caledonicus, endemic to Grande Terre, New Caledonia, has duller and greyer upperparts.
Elsewhere, other subspecies breed from Philippines to Micronesia.

STRIATED HERON *Butorides striata* — Plate 12

(Héron strié)

Description 45 cm. Very small dark heron with short, often hunched neck, black cap and paler underparts. Has slim dark grey bill with variable dull yellow base. In flight, yellowish legs conspicuous and wing-coverts slightly paler than primaries and secondaries. Adult has dark grey mantle and wings, plain grey neck and underparts with black spots along white throat. Breeding adult has orange feet. Juvenile has browner upperparts with slight pale streaking on crown, pale tips on wing-coverts, heavily streaked buffy underparts and duller legs.
Similar species Differs from Nankeen Night Heron by smaller slighter shape; adult is much greyer, immature slightly greyer and darker, especially on underparts, with plainer mantle. From Black Bittern by paler, more contrasting plumage which lacks buffy throat-stripe. From Yellow and Black-backed Bittern by larger, more thickset shape, greyer plumage and no contrasting pale upper wing-coverts. From Australasian Bittern by smaller size and grey-brown plumage.
Voice Usually calls when flushed. Explosive nasal *tchew!* Also series of high-pitched rasping *kit-kit-* notes.
Habits Beside water, especially reefs, coastal creeks and mangroves but also inland along rivers, swamps and sometimes dry thickets. Solitary, creeping along water's edge or perched on branch low over water. Usually perches hidden in undergrowth but also on open reefs.
Conservation status Rare in Bismarcks and locally common in Solomons and Vanuatu. Vagrant or extremely rare in New Caledonia. Not globally threatened.
Range Across Melanesia but rare or absent from many islands.
B. s. solomonensis breeds on Lavongai and New Ireland, with scattered records of unknown subspecies from Manus, Mussau and New Britain, and breeds across Solomons (except Rennell and the most isolated tiny islands) to south Vanuatu (but absent from many islands), and elsewhere breeds only in Fiji.

B. s. macrorhynchus, very rare, perhaps vagrant, on Grande Terre and Ouvéa, is larger with fewer throat-spots and narrower buff fringes on wing-coverts, and elsewhere breeds in east Australia.
Elsewhere, other subspecies breed across South America, Africa and Eurasia.

EASTERN CATTLE EGRET *Bubulcus coromandus* Plate 11

(Also treated as a subspecies of Cattle Egret *B. ibis*; Héron garde-boeufs)

Description 50 cm. A small dumpy white egret with distinctive 'jowl' or bulge under bill-base and chin, and short yellow bill. Legs are usually dull green but may be grey or black. Non-breeding adult is all white. Breeding adult has orange-buff on head, neck and mantle, orange-red bill and dull red legs. Juvenile as non-breeding adult but has duskier legs and bill.
Similar species Jowl of bulging chin feathers and buff plumage of adult distinctive. Also differs from Intermediate Egret and other egrets by smaller dumpier size and shorter neck, bill and legs.
Voice Usually silent.
Habits Gregarious, usually foraging for insects in short grassland, often with cattle. Vagrants are often on airfields.
Range Vagrant, with single records from Manus, New Ireland, New Britain and Guadalcanal, and a few records from Grande Terre, Lifou and Maré. May remain for some years and might breed in future. Elsewhere, breeds from South-East Asia to Australia and New Zealand.

EASTERN GREAT EGRET *Ardea modesta* Plate 11

(*Casmerodius modestus*; *Egretta modestus*; also treated as a subspecies of Great [White] Egret *A. alba*; Grande Aigrette)

Description 84 cm. Tall all-white egret with long slender neck, often kinked and longer than body when outstretched. Non-breeding and immature birds have long slender yellow bill with variable dusky tip and dark yellowish legs. Breeding adult has plumes on mantle, black bill, greenish or blue facial skin and black or reddish legs. In flight, has slowest wing-beats, most bulging neck and longest leg projection of any egret.
Similar species Differs from other egrets by being taller and more elegant, with longer, more kinked neck, and diagnostic extension of gape-line just onto cheeks beyond eye. From Royal Spoonbill by pointed bill.
Voice Repeated deep rasping *arh-arh-* when flushed.
Habits Open lakes and rivers, occasionally on coasts, rarely on short grassland and not in wetlands shaded by forest. Singles or small flocks walk slowly in shallow water.
Conservation status Breeding status in Melanesia is unknown; possibly breeds on New Britain where locally common, and probably an irregular and uncommon non-breeding visitor elsewhere from Australia. Not globally threatened.
Range New Britain, and migrant to Solomons and New Caledonia, with many records from Bougainville, New Georgia island group, Guadalcanal, Rennell and Grande Terre, and a vagrant to Manus, Unea, Buka, Isabel, Bellona, Tanna, Lifou and Chesterfield, mostly April–October. Elsewhere, breeds from India to Australia and New Zealand.

INTERMEDIATE EGRET *Egretta intermedia* Plate 11

(*Ardea intermedia*; *Mesophoyx intermedia*; Héron intermédiaire)

Description 64 cm. Medium-sized all-white egret with long neck about same length as body when fully stretched and slight jowl under bill-base. Medium-length yellow bill with variable dusky or black tip. Legs usually black but may be yellow, dusky, black or red. Breeding adult has plumes on breast and back, red bill, greenish facial skin, red upper legs and black lower legs.
Similar species Often confused with Eastern Cattle Egret but much larger with longer bill, neck and legs. Differs from Little Egret by bulkier shape and bulkier yellow bill. From white-morph Pacific Reef Heron by different bare-part colours, finer bill, longer legs and neck, and different habitat. From non-breeding Eastern Great Egret by smaller size, shorter stouter bill, shorter neck and gape not extending beyond eye.
Voice Usually silent.
Habits Singles or small flocks beside freshwater and damp grassland, sometimes with cattle.
Range Vagrant to Manus, Umboi, New Britain, Buka, Bougainville and Makira. Elsewhere, *E. i. plumifera* breeds in east Indonesia, New Guinea and Australia, and two other subspecies in Africa and south Asia.

PIED HERON *Egretta picata* (not illustrated)

(Pied Egret; Héron pie)

Description 47 cm. Small pied heron. All dark slaty-grey with white throat, neck and upper breast, including long plumes on breast, yellow bill and medium-long legs. Adult has slaty-grey cap, with longer crest feathers in breeding plumage. Immature has plain white head, often darker mottling on head and neck, and browner body and wings.
Similar species Distinctive pattern but see Straw-necked Ibis.
Voice A loud croaking *awk* when flushed.
Habits Solitary or in flocks beside lakes, river and coasts, especially in shallow water beside lakes, and sometimes in grassland. Stands still or actively chases after prey.
Range One recent record from Surprise, New Caledonia. Breeds in northern Australia and Sulawesi, some migrating to New Guinea and eastern Indonesia.

WHITE-FACED HERON *Egretta novaehollandiae* Plate 11

(*Ardea novaehollandiae*; Aigrette à face blanche)

Description 66 cm. Large elegant blue-grey heron with irregular white face-patch and reddish-pink wash on breast. In flight, shows darker upper primaries and secondaries than wing-coverts. Juvenile is browner with less distinct white face-patch.
Similar species Differs from dark-morph Pacific Reef Heron by white face and slender build. From Striated Heron by larger size, paler grey plumage and white face.
Voice A repeated loud croaking *graaw* when flushed.
Habits Solitary or in small loose groups beside lakes, rivers, mangroves, coasts, reefs and also grasslands including airfields. Often perches conspicuously on trees, posts and other artificial structures. Flies short distances with neck outstretched, and longer distances with neck retracted, as other herons.
Conservation status Locally common. Not threatened.
Range Breeds on New Caledonia; vagrant across Solomons and Vanuatu. Breeds on Grande Terre and Ile des Pins, where sometimes separated as smaller endemic subspecies *E. n. nana*. Rare vagrant to Bougainville, Guadalcanal, Nendo and Torres Is, and commoner on Tanna, Aneityum, Ouvéa and Lifou. Appears to be expanding range and may occur more commonly. Elsewhere, breeds in Indonesia, Australia, New Guinea and New Zealand, and colonised Fiji in 2002.

LITTLE EGRET *Egretta garzetta* Plate 11

(Aigrette garzette)

Description 56 cm. A small elegant white egret. All-white with slim black bill, bright yellow facial skin, black legs and greenish-yellow soles to feet. Breeding adult has plumes on mantle and breast and a pair of streamers from crown. Immature has duller facial skin and may have dull yellow on bill-base and dull yellow on lower legs or grey-green legs.
Similar species Differs from all other egrets by slimmer black bill, more elegant shape, smaller size and active feeding habits. Black bare parts are shared only by some Eastern Great Egrets, but Little much smaller, finer-billed, appears shorter-legged and more compact and buoyant in flight. Immature with grey-green legs differs from Pacific Reef Heron by finer bill and longer legs.
Voice A short croak *kark*.
Habits Singles stalk in shallow fresh water, estuaries and creeks, often actively chasing and darting after prey, sometimes paddling feet in water, and often mixed with other waterbirds.
Range *E. g. nigripes* is a rare vagrant to New Britain, Buka, Bougainville and Vonavona. Elsewhere, it breeds in South-East Asia and New Guinea, and other subspecies breed patchily across Africa and south Eurasia.

PACIFIC REEF HERON *Egretta sacra* Plate 11

(Eastern Reef Egret; Aigrette sacrée)

Description 64 cm. A thick-set stout-billed egret with relatively short stout legs. Most birds are either all white or uniformly dark grey except for a small white chin-patch. Patchy intermediate morph uncommon. Breeding adult has plumes on nape and short plumes on mantle and breast. Bill colour varies from yellow, through dusky on tip, to dark, sometimes with a yellowish base. Legs are usually greenish, sometimes yellowish to pale brown, and relatively short, with only feet projecting from tail in flight.

Similar species Usually the only heron on exposed coasts apart from Striated and White-faced Herons. Dark morph differs from White-faced Heron by being darker and more uniform, without an obvious white face-patch. White morph differs from Eastern Cattle Egret by being larger with longer neck, longer bill, greenish legs and less jowl. Differs from other egrets by stouter blunter bill and shorter stouter greenish legs.
Voice Usually silent but occasional harsh frog-like croaks.
Habits Usually solitary or in pairs along all coasts, especially reefs, rocky coasts and mangroves. Occasionally several kilometres inland up rivers to 400 m altitude. Single pairs nest in treetops, usually on small islets. Usually walks slowly along water's edge in hunched bent-over stance.
Conservation status Common and not threatened.
Range *E. s. sacra* occurs across Melanesia, including most tiny and remote islands, and the larger *E. s. albolineata* is endemic to New Caledonia and Loyalties. Elsewhere, *E. s. sacra* breeds along coasts from India to Polynesia.

FRIGATEBIRDS Fregatidae

Very large black and white seabirds with long flexed wings and long narrow tail, deeply forked when spread. Soar to great heights over the sea or coast, occasionally inland especially after strong winds, snatching food from sea or chasing other seabirds for their food. Gregarious and often found in mixed-species feeding flocks. Usually less than 80 km from land, as flocks return nightly to roost on small islands, and never sit on sea. Nest colonially in trees, often mixed with other seabird species. Male inflates red throat-pouch during display.

[CHRISTMAS FRIGATEBIRD *Fregata andrewsi*] Plate 9

(Christmas Island Frigatebird; Frégate d'Andrews)

Description Male 91 cm, female 100 cm. Large frigatebird with white extending onto rear belly and prominent pale bars on upperwing. Adult male is all black with white shield on lower breast and belly, sometimes with white extending onto axillaries. Adult female has black head and throat, narrow white collar, black spur on upper breast, straight white spur onto underwing and white extending onto lower belly. Juvenile has hexagonal-shaped white belly-patch, black breast-band and buff or white head, usually with narrow parallel-edged white extension onto axillaries from behind breast-band. Immature intermediate but usually shows narrow, parallel-edged white on axillaries, behind short black extensions onto breast-sides.
Similar species Adult male has distinctive belly-patch but beware juvenile Great Frigatebird with slightly higher belly-patch in combination with brown head. Female differs from Lesser Frigatebird by white extending onto lower belly, black spurs on breast-sides and larger straighter white axillary spurs. Juvenile differs from juvenile Great Frigatebird by hexagonal belly-patch and shape of axillary spurs, usually present, with second-year birds attaining black breast-spurs.
Habits Pelagic, as other frigatebirds.
Range No definite records from Melanesia but several birds with plumage of this species seen in flocks of other frigatebirds in Solomons. Rare breeder on Christmas I, Indian Ocean, and vagrant to south New Guinea.

GREAT FRIGATEBIRD *Fregata minor* Plate 9

(Frégate du Pacifique)

Description Male 86 cm, female 93 cm. Large frigatebird without white spurs on underwing. Adult male is all black, with red throat-sac, usually only visible when displaying. Adult female is all black except white from chin to upper belly, with prominent black cap, and white extending further back along flanks than on belly midline. Juvenile has buff or white head and neck, black breast-band, egg-shaped white lower breast- and belly-patch; about 30% have short axillary spurs from centre of breast patch. Immature is intermediate with mottled plumage but never has any white on axillaries.
Similar species Adult male is only entirely black frigatebird. Female and immature are distinctive in lacking white axillary spurs, but these are also lacking in some juvenile or adult male Christmas Frigatebirds, from which female differs by pale throat and black point on belly, juvenile differs by shape of spurs and egg-shaped belly-patch, and immature male lacks black breast-spurs.
Voice Various whinnying and reeling calls and bill-snapping and rattling given by perched birds on breeding sites.
Habits Pelagic but often flies over land. Usually rarer than, but mixed with, Lesser Frigatebirds. Nests colonially in tree-tops, often with boobies and other seabirds.
Conservation status Fairly common at sea but a rare breeder. Not globally threatened but breeding status in Melanesia may be under threat.

Range Widespread at sea; breeds only on Tench, Nuguria, Surprise, Chesterfield and Walpole, but roosts more commonly on small islands across Melanesia. Monotypic, but sometimes treated as five subspecies, of which *F. m. palmerstoni* is endemic to west and central Pacific. Elsewhere, pantropical.

LESSER FRIGATEBIRD *Fregata ariel* — Plate 9

(Least Frigatebird; Frégate ariel)

Description 76 cm. Smallest frigatebird, always with white spurs extending onto axillaries. Adult male is all black except for narrow white bar from sides of flanks onto underwing-coverts and red throat-patch visible in display. Adult female has black hood and throat, white breast with triangular spurs and white extending further back along flanks than on belly midline. Juvenile has buff or white head, black breast-band and triangular white breast-patch with triangular or parallel-edged white spurs. Immature is intermediate and mottled.
Similar species Adult male has distinctive white bars, but these are sometimes dull and obscure at long range. Female differs from Great Frigatebird by white spurs and black throat, and from Christmas Frigatebird by black extending up central belly, and white spurs more triangular and behind breast. Juvenile differs from both by its triangular breast-patch.
Voice Various whistles, squeals, shrieks and bill-clapping at breeding sites.
Habits Gregarious and often common at sea and occasionally gliding over land. Nests colonially in tree-tops, bushes or on ground, often with boobies and other seabirds.
Conservation status Common at sea but localised breeder in Melanesia. Some colonies may be locally at risk, but species not globally threatened.
Range Across Melanesia, breeding on Tench, Nuguria, Chesterfield, Surprise and Walpole but roosting more commonly on many small islands. Elsewhere, *F. a. ariel* also breeds from tropical central Indian Ocean to central Pacific, and other subspecies are pantropical.

PELICANS Pelecanidae

Massive gregarious waterbirds with a huge pink bill, short legs and short tail. Dive for fish from the air or water surface.

AUSTRALIAN PELICAN *Pelecanus conspicillatus* — Plate 9

(Pélican à lunettes)

Description 170 cm. Huge black and white waterbird with very long pink bill. White with black tail and upperwing, and white patch on secondary coverts. Female smaller with shorter bill. Immature has browner wing, tail and bill. In flight, shows black upperwing, rump and tail except for white patch on wing-coverts and narrow rump-band, and white underwing with black primaries and secondaries.
Similar species Unmistakable. Differs from boobies and White-bellied Sea Eagle by very different flight actions and proportions.
Habits Usually seen perched on water, shoreline, or trees beside lakes or brackish water including estuaries. Flies slowly in V-formation, with retracted neck and deep slow wing-beats, gliding and soaring.
Range Vagrant, often blown by cyclones, across Melanesia, with individuals sometimes staying for years. Breeds in New Guinea and Australia.

GANNETS AND BOOBIES Sulidae

Medium-sized seabirds, feeding by spectacular dives into the sea. Usually fly high above the sea, alternating slow powerful wing-beats with glides; congregate at mixed-species feeding flocks, and sometimes settle on water. Rarely found more than 50 km from land, and return nightly to roost on small islands. Robust body with long straight bill, neck, wings and pointed tail. All are black or brown and white with brightly coloured bare parts.

AUSTRALASIAN GANNET *Morus serrator* — Plate 8

(Australian Gannet; *Sula serrator*; Fou austral)

Description 88 cm. Large pied or greyish booby. Adult is white with black primaries and secondaries except white innermost secondaries, black central tail feathers, yellowish head and grey bill. Juvenile has grey-brown upperparts with white spots, grey-brown head and neck contrasting with off-white breast and belly, and off-white underwing with broad dark grey-brown margins. Immature as adult but has variable mottling of juvenile feathers, often retaining all-dark tail.

Similar species Adult differs from Masked Booby by white outer tail and inner secondaries, yellow head and grey bill. From pale-morph Red-footed Booby by black on tail, white underwing primary coverts, yellow head and dark grey feet. Juvenile differs from Masked Booby by lacking paler nape and upper back. From other immature boobies by greyer, spotted upperparts. Plumage similar to many albatrosses but is smaller and has different flight and habits.

Habits Pelagic but more often inshore than other boobies.

Range One record from Belep off New Caledonia, and may occur more frequently as a vagrant to southern Melanesia. Breeds off south-east Australia and New Zealand, and ranges around coast of Australia to latitude of New Caledonia.

[ABBOTT'S BOOBY *Papasula abbotti*] Plate 8

(*Sula abbotti*; Fou d'Abbott)

Description 79 cm. Small booby with all-black upperwings. Off-white head, body and underwing, with black upperwing and tail, white spots on wing-coverts, a few black spots on flanks and rump, and narrow black margins on underwing. Black eye-patch. Male and juvenile have pale grey bill with black tip. Female has pink bill with black tip. In flight, has narrower head, neck and wings than other boobies.

Similar species Distinctive black upperwings contrasting with white head and body is shared only by much larger albatrosses. Pink or grey bill with black tip is usually distinctive but very rarely shared by Red-footed Booby.

Habits Probably as other boobies.

Range No recent records from Melanesia but known from subfossil bones on Tikopia in Temotu, and Efate in Vanuatu, where it probably bred until hunted to extinction. Now breeds only on Christmas I in Indian Ocean, dispersing to adjacent seas.

MASKED BOOBY *Sula dactylatra* Plate 8

(Fou masqué)

Description 80 cm. Large pied booby. Adult is white with black tail and flight feathers, black mask around eye and bill-base, dark grey or green legs, and yellow bill sometimes greenish-yellow, orange or pink, especially in female. Juvenile has brown hood separated from mottled brown upperparts by whitish collar and upper mantle.

Similar species Adult differs from similar white morph Red-footed Booby by bare-part colours, only a tiny black spot on underwing-coverts, black on inner wing extending to tertials, always a black tail and larger size. Whitish collar and brown hood of juvenile is distinctive, as are mottled upperparts, but underwing pattern similar to juvenile Brown Booby. See Australasian Gannet and Abbott's Booby.

Voice Honking and whistling at nest.

Habits Generally more pelagic than other boobies, often solitary, and flying and diving from greater heights. Nests colonially on ground.

Conservation status Rare and localised in Melanesia. Probably threatened in Melanesia but not globally threatened.

Range Rare at sea across Melanesia, and breeds off New Caledonia.

S. d. personata breeds on Chesterfield and Surprise off New Caledonia and occasionally on Carrey in the New Caledonian lagoon and perhaps some distant Bismarck atolls, and occurs at sea across Melanesia; has orange-yellow eyes; elsewhere, it breeds in east Indian Ocean and west Pacific.

Tasman Booby *S. d. tasmani* or *S. d. fullagari* has been recorded in Vanuatu and New Caledonia, and may occur elsewhere in as a non-breeding migrant; has dark brown eyes, and breeds on Lord Howe, Norfolk and Kermadec Is, just south of Melanesia.

Elsewhere, other subspecies are pantropical.

RED-FOOTED BOOBY *Sula sula* Plate 8

(Fou à pieds rouges)

Description 75 cm. Small booby with distinctive red feet but variable plumage. Adult has blue bill, pink around bill-base and bright red feet. Most are white morphs, with black primaries, secondaries and patch on underwing primary coverts only visible at close range. Some have black tail. Intermediate morph has brown head and body, variably paler than wings, with white tail, rump and vent. Dark morph is all chocolate-brown. Juvenile is all dark brown with variably pale belly and centre to underwing, grey-brown bill and facial skin and grey feet. Immature is often mottled greyish-brown.

Similar species Adult has distinctive red feet. White morph has distinctive black primary-covert patch on underwing, but see Masked Booby and Australasian Gannet. Intermediate morph has distinctive plumage. Brown morph and juvenile differ from Brown Booby by poorly defined paler belly and central underwing, and bare-parts colour. From Australasian Gannet by plain warmer brown plumage, often with less white on underparts.

Voice Sharp metallic *karrk* and other guttural cackles at nest.

Habits Gregarious at sea close to colonies. Breeds in colonies in tree-tops or cliffs, often with other seabirds. Perches high in large trees or artificial structures at colonies and roost sites. Small numbers at sea across region, often flying medium-low over sea in small loose groups and usually slightly further offshore than Brown Booby.

Conservation status Fairly common at sea but localised breeder in small numbers. Locally threatened by harvesting for food, but not globally threatened.

Range Widespread at sea and breeds locally on small, often inhabited, islands across Melanesia. *S. s. rubripes* breeds on Tench, Nuguria, Takuu, Nukumanu, Ontong Java, Sikaiana, Rennell, Tikopia, Anuta, Nupani, Ilot Coco in Grande Terre lagoon, Surprise, Hunter, Chesterfield and Walpole; elsewhere, breeds in tropical Indian Ocean and central Pacific. Other subspecies breed in east Pacific and west Atlantic.

BROWN BOOBY *Sula leucogaster* — Plate 8

(Fou brun)

Description 69 cm. Adult is dark chocolate-brown with sharply marked white belly and underwings. Feet are greenish-yellow and bill is yellowish-grey, with bill-base and facial skin blue in male and yellow in female, brighter during breeding season. Juvenile is slightly paler, with brown mottling on less well marked white belly and underwing.

Similar species Adult differs from other boobies by sharp demarcation of white belly and centre to underwing. Juvenile differs from other boobies, especially juvenile and dark-morph Red-footed Booby, by more contrasting paler belly and underwing, plain upperparts and yellowish legs.

Voice Honking, growling and whistling at nest.

Habits Usually the commonest booby in inshore waters. Breeds in tree-top or ground colonies, often with other seabirds. Roosts on nesting islands, high in trees on small islands or on artificial structures at sea. Occurs in small numbers at sea across the region, usually close inshore. Flies fairly low over sea, often mixed with other feeding seabirds.

Conservation status Fairly common to rare at sea, and rare breeder. Melanesian threat status unknown, but not globally threatened.

Range At sea across Melanesia, but a very local breeder. *S. l. plotus* breeds on Nuguria, Ramos, Ontong Java, Monument Rock north of Efate, Tiga, Carrey in New Caledonian lagoon, Chesterfield, Walpole, Matthew and Hunter and perhaps elsewhere in Red-footed Booby colonies. Elsewhere, breeds in Red Sea, tropical Indian Ocean and central Pacific and other subspecies are pantropical.

CORMORANTS Phalacrocoracidae

Large black or pied waterbirds with long neck, wings, tail and hooked bill. Cormorants swim low on the water, often with bill held up high, diving from the surface for fish. Perch upright on bare ground or exposed tree branches, often sunning or preening with wings held partly open. Gregarious and mobile, flocks flying in straggling lines with outstretched, slightly uplifted, necks and occasional glides between steady flaps.

LITTLE PIED CORMORANT *Microcarbo melanoleucos* — Plate 10

(Little Shag; *Phalacrocorax melanoleucos*; Cormoran pie)

Description 61 cm. Small cormorant with white face and underparts and short yellow bill. White feathers sometimes stained orange. Breeding adult has short crest on forehead, white plumes on crown-sides and grey facial skin. Immature has black on thighs and above eyes, duller bill and browner plumage.

Similar species Differs from other cormorants by white underparts, except some immature Great Cormorants but Little Pied smaller, shorter-billed and white sharply cut off from blacker upperparts. See also Australasian Darter. Larger and longer-tailed than ducks.

Voice Usually silent. Quiet cooing and clicking at nest.

Habits Usually on lakes but also swamps, backwaters of rivers, mangroves and brackish coastal waters. Singles or in small loose groups. Nests colonially in trees overhanging water or sometimes on cliffs.
Conservation status Locally common on lakes and a few large rivers. Not threatened.
Range Scattered across Melanesia, mostly on islands with lakes.
M. m. melanoleucos breeds only on New Britain, Bougainville, Guadalcanal, Three Sisters, Santa Anna, Tikopia and Grande Terre, New Caledonia, but disperses more widely, including to Choiseul, larger islands in New Georgia group, Makira, Vanikoro, Efate and Ambae.
M. m. brevicauda, endemic to Rennell where common on the lake, is smaller with more white on head.
Elsewhere, *M. m. melanoleucos* breeds from Indonesia to Australia and *M. m. brevirostris* on New Zealand.

LITTLE BLACK CORMORANT *Phalacrocorax sulcirostris* Plate 10

(Little Black Shag; Cormoran noir)

Description 60 cm. Small all-black cormorant. Black with a green gloss, dark scalloping on mantle and wings, dark grey bill and facial skin. Breeding adult has fine white streaking on head and bronze-washed upperparts. Immature is duller and browner.
Similar species Differs from Great Cormorant by small size, plain plumage and finer bill. From flying Glossy Ibis by straight bill and shallower beats on narrower wings.
Habits Usually in small flocks on lakes but also on large rivers and coasts, especially estuaries. May feed communally in dense coordinated flock. Perch and roost in large, often dead, trees and nest in large *niaouli* trees beside water.
Conservation status Very localised but increasing in Melanesia. A colony of *c.*20 nests found in New Caledonia in 2009. Not threatened.
Range Breeds on Grande Terre, New Caledonia, and vagrant to Manus, New Britain, Bougainville, Ile des Pins and Chesterfield. Elsewhere, breeds in Indonesia, New Guinea, Australia and New Zealand.

GREAT CORMORANT *Phalacrocorax carbo* Plate 10

(Black Cormorant; Black Shag; Grand Cormoran)

Description 83 cm. Large thickset black cormorant. Adult is all black with a green gloss, bronzed wings with dark scallops and an orange-yellow and white patch under the eye. Breeding adult has white flank-spot, white streaks on neck-sides and short black crest. Immature is dull dark brown, with variably dirty-white or pale brown underparts and smaller indistinct dull yellow bill-base.
Similar species Differs from Little Black Cormorant by larger size, yellow facial skin and, if present, white patches. From Australasian Darter by thick neck and bill. Immature differs from Little Pied Cormorant by ill-defined paler underparts, longer darker bill and larger size.
Voice Loud raucous calls at nesting colony.
Habits Gregarious on large lakes and also in brackish waters and coasts. Nests colonially in tops of large trees beside water. May feed communally in dense coordinated flock.
Conservation status Very localised but increasing in Melanesia. Not threatened.
Range Breeds on Rennell and Grande Terre, New Caledonia, where colonised in about 1993 and 2002 respectively. One record from Gizo, and vagrants of this dispersive species are possible anywhere in Melanesia. Elsewhere, *P. c. novaehollandiae* also breeds on Australia and New Zealand, and is a rare visitor to New Guinea, and other subspecies occur patchily across North America and the Old World.

DARTERS Anhingidae

Similar to cormorants but with very long narrow bill and neck, often held kinked. Swim extremely low on water, sometimes with only head and upper neck exposed; perch on dead branches beside water and soar high in sky.

AUSTRALASIAN DARTER *Anhinga novaehollandiae* Plate 10

(Also treated as a subspecies of Darter *A. melanogaster*; Anhinga d'Australie)

Description 90 cm. Cormorant-like with very slender bill, head and neck, and long tail. Dark brown upperparts with silvery plumes and fringes on wing-coverts. Adult male is glossy brown-black with fine white stripe on face. Adult female has grey-brown upperparts, narrow white and black stripes on face, and white underparts, washed buff on neck. Immature as female but paler and less well marked.

Similar species From cormorants by slender bill and neck, striped face and long tail.
Habits Singles or loosely gregarious on swamps, lakes and large rivers, occasionally sheltered coasts. Flies with rapid shallow wing-beats and glides, or soars, often fanning its long tail.
Range One recent record from Long and one historical record from New Britain. Elsewhere, breeds New Guinea and Australia.

OSPREY Pandionidae

Ospreys are large fish-eating birds of prey, similar to some eagles and hawks.

EASTERN OSPREY *Pandion cristatus* — Plate 14

(Also treated as a subspecies of Osprey *P. haliaetus*; Balbuzard pêcheur)

Description 57cm. Large raptor with striped head and largely white underparts. Chocolate-brown upperparts, hindneck and broad eye-stripe, and white crown and white underparts with faint or prominent band of streaks across breast. Underwing is white with dark carpal patch and barred wing and tail feathers. Short tail. Long thin wings are usually angled at carpal joints and held flat or bowed. Juvenile is paler with pale fringes on upperparts and has more obvious breast-band.
Similar species Distinctive striped head pattern and flight shape. Larger than any raptor except sea eagles. Differs from immature White-bellied Sea Eagle by level or bowed wings, longer tail and plumage pattern. From juvenile Brahminy Kite by longer wings, shorter tail and largely white underparts and underwing.
Voice Series of quiet drawn-out *kee-ee, kee-ee* whistles.
Habits Coasts, inshore waters, small islets and some large lakes. Singles, pairs and family groups are territorial, often perching conspicuously in dead trees. Usually flies with loose flaps, interspersed with glides on bowed wings, but also soars and hovers heavily over water before plunging feet-first and flying back with large fish in talons.
Conservation status Conspicuous and widespread, but in small numbers. Not threatened.
Range Across Melanesia except Temotu, Vanuatu and Loyalties. Breeds from Admiralties to Rennell and Makira including most small islands but not the most isolated groups such as Hermit Is and Kaniet, and breeds on Grande Terre in New Caledonia. Melanesian birds are sometimes split as *P. c. melvillensis*. Elsewhere, breeds from Indonesia to New Guinea and Australia.

HAWKS AND EAGLES Accipitridae

A diverse range of diurnal birds of prey, or raptors, with hooked bills and powerful feet. Females are larger than males, but average length is given in text. Bazas *Aviceda* and honey buzzards *Henicopernis* are rather sluggish broad-winged forest raptors. Kites *Milvus* and *Haliastur* are large scavengers of open habitats, characteristically flexing and manoeuvring their angular wings and long tails in flight. Sea eagles *Haliaeetus* are very large top predators and scavengers which soar on sharply uptilted wings. Harriers *Circus* patrol slowly low over open habitats on long wings and tail. Hawks *Accipiter* are small to medium active hunters with relatively short rounded wings and long tails.

PACIFIC BAZA *Aviceda subcristata* — Plate 17

(Crested Baza; Baza huppé)

Description 39 cm. Medium-sized short-tailed raptor with barred underparts. Grey head with a short upstanding crest and yellow eye, conspicuous black-and-white-barred breast and belly, and rufous vent. In flight, very broad wings are pinched in at bases and have deep fingered hands. Several dark bars along primaries and secondaries, more prominent on outer primaries. Tail has narrow bars at base, and in adults wide pale subterminal and black terminal bands. Juvenile has pale rusty fringes on upperparts, whiter throat and buff wash on less heavily barred underparts. Patterns and colouring vary considerably with subspecies, age and sex.
Similar species Only raptor with a projecting crest. Barred underparts distinctive, except shared by some juvenile *Accipiter* hawks, from which Pacific Baza differs by short tail and no buff and dark brown tones. Broad outer wing distinctive, except shared by Black Honey Buzzard, but Pacific Baza smaller, with shorter wings and largely white underwing.
Voice Repeated high-pitched *ki-yu*, often repeated at one second intervals in short series, especially in flight and

display, slower than *Accipiter* hawks and a clearer whistle than Ultramarine Kingfisher. Repeated weak piping.
Habits Most common in open and degraded forest but also closed forest and open habitats with scattered trees, usually in lowlands but to 800 m. Solitary or in pairs, hunting from perches within forest canopy, and sometimes soaring on flat wings. Has distinctive display flight, climbing steeply with exaggerated slow flaps, and diving down to level out and repeat.
Conservation status Fairly common in small numbers. Not threatened.
Range Admiralties, Bismarcks and Solomons.
A. s. coultasi, endemic to Manus and San Miguel, where uncommon or rare, has broad browner bars down to thighs.
A. s. bismarckii, endemic to New Ireland and New Britain, including Lavongai, Djaul, Lolobau and Tabar, where fairly common, has broad bars on underparts, dark grey in male and brown-black in female.
A. s. gurneyi, sometimes split into three subspecies *gurneyi*, *proxima* and *robusta* differing slightly in size and barring, endemic to Solomons where absent from smaller islands and Rennell, has narrower blackish bars on underparts and female has browner upperparts and narrower bars.
Elsewhere, other subspecies breed from east Indonesia to Australia

BLACK HONEY BUZZARD *Henicopernis infuscatus* Plate 13

(New Britain [Honey] Buzzard; Bondrée noire)

Description 50 cm. Medium-large very dark forest raptor. Plumage is sooty-brown with paler silvery-brown bars on wings and tail, visible when perched. In flight, has three broad pale bars across wings and tail but often only a single pale subterminal wing-bar is visible. In flight, has long tail, broad wings held forward, pinched in at base and with bulging outer primaries. Juvenile unknown but may have an extra bar on wings and tail.
Similar species Wing shape distinctive, but closest to Pacific Baza. Only other black raptor on New Britain is Meyer's Goshawk, from which it differs by conspicuous wing-bars and long bulging wings. From juvenile Brahminy Kite and vagrant Black Kite by blackish plumage with pale bars.
Voice About 12 piping notes, upslurred, accelerating and shortening over about three seconds, repeated at three-second intervals, reminiscent of Collared Kingfisher.
Habits Usually primary hill forest but also from sea-level to 1300 m. Solitary and unobtrusive. Perches upright within forest canopy, and glides but rarely soars over forest.
Conservation status Uncommon or rare. Probably has a low population density and declining from lowland forest loss. IUCN: Vulnerable.
Range Endemic to New Britain, where probably widespread, including Lolobau.

BLACK KITE *Milvus migrans* Plate 13

(Milan noir)

Description 55 cm. Large raptor with a long, shallow-forked tail which appears square when fully spread. Plain dark brown plumage with obscure streaks. In flight, paler window over base of outer primaries, long wings usually angled at carpals and with spread primary tips; droops and flexes long tail. Juvenile is streaked paler and has pale tips to upperparts.
Similar species Forked tail is distinctive but beware other species in moult. Differs from juvenile Brahminy Kite by longer tail, darker brown plumage and plainer underwing. From Black Honey Buzzard by paler unbarred wings and tail.
Voice High-pitched whinny *pee-err*. Trilled whistles.
Habits Usually perched or gliding over open, wetland and urban habitats.
Range One recent record from New Caledonia and one historical record from New Britain. *M. m. affinis* breeds in Indonesia, New Guinea and Australia, and other subspecies breed across Africa and Eurasia.

WHISTLING KITE *Haliastur sphenurus* Plate 13

(Milan siffleur)

Description 56 cm. Large sandy-brown raptor with obscure streaks on body and spots on wing-coverts. In flight, long wings have characteristic blackish secondaries and outer primaries, contrasting with pale brown inner primaries and remainder of underparts. Long pale tail is slightly rounded. Juvenile is more streaked and spotted.
Similar species Differs from Swamp Harrier by underwing pattern, lack of white rump and flight action, flying on flat or drooped wings. From juvenile Brahminy Kite by dark secondaries and outer primaries, and longer wings and tail. From juvenile White-bellied Sea Eagle by flight action, small size and long all-brown tail.

Voice Slow descending whistle, often followed by rapid rising series of staccato whistles.
Habits Beside lakes and swamps, open habitats including farmland, and less often coasts. Singles or pairs, sometimes small flocks, exceptionally up to 50 birds, usually at carrion. Usually glides between several deep flaps, or soars on flat or drooped wings. Flies fairly high over roads and open habitats, and perches on exposed branches and poles.
Conservation status The commonest large raptor on New Caledonia. Not threatened.
Range New Caledonia, where restricted to Grande Terre. Elsewhere, breeds in New Guinea and Australia.

BRAHMINY KITE *Haliastur indus* Plate 13

(Milan sacré)

Description 48 cm. Medium-large raptor with fairly short tail and long broad wings. Adult is rich chestnut with white head, neck and breast, black primary tips and narrow white tail-tips. Juvenile is untidy, mottled and streaked brown, paler on head and belly. Juvenile in flight has patchy plumage, with prominent black tips to outer primaries and pale bases to primaries extending along secondaries to body. Immature has blotches of adult plumage.
Similar species Adult distinctive. Juvenile differs from Whistling Kite by shorter wings and tail, and underwing pattern of patchy pale and brown offset by dark primary tips. From Eastern Osprey, Black Kite, White-bellied Sea Eagle and Swamp Harrier by wing and tail proportions and primary pattern.
Voice Weak downslurred mewing *pee-yah*. Various squeals and mews.
Habits All habitats but particularly coasts, wetlands and plantations, usually in lowlands but up to 1000 m. Generally the commonest large raptor, gregarious where common. Soars with carpals angled forward, wings bowed and tail often twisted, or flaps buoyantly. Flies fairly high over rivers, coasts, roads and open habitats, and perches on exposed branches.
Conservation status Fairly common to very common. Not threatened.
Range Admiralties, St Matthias Is, Bismarcks and Solomons, and an unconfirmed report from Vanuatu.
H. i. girrenera breeds throughout the Admiralties, St Matthias and Bismarcks, but not the most isolated groups such as Hermit Is; elsewhere, breeds in Indonesia, New Guinea and Australia.
H. i. flavirostris, endemic to the Solomons, including Feni and Nissan and all small islands but not Rennell or Temotu, has plainer yellower bill.
Elsewhere, other subspecies breed from Pakistan to Indonesia.

WHITE-BELLIED SEA EAGLE *Haliaeetus leucogaster* Plate 14

(Pygargue blagre)

Description 75 cm. Largest raptor in region. Massive eagle with heavy bill. Distinctive flight shape of thin head and neck, bulging secondaries, slightly pointed wings and very short wedge-shaped tail. Adult is white with grey upperparts and black primaries and secondaries on upper- and underwing. Juvenile is untidy buff and mid-brown, often with paler head. Upperwing has pale covert panel and pale inner primaries. Underwing is patchy, with greatest contrast between white patch at base of primaries and black outer primary tips and secondaries. Brownest juvenile always has some white on axillaries and tail-base, and lower breast and belly is paler and more mottled than upper breast. Immature retains pale base to primaries and buff wash to white plumage for three years.
Similar species Flight action and shape shared only by Solomons Sea Eagle, from which juvenile differs in having white on tail and axillaries, and more mottled underparts. Underwing of juvenile resembles Whistling Kite but is patchier; tail much shorter. Differs from Eastern Osprey by narrowly barred wings and tail, and lacks dark carpal patch and eye-stripe.
Voice Goose-like nasal cackling *ang-ang-ang-* and high-pitched faster variants.
Habits Coasts and occasionally large lakes, rivers and forest, ranging far inland to 850 m. Singles or pairs perch in dead trees and soar high with wings swept up into V. Hunts, scavenges along coasts, and robs other raptors.
Conservation status Fairly common but in small numbers. Not threatened.
Range Admiralties, St Matthias Is and Bismarcks as far east as Nissan, including many tiny islands but not isolated islets such as Hermit Is. Elsewhere, breeds from India to Australia.

SOLOMONS SEA EAGLE *Haliaeetus sanfordi* Plate 14

(Sanford's [Sea] Eagle; Pygargue de Sanford)

Description 73 cm. Largest raptor in Solomons. Massive, often scruffy brown eagle with heavy bill. Warm brown plumage with black tail, dark brown primaries, paler head and, depending on stage of moult, paler buff patches on wings. Head may become paler with age. Juvenile darker colder brown with pale tips and fringes, and slightly longer

tail. Flight action and shape as White-bellied Sea Eagle but has slightly broader wings.
Similar species Distinctive size, flight shape and action. Differs from juvenile White-bellied Sea Eagle by absence of any white on blacker tail or on slightly rufous axillaries, and darker belly is uniform with upper breast.
Voice Series of cackles *guak, guak, guak...*
Habits Coasts, especially adjacent to forest and reefs, and inland to at least 1500 m. More of a forest species than White-bellied Sea Eagle, where it preys mostly on mammals. Singles and pairs cruise high over coasts and land and often perch on or near their massive nest near top of large tree, often at forest edge. Displaying pairs call while rocking from side to side with wings held high and legs dangling.
Conservation status Fairly common to rare but always in small numbers, and rarer on larger islands, especially Guadalcanal and Malaita, where possibly hunted. IUCN: Vulnerable.
Range Endemic to the Solomons, including all small islands from Buka to Makira, but not Rennell.

SWAMP HARRIER *Circus approximans* — Plate 13

(Pacific Marsh-Harrier; Busard de Gould)

Description 55 cm. Large brown raptor with white rump. Slimmer, with longer wings and tail than other medium-large raptors. Dark warm brown, streaked on head and underparts, with conspicuous white rump-band in flight and owl-like facial disc. Wings and tail become greyer with age, especially males. Female is darker, more rufous on underparts and less grey. Juvenile is uniform dark brown, more chestnut on underparts, with some white streaking on nape, extensive pale grey bases to underwing primaries but rump-patch narrow or pale brown.
Similar species Distinctive white rump and flight action with wings held up. Also differs from Brown Goshawk by longer, less pointed wings. From Whistling Kite and juvenile Brahminy Kite by long tail and plainer underwing pattern.
Voice High mewing *kyeow!* Quiet repeated piping.
Habits Open habitats and forest at all altitudes but commoner in open lowland habitats. Singles or pairs glide and flap slowly and buoyantly low over ground or canopy with long wings held in shallow V. Also soars high and displaying pairs circle and dive high in sky, holding wings high and calling. Perches low on fences and ground, and nests on ground.
Conservation status Fairly common. Not threatened.
Range Vanuatu and New Caledonia, but rare on Solomons. Fairly common across Vanuatu, except for a few of the smallest islands, Loyalties, Grande Terre and Ile des Pins. Several recent records from Guadalcanal and one old record from Three Sisters. Elsewhere, breeds Australia, New Zealand, Fiji and Tonga.

VARIABLE GOSHAWK *Accipiter hiogaster* — Plate 15

(Varied Goshawk; also treated as a subspecies of Grey Goshawk *A. novaehollandiae*; Autour blanc)

Description 40 cm. Variable medium-sized hawk with relatively short rounded wings. Adult has mid-grey head and upperparts and sometimes throat, sometimes with paler head, and rich rufous underparts and underwing-coverts. Rufous underparts extend onto sides of neck, sometimes appearing as half-collar, especially in immatures, and may appear barred. Bismarck subspecies have paler upperparts, and underparts more reddish than orange-rufous of Solomons subspecies, with paler throat. Eye red, brown in juveniles, usually appearing dark. Cere, loral skin and legs rich yellow or orange, paler in juveniles. In flight, shows rufous underwing-coverts. Juvenile upperparts are rather uniformly dark brown with fine rufous fringes, and undertail has c.10 obscure dark bars. Juvenile and immature underparts vary considerably within and between subspecies. Usually have strong brown streaks on creamy throat, dark brown spots or tear-marks on breast, narrow bars on lower breast and upper belly, plain orange-buff thighs and white vent. Some, perhaps immatures, have unmarked pale grey throat and barring from upper breast to belly. Bars may be broken into spots. Bars and streaks may be blackish, dark brown or dark rufous. Extreme individuals, especially on Manus, have almost unmarked underparts. Immature soon develops grey wash to head and upperparts and rufous wash to underparts, especially breast. Subadult may retain barred tail and duller upperparts.
Similar species Adult differs from other hawks by rich rufous underparts, pale grey upperparts and shorter wings, but see descriptions of other species. Juvenile differs from juvenile Slaty-mantled Goshawk by almost unbarred upperparts and usually some streaks on underparts. From juvenile New Britain Sparrowhawk by plainer upperparts and usually some bars on belly. However, note that Variable Goshawk may have other plumage morphs which are not safely identifiable from the poorly known Slaty-mantled Goshawk and New Britain Sparrowhawk. From juvenile Pied Goshawk by yellow-orange cere, hardly barred upperparts, brown uppertail and indistinctly barred undertail. From immature Meyer's Goshawk by smaller size and bars on underparts. From New Britain Goshawk by rufous or patterned underparts.

Voice Territorial call, often given by pairs at dawn, is a repeated squealing *quee-he?* in Bismarcks, but faster in Solomons: *ya-ya-* or *hya-ya*, and is lower-pitched, slower and more drawn out than Pied Goshawk and falcons, faster and less slurred than Collared Kingfisher. Rapid series of *ki-ki-* notes is also lower-pitched than Pied Goshawk.
Habits Solitary or in pairs in all forested habitats but usually forest edge in lowlands, up to 800 m. Usually hunts from perch but often soars and has deep-flapping and diving display flight.
Conservation status Generally the commonest hawk. Not threatened.
Range Admiralties, Mussau, Bismarcks and Solomons, but not Makira or Rennell. Subspecies characters are documented only for adults and each is compared to the preceding subspecies.
A. h. manusi, endemic to the Admiralties, where recorded from Manus, Rambutyo, San Miguel and Nauna, is small with a contrasting paler head.
A. n. matthiae, endemic to Mussau, is smaller with paler upperparts.
A. n. dampieri, endemic to New Britain, including Umboi, Lolobau, Duke of York and vagrant to Watom, is smaller and paler with faint barring on underparts and paler, almost white, thighs and undertail-coverts.
A. n. lavongai, endemic to New Ireland, including Lavongai, Djaul and probably Tabar where subspecies is uncertain, is larger and darker.
A. n. lihirensis, endemic to Lihir and Tanga, is larger, darker grey, with more grey on throat and females have lower flanks and undertail-coverts barred white.
A. n. bougainvillei, endemic to Bougainville, including Buka and Shortland, has deeper, more orange unmarked underparts and a grey throat uniform with paler upperparts.
A. n. rufoschistaceus, endemic to Choiseul, Isabel and Florida Is, is larger and slightly darker.
A. n. rubianae, endemic to New Georgia group, including most large islands but not Ranongga, where uncommon, is smaller and richer chestnut below.
A. n. pulchellus, endemic to Guadalcanal, has paler, almost white, thighs and undertail-coverts, and paler, greyer underwing-coverts.
A. n. malaitae, endemic to Malaita, is similar to *A. h. rubianae* but has much darker upperparts and sometimes faint white bars on underparts.
Elsewhere, other subspecies breed from east Indonesia to New Guinea.

BROWN GOSHAWK *Accipiter fasciatus* — Plate 16

(Autour australien)

Description 45 cm. Medium-large hawk with long tail and long wings. In flight, has slightly bulging secondaries and more pointed wings than other *Accipiter* hawks. Adult has dull grey-brown upperparts with rufous collar. Underparts are rufous with fine off-white bars except for grey throat. Juvenile has dark brown upperparts and off-white underparts with dark brown streaks on throat, becoming heavy spots on upper breast, and bars on lower breast and belly, and fine rufous bars on thighs.
Similar species Differs from Swamp Harrier by plumage, flight action and shorter wings which are often held with pointed tips. From juvenile White-bellied Goshawk on New Caledonia by coarser markings on underparts and finely barred rufous thighs. From juvenile Peregrine Falcon by flight shape and action and underparts pattern. Does not overlap in range with Variable Goshawk.
Voice Male gives a rapid *kikiki...* Female gives a mellow *yuik-yuik-yuik*.
Habits Prefers open habitats with scattered trees, forest edge and degraded forest at all altitudes, but also primary forest on Rennell. Hunts actively with deep flaps and glides or soars on flat or slightly upswept wings, and may fan tail. Often hunts from hidden perch within canopy and flies rapidly through trees.
Conservation status Usually common. Not threatened.
Range Rennell, south Vanuatu and New Caledonia.
A. f. fasciatus breeds on Rennell and Bellona, and elsewhere breeds on Timor and Australia.
A. f. vigilax, endemic to New Caledonia, including Grande Terre, Ouvéa, Lifou and Maré, and Vanuatu, where historically known only from Aneityum but recent records from Tanna, Efate and possibly Santo, is smaller.
Elsewhere, other subspecies breed in east Indonesia and New Guinea.

PIED GOSHAWK *Accipiter albogularis* — Plate 16

(Autour pie)

Description 36 cm. Medium-sized polymorphic pied hawk. In flight, has fairly long tail and wings. Furrowed brow gives fierce expression. Pale morph has mid-grey upperparts with rufous hind-collar and white underparts, and white underwings with grey tips to primaries and secondaries. Pied morph has glossy slaty-black upperparts and white underparts, and white underwings with dark grey tips to primaries and secondaries, sometimes with black primary tips which may be faintly barred; variable rufous hind-collar often absent. Sometimes appears hooded with some extension of dark onto neck-sides but always has white chin and central throat. Intermediates between pale and pied morphs may occur. Black morph is entirely glossy black with either silvery bases to underwing primaries or all-silvery underwing primaries and secondaries. Legs are yellow or orange-yellow, eye is yellow, orange or orange-red, cere and bill-base dull green or yellow. Juvenile has rufous-brown upperparts with darker, often blackish crown and mantle, and heavy black barring and mottling, including on wings and undertail. Underparts are off-white with dark brown streaks on lower throat, becoming spots and bars on breast and belly. Dark-morph juvenile has dark rufous underparts, with dense darker streaks and bars. Immature soon loses streaking and develops white throat, then grey upperparts.

Similar species Adult differs from Meyer's Goshawk by smaller size, slimmer shape, and pied morph has unmarked underparts. Pied-morph adult from very similar Imitator Goshawk by greyer upperparts, grey undertail, silvery-grey underside of primaries with darker outer tips, orange or yellow eye, larger and longer-winged. Note that Imitator never has rufous collar but often has black throat. Black-morph adult from Imitator by bare parts and structure. Juvenile from Variable Goshawk by stronger blacker barring on upperparts and undertail, greyer uppertail and no plain buff or rufous on thighs. Juvenile from Imitator Goshawk by heavy streaks on throat, coarser bars on underparts to vent, crown uniform with mantle unless a moulting immature, heavy barring on uppertail, and structure.

Voice Series of 7–50 high-pitched nasal *ki-ki-ki-* notes which initially rise, louder, faster and more penetrating than Variable Goshawk, slower and lower than falcons, faster and less slurred than Collared Kingfisher. One or two forced nasal upslurs, repeated several times at about one second intervals.

Habits All forest habitats, sometimes including coconut plantations and open parkland with scattered trees, from sea-level to 1800 m. Active hunter, in flight or from perches, also frequently soars, and sometimes hunts grassland insects from low perches.

Conservation status Fairly common. Not threatened.

Range Endemic to Solomons including Feni, Utupua and Vanikoro.

A. a. eichhorni, endemic to Feni, off New Ireland, may all be pale morph with broad pink-rufous collar and faint grey barring on upper breast-sides.

A. a. woodfordi, endemic to Bougainville, Choiseul, Isabel, Guadalcanal and Malaita, including Buka, Shortland, Florida Is, and Ulawa, lacks the palest morphs, and pied-morph juvenile has paler underparts with heavier dark markings.

A. a. gilvus, endemic to New Georgia group, including all larger islands and Simbo, may have only pied morphs without a rufous collar, and juvenile has fewer, finer markings on buffier underparts.

A. a. albogularis, endemic to Makira, including Ugi, Santa Ana and Santa Catalina, where common in the absence of Variable Goshawk, has all-dark and dark pied morphs with no collar, and juveniles have more tawny on underparts.

A. a. sharpei, endemic to Utupua and Vanikoro, in Temotu, has pale morph with narrow rufous collar and faint grey barring on upper breast and/or pink-rufous wash on neck-sides and thighs.

WHITE-BELLIED GOSHAWK *Accipiter haplochrous* Plate 16

(Autour à ventre blanc)

Description 34 cm. Medium-sized, fairly stocky pied hawk with relatively short broad wings in flight. Adult has slate-grey upperparts and head, slightly paler on throat and upper breast, white lower breast and belly, and white underwing with black wing-tip. Cere and legs yellow, and eye orange-red in adult and yellow in juvenile. Juvenile has dark brown upperparts with fine rufous barring and paler collar. Underparts are creamy with blackish-brown streaks on throat and upper breast, becoming spots and bars on lower underparts.

Similar species Adult plumage is distinctive. Shape differs from Brown Goshawk by small size and shorter wings and tail. Juvenile also differs from juvenile Brown Goshawk by coarser markings on underparts and coarse dark barring on off-white thighs.

Voice Series of *ki-ki-ki-* notes, very similar to Brown Goshawk.

Habits Singles and pairs occur in all forested habitats, but less common in heavily degraded forest, up to 1300 m. Rather sluggish and usually hunts from perches, often within forest canopy. Often soars and calls above territory. Fluttering wing-beats in level flight.

Conservation status Fairly common, with an estimated population of 2500–5000 pairs. IUCN: Near Threatened.

Range Endemic to Grande Terre, New Caledonia.

SLATY-MANTLED GOSHAWK *Accipiter luteoschistaceus* Plate 15

(Slaty-mantled Sparrowhawk; Autour bleu et gris)

Description 34 cm. Medium-small hawk with rather short wings and tail and long legs. Adult has slaty-black upperparts and undertail, and white to pale cinnamon underparts, sometimes with faint grey barring on upper breast. Female has richer buffy underparts and more barring on breast. Eye is orange-yellow, cere, loral skin and eye-ring are yellow-orange to reddish-orange and legs yellow-orange to orange-red. Juvenile has black crown, heavily barred rufous-and-black upperparts like a Kestrel, very prominent black bars on orange uppertail and undertail, coarse rufous-brown bars on off-white underparts, becoming more broken, almost streaked, on throat and sometimes a narrow midline chin- and throat-stripe. Juvenile bare parts are all yellow.
Similar species Adult differs from New Britain Sparrowhawk by larger size, longer tail, darker upperparts, more orange bare parts, underparts washed buff rather than grey, and no rufous collar. From Variable Goshawk by darker upperparts and generally much paler underparts; individuals with richer underparts usually have faint barring on breast, also pale eye and head is uniform with upperparts. From Meyer's Goshawk by smaller and slimmer size, grey upperparts and plain breast. Juvenile has distinctive heavy blackish barring on rufous upperparts and tail, and also has heavier barring on underparts than other hawks, extending onto thighs and undertail-coverts.
Voice Unknown.
Habits Very poorly known but appears to be a lowland forest species from sea-level to 700 m. There are so few records that it is difficult to assess its true habitat requirements and status. Probably replaced by Variable Goshawk in all degraded forest habitats and reported to be restricted to interior forest on Umboi.
Conservation status Very rarely recorded, but possibly overlooked through confusion with Variable Goshawk. Likely to be threatened by forest loss. IUCN: Vulnerable.
Range Endemic to New Britain, including Umboi. Unconfirmed records from New Ireland probably refer to New Britain Sparrowhawk.

IMITATOR GOSHAWK *Accipiter imitator* Plate 16

(Imitator Sparrowhawk; Autour imitateur)

Description 30 cm. A small polymorphic hawk which closely resembles Pied Goshawk. Adult pied morph has glossy black upperparts, including undertail. Throat and upper breast is black or white or sometimes streaked black, and underparts to vent are white, pale buff or pale grey. Underwing is white, with a few black bars bordering black flight feathers. Red, brown or golden-brown eye, orange-yellow or yellow cere and bill-base, and paler orange-yellow or yellow legs. Dark morph is entirely glossy black except for silvery bases to underside of primaries and outer secondaries. Juvenile has yellow eye, black crown and nape often with white feather bases, contrasting with warm brown upperparts with pale rufous fringes and indistinct dark bars, and indistinct bars on tail. Underparts are buff with fine rufous bars, often fading away on lower breast.
Similar species Very like Pied Goshawk but smaller, with shorter wings, stockier legs and dark eye. Black or streaked throat of pied adults should be distinctive but beware Pied Goshawk may appear hooded when seen in flight. Otherwise, differs by jet-black upperparts, black undertail, black undersides to outer primaries, no rufous on collar and sometimes off-white underparts. From Meyer's Goshawk by smaller size, slimmer shape and pied morph has unstreaked flanks. Juvenile differs from juvenile Pied Goshawk by finely barred underparts, paler brown upperparts contrasting with crown, and faint barring on uppertail. Juvenile from juvenile Variable Goshawk by finely barred underparts including thighs and more barring on upperparts.
Voice Poorly known but probably has a similar repertoire to Pied Goshawk.
Habits Very poorly known. All records are from lowland and hill rainforest, usually perched inside or gliding over closed-canopy forest, to at least 1000 m.
Conservation status Rare, locally uncommon, but probably overlooked. Recent records only from one area on Isabel and three specimens and one sighting on Bougainville. May be threatened by lowland forest loss. IUCN: Vulnerable.
Range Endemic to Bougainville, Choiseul and Isabel, where presumed to be resident across all three islands.

NEW BRITAIN GOSHAWK *Accipiter princeps* Plate 15

(Autour de Mayr)

Description 40 cm. Medium-large blue-grey hawk, appearing bulky with a slightly bulging chest and short rounded wings. Adult is pale blue-grey with slightly paler head and neck, paler breast and belly, and darker primary tips. Rich red-orange eye, lores and cere, heavy black bill and short orange-yellow legs. Faint barring on breast may be related to age or sex. Juvenile unknown, possibly has faintly streaked underparts and duller bare parts as Grey-headed Goshawk *A. poliocephalus* of New Guinea. Grey-headed Goshawk also has a dark morph, all dark slaty-black with normal bare-part coloration, which is possible in New Britain Goshawk.

Similar species Distinctive uniform blue-grey plumage, with slightly paler breast and belly, and without rufous or white on underparts. From other New Britain *Accipiter* hawks by larger bulkier size, except the even larger Meyer's Goshawk.

Voice Stronger and deeper than Variable Goshawk.

Habits Hill and montane forest from 750 to 1400 m, with occasional records from lowland forest, including unconfirmed records down to sea-level. Single birds usually seen perched in subcanopy or flying rather slowly but powerfully through mid-mountain forest.

Conservation status Uncommon to rare but may be secure in montane forest. IUCN: Vulnerable.

Range Endemic to New Britain, where probably widespread but little known.

NEW BRITAIN SPARROWHAWK *Accipiter brachyurus* — Plate 15

(Bismarck Sparrowhawk; Épervier de Nouvelle-Bretagne)

Description 30 cm. Small hawk with relatively short tail, fairly pointed wings and long legs and toes. Adult has slaty-grey upperparts with orange-rufous collar which, although broad, is sometimes difficult to discern. Very pale grey underparts, sometimes with rufous tint to sides of breast. Eye red-brown, cere and loral skin yellow or greenish-yellow, legs yellow, and all bare parts duller in juvenile. Pale grey underwing with black primary tips. Juvenile has rufous upperparts with black blotches and plainer black crown. Underparts are pale buff with heavy dark rufous streaks, becoming more drop- or arrow-shaped on belly and finely barred on thighs. Uppertail has 7–8 indistinct darker bars but undertail has prominent dark bars of similar width to pale bars. However, this species is poorly known and may show more variation than presently known.

Similar species From other Bismarck *Accipiter* hawks by shorter tail and relatively more pointed, longer wings. Adult differs from very similar Slaty-mantled Goshawk by rufous collar, paler yellow facial skin, cere and legs, and greyish-white underparts. From much larger Meyer's Goshawk by rufous collar and no streaks on underparts, and juvenile has blotched upperparts and streaks on underparts becoming broken. Juvenile from other *Accipiter* hawks by no bars on underparts. From immature Variable Goshawk, which often shows dull rufous half-collar, by streaked underparts, more rufous upperparts, and yellow cere, facial skin and legs.

Voice Unknown.

Habits Very poorly known species with few specimen or sight records. Most records from montane forest to 1800 m but possible sight records down to sea-level.

Conservation status Uncommon or rare, however montane forest habitat is probably not threatened. IUCN: Vulnerable.

Range Endemic to New Britain and New Ireland. Recently discovered on New Ireland where only known from montane forest in far south.

MEYER'S GOSHAWK *Accipiter meyerianus* — Plate 15

(Autour de Meyer)

Description 52 cm. Large bulky pied hawk, usually with an obvious bulging chest in flight and relatively short wings and tail. Adult is black above and white below, with fine black streaking or barring on underparts, broad grey-and-black bars on tail, and black-and-white barring on outer underwing. Dark morph is glossy black with grey bars on tail and underwing. Eye is red-brown, cere yellow or grey, legs yellow. Juvenile has dark brown upperparts with buff and tawny streaks and fringes, barred dark and tawny-brown tail, rich buff underparts with fine dark brown streaks and pale eye.

Similar species About twice the bulk of all other *Accipiter* hawks except New Britain Goshawk, which has orange bare parts. Pied adult plumage differs from Pied Goshawk, Slaty-mantled Goshawk and New Britain Sparrowhawk by markings on breast, tail and underwing, and bare-part colours. Also differs from Slaty-mantled by blacker upperparts and from New Britain Sparrowhawk by blacker upperparts and lack of collar. Black adult also differs from Pied Goshawk by barred tail and underwing. Black adult from Black Honey Buzzard by smaller size, flight action, short rounded non-bulging wings and less conspicuously barred wings. Juvenile from other juvenile hawks by uniform rich rufous underparts with heavy streaks but no bars.

Voice A series of 8–10 loud nasal upslurs over three seconds, often answered by mate with more strident and hurried *k-ke* over one second. (Call description from New Guinea.)

Habits Forest and especially forest edge, usually in lowlands and hills but from sea-level to 1800 m. Singles usually seen perched or in powerful flapping or gliding flight.

Conservation status Usually rare, but locally uncommon. Possibly threatened on some islands but not globally threatened.

Range Scattered across Manus, Bismarcks and Solomons. Rare, with few records on Long (where unconfirmed), Umboi, New Britain, Watom (where vagrant), Buka (where unconfirmed), Kolombangara and Guadalcanal, but recent sightings on Manus, New Ireland and Vella Lavella suggest that it may be overlooked on other islands. Elsewhere, scattered and usually rare on New Guinea and east Indonesia.

FALCONS Falconidae

Diurnal raptors which drop onto prey on ground or catch birds and insects in flight. Hunt in open space, often over forest. Skilled fliers on long narrow wings, wing-tips usually pointed but appearing slightly rounded when soaring. Fly with long glides interspersed with a few shallow fluid wing-beats, or chasing prey in fast highly manoeuvrable pursuits, and sometimes soar high. Females are larger than males, but an average length is given in the text.

NANKEEN KESTREL *Falco cenchroides* — Plate 17

(Australian Kestrel; Crécerelle d'Australie)

Description 32 cm. Small slim falcon, often seen hovering. Dark moustachial stripe across pale throat and cheeks, rufous-brown upperparts with black spots, black primaries and secondaries, off-white underparts with fine black streaks, and broad black terminal tail-bar. Underwing is white with fine dark barring and dark wing-tips. Dark eye, but other bare parts are bright yellow. Adult male has grey crown, nape and tail. Adult female has crown, nape and finely barred tail the same rufous-brown as upperparts. Juvenile as female but has more heavily spotted upperparts and barred tail.

Similar species Differs from Peregrine Falcon by smaller, slimmer size and rufous upperparts. From juvenile Oriental and Australian Hobby by fine dark moustachial stripe and warm rufous upperparts. From hawks by moustachial stripe, rufous upperparts, white underparts and more pointed wings. Hovering is shared only by Brown Falcon, restricted to Long I.

Voice Rapid shrill *kekeke-*. Longer, wavering *ke-er, ke-er -*.

Habits Open habitats, usually grasslands. Singles and pairs characteristically hover, but also hunt from exposed perches, especially poles and wires, and soar high in sky.

Range Three records of vagrants on New Caledonia, on Grande Terre and Lifou in April and July. Elsewhere, breeds across New Guinea and Australia, including Lord Howe and Norfolk Is, and migrates irregularly to Indonesia and New Zealand.

ORIENTAL HOBBY *Falco severus* — Plate 17

(Faucon aldrovandin)

Description 28 cm. The smallest Melanesian raptor. Small slender falcon with long narrow pointed wings and medium-long tail. Long pointed wings project beyond tail when perched. Dark eye, but other bare parts are bright yellow. Adult has dark grey upperparts, often appearing black, with hood extending as point onto buff-white cheeks and throat, rich orange-rufous underparts and underwing-coverts, and indistinct barring on tail. Juvenile duller, with pale buff fringes on dark brown upperparts, short broad black streaks on buff breast and belly, and orange-buff underwing-coverts.

Similar species Differs from all except Peregrine Falcon and Australian Hobby by narrow pointed wings, and prominent pointed hood. From Peregrine Falcon by orange on underparts, but beware distant birds which often look dark below, smaller and slimmer size with narrower longer wings. See very similar vagrant Australian Hobby below.

Voice Calls frequently. Long rapid series *ki-ki-ki-*, faster and shriller than *Accipiter* hawks.

Habits Forest edge and gardens, sometimes closed forest, from sea-level to 1000 m. Singles and pairs perch in dead tree-tops and sally out after flying insects or birds, or glide or soar over forest. Often crepuscular.

Conservation status Uncommon to rare. Not threatened.

Range Admiralties, Mussau, Bismarcks and Solomons, where scattered and localised. Recorded from Manus, Tong, Mussau, Tanga, New Ireland, New Britain, Watom (where vagrant), Duke of York, Buka, Bougainville, Choiseul, Santa Isabel, Kolombangara, Gizo, Guadalcanal, Malaita and Makira. Status poorly known; breeds on New Britain but also may be a migrant from New Guinea. Elsewhere, breeds from India to New Guinea, sometimes divided into subspecies including *F. s. papuanus* in Melanesia.

AUSTRALIAN HOBBY *Falco longipennis* Plate 17

(Petit Faucon)

Description 33 cm. Small slender falcon, similar to Oriental Hobby. Adult has grey upperparts with narrow black bars on tail. Darker head has short moustachial stripe, white on cheeks and throat, and pale orange underparts with fine black streaks. Eye is dark, cere and eye-ring pale blue, and legs yellow. Juvenile has browner upperparts with rufous fringes and brown wash to face and underparts.

Similar species Narrow pointed wings and prominent pointed moustachial stripe differ from all except Peregrine Falcon and very similar Oriental Hobby. Differs from Oriental Hobby by longer tail which usually projects beyond wing-tips when perched, pale collar extending further onto neck, streaked underparts although streaks may be difficult to see, often paler upperparts, barred tail, paler lores, blue cere and eye-ring. Juvenile also lacks heavy broad streaks on underparts. Differs from Peregrine Falcon by streaked buffy-orange underparts and is smaller, slimmer and longer-winged.

Voice Shrill *kek-kek-kek-* or faster *ke-ke-ke-*.

Habits Usually in lowland open country, especially grasslands. Flight and habits as Oriental Hobby.

Range Single historical records from New Britain and Watom and one probable recent record on Grande Terre, New Caledonia. *F. l. longipennis* breeds across Australia, some migrating to southern New Guinea, and *F. l. hanieli* breeds in southern Indonesia.

BROWN FALCON *Falco berigora* Plate 17

(Faucon bérigora)

Description 45 cm. Large sluggish, scruffy and rather round-winged atypical falcon. Polymorphic adult plumage always has dark moustachial and cheek-stripes, contrasting with paler throat, mid-cheeks and hind-cheeks. Darkest birds are otherwise uniform sooty-brown. Palest birds have pale rufous upperparts and white underparts with warm brown thighs. Dark eye, grey-green cere and legs, occasionally yellow in pale birds. Juvenile has buff fringes on upperparts, yellow wash to head and blotched underparts.

Similar species Flight action is distinctive. From Peregrine Falcon by broader-based wings and different head and underparts plumage.

Voice Variable, usually a loud chattering cackle unlike any other falcon. Also screeches and rattles.

Habits Usually in grasslands but also secondary scrub at all altitudes on Long I. Singles and pairs perch upright on long legs on exposed perches, glides down onto prey on ground, hovers clumsily, flies slowly with deep wing-beats on broad-based wings, glides with wings in a shallow V, or soars with fanned tail on upswept wings. Dashing, diving display flight but lacks rapid flickering flight action of other falcons.

Conservation status Fairly common. Not threatened.

Range *F. b. novaeguineae* breeds on Long I., between New Britain and New Guinea. Elsewhere, breeds across New Guinea and far north Australia, and two other subspecies across Australia.

PEREGRINE FALCON *Falco peregrinus* Plate 17

(Faucon pèlerin)

Description 44 cm. Large stocky falcon, with wing-tips almost as long as tail when perched. In flight, often shows bulging chest and distinctive anchor shape with broad-based pointed wings and medium-length tail. Adult has blue-grey upperparts, darker on head and cheeks, with white throat and half-collar. White breast, belly and underwing with dense black bars, sometimes appearing solid black on distant birds. Underparts of Vanuatu and New Caledonia birds are buff or even rufous, with black bars. Eye-ring, cere and legs are yellow in adult but blue-grey in juvenile. Juvenile has dark brown upperparts, with fine paler fringes, and pale buff underparts with heavy dark brown streaks.

Similar species Flight action, wing shape, short tail and dark cheeks are distinctive, similar only to other falcons. Differs from Brown Falcon by flight action and head pattern. From Oriental and Australian Hobby by heavier shape, bulkier chest and broader-based shorter wings. Adult also differs by black bars on white or buff underparts. Juvenile also differs by heavy streaking on buff underparts. Juvenile differs from Brown Falcon by more heavily streaked underparts and single point on cheeks. Juvenile plumage recalls juvenile Meyer's Goshawk but has different shape and flight action and more prominent moustachial stripe. See Nankeen Kestrel on New Caledonia.

Voice Series of *ki-ki-ki-* notes deeper than Oriental Hobby. Series of rising hoarse screams *airck, airck…* Clucking *tchuk* contact call.

Habits Usually seen over coasts and open country but also forest, especially where close to cliffs, and wanders over any habitat. Singles or pairs are often seen close to breeding sites on cliffs. Often soars high or climbs rapidly when prey is sighted, then dives down at great speed onto medium-sized birds such as seabirds, waders and pigeons.

Conservation status Rare in Bismarcks and Solomons, and uncommon in Vanuatu and New Caledonia. Local populations possibly threatened, but status obscured by nomadic and vagrant habits. Not globally threatened.
Range Scattered and localised across Melanesia. Wanders long distances, and records, especially from small islands, may not indicate breeding.
F. p. ernesti is rarely recorded on New Ireland, Lihir, Feni, Long, Umboi, New Britain and Witu, with birds of unknown subspecies on Bougainville, Kolombangara, Guadalcanal, Makira and Three Sisters; elsewhere, breeds from Thailand and Philippines to New Guinea.
F. p. nesiotes breeds but uncommon in Vanuatu and New Caledonia, where recorded from Torres Is, Vanua Lava, Gaua, Santo, Malo, Ambae, Malekula, Ambrym, Tongoa, Efate, Erromango, Aniwa, Tanna, Futuna, Aneityum, Grande Terre, Ouvéa, Lifou and Walpole; has buff or rufous wash on underparts; elsewhere, breeds only on Fiji, where rare. Elsewhere, other subspecies (larger paler birds) have occurred as vagrants to Indonesia and may occur in Melanesia.

KAGU Rhynochetidae

Endemic family. One extant species but another New Caledonian species is known only from subfossils.

KAGU *Rhynochetos jubatus* — Plate 12

(Cagou; Kagou huppé)

Description 55 cm. Large pale grey ground bird, somewhat intermediate between a heron and a rail. Plumage is uniformly pale ash-grey with slightly darker mantle, closed wings and tail, and strong dark grey-and-white barring on spread wings. Long wispy crest usually droops over nape but is erected fan-like in display. Medium-long orange-red bill and legs, and dark red eye. Female has fine bars on upperwing. Juvenile is faintly barred, browner and has browner or orange bill and legs.
Similar species Grey plumage, red bill and legs and habits are distinctive.
Voice Loud territorial duet of up to 15 minutes of crowing or small dog barking notes, usually given every dawn, rarely during day. Male often gives a long series of *gwa-gwa-* notes. Female often gives a series of *gwa-gwa—wha-wha-whaa* phrases. Hisses as a threat. Screaming cluck *rrHAA*.
Habits Commonest in wet forests with open understorey, often in undisturbed areas at mid-altitudes but ranges from sea-level to 1400 m and occasionally in patches of scrub. Walks a few steps and pauses motionless or runs fast on forest floor. Flightless but flaps wings to aid climbing steep slopes and usually roosts on understorey branches. In display, spreads or droops wings and erects crest.
Conservation status Generally rare and localised but fairly common where dogs are controlled in the Rivière Bleue park. Total population is estimated to be over 1000 birds. Threatened by predation by dogs and perhaps rats, cats and pigs. IUCN: Endangered.
Range Endemic to New Caledonia where locally distributed in suitable habitat on Grande Terre.

RAILS Rallidae

Ground birds with relatively long legs, neck and often long bill, usually found in wet or grassland habitats. Shy and furtive, often crepuscular or nocturnal. Commonly flick tail and head when alarmed before running into cover or flying with weak fluttering wing-beats and trailing legs. However, can fly long distances with stronger wing-beats and retracted legs, and disperse to isolated islands. Several species are flightless and others are often reluctant to fly. Most species can swim but only moorhens swim habitually. Precocial chicks and juveniles are black with shorter bills than adults.

RED-NECKED CRAKE *Rallina tricolor* — Plate 18

(Red-necked Rail; Râle tricolore)

Description 28 cm. Medium-sized chestnut and olive rail. Mostly dark olive-brown with chestnut head and neck, and variable faint pale barring from belly to undertail-coverts. Red eye, green bill and olive legs. Juvenile is uniformly dark olive-brown, soon developing a paler buffy face. White bars on wing are usually seen only in flight, and more conspicuous on juveniles.
Similar species Juvenile differs from Pale-vented Bush-hen by pale bars on dark undertail, and plainer head lacking paler throat. From Buff-banded Rail by only faintly barred underparts, plain head pattern and shorter green bill. From

Bare-eyed Rail by shorter bill and shorter non-contrasting tail.
Voice Territorial call is a rapid descending series of loud harsh *neek-neek-neek-* or *nak-nak-nak-* notes. Monotonous repeated *tok-tok-tok-*. Repeated soft *plop*. Low grunts. Pig-like squeals.
Habits Rainforest with wet ground, especially where understorey dense, in lowlands and sometimes in hills. Singles, pairs and small groups.
Conservation status No Melanesian records since 1944, and current status is unknown. Not globally threatened.
Range Records from Mussau, Lavongai and New Ireland, and possible historical records from Duke of York and New Britain. Usually regarded as monotypic but has been split as subspecies *R. t. laeta* on Mussau, which is paler orange on head and neck with greyer upperparts, and *R. t. convicta* on Lavongai and New Ireland, which is browner above with heavy buff barring on belly. Elsewhere, a dispersive breeder in New Guinea, north Queensland and perhaps east Indonesia.

WOODFORD'S RAIL *Nesoclopeus woodfordi* Plate 20

(*Rallus woodfordi*; Râle de Woodford)

Description 30 cm. Large dark flightless rail. Adult has very dark brown upperparts and slightly greyer underparts, often appearing uniformly blackish, but some birds have tawny or brown or grey patches, especially on head. Variable faint buff or white barring on flanks, vent and undertail-coverts and stronger barring and spotting on underwings. Stout, medium-long bill is usually ivory but has variable dark tip and may be yellowish, or all-dark on Guadalcanal and perhaps immatures on other islands. Medium-long legs are pale grey or greenish; eye chestnut-red. Immature has paler chin.
Similar species Plain blackish and flightless. Differs from all-black juvenile Purple Swamphen and Buff-banded Rail by longer, usually pale bill, pale legs, reddish eye and often white spots on underwing. From Pale-vented Bush-hen by darker plumage, longer, less green bill, often white spots on wing and no buff vent or undertail-coverts.
Voice Series of *kik-kik-kik-* notes fluctuating in tone and volume, probably a duet. Single *kik* and *keek* notes slower and deeper than Buff-banded Rail. Nasal rasp *ngowh* similar to Purple Swamphen but less nasal, shorter and without terminal echoing. Very quiet growl like a distant chain-saw.
Habits Damp grassland and grassy thickets, rarely in forest except thickets along rivers or abandoned gardens, with reports to 600 m. Shy. Singles and pairs stand rather upright and flick tail. Runs and may flap stubby wings when alarmed.
Conservation status Generally rare or absent but locally common. Status poorly known. Has increased where damp grasslands are no longer maintained and become overgrown, but possibly threatened by introduced mammals. IUCN: Near Threatened.
Range Endemic to the Solomons. Plumage and especially bare parts appear to vary considerably within subspecies as well as between subspecies.
N. w. tertius, endemic to Buka and Bougainville, has faint buff-and-white barring on underparts and primaries and a yellow-horn bill or bill-base.
N. w. immaculatus, endemic to Isabel, and possibly Choiseul where there are local reports of this species, has little or no white markings and has an ivory or pale horn bill, often darker at base.
N. w. woodfordi, endemic to Guadalcanal, has dark grey bill, many white spots on wings, and often a pale grey head.
An undescribed population, probably an endemic subspecies, on Malaita, is sooty-brown with some white barring on greyer flanks and vent, many pale buffy-orange spots on wings, dark bill and mid grey legs.

NEW CALEDONIAN RAIL *Gallirallus lafresnayanus* Plate 19

(*Tricholimnas lafresnayanus*; Râle de Lafresnaye)

Description 47 cm. Large flightless rail with a long bill and relatively long tail. Plain brown upperparts, greyer on underparts and some faint barring on thighs, undertail-coverts and especially axillaries. Long bill is dark horn, and legs dark horn or brown. Juvenile is largely black, washed chestnut on upperparts and grey on head and throat. Feathers, especially wings, are shaggy and hair-like, without the barb structure of flight feathers.
Similar species From immature Purple Swamphen by browner plumage and longer bill. From Buff-banded Rail by larger size, plainer plumage and longer bill. From Red Junglefowl by habits, long bill and darker plainer plumage.
Voice Unknown. Likely to be similar but deeper than Buff banded Rail.
Habits A rainforest species, reported to be crepuscular, even nocturnal. May possibly survive in remote montane forest massifs.
Conservation status Possibly extinct, with no definite records since 1890 but some unconfirmed recent reports. Presumably declined through predation by introduced mammals. IUCN: Critically Endangered.
Range Endemic to New Caledonia, on Grande Terre and possibly Ile des Pins.

PINK-LEGGED RAIL *Gallirallus insignis* Plate 19

(New Britain Rail; *Habropteryx insignis*; Râle de Nouvelle-Bretagne)

Description 33 cm. Medium-large stout flightless forest rail. Plain rufous-brown upperparts are more rufous on head, and strongly barred black-and-silver underparts including underwing but plain black thighs and central vent. Very short tail never flicked. Medium-length heavy dark bill; pink legs sometimes appear red or even orange. Juvenile unknown.
Similar species Often occurs alongside Pale-vented Bush-hen from which it differs by its barred underparts and heavy bill on plain rufous head. Rarely alongside Buff-banded Rail from which it differs by plain head, more prominent bars extending up to chin, and pink legs. Differs from similar-sized Melanesian Megapode by barred underparts, pink or red legs and no crest.
Voice Varied but poorly known and probably has undescribed calls. Pig-like squeal, *yeeow!* Low nasal gulping. Dog-like yaps. Extended duets.
Habits Most forest habitats but seemingly commoner in thickets and damp areas in hills and mountains, to 1250 m. Usually in pairs, but sometimes singles or small groups. Reports from grassland and of bird in flight are unconfirmed.
Conservation status Uncommon and possibly declining through predation by introduced mammals and trapping. IUCN: Near Threatened.
Range Endemic to New Britain, where widespread.

BUFF-BANDED RAIL *Gallirallus philippensis* Plate 19

(Banded Landrail; *Rallus philippensis*; Râle tiklin)

Description 28 cm. Medium-length slightly decurved bill is dull pink with dusky tip, and legs are pale yellow-pink; head orange-rufous with conspicuous pale supercilium and faint pale moustachial stripe. Upperparts brown with black mottling and variable small white spots. Throat very pale grey, upper breast pale grey, underparts with black-and-white bars; many subspecies have orange breast-band. Juvenile black, becoming pale on throat. Immature paler and duller than adult, with less contrasting underparts and no rufous on head.
Similar species Differs from most other rails by barred underparts. From Pink-legged Rail by pale supercilium. From Roviana Rail by patterned upperparts. From Red-necked Crake, which sometimes show faint barring, by patterned upperparts and medium-long pink-brown bill. From Pale-vented Bush-hen, which it often occurs alongside, by pale supercilium, longer bill and patterned body.
Voice Several distinct calls. Fluctuating series of *ki-ki-ki-* pipings. Loud nasal *tchou!* Yelping *tchu-tchu-tchu*. Squeal increasing in pitch but decreasing in volume. Series of mechanical rattles *trrr, trrr,...* Very deep, quiet gulping or rumbling.
Habits Damp and dry grassland including grassy thickets, gardens, overgrown urban yards and coconut plantations, to 500 m. Often in pairs and family parties. Has rather horizontal posture, often flicking its fairly long tail. More diurnal, confiding and ready to fly than most rails.
Conservation status Fairly common, but subspecies *G. p. lesouefi* and *G. p. meyeri* are rare and localised and status of *G. p. anachoretae*, *G. p. admiralitatis* and *G. p. praedo* is unknown. All are possibly threatened. Not globally threatened.
Range Across Melanesia but patchy occurrence and variable abundance, often commoner on small islands. The exact distribution, abundance, conservation status and taxonomic validity of the north Melanesian subspecies are poorly known.
G. p. reductus, breeding on Long, has little or no breast-band, blackish mantle with bars, and unmarked tertials and uppertail; elsewhere it breeds in adjacent New Guinea.
G. p. anachoretae, endemic to Kaniet and this or *G. p. admiralitatis* across Wuvulu, Hermit and Ninigo Is, has broad unbarred breast-band, fewer bars on underparts, heavy white bars on mantle, but unmarked lower back to uppertail.
G. p. admiralitatis, endemic to Papenbush and Pityili, off Manus, has white barring on entire upperparts, wider white barring on underparts and buff unbarred central belly.
G. p. praedo, endemic to Skoki close to Manus, has dark upperparts spotted with white especially on upper mantle, and an uninterrupted breast-band
G. p. lesouefi, endemic to Lavongai but with populations probably of this subspecies also on New Ireland, Tingwon, Tabar and Tanga, has black upperparts with heavy white spotting and streaking on lower back and rump, narrow breast-band and broad black bars on underparts.
G. p. meyeri, endemic to New Britain, including Witu, Watom and Duke of York, has browner upperparts with very few white spots, a broad uninterrupted breast-band and large unbarred buff central belly-patch.

G. p. christophori, endemic to east Solomons, including Florida Is, Guadalcanal, Malaita, Ulawa, Makira, Ugi, Three Sisters, Santa Catalina and Santa Ana, has white spots and bars on uppertail-coverts and central tail feathers, and heavily barred underparts with an obscure breast-band.
G. p. sethsmithi, breeding in Vanuatu, where recorded from all large islands and many smaller islands, and probably Nendo in Temotu where of unknown subspecies, has browner upperparts and narrower bars on underparts extending over belly and a variable reduced breast-band; elsewhere, breeds in Fiji.
G. p. swindellsi, endemic to New Caledonia, including Grande Terre, lagoon islets, Ouvéa, Lifou, Maré and perhaps other small islets, is dark with few white spots on upperparts, narrow white bars on underparts and virtually no breast-band.
G. p. touneliere, breeding on Surprise and perhaps other islets off west New Caledonia, is paler with more white spots and bars on upperparts and a variable breast-band; elsewhere breeds in other Coral Sea islets off New Guinea and Australia.
Elsewhere, other subspecies breed from Philippines to New Zealand and Samoa.

ROVIANA RAIL *Gallirallus rovianae* — Plate 19

(Râle roviana)

Description 30 cm. Medium-sized flightless rail. Dark sooty-brown upperparts with brighter rufous nape, crown and mask contrasting with long pale grey supercilium and paler grey throat. Dark grey underparts, paler on throat and with variable fine black-and-silvery barring on sides of neck and flanks. Barring may extend across whole breast, and some birds, especially on New Georgia, have pale tawny patch on central breast. Stubby wings with some white and rufous spots or bars on primaries. Medium-long bill is dark grey, often with dull pinkish-red base. Legs are stocky and dull grey. Plumage and bare-part colours may be more variable than documented.
Similar species Differs from juvenile Purple Swamphen by barred underparts, paler supercilium and longer bill. From Pale-vented Bush-hen by longer darker bill, pale supercilium, barred underparts and more upright posture. From Buff-banded Rail, which does not occur on same islands, by shorter tail, longer neck, more upright posture, darker and plainer plumage.
Voice Varied and poorly known. Staccato chattering *kik-kik-kitikek-kitikek-* with calls becoming more rapid up to ten notes/second. Loud nasal *tchu-ku*. Note the onomatopoeic local names *kitikete*, *kermete* and *pio-piu*. Sneezed *tchu*, often repeated every few seconds. Deep gulping.
Habits Dense ground vegetation, especially grassy areas in overgrown plantations and abandoned gardens but also secondary and riverside forest. All records from close to sea-level. Singles, pairs and family groups forage in thick undergrowth and sometimes emerge onto open grassland and roads. Flightless but can flutter a few metres.
Conservation status Localised and rare except on Kolombangara where locally fairly common. Possibly declining through predation by introduced mammals. IUCN: Near Threatened.
Range Endemic to Solomons, where known from New Georgia and Kolombangara and reported from Kohinggo, Vonavona and Rendova.

BARE-EYED RAIL *Gymnocrex plumbeiventris* — Plate 19

(Râle à ventre gris)

Description 32 cm. Medium-sized long-billed and long-legged rail. Bright chestnut head, neck, upper mantle and breast, olive-brown wings and lower mantle, ashy-grey lower breast and belly and black tail. Bill green, yellowish or brown-olive, legs and bare skin around eye pink. Juvenile unknown.
Similar species Erect black tail, long greenish bill and pink-red legs distinctive. Differs further from Red-necked Crake by no barring on belly and undertail, and from Pale-vented Bush-hen by chestnut head and neck.
Voice Probable territorial call is a loud gulping *wow-wow-wow-*. Gulping *uw-uw-uw-* when foraging or flushed. Repeated pig-like grunt.
Habits Inhabits wet forest and sometimes wet grasslands and swamps in lowlands but also hills and low mountains, but migrants appear in atypical habitats. Shy. Singles walk rather horizontally with erect black tail.
Range Uncertain status. One specimen, with darker upperparts, more maroon neck and slightly paler belly, is labelled as New Ireland or Solomons and has been described as *G. p. intactus*. Elsewhere, *G. p. plumbeiventris* and *G. p. hoeveni* breed across New Guinea, Aru Is, Moluccas and Karkar and, as a dispersive species, may reach Melanesia as a vagrant.

PALE-VENTED BUSH-HEN *Amaurornis moluccana* — Plate 19

(Rufous-tailed Bush-hen; also treated as a subspecies of Bush-hen *A. olivaceus*; Râle des Moluques)

Description 26 cm. Medium-sized, rather dumpy rail with greenish-yellow legs and bill. Olive-brown upperparts contrast slightly with grey underparts and pale buffy-rufous vent and undertail-coverts. Medium-length legs and stout bill are greenish-yellow, brighter green when breeding. Juvenile has paler throat and duller bare parts and plumage.
Similar species Distinctive rich buff undertail shared only by White-browed Crake, from which it differs by being much larger with unmarked head and upperparts. Differs from Red-necked Crake by unmarked underparts and lack of chestnut on head and neck. From Bare-eyed Rail by shorter bill, non-contrasting tail and lack of chestnut head and neck. From Woodford's Rail by shorter green bill, paler plumage and lack of any white on underwing. From immature Dusky Moorhen by undertail pattern and bill and leg colour. Often occurs alongside Buff-banded Rail, from which it differs by lacking the pale supercilium and barred underparts.
Voice Loud distinctive and often nocturnal duetting *whee-kyoou* of paired cat-like wails, usually upslurred then downslurred, repeated at about one second intervals about ten times, sometimes interspersed with clucking. Long regular series of *chat-chat-chat-* and other simple repeated clicking and piping notes.
Habits Dense grassland and overgrown gardens and thickets, especially where wet, sometimes within forest, to 900 m. Singles and pairs are secretive, rarely leaving cover, and often crepuscular.
Conservation status Fairly common but localised. Not threatened.
Range Bismarcks and Solomons.
A. m. moluccana, breeds on Long I., has green or green-yellow bill with brownish culmen and no red at base; elsewhere breeds across north New Guinea and Moluccas.
A. m. nigrifrons, endemic to New Ireland, New Britain and Bougainville, including Lavongai, Lihir, Tabar, Tanga, Tolokiwa, Umboi, Sakar, Watom, Witu, Duke of York and Buka, is darker with tawny undertail-coverts, blackish culmen and small red line at base of bill.
A. m. ultima, endemic to eastern Solomons, including Ndai, Malaita, Makira, Ugi, Santa Ana and Santa Catalina, is smaller and paler with whitish throat, deep vinaceous undertail-coverts and no red on bill-base.
Records from Choiseul, Isabel, most of New Georgia group (where rare) and Guadalcanal are of unknown subspecies which may be intermediate.
Elsewhere, *A. m. ruficrissa* breeds in southern New Guinea and Australia.

BAILLON'S CRAKE *Porzana pusilla* — Plate 18

(Marouette de Baillon)

Description 16 cm. Tiny rail with grey face, throat and breast, black-and-white-barred belly and undertail, and tawny upperparts with black and white streaks. Green bill and legs, red eye. Juvenile has pale buff face, throat and breast.
Similar species Differs from White-browed Crake by barred belly and undertail and plain face pattern. From Spotless Crake by paler buffier plumage with mottled upperparts. Much smaller than Buff-banded Rail and other rails.
Voice Rapid repeated clicks. Harsh *krek-krek*. Whirring *chir*. Soft whining notes. (Call descriptions from Australia.)
Habits Dense vegetation alongside fresh water, usually swamps. Singles creep unobtrusively in dense vegetation and walk on floating leaves.
Range New Caledonia, where known only from a breeding pair collected from Grande Terre in 1880, probably *P. p. affinis* of New Zealand. Other subspecies are scattered across Africa and Eurasia to Australia and New Guinea.

SPOTLESS CRAKE *Porzana tabuensis* — Plate 18

(Marouette fuligineuse)

Description 17 cm. Tiny plain dark rail. Plumage sooty except for olive-brown mantle and wings, and white bars on undertail-coverts. Bright red eye, pink-red legs and dark grey bill. Juvenile has paler underparts, especially on throat, is browner on head, sometimes with narrow white supercilium, and has duller eye and legs.
Similar species Differs from other tiny rails by plain dark upperparts. From all-black rail chicks by red eye and legs. From much larger Pale-vented Bush-hen by barred vent and undertail, and bare-part colours.
Voice Rapid machine-gun chatter. Loud explosive motorcycle purring for 1–3 seconds, often preceded by a soft quarrelling. Sharp *kek!* Harsh nasal *harr*. Dove-like *croo*. (Call descriptions from Australia.)
Habits Dense vegetation alongside fresh water, often beside small ponds and streams. Also in dry scrubby habitats on small islands. All Melanesian records are from near sea-level but may occur in mountains, as in New Guinea. Singles, pairs and small groups usually keep hidden in vegetation, sometimes coming onto mud beside waterside vegetation.
Conservation status Rare and locally threatened but poorly known. Not globally threatened.

Range Across Melanesia, where *P. t. tabuensis* is a rare and localised breeder but dispersing over wider area, with records from Wuvulu, Watom, tiny islets off New Georgia, Guadalcanal, Rennell, Makira, Tinakula, Erromango, Tanna, Aneityum, Lifou, Maré, Ouvéa and Grande Terre; elsewhere occurs from Philippines to Australia, New Zealand and Polynesia with other subspecies in New Guinea.

WHITE-BROWED CRAKE *Porzana cinerea* — Plate 18

(*Poliolimnas cinereus*; Marouette grise)

Description 17 cm. Tiny rail with distinctive face pattern of two white stripes on dark grey face. Rich buff upperparts have black mottling, pale grey throat and neck to belly, and plain buff vent and undertail-coverts. Juvenile has similar but less contrasting buff-striped head-pattern, and pale buff neck and underparts.
Similar species Distinctive face pattern. Other tiny rails, Spotless Crake and Baillon's Crake have barred undertail-coverts.
Voice Chorus of rapid nasal chattering *chika-chika-chika-*. Slower clockwork *chika, chika,...* Churrs, grunts and squeaks.
Habits Densely vegetated margins of lakes, ponds and swamps. All Melanesian records are from close to sea-level but it also occurs in mountains of New Guinea. Singles and pairs walk under and climb into thick grassy vegetation, and walk over floating vegetation or on muddy margins.
Conservation status Uncommon and localised. Not globally threatened.
Range Scattered across Melanesia, with records from Mussau, Emirau, Lavongai, New Ireland, Lihir, Umboi, New Britain, Buka, Bougainville, Guadalcanal, Makira, Three Sisters, Nendo, Gaua, Erromango, Tanna, Lifou and Grande Terre. Has been split into subspecies including *P. c. meeki* endemic to Mussau, which has dark grey underparts, but generally regarded as monotypic.
Elsewhere, breeds from Malaysia and Philippines to north Australia, Fiji and Samoa.

PURPLE SWAMPHEN *Porphyrio porphyrio* — Plate 20

(Also treated as Black-backed Swamphen *Porphyrio melanotus*; Talève sultane)

Description 41 cm. Large thickset chicken-like rail. Bright red massive bill, frontal shield, eye and legs. Head and body deep blue-purple except dull dark brown on mantle, wings and uppertail, and white undertail-coverts. Juvenile is all-black including bare parts, but has paler chin.
Similar species Large size, purple plumage and massive red bill distinctive. Also differs from Dusky Moorhen by more white on undertail-coverts. When flushed, differs from megapodes and Nicobar Pigeon by longer neck and weaker flight.
Voice Varied. Wheezy yelp *kee-yhow*, often repeated. Explosive *pruuk*. Short sharp yelps. Deep sonorous calls and trumpeting. High-pitched squeals.
Habits Any wet freshwater habitat and often in dry forest thickets, gardens and grassland, usually in lowlands but up to 600 m. Usually on ground but also climbs clumsily up dense vegetation. Often gregarious. Shy where hunted. When flushed, flies with heavy broad wings, similar to megapode.
Conservation status Locally common but rare on New Britain and very rare on New Ireland and Nendo. Often persecuted for raiding gardens. Not threatened.
Range Across Melanesia, where *P. p. samoensis* is recorded from Manus, Rambutyo, Lavongai, New Ireland, Tabar, Umboi, New Britain, Watom, across Solomons (except Ulawa), Nendo, Vanuatu (except Torres Is and Bank Is), Ouvéa, Maré and Grande Terre. Considerable variation has led to description of many subspecies such as *P. p. caledonicus* endemic to New Caledonia, but variation also occurs within populations. Elsewhere, *P. p. samoensis* breeds in Fiji, Samoa and Tonga and other subspecies are scattered across Africa and Eurasia to New Zealand.

MAKIRA WOODHEN *Gallinula silvestris* — Plate 20

(Makira Moorhen; San Cristobal Moorhen; *Edithornis silvestris*; *Pareudiastes silvestris*; Gallinule d'Édith)

Description 26 cm. Short-winged flightless rail with almost no tail. Black plumage with blue gloss on neck, and browner on underparts and especially wings. Bright scarlet legs and bill, blue-grey frontal shield over forehead onto base of upper mandible, and yellow facial skin.
Similar species Differs from other rails on Makira by not flicking tail and being flightless. From Purple Swamphen by smaller size, black undertail-coverts, blue shield and finer bill. From Buff-banded Rail and Pale-vented Bush-hen by darker plumage, although all three species can appear dark in poor light, and red legs and bill. From Spotless Crake by much larger size, unmarked undertail and red bill.

Voice Unknown but may resemble local name *kia*.
Habits Reported to inhabit primary hill and lower montane forest with dense undergrowth on steep slopes from below 500 m to 600 m. Reported to run fast and flap up trees when hunted by dogs.
Conservation status Known from one specimen in 1929, one report in 1953 and local reports in 2002. Probably exterminated by predation by introduced mammals. IUCN: Critically Endangered.
Range Endemic to Makira where known from the central mountains.

DUSKY MOORHEN *Gallinula tenebrosa* — Plate 20

(Gallinule sombre)

Description 31 cm. Blackish rail, usually seen swimming. Adult is dark blue-grey with browner mantle and wings and conspicuous white outer undertail-coverts. Breeding adult bill and frontal shield red with yellow bill-tip, and legs often red; non-breeding adult has greenish or black bill and shrunken shield, legs greenish below knee. Juvenile is duller and browner, with dull, often olive-brown bill and legs.
Similar species White undertail is distinctive, as are adult bare parts. White on undertail is shared only with Purple Swamphen, from which it differs by blacker plumage, although immature swamphen is also black, smaller bill with yellow tip, and black central stripe on undertail.
Voice Repeated resonant *kok*. Strident crowing *kerk!* Shrieks, squawks and various sharp alarm calls.
Habits Well-vegetated lakes and swamps. Pairs and small groups usually feed on floating vegetation while swimming but also graze waterside vegetation, returning to water when disturbed. Swims jerkily, usually flicking tail.
Conservation status Rare and localised but probably increasing. Not threatened.
Range Very local resident on New Britain, where known from Lake Lalili, and Grande Terre, New Caledonia. Probably a recent colonist on both islands and may spread further. One record from Guadalcanal. Subspecies unknown; may be *G. t. frontata* of east Indonesia and south New Guinea, the smaller darker *G. t. neumanni* of north New Guinea, or the larger *G. t. tenebrosa* of Australia.

BUTTONQUAILS Turnicidae

Very small dumpy ground birds of grasslands, superficially similar to quails. Usually seen only when flushed, flying a short distance with low whirring flight and glides, but sometimes seen emerging out of grassland edge especially on paths and beside roads. Sexually role-reversed; females have brighter plumage than males.

RED-BACKED BUTTONQUAIL *Turnix maculosus* — Plate 18

(Turnix moucheté)

Description 14 cm. Very small dumpy ground bird. Rufous or buff face and underparts with a few black spots and grey bars on breast and flanks. Dark crown and upperparts are barred and mottled grey, buff, rufous and black, and has white eye, yellow legs and bill. Male has less rufous on face and neck and buff wash on underparts. Female is brighter with more extensive richer rufous and brighter yellow bill. Juvenile darker with more black mottling on underparts, dull bare parts and uniform upperwing in flight. In flight, appears streaky brown and buff, with paler buff inner wing-coverts contrasting with darker primaries and secondaries.
Similar species Very like female King Quail but longer-winged and plumage always mottled brown with paler upperwing-coverts; on ground, differs by larger yellow bill and black spots on buff breast, flanks and wing-coverts. From small crakes and rails by short legs hardly visible in flight and faster wing-beats on narrower wings.
Voice Deep upslurred boom *hoooOOM*, repeated *c.*15 times between short pauses, initially one note per second, then accelerating slightly. Very quiet and may be overlooked as a distant fruit dove. Silent when flushed.
Habits Short and long dry grasslands, especially dry ridge-tops, and weedy cultivated areas. Singles and pairs flush at very close distance with fast whirring wings, gliding back into grassland a few metres away.
Conservation status *T. m. saturata* is uncommon, with very few recent records, and may be threatened. *T. m. salomonis* is locally common but may be threatened by ongoing declines in its small area of habitat. Not globally threatened.
Range New Britain and Guadalcanal.
T. m. saturata, endemic to New Britain and Duke of York, has slight rufous wash on collar, and blacker upperparts and deeper rufous underparts than New Guinea subspecies.
T. m. salomonis, endemic to the north coastal plain of Guadalcanal and recently reported from Florida Is, has more rufous on collar and more rufous and black on upperparts. Elsewhere, other subspecies breed from east Indonesia to Australia.

PAINTED BUTTONQUAIL *Turnix varius* — Plate 18

(Turnix bariolé)

Description 16 cm. Very small dumpy ground bird. Upperparts have orange-rufous, grey, black and white mottling, head is greyer with pale grey supercilium and throat, shoulders more rufous, and underparts pale grey with white spots and white belly. Red eye, grey bill and yellow legs. Female is brighter and more rufous on upperparts. Juvenile as male but has more black on underparts, less creamy streaking on upperparts and dull bare parts.
Similar species Differs from Spotless and White-browed Crakes, the only other tiny ground birds on New Caledonia, by short legs hardly visible in flight and faster wing-beats on narrower wings.
Voice Territorial call is an accelerating, rising series of 10–30 *oom* booms at one second intervals. Contact call is a rapid soft drumming. (Call descriptions from Australia.)
Habits No Melanesian field records. In Australia, it inhabits savanna and open forest, especially dry forest with open understorey but thick litter-layer. Singles, pairs and small groups usually run from danger, rarely flushing into fast flight low between trees. Often detected by presence of round feeding depressions created by clearing regular circles in leaf-litter.
Conservation status *T. v. novaecaledoniae* is known from a handful of old specimens, last taken in 1912, and no sightings. The subspecies is likely to be Critically Endangered or Extinct but the species is not globally threatened.
Range *T. v. novaecaledoniae* is endemic to Grande Terre, New Caledonia, and is smaller with more black and rufous on upperparts than other subspecies. Elsewhere, two other subspecies breed in Australia.

STONE-CURLEWS (THICK-KNEES) Burhinidae

Large stout shorebirds with heavy bill and legs and cryptic brown plumage. Often crepuscular or nocturnal, hiding in shade during day.

BEACH STONE-CURLEW *Esacus magnirostris* — Plate 21

(Beach Thick-knee; *Burhinus magnirostris*; *E./B. giganteus*; *E./B. neglectus*; Grand Oedicnème)

Description 56 cm. Large stout brown wader with a very heavy yellow-based black bill and dull yellow legs. Grey-brown with dark brown and white stripes on face, paler underparts, and dark bar and grey panel on closed wing. In flight, underwing is largely white with black tips, and upperwing has two white patches on black outer primaries, white inner primaries and pale grey secondaries. Immature has duller bare parts and buff fringes to upperparts.
Similar species Distinctive bill and head-pattern, but note surprisingly white appearance in flight.
Voice Shrill wailing *keer-lee* sometimes repeated or chorused. Rather quiet sharp single or repeated piping *klee*.
Habits Beaches, reefs and mangroves, and sometimes short coastal grassland. Commonest on small islands close to large islands. Pairs, sometimes singles or small groups, stand motionless, walk slowly or run and pause on beaches. Crepuscular, often standing in shade through day. Shy, preferring undisturbed beaches and islets, flying far when flushed. Heavy flight with slow wing-beats.
Conservation status Uncommon or rare, and possibly declining through disturbance. IUCN: Near Threatened.
Range Widespread resident breeder across Melanesia, including Manus, Mussau, New Britain and most satellite islands, New Ireland, including Lavongai and Lihir, across the Solomons except Rennell, but very rare on Vanuatu and New Caledonia, where recorded from Santo and the northern lagoon of Grande Terre. Elsewhere, breeds from South-East Asia to Australia.

OYSTERCATCHERS Haematopodidae

Large stout coastal shorebirds with pied plumage and long red straight bill and legs.

SOUTH ISLAND OYSTERCATCHER *Haematopus finschi* — Plate 21

(Huîtrier de Finsch)

Description 46 cm. Large black wader with white from lower breast to vent, white rump extending onto upper back and broad white wing-bar. Long straight orange-red bill and fairly short pink-red legs. Immature has duller bare parts and brown fringes to upperparts.
Similar species Plumage, bare parts and stout proportions distinctive. Differs from Australian Pied Oystercatcher *H. longirostris*, not yet recorded in Melanesia but visitor north to New Guinea, by white on back, broad white rump-band and longer broad white wing-bar.

Voice Loud ringing *kleep, kleep...* or *peepapep, pepapeep...*
Habits Sandy and muddy coasts, and sometimes adjacent short grassland. Walks slowly, probing or picking at ground.
Range Single record from Vanuatu and two from New Caledonia in September–October. Breeds on South Is, New Zealand, and winters north to North Is with occasional records to Norfolk Is.

STILTS AND AVOCETS Recurvirostridae

Slender pied shorebirds with long neck, legs and bill.

WHITE-HEADED STILT *Himantopus leucocephalus* Plate 21

(Also treated as a subspecies of Black-winged Stilt *H. himantopus*; Échasse d'Australie)

Description 37 cm. Elegant slender pied wader with exceptionally long pink legs and long fine black bill. Adult is white with black wings, mantle and hindneck. Female has browner upperparts. In flight, long legs hang beyond tail, and black wings contrast with white underwing-coverts and lower mantle. Immature lacks neck-patch but has blackish smudging on face and crown, variable grey smudging on neck and browner upperparts.
Similar species Long legs and plumage pattern are distinctive.
Voice Repeated loud yapping *kyap, kyap...*, especially in alarm. Immature gives a thin whistle.
Habits Shallow muddy waters. Gregarious in shallows of lakes and sometimes on coasts. Walks slowly, pecking at insects on surface of water, often calling and chasing around breeding sites.
Conservation status Rare and possibly threatened in Melanesia but not globally threatened.
Range Very localised on New Britain, Long and Umboi where breeding confirmed only on Lake Dakatoa, New Britain. One record from Vanikoro. Elsewhere, breeds in Indonesia, New Guinea, Australia and New Zealand.

MIGRATORY SHOREBIRDS (PLOVERS, CURLEWS AND SANDPIPERS)

Shorebirds (or waders) are poorly studied in Melanesia, with more observations on Bougainville and New Caledonia, but many species are likely to occur more widely than currently documented. However, some species commonly migrating to Australia are extremely rare in Melanesia. Other migrant species, including American species, have not yet been recorded but are likely to occur as rare vagrants. Most species are commoner during their southerly migration in September to November, some staying for the northern winter to about April when there is a less marked return migration, and smaller numbers of all species spend the northern summer in Melanesia. Most are coastal species and roost communally in dense mixed species flocks when feeding grounds are covered at high tide.

PLOVERS Charadriidae

Similar to curlews, sandpipers and allies but with rounded head, large eye, short, straight bill and distinctive gait of running a few paces then stopping abruptly. Lapwings *Vanellus* are large and boldly patterned. Golden and Grey Plovers *Pluvialis* are medium-sized with spangled upperparts. Other plovers or dotterels *Charadrius* are rather dumpy, small or medium-sized shorebirds. Most are non-breeding migrants to Melanesia, breeding in northern Eurasia and migrating south for the northern winter, often to Australia. A few species breed in Australia and New Zealand and migrate north in the southern winter.

MASKED LAPWING *Vanellus miles* Plate 21

(Yellow-wattled Lapwing; Masked Plover; Vanneau soldat)

Description 37 cm. Large plover with yellow bill and facial wattle. Black cap extends onto nape and down breast-sides, otherwise uniformly grey-brown above and white below. In flight, brown mantle and upperwing-coverts contrast with black primaries and secondaries, white rump and black tail-band, and white underwing-coverts. Immature has small wattles and buff fringes to upperparts.
Similar species Distinctive behaviour, yellow bill and wattle, and flight pattern.
Voice Loud grating staccato *kree-kree-kree-* repeated constantly when disturbed.
Habits Pairs and small flocks inhabit open short grasslands. Noisy and aggressive, diving at intruders.

Conservation status Increasing. First recorded in New Caledonia in 1994 where small numbers have bred since 1998. Not threatened.
Range Rare breeder on New Caledonia, around Dumbéa, Boulouparis and Koné, and single records from New Georgia and Tanna. Elsewhere, *V. m. novaehollandiae* also breeds in east Australia and New Zealand, and *V. m. miles*, which has black restricted to a small cap, breeds in New Guinea and northern Australia.

PACIFIC GOLDEN PLOVER *Pluvialis fulva* Plate 22

(Also treated as a subspecies of Lesser Golden Plover *P. dominica*; Pluvier fauve)

Description 25 cm. The commonest wader in Melanesia, especially inland. Medium-small short-billed wader with golden spangling on crown and upperparts, fading with time to creamy-buff. Short black bill and medium-long dark grey legs. In flight, plain with indistinct narrow white wing-bar and dusky underwings. Non-breeding adult and immature have buffy-grey streaked and mottled head, neck and breast, whiter belly and ill-defined short broad silvery supercilium and dark spot on rear ear-coverts. Breeding adult has black underparts from face to belly, bordered by broad white band from bill to vent. Intermediates with patchy underparts are common.
Similar species Differs from Grey Plover by golden to creamy plumage, uniformly dusky underwings, indistinct wing-bar and plain tail, slighter bill, longer legs and slimmer shape. From other plovers by black legs, spangled upperparts and uniformly patterned buffy chin to breast. Differs from very similar American Golden Plover *P. dominica*, not yet recorded from Melanesia, by its yellower upperparts spots, less prominent white supercilium, finer bill, blunter rear end in which the tertials cover nearly all the primary tips which hardly extend beyond the tail tip, and the feet project beyond the tail in flight.
Voice Clear hurried *chew-it*. Slower slurred *clu*-ee.
Habits Short grassland, particularly airfields and playing fields, and smaller numbers along all coasts. Usually in small flocks, sometimes in hundreds. More upright posture than other plovers.
Range Widespread and fairly common across Melanesia, especially September–April. Breeds in Arctic Asia and migrates to South-East Asia, Australasia and west Pacific.

GREY PLOVER *Pluvialis squatarola* Plate 22

(Black-bellied Plover; Pluvier argenté)

Description 29 cm. Medium-sized short-billed wader with cold black, grey and white plumage. Short, fairly stout black bill and medium-long dark grey legs. In flight shows white wing-bar, white rump, black bars on tail and whitish underwing with black armpits. Non-breeding adult has grey streaked and mottled head, neck and breast, whiter belly, short broad white supercilium and grey upperparts with paler spangling. Immature may have slight buff wash. Breeding adult has black underparts from face to belly, bordered by broad white band from bill to upper flanks, and black and silvery spangled upperparts. Intermediates with patchy underparts are common.
Similar species Distinctive black armpits in flight. Differs from Pacific Golden Plover also by cold grey plumage, rarely with slight buffy wash, distinct wing-bar and barred white uppertail, stouter bill and dumpier shape. From other plovers by black legs, spangled upperparts and uniformly patterned grey chin to breast.
Voice Loud plaintive drawn-out *klee-oo-wee*.
Habits Along all coasts, especially mud and sand. Usually solitary or in small well-spaced groups. Usually rather hunched and horizontal.
Range Widespread but uncommon visitor across Melanesia, but only one record from Vanuatu, especially September to April. Breeds in Arctic and migrates south to coasts world-wide.

COMMON RINGED PLOVER *Charadrius hiaticula* Plate 22

(Pluvier grand-gravelot)

Description 19 cm. Small plover with a bold breast-band, white collar, very short bill and short dull orange legs. In flight shows broad white wing-bar and white sides to rump. Non-breeding adult has dark brown breast-band and mask, sandy-brown crown, mantle and wings, and dull orange base to blackish bill. Immature similar, but has narrower breast-band, sometimes broken in centre, buffy fringes to upperparts and duller bare parts. Breeding adult has black breast-band, mask from bill to ear-coverts and over forecrown, and black-tipped orange bill.
Similar species See Semipalmated Plover. Differs from Little Ringed Plover by orange bill and legs, lack of yellow eye-ring, dumpier shape, larger size, broader breast-band, distinct wing-bar and call. From other plovers, especially Double-banded Plover and Lesser Sand Plovers, by small size, white collar, distinct breast-band, orange bare parts, and bold head markings.

Voice Soft mellow rising *too-lee*.
Habits Coasts, especially sand and mud, and sometimes short grassland and occasionally along rivers and lakes.
Range Two records from New Ireland, at Kavieng in October and November. May occur as rare vagrant anywhere in Melanesia. Two subspecies breed in the Arctic and migrate to Africa and south-west Asia.

SEMIPALMATED PLOVER *Charadrius semipalmatus* — Plate 22

(Pluvier semipalmé)

Description 17 cm. Small plover, almost identical to Common Ringed Plover.
Similar species Differs from Common Ringed Plover by call, tiny webs between toes, shorter thicker bill, narrower breast-band and very thin pale eye-ring. Immature also has a tiny extension of white above gape at bill-base. See Common Ringed Plover for differences from other plovers.
Voice A clear sharp rising *chewee* or more disyllabic *che-weee*.
Habits Coasts, especially sand and mud.
Range Two recent records from New Caledonia. May occur as rare vagrant anywhere in Melanesia. Breeds in Arctic America, migrates to coastal North and South America and is a rare vagrant to Polynesia.

LITTLE RINGED PLOVER *Charadrius dubius* — Plate 22

(Pluvier petit-gravelot)

Description 15 cm. Very small plover with bold breast-band, white collar, short pinkish legs and narrow yellow eye-ring. In flight shows white sides to rump and very fine white wing-bar. Adult has black breast-band and mask from bill to ear-coverts and over forecrown, bordered by a narrow white band, sandy-brown hindcrown, mantle and wings, blackish bill with yellow or pink base and a broad yellow eye-ring which flushes red when breeding. Immature has black markings replaced by less defined dark brown and a narrower eye-ring.
Similar species Differs from Common Ringed Plover and Semipalmated Plover by yellow eye-ring, pink legs, more elongate shape, narrower breast-band, plain upperwing and call. Adult also has narrow white bar across mid-crown. From other plovers, especially Double-banded Plover and Lesser Sand Plover, by small size, white collar, distinct breast-band, yellow eye-ring, pinkish legs and bold head markings.
Voice Harsh *chit, chit, chit*.
Habits Breeds on gravel beds in rivers. May also occur beside lakes and swamps, short grassland and occasionally coasts. Singles and pairs usually feed on their own, ignoring any other waders.
Conservation status Very rare and possibly threatened in Melanesia, but not globally threatened.
Range *C. d. dubius* breeds locally on New Ireland and New Britain. Elsewhere, it breeds in the Philippines and New Guinea. *C. d. jerdoni* breeds in India and South-East Asia. *C. d. curonicus* breeds across Eurasia, migrating south to Africa, occasionally to New Guinea and may occur in Melanesia. Differs from *C. d. dubius* in narrower eye-ring which never flushes red, less pale at bill-base, black bar on outer tail feathers; non-breeding adult as immature but brighter eye-ring and lacking buffy fringes to upperparts; immatures have browner breast-band and less white on forehead; call a clear whistled *piu*.

DOUBLE-BANDED PLOVER *Charadrius bicinctus* — Plate 22

(Pluvier à double collier)

Description 19 cm. Small plover with two breast-bands or extensions from sides of breast, and short yellow-green legs. In flight shows narrow white wing-bar, white sides to rump and white outer tail feathers. Non-breeding adult has grey-brown head with broad square-ended buffy or creamy supercilium, buffy collar and nape, and two ill-defined buffy patches on breast-sides. Immature similar, but breast-patches often ill-defined and sometimes no more than a wash, and wing-coverts may have mixture of buff-fringed immature feathers and chestnut-fringed adult feathers. Breeding adult has narrow blackish upper breast-band, broad chestnut lower breast-band, and white forehead and supercilium. Upper breast-band, forecrown-bar and lores are black in male and dark brown in female.
Similar species Double breast-bands of adult are distinctive. Non-breeding and immature differ from Lesser and Greater Sand Plovers by double breast-band if discernible, more creamy-buff on head and neck, darker upperparts, shorter legs, finer bill, smaller size and call. From Oriental Plover by breast pattern, dumpy shape, smaller size and call.
Voice Clear incisive *chip*, often repeated 3–4 times.

Habits Coasts and short grassland. Singles and loose groups. Stands more upright than other small plovers.
Range Uncommon but regular migrant to New Caledonia and one record from Aniwa, Vanuatu, mostly March–August. Breeds in New Zealand; some disperse to east Australia.

LESSER SAND PLOVER *Charadrius mongolus* Plate 22

(Mongolian [Sand] Plover; Pluvier de Mongolie)

Description 20 cm. Small plover with black bill and medium-long greenish-grey legs. Stout bill is as long as bill-base to rear of eye. In flight shows narrow white wing-bar and sides to rump, and toes only project slightly beyond tail. Non-breeding adult has sandy-brown upperparts and broad lateral breast-patches, with whitish forehead and supercilium. Immature similar, but breast-patches and supercilium buffier, with pale fringes on upperparts. Breeding adult male has black ear-covert mask, black borders to white forehead-spot and throat, orange-rufous neck-sides and upper breast, white lower breast and belly, and grey-brown crown and upperparts. Female is duller and lacks black border to throat-patch and lacks black forehead-line.
Similar species Differs from very similar Greater Sand Plover by smaller size, being about Common Sandpiper sizes versus tattler size, shorter and slightly finer bill, rounder head, less distinct mask, paler upperparts, less white on rump-sides, no dark subterminal tail-band, clearer wing-bar, and shorter duller legs. Breeding adult male also has black border to throat. From Oriental Plover by dumpy shape, shorter wings, shorter darker legs and breast markings. From Little Ringed Plover by larger size, longer greyish legs, and lack of white collar, eye-ring, distinct breast-band and distinct head markings. See Double-banded Plover.
Voice Sharp hard *drrit*. Hard *chitik*, or *chi-chi-chi* trills.
Habits Coasts, especially mud and sand, and sometimes short grassland. Singles and small scattered groups, often mixed with other waders.
Range Widespread but uncommon migrant and non-breeding visitor across Melanesia, with only one record from Vanuatu, usually September to April. *C. m. mongolus* and *C. m. stegmanni* breed in Siberia and migrate to east Asia and Australia. Elsewhere, other subspecies breed in central Asia and migrate to Africa to Indonesia.

GREATER SAND PLOVER *Charadrius leschenaultii* Plate 22

(Pluvier de Leschenault)

Description 23 cm. Medium-small plover with long greenish or yellowish legs. Heavy black bill is longer than bill-base to rear of eye. In flight, shows narrow white wing-bar, white sides to rump, and toes project distinctly beyond tail. Non-breeding adult and immature plumages are very like Lesser Sand Plover. Breeding adult male plumage as Lesser Sand Plover but breast-band narrower and slightly paler, no black border to throat-patch. Breeding adult female as non-breeding but with narrow orange-brown breast-band.
Similar species See Lesser Sand Plover above.
Voice Trilled *prrit*, *trri* etc, softer and longer than Lesser Sand Plover.
Habits Coasts, especially mud and sand, but rarely short grassland. Usually singles or small numbers mixed with other waders.
Range Widespread but scattered and uncommon migrant and non-breeding visitor across Melanesia, especially the north, usually September–April. *C. l. leschenaultii* breeds in eastern central Asia and migrates to south Asia as far as Australia. Elsewhere, other subspecies breed in west and central Asia and migrate to Africa.

ORIENTAL PLOVER *Charadrius veredus* Plate 22

(Pluvier oriental)

Description 24 cm. Medium-small elongate plover with long yellowish legs and long wings projecting well beyond tail-tip. In flight, shows long plain wings and dusky underwings. Non-breeding adult has plain buffy-brown neck, upper breast and upperparts with a buffy-white broad supercilium, bill-base and chin, and white lower breast to vent. Adult breeding male has buffy-white head and neck except for a small brown cap, orange-rufous upper breast, dark lower breast-band and white belly. Female has buffy-brown head and neck, darker on crown and ear-coverts, and rufous-washed upper breast. Immature and fresh non-breeding adult has rufous to buff fringes on upperparts.
Similar species Differs from other plovers, especially Lesser Sand Plover, Greater Sand Plover and Pacific Golden Plover by slimmer shape, longer wings, longer pale legs and unmarked breast and upperparts. From Australian Pratincole by head pattern, longer straight bill and shorter plain wings.
Voice Sharp whistled *tink, tink, tink*. Short piping *klink*. Trills.

Habits Short dry grassland, especially with rocks, and sometimes beside water. Singles and scattered groups walk and run. Flies high and erratically.
Range Single records from New Ireland, Bougainville, New Georgia, Rennell, New Caledonia and probably Vanuatu, in October–December. Breeds in north-east Asia and migrates to Australia for September–March.

JACANAS Jacanidae

Wading birds with long legs and exceptionally long toes, which walk on top of floating vegetation on swamps and lakes. Sexually role-reversed, and often chase noisily and excitedly.

COMB-CRESTED JACANA *Irediparra gallinacea* Plate 20

(Jacana à crête)

Description 23 cm. Short-tailed rail-like bird with exceptionally long toes. White underparts and brown upperparts. Adult has bright red comb on a frontal shield, buff wash on neck and broad black breast-band. Comb is pinker in breeding adults, more orange when non-breeding. Male is smaller and duller. In flight, shows darker flight feathers and very long trailing legs and feet. Juvenile lacks shield and comb, has chestnut crown and entirely white underparts.
Similar species Habit of walking on floating vegetation is shared only by a few small rails and waders. Very long toes and adult's comb distinctive.
Voice Shrill trilling, especially in flight. Explosive soft bugle.
Habits Floating vegetation, especially lilies, on large lowland swamps and lakes. Walks slowly and deliberately. Gregarious, often chasing and flying. When disturbed, flies low over water with rather rail-like flight but stronger and faster, usually landing again on open vegetation.
Conservation status Rare and localised. Not globally threatened.
Range Breeds locally on New Britain, around Lake Lalili, probably *I. g. novaeguineae*. Elsewhere, *I. g. novaeguineae* breeds in north and south-east New Guinea and Aru Is, and two other subspecies breed in Philippines, east Indonesia, south-west New Guinea and Australia.

CURLEWS AND SANDPIPERS Scolopacidae

Varied group of shorebirds, generally with long legs and bills. Most walk along the shore, probing into mud and sand but also pick from surface of rocky coastal substrates, inland wetlands and grassland. Many species look similar and variable plumages create additional difficulties with identification: note relative size, bill size, shape and colour, leg length and colour, and wing and tail pattern in flight. Snipes *Gallinago* have very long straight bills and cryptic plumage and forage furtively in grassland. Godwits *Limosa* are large and elegant with long straight bills. Curlews and whimbrels *Numenius* are large, with mottled brown plumage and long decurved bills. Shanks and tattlers *Tringa* are medium-sized with medium-length straight bills. Terek Sandpiper *Xenus* is similar but with upturned bill, and Common Sandpiper *Actitis* has distinctive habits and flight. Turnstone *Arenaria* has bold neck markings and a short bill. Sandpipers *Calidris* are a large group of medium-small shorebirds with medium-short, sometimes slightly decurved bills. Ruff *Philomachus* is similar but larger and elegant. Phalaropes *Phalaropus* are small, straight-billed and often pelagic. All are non-breeding migrants to Melanesia: see discussion of migratory shorebirds before plovers Charadriidae.

[LATHAM'S SNIPE *Gallinago hardwickii*] Plate 25

(Japanese Snipe; Bécassine du Japon)

Description 29 cm. Very similar to Swinhoe's Snipe.
Similar species Differs from Swinhoe's and Pintail Snipe by larger size (29 cm), often in wetter habitats, zigzags more and climbs more steeply when flushed, toes not projecting beyond tail in flight, and has shorter lower-pitched flush call *rak*. At rest, has relatively long tail projection beyond wings, short or no primary projection beyond tertials, and greyer legs. In hand, differs by having only one pair of pin-like outer tail feathers, and wing length of 157–168 mm.
Range No confirmed Melanesian records. Suspected on New Ireland, New Britain and Bougainville. In New Guinea, commonest as migrant in October–November and April–May. Breeds in Japan and adjacent Russia, and migrates to Australia.

[PINTAIL SNIPE *Gallinago stenura*] Plate 25

(Bécassine à queue pointue)

Description 26 cm. Very like Swinhoe's Snipe.
Similar species Differs from Swinhoe's and Latham's Snipe by smaller size (26 cm), shorter bill, shorter rounder wings, almost full length of toes projecting beyond tail, less white on tail-tips, and less heavily barred neck-sides and flanks; often inhabits wetter habitats, flushing low without zigzagging and dropping back down after short flight, rarely calling, but has louder and slightly harsher call. At rest, tail projects very little beyond wings, has short primary projection beyond tertials, legs greyer. In hand, differs by having 6–9 pairs of pin-like outer tail feathers 1–2 mm wide, and wing length of 124–143 mm.
Range No confirmed Melanesian records. Suspected on New Ireland in January but most New Guinea reports are in October–November. Breeds in north Russia and migrates to tropical Asia as far east as Indonesia.

SWINHOE'S SNIPE *Gallinago megala* Plate 25

(Chinese Snipe; Bécassine de Swinhoe)

Description 28 cm. Stocky medium-sized wader with extremely long straight bill, short legs and mottled brown plumage. Head has broad dark lateral crown-stripe and narrower dark eye-stripe and throat-bar. Mantle and wing-coverts are dark with rufous and buff fringes, and two clear pale yellow stripes on mantle. Neck and breast buff with indistinct striped mottling, whiter and more barred on flanks. In flight, dumpy with short dark grey wings, and toes only project slightly beyond short tail which has orange-rufous central feathers and broad white tips.
Similar species Snipe have a relatively longer bill and more heavily patterned head and upperparts than other waders. See Latham's and Pintail Snipe but often impossible to identify these species in field. In hand, has four pairs of pin-like outer tail feathers 2–4 mm wide, and wing-length of 137–151 mm.
Voice Harsh *raaap* when flushed.
Habits Damp grassland and edges of lakes, swamps and rivers. Singles and small groups probe into soil. Secretive and crepuscular, rarely seen until flushed from very close range into explosive flight. More active at dusk and after dark when often flies.
Range Scarce non-breeding visitor across Admiralties, Bismarcks and Solomons east to Guadalcanal, usually September–April. Breeds in central north Asia and migrates to tropical Asia including New Guinea, but uncommon in Australia.

ASIAN DOWITCHER *Limnodromus semipalmatus* (not illustrated)

(Asiatic Dowitcher; Bécassin d'Asie)

Description 34 cm. Large rather dumpy wader with medium-long black legs and long straight black bill with slightly swollen tip. In flight, shows rather plain upperparts with fine white wing-bar and pale grey rump becoming more heavily barred on uppertail, and white underwings. Non-breeding adult has white underparts and supercilium with fine dusky grey barring on throat and breast that becomes prominent bars along flanks and undertail. Dusky-grey crown and upperparts, with pale fringes to wing-coverts. Immature similar but has orange wash to neck and breast, and buff fringes to wing-coverts. Breeding adult has plain brick-orange supercilium, face, neck and underparts to belly, and white undertail-coverts.
Similar species Long straight bill and rather dumpy body differ from all except godwits and snipe. From Black-tailed Godwit by plain wing pattern, all-dark bill and barring on underparts. From Bar-tailed Godwit by completely straight all-dark bill, stronger mottling and indistinct grey rump and lower back. From snipe by lack of heavy black and buff striping on upperparts.
Voice Usually silent. Quiet plaintive *yow*. Yelping *chep-chep*.
Habits Wades in shallow waters, mostly mudflats, probing deeply, often with rapid mechanical 'sewing-machine' action. Singles or small groups mixed with other waders.
Conservation status IUCN: Near Threatened.
Range One record from the Solomons, on Isabel in September, but could occur across northern Melanesia. Breeds in central north Asia and migrates to tropical Asia and, uncommonly, in New Guinea and Australia, mostly September–April.

BLACK-TAILED GODWIT *Limosa limosa* Plate 23

(Barge à queue noire)

Description 40 cm. Large elegant wader with long black legs and very long straight black-tipped pinkish bill. In flight, shows black wings and tail with white rump and uppertail-coverts, and broad white wing-bar and underwing-coverts. Non-breeding adult has plain grey-brown head, neck and breast with paler supercilium and darker wings. Immature similar, but has buffy wash to head, neck and underparts, and buff fringes to upperparts. Breeding adult has orange-rufous head, neck and breast, white belly, black bars on lower breast and belly, and mottled mantle and wings. Breeding female is paler rufous with fewer black bars and more brown and grey mottling on upperparts.
Similar species Distinctive flight pattern. Also differs from Bar-tailed Godwit by longer legs and neck, straighter bill, plainer greyer plumage and less distinct supercilium and, in breeding plumage, bars on breast and white on belly. From other waders by larger size, more elegant and longer straight bill.
Voice Chattering repeated *rita*. Yelping *kip*, often repeated.
Habits Prefers estuaries and muddy swamps but sometimes on open coasts and sand. Small flocks walk slowly probing in mud, often in deep water.
Conservation status IUCN: Near Threatened.
Range Rare migrant to New Britain, Buka, Bougainville, Vanuatu, New Caledonia and possibly Three Sisters, mostly September–May. *L. l. melanuroides* breeds in north-east Asia and migrates to tropical Asia and Australia. Elsewhere, other subspecies breed in Eurasia and migrate to southern Europe and Africa.

BAR-TAILED GODWIT *Limosa lapponica* Plate 23

(Barge rousse)

Description 40 cm. Large elegant wader with long black legs and very long slightly upcurved black-tipped pinkish bill. In flight, shows plain upperwings with brown-and-white barring on rump, uppertail-coverts and underwing-coverts. Non-breeding adult has slightly streaked buffy-brown head, neck and breast with paler supercilium and darker wings. Immature similar but has darker blotches and buff fringes on upperparts and more distinct streaking on breast-sides. Breeding adult has reddish-chestnut head, neck and underparts, and mottled mantle and wings. Breeding female has pale chestnut or buffy-orange head, neck and breast.
Similar species Differs from Black-tailed Godwit by shorter legs and neck, upcurved bill, buffier, slightly streaked plumage, more prominent supercilium and plain pattern in flight. Breeding male is reddish to vent and lacks dark bars. From Common Greenshank by longer bill and warmer brown plumage. From other waders by larger size and longer straight bill.
Voice Flight calls include *kit*, *kew-kew*, *kiv-ik*, barking *kak-kak* and nasal *ke-wu*.
Habits Sandy and sometimes muddy coasts. Loose flocks, usually mixed with other waders, walk slowly, probing in mud and sand, often in shallow water.
Range Widespread, fairly common migrant and non-breeding visitor across Melanesia, mostly September–April. *L. l. baueri* breeds in the Arctic Pacific and migrates to tropical east Asia and Australasia. Elsewhere, other subspecies breed in Arctic Eurasia and migrate to Europe and Africa to west Australia.

LITTLE CURLEW *Numenius minutus* Plate 23

(Little Whimbrel; Courlis nain)

Description 30 cm. Medium-sized wader with a decurved bill. Bill longer than head, blackish with pinkish base. Legs medium-long, greyish or yellowish. Pale narrow central crown-stripe bordered by broad dark lateral crown-stripe contrasting with broad buffy supercilium and short eye-stripe not reaching bill. Rest of plumage warm buff with fine dark streaks on neck and breast, whiter and unmarked on belly, and heavy dark mottling on upperparts. In flight, shows dark brown upperwings with paler inner wing-coverts, body and tail, mottled brown underwing, and white restricted to belly and vent. Immature may retain some juvenile covert or tertial feathers which are darker with smaller, well-defined pale spots.
Similar species Differs from Whimbrel and Bristle-thighed Curlew by smaller size, shorter thinner straighter bill, warm buff plumage, incomplete loral stripe, uniformly dark upperparts and call. From Pacific Golden Plover by longer bill and legs. From Ruff by head pattern, longer bill, and streaked neck and breast.
Voice Soft whistled *te-te-te* rising slightly in pitch, shorter, higher-pitched and more metallic than Whimbrel. Harsher *tchew-tchew-tchew* and *kweek-ek* when alarmed.
Habits Short grassland, especially airfields. Singles and loose flocks pick items from ground.
Range Uncommon migrant to New Britain, rare vagrant to Manus, Bougainville, Guadalcanal and New Caledonia and may occur more widely in north Melanesia, especially October–November. Breeds in Siberia and migrates to Australia.

WHIMBREL *Numenius phaeopus* Plate 23

(Courlis corlieu)

Description 43 cm. Large wader with long grey legs and long decurved black bill with pink-brown base. Broad dark lateral crown-stripe contrasts with broad buffy supercilium and dark eye-stripe. Rest of plumage is warm buff, fading to creamy or even greyish-white, with fine dark streaks on neck, breast and flanks, and darker wings with buff or white spots. In flight, shows rather plain upperparts with fine barring on white rump and upper back, and white belly to vent. Immature has clearer buff spots on upperparts.
Similar species Distinctive calls. Differs from Bristle-thighed Curlew by greyer plumage, less strongly spotted upperparts, more flank-bars, shorter finer bill with less distinct pink base, and no warm buff or cinnamon rump and underwing-coverts. From Little Whimbrel by larger size, longer bill and complete dark loral stripe. From Eastern Curlew by striped head, shorter bill and no clear white rump.
Habits Muddy and sandy shores, often in mangroves, sometimes on reefs or short grassland. Singles and small loose flocks pick and probe.
Voice Rapid rippling titter of equal notes *quiquiquiquiqui…* Liquid upslurred *kur-lu* or *kur-lee*. Series of bubbling *kur-lu* notes.
Range Widespread and common non-breeding visitor across Melanesia, mostly August–April but some present all year.
N. p. variegatus has white on upper back and rump; breeds in Siberia and migrates to tropical Asia and Australasia.
Hudsonian Whimbrel *N. p. hudsonicus* lacks white on rump; breeds in North America and migrates to southern America, occasionally occurring in New Zealand, and is known from one record on New Caledonia.
Other subspecies breed across the Arctic and migrate to coasts worldwide.

BRISTLE-THIGHED CURLEW *Numenius tahitiensis* Plate 23

(Courlis d'Alaska)

Description 42 cm. Large wader with long bristles projecting from thighs. Long grey legs and long decurved black and pinkish bill. Broad dark lateral crown-stripe contrasts with broad buffy supercilium and dark eye-stripe. Rest of plumage warm buff, but fades to creamy in worn plumage, with fine dark streaks on neck and breast, a few dark brown bars on flanks, and blackish wings with large buff spots. In flight, shows cinnamon underwing, and buffy rump and tail with fine dark barring. Immature has larger spots on upperparts and less streaking on breast.
Similar species Diagnostic bristles on thighs visible only at very close range. Differs from Whimbrel by warmer buff plumage when fresh, bolder spots on upperparts, less marked on flanks, longer thicker bill with extensive pink base, cinnamon on rump and underwing-coverts, and call.
Habits Coasts, reefs and grasslands, especially on small, isolated islands. Singles and small groups pick and probe and often perch on trees. Many adults are flightless during moult in September–November.
Voice Long trisyllabic whistle *chi-u-wit* like human whistle. Less commonly, a short rippling whistle *whe-whe-whe-whe* and ringing *whee-wheeoo*.
Conservation status Threatened by hunting and predation. IUCN: Vulnerable.
Range Rare in eastern Solomons and Temotu, where recorded from Malaita, Three Sisters, Reef Is, Duffs Is and Tikopia, as a non-breeding visitor September–April, perhaps commoner on migration in September–October. One record from Manus and may occur elsewhere in Melanesia, especially tiny out-lying islands. Breeds in Alaska and migrates to central Pacific September–May.

EASTERN CURLEW *Numenius madagascariensis* Plate 23

(Far Eastern Curlew; Courlis de Sibérie)

Description 63 cm. Very large brown wader with an exceptionally long 18 cm decurved bill. Head, neck and breast buffy-brown with fine dark streaks but no distinct head markings, some streaks extending onto paler belly, and heavy dark mottling on mantle and wings. In flight, shows plain upperparts with darker primaries, and finely barred brown underwings. Breeding adult has rufous fringes on upperparts and warmer underparts.
Similar species Very long bill and large size distinctive. Differs from Whimbrel and Bristle-thighed Curlew by plain head, longer bill, larger size and call.
Voice Loud, slow and haunting *ker-leee*, often repeated. More strident *cur-ee*. Musical bubbling trill.
Habits Muddy and sandy coasts, and sometimes adjacent short grasslands. Singles and scattered flocks are wary, flying before other waders flush.
Conservation status Threatened by habitat loss, especially along East Asian migration route. IUCN: Vulnerable.

Range Rare migrant recorded from scattered islands across Bismarcks, Solomons, New Caledonia and possibly Vanuatu, mostly September–April. Breeds in east Siberia and migrates mainly to Australia.

MARSH SANDPIPER *Tringa stagnatilis* Plate 24

(Chevalier stagnatile)

Description 23 cm. Slender, graceful medium-small wader with medium-long very fine straight bill and long fine greenish-yellow legs. In flight, shows plain upperwing with white rump-wedge extending onto lower mantle and finely barred tail. Toes and end of legs extend beyond tail. Non-breeding adult is very pale with pale grey upperparts, indistinct fine streaking extending onto neck- and breast-sides, blackish lesser wing-coverts and primaries sometimes visible, poorly contrasting white supercilium, white underparts and greenish legs. Immature browner with pale fringes on upperparts. Breeding adult has warm brown upperparts and breast and white underparts, with dark spots on upperparts extending onto lower breast and flanks, and yellowish legs.
Similar species Differs from Common Greenshank by smaller size, slimmer build, finer straight black bill, longer yellower legs, whiter lores and lighter streaking. From Wood Sandpiper by longer finer bill, longer legs, greyer plumage, whiter lores, no white spots on upperparts and white wedge extending onto mantle in flight. From Common Sandpiper, Terek Sandpiper and other waders by proportions, and markings in flight.
Voice Short plaintive *plew*, higher-pitched, less ringing and not rapidly repeated in short series as in Common Greenshank. Series of loud *yip* notes when alarmed.
Habits Swamps, lakes, rivers and rarely coasts. Singles and small flocks actively probe, sweep, pick and sometimes swim.
Range Rare migrant and non-breeding visitor recorded from New Ireland, New Britain, Bougainville, Rennell and New Caledonia, especially September–November but also through to February. Breeds in central Asia and migrates to Africa and Australia.

COMMON GREENSHANK *Tringa nebularia* Plate 24

(Chevalier aboyeur)

Description 32 cm. Medium-large wader with fairly long neck, long greenish legs and slightly upturned long black bill with a dull green base. In flight, shows plain upperwing with white rump-wedge extending onto lower mantle and finely barred tail. Toes extend slightly beyond tail. Non-breeding adult has pale grey-brown upperparts with indistinct fine streaking extending onto neck and breast-sides, darker lesser wing-coverts and primaries sometimes visible, faint dark eye-stripe, white supercilium not extending behind eye, and white underparts. Immature is browner with pale fringes on upperparts. Breeding adult has grey upperparts with some heavy black spots and blackish streaking on head, neck, breast and flanks.
Similar species Differs from Marsh Sandpiper by larger size, more robust build, stout, slightly upturned bill with greenish base, shorter stouter greenish legs and heavier streaking. From Wood, Common and Terek Sandpipers, tattlers and other waders by large size, bill and leg proportions, pale plumage, white rump-wedge extending onto mantle in flight, and call.
Voice Loud rushed series of ringing *tew-tew-tew*, lower-pitched and more ringing than Marsh Sandpiper.
Habits Swamps, lakes, rivers and muddy coasts. Singles and small loose flocks actively probe and pick, often rushing and sometimes sweeping and swimming. Nervous, often bobbing, and calls loudly when flushed.
Range Rare migrant and non-breeding visitor to New Britain, Bougainville, Ontong Java in Solomons and New Caledonia, commonest in August–December. Breeds in sub-Arctic Eurasia and migrates to southern Europe and Africa to Australia.

WOOD SANDPIPER *Tringa glareola* Plate 24

(Chevalier sylvain)

Description 21 cm. Small slim wader with pale-spotted brown upperparts, medium-long straight bill and medium-long greenish-yellow legs. In flight, shows plain upperwing, white rump and uppertail-coverts and finely barred tail. Toes extend beyond tail. Non-breeding adult and immature have grey-brown upperparts with small buff spots, dark eye-stripe, long pale supercilium and pale streaks on brown-washed neck and breast. Breeding adult has warmer brown upperparts with more distinct white spots, and fine dark streaking on neck and breast.
Similar species Differs from Marsh Sandpiper by shorter legs, shorter stouter bill, brown plumage with pale spots, dark eye-stripe and dark mantle in flight. From Common Sandpiper by longer bill and legs, spotted upperparts, streaked breast, white rump and habits.

Voice Rushed *chiff-iff-iff* usually given in flight. Sharp *chip*.
Habits Muddy and grassy freshwater wetlands. Singles and small groups pick around wetland margins, often remaining close to grassy and other cover. Nervous; bobs, and flies up steeply and high when flushed, usually calling.
Range Single records from New Britain and Bougainville in October and December. May occur elsewhere, especially in Bismarcks, September–April. Breeds in Arctic and migrates to Africa and Asia but uncommon in Australia.

GREY-TAILED TATTLER *Tringa brevipes* Plate 24

(*Heteroscelus brevipes*; Chevalier de Sibérie)

Description 25 cm. Medium-small stocky grey wader with medium-short yellowish legs and medium-length dark-tipped yellowish bill. Plain mid-grey upperparts with distinct darker eye-stripe and white supercilium to end of ear-coverts. In flight, shows plain grey upperparts and underwing. Non-breeding adult has smooth grey wash from face to breast and flanks, whiter on throat, and often retaining a few obscure bars along flanks. Immature has fine white spots on upperparts. Breeding adult has white underparts with fine dense black stripes on sides of neck and bars on breast and flanks.
Similar species Differs from Wandering Tattler by call, paler greyer plumage, longer supercilium usually joining above bill and extending as far beyond the eye as in front, more contrasting dark eye-stripe, and wing-tips hardly extending beyond tail. In breeding plumage, also differs by paler, finer barring and unbarred central belly, vent and undertail-coverts, but beware moulting Wandering. In hand, also differs by nasal groove extending along half or just over half length of bill (three-quarters of bill in Wandering). From other waders, notably Wood, Common and Terek Sandpipers, by unmarked grey upperparts, grey-washed or finely barred underparts, medium bill and leg length and plain flight pattern.
Voice Soft liquid rising *tloo-eep*. Scratchy faster *tu-wi* or *twiwiwi* or strident *klee*. Notes variable but always slurred and often similar to Pacific Golden Plover.
Habits Muddy and rocky coasts and reefs. Singles and small scattered groups forage slowly, picking and probing. Often bobs rather like Common Sandpiper and holds wings raised after landing.
Range Widespread non-breeding visitor across Melanesia, common in Bismarcks and Solomons and fairly common in Temotu, Vanuatu and New Caledonia, especially September–May. Breeds in east Siberia and migrates to Indonesia, Philippines, New Guinea and Australia.

WANDERING TATTLER *Tringa incana* Plate 24

(*Heteroscelus incanus*; Chevalier errant)

Description 27 cm. Medium-small stocky grey wader, very like Grey-tailed Tattler. Plain brown-grey upperparts with short narrow supercilium which tapers to point at bill-base and hardly extends behind eye. Breeding adult has white underparts with fine dense black stripes on neck-sides and heavy broad bars across all underparts except central belly.
Similar species See Grey-tailed Tattler.
Voice Fast rippling trill of about ten notes, accelerating, descending and decreasing in volume, similar to Whimbrel but quieter, faster and more slurred. Often fewer notes, sometimes only two, but always staccato unlike slurred notes of Grey-tailed Tattler. Warbling trills given in territorial or aggressive interactions.
Habits As Grey-tailed Tattler but rarely away from rocky coasts, reefs and small islets.
Range Widespread non-breeding visitor across Melanesia, uncommon in Bismarcks but increasingly common east to Temotu, Vanuatu and New Caledonia, especially September–May. Commoner than Grey-tailed Tattler in east and on small rocky islets. Breeds in Alaska and far north-east Siberia and migrates to coasts of tropical west America and Pacific islands.

TEREK SANDPIPER *Xenus cinereus* Plate 24

(*Tringa cinerea*; *Tringa terek*)

Description 23 cm. Small wader with long upcurved bill and fairly short legs. Legs and bill-base are orange-yellow. Grey-brown upperparts with darker lesser wing-coverts, white supercilium and white underparts with grey-brown wash, slightly streaked, on neck and breast-sides. In flight, plain upperparts including rump and tail, with broad white trailing edge to secondaries. Breeding adult has blackish stripe on scapulars and darker bill.
Similar species Distinctive long upturned bill, short yellowish legs, upper wing pattern and behaviour. Also from Common Greenshank by much smaller size, and from Common Sandpiper by indistinct white breast-patches.
Voice Rippling trilled *du-du-du-*. Sharper *tee-te-tee-* or *twit-wit-wit-*.

Habits Coasts, especially muddy channels, but sometimes reefs and freshwater. Distinctive rushing feeding action with head and bill held low; often bobs head and tail; posture usually hunched but sometimes stands upright extending medium-long neck. Forages alone but roosts with other waders.
Range Uncommon migrant and non-breeding visitor, recorded from Bismarcks, Bougainville and New Caledonia, mostly September–May. Breeds in north Russia and migrates to Africa, Asia and Australia.

COMMON SANDPIPER *Actitis hypoleucos* — Plate 24

(*Tringa hypoleucos*)

Description 20 cm. Small wader with distinctive habits and flight. Medium-length straight bill, short greenish legs and long tail projecting beyond wing-tips. Greyish-brown or olive-brown upperparts with fine mottling, extending onto breast-sides where sharply cut off from white underparts which extend as a white spur in front of shoulder. Short white supercilium, narrow white eye-ring, dark eye-stripe and white chin and throat. In flight, shows long narrow white wing-bar and white sides to tail.
Similar species Distinctive sharp white shoulder-crescent, flight and habits. Habits most similar to Terek Sandpiper, but differs by straight shorter bill and greenish legs. From Wood Sandpiper by shorter bill and legs, plain upperparts and wing pattern.
Voice Plaintive piping *tswee-wee-wee-* often repeated. Single rising *weep*.
Habits Usually coastal but also common far inland along rivers and sometimes lakes, puddles, roads and short grassland. Stands horizontally, rarely standing still, usually bobbing head and tail. Flies with characteristic flicking shallow wing-beats and gliding on downswept wings. Usually solitary.
Range Widespread non-breeding visitor across Melanesia. Very common migrant and non-breeding visitor to Bismarcks and Solomons but uncommon in Temotu, Vanuatu and New Caledonia, recorded in all months but very few in May–June. Breeds across northern Eurasia and migrates to Africa, Asia and Australia.

RUDDY TURNSTONE *Arenaria interpres* — Plate 23

(Tournepierre à collier)

Description 23 cm. Small dumpy wader with black or dark brown, pale brown and white patches across head and breast. Short straight black bill and short orange legs. In flight, shows black tail-band, white lower mantle and rump, white shoulder-stripe, white wing-bar, and white underwing with black margins. Non-breeding adult has broad sooty stripes on neck and breast, paler brown head and upperparts, and white lower breast to vent. Immature duller with duller legs. Breeding adult has broader blacker stripes, black and white head, and black stripes on orange-rufous mantle and wings.
Similar species Distinctive sooty-black and white pattern on breast and neck. Dullest birds differ from plovers, which share short black bill and black breast-band, by habits, head pattern, leg colour and bill shape.
Voice Low-pitched grating rattle, combinations of *tuk, tuk* and *tuk-i-tuk*.
Habits Coasts with rocks and reefs, especially strand-line, picking and turning over seaweed and stones. Small flocks walk and run, often defend feeding territories, displaying and chasing each other.
Range Fairly common non-breeding visitor across Melanesia, especially September to April. *A. i. interpres* breeds in Arctic Canada and Eurasia and migrates to coastal Europe to Pacific islands, and *A. i. morinella* breeds in Arctic Alaska and Canada and migrates south to American coast.

GREAT KNOT *Calidris tenuirostris* — Plate 25

(Bécasseau de l'Anadyr)

Description 27 cm. Medium-sized wader with medium-short dark or greenish legs and medium-long, very slightly decurved black bill. In flight, shows grey upperparts with narrow white wing-bar and white uppertail-coverts. Non-breeding adult is grey with fine dark streaking on upperparts and breast, some streaky spots on white belly, and indistinct eye-stripe and supercilium. Immature similar but has stronger black mottling and streaks on upperparts and buff-washed breast. Breeding adult has fine black streaks on crown, neck and mantle, heavy black spots on upper breast, scattered black spots on white lower breast and belly, and some chestnut and black on wing-coverts.
Similar species Non-breeding and immature differ from Red Knot by longer, slightly decurved bill, more heavily marked breast, less distinct head pattern, unmarked white uppertail-coverts, larger size and less compact shape. From Sharp-tailed and Pectoral Sandpipers by cold grey plumage, longer black bill, more heavily marked breast, and white uppertail-coverts. From Ruff by shorter neck, more heavily marked breast, and white uppertail-coverts. Breeding adult has distinctive black on underparts, but see Pectoral Sandpiper and Ruff.

Voice Throaty *nhut* or *nyut-nyut*, second note shorter and lower.
Habits Muddy and sandy coasts. Gregarious, usually mixed with other waders.
Conservation status Threatened by habitat loss, especially along East Asian migration route. IUCN: Vulnerable.
Range Three records from New Caledonia, between October and March. Breeds in east Siberia and migrates to South-East Asia, New Guinea and Australia, especially September–April.

RED KNOT *Calidris canutus* Plate 25

(Bécasseau maubèche)

Description 24 cm. Medium-small compact wader with short greenish legs and medium-length straight black bill. In flight, shows grey upperparts with narrow white wing-bar and finely barred uppertail which appears plain at a distance. Non-breeding adult has uniform grey upperparts with fine streaking on breast, some dark crescents on flanks, darker eye-stripe and white supercilium. Immature similar but has pale fringes on upperparts and buff-washed breast. Breeding adult has plain orange-chestnut face and underparts, and chestnut and black spots on upperparts.
Similar species See Great Knot above. Non-breeding and immature differ from Sharp-tailed and Pectoral Sandpipers by greyer plainer upperparts, black bill and streaks on flanks. From tattlers by markings on underparts and black bill. From Sanderling and stints by larger size, more marked underparts, indistinct wing-bar and habits. Breeding adult has distinctive brick-red plumage, shared only by Curlew Sandpiper and godwits, which are elegant with longer bill and legs.
Voice Throaty *knut*.
Habits Muddy and sandy coasts. Usually mixed with other waders, walking slowly and probing.
Range Rare migrant to New Caledonia but also likely to occur elsewhere. *C. c. rogersi* and *C. c. piersmai* breed in east Siberia and migrate to Australia and New Zealand, especially August–April, and other subspecies breed elsewhere in Arctic and migrate to America, Europe and Africa.

SANDERLING *Calidris alba* Plate 26

(Bécasseau sanderling)

Description 20 cm. Small stocky wader with pure white underparts, medium-short straight black bill and short black legs. In flight, shows very prominent white wing-bar and white sides to rump. Non-breeding adult has pale grey upperparts and head with blackish shoulders, indistinct white supercilium and unmarked white underparts except for some grey on breast-sides. Immature similar, but has black mottling on mantle and wings and some blackish streaking on buffy breast-sides. Breeding adult has variably bright rufous upperparts, head, neck and breast, with fine black streaks and black spots on scapulars, and unmarked white lower breast and belly.
Similar species Differs from Red-necked Stint by larger size, slightly longer blunter bill, broader wing-bar, lack of hind-toe and habits. Breeding adult differs further by more streaked face and upper breast; non-breeding adult by less streaking and more prominent black shoulder. From knots by almost unmarked white underparts, longer legs, smaller size and distinct wing-bar.
Voice Quiet liquid *kwik* or *ket* sometimes repeated as trill.
Habits Sandy beaches. Singles or small parties run with steady fast gait along waterline, picking at sand.
Range Uncommon migrant and non-breeding visitor recorded from New Britain, Bougainville, Gizo, Temotu, New Caledonia and possibly Three Sisters, mostly September–April, but undoubtedly more widespread. Breeds in high Arctic and migrates to coasts worldwide.

RED-NECKED STINT *Calidris ruficollis* Plate 26

(Rufous-necked Stint; Bécasseau à col roux)

Description 15 cm. Very small wader with pure white underparts, short straight black bill and short black legs. In flight, shows grey upperparts with white wing-bar and white sides to rump. Non-breeding adult has pale grey upperparts and head, faintly streaked darker, white supercilium and some grey streaks on breast-sides, underparts otherwise unmarked white. Immature similar, but has some black-and-rufous mottling on upperparts. Breeding adult has variably bright rufous head, neck, breast and mantle, streaked on crown and mottled darker on mantle, and with some dark spots on sides of breast.
Similar species Differs from Sanderling by smaller size, slightly shorter, more pointed bill, narrow wing-bar, habits and normal tiny hind-toe. Non-breeding also differs by more streaked breast and no black shoulder. Adult breeding differs further by unmarked rufous face and upper breast. From Long-toed Stint by shorter black legs, greyer plainer plumage, less streaking on breast-sides, blunter all-black bill and shorter neck. From other waders by tiny size, short bill and black legs.

Voice Thin *kreep* or *chit*, sometimes trilled.
Habits Muddy and sandy coasts and sometimes freshwater margins. Gregarious, mixing with other waders, actively and rapidly pecking and probing.
Range Widespread but fairly uncommon non-breeding visitor across Bismarcks, Solomons, Temotu and New Caledonia, but only one possible record from Vanuatu, especially August–April. Breeds in Arctic Siberia and migrates to South-East Asia and Australasia.

LONG-TOED STINT *Calidris subminuta* Plate 26

(Bécasseau à longs doigts)

Description 15 cm. Very small wader, similar to tiny elongate Sharp-tailed Sandpiper. Short, slightly decurved black bill with pale base to lower mandible, yellowish-brown to greenish legs and long toes. Brown upperparts with finely streaked darker crown, pale supercilium, coarse streaks on neck, broad breast-band and mantle, and rather mottled wings. In flight, shows greyish upperparts with faint white wing-bar, white sides to rump and toes extending beyond tail. Non-breeding adult has greyer upperparts with buff wash especially on breast-sides, and darker spots on wings. Immature has rufous crown, buffy sides to breast, rufous fringes on upperparts and fine white lines on mantle. Breeding adult similar to immature but lacks fine lines on upperparts.
Similar species Differs from Red-necked Stint by longer pale legs, browner plumage, more extensive breast-band, more heavily marked upperparts, finer, slightly decurved bill with pale base and longer neck. From Sharp-tailed Sandpiper by smaller size, less contrasting rufous cap and finer breast-streaks not extending along flanks. From other waders by tiny size, short bill and pale legs.
Voice Trilling *chee* or *prrrt*. Soft rolling *kurrip* rather like a sparrow. Short *prit*.
Habits Wet grassy margins of freshwater wetlands, often amongst vegetation, less often short damp grassland and coasts. Singles creep and run, standing rather horizontally, but sometimes stretch erect, showing long neck. Towers high when flushed.
Range Rare vagrant to New Ireland, New Britain and Bellona. Likely to be a widespread rare migrant and possibly non-breeding visitor August–May. Breeds in Siberia and migrates to South-East Asia and Australasia.

PECTORAL SANDPIPER *Calidris melanotos* Plate 26

(Bécasseau à poitrine cendrée)

Description 21 cm. Small wader with sharply defined lower border to streaked brown neck and breast. Upperparts brown, scaled with paler fringes, with slightly darker, more rufous and finely streaked crown, and distinct white supercilium. Medium-length slightly decurved bill with pale olive-yellow base and medium-length greenish-yellow legs. In flight, shows faint white wing-bar and white sides to rump. Non-breeding adult may lack all warm tones except on crown. Immature has buff-washed head and neck, buff to chestnut fringes on upperparts, fine white lines on mantle and scapulars and perhaps some streaking on flanks. Breeding adult as dull immature, but without white lines on upperparts. Breeding male may have black breast with white mottling.
Similar species Sharp lower border to brown breast distinctive. Differs from Sharp-tailed Sandpiper by less rufous cap, more heavily streaked breast, longer bill with obvious pale base, yellower legs, more upright posture and call. From Ruff by streaked breast, shorter legs and neck and more patterned head. From Long-toed Stint by larger size.
Voice Dry croaky trilling *prrt*.
Habits Wet grassy margins of freshwater swamps and lakes but sometimes on short dry grassland and muddy coasts. Usually solitary or with Sharp-tailed Sandpipers. Often shy; posture commonly hunched but sometimes stretches showing long neck.
Range Single records from New Ireland, New Britain, Buka, Bougainville, Rennell and possibly Efate, most often in October–November. Breed in Arctic east Siberia and America, migrating to South America with small numbers to Australia and New Zealand.

SHARP-TAILED SANDPIPER *Calidris acuminata* Plate 26

(Bécasseau à queue pointue)

Description 20 cm. Small wader with broad white supercilium and finely streaked rufous crown. Neck and upper breast brown with faint streaks and spots, merging into white lower breast and belly. Mantle and wing-coverts scaled with paler fringes. Medium-length greenish legs and slightly decurved bill with an indistinct pale base. In flight, shows faint white wing-bar and white sides to rump. Non-breeding adult greyer with pale buff fringes on upperparts and dull rufous crown. Immature has bright rufous crown, plain white throat and warm buff wash on sparsely streaked breast. Breeding adult has scattered black arrowhead markings along flanks, buff-washed head and neck and buff to chestnut fringes on upperparts.

Similar species Differs from Pectoral Sandpiper by sparsely streaked breast without clear-cut lower border, rufous cap, shorter bill with indistinct pale base, greenish legs, less upright stance, and call. From Ruff by streaked breast, shorter legs and neck and more patterned head. From Long-toed Stint by larger size. Arrowhead markings on flanks of breeding adult are distinctive.

Voice Dry *trit-trit-*. Twittering *prtt-wheet-eet-*.

Habits Short grassland or margins of freshwater swamps and lakes, sometimes on coast especially in seaweed. Usually in small groups, often mixed with other waders.

Range Widespread and fairly common migrant and winter visitor across Melanesia but less common in Vanuatu and New Caledonia, commonest September–November with fewer birds staying to April. Breeds in north-east Siberia and migrates to Australasia.

CURLEW SANDPIPER *Calidris ferruginea* — Plate 26

(Bécasseau cocorli)

Description 21 cm. Small elegant wader with long fine decurved black bill, medium-long black legs and prominent pale supercilium. In flight, shows plain white rump and white wing-bar. Non-breeding adult has plain grey upperparts and smudged breast-sides. Immature has pale buff scales on upperparts and orange-buff wash to faintly streaked breast. Breeding adult has orange-chestnut head and underparts, with white vent and black, chestnut and white patches on mantle and scapulars. Breeding female has paler underparts with white fringes. Intermediates with scattered chestnut feathers on underparts are common.

Similar species Long decurved bill and white rump are distinctive. Also differs from Sanderling, Red-necked Stint and Broad-billed Sandpiper by longer more elegant bill, neck and legs. Adult breeding colours similar to Red Knot.

Voice Liquid *chirup*. Musical *tirri-tirri-tirri*.

Habits Usually estuaries but also freshwater and muddy coasts. Gregarious, mixing with other waders, actively probing in mud and waterside vegetation, sometimes wading in deep water.

Range Uncommon migrant to New Ireland, New Britain, Buka, Bougainville and New Caledonia and possibly Three Sisters, especially September–November and April–May. Breeds in Arctic Siberia and migrates to Africa and Australasia.

[BROAD-BILLED SANDPIPER *Limicola falcinellus*] — Plate 26

(Bécasseau falcinelle)

Description 17 cm. Very small wader with long black bill slightly drooping at tip, and striped head with white lateral crown-stripe joining white supercilium in front of eye. White underparts with fine dark grey streaks on neck and breast, grey mantle and wings with paler fringes, and short greenish legs. In flight, shows narrow white wing-bar, white sides to rump and darker bar on lesser wing-coverts. Non-breeding adult is pale grey and white, sometimes showing darker shoulders, with a little fine streaking on breast-sides. Immature has blackish markings and rufous fringes on mantle and wings, fine white lines on mantle and scapulars and fewer streaks on buff-washed breast-sides. Breeding adult duller with heavy streaks on breast and along flanks.

Similar species Distinctive bill shape and crown pattern. See Pectoral, Sharp-tailed and Curlew Sandpipers, Red-necked and Long-toed Stints and Sanderling.

Voice Dry buzzing trilled *triit*, often repeated.

Habits Prefers muddy estuaries but also grassy and sometimes sandy freshwater and coastal margins. Singles mix with other waders, probing deep into mud, often in deep water, and run, but not as active as stints.

Range Unconfirmed report from Three Sisters, Solomons. Breeds Arctic Eurasia, migrating to Africa and Australia, and is an uncommon migrant to New Guinea and Australia September–May.

RUFF *Philomachus pugnax* — Plate 25

(Combattant varié)

Description Male 29 cm; female 23 cm. Medium-small elegant wader with long neck, small head and plain head pattern with pale lores. Medium-short almost straight bill is usually blackish but may have greenish or orange base, even entirely orange in breeding plumage. Medium-long legs are usually yellowish but may be orange, grey or greenish. In flight, shows broad white oval on rump-sides, narrow white wing-bar and toes projecting beyond tail. Non-breeding adult has buff-brown or grey-brown upperparts and breast with fine scaling on mantle and wings and fine streaking on breast-sides. Immature has darker brown upperparts with prominent buff scaly fringes and buff head, neck and breast with finely streaked breast-sides. Breeding adult, unlikely to occur in Melanesia, is variable, with black, white, grey and/or orange-chestnut patches, bars or mottles on upperparts and bright bill and legs. Breeding male has long shaggy ruff of feathers over neck.

Similar species Uppertail pattern, long neck and small head are distinctive. Immature differs from Pectoral and Sharp-tailed Sandpipers by plainer head, almost unmarked warm buff neck and breast, and longer legs. Non-breeding adult differs from Great Knot, Curlew Sandpiper and other pale grey waders by bill shape and often bright legs. Breeding male is distinctive. Breeding female differs from Great Knot and darkest Pectoral Sandpiper by messy black markings and bright legs.

Voice Usually silent.

Habits Wet grassland and muddy freshwater margins and estuaries, uncommonly on coasts or dry grasslands. Gregarious, often walking slowly with other wader species.

Range Rare migrant and non-breeding visitor to Manus, New Ireland, New Britain and Bougainville, most likely in September–November but also through to April. Breeds north Eurasia and migrates to Africa, south Asia and small numbers to Australia.

RED-NECKED PHALAROPE *Phalaropus lobatus* — Plate 25

(Phalarope à bec étroit)

Description 18 cm. Small wader with a dark mask through eye and ear-coverts, usually seen swimming. Very fine short black bill and short dark grey legs. In flight, shows prominent white wing-bar and white sides to rump. Non-breeding adult has pale grey crown, hindneck and upperparts, with paler fringes on mantle and coverts, and faint streaking on breast-sides; distinctive dark grey ear-covert patch surrounded by white. Immature has darker brown upperparts with rich buff fringes and orange-washed breast-sides. Breeding female has dark upperparts with buff stripes, slate-grey head and neck with rufous-chestnut neck-stripe, white throat, and grey spotted flanks. Breeding male is duller with orange neck-stripe.

Similar species Distinctive habits and dark mask. Also differs from other waders by short fine bill.

Voice Soft *chuk*. Sharp *twit*.

Habits Swims on sea or on coastal lakes, and occasionally wades in grassy or muddy margins of swamps, lakes and coasts. Gregarious, sits high on water, swimming and often spinning in circles and picking at surface. Fluttering flight low over sea.

Range Non-breeding visitor to north Bismarcks where scattered and erratic in occurrence, usually small numbers offshore October–April but one record of c.4500 on Lake Dakatoa, New Britain. Breeds in Arctic and migrates to restricted areas of tropical oceans.

COURSERS AND PRATINCOLES Glareolidae

Long-winged waders with short, slightly decurved bills and relatively short legs. Inhabit open inland habitats and run or fly after food; usually gregarious and crepuscular. Migratory: see account under plovers Charadriidae.

AUSTRALIAN PRATINCOLE *Stiltia isabella* — Plate 21

(Glaréole isabelle)

Description 23 cm. Slim graceful wader with very long wings which project far past tip of short tail. Non-breeding adult is sandy-brown with paler face and throat with fine black spots, dusky flank-patches on white belly, and dull greyish bill and legs. In flight, has very long pointed wings, black primaries contrasting with sandy upperwings, black underwing primaries and coverts and dark flank-patches contrasting with paler underparts and broad inner trailing edge to wings, and legs project beyond short black-centred white tail. First-year shorter-winged and browner with sandy fringes to upperparts. Breeding adult has black and chestnut band across flanks, unmarked face, red bill-base and grey or reddish-brown legs.

Similar species Flight action and exceptionally long wings are shared only by Oriental Pratincole, but is longer-legged and paler sandier-brown with uniform throat and dark flank-patches; in flight it differs by contrasting upperwing, black underwing-coverts, dark flank-patches and square tail.

Voice Liquid *weetweet*, repeated. Tern-like trilling *quirree-quirree* or *quee-quee*.

Habits Grassland or bare habitats, often on airfields. Runs after arthropods, bobs head when disturbed, and hawks adeptly after flying insects, often high in sky.
Range Single records from New Ireland, New Britain, Buka, Bougainville and New Caledonia in June to August but may occur as a vagrant anywhere in Melanesia. Breeds in Australia and migrates north including southern New Guinea, usually May–November.

ORIENTAL PRATINCOLE *Glareola maldivarum* Plate 21

(Glaréole orientale)

Description 23 cm. Small slender wader with rather tern-like short legs, long wings and graceful flight. Olive-brown upperparts, buffier and paler on underparts, shading into off-white belly. Yellow-buff throat-patch has black border, indistinct and streaky in non-breeding adult. Short black bill has red base in breeding adult. In flight, long pointed wings are all dark with chestnut underwing-coverts, white rump and belly, and black fork on short white tail. Immature has black and buff fringes to upperparts, paler throat with no border, and obscure streaks on neck and breast.
Similar species Throat-patch, shape and flight action are distinctive; see Australian Pratincole for differences.
Voice Harsh tern-like chattering *kyik* or *chet*, repeated. Loud *cherr.* Rising *trooeet*.
Habits Short grassland and mud, often on airfields. Runs on ground. Hawks acrobatically, often high in sky, with easy fluid wing-beats on long sickle-shaped wings.
Range Rare migrant to north Melanesia, with records from New Ireland, New Britain, Buka, Bougainville and possibly Three Sisters, Solomons, in April, July and November. Breeds from India to Siberia, migrating south as far as Australia but scarce in New Guinea, usually October–March.

GULLS AND TERNS Laridae

Small to medium-sized gregarious seabirds, mostly pale grey and white but some sooty. Fly buoyantly with deep beats of long wings. Terns and noddies dive for fish and pick items off water surface. Gulls are generalist feeders, scavenging and picking up food items from the ground, sea or air. Usually breed in colonies on isolated islets and forage up to 50 km offshore but return to land to roost. Noddies *Anous* are sooty with pale caps, pelagic, picking from the sea surface and nesting on trees. Grey Noddy *Procelsterna* and White Tern *Gygis* are plain grey or white and remain close to their nesting islands. Gulls *Chroicocephalus* and *Larus* are larger and stouter coastal birds. Typical terns have forked, often elongated, tails and often bright bills, and are usually coastal and nest on beaches. Marsh terns *Chlidonias* have short notched tails, hawk low over freshwater and are non-breeding migrants.

BROWN NODDY *Anous stolidus* Plate 29

(Common Noddy; Noddi brun)

Description 42 cm. Dark chocolate-brown tern with silvery crown, whiter on forehead, and broken white eye-ring. In flight, has paler central upperwing-bar and paler underwings with dark margins, and slightly darker long wedge-shaped tail may appear slightly forked when spread. Juvenile has browner, sometimes indistinct cap, and buffy fringes on upperparts.
Similar species Differs from Black Noddy by larger size, proportionately shorter stouter bill (usually shorter than white cap), less definite pale cap, browner plumage, paler underwings contrasting more with darker margins, more contrasting pale upperwing-bar, longer tail which sometimes projects beyond wing-tips at rest, darker tail and slower wing-beats. Juvenile also has less white on crown and broader pale fringes. From other dark seabirds, including juvenile Sooty Tern, Bulwer's Petrel and small shearwaters, by white crown, flight action and habits.
Voice Calls at nesting sites including various croaking, growling and clicking. Harsh grunting and croaking *karrrk* or *kwok*.
Habits Inshore and offshore seas. Flocks, often hundreds of birds and sometimes mixed with other species, fly low over sea, flapping steadily with occasional short glides, to pick from surface. Usually in separate, smaller, flocks to Black Noddy but may mix when feeding. Sometimes sits on sea or flotsam. Colonies nest on trees, bushes, ground or cliffs on small isolated islands.
Conservation status Common along most coasts but rarer in Vanuatu. Hunted at some colonies and breeding status poorly known, except 1500 pairs estimated in New Caledonia southern lagoon in 2002. Not globally threatened.
Range Widespread across Melanesian seas, and nesting colonies scattered across region, but not confirmed in Vanuatu. Elsewhere, *A. s. pileatus* breeds in Indian Ocean and Pacific, and other subspecies breed in east Pacific, Atlantic and Red Sea.

BLACK NODDY *Anous minutus* Plate 29

(Noddi noir)

Description 34 cm. Dark sooty-brown tern with white cap, broken white eye-ring, and long slender bill (longer than cap). In flight, has uniform upperwings, but underwing-coverts are slightly darker than primaries and secondaries. Long wedge-shaped tail may appear slightly forked when spread, sometimes paler or greyer than rest of upperparts, and shorter or equal to wing-tips at rest. Juvenile has smaller cap on forecrown with variable sooty wash, and buffy fringes on upperparts.
Similar species See Brown Noddy.
Voice Calls at nesting sites including various croaking, crackling and screeching. Nasal rattling *chrrr*. Tern-like *kik-kirrik*.
Habits Inshore and offshore seas. Highly gregarious, often in large flocks, flapping steadily, with very brief glides, low over sea, towards mixed-species feeding flocks. Rests on sea and flotsam. Breeds in large colonies on trees, usually on well-vegetated small isolated islands.
Conservation status Common along most coasts but rarer in Vanuatu. Hunted at some colonies and breeding status poorly known, but c.80,000 pairs estimated in New Caledonia southern lagoon in 2002. Not threatened.
Range Widespread across Melanesia, but uncommon in Vanuatu. Breeding colonies scattered across region, but not confirmed in Vanuatu. Elsewhere, *A. m. minutus* breeds in south-west Pacific from east Australia to Polynesia, and other subspecies breed elsewhere in the Pacific and Atlantic Oceans.

[BLUE NODDY *Procelsterna cerulea*] Plate 29

Description 26 cm. Small uniform blue-grey tern with prominent eyes. Mid blue-grey head and body, slightly darker blue-grey mantle and wing-coverts, blackish primaries and black legs. Large black eye, fairly long slender black bill and fine white crescent behind eye. In flight, shows short notched darker grey tail.
Similar species See Grey Noddy.
Habits As Grey Noddy.
Range May occur as a vagrant to Melanesia. Breeds in central and east Pacific, with small numbers as far west as Samoa.

GREY NODDY *Procelsterna albivitta* Plate 29

(Also treated as a subspecies of Blue Noddy *P. cerulea*; Noddi gris)

Description 29 cm. Small uniform pale grey tern with prominent eye. Very pale grey head and underparts, blue-grey mantle and wings and black legs. Large black eye and fairly long slender black bill create facial expression similar to White Tern. In flight, shows short notched tail and darker primaries. Juvenile has blacker primaries and secondaries and brown-washed upperparts.
Similar species Differs from Blue Noddy by head and underparts much paler than upperparts, and primaries and secondaries darker than wing-coverts, especially on underwing. From White Tern by contrasting darker primaries and grey on upperparts. From other terns by unmarked head pattern.
Voice Calls at nesting sites. Occasional squeals and purrs.
Habits Inshore seas, usually very close to breeding islands. Compact flocks fly buoyantly low over sea, hovering, dipping and pattering low over surface. Nests in rock crevices on small islets and often flies around cliffs and rock stacks.
Conservation status Very rare and localised in Melanesia where status is poorly known. Not globally threatened.
Range Breeds on Matthew, Hunter and Walpole Is off New Caledonia. Rarely wanders far from breeding islands and very few records at sea from New Caledonia and Vanuatu. Elsewhere, breeds on Norfolk, Lord Howe, Kermadec and Tonga Is.

WHITE TERN *Gygis alba* Plate 29

(Common White Tern, Fairy Tern; Gygis blanche)

Description 31 cm. Small stocky pure white tern with large black eye and slightly upturned slender black-tipped blue bill. In flight, shows short forked tail and fine dark primary shafts. Primaries, secondaries and tail appear translucent from below. Juvenile has dark spot behind eye, brown and buffy wash on body, wing-coverts and tail, and broader black primary shafts.
Similar species Distinctive white plumage and facial expression. Differs from Grey Noddy by lacking grey upperparts and darker primaries. From other terns by unmarked head pattern, with indistinct postocular spot and other very faint marks on juvenile, relatively short wings and tail, and buoyant flight.

Voice Calls at nesting sites. Guttural chattering e.g. *heech, heech...* Rattles, chatters and wheezes.
Habits Inshore seas, close to breeding islands. Light buoyant flight a few metres over sea, hovering and dipping to surface. Colonies nest on small islets, laying eggs directly on tree branches.
Conservation status Uncommon and localised breeder in Melanesia where breeding status poorly known. Not globally threatened.
Range Widespread but restricted to (and rarely seen away from) a few far-flung small islands, including atolls north of Bismarcks and Solomons, islets in Temotu, and Walpole and perhaps Hunter off New Caledonia. Elsewhere, *G. a. alba* breeds in central and east Pacific and Atlantic, and other subspecies breed in Indian Ocean and Polynesia.

SILVER GULL *Chroicocephalus novaehollandiae* — Plate 27

(*Larus novaehollandiae*; Mouette argentée)

Description 42 cm. Medium-small white-headed gull with bright red bill and legs. Adult is white with pale grey mantle and wings, white outer primaries and black wing-tips with white central patch. Juvenile has pinkish to black bare parts, brown mottling on mantle and wings, brown smudge on ear-coverts, brown terminal tail-band and broken black trailing edge to wing. Immature has a little brown on upperparts and dull brownish bill and legs.
Similar species Differs from Black-headed Gull by head pattern and wing-tip pattern. Differs from terns by white head, wing-tip pattern, short bill and tail, and habits. Other gull species may occur as vagrants to Melanesia.
Voice Harsh screaming, e.g. *korr, keow* and *karr.*
Habits Coasts, especially beaches, and sometimes parks and short grasslands beside sea. Nests on small islets. Often tame and scavenges human trash. Usually in small flocks.
Conservation status Locally common and under no apparent threat. Not threatened.
Range *C. n. forsteri* is endemic to New Caledonia, on Grande Terre on many inshore islets, Surprise and Ile des Pins but rare outside the lagoon, and a rare vagrant to Lifou, seas to north and Efate; elsewhere the smaller *C. n. novaehollandiae* breeds in Australia.

BLACK-HEADED GULL *Chroicocephalus ridibundus* — Plate 27

(Common Black-headed Gull; *Larus ridibundus*; Mouette rieuse)

Description 40 cm. Medium-sized gull with dark brown head in breeding plumage. Adult is white with pale grey mantle and wings, white wedge along outer primaries, narrow black trailing edge to all primaries, and dusky underside to primaries. Breeding adult has chocolate-brown hood with white eye-lids, red bill and legs. Non-breeding adult has white head with dark smudge behind eye and obscure smudge on crown-sides, duller legs and blackish tip to bill. Immature similar, but mottled brown on wing-coverts, creating brownish band across wings in flight, with broad blackish trailing band across wings and tail, and duller bill and legs. Second-year subadult retains some brown on upperparts and develops incomplete hood.
Similar species Differs from Silver Gull by head markings and wing-tip pattern. Immature differs from Black-tailed Gull by upperwing pattern and bare-parts colours. Differs from non-breeding Gull-billed Tern by smaller ear-covert spot, reddish bill and legs, wing-tip pattern and square tail. From other terns by short bill and tail, lacking black cap and habits. Other gull species may occur as vagrants to Melanesia.
Habits Coasts, especially muddy shores. Singles and small flocks.
Range Vagrant to Bougainville where one record of up to six birds staying several months. Breeds across north Eurasia and north-east America, dispersing south to equator, and vagrant to New Guinea and Australia.

BLACK-TAILED GULL *Larus crassirostris* — Plate 27

(Goéland à queue noire)

Description 46 cm. Large stocky gull with broad black subterminal tail-band. Breeding adult has white head, underparts, rump and tail, dark grey mantle and wings, black wing-tips, heavy dark-tipped yellow bill and yellow-green legs. Non-breeding adult has grey streaks on head and nape. First-year immature is greyish-brown with whitish forehead, throat, rump and vent, blackish tail with narrow white terminal band, and pinkish legs and bill with dark tip. Second-year immature is similar to adult but mottled brown.
Similar species Adult differs from other gulls by prominent black tail-band, darker grey upperparts and yellowish bill and legs. From Crested Tern by stocky shape, tail-band, white head and yellow legs. Immature differs from skuas by plain wings, pale rump and pinkish legs. Other gull species may occur as vagrants to Melanesia.
Range One report from Bougainville in May. Breeds coastal north Asia, dispersing south to Taiwan with vagrants to Australia.

[GULL-BILLED TERN *Gelochelidon nilotica*] Plate 27

(*Sterna nilotica*; Sterne hansel)

Description 39 cm. Medium-large stocky tern with black stout gull-like bill. White with short, shallowly forked tail, pale grey mantle and wings and ill-defined dusky trailing edge to primaries. Breeding adult has black cap from forehead to nape. Non-breeding adult has black patch on ear-coverts, often mottled black up onto hindcrown. Immature has darker upperwings, faintly fringed and mottled brown, and dusky tail-tip.
Similar species Distinctive stout bill. Differs from Whiskered Tern by stouter bill, larger size, paler upperparts and dusky trailing edge to wings. From Common, Roseate and Black-naped Terns by stouter bill, more defined ear-covert patch on non-breeding birds, plain upperwings with dusky trailing edge and short tail.
Voice Throaty rising *ger-wik* and *tirruk*.
Habits Sheltered and shallow coasts and inland waters. Singles and small groups fly a few metres above water, usually picking prey from surface, rarely diving.
Range Single unconfirmed reports from Duke of York and Guadalcanal. May occur as rare vagrant anywhere in Melanesia. *G. n. nilotica* breeds patchily in Eurasia and Africa, dispersing south including north New Guinea and Australia; *G. n. macrotarsa* breeds in Australia, dispersing to south New Guinea; and other subspecies breed patchily in America.

GREAT CRESTED TERN *Thalasseus bergii* Plate 27

(Swift Tern; Crested Tern; *Sterna bergii*; Sterne huppée)

Description 46 cm. Large tern with long cold yellow or greenish-yellow bill, grey mantle and wings and paler grey rump and tail. Breeding adult has shaggy black cap separated from bill by narrow white band, and indistinct dark trailing edge to outer primaries. Non-breeding adult has white forehead, black mask and streaky black hindcrown. Juvenile similar, but has heavy brown mottling on upperparts including tail, rather plain dark grey primaries but four dark bars across inner wing, a duller bill and sometimes orange legs. Immature similar, but has uniform grey mantle, loses mottled wing-coverts, and other wing-bars fade.
Similar species Differs from Lesser Crested Tern by stouter yellow bill, slightly darker upperparts, paler rump and tail, larger size, and heavier structure and flight; immature has more heavily barred inner wings, and breeding adult has white above bill-base. Differs from other terns by yellow bill, darker upperparts and large size. Differs from gulls by longer yellow bill, head pattern and structure.
Voice Harsh notes e.g. *kreek* and *kerrak*.
Habits Inshore seas, following ships further out to sea, and loitering around harbours and ports. Colonies breed on small islets. Singles and small groups, rarely up to 200 birds, usually fly steadily several metres above sea, diving occasionally, and sometimes join mixed seabird flocks.
Conservation status Common along coasts of most islands. Breeding status poorly known, except 1500 pairs in New Caledonia southern lagoon in 2002. Some colonies may be locally threatened, but not globally threatened.
Range Widespread across Melanesia. Breeding records are few and scattered, perhaps only on New Caledonia. Elsewhere, *T. b. cristata* also breeds from Malaysia to Australia and Polynesia, and other subspecies breed around the Indian Ocean and Red Sea.

LESSER CRESTED TERN *Thalasseus bengalensis* Plate 27

(*Sterna bengalensis*; Sterne voyageuse)

Description 39 cm. Medium-large tern with long slender yellow-orange bill and medium-grey mantle, wings and tail. Breeding adult has shaggy black cap from bill to nape. Non-breeding adult has white forehead, black mask, streaky black hindcrown and paler bill. Fresh adult has plain upperwing with faint dusky trailing edge to outer primaries. Worn adult has darker outer primaries and subterminal secondary bar. Immature as non-breeding adult, but has darker grey primaries, dusky subterminal secondary bar, faint dusky-brown lesser-covert and secondary-covert bars, some mottling on upperparts including tail and duller bill. Wing pattern fades greatly before moulting into adult plumage.
Similar species Differs from Crested Tern by slenderer, more orange bill, slightly paler upperparts, darker rump and tail, smaller size and more graceful flight; immature has plainer, largely grey inner wings except for strong secondary bar, and breeding adult has black cap reaching bill. Differs from other terns by orange bill and large size. Differs from gulls by longer orange bill, head pattern and structure.
Voice Quiet high-pitched *kreek*.
Habits Inshore seas. Singles and small groups fly a few metres above sea, diving for small fish.
Range Rare vagrant to Bougainville and possibly Manus and New Ireland but may occur as a vagrant anywhere in

Melanesia. *T. b. torresii* breeds in Indonesia, New Guinea and north Australia, and other subspecies breed in Africa, Middle East and Indian Ocean.

LITTLE TERN *Sternula albifrons* — Plate 28

(*Sterna albifrons*; Sterne naine)

Description 23 cm. Small tern with longish bill and short tail, much shorter than wing-tips at rest. Breeding adult has black-tipped yellow bill, orange-yellow legs and black cap broken by white forehead extending sharply over black lores and eye. Mantle and wings mid-grey with blackish outer primaries and short forked white tail. Non-breeding adult and immature have dark bill and legs, streaky white mid-crown and dark lesser-covert bar. Juvenile similar, but has dark crescents and bars on mantle, wing-coverts and tertials, and initially a yellow bill-base and buff wash on forehead and breast.

Similar species Differs from other terns by small size, flight action, proportionately longer bill, blackish outer primaries and lack of dark secondary bar. From small Whiskered and White-winged Terns also by narrower, more pointed wings. See very similar Fairy Tern of New Caledonia.

Voice Short sharp notes, often repeated, e.g. *kik, kweek, kee-ik*. Harsh *kirri-kiki-...*

Habits Inshore shallow water seas, often muddy and sandy bays. Breeds in small colonies on beaches close to estuaries. Small flocks fly buoyantly with rapid deep wing-beats, wings held forward at carpals, often hovering and sometimes plummeting between hovers, before diving into sea.

Conservation status Locally fairly common non-breeding visitor, and rare and localised breeder in Melanesia; perhaps threatened by disturbance and predators at colonies. Not globally threatened.

Range Widespread across the Bismarcks and Solomons, but rare in Vanuatu, where recorded from Malekula and Efate, and fairly common in New Caledonia. Breeds very locally on New Britain, Bougainville and perhaps Isabel. Otherwise, occurs as a migrant usually September–April. Elsewhere, *S. a. sinensis* also breeds patchily through east Asia to Micronesia, and other subspecies breed in Eurasia, Africa and Australia.

FAIRY TERN *Sternula nereis* — Plate 28

(*Sterna nereis*; Sterne néréis)

Description 23 cm. Small tern with rather long bill and short tail, much shorter than wing-tips at rest. Breeding adult has orange-yellow bill and legs, black cap extending slightly and bluntly along midline over well-defined white forehead, and black through eye but not reaching bill. Mantle and wings are unmarked mid-grey. Non-breeding adult has dull yellow and black bill, dull yellow legs, some white streaks on crown and faint dark lesser-covert bar. Juvenile has black bill, dull orange-brown legs, black mask and hindcrown, streaky white mid-crown, dark crescents and bars on mantle, wing-coverts and tertials, darker lesser-covert bar and darker outer primaries. Immature is similar, but lacks barring on upperparts and streaks on white crown.

Similar species Differs from other terns by small size, flight action, proportionately longer bill, and lack of dark secondary bar. From very similar Little Tern by paler plumage and shorter legs. Adult also differs by forehead pattern, uniform outer primaries and often no black bill-tip. Juvenile and immature extremely like Little Tern, but have less contrasting lesser-covert bar and outer primaries.

Voice Short sharp notes, often repeated, e.g. *kik, ket* and *tchi-wik*. Harsh *kirri-kiki-...*

Habits Inshore seas, as Little Tern, but breeds in small colonies on small islets.

Conservation status Rare breeder, locally threatened by disturbance and predators. An estimated 65–200 pairs nested in New Caledonia in 2006–8, mostly in northern lagoon, with smaller numbers in southern lagoon, Chesterfield Reefs and possibly breeding on Entrecasteaux. IUCN: Vulnerable.

Range *S. n. exsul* is endemic to New Caledonia where it breeds on islets around Grande Terre, Chesterfield and Entrecasteaux. Other slightly smaller subspecies breed in Australia and New Zealand.

SPECTACLED TERN *Onychoprion lunatus* — Plate 29

(Grey-backed Tern; *Sterna lunata*; Sterne à dos gris)

Description 38 cm. Medium-sized tern with dark grey upperparts. Adult has black cap with clear-cut white forehead and supercilium to behind eye, grey upperparts including tail, slightly paler on upper mantle, and narrow white on outer tail feathers. Worn birds often have brown wash to upperparts, especially wings. Non-breeding adult has fine white streaks on forecrown. Juvenile, probably not occurring in Melanesia, has broad white fringes on upperparts, especially tertials and tail, and fine streaking on crown. Immature as adult but has browner crown and nape with some white streaking.

Similar species Differs from Bridled Tern by blue-grey mantle or entire upperparts, less white on outer tail, purer white underparts, black tips of primaries on underwing, and finer bill; juvenile has more heavily scaled upperparts. Note, however, appearance of upperparts varies with wear and light, and identifications need great caution. From adult Sooty Tern by black cap contrasting with blue-grey upperparts, white forehead extending beyond eye, and shorter wings.
Voice High-pitched screeches, softer than Sooty Tern.
Habits Open oceans. Similar to Bridled Tern, but more pelagic. Often perches with wings and tail raised high above back.
Range Uncertain status with very few reports (and some confusion with Bridled Tern) from Bismarcks, Solomons and Temotu, where probably vagrant. Breeds in central tropical Pacific including Micronesia.

BRIDLED TERN *Onychoprion anaethetus* Plate 29

(*Sterna anaethetus*; Sterne bridée)

Description 38 cm. Medium-sized tern with brown upperparts. Adult has black cap with clear-cut white forehead and supercilium to just behind eye, almost separated from brown mantle by pale collar, brown or grey-brown upperparts including tail, white on outer tail, and very pale grey on breast. Non-breeding adult is paler with black and white streaks on crown and paler tips on upperparts. Juvenile similar, but has messier head pattern, distinct buff and white fringes on upperparts, and brown wash on breast-sides.
Similar species Differs from Grey-backed Tern by browner upperparts, but this varies with wear and depends on viewing conditions, more white on outer tail, pale grey breast, white-centred black underwing primaries and stouter bill; juvenile has less scaling on upperparts. From adult Sooty Tern by black cap almost separated from and contrasting with brown upperparts, white forehead extending beyond eye, paler underside of primaries and secondaries contrasting less with white underwing-coverts, shorter wings, smaller size and distinctive calls.
Voice Typically a sharp yelping *yap-yap*.
Habits At sea, usually close inshore. Small flocks often join mixed seabird flocks. Lighter, more graceful flight, more often settling on sea and flotsam than Sooty Tern, and flies lower over water; less pelagic and less gregarious. Breeds colonially on small islets.
Conservation status Fairly common at sea but rare as breeder away from New Caledonia, where some 1000 pairs in southern lagoon in 2002. Locally affected by disturbance and perhaps predators, but not globally threatened.
Range Widespread across Melanesia but uncommon in Vanuatu. Known to breed on Admiralties, Rennell and around New Caledonia but probably more widespread on isolated islets. Elsewhere, *O. a. anaethetus* also breeds from Japan and Indonesia to Australia, and other subspecies breed in tropical America and Africa.

SOOTY TERN *Onychoprion fuscatus* Plate 29

(*Sterna fuscata*; Sterne fuligineuse)

Description 43 cm. Medium-sized tern with blackish upperparts. Adult has black cap with clear-cut white forehead not extending above eye, sooty-black upperparts including tail, white on outer tail, and white underparts. Non-breeding adult has white tips on crown and paler fringes on upperparts. Juvenile is all sooty-black except off-white underwing-coverts, lower belly and vent, and fine bars and tips on upperparts. Immature intermediate, with patchy brown on underparts.
Similar species Adult differs from Bridled and Grey-backed Terns by black cap continuous with sooty-black upperparts, white forehead not extending above eye, uniformly dark undersides of primaries and secondaries contrasting more with white underwing-coverts, longer wings, larger and distinctive calls. Juvenile differs from noddies by pale vent and tail shape, but also see skuas.
Voice Commonly calls at sea. Loud high-pitched *ker-wack-wack* and shorter *kraak*.
Habits Highly pelagic, rarely seen from shore. Gregarious, often wheeling or soaring high over sea, diving to surface but rarely into sea or sitting on it. Breeds in large colonies on isolated islands.
Conservation status Fairly common at sea. Breeding colonies include thousands on Matthew, Chesterfield and Entrecasteaux Is off New Caledonia but breeding is poorly known elsewhere. May be at risk in Melanesia but not globally threatened.
Range Widespread across Melanesian seas, but uncommon in Vanuatu. Breeds on islets around New Caledonia and distant atolls, and possibly elsewhere such as Ontong Java in the Solomons. Elsewhere, *O. f. serratus* breeds in south New Guinea and Australia, and other subspecies are pantropical.

ROSEATE TERN *Sterna dougallii* — Plate 28

(Sterne de Dougall)

Description 38 cm (including 10 cm tail-streamers). Medium-sized elegant pale tern. Breeding adult is white with black cap, long red bill with variable black tip, red or dark red legs, very pale grey upperparts, long tail-streamers projecting well beyond wing-tips at rest, and sometimes pink-washed underparts. Wings plain except for few darker outer primaries. Non-breeding adult similar but has white forecrown, black bill, darker legs and outer primaries, shorter tail-streamers and sometimes a faint dark lesser-covert bar. Juvenile has black bill and legs, dark mask, hindcrown and initially forecrown, heavy brown and black crescents or bars on mantle, wing-coverts and especially tertials, mid-grey upperwings with darker secondary bar and outer primaries, and short tail-streamers. Immature as adult non-breeding but darker lesser-covert bar, slightly darker secondary bar, shorter tail-streamers and dark outer primaries when worn.
Similar species Differs from very similar Common Tern by call, paler upperparts, longer tail-streamers, wing pattern, longer bill sometimes with red base, slimmer structure, flight action and sometimes pink on underparts. From Black-naped Tern by greyer upperparts, head pattern and faint upperwing markings. Juvenile differs from other juvenile terns by initially dark forehead and heavy brown mottling on mantle. From juvenile Black-naped Tern by dusky forehead and crown, indistinct dark trailing edge on underwing primaries and more coarsely barred mantle.
Voice Distinctive upslurred *chu-vee*, similar to Pacific Golden Plover. Harsh rasping *kraak*. Sharp *kik-kik-kik*.
Habits Inshore and offshore coastal seas, often close to extensive reefs. Patrols with shallow, stiff, fast wing-beats intermediate between Common and Little Terns, often joining mixed seabird flocks. Nests in colonies on small islets.
Conservation status Usually rare but locally common around colonies. Small colonies known in Bismarcks and Solomons, but c.5000 pairs estimated in New Caledonia southern lagoon in 2002 and small numbers in north. Regionally affected by disturbance and perhaps predators, but not globally threatened.
Range Widespread but localised across Melanesia. Few scattered records across Bismarcks, including Hermit, Long and New Britain and Solomons, especially New Georgia island group and Florida Is; no confirmed records from Vanuatu, but locally common on islets around New Caledonia. Elsewhere, *S. d. bangsi* also breeds from Arabian Sea and Japan to New Guinea, and other subspecies in Atlantic and Indian Oceans including Australia.

BLACK-NAPED TERN *Sterna sumatrana* — Plate 28

(Sterne diamant)

Description 31 cm (including 5 cm tail-streamers). Medium-sized tern with distinctive black eye-mask joining across upper nape, very pale grey mantle and upperwing marked only by dark-edged outer primary, and long white tail-streamers; bill and legs black. Breeding adult sometimes has pink wash on underparts. Non-breeding adult has some streaks on hindcrown. Juvenile has dirty yellow bill soon turning black, dark mask, some white spots on head and dark streaks on crown, black crescents and bars on mantle, wing-coverts and tertials, darker secondaries and primaries, and greyer shorter tail. Immature as non-breeding adult but has darker lesser-covert bar and slightly darker primaries, tertials and tail.
Similar species Differs from other terns by head pattern, unmarked very pale upperwings, and black bill and legs. Immature differs from Roseate Tern by whiter crown and whiter upperparts. Juvenile from Roseate Tern by dusky mask through eye onto nape but pale crown, all-white underwing and finer barring on mantle. Immature from Little and Fairy Terns by larger size, darker bill and only slightly darker outer primaries.
Voice Combinations of sharp *kik*, *chit-er*, *tsee-cher*, often harsher than other terns.
Habits Coasts and inshore seas, especially around coral islets. Breeds in small colonies on isolated coral beaches, especially tiny islets. Small flocks fly buoyantly, and dive steeply to pick from sea, sometimes diving.
Conservation status Common, usually in small numbers, rarely up to 1000 birds. Overall breeding status poorly known, except c.1000 pairs estimated in New Caledonia southern lagoon in 2002. Not globally threatened.
Range Widespread across Melanesia but breeding records localised. Elsewhere, *S. s. sumatrana* also breeds across coastal Asia to north Australia and Polynesia, and *S. s. mathewsi* breeds in west Indian Ocean.

COMMON TERN *Sterna hirundo* — Plate 28

(Sterne pierregarin)

Description 34 cm (including 7 cm tail-streamers). Medium-sized tern with black bill and dark red legs, not breeding in Melanesia. Breeding adult has black cap, mid-grey upperparts, very pale grey underparts contrasting slightly with white chin and cheeks, white rump and tail with tail-streamers equal to wing-tips at rest. Upperwing has dark trailing

edges to primaries, often a wedge of darker outer or middle primaries, and a narrow white trailing edge to mid-grey secondaries. Underwing has translucent secondaries contrasting with darker primaries which have a smudged dark trailing edge. Non-breeding adult has black mask and hindcrown, distinct lesser-covert bar, shorter tail-streamers and greyer outer tail. Immature as adult non-breeding but has darker lesser-covert and secondary bars, shorter tail-streamers and darker outer primaries especially in worn first-summer plumage.
Similar species See similar Roseate and Arctic Terns. Differs from Whiskered Tern by habits, larger size, sleeker shape, narrower wings, long white tail, and more patterned upperwings. From Black-naped Tern by head pattern and darker, patterned wings. From Little Tern by larger size, flight action, black bill, dark secondary bar and less contrasting outer primaries.
Voice Strident *ker-yah*. Sharp *kik-kik-*. Quieter *kek*.
Habits Sheltered waters, especially shallow bays, but may occur along any coasts and inland at large lakes. Gregarious, usually small flocks, rarely up to 200. Flies buoyantly a few metres above water, diving shallowly for fish in sea but usually picking from surface at lakes, and sometimes hovering.
Range Widespread non-breeding visitor to Bismarcks and Solomons, much less common in Temotu and possibly Vanuatu, from September to April, with fewer May–August. *S. h. longipennis* breeds in north-east Asia and disperses south to Australia, and other subspecies breed across north America and Eurasia, dispersing to tropical and southern oceans.

[ARCTIC TERN *Sterna paradisaea*] Plate 28

(Sterne arctique)

Description 34 cm (including 7 cm tail-streamers). Very similar to Common Tern. Breeding adult has black cap, dark red bill and legs, mid-grey upperparts, very pale grey underparts contrasting with white chin and cheeks, and white rump and tail, with tail-streamers slightly longer than wing-tips at rest. Upperwing is uniform except for fine darker margin to the primaries. Underwing is uniformly translucent. Non-breeding adult has black bill, black mask and hindcrown, faint dark lesser-covert bar, and shorter tail-streamers. Immature similar, but has distinct narrow dark lesser-covert bar and shorter tail-streamers.
Similar species From very similar Common Tern by primaries marked only by well-defined narrow dark margins, uniformly translucent underwing, shorter bill and legs, slimmer shape and shorter narrower wings. Immature also lacks dark secondary bar, has fainter lesser-covert bar and whiter rump. Breeding adult also has all-red bill and longer tail-streamers. See Common Tern for other similar species.
Voice Short clear *kriii-ah*.
Habits Gregarious, usually mixed with other tern species. Usually pelagic but often roosts on beaches.
Range One report from Bougainville but may occur as vagrant anywhere in Melanesia, most likely on migration in September–November or March–May. Breeds across the Arctic, migrating through east Pacific to Antarctic seas.

WHISKERED TERN *Chlidonias hybrida* Plate 28

(Guifette moustac)

Description 26 cm. Small compact freshwater tern with broad plain wings and short, slightly forked grey tail. Breeding adult has black cap, mid-grey upperparts, white throat and face, dark grey underparts contrasting with white vent and underwing-coverts, and dark red bill and legs. Non-breeding adult has black bill, dark red legs and black mask from eye to nape with dark streaks on hindcrown, but sometimes black is restricted to ear-covert patch. Juvenile similar, but mantle has buff wash and black-and-buff bars.
Similar species Breeding adult has distinctive grey underparts. Habits are shared only with White-winged Tern, from which differs by horizontal shape of ear-covert patch, grey rump and uppertail, plainer upperwing, larger size and stockier stouter bill. From all other terns by dumpier shape, broader wings, short grey tail, plainer upperwings; smaller than all except Little and Fairy Tern. Head pattern may resemble Gull-billed Tern but is much smaller with smaller bill.
Voice Hoarse *kreeep*. Short sharp *kek* or *ki-ik*.
Habits Prefers large well-vegetated lakes and swamps, slow rivers and deltas but rarely along coasts. Small flocks, often mixed with other terns, fly slowly and gracefully low over fresh water, swooping to pick from surface. Perches on waterside dead trees, wires and open ground.
Range Uncommon non-breeding migrant to New Britain, Bougainville and New Caledonia. May occur elsewhere in Melanesia but limited by lack of suitable habitat. *C. h. fluviatilis* breeds in Australia and migrates north to New Guinea and east Indonesia mostly April–December. Elsewhere, other subspecies breed patchily in Eurasia and Africa, most migrating to tropics.

WHITE-WINGED TERN *Chlidonias leucopterus* Plate 28

(White-winged Black Tern; Guifette leucoptère)

Description 23 cm. Small freshwater tern with distinctive head pattern. Breeding adult has black head, body and underwing-coverts contrasting with pale grey upperwing, tail and underwing primaries and secondaries, and white rump and uppertail-coverts. Legs and bill dark red in breeding adult, black in other plumages. Non-breeding adult lacks black, and has rounded black patch on ear-coverts and central nape, connected by narrow band over hindcrown, appearing like head-phones, and pale grey upperparts with darker primaries, lesser-covert and secondary bars. Moulting birds have black spots on underwing-coverts. Immature has darker primaries, lesser-covert and secondary bars.
Similar species Breeding adult has distinctive black body and underwing-coverts. Habits shared only with Whiskered Tern (which see for differences). From other terns by broader wings, head pattern, short tail, and smaller than all except Little and Fairy Tern.
Voice Harsh *kreek* or *kersch*. Short sharp *kik*.
Habits Well-vegetated lakes and swamps, slow rivers and deltas, and sometimes close inshore along coasts. Small flocks, often mixed with other terns, fly slowly and gracefully low over water, picking from the surface, and settle on any nearby open perches.
Range Uncommon or rare non-breeding migrant to Wuvulu, New Britain, Bougainville, Rennell and Grande Terre, New Caledonia. May occur elsewhere in Melanesia but limited by lack of suitable habitat. Breeds in temperate Eurasia and migrates south to tropics including New Guinea and Australia in October–May.

SKUAS Stercorariidae

Medium-large seabirds, similar to heavily built terns. Plumage is brown with white flash at base of primaries and often pale on head and underbody. Usually solitary, in level and steady flight low or at mid-height over sea, rarely gliding, or floating high on sea. Pirates, agile in pursuit of other seabirds for their food. Breed in extreme latitudes, otherwise ranging widely across oceans. All are poorly known and under-recorded in Melanesia and likely to be widespread but uncommon at sea.

SOUTH POLAR SKUA *Stercorarius maccormicki* Plate 30

(*Catharacta maccormicki*; Labbe de McCormick)

Description 53 cm. Large stocky skua with prominent white flash on upperwing and underwing. Dark cold brown or grey-brown mantle and wings with very large white primary bases on dark upperwing and underwing. Head and body plumage usually paler than wings but vary from uniformly dark grey-brown to having a pale greyish or milk-coffee-coloured collar or nape or head and breast. Immature usually lacks pale on head and neck, has fine pale fringes on upperparts, blue-grey base to black bill and sometimes smaller white flash on upperwing. At rest, appears very stocky with heavy hooked black bill.
Similar species Distinctive white wing-flash shared only by other skuas and some petrels. See Brown Skua. Differs from other skuas and jaegers by larger size, more thickset body and wings, broader wing-flash especially on upperwing, shorter tail without streamers, and lack of black cap or pale barring on underside. Differs from petrels by equally large wing-flash on upper- and underwing, short broad-based wings and steady flapping flight.
Habits Usually offshore. Flies powerfully with regular, rather heavy flaps like a large hawk, usually c.10–15 m above sea, or chasing and harassing large seabirds.
Range Rare migrant or non-breeding visitor recorded once from Solomons and twice from New Caledonia in September–April. Breeds around sub-Antarctic and disperses north, many to north Pacific Ocean.

BROWN SKUA *Stercorarius antarcticus* Plate 30

(Subantarctic Skua; *Catharacta antarctica*; *S. lonnbergi*; Labbe brun)

Description 63 cm. Large stocky skua, all dark brown except for prominent white wing-flash. Whole plumage is plain chocolate-brown, often with some rufous tones, with very large white primary bases on upperwing and underwing and some indistinct yellow streaking on hindneck or across upperparts and breast. Immature has less streaking, less white on wing and may have paler hindneck. At rest, appears very stocky with heavy hooked black bill.
Similar species See other similar species under South Polar Skua. Differs from pale-phase South Polar Skua by head and underparts uniform with wings. From very similar dark-phase South Polar Skua by larger bill, warmer brown plumage, often yellow streaking on neck or upperparts, and less distinctly pale hindneck which never forms a collar.

Adult moults wings from February to October and juvenile from September to February, whereas South Polar Skua moults from April to October. Some may be hybrids.
Habits As South Polar Skua.
Range Rarer vagrant, with two records off Lifou in July and August. Breeds around sub-Antarctic and disperses locally, including to seas off New Zealand and southern Australia.

POMARINE SKUA *Stercorarius pomarinus* Plate 30

(Pomarine Jaeger; Labbe pomarin)

Description 45 cm (plus up to 11 cm tail-streamers). Fairly stocky skua, often with prominent chest. Black cap, dark brown mantle, wings and tail, broad silvery flash on underwing and more streaky flash on upperwing. Distinctive additional narrow silvery crescent at base of underwing primary coverts. Pale-morph breeding adult has yellow-washed cheeks, white face, neck and underparts with variable brown bars on breast-band, flanks and vent. Distinctive long central tail feathers are twisted to appear spoon-shaped, but often broken or absent. Rare dark-morph adult has sooty-brown underparts, paler on chest and palest on face. Non-breeding adult shows variable signs of immature plumage, often barred tail-coverts, shorter tail-streamers and more extensive brown on underparts. Pale morph immature is cold brown with white or buff barring and tips on body and wings, prominent barring on underbody, uppertail-coverts and underwing-coverts, and very short blunt projection of central tail feathers. Immatures showing uniform dark head and strongly barred uppertail-coverts are distinctive; dark-morph immature sooty-brown with pale barring restricted to tail-coverts. Second- and third-year immatures are similar to adults but often retain barring on underwing-coverts.
Similar species White wing-flash is shared only by other skuas and some petrels. Distinctive additional white bases on underwing primary coverts of immature. See very similar Arctic and Long-tailed Skuas. Differs from South Polar and Brown Skuas by slighter structure, less white on primaries, longer tail often with streamers, more prominent cap, and often barred or white-bodied plumage. Differs from petrels by prominent white flash on upperwing, shorter broader-based wings and steady flapping flight.
Habits Offshore seas. Single birds often follow tern flocks with rather heavy slow direct flight.
Range Uncommon non-breeding visitor across Melanesia, September–May. Breeds across Arctic and disperses to southern oceans, especially tropical latitudes.

ARCTIC SKUA/PARASITIC JAEGER *Stercorarius parasiticus* Plate 30

(Labbe parasite)

Description 41 cm (plus up to 7 cm tail-streamers). Plumages similar to Pomarine Skua. Breeding adult is chocolate-brown with white wing-flash, black cap and long pointed central tail feathers, dark morph has brown body, but pale morph has yellow-washed face and white underbody, and all stages of intermediates occur. Non-breeding adult has dark barring on body and tail, but usually a plain white lower breast and belly, and shorter tail projection. Immatures and subadults are variable, but have more extensive barring on underbody and underwing, and shorter tail projection.
Similar species Distinctive white wing-flash is shared only by other skuas and some petrels. See Long-tailed Skua. Differs from Pomarine Skua by slighter build without prominent chest, slighter bill, narrower wings and more buoyant tern-like flight. Pale-morph breeding adult also differs by pointed central tail-streamers, less extensive, greyer and less barred breast-band, flanks and vent, paler greyer mantle and upperwing-coverts and paler yellow on face. Some non-breeding and immature birds also have more pointed central tail projection. Immature also has dark streaking on head and neck, less prominent barring on underwing, flanks, vent and tail-coverts, no white bases to underwing primary coverts, and often a distinctive rusty or cinnamon tone to head and especially nape. Differs from petrels by prominent flash on upperwing, shorter wings and steady flapping flight.
Habits Offshore seas. Lighter flight than larger skuas, reminiscent of Peregrine Falcon, especially when chasing terns.
Range Scattered records across Melanesia. Probably a widespread but uncommon non-breeding visitor September–May. Breeds across Arctic and disperses to southern oceans, especially temperate latitudes.

LONG-TAILED SKUA/LONG-TAILED JAEGER *Stercorarius longicaudus* Plate 30

(Labbe à longue queue)

Description 38 cm (plus up to 22 cm tail-streamers). Very like Arctic Skua but smaller. Breeding adult has grey upperparts, black primaries and secondaries, very long central tail feathers, black cap, yellowish face, white head and

body, and grey vent and lower belly. Dark morph is very rare. Non-breeding adult has dark bars on upper body and pale bars on tail. Immatures are variable but usually greyish with heavy barring, especially on underwing and tail.
Similar species Differs from Arctic and Pomarine Skuas by slighter build, shorter bill (proportionately stouter than Arctic Skua), and more elongated body and tail behind narrower wings. On sea, or perched, wings project beyond main tail. Breeding adult further differs by very long pointed tail-streamers, paler greyer mantle and upperwing-coverts contrasting with blackish primaries and secondaries, white wing-flash restricted to white shafts on outer two primaries on upperwing and outer one on underwing, and grey vent extending onto lower belly. Immatures variable but lack rusty or cinnamon tones, underwing-coverts and tail-coverts usually more heavily barred than Arctic Skua, upperwing has pale shafts on outer two primaries, underwing has small white flash at base of primaries, and central tail-projection is rounded and usually longer than Arctic Skua. Immatures with pale grey or white head and belly are distinctive. Differs from terns, especially Sooty Tern, by dark underwing of adult, and white wing-flash and extensive pale barring of immature.
Habits Offshore seas. Light, buoyant and rather weak flight. Often picks from sea or briefly chases terns.
Range Known only from a scatter of records, mostly in northern Melanesia, but probably an uncommon non-breeding visitor across Melanesia September–May. *S. l. longicaudus* breeds in Arctic Eurasia and *S. l. pallescens* breeds in Arctic America and east Siberia, both dispersing to southern oceans, especially sub-Antarctic latitudes.

PIGEONS Columbidae

Pigeons and the usually smaller doves are common, diverse and conspicuous in Melanesian forests. All are relatively dumpy birds with small heads and bills. Arboreal species have short legs, and many are nomadic in search of seasonal fruits. Terrestrial species have medium-length legs and are reminiscent of game-birds. Although often brightly coloured, pigeons spend long periods sitting still and may be very unobtrusive unless calling or flushed. Most have one or more distinctive advertising calls, and are best detected by them. All fly fast and direct, rarely gliding, many smaller species producing an audible whirring. Display flights usually involve flying up at a steep angle and gliding back down, often accompanied by wing-claps. 'Typical pigeons' Columba are large and dark with relatively pointed wings. Cuckoo-doves Macropygia are fairly small, long-tailed and rufous-brown, flying with deep wing-beats. Reinwardtoena are larger cuckoo-doves with dark and pale grey plumage. Ground doves Gallicolumba are usually seen when flushed on rapidly whirring wings, sometimes landing on a low branch, bobbing in alarm. Other ground doves include the usually common green and rufous Chalcophaps, rare bronzewing Henicophaps, large black Nicobar Pigeon Caloenas and the introduced Spilopelia and Geopelia of open habitats in New Caledonia. The commonest arboreal species are fruit doves Ptilinopus and Drepanotila, which are medium-sized short-tailed green doves, very inconspicuous despite patches of bright yellow and red. Imperial pigeons Ducula are common, large, usually grey canopy pigeons with loud booming or barking calls. Mountain pigeons Gymnophaps are slenderer species of high mountainous islands.

ROCK DOVE *Columba livia* — Plate 36

(Feral/Domestic Pigeon, Pigeon biset)

Description 33 cm. Medium-sized grey pigeon closely associated with buildings. Variable plumage is typically grey with double black wing-bar, white rump, and green and purple gloss on neck. Other common colour morphs are similar but darker, sometimes blackish, or paler or all-white. Juvenile has less iridescence, pale fringes to many feathers and greyer legs.
Similar species Plumage variability may cause confusion but its distinctive habits, notably dependence on human dwellings, are shared only with Spotted and Peaceful Doves, which are smaller and longer-tailed. Differs from Metallic Pigeon, imperial pigeons and mountain pigeons by being smaller and shorter-tailed, and usually shows dark wing-bars and white rump. Black birds differ from Nicobar Pigeon by tail longer than wing-tip and iridescence restricted to neck-sides.
Voice Calls infrequently and quietly. Deep moaning *coo*. Bubbling display call *oo-rooo-coo-coo*.
Habits Breeds only in and around towns and other buildings but may be released around villages or houses. Feeds on ground and often perches on buildings, sometimes in small flocks. Fast flight with deep wing-beats.
Conservation status Rare non-native in Melanesia. Not threatened.
Range Sporadically introduced across Melanesia, mostly in large towns but occasionally in villages, with recent records from Manus, Vila and Luganville on Vanuatu, and Nouméa and nearby towns on New Caledonia, but newly released birds may occur anywhere.

METALLIC PIGEON *Columba vitiensis* Plate 36

(White-throated Pigeon; Pigeon à gorge blanche)

Description 37 cm. Large blackish pigeon with white throat, and green, purple and pink gloss. Pure white throat-patch includes chin and ear-coverts. Upperparts, including crown, are dark grey or blackish, and underparts vary between subspecies from chestnut to blackish. Juvenile has browner underparts and less gloss, especially on head and neck.
Similar species Differs from Yellow-legged Pigeon on Bismarcks and Solomons by dark crown and neck and dark legs. From Black Imperial Pigeon by white throat and dark undertail. From New Britain Bronzewing by blackish crown, neck, breast and belly, and iridescence not restricted to wing-coverts. From other imperial pigeons by uniform blackish upperparts.
Voice Calls infrequently. A series of 2–3 deep notes, *c.*3–4 seconds apart, the first rising slightly, the second and third at lower pitch *uwoo....woo* or *whoo...ooo...ooo*, repeated 3–5 times. On Vanuatu, the second note may be longer, multisyllabic and trailing off in volume. On New Caledonia, usually trisyllabic, the first and second notes quavering and rising in pitch, the third dropping in pitch and volume: *poo-roo, hoo* or *poo-hooroo, hoo*. Last note may be difficult to hear at long distance. May give single notes such as a loud booming *hoo!*
Habits Unobtrusive, especially in north Melanesia. Usually restricted to forest but also in open forest and savanna in Vanuatu and New Caledonia. From sea-level to 1760 m, but largely restricted to mountains in Solomons. Usually singles or very small flocks but historic records of flocks of up to 80 on New Caledonia. Forages at all levels from canopy to ground, often feeding on rough roads. Bobs head when alarmed. Rather heavy flight with deeper wing-beats and longer, more pointed wings than imperial pigeons.
Conservation status Fairly common in New Caledonia, Vanuatu and Makira, uncommon elsewhere in Solomons and rare on Bougainville and Bismarcks. Not threatened.
Range Larger islands across Melanesia but not Manus or Mussau.
C. v. halmaheira breeds across the Bismarcks and Solomons, including New Ireland, New Britain, where very few records, Bougainville, Isabel, Vella Lavella, Kolombangara, Vangunu, Nggatokae, Florida Is, Guadalcanal, Malaita and Makira; has black underparts with purple and green gloss; elsewhere this subspecies occurs in Indonesia and New Guinea.
C. v. leopoldi, endemic to Vanuatu, where widespread but no records from Gaua, has rich chestnut to dark brownish-grey underparts, weakly glossed with green, and more purple iridescence on upperparts.
C. v. hypoenochroa, endemic to New Caledonia, including Grande Terre, Ouvéa, Maré and Lifou, has brighter chestnut underparts, purple gloss on breast, strong purple gloss on head, neck and mantle, and often a grey wash on throat.
Elsewhere, other subspecies range from the Philippines and Indonesia through New Guinea to Fiji and Samoa.

YELLOW-LEGGED PIGEON *Columba pallidiceps* Plate 36

(Pigeon à tête pale)

Description 37 cm. Iridescent black pigeon with silvery-grey head and throat. Fairly long yellow legs. Broad green, purple and pink iridescent fringes are most prominent on wings and breast, greener on breast and upperparts, and pinker on belly. Head may appear white at distance. Female has duller grey head, sometimes slightly mottled on hindcrown. Juvenile has browner head and less iridescence.
Similar species Differs from Metallic Pigeon by crown uniform with cheeks, yellow legs and brighter greener iridescence. From New Britain Bronzewing by plumage except head wholly iridescent blackish and yellow legs. From Chestnut-bellied Imperial Pigeon by strongly contrasting head, blackish underparts and yellow legs. Note that many imperial pigeons appear to be dark with pale heads when seen from above in flight.
Voice A stuttered deep throaty boom *h-h-h-h-hooo* or *hu-vrrrrru*. Wings whistle in flight.
Habits Most records from hills up to *c.*650 m but also in lowlands and one record at 1300 m. Usually solitary but groups of up to five recorded in fruiting trees. Most commonly in understorey fruiting trees or on ground but sometimes in (and occasionally seen flying above) canopy.
Conservation status Rare on all islands except for Makira where locally uncommon. Appears to have declined, perhaps through predation by introduced mammals, over-hunting and habitat loss. IUCN: Vulnerable.
Range Endemic to Bismarcks and Solomons. Recorded from New Ireland, New Britain, Bougainville, Choiseul, Vella Lavella, Ndai, Florida Is, Ramos, Guadalcanal, Makira, and possibly Duke of York and Ugi, but recent records from only New Ireland, New Britain, Guadalcanal and Makira.

SPOTTED DOVE *Spilopelia chinensis* Plate 36

(Spotted Turtle-Dove; *Streptopelia chinensis*; Tourterelle tigrine)

Description 30 cm. Small slim long-tailed ground dove with white-spotted black neck-patch. Grey head, dull brown upperparts, pale pinkish neck and underparts, and white undertail-coverts. In flight, has short wings and long tail with broad white tips to outer tail feathers. Juvenile is dull greyish-brown with ill-defined marks on neck-patch and pale fringes on mantle and wing-coverts.

Similar species Differs from Zebra Dove by larger size, neck-patch in adults, no barring on neck and underparts, uniform brown underwing, and call. From other New Caledonian pigeons by small size, long tail and flight action.

Voice Mournful *coo, coo-ooo-crouk, coo-coo-crrrooo* and shorter variants.

Habits Commonest around parks, villages and cultivation but sometimes in native savanna and scrubby or open habitats. Feeds on ground, often in small flocks. Fast flight with rapid, flicking wing-beats similar to cuckoo-doves.

Conservation status Locally common non-native on New Caledonia. Not threatened.

Range Introduced to Grande Terre, New Caledonia, where in villages across the island. Three specimens, perhaps escapes, from Rabaul, New Britain, in 1932–1933. Presumed to be *S. c. tigrina* of South-East Asia, Philippines and Indonesia. Elsewhere, other subspecies are native to Indian subcontinent and south China, with scattered introduced populations including Australia and Hawaii.

SLENDER-BILLED CUCKOO-DOVE *Macropygia amboinensis* — Plate 31

(Also treated as a subspecies of Brown Cuckoo-Dove *M. phasianella*; Phasianelle d'Amboine)

Description 36 cm. Medium-sized plain brown cuckoo-dove with fine black barring on neck and breast. Male has paler buffy underparts with pink gloss, green or purple-pink gloss on neck-sides, and black barring on foreneck, neck-sides and especially breast. Female lacks iridescence, has darker browner underparts, black mottling on ear-coverts, black barring on hindneck, and stronger barring on foreneck and breast. Juvenile is like female but has black mottling on crown, stronger barring on nape and mantle, and mottled foreneck and breast.

Similar species Cuckoo-doves differ from other pigeons by their long tail and plain brown plumage. Differs from Bar-tailed Cuckoo-Dove by unbarred tail and larger size; also, males have paler underparts and barred breast and females have finer barring only on neck and breast, but beware that tail-bars may be difficult to see in some Bar-tailed Cuckoo-Doves. From Mackinlay's Cuckoo-Dove by barred not mottled breast, larger size, paler duller plumage, and paler underparts of male. From Pied Cuckoo-Dove by pale brown head and underparts contrasting less with browner upperparts, and smaller size. From juvenile Pied Cuckoo-Dove by warm brown plumage and barring on neck and breast.

Voice Monotonously repeated *whop-whop-whop-whop...*, each note increasing in pitch but decreasing in volume, given at a rate of 2–2.5 notes per second for 2–12 seconds. Higher-pitched and less resonant than similar fruit dove calls, and faster and higher-pitched than Stephan's Emerald Dove. Sometimes just single notes, sometimes a longer *whooop-*. Growling display call *crOOOuw*.

Habits Forest, especially forest edge and secondary forest, in lowlands and hills up to 1200 m. Usually singles or pairs in forest mid-storey but sometimes feeds on ground. Flies with fairly slow deep wing-beats, often two birds chasing through forest.

Conservation status Fairly common, but uncommon on Manus, and tolerant of degraded forest. Not threatened.

Range Admiralties, Mussau and Bismarcks.

M. a. admiralitatis, endemic to Manus, other small Admiralty Is and probably this subspecies on Mussau, is barred on entire underparts.

M. a. carteretia, endemic to the Bismarcks including New Ireland, Djaul, Tabar, Lihir, Tanga, Feni, New Britain, Lolobau, Watom and Duke of York; male has pale breast with very fine bars or no barring. Birds on Feni have duller, darker, cold brown upperparts and may represent a new subspecies.

Birds on Long, Tolokiwa, Umboi and Sakar are included within *M. a. carteretia* or *M. a. cinereiceps* of New Guinea, the male having a greyer head.

M. a. huskeri, endemic to Lavongai, has darker colder-brown upperparts and tail, redder wing-coverts, and distinct fine blackish bars on breast and flanks.

Elsewhere, recorded from Indonesia and New Guinea.

BAR-TAILED CUCKOO-DOVE *Macropygia nigrirostris* — Plate 31

(Black-billed Cuckoo-Dove; Phasianelle barrée)

Description 29 cm. Small cuckoo-dove with ruddy-brown plumage and narrow black bars on uppertail. Wings are darker and underparts slightly paler rufous-brown. Female has black spots on head and black bars on neck, upperparts and breast, and more obscure bars on belly. Juvenile like female but has irregular tail barring.

Similar species Differs from other cuckoo-doves by barring on uppertail which however may be faint, absent or difficult to see in dark forest. Differs from Slender-billed Cuckoo-Dove by rich ruddy-brown plumage with only slightly paler underparts and smaller size; males further lack iridescent pale neck, and females have barring on upperparts. From Mackinlay's Cuckoo-Dove by barred not mottled breast, but range rarely overlaps.

Voice Similar to Slender-billed Cuckoo-Dove but higher-pitched and faster: a series of c.12 *kwok* notes at rate of c.3–4 per second. Decreases slightly in volume but has constant pitch and rate. Similar to some fruit doves but faster, does not accelerate at end and has harder, less resonant quality.
Habits Singles or pairs feed unobtrusively in forest and forest edge, sometimes in small flocks in fruiting tree. Locally commoner in hills and mountains, up to at least 1700 m.
Conservation status Uncommon in Melanesia. Not threatened.
Range *M. n. major* is endemic to the Bismarcks, including Lavongai, New Ireland, Tabar, New Britain and Duke of York with one record on Watom; has slenderer bill, paler underparts, and finer black bars on breast than *M. n. nigrirostris* which occurs across New Guinea and offshore islands.

MACKINLAY'S CUCKOO-DOVE *Macropygia mackinlayi* Plate 31

(Spot-breasted Cuckoo-Dove; Phasianelle de Mackinlay)

Description 32 cm. A small rufous-brown or grey-brown cuckoo-dove with distinct black spots on breast. Slightly paler head and underparts and darker wings. Female has slightly greyer upperparts. Grey morph is dark ash-grey with paler fringes on wings and paler grey underparts. Some females are intermediate between normal and grey morphs. Juvenile has finely barred underparts.
Similar species Differs from other cuckoo-doves by breast-spots. From Slender-billed Cuckoo-Dove, on Manus and larger Bismarck Is, by rich ruddy-brown plumage with only slightly paler underparts, spotted breast and smaller size. From Bar-tailed Cuckoo-Dove by spotted breast, unmarked tail, and juvenile differs by irregular barring on underparts and plain tail, but range rarely overlaps.
Voice A quiet but far-carrying *cuc-ku* or *whah-who*, first syllable higher-pitched than second, latter quavering as it descends pitch, repeated every 1–2 seconds, similar to Common Cuckoo *Cuculus canorus* of Eurasia. Rarely, just first note; or second note is upslurred *whah-whooah*. Rising rasping *vrrhhuu* in courtship.
Habits Forest and gardens from sea-level to 1600 m. Often commoner in secondary regrowth, mangroves and mountains. Usually in singles, pairs or small groups in small fruiting trees. Occasional records on large islands suggest wide dispersal or nomadism.
Conservation status Generally common throughout most of range but abundant on some islands and rare on others, including those where it may be non-breeding visitor, such as Manus and New Britain. Not threatened.
Range Endemic to Bismarcks, where only on smaller islands, Solomons and Vanuatu. Grey morph occurs across Vanuatu but is common only on Tanna.
M. m. arossi is endemic to north Melanesia including Manus, Rambutyo, Nauna, San Miguel, Tong, Mussau, Emirau, Crown, Long, Tolokiwa, Umboi, Sakar, Witu, Kimbe Bay islands, Watom, Lihir, Nissan and the Solomons from Buka and Bougainville to Makira including most small islands and Rennell. Occasional records from New Britain and New Ireland, where probably not resident.
M. m. mackinlayi, endemic to Temotu, where recorded from Nendo, Reef Is, Utupua, Vanikoro, and across Vanuatu except the Torres Is and Aniwa, and very rare on Aneityum, has paler plumage and larger black breast-spots.
Elsewhere, *M. m. krakari* occurs on Karkar just west of Melanesia and possibly once on the New Guinea mainland.

PIED CUCKOO-DOVE *Reinwardtoena browni* Plate 31

(Phasianelle de Brown)

Description 45 cm. Large long-tailed pigeon with blackish upperparts and off-white head and underparts. Slightly greyer on crown, nape, flanks and undertail-coverts. Upperparts are otherwise dark slate-grey with blue gloss. Juvenile is poorly known but probably predominantly sooty-grey, slightly paler on underparts.
Similar species Long tail differs from all other pigeons except cuckoo-doves, from which (notably male Slender-billed Cuckoo-Dove) it differs by blackish upperparts, whitish underparts and larger size. From Papuan Mountain Pigeon by pale head not contrasting with breast, and longer tail.
Voice Short note followed by long mournful note rising in pitch and finishing with two more short lower notes, the last at lower pitch. Sometimes just middle two notes. Repeated for long periods, at intervals of about four seconds. Far-carrying, birds often calling at each other across valleys.
Habits Primary or old-growth forest from sea-level to 1760 m but commonest in hills up to 1000 m. Usually solitary in mid-storey forest. Unobtrusive, usually seen in flight or when calling from an exposed subcanopy perch. In flight, has slow, deep wing-beats, especially in display flight when it flies up and dives almost vertically.
Conservation status Generally uncommon, locally fairly common. Possibly threatened by lowland forest loss and degradation, but probably secure in its preferred steep hills. IUCN: Near Threatened.

Range Endemic to the Admiralties and Bismarcks.
R. b. solitaria, endemic to Manus, Rambutyo and Nauna, is smaller and has darker grey upperparts and grey-blue wash on underparts.
R. b. browni is endemic to Lavongai, New Ireland, Djaul, Lihir, Tabar, Umboi, where possibly a separate subspecies as smaller and darker, New Britain, Lolobau, Watom, where vagrant, and Duke of York.

CRESTED CUCKOO-DOVE *Reinwardtoena crassirostris* Plate 31

(Phasianelle huppée)

Description 42 cm. Large long-tailed pigeon with wispy upswept crest along nape. Mid-grey head, neck and underparts, slightly darker on breast, shading to dark grey undertail-coverts. Dark blue-black wings, back and tail with slight gloss. Thick, strongly hooked bill. In flight, appears robust and shorter-tailed than smaller cuckoo-doves but crest not visible. Juvenile has slight crest, darker grey head and underparts, and rusty fringes to most feathers.
Similar species Differs from Pale Mountain Pigeon by crest, unmarked upperparts, longer tail and shorter wings. From MacKinlay's Cuckoo-Dove by much larger size and no rufous in plumage.
Voice Rather subdued but far-carrying mournful pair of double notes *hoo-woot, hoo-whoooo*, the first double-note rising in pitch, the second double-note rising in pitch then dropping as it trails off. Sometimes drops one or more of these syllables, e.g. *hoo, hoo-whooo* or *hoo-whoo, wuu*. Repeated for long periods at about five second intervals. Sometimes mimicked by imperial pigeons with calls that are more slurred and flatter in tone.
Habits Primary and secondary forest and forest edge, from lowlands to c.1500 m. Commonest in steep hills at 500–900 m. Usually solitary and unobtrusive in mid-storey but most often seen in flight or when calling from more exposed perch.
Conservation status Locally fairly common but rare or absent from large areas. Its preferred steep hill forest is under less threat from logging and clearance. IUCN: Near Threatened.
Range Endemic to the Solomons, including Bougainville, Choiseul, Isabel, Ranongga, Vella Lavella, Kolombangara, Kohinggo, New Georgia, Vangunu, Nggatokae, Gizo where a visitor, Rendova, Tetepare, Guadalcanal, Florida Is, Malaita, Makira, Ugi, Three Sisters, Santa Ana and Santa Catalina.

PACIFIC EMERALD DOVE *Chalcophaps longirostris* Plate 32

(Also treated as a subspecies of Green-winged Dove or [Common] Emerald [Ground] Dove *Chalcophaps indica*; Colombine turvert)

Description 26 cm. Small fat ground dove with shiny green wings and mantle, bright pale blue shoulder, muddy purple-rufous head and underparts, and bright orange-red bill. In flight, appears fat and bulky with fairly long wings and strong wing-beats, with two pale grey bars on back and pale outer tail feathers with black subterminal band, but green wing-coverts can be difficult to see. Female has smaller duller blue shoulder-patch, browner head and underparts, more orange bill and more rufous rump and tail. Juvenile similar to female, but has much less green on mantle, broad rufous wing-bars, brownish bill, and dark fringes and bars on underparts, especially breast.
Similar species The only small ground pigeon on most islands. Adult differs from Santa Cruz Ground Dove, on Santo and some Temotu islands, by more distinct green on wings, bars on back and orange bill, and by slower wing-beats when flushed. Juvenile differs from juvenile Santa Cruz Ground Dove by pale bars on back, although sometimes obscure, and paler outer tail feathers.
Voice Calls often, from low perch. Mournful, slightly upslurred and rising series of *hwoooa* notes monotonously repeated 3–12 times at about one per second. Often preceded by short *tk*, either once or before each note, audible only at close range, like sharp intake of breath. Sometimes increases in volume through series, which is usually repeated after a few seconds.
Habits Forest, most commonly in secondary forest, coconut plantations and under scattered trees around villages, but also in primary forest. Usually in lowlands and hills, rarely above 600 m. Walks on forest floor, usually in pairs, but sometimes in small groups under fruiting trees. Often flushed from forest trails, flying off low and fast, either landing out of sight or on understorey perch.
Conservation status Usually common. Not threatened.
Range Temotu, Vanuatu and New Caledonia.
C. l. sandwichensis, endemic to Temotu but not the smallest islands such as Tinakula, Vanuatu where on all islands, and Ouvéa, Maré and Lifou, has richer, more uniform body colour than other subspecies.
C. l. chrysochlora, on Grande Terre, New Caledonia, has less pink underparts and slight purple wash to crown and mantle; elsewhere it occurs in eastern Indonesia, New Guinea and eastern Australia.
Elsewhere, *C. l. longirostris* occurs in north Australia.

STEPHAN'S EMERALD DOVE *Chalcophaps stephani* — Plate 32

(Stephan's [Ground] Dove; Colombine d'Étienne)

Description 23 cm. Small fat ground dove, rich rufous-brown with shiny green wings. Orange-red bill in adults, blackish in juveniles. In flight, shows green wing-coverts, rufous outer wings, blackish back with two pale buff bars, and rufous tail except for grey outer tail with blackish subterminal band and rufous tips. Male has clear white forehead and purple wash to crown and nape. Female has soft grey less defined forehead and no purple. Juvenile has green initially only on median wing-coverts, paler buff around eye, and some black barring especially on wings and breast.
Similar species Adult has distinctive white forehead, orange bill and extensive green iridescence on wings. Also differs from *Gallicolumba* ground doves by brighter rufous plumage, and in flight by longer tail and wings, slower wing-beats and pale bars on back. Juvenile differs from other ground doves by being more rufous, and larger than Bronze Ground Dove.
Voice A long series of mournful *pu* notes, starting softly and sounding distant, but swelling in volume for a few notes before continuing monotonously *oo-oo-oo-oo-pu-pu-pu-pu-pu-* at about three notes per second for 10–20 seconds. Usually preceded by low mournful *woooah* 1–2 seconds beforehand.
Habits Forest, especially degraded forest including coconut plantations, but uncommon in old-growth forest; commonest in extreme lowlands but recorded up to at least 750 m. Almost always terrestrial but occasionally in low fruiting shrubs and often seen flying c.2–4 m above ground. Quiet and unobtrusive, usually seen singly or in pairs, sometimes small groups below fruiting trees or Metallic Starling colonies. When flushed, often perches on understorey perch, where sometimes bobs head but more slowly than *Gallicolumba* ground doves.
Conservation status Common. Not threatened.
Range Admiralties, St Matthias, Bismarcks and Solomons.
C. s. stephani occurs across the Bismarcks including Admiralties and St Matthias but not the most isolated islands such as Ninigo, Hermit and Tench; elsewhere it occurs on New Guinea and nearby islands.
C. s. mortoni, endemic to the Solomons, including most small islands from Nissan and Buka to Makira and Santa Ana, but not Rennell, is slightly larger and darker, especially on underparts.
Elsewhere, *C. s. wallacei* occurs in Indonesia.

NEW BRITAIN BRONZEWING *Henicophaps foersteri* — Plate 36

(Colombine de Nouvelle-Bretagne)

Description 39 cm. Large terrestrial pigeon with brilliant purple, bronze and green iridescence on wing-coverts. Iridescent blackish mantle, wings and tail with strong gloss on wing-coverts, and orange-brown crown, nape and neck-sides with buffy-white face and underparts. Male has almost white face, throat, lower breast and belly, bright orange-brown crown, neck and sometimes upper breast-band, and rich maroon on lesser wing-coverts. Female has rich rufous-brown crown to upper mantle, paler orange-brown on neck-sides and across breast, creamy-white throat and ear-coverts, and darker lower breast and belly. Juvenile unknown.
Similar species Differs from Metallic and Yellow-legged Pigeons, which also feed on ground, by brown neck and underparts, no clearly contrasting white throat or uniformly pale head, and iridescence restricted to wings. Differs from other ground doves by larger size, longer tail and plumage.
Voice Two unconfirmed descriptions. (1) A monotonously repeated *pip-yia*, the second note higher-pitched and upslurred. (2) A long monotonous series of deep flat *hoop-hoop-* notes very like White-breasted Ground Dove.
Habits Old-growth forest in lowlands and hills to at least 700 m. Retiring and elusive, usually seen when flushed from forest floor, when flies up silently on broad rounded wings with rather slow floppy wing-beats. Often lands on perch and bobs head. Largely terrestrial but may possibly feed in low bushes like New Guinea Bronzewing *H. albifrons*.
Conservation status Few recent records, and appears to be rare. Presumably threatened by lowland forest loss and degradation. IUCN: Vulnerable.
Range Endemic to New Britain, including Umboi and Lolobau.

ZEBRA DOVE *Geopelia striata* — Plate 36

(Géopélie zébrée)

Description 21 cm. Tiny long-tailed dove with fine black barring. Grey-brown nape, mantle, wings and tail, blue-grey head, dull pink central underparts and white belly to vent, with coarse black barring on wings and tail and fine black barring on nape, mantle, breast-sides and flanks. In flight, shows long graduated tail with white tips to outer tail feathers, and chestnut underwing-coverts. Female has barring extending closer to mid-line on breast. Juvenile duller with less distinct bars, barring almost to centre of breast, and pale fringes on wings.

Similar species Differs from Spotted Dove by smaller size, call, barring on neck and underparts, plain neck, and chestnut underwing-coverts. From other New Caledonian pigeons by very small size, long tail and flight action, and from buttonquail by long tail.
Voice Calls often. Soft trill *croodle* followed by rapid series of c.6–8 *croo* notes.
Habits Open habitats, usually grassland, especially in parks, alongside roads and towns. Pairs or small flocks feed on ground. Fast flight with very rapid, flicking wing-beats interspersed with brief closing of wings.
Conservation status Locally common non-native on New Caledonia. Not threatened.
Range Introduced to New Caledonia where currently restricted to the Nouméa and La Foa areas, but may spread. Elsewhere, native in Thailand to Java, with scattered introduced populations including Tahiti and Hawaii.

NICOBAR PIGEON *Caloenas nicobarica* — Plate 37

(Nicobar à camail)

Description 34 cm. Large fat black pigeon with extremely short tail, white in adults and black in immatures. Long chicken-like hackles on neck. Upperparts, especially neck and wing-coverts, have iridescent green and blue gloss. Female has smaller knob on bill and shorter hackles. Juvenile and immature have black tail, juvenile also lacks neck-hackles and gloss. Distinctive flight shape of very short tail, deep chest, long broad wings and rather long neck with head held up.
Similar species Distinctive short tail, white tail of adult, neck-hackles and flight shape. When flushed, flies up noisily with cracking wing-beats, at steeper angle than Melanesian Megapode and Purple Swamphen.
Voice Usually silent. Occasionally a harsh guttural croak or bark *ku-RRAU*. At breeding colonies, may give a very deep, reverberating, pulsing *rrr-rrr-rrr-rrr-*.
Habits Prefers flat coastal primary forest but locally in secondary forest, bamboo thickets and rubber plantations, and uncommonly in hills to 500 m. Breeds in loose colonies on small forested islets, usually uninhabited and remote with low hunting levels. Small flocks fly high over sea to feed on adjacent larger islands, leaving at dawn and returning in late afternoon. Non-breeding birds occur further from breeding colonies and may be nomadic. Melanesian colonies usually number tens or hundreds of birds. Away from colonies, usually forages singly or in loose groups of up to ten on forest floor. Shy, commoner in uninhabited areas, and flushes at long range, flying up steeply, sometimes with dangling legs, to distant subcanopy perch.
Conservation status Usually rare on large islands, uncommon on small islands and locally common at breeding colonies and adjacent forest. Heavily hunted, especially at colonies, and declining through loss of lowland forest. Some Melanesian colonies are seriously threatened but overall status poorly known. IUCN: Near Threatened.
Range Admiralties, St Matthias Is, Bismarcks and Solomons.
Recorded from most islands from Wuvulu, Hermit Is, and St Matthias Is east through the Bismarcks and Solomons to islands off Makira, including Ndai, Ontong Java and Rennell. However, no recent records from many islands, especially in east Solomons. Elsewhere, occurs on small islands from Andaman Is and Philippines to New Guinea, with subspecies *C. n. pelewensis* on Palau.

[SPOTTED PIGEON *Caloenas maculata*] — Plate 31

This species may have inhabited Melanesia but is probably now extinct. It is known only from a single specimen of unknown provenance. It appears to be too small for the extinct species known only from subfossils on New Caledonia. It was a black pigeon with large yellow-buff spots on wings and rump and a fairly long buff-tipped tail. Its size and shape was similar to an imperial pigeon *Ducula* but it had elongated neck-hackles like Nicobar Pigeon.

WHITE-BREASTED GROUND DOVE *Gallicolumba jobiensis* — Plate 32

(White-bibbed Ground-Pigeon; Gallicolombe de Jobi)

Description 25 cm. Small fat blackish ground dove with white supercilium, throat and breast, and purple gloss on mantle and wing-coverts. In flight, shows plain blackish upperwing and tail with paler grey-brown tips to outer tail feathers. Female variable, often with greyish wash on breast, less purple gloss and grey wash to blackish areas. Single female specimen from Solomons was plain dark brown. Juvenile is dark brown, slightly olive on mantle and wing-coverts, with distinct rufous edgings to most feathers particularly wing-coverts, faint pale supercilium and paler greyish throat. Purple feathers soon appear on wing-coverts and mantle, and grey or white feathers on breast.
Similar species White breast of adult distinctive. Differs from Bronze Ground Dove by white patterns, no green on upperparts and larger size. Juvenile plumage similar but often shows scattered purple or grey-white feathers. Adult differs from Stephan's Emerald Dove by distinctive plumage including plain rump in flight; juvenile differs by rufous

restricted to fringes, often showing purple or grey-white feathers, no green, plain rump and shorter tail. Differs from other ground pigeons, notably White-throated Pigeon and New Britain Bronzewing, by plumage pattern, small size and dumpy shape. See Thick-billed Ground Dove in eastern Solomons.
Voice Long monotonous series of deep flat *hoop-hoop-* notes, starting slightly slower, and pausing for a few seconds before another series. May call from low perch. Slightly louder and harder than Bronze Ground Dove.
Habits Forest, especially secondary growth and garden regrowth, from sea level to 1550 m, but may be nomadic. Usually singles, sometimes pairs, walk on forest floor, but seen flying low through forest and occasionally forages in low bushes. Most often seen when flushed, when often perches on nearby low branch or log, bobbing head nervously.
Conservation status Uncommon or rare in Admiralties and Bismarcks. In the Solomons, *G. j. chalconota* is known from only four specimens and one sighting, and this subspecies is presumed to be Critically Endangered. The species is not threatened.
Range Admiralties, Bismarcks and Solomons.
G. j. jobiensis recorded from Hermit, Tong, Lavongai, New Ireland, Lihir, Tabar, Umboi, Sakar, New Britain, Lolobau, Watom and possibly Duke of York; may occur more widely. Elsewhere, occurs across New Guinea and nearby islands.
G. j. chalconota endemic to Vella Lavella, Guadalcanal and Makira, is 23 cm, male with less white on supercilium and less purple gloss, female dark grey-brown with slight green gloss on upperparts and cinnamon on throat and breast. Could be treated as separate species.

SANTA CRUZ GROUND DOVE *Gallicolumba sanctaecrucis* Plate 32

(Gallicolombe de Santa Cruz)

Description 23 cm. Small fat ground dove with grey or orange-brown head and underparts. Male has ashy-grey head and nape, brown upperparts with purple gloss on back and wings, especially on shoulder, pale pinkish-buff (almost white) throat and breast-patch, and dark brown belly. Female duller, with rufous-brown head, neck and breast, greyish belly and dark olive upperparts with greenish gloss. Juvenile uniform brown, sometimes with glossy purple shoulder-patch. In flight, male has uniform uppertail with obscure broad blackish subterminal band and paler tips, especially at corners.
Similar species Differs from Pacific Emerald Dove by brown mantle and wings with purple or dull green gloss, plain back and black bill.
Voice Monotonous series of identical low upslurred *wuuuu-up* notes given at 0.5–1 second intervals, often continuing for several minutes. May also have more rapid calls, with up to five notes per second.
Habits Recent Santo records are from old-growth forest between 300–1100 m, but may also occur down to sea-level. A shy terrestrial species, solitary or in pairs. When flushed, usually runs away with tail erect, but also flies up with loud wing-whirring and lands out of sight. Sometimes perches on low branches.
Conservation status Uncommon or rare on Santo. Possibly extinct in Temotu but survey effort on Nendo and Utupua has been limited, and many small islands including Tinakula have not been visited in recent years. Probably predated by introduced mammals, notably cats. IUCN: Endangered.
Range Endemic to Temotu and Santo, Vanuatu. Recorded from Tinakula, Utupua and Santo, with sightings on Nendo, but may also occur on other islands.

TANNA GROUND DOVE *Gallicolumba ferruginea* Plate 32

(Also treated as a subspecies of Santa Cruz Ground Dove *G. sanctaecrucis* or Shy Ground Dove *G. stairi* of Fiji and Samoa; Gallicolombe de Tanna)

Description 27 cm. Small ground dove. Male has white head, throat and breast, and reddish-black upperparts and belly. Female has rusty-brown head and breast, reddish-purple back, dark green wings and grey belly.
Similar species Differs from Pacific Emerald Dove by plain reddish-black upperparts and black bill. From Santa Cruz Ground Dove, on other islands in north Vanuatu, by male's white head and breast, and dark crown and nape, and female's reddish-purple back.
Habits Unknown but probably a terrestrial forest species, as other ground doves.
Voice Unknown but probably like other ground doves.
Conservation status Extinct. Known only from two historical specimens collected around 1774, which have been lost, but descriptions and a painting remain. Probably exterminated by predation by introduced mammals such as cats.
Range Endemic to Tanna, Vanuatu. May have previously occurred more widely.

THICK-BILLED GROUND DOVE *Gallicolumba salamonis* Plate 32

(Gallicolombe des Salomon)

Description 26 cm. Relatively large brown ground dove with paler head and breast, and heavy dark bill. Rich chestnut upperparts with faint purple iridescence on scapulars and lesser wing-coverts. Paler head and pale buff throat and breast-shield, sharply contrasting with chocolate-brown belly. In flight, shows dark chestnut uppertail with narrow pale rufous tip.
Similar species Distinctive pale buff breast, large size and thick bill. Differs from female and juvenile White-breasted Ground Dove by warmer brown plumage, plain head pattern and no contrasting rusty fringes. From Bronze Ground Dove by warm brown plumage and longer plain tail with only slightly paler rufous corners. From Stephan's Emerald Dove by plain chestnut upperparts.
Voice Unknown but probably similar to other *Gallicolumba* ground doves.
Habits The only known specimens were collected close to sea-level on Ramos and c.300 m on Makira. Habits probably similar to other ground doves.
Conservation status Known only from two specimens taken in 1882 and 1927. No recent records or local reports from either island despite targeted searches. Probably exterminated by predation by introduced mammals, especially cats. Presumed Extinct.
Range Endemic to the Solomons, where known from Makira and Ramos, a tiny island north of Isabel and Malaita. May have occurred more widely, especially on small islands.

BRONZE GROUND DOVE *Gallicolumba beccarii* Plate 32

(Beccari's Ground Dove; Gallicolombe de Beccari)

Description 19 cm. Small, plump ground dove with grey head and breast. Pale ashy-grey head, neck and breast, becoming paler on lower breast, sharply contrasting with blackish belly-band. Many, perhaps all in Bismarcks, have broad white eye-ring. Dark rufous-brown mantle and wings with bronze-green gloss and maroon on lesser wing-coverts. In flight, appears uniform but outer tail has brighter rufous terminal band and blackish subterminal bar. Female is duller and browner, especially on breast where dark grey upper breast merges into rufous lower breast, and lacks maroon on wing-coverts. Juvenile is uniform warm brown, lacking any grey, with rusty-orange fringes on wings and chestnut fringes on much of breast and belly.
Similar species Distinctive clearly marked grey head and breast-shield. When present, white eye-ring is also distinctive. Smaller and shorter-tailed than other ground doves. Differs from White-breasted Ground Dove by plain grey head and breast, contrasting with dark belly, no face markings except eye-ring, and no purple on mantle. From Thick-billed Ground Dove on Makira by grey head and breast and smaller size. From Stephan's Emerald Dove by duller green wings, duller rufous body, unmarked rump, black bill and smaller size. When flushed, differs from *Zoothera* ground-thrushes by fast whirring flight, then a glide, and shorter tail.
Voice Long monotonous series of deep flat *hoop-hoop-* notes, fluctuating slightly in speed and volume, and pausing for a few seconds before another series. Often calls from concealed perch within understorey thicket. Slightly quieter and softer than White-breasted Ground Dove.
Habits Forest, usually old-growth forest in hills, to 1250 m, but on small islands more often in secondary habitats. An unobtrusive forest-floor species, usually in singles or pairs. Walks erratically on ground, sometimes with cocked tail. Shy, flushing from ground with whirring wings and usually gliding back to ground out of sight, rather like a quail, or sometimes to low perch. Bobs head when alarmed.
Conservation status Usually rare but often overlooked and locally fairly common, for instance on Makira. Not threatened.
Range Admiralties, St Matthias Is, Bismarcks and Solomons.
G. b. admiralitatis, endemic to Manus; male has pure grey nape and female has dark grey head, neck and breast.
G. b. eichhorni, endemic to Mussau and Emirau, is slightly smaller and male has white eye-ring and paler breast.
G. b. johannae is almost endemic (elsewhere only on Karkar just west of Melanesia) to New Ireland and New Britain, including Lavongai, New Ireland, Lihir, Tanga, Feni where the subspecies is unconfirmed, Crown, Long, Tolokiwa, Umboi, Sakar, New Britain, Witu, Lolobau and Duke of York; male has white eye-ring and paler breast.
G. b. masculina, endemic to Nissan, has paler grey-brown lower breast and belly, no pale eye-ring; female similar to male but lacks purple on shoulder and has an ill-defined lower border to grey breast.
G. b. intermedia, endemic to Bougainville, Kolombangara, Gizo and New Georgia, has darker, more purplish-bronze belly.
G. b. solomonensis, endemic to Ndai, Guadalcanal, Makira, Three Sisters, Santa Ana, Rennell and Bellona, has slightly bronzier upperparts.
Elsewhere, *G. b. beccarii* occurs across the New Guinea mountains.

CHOISEUL PIGEON *Microgoura meeki* Plate 37

(Solomon Islands Crowned Pigeon; Microgoura de Choiseul)

Description 31 cm. Very distinctive medium-sized ground pigeon with long pale blue crest. Pale blue head with black around bill-base and pale pink on cheeks. Darker blue-grey neck, mantle and breast, orange belly, brown wings and short purple-black tail. Exact shape of crest unknown but may be held flat or fanned as Goura crowned-pigeons of New Guinea. Female slightly smaller. Juvenile unknown.
Similar species Differs from Crested Cuckoo-Dove by many features, notably short tail and terrestrial habits, but sometimes confused as both have crest.
Voice Unknown, but possible reports include 'a beautiful rising and falling whistling call given from the roost site every evening' or a low *c-r-r-ooo, cr-ooo, cr-o-o-o*.
Habits Lowland forest, including coastal limestone areas with sparse vegetation, and swamp forest but not mangroves. Terrestrial, reported to be tame, occurring in small groups and roosting together in low branches.
Conservation status Extinct. Last specimens taken in 1904 and possible reports until 1940s. It seems unlikely that this very distinctive species still survives given several unsuccessful searches for it. Probably predated by introduced cats.
Range Endemic to Choiseul in the Solomons. May possibly have occurred on Bougainville and Isabel, and even Malaita.

TANNA FRUIT DOVE *Ptilinopus tannensis* Plate 33

(Vanuatu/New Hebrides/Yellow-headed Fruit Dove; Ptilope de Tanna)

Description Length 26 cm. Large green fruit dove with yellowish crown and yellow wing-spots. Uniformly green except variable yellowish wash on crown, bright yellow tips to tertials and inner greater-coverts, silvery shoulder-patch of grey spots, and lemon-yellow vent and undertail-coverts. Relatively long bill, neck and tail. In flight, shows obscure greyish terminal tail-band. Female has fewer grey shoulder-spots and more extensive paler yellow on lower belly. Juvenile has yellow fringes on mantle, wings and underparts, less yellow on crown, and no grey shoulder-spots.
Similar species Differs from Red-bellied Fruit Dove by underparts not paler than upperparts, yellow wing-spots, different shape and larger size, and no purple patches of adult Red-bellied Fruit Dove.
Voice Slow series of about six upslurred *whu-ho, whu-ho…* notes, accelerating slowly, and repeated after 1–5 minutes. Also single deep notes.
Habits Forest, primarily old-growth rainforest, but also degraded habitats with large fruiting trees, including open woodland, parkland, plantations and gardens. Commonest in lowlands and hills, becoming rarer in mountains to at least 1500 m. Singles and pairs are unobtrusive and easily overlooked in forest canopy. Small parties, often mixed with Red-bellied Fruit Doves, are more active in fruiting trees, especially figs. May be locally nomadic, possibly moving between islands.
Conservation status Generally fairly common but rarer on southern islands and very rare on Aneityum. Declining through over-hunting and clearance of lowland forests.
Range Endemic to Vanuatu, where widespread except the Torres Is.

SUPERB FRUIT DOVE *Ptilinopus superbus* Plate 33

(Ptilope superbe)

Description 23 cm. Fairly large fruit dove with boldly coloured male. All plumages have distinct bars on white belly and, in flight, a broad pale grey terminal tail-band. Male has purple crown, rusty-orange nape and shoulders, silvery throat and breast, black lower breast-band and white belly with two broad green flank-bars. Female is green, often with grey wash especially on underparts, with green breast-band and two flank-bars on white belly, creamy undertail-coverts with broad green stripes, paler throat, yellow fringes on wing-coverts, dark spots on scapulars and small dark nape-patch. Juvenile similar to female but lacks nape-patch and scapular spots and has more yellow fringes on wings.
Similar species Male has distinctive orange nape and barred breast and belly. From other fruit doves by clearer tail-band, longer tail and slightly larger size. Female and juvenile also differ from other fruit doves by white belly with two green bars, greyer breast and pale throat; dark nape-patch is difficult to see.
Voice Slower and deeper than other fruit doves. Typically, a steady series of 3–6 double *who-up* notes at about one second intervals, the first note often shorter and quieter, and usually preceded by a quiet mumbled *mm*, sometimes accelerating and sometimes as triple-noted *oo-ooku*. Also a slow steady series of 3–8 single upslurred notes *hwoop, woop, woop*. Single loud guttural *whoot* and double or single *coo(-coo)*.
Habits Lowland forest, including degraded forest with tall trees, and less common in mountains up to 1250 m. Usually singles or pairs sit unobtrusively in canopy or subcanopy but occasionally in small groups at fruiting trees, and rarely flushed from ground.

Conservation status Common on most islands, but uncommon on some such as Mussau and Gizo. Not threatened.
Range Admiralties, Mussau, Bismarcks and Solomons. *P. s. superbus* occurs on Manus, Rambutyo, Tong, Mussau, Lavongai, New Ireland, Tabar, Lihir, Tanga, Feni, Tolokiwa where montane, Umboi, New Britain, Lolobau, Watom where vagrant, and Solomons from Buka east to Malaita but absent from Ulawa, Makira and Rennell, and in Indonesia, New Guinea and east Australia, with *P. s. temminckii* on Sulawesi.

SILVER-CAPPED FRUIT DOVE *Ptilinopus richardsii* Plate 33

(Ptilope de Richards)

Description 21 cm. Small fruit dove with bright orange belly to vent. Grey-green head and breast, silvery-grey crown, dark green upperparts with pink spots and fringes on scapulars and tertials, and pale yellow terminal tail-band. Female has duller pink spots, less extensive orange on belly, and no pinkish wash on undertail-coverts. Juvenile is uniform green with grey-washed head, yellow fringes on upperparts, pale yellow throat, bright yellow belly and undertail-coverts with a few orange feathers, and obscure grey tail-band.
Similar species The only fruit dove on Rennell. On Ugi, Three Sisters and Santa Ana, differs from female and juvenile White-headed and Yellow-bibbed Fruit Doves by the yellow and orange on the belly.
Voice One or two slow upslurred single notes, then a series of shorter notes, often double notes or quicker stuttered phrases of 3–4 notes e.g. *woo-hahaha* or *hoowoop, hoowoop, hoop-hoop, hoop-hoop, hoop-hoop*, slowly decreasing in volume and pitch, sometimes accelerating and becoming irregular. The series is repeated several times, often becoming longer. A quiet growl *vhoo*.
Habits Forest, including degraded forest and large isolated trees. Usually in singles or pairs, occasionally in small parties, especially in figs. In canopy and understorey, often perching on open branches above the canopy.
Conservation status Common and under no apparent threat despite its small range. Not threatened.
Range Endemic to Rennell and small islands off Makira.
P. r. richardsii is endemic to Ugi, Three Sisters, Santa Ana and Santa Catalina, and may occur as a vagrant to Makira.
P. r. cyanopterus, endemic to Rennell and Bellona, has darker grey forehead and crown, brighter yellow chin and throat, and less orange on centre of belly not extending onto flanks.

RED-BELLIED FRUIT DOVE *Ptilinopus greyii* Plate 33

(Ptilope de Grey)

Description 23 cm. Fairly large fruit dove, with purplish-red crown and belly-patch. Generally green with greyer wash on head, neck and breast, fine black streaks on breast, yellow fringes on wings, clear purple forecrown with yellowish border, some purple on belly and orange-pink on vent and undertail-coverts, pale grey terminal band on undertail and yellow-grey on uppertail. Female has darker upperparts and smaller purple belly-patch. Juvenile lacks purple patches, is uniform green with paler and yellower undertail-coverts and has yellow fringes to most feathers.
Similar species Differs from Tanna Fruit Dove by purple and orange patches, greyer head, yellow fringes but not large spots, and smaller size. From Pacific Emerald Dove by green head and underparts, and habits.
Voice Series starting with two or three short or paired notes, running into an accelerating series of stuttered notes, decreasing in volume towards end: *coo-coo-coo-coocoocococo* or *hoo-hoo, hoo-hoo, ho-ho-hohohoho*. The series is usually repeated several times. Also single short notes.
Habits Forest, including secondary growth, and less common in savanna, isolated trees especially figs in open country, and mountains up to 1500 m. Often seen singly or in pairs but sometimes in flocks of up to 30 birds, often with other pigeons, in forest canopy. Local nomadism is recorded; probably capable of travelling between islands.
Conservation status Generally common, but uncommon to rare on Grande Terre.
Range Endemic to Temotu, Vanuatu and New Caledonia, where throughout Temotu and Vanuatu to Loyalties and Ile des Pins but uncommon and localised on Grande Terre. Also on Ndai, north of Malaita in the Solomons, without any records from intervening islands.

WHITE-BIBBED FRUIT DOVE *Ptilinopus rivoli* Plate 33

(White-breasted Fruit Dove; Ptilope de Rivoli)

Description 23 cm. Fairly large chunky fruit dove, with broad white breast-band in males. Male has deep purple forehead, broad white breast-bib, dark purple central belly and yellow rear-belly to undertail-coverts. Conspicuous yellowish bill and lores and greenish skin around deep orange eye. Indistinct pale terminal tail-band, clearer from below. Female plain dark green with yellow vent and undertail-coverts. Juvenile as female but with yellow fringes on underparts.

Similar species White bib of male distinctive although similar yellow bib in Yellow-bibbed Fruit Dove. Female and juvenile differ from latter by yellow bill and lores, less extensive orbital skin, orange eye and larger size. From juvenile Knob-billed Fruit Dove by clear yellow vent and undertail-coverts, all-green head and no orange belly feathers or red knob on bill-base. From juvenile Claret-breasted Fruit Dove on Lihir by clear yellow vent and undertail-coverts, yellow bill-base and lores, and no grey spots on shoulder and tertials.
Voice Series of rather loud clear *woa* notes, accelerating and dropping in pitch at end: *woa—woa—...-woa-woa-...-wo-wo-...-o-o*; or rising slightly in pitch and volume then falling back again: *woo—woo-woo-wo-wo-wo-woo-woo—woo*. Sometimes preceded by one or more high-pitched *wooaa* notes, rising then falling in pitch, and occasionally given on own. Differs from other fruit doves by fast accelerating end. A long series of *whoa* notes, evenly spaced about five seconds apart. Short growling *vrrruuh*.
Habits Forest from sea-level to highest mountains, but rare in lowlands of largest islands. Unobtrusive, usually perched alone or in pairs in forest understorey, also canopy and occasionally several at fruiting tree. Uncommon in secondary forest.
Conservation status Common in mountains of New Britain and fairly common in lowlands of smaller islands. Not threatened.
Range *P. r. rivoli* is endemic to Bismarcks, including Lavongai, New Ireland, Djaul, Tabar, Lihir, Tanga, Umboi, New Britain, Lolobau and Duke of York. Elsewhere, other subspecies occur in Indonesia and New Guinea and nearby islands.

YELLOW-BIBBED FRUIT DOVE *Ptilinopus solomonensis* — Plate 33

(Ptilope des Salomon)

Description 21 cm. Small compact fruit dove, with broad yellow breast-band in males. Male is uniform green with small dark pink-purple forehead-spot, broad yellow crescent across breast, large pink-purple belly-patch, and yellow vent and undertail-coverts. Greyish-green bill, broad naked blue-green eye-ring and orange or yellow eye. Indistinct grey terminal tail-band, clearer from below. Female is all-green with yellow vent and undertail-coverts and yellow fringes on belly. Juvenile as female but with narrow yellow fringes, especially on wing-coverts.
Similar species Yellow bib of male is distinctive although similar in shape to White-bibbed Fruit Dove on New Britain, Umboi and Lavongai. Female and juvenile differ from White-bibbed Fruit Dove by greyish-green bill, non-contrasting lores, extensive blue-green orbital skin, yellow eye and smaller size. From Claret-breasted Fruit Dove by yellow or green breast, brighter yellow undertail-coverts and no pale grey shoulder-patch or tertial spots. From female Superb Fruit Dove by plain yellow vent and undertail-coverts. From adult Knob-billed Fruit Dove by no red knob, orange on belly nor grey spots on shoulder or tertials. From juvenile Knob-billed Fruit Dove by clear yellow vent and undertail-coverts, all-green head.
Voice Series of notes starting slowly, rising in volume and speed, then dropping in volume and pitch: *hu, hoo, hoo-hoo-hoo-hoo-hoo-ho-ho-ho-hu-hu-u-u-uuuuu*. Also a series of unvaried *hoo* or *woop* notes, often double *hoo* notes when heard at close range. Sometimes calls at night.
Habits Forest, often restricted to old-growth forest on larger islands but also secondary growth on small islands. Some subspecies of larger islands are restricted to mountains, e.g. usually above 600–700 m on Bougainville, Kolombangara and Guadalcanal, but common down to sea-level on Malaita and Makira. Singles and pairs are unobtrusive in all levels of forest, occasionally in small flocks in fruiting trees, sometimes with other species.
Conservation status Common on some islands such as Bougainville and Makira but rare on Manus and New Britain. Not threatened.
Range Admiralties, St Matthias Is, Bismarcks and Solomons.
P. s. johannis, endemic to Wuvulu, Ninigo, Hermit, Kaniet, Manus, San Miguel, Rambutyo, Tong, Nauna, Mussau, Emirau, Tench and Lavongai, has large paler lilac-mauve cap back to level of rear of eye, and paler mauve belly-patch separated from yellow bib by purplish band.
P. s. meyeri, endemic to islands off New Britain, where recorded from Crown, Long, Tolokiwa, Umboi, Malai, Sakar, Witu and Watom but rare and may not breed on New Britain itself, has extensive cap as *P. s. johannis* and a more extensive and deeper yellow breast-band.
P. s. neumanni, endemic to Nissan, is like *P. s. meyeri* but with shorter bill.
P. s. bistictus, endemic to Buka and Bougainville, has forehead-patch split into large super-loral spots, almost meeting above bill, and whole plumage is slightly paler.
P. s. vulcanorum, endemic to Vella Lavella, Vangunu, Nggatokae, Kolombangara, Rendova, Florida Is, and probably this subspecies on Russell Is and Ramos, has large purple cap and a more violet belly-patch.
P. s. ocularis, endemic to Guadalcanal, has purple cap reduced to small spot in front of eye.
P. s. ambiguus, endemic to Malaita, has larger purple eye-spots than *P. s. ocularis*, sometimes meeting on forehead.

P. s. solomonensis, endemic to Makira, Ugi and Three Sisters, has broader belly-patch and more prominent dark band behind yellow bib.
Elsewhere, *P. s. speciosus* occurs on Geelvink Bay islands off north-west New Guinea.

CLARET-BREASTED FRUIT DOVE *Ptilinopus viridis* Plate 33

(Ptilope turvert)

Description 21 cm. Small compact fruit dove with large purple-red breast-patch. Green with variably grey head, pale grey shoulder-patch and spots on tertials, grey terminal tail-band, red throat and breast and pale yellow undertail-coverts with green streaks. Yellow bill has red base. Juvenile often has smaller red breast-patch mottled with olive, less distinct grey shoulder-patch and broader paler yellow wing-covert fringes.
Similar species Adult's red breast-patch distinctive. Differs from similar Knob-billed Fruit Dove, on Lihir and Tanga, by lacking red knob and orange belly of adult, and from juvenile by grey on head and pale yellow undertail-coverts with green spots. Juvenile differs from Yellow-bibbed and White-bibbed Fruit Doves by pale grey shoulder-patch and spots on tertials, patterned dull yellow undertail-coverts, red bill-base and non-contrasting lores. From female Superb Fruit Dove by plain belly pattern, and grey on shoulder or tertials.
Voice Series of about five soft double *whoo-hoooo* notes, with longer higher-pitched second note, sometimes preceded or followed by series of upslurred double or single *whoo* notes, accelerating and dropping in pitch and volume. A quiet *brrr* trill.
Habits Lowland forest, especially degraded forest with figs including secondary growth, gardens, overgrown plantations and fringes of towns. Commonest in coastal lowlands but occurs rarely up to 950 m. Usually seen singly, in pairs or in flocks at fruiting figs, where often with imperial pigeons and other species. Often conspicuous, perching in open and chasing other species away from fruiting trees.
Conservation status Common on most islands.
Range *P. v. lewisii* is endemic to Manus, islands east of New Ireland and Solomons, including Manus, Lihir, Tanga, Nissan, Buka, Bougainville and the Solomons east to Ulawa, including Shortland, Choiseul, Isabel, Vella Lavella, Ranongga, Gizo, Kolombangara, New Georgia, Vangunu, Nggatokae, Rendova, Russell Is, Florida Is, Guadalcanal, Malaita, Ndai and Ulawa, but appears to be expanding its range and may occur on other islands. Elsewhere, other subspecies occur in Indonesia, New Guinea and nearby islands.

WHITE-HEADED FRUIT DOVE *Ptilinopus eugeniae* Plate 33

(Also treated as a subspecies of Claret-breasted Fruit Dove *P. viridis*; Ptilope d'Eugénie)

Description 20 cm. A small compact fruit dove with a white head and purple-red breast-patch. Plumage is otherwise green, greyer on lower breast and belly, with grey spots on shoulder and tertials, grey terminal tail-band, and yellowish vent and undertail-coverts with green streaks. Juvenile has green head with whitish forehead and throat, a few red feathers on breast, often no grey wing-spots and broader yellow fringes on wing-coverts.
Similar species Distinctive white head and red breast. Juvenile differs from Yellow-bibbed and Silver-capped Fruit Doves by pale grey shoulder-patch and tertial spots, grey-green belly, dull yellow undertail-coverts and yellow-green bill with red base.
Voice As Claret-breasted Fruit Dove.
Habits Forest, where locally common in degraded forest especially on small islands and hills to at least 700 m. Usually in singles or pairs, less often small flocks especially at figs and fruiting trees.
Conservation status Fairly common and locally tolerant of forest degradation. IUCN: Near Threatened.
Range Endemic to Makira and the adjacent small islands of Ugi and Three Sisters.

KNOB-BILLED FRUIT DOVE *Ptilinopus insolitus* Plate 33

(Red-knobbed Fruit Dove; Ptilope casqué)

Description 23 cm. Small fat fruit dove with large swollen bright red cere and bright orange belly-patch. Generally green with ashy-grey shoulder-patch and spots on scapulars and tertials, grey terminal tail-band, yellow vent and pale yellow undertail-coverts with green streaks. Very pale eye, often whitish. Juvenile unknown but likely to have small knob and all-green plumage except for yellow fringes, especially on belly and undertail-coverts.
Similar species Red knob and orange belly distinctive. Juvenile differs from juvenile Claret-breasted Fruit Dove on Lihir and Tanga by variably sized red knob, uniform green head and green underparts with yellow fringes and often some orange belly feathers.

Voice Varied, including a distinctive, slow, rather mournful four-note phrase, softer than Red-knobbed Imperial Pigeon, consisting of a long-drawn-out upslurred note, short falling note, medium-long upslur and downslur: *hwooooo-hu-wooo-huu*, lasting c.3.5 seconds and repeated about every 15 seconds; may be shortened by missing or slurring notes. Also an accelerating series of about ten notes becoming quieter, often preceded by one or two slower notes, *hoop—hoop—hoop-hoop-oop-oop-opopopopopop*, or preceded by long upslurred *hwoooo*. Single *hoo* notes. Mewing *arrrh*. Surprised *vrrroo!*
Habits Lowland forest, often commoner in secondary habitats including secondary growth and open habitats with large trees, even in villages. Habitat varies, occurring in all types on Sakar and Lavongai, mostly in secondary habitats on New Britain and New Ireland, and restricted to hills on Long, Crown and Tolokiwa. Common in lowlands and hills, uncommon in low mountains to 1200 m. Gregarious, sometimes in flocks of up to 40 but often singly or small parties. Often perches conspicuously on open branches above canopy and flies over canopy.
Conservation status Common but uncommon on Mussau.
Range Endemic to St Matthias Is and Bismarcks.
P. i. inferior, endemic to Mussau and Emirau, is smaller with rusty-brown on neck and lesser coverts beside the grey shoulder-patch, and possibly a smaller cere.
P. i. insolitus is endemic to the Bismarcks including Lavongai, New Ireland, Djaul, Tabar, Lihir, Feni, Crown, Long, Tolokiwa, Umboi, Sakar, New Britain, Lolobau, Watom and Duke of York. Elsewhere, records of probable vagrants on Purdy Is and at Bogia on New Guinea.

CLOVEN-FEATHERED DOVE *Drepanoptila holosericea* — Plate 37

(*Ptilinopus holosericea*; Ptilope vlouvlou)

Description 28 cm. Distinctive large bright green dove with vertical forehead and short tail. Two broad silver-grey bars on tail and wing-coverts, and about five bars on tertials, white central throat, and white and black breast-band. Yellow belly to undertail-coverts, with green flanks and thighs, and fluffy white legs. In flight, has short broad tail and very broad rounded wings. Female duller green with less defined wing-covert bars, tail bars and breast-band, and strong green wash on yellowish belly. Juvenile almost lacks the silvery bars and has broad yellow fringes on wings.
Similar species Distinctive, although see Red-bellied Fruit Dove and Pacific Emerald Dove.
Voice Deep slow and regular *oo-oo-oo-oo*. Or *woo-waaow—oo—oo—oo* with lower and softer first double-note falling then rising in tone. Disyllabic *whoo-oo*, first note long, deep and vibrant for about two seconds, second short and higher for fraction of second.
Habits Forest, especially humid forest in hills up to 1000 m, including degraded forest and open *Melaleuca* savanna close to humid forest. Usually singles but sometimes in large flocks at fruiting trees. Unobtrusive in canopy and rarely seen unless calling or in flight, when cloven or notched wing feathers create a distinctive loud whistling or hissing sound.
Conservation status Locally common, but sometimes rare, and rarely hunted. IUCN: Near Threatened.
Range Endemic to New Caledonia, on Grande Terre and Ile des Pins.

PACIFIC IMPERIAL PIGEON *Ducula pacifica* — Plate 34

(Carpophage pacifique)

Description 39 cm. Large grey pigeon with large black cere. Ashy-grey head and neck, faint white ring around eye and bill-base, pink wash on breast and belly, and dull chestnut vent and undertail-coverts. Green gloss on dark mantle, wings and tail, sometimes with blue and bronze gloss. In flight, underwing-coverts dark grey, only slightly paler than flight feathers. Flight is fast and direct with slow deep wing-beats and relatively long tail. Female duller with smaller cere. Juvenile lacks enlarged cere and is duller, lacking pink wash.
Similar species Enlarged black cere of adult distinctive, but note that Red-knobbed Imperial Pigeon, on larger islands in Bismarcks and Solomons, has red enlarged cere. Also from Island Imperial Pigeon, on Wuvulu, Hermit Is, Mussau, Ramos and Three Sisters, by darker underparts, more contrasting darker wings, uniform underwing, and indistinct paler patches around bill-base and eye.
Voice Most commonly, a growling or rolling *crrrrrooo* with rising inflection. Many variants including a similar but double note *rooo-prrrooooooo*, sometimes rising then falling in pitch. A 'wetter', more bubbling call *br-r-r-r-r-r-r-*. A deep drawn-out *hooOOOoo*.
Habits Typically on small remote islands without other imperial pigeon species, but also on larger islands in Vanuatu. Forest including primary forest, secondary growth, cultivated areas, parkland, dry coastal forest and scrub and overgrown coconut plantations. Less common on hills and rarely found in montane forest up to 1000 m except where Vanuatu Imperial Pigeon is absent. Fairly gregarious, including flocks of over 50. Nomadic and often seen flying high above forest or between islands.

Conservation status Common on most islands, but locally rare where hunted, and rare on islands with other large pigeon species including Mussau, Nissan and New Caledonia. Not threatened.
Range Temotu, Vanuatu and New Caledonia, and remote islands in north Melanesia. May be vagrant to Grande Terre and other islands, including coasts of larger islands in north Melanesia.
D. p. sejuncta on Wuvulu, Ninigo, Hermit, Kaniet, Mussau, Tench and Nissan is smaller with a paler, lighter grey crown, hindneck and underparts; elsewhere it occurs on tiny islands off north New Guinea.
D. p. pacifica inhabits Nukumanu, Ontong Java, Ramos, Ndai, Rennell, Bellona, Sikaiana, Three Sisters, throughout Temotu and Vanuatu, Lifou, and visits Ouvéa and Grande Terre; elsewhere it occurs on islands off eastern Papua New Guinea and east through Fiji and Tonga to the Cook Islands.

RED-KNOBBED IMPERIAL PIGEON *Ducula rubricera* Plate 34

(Red-knobbed Pigeon; Carpophage à cire rouge)

Description 41 cm. Large pigeon with enlarged red cere. Pale grey head, neck and breast with pink wash on face and breast. Dark rufous belly to undertail-coverts. Bright metallic green upperparts, wings and tail with blue reflections, especially on tail. In flight, underwing-coverts are pale grey contrasting with darker flight feathers. Male has more bronze gloss on mantle. Juvenile has smaller paler cere and, at least in the Solomons, some narrow rufous fringes on grey breast.
Similar species Enlarged red cere differs from all except Knob-billed Fruit Dove, from which it differs by pale grey head, neck and breast and larger size. From Pacific Imperial Pigeon by red cere and rufous belly. Juvenile differs from Island Imperial Pigeon by rufous belly and darker glossier upperparts.
Voice Calls often. Variable. A loud barking *wrarh!* or more disyllabic *ku-wau*, often repeated as series of 3–6 notes, lower-pitched and more rolling than Bismarck Crow. A deep slow rolling *brrrOOow* or *hooOOah* rising then falling in pitch and volume, lasting one or two seconds and repeated every 7–8 seconds. May be more clearly trisyllabic *hoo-woo-hoo* or four notes *oo-woo-oo-hoo*. Longer laughing series of about seven *brrr* growls, accelerating and increasing then decreasing in pitch and trailing off in volume, lower-pitched and much rarer than similar call of Island Imperial Pigeon. Very deep *vroooo* boom. May also mimic calls of other large pigeons.
Habits Forest, including forest edge, old secondary forest and sometimes overgrown plantations and isolated trees in gardens when close to old-growth forest. Commonest in lowlands and hills up to c.500 m, rarely to 1250 m. Fairly gregarious, usually singles or pairs but also in small flocks of up to 40 in figs and fruiting trees and flying to communal roosts. Usually high in forest canopy, rarely perching in open.
Conservation status Common on most islands but threatened by logging of lowland forests. IUCN: Near Threatened.
Range Endemic to the Bismarcks and Solomons.
D. r. rubricera is endemic to New Ireland and New Britain, including Lavongai, Djaul, Tabar, Lihir, Tanga, Feni, Umboi, Sakar, Lolobau, Watom and Duke of York.
D. r. rufigula, endemic to the Solomons, including Buka, Bougainville, Shortland, Choiseul, Isabel, Vella Lavella, Ranongga, Simbo, Gizo, Kolombangara, New Georgia, Vangunu, Nggatokae, Rendova, Florida Is, Guadalcanal, Malaita, Ulawa, Makira, Ugi, Three Sisters and Santa Ana, but not Rennell or Temotu, has a darker grey head, neck and breast, pink restricted to throat and ear-coverts, darker rufous-pink lower breast, darker deep chestnut belly to undertail-coverts and darker grey underwing-coverts.

FINSCH'S IMPERIAL PIGEON *Ducula finschii* Plate 34

(Carpophage de Finsch)

Description 36 cm. Small imperial pigeon with conspicuous silvery tail-band. Pale grey crown to nape, pinkish-grey face to breast, paler spectacles, and orange-rufous belly to undertail-coverts. Dark metallic green upperparts, with distinct bronze tone on mantle and blue on wings and tail, and well-defined pale grey subterminal tail-band. Female darker and greyer on head, neck and breast. Juvenile has duller browner wing-coverts.
Similar species Distinctive tail-band and rufous belly, but some fruit doves and Papuan Mountain Pigeon have pale grey terminal tail-bands. Differs from other imperial pigeons by smaller size. Differs from fruit doves by pale grey head and breast.
Voice A long deep tremulous *vrrrRRRRoooo*, falling then rising in pitch, and trailing off in volume, reminiscent of distant klaxon or air-raid siren. Often preceded by one or two short gruff *wra* notes. Rarely just a single *wra*.
Habits Old-growth forest and forest edge in lowlands, hills and lower mountains to 1500 m, especially between 200–900 m. Less common in degraded or drier forest. Usually solitary and unobtrusive in mid-storey or canopy, rarely in fruiting figs or flying above canopy.

Conservation status Fairly common in old-growth forest in hills, otherwise uncommon or rare. IUCN: Near Threatened.
Range Endemic to New Ireland and New Britain, including Lavongai and Umboi, and vagrant to Watom.

ISLAND IMPERIAL PIGEON *Ducula pistrinaria* Plate 34

(Grey Imperial Pigeon; Carpophage meunier)

Description 43 cm. Large pale grey pigeon with pale eye-ring. Pale grey head, neck and underparts with white around bill-base and white spectacles, slight pink wash to face and breast, and dark chestnut undertail-coverts. Dark glossy grey-green upperparts, merging into grey hindneck. In flight, pale grey underwing-coverts contrast strongly with dark wing feathers and tail. Juvenile duller, lacks pink but has some buff fringes on underparts, and is less glossy on upperparts.
Similar species Differs from Red-knobbed Imperial Pigeon by lacking large red cere of adults, and by grey belly extending to vent and duller greyer upperparts. From Pacific Imperial Pigeon, on Wuvulu, Hermit, Ramos, Three Sisters and vagrant to many other islands, by lacking large black cere of adults, otherwise by clearer white around bill-base and eyes, and underwing-coverts paler than flight feathers.
Voice Typically a deep laughing series of throaty notes, starting with a few emphatic upslurred notes, then dropping in pitch and volume, *wuup-wuup-woo-woo-wo-wo-wo-o-o-o-o*, faster and high-pitched than Red-knobbed Imperial Pigeon. A slow *c-wooooohooo* rising in pitch and volume then trailing off, repeated every 10–20 seconds, but initial note difficult to hear. A rather high-pitched purring *crrrrrurrr.* rising then falling in pitch and volume. May also mimic calls of other pigeon species.
Habits Typically a species of small islands and coasts of larger islands which have other species of imperial pigeon. Forest including mangroves, coastal forest, primary lowland forest, overgrown coconut plantations and degraded habitats with tall trees. Uncommon away from coast on large islands but recorded to 250 m on New Britain and, exceptionally, 600 m on Bougainville. Usually seen singly, in pairs or small flocks; in larger flocks at communal roost and breeding sites, often on small islets off larger islands. Nomadic, often flying over sea with strong direct flight.
Conservation status Locally common but rarer in east Solomons, and declining through loss of coastal forest and perhaps hunting. Not threatened.
Range Admiralties, St Matthias Is, Bismarcks and Solomons.
D. p. rhodinolaema, almost endemic to the Admiralties, including Wuvulu, Hermit Is, Manus, Lou, Nauna and Tong and perhaps St Matthias, has dark, more intensely glossy green upperparts with bronze and blue reflections, and greyer underparts with pink restricted to throat and ear-coverts; elsewhere it occurs on some small islands off north New Guinea.
D. p. vanwyckii, endemic to the Bismarcks, including Lavongai, New Ireland, Djaul, Tabar, Crown, Long, Tolokiwa, Umboi, New Britain, Bali, Witu, Lolobau, Watom, Duke of York and probably Mussau and Emirau, is slightly less glossy above than *D. p. rhodinolaema*, but these may intergrade.
D. p. pistrinaria, endemic to Lihir, Tanga, Feni, Nissan, and the Solomons from Buka and Bougainville east through to Makira, including Ulawa, Ugi, Ulawa, Three Sisters and Santa Ana but not Ndai, Ontong Java, Rennell or Temotu, has paler grey upperparts with slight green gloss and paler pinker underparts.
Elsewhere, *D. p. postrema* occurs on small islands off east New Guinea.

CHESTNUT-BELLIED IMPERIAL PIGEON *Ducula brenchleyi* Plate 34

(Carpophage de Brenchley)

Description 38 cm. Large dark pigeon with paler greyer head and purple-washed underparts. Sooty-grey upperparts, grey head and upper neck, deep purple-grey throat shading into deep purple breast and purple-chestnut belly to undertail-coverts. Some birds have contrasting silvery-grey cap, others have all-dark head. In flight, chestnut belly extends onto underwing-coverts, contrasting with dark grey underwing. Juvenile has yellowish-buff chin and throat, shading into sooty-grey head and breast which lack any purple tones.
Similar species Differs from other large pigeons by relatively slender build and long tail; in flight, chestnut underwing-coverts are distinctive. Differs from Island Imperial Pigeon by darker, more purple tones, chestnut belly and no pale spectacles. From Yellow-legged Pigeon by less contrasting pale head, and paler underparts.
Voice Calls rather infrequently. A deep, smooth, prolonged *ooOOOoo*, rising then falling in pitch, often repeated three times, sometimes double-notes. A rather quiet cat-like *gaooo*.
Habits Old-growth forest, sometimes also secondary forest, from sea-level to at least 700 m, commonest in hills. Canopy, often on exposed perches. Rather gregarious, often with other pigeon species at fruiting trees, but also frequently seen singly or in pairs. Locally nomadic in search of fruiting trees.

Conservation status Locally uncommon on Makira but rare elsewhere. Confiding gregarious habits make it susceptible to hunting, exacerbated by forest loss. IUCN: Vulnerable.
Range Endemic to east Solomons, including Guadalcanal, Malaita, Makira and the smaller islands of Ulawa, Ugi and Three Sisters.

VANUATU IMPERIAL PIGEON *Ducula bakeri* Plate 35

(Baker's [Imperial] Pigeon; Vanuatu Mountain Pigeon; Carpophage de Baker)

Description 40 cm. Large dark grey pigeon with paler head and purplish breast. Blue-grey head contrasts with dark sooty-grey upperparts and dark purple-chestnut collar, neck and breast, which merges into deep chestnut belly and slightly paler rufous undertail-coverts. In flight, shows chestnut underwing-coverts and slightly paler rufous flight feathers. Juvenile much duller, without no gloss but rufous fringes on upperparts.
Similar species Differs from Pacific Imperial Pigeon by much darker purple-chestnut underparts and underwing-coverts and no black knob. From Metallic Pigeon by purple-chestnut in plumage and no white throat.
Voice A series of 1–5 long powerful, booming notes *hoow-hoow-hoow-*, repeated at irregular intervals. Occasional deep purring *br-r-r-r-r*.
Habits Hill and montane forest, from sea-level in Banks Is but above 300 m on larger islands. Usually in singles or pairs but sometimes small flocks at fruiting trees. Unobtrusive and shy in canopy and sometimes in understorey, but may perch on exposed branches in early morning. Nomadic within larger islands.
Conservation status Fairly common in remote mountains, but uncommon or rare where hunted. IUCN: Vulnerable.
Range Endemic to north Vanuatu, on Ureparapara, Vanua Lava, Gaua, Santo, Maewo, Ambae, Pentecost and Ambrym.

GOLIATH IMPERIAL PIGEON *Ducula goliath* Plate 35

(New Caledonian/Giant Imperial Pigeon; Carpophage géant)

Description 51 cm. Very large dark brown and grey pigeon. Relatively long, slightly decurved bill and long tail. Streaky blue-grey head, neck and breast, and deep chestnut belly shading into paler buffy undertail-coverts. Sooty-grey upperparts with pale grey panel on bases of primaries and dark chestnut subterminal tail-band. Juvenile duller and browner with chestnut fringes on wing-coverts, lacks streaks on neck and breast and has less distinct tail-band.
Similar species Differs from Metallic Pigeon by larger size, pale undertail-coverts, broader wings and no white throat.
Voice Series of very deep booms, often with longer pause after first two notes *oom, oom, oom—oom—oom—oom*, not varying in pitch or volume, tone similar to blowing over an empty bottle. A very deep loud croaking roar.
Habits Forest, especially in more remote areas with less hunting. Usually in singles or pairs, tame in forest canopy and mid-storey or flying noisily within forest or above canopy.
Conservation status Fairly common where not hunted. IUCN: Near Threatened.
Range Endemic to New Caledonia, on Grande Terre and Ile des Pins.

BLACK IMPERIAL PIGEON *Ducula melanochroa* Plate 35

(Bismarck Imperial Pigeon; Carpophage noir)

Description 43 cm. Large stout black pigeon. All glossy black except for pale grey scalloping on wings, very dark chestnut undertail-coverts and silver-grey undertail. Conspicuous red eye and eye-ring. In flight, appears heavy with slow wing-beats and deep chest. Juvenile has slightly paler undertail-coverts.
Similar species Distinctive all-black plumage. Differs from flying juvenile Nicobar Pigeon by longer tail, shorter wings and short thick neck. From Metallic Pigeon by pale undertail and lack of white throat.
Voice Series of usually three very deep booming notes *vrrrhu-hoo-ooo*, first note loudest, longest and rising in pitch, the others falling in pitch and quavering in volume. Or a series of about three paired notes *vrrhu-hoo, vrrhu-hoo, vrrhu-hoo*. Hornbill-like *arh!*
Habits Forest, especially old-growth hill forest, including moss forest and forest edge. From sea-level and lowlands, where rare, to 1850 m. Singles, pairs or flocks in fruiting trees, often conspicuously perched above canopy or flying high over forest. Probably nomadic especially to lowlands, with flocks occasionally seen flying downhill with Papuan Mountain Pigeons.
Conservation status Often commonest large pigeon in hills of New Britain, New Ireland and Umboi but rare in lowlands and probably vagrant to Watom and Duke of York.
Range Endemic to New Britain and New Ireland, including Umboi, Watom and Duke of York.

TORRESIAN IMPERIAL PIGEON *Ducula spilorrhoa* Plate 35

(Torres Strait Imperial Pigeon; also treated as a subspecies of Pied Imperial Pigeon *D. bicolor*; Carpophage argenté)

Description 38 cm. Large pied pigeon. Creamy-white, sometimes yellowish on nape, with black greater primary coverts, alula, primaries and secondaries. Vent and thighs have large black spots, forming bars on undertail-coverts. Tail-tip black, broadest centrally, and hardly any black on outer feathers. Underwing-coverts entirely white. Juvenile is greyer on head and neck and yellower on underparts, with yellow fringes all over, and may lack black tips to outer tail feathers.
Similar species Distinctive white plumage, shared only by Blue-eyed Cockatoo. Differs from Yellowish Imperial Pigeon by no yellow or limited pale yellow wash, white lesser primary coverts contrasting with black alula, less black on undertail-coverts, very little black on outer tail feathers, and white primary underwing-coverts.
Voice Usually silent. Loud, deep disyllabic, sometimes trisyllabic, *who-WHOOO*, repeated at intervals of several seconds. (Call description from New Guinea and Australia.)
Habits Small forested islands and coastal forest, including mangroves and degraded forest. Gregarious, usually seen in small flocks but flocks can be very large when flying to and from roost, often in mangroves or small islands. Usually nomadic and often fly long distances high over sea.
Conservation status Poorly known in Melanesia, where confused with Yellowish Imperial Pigeon. Probably rare vagrant but may be regular visitor or even breed on westernmost islands. Common elsewhere in range. Not threatened.
Range One specimen from Umboi and another possibly from New Britain. May have been overlooked elsewhere in Bismarcks, especially islands west of New Britain. Elsewhere, *D. s. spilorrhoa* occurs across lowland New Guinea, nearby islands and north Australia.

YELLOWISH IMPERIAL PIGEON *Ducula subflavescens* Plate 35

(Yellow-tinted Imperial Pigeon; also treated as a subspecies of Torresian Imperial Pigeon *D. spilorrhoa* or Pied Imperial Pigeon *D. bicolor*)

Description 38 cm. Large black and creamy-yellow pigeon. Relatively small, short-tailed and compact compared to other imperial pigeons. Black primary coverts, primary underwing-coverts, primaries and secondaries. Vent and thighs have large black spots, forming broad bars on undertail-coverts. Black tail-tip, broader in centre and narrower on outer feathers. Juvenile unknown but may be greyer on head and neck, and lack black tips to outer tail feathers, like Torresian Imperial Pigeon.
Similar species Distinctive creamy-white plumage, shared only by Blue-eyed Cockatoo. Differs from Torresian Imperial Pigeon by deep yellow wash over all white plumage, black lesser primary coverts and alula, broader black undertail-covert bars, broad black tips to outer tail feathers, and underwing primary coverts black beyond carpal.
Voice Usually silent. Quiet nasal hoot *vroo*. Probably also a deep resonating *oo-oom*, first note upslurred, second slightly dropping in pitch.
Habits Forest, including primary forest, forest edge, logged forest and scattered large trees in more open habitats. Commonest close to coast but wanders widely to 900 m on New Britain, 560 m on New Ireland and across Manus. Usually in small flocks but may occur singly or in pairs. Often forages with other imperial pigeon species but flies in separate flocks. Sometimes flocks roost coastally and fly inland each day.
Conservation status Locally fairly common but rare or absent in places. May be threatened by loss of coastal and lowland forest. IUCN: Near Threatened.
Range Endemic to the Admiralties and Bismarcks, including Manus, Lou, Nauna, Lavongai, New Ireland, New Britain, Lolobau, Watom and Duke of York. Probably on Crown, Long, Tolokiwa, Umboi and Sakar, but these may be Torresian Imperial Pigeon.

PAPUAN MOUNTAIN PIGEON *Gymnophaps albertisii* Plate 37

(Carpophage d'Albertis)

Description 34 cm. Relatively slender long-tailed medium-large pigeon. Large red bare patch around eye and bill. Dark grey head, neck and upperparts with black scalloping on wings and paler grey terminal tail-band. White or pale pink or pale grey lower throat and breast, purple-chestnut belly and grey undertail-coverts. Male has dark purple-chestnut throat and ear-coverts. Female has greyer throat and ear-coverts, and grey mottling on breast. Juvenile duller and browner, mottled with grey on breast, with pale brown fringes on belly to undertail-coverts.
Similar species Long wings and tail, pale breast and pale terminal tail-band are distinctive.
Voice Usually silent. Muted, deep *woooooom* or *woom* which rises in pitch, and soft querulous whistles in breeding season. (Call description from New Guinea.)

Habits Hill and mountain forest up to tree-line, occasionally seen flying over flat lowlands, but rarely feeds in lowlands. Gregarious, usually seen in small flocks in canopy, not mixing with other species. Highly mobile and partially nomadic. Usually roosts at high altitudes, flocks swooping steeply downhill in morning, producing loud 'whooshing' on swept-back wings. In display, male plummets vertically with closed wings from high perch, then suddenly flies up almost vertically, and repeats high above forest.
Conservation status Generally uncommon or rare, but locally common elsewhere in range. Not threatened.
Range *G. a. albertisii* breeds on New Britain and New Ireland, and elsewhere on New Guinea including Yapen and Goodenough, and *G. a. exul* on Bacan in Indonesia.

PALE MOUNTAIN PIGEON *Gymnophaps solomonensis* Plate 37

(Solomons Mountain Pigeon; Carpophage des Salomon)

Description 38 cm. Slender long-tailed pale grey and blackish pigeon. Pale ash-grey head, neck, underparts and tail, slightly darker on belly to undertail-coverts. Dark grey mantle and wings scalloped with darker fringes on coverts. Upperparts vary from glossy greenish-black to dull greyish-black, and underparts vary from pale grey to white or with a distinct pink wash. Juvenile has buff on crown, wing-coverts and undertail-coverts, and no pink on underparts.
Similar species Differs from Crested Cuckoo-Dove by longer wings and shorter tail, lack of crest, scaly upperparts, and habits. Differs from imperial pigeons by longer off-white tail, longer wings and paler head and underparts.
Voice Usually silent. Nasal pig-like wheeze *vrrhee!* Quiet throaty *vrrhu*.
Habits Breeds in mountain forest including stunted moss forest between *c*.500–1565 m but feeds down to sea-level, including in degraded and old growth secondary forest. Gregarious, usually seen in small flocks in canopy but occasionally in understorey. As with Papuan Mountain Pigeon, flocks roost high in mountains and many 'whoosh' down to lowlands in early morning.
Conservation status Locally fairly common on Bougainville and Kolombangara, but uncommon on Guadalcanal and Malaita.
Range Endemic to the Solomons, where recorded from Bougainville, Kolombangara, Vangunu, Guadalcanal and Malaita.

COCKATOOS Cacatuidae

Very large parrots with massive bills, medium-length tail and erectile crest. Melanesian species are entirely white except for some yellow on crest and vent, blue naked facial skin and grey bill and legs.

SOLOMONS COCKATOO *Cacatua ducorpsii* Plate 38

(Ducorps's Cockatoo; Solomon Islands Corella; Cacatoès de Ducorps)

Description 34 cm. Large white parrot with erectile crest on crown. All white except for yellow wash on underwing and undertail, broad pale blue eye-ring, and dark grey bill and feet. Short crest often erected into raised helmet. Eye dark brown in male, reddish in female and dark grey in juvenile.
Similar species Only white parrot in Solomons. Blue-eyed Cockatoo on New Britain is larger with yellow on crest.
Voice Repeated loud harsh screeching *eerk* or *arrk* notes. Nasal *tcha-tchow*. Harsher and more discordant than Eclectus Parrot.
Habits Lowland forest including degraded forest and gardens with large trees, sometimes wandering into open habitats. Usually in pairs or flocks up to 15 in lowlands and hills, rare in mountains above 700 m, rarely up to 1800 m. Noisy and conspicuous, often mobbing observer or perching on exposed branches. Flies high over forest with buoyant but erratic flight, including shallow fluttering wing-beats, short glides on down-swept wings, deep wing-beats with wings held high above body, and banking or flopping from one side to another.
Conservation status Generally common but uncommon in some of the New Georgia group. Not threatened.
Range Endemic to Solomons, from Bougainville to Malaita and Guadalcanal, including Buka, Shortland, most small islands in New Georgia group and Russell Is but not Ranongga or Makira group.

BLUE-EYED COCKATOO *Cacatua ophthalmica* Plate 38

(Cacatoès aux yeux bleus)

Description 50 cm. Very large white parrot. All white except for yellow wash on underwing and undertail, and yellow on crest, often hidden under white crown feathers until erected as rounded back-swept crest. Broad pale blue eye-ring, and dark grey bill and feet. Eye dark brown in male, red-brown in female and grey in juvenile.

Similar species The only other large white forest bird in the Bismarcks is Yellowish Imperial Pigeon. Solomons Cockatoo is smaller and lacks yellow in crest, and other species of escaped cockatoo, particularly Sulphur-crested Cockatoo *C. galerita* of New Guinea, have different, often upturned, crest.
Voice Loud hoarse screeching, often repeated in long series, including chimpanzee-like screaming. Harsher and more discordant than Eclectus Parrot.
Habits Lowland forest including degraded forest and gardens, sometimes wandering into open habitats. Usually singles, pairs or small flocks in lowlands and hills, rare in mountains above 1000 m. Conspicuous and obtrusive, often mobbing observer or flushing a short distance to perch and screech. Flies with shallow fluttering wing-beats, interspersed with short glides on down-swept wings, occasionally wings held up in shallow V.
Conservation status Fairly common, but threatened by lowland forest loss and may be dependent on large trees for nesting. IUCN: Vulnerable.
Range Endemic to New Britain. (A cockatoo, probably this species, occurred prehistorically on New Ireland and Mussau.)

PARROTS Psittacidae

Conspicuous, noisy, stocky forest birds which are usually bright green and red. Parrots have stout hooked bills and short but strong legs and feet, and climb acrobatically within trees. Often wander far in search of seasonal fruits, seeds and nectar. Many species roost gregariously with conspicuous evening and dawn flights. Hanging parrots *Loriculus* are tiny, short-tailed, acrobatic and partly nectarivorous like lorikeets. Pygmy Parrots *Micropsitta* are tiny, short-tailed, gregarious, and creep up and down tree-trunks and branches, feeding on lichens and fungi, with widely splayed feet and tail acting as prop. Lories and lorikeets are fast-flying nectar-feeders and often aggregate at flowering trees including coconuts. Lories *Lorius* are stout, short-tailed and usually in pairs. Lorikeets *Chalcopsitta*, *Trichoglossus* and *Charmosyna* are long-tailed and gregarious. Parakeets *Eunymphicus* and *Cyanoramphus* are long-tailed green parrots, restricted in Melanesia to New Caledonia. *Geoffroyus* and *Eclectus* are large parrots with short tails, usually in pairs or small flocks.

BISMARCK HANGING PARROT *Loriculus tener* — Plate 40

(Green-fronted Hanging Parrot; Coryllis des Bismarck)

Description 10 cm. Tiny bright green parrot with large red throat-spot. Uniform grass-green except for orange-red throat-patch, yellowish-green rump and uppertail-coverts, pale blue underwing and undertail, black bill, whitish eye and red legs. Female has blue wash on forehead, forecrown and cheeks. Immature lacks red throat-spot and has pale brown bill.
Similar species Differs from pygmy parrots by cleaner brighter green plumage, plainer tail-pattern, habits and, in adults, a clear red throat-spot. In flight, appears longer-tailed and less dumpy, more like a short-tailed lorikeet.
Voice High-pitched repeated *tsip, tsip* or *tse, tse*, lower-pitched and slower than pygmy parrot calls. Also a longer buzzing *tseee-up*.
Habits Restricted to lowland forest to c.500 m, but recorded once at 900 m; usually seen around forest edge, perhaps because it is otherwise difficult to see. Singles and pairs forage unobtrusively in forest canopy, usually in or around flowers and small fruit. Usually perches upright or with body leaning forward. Often acrobatic, hanging upside-down when foraging.
Conservation status Uncommon or rare but probably under-recorded. Possibly at risk from forest clearance and logging but is apparently commoner or easier to see in degraded habitats. IUCN: Near Threatened.
Range Endemic to the Bismarcks, where known only from Lavongai, New Ireland, New Britain and Duke of York.

BUFF-FACED PYGMY PARROT *Micropsitta pusio* — Plate 40

(Micropsitte à tête fauve)

Description 8 cm. Tiny parrot, largely bright green with yellow-buff face. Dark blue crown over buff face, which extends from forehead and throat to upper neck. Body and wings bright green, slightly paler yellowish on underparts. Black and blue uppertail with yellow spots on outer tail feathers, and yellow undertail-coverts. Female has paler face and crown. Immature has greener crown and less extensive, more yellowish face-patch.
Similar species Differs from female Red-breasted Pygmy Parrot, which is usually in flocks including distinctive males, by lowland distribution, less blue on cap not extending down to eyes, and richer darker face-patch. From Bismarck Hanging Parrot by pale face-patch, no red on throat, tail-pattern and habits.

Voice Quiet, indistinct and easily overlooked. Very thin high-pitched wheezy, often repeated notes e.g. *tzip, tzeee*. Higher-pitched than Red-breasted Pygmy Parrot, more drawn-out and sibilant than Bismarck Hanging Parrot, but similar to myzomelas and Blue-faced Parrotfinch.
Habits Lowland and hill forest, including degraded and secondary forest, to at least 950 m. Singles, pairs and small flocks graze on trunks and branches. Unobtrusive, often overlooked unless calling.
Conservation status Fairly common but under-recorded. Not threatened.
Range New Britain and nearby islands.
M. p. pusio occurs in New Britain, including Witu, Lolobau, Watom and Duke of York, and south-east New Guinea.
M. p. beccarii, on Sakar, Tolokiwa and Umboi, and north New Guinea, is darker, especially on face.
Elsewhere, other subspecies occur on Fergusson, Misima and Tagula off New Guinea.

MEEK'S PYGMY PARROT *Micropsitta meeki* — Plate 40

(Yellow-breasted Pygmy Parrot; Micropsitte de Meek)

Description 10 cm. Tiny bright green parrot with yellow-buff head and breast. Variable head pattern, usually with dull grey-brown crown, face and throat, and yellow supercilium, sides of neck, breast, central belly and undertail-coverts. Head and underparts have variable darker scaly fringes. Female is similar to male but immature is unknown.
Similar species Distinctive, the only tiny parrot in its range.
Voice Very high-pitched repeated thin *tsst*, often repeated at different pitches, e.g. *tseep*. Shorter, with better-defined end to note, and more variable in pitch than Blue-faced Parrotfinch. Higher-pitched and thinner than Bismarck Black Myzomela or Olive-backed Sunbird.
Habits In all forest habitats, including highly degraded forest and scrub. Usually in small vocal flocks moving through forest, often in thickets and on small branches.
Conservation status Fairly common on Manus but seems uncommon on St Matthias. Not threatened.
Range Endemic to Admiralties and St Matthias Is.
M. m. meeki is endemic to Manus and Rambutyo.
M. m. proxima, endemic to St Matthias Is, including Mussau, Eloaua and Emirau, has more yellow on face, including distinct yellow supercilium meeting on forehead.

FINSCH'S PYGMY PARROT *Micropsitta finschii* — Plate 40

(Green Pygmy Parrot; Micropsitte de Finsch)

Description 9 cm. Tiny green parrot. Variably red eye and eye-ring and blue-washed cap. Black and blue uppertail with yellow spots on outer tail feathers and yellow undertail-coverts. Male has blue-washed chin, pink-red cere and eye-ring, and may have orange-red central breast-patch. Female has buff-pink wash on chin, grey cere and no red on belly.
Similar species Differs from female Red-breasted Pygmy Parrot on New Ireland, Bougainville, Kolombangara and Guadalcanal by lowland distribution, no pale buff face and less blue on cap not extending close to eyes. From Bismarck Hanging Parrot on New Ireland by blue patches on head, lack of large clear red throat-spot, tail-pattern and habits.
Voice Repeated very thin high-pitched *tseet*, *zzzee*, or *zeeheee* notes, easily overlooked. Higher-pitched and more buzzing in flight. Similar to Island Thrush but a single tone, not upslurred, more sibilant and quavered. Shriller than flowerpeckers.
Habits Lowland forest, scrubby regrowth, and sometimes coconuts and casuarinas, to at least 1050 m but often replaced above 500 m by Red-breasted Pygmy Parrot where both species occur. Often in pairs, creeping along trunks and branches, sometimes small twigs.
Conservation status Fairly common to common. Not threatened.
Range Endemic to New Ireland and Solomons.
M. f. viridifrons, endemic to New Ireland, including Lavongai, Djaul, Tabar and Lihir; male has extensive blue on crown and cheeks, more blue on uppertail and variable orange-red patch on central belly.
M. f. nanina, endemic to Buka, Bougainville, Choiseul and Isabel; male has small greenish blue crown-patch and plain underparts.
M. f. tristrami, endemic to Vella Lavella, Gizo, Kolombangara, New Georgia, Vangunu, Rendova and Tetepare; male has blue-washed crown and plain underparts.
M. f. aolae, endemic to Guadalcanal and Malaita, including Russell Is and Florida Is; male has pale blue on crown, plain underparts and darker upperparts.
M. f. finschii, endemic to Rennell and Makira, including Ugi; male has green crown and red on central breast.

RED-BREASTED PYGMY PARROT *Micropsitta bruijnii* Plate 40

(Micropsitte de Bruijn)

Description 9 cm. Tiny montane parrot, with distinctive male plumage. Male has orange face and crown, orange-red breast to undertail, and broad dark blue-grey eye-stripe and breast-band joining on nape. Bright green upperparts and flanks. Black and blue uppertail with yellow-orange spots on outer tail feathers. Female is green with orange-buff face and forehead, dark blue crown extending down to eye, yellower underparts and yellow undertail-coverts. Immature as female but has whiter forehead and face, and immature male has orange-red on underparts.
Similar species Overlaps at mid-altitudes with Buff-faced Pygmy Parrot on New Britain and Finsch's Pygmy Parrot on other islands. Usually in larger flocks at higher altitudes than other pygmy parrots. Male is distinctive. Female differs from Buff-faced Pygmy Parrot by blue crown extending down close to eyes and paler buff face, and from Finsch's Pygmy Parrot by buff face-patch and dark blue crown, and from both by more black on wing-coverts. From Bismarck Hanging Parrot in Bismarck lowlands by head and underparts pattern and habits.
Voice Incessant twittering notes, e.g. *tzee, tzu*. Slightly lower-pitched and more paired notes than Buff-faced and Finsch's Pygmy Parrots.
Habits Commonest in tall mid-montane forest, including logged and degraded forest, but rarely mossy montane forest, from 720 m to highest summits, occasionally lower. Usually in flocks, often foraging high in forest canopy and flying above canopy.
Conservation status Uncommon to locally common. Not threatened.
Range Mountains of New Britain, New Ireland, Bougainville, Kolombangara and Guadalcanal.
M. b. necopinata, endemic to New Britain and New Ireland; male has brownish-yellow cap, orange-red cheeks, central breast and belly and yellow undertail-coverts.
M. b. rosea, endemic to Bougainville, Kolombangara and Guadalcanal; male has pinker cap and cheeks, and is red from breast to undertail-coverts.
Elsewhere, other subspecies occur in Indonesia and New Guinea.

CARDINAL LORY *Chalcopsitta cardinalis* Plate 38

(Lori cardinal)

Description 31 cm. Medium-sized lanky red parrot with long wedge-shaped tail. Plumage dull crimson, darker on wings and mantle, with faint barring on underparts. Orange-red bill, dark grey cere and eye-ring, and grey feet. In flight, tail appears long and rounded or graduated diamond shape. Immature paler with yellowish eye and duller bill with black markings.
Similar species Distinctive red plumage is shared only by female Eclectus Parrot, from which it differs by slender shape, long tail and no purple-blue on body and wings. In flight, differs from Coconut Lorikeet, the other medium-sized long-tailed parrot, by red plumage, rounded cuckoo-like tail, often held slightly open showing wedge shape, rounder wings, stouter shape and larger size.
Voice Shrill harsh screeching *zheet-zheet*, usually lower-pitched, more buzzing, less harsh and louder than Coconut Lorikeet, but with some overlap in calls.
Habits Open lowland forests with flowering trees and open habitats with scattered trees and coconuts. Less common in primary forest, uncommon in hills, and rare to 1200 m. Usually in flocks of 6–30 in red flowering trees or coconuts, often mixing with Coconut Lorikeets. Often flies large distances, often high overhead, over short sea crossings and to and from large roosts.
Conservation status Generally common and often abundant, but rare on the Makira group. Not threatened.
Range Endemic to Solomons and islands east of New Ireland, including Tabar, Lihir, where only Mahir, Masahet and possibly other small islands, Tanga, Feni, Nissan, Ontong Java and all small islands in the Solomons from Buka to Ulawa, Makira, Ugi and Three Sisters, but not Rennell.

COCONUT LORIKEET *Trichoglossus haematodus* Plate 39

(Also combined with other lorikeets as Rainbow Lorikeet *T. haematodus*; Loriquet à tête bleue)

Description 27 cm. Medium-sized green, red and purple lorikeet with long pointed tail. Bright green with red breast and dark violet head contrasting with orange-red bill and yellowish hind-collar. Appears green in flight, with red breast and underwing-coverts and broad yellow underwing-bar from below. Immature is duller with dark bill.
Similar species Differs from *Charmosyna* lorikeets by larger size, bulkier body, calls and red on plumage. Only male Red-flanked Lorikeet of the Bismarcks has some red on face and wings. Differs from Cardinal Lory in the Solomons and islands east of New Ireland by more pointed tail, slimmer shape, and green in plumage. Differs from parakeets

on New Caledonia by dark purple head, red breast, faster shallower wing-beats, more pointed tail and wings, and different habits.

Voice Very noisy. Often scolds people. Commonest calls are single or double high-pitched screeches when alarmed, about to fly or flying. Higher-pitched and harsher than larger lorikeets and parakeets. Harsher and more sibilant than *Charmosyna* lorikeets. Occasionally gives other softer, lower-pitched calls. Short high-pitched contact calls.

Habits Often the commonest parrot, especially in lowlands. Commonest in open lowland forests with flowering trees but also in open habitats with scattered trees, coconuts and primary forest patches, and uncommon in montane forest to at least 1900 m. Usually in pairs in forest or in flocks in flowering trees, often mixing with other lorikeet species but flying in separate flocks. Often flies large distances over land and sea. Roosts in rocky crevices on small islets in Admiralties and perhaps elsewhere.

Conservation status Generally common and often abundant. Not threatened.

Range Across Melanesia except some small and isolated islands.

T. h. nesophilus, endemic to Ninigo Is and possibly Hermit Is, has little dark barring on red breast and black head with some greyish-green streaks and violet around forehead and eye.

T. h. flavicans, endemic to Admiralties and Lavongai, and possibly this subspecies on St Matthias group, Nuguria and Hermit Is, as *T. h. nesophilus* but with green or bronze-yellow upperparts.

T. h. massena, endemic to rest of the Bismarcks, Solomons, Temotu and Vanuatu, probably including all the small islands, except Rennell and Duff Is, has green upperparts and smaller red breast-patch; elsewhere this subspecies occurs just outside Melanesia on Karkar.

T. h. deplanchii, endemic to New Caledonia, on Grande Terre, Ile des Pins and introduced on Ouvéa, has more blue on head and less yellow on thighs and undertail.

Elsewhere, other subspecies range from east Indonesia to New Guinea (and closely related forms, previously included within Rainbow Lorikeet *T. haematodus*, occur in central Indonesia and Australia).

PURPLE-BELLIED LORY *Lorius hypoinochrous* — Plate 38

(Eastern Black-naped Lory; Lori à ventre violet)

Description 26 cm. A stocky medium-sized short-tailed parrot. Bright red with green wings and tail, purple belly, black cap and white cere above orange bill. In flight, red body, fairly short broad green wings with broad yellow underwing-bar, red underwing-coverts and yellowish underside to short tail. Immature has brownish bill.

Similar species Distinctive plumage and shape is shared only by White-naped Lory on montane New Ireland. Largely red plumage is shared only by larger female Eclectus Parrot, which lacks green wings and black cap, and long-tailed all-red Cardinal Lory on Tabar and Lihir. In flight, has dumpier shape, shorter tail, broader wings and more whirring wing-beats than Song Parrot.

Voice Varied and similar to but softer than Eclectus Parrot and Coconut Lorikeet, and less melodious than Song Parrot. Most commonly, a long nasal wail *eee-ah* or *we-we-we-we-arr*, rising then falling in pitch. Soft *vraa-raa-raa*. Yelping hawk-like calls.

Habits Lowland forest, including degraded forests and sometimes coconut plantations. Usually in lowlands but rarely in mountains up to 1120 m on New Britain and c.750 m on New Ireland. Pairs and sometimes small flocks are noisy and conspicuous in forest canopy, often in flowering trees. Flies with rapid shallow beats of short wings.

Conservation status Fairly common and tolerant of degraded habitats. Not threatened.

Range *L. i. devittatus* breeds in Bismarcks, including Lavongai, New Ireland, Djaul, Tabar, Lihir, Long, Umboi, Sakar, New Britain, Witu and Lolobau, lacks the black underwing-covert bar of other subspecies; elsewhere, this subspecies occurs in far south-east of New Guinea and D'Entrecasteaux Is, and other subspecies occur in the Louisiade Is off east New Guinea.

[STRESEMANN'S LORY *Lorius amabilis*] — (not illustrated)

Known from one specimen from south New Britain, probably an aberrant Purple-bellied Lory. Differs from that species by lacking the black cap, and has brownish-red eye and yellowish-brown legs.

WHITE-NAPED LORY *Lorius albidinucha* — Plate 38

(Lori à nuque blanche)

Description 26 cm. Medium-sized short-tailed parrot. Appears red with green wings and tail, and black cap. White triangle on nape is visible only at close range, and has black cere above orange bill. In flight, red with rather short broad green wings and broad yellow bar on underwing. Immature unknown but may have brownish bill as Purple-bellied Lory.

Similar species Distinctive plumage and structure is shared only by Purple-bellied Lory, from which it differs by slimmer shape, red belly, white on nape not cere, and yellow narrow broken breast-band. Differs from female Eclectus Parrot by plumage, smaller size, shorter wings, longer tail and faster wing-beats. In flight, has dumpier shape, shorter tail, broader wings and more whirring wing-beats than Song Parrot.
Voice Weak rising whistle *schweet* or *wea*, sometimes repeated. Less harsh than other parrots.
Habits Hill and montane forest between 500–2000 m, overlapping with Purple-bellied Lory between *c.*500–750 m. Singles and pairs. Often flies fast with rapid wing-beats just above forest canopy.
Conservation status Locally fairly common but in small numbers. Occurs mostly above the altitudes threatened by logging. IUCN: Near Threatened.
Range Endemic to New Ireland. Probably occurs in suitable altitudes in central and southern New Ireland but records only from southern massif and Limbin in central New Ireland.

YELLOW-BIBBED LORY *Lorius chlorocercus* — Plate 38

(Lori à collier jaune)

Description 28 cm. Stocky medium-sized short-tailed parrot. Red head and body, green wings and tail, black cap, yellow bib with black extension onto neck-sides and blue thighs. In flight, has rather short broad wings with purple-blue underwing with red central underwing-bar and dirty yellow tail-tip. Immature lacks black on neck-sides and has indistinct yellow bib.
Similar species Distinctive plumage and structure. Differs from Duchess Lorikeet by larger size, stockier build, shorter, more rounded tail, black forehead and yellow restricted to breast. From female Eclectus Parrot by smaller size, green wings and black cap. From Song Parrot in flight by dumpier shape, shorter tail, broader wings and more whirring wing-beats.
Voice Generally lower-pitched and harsher than Cardinal Lory. Varied calls and probably mimics other birds. Creaking nasal *hau, hau…* Slurred multisyllabic shrill wheezy squeals, sometimes mewing like cat. Rising screech *waeek*. Rapid high-pitched *ki-ki-ki-* series similar to *Accipiter* hawk. Typical lorikeet chatters.
Habits Lowland and montane forest, including degraded forest but uncommon in coconuts, to 1550 m, but commonest in mid-altitude hills. Usually in pairs, but also singles and small flocks. Flies with rapid shallow beats of short wings.
Conservation status Common, but uncommon on Rennell where it may have been introduced. Possibly threatened by logging.
Range Endemic to east Solomons, including Guadalcanal, Savo, Malaita, Ulawa, Makira, Ugi, Santa Ana, Santa Catalina and Rennell. Often kept as cage-bird and occasional escapes may occur on other islands in the Solomons.

PALM LORIKEET *Charmosyna palmarum* — Plate 40

(Green Palm Lorikeet; Lori des palmiers)

Description 16 cm. Small grass-green lorikeet. At close range shows orange-red bill and legs, variable-sized small red patch from bill-base to chin, yellow tail-tip and slightly darker upperparts with bronze wash on upper mantle. In flight, shows narrow yellow underwing-bar. Female has less red on chin and lacks bronze on upper mantle. Immature duller, especially bill and eye.
Similar species Differs from Coconut Lorikeet by all-green plumage, smaller size, slimmer body and calls.
Voice Very high-pitched screeching *tsweet-tsweet-* or *shi-shi-* in flight. Slightly harsher and louder when alarmed. Higher-pitched, quieter and less harsh than Coconut Lorikeet, but louder than parrotfinches. Incessant quiet high-pitched twittering when feeding: repeated high thin *tseep* or *srrri*. Chattering *ch-ch-ch-* similar to Cardinal Myzomela but harsher and more varied in tone.
Habits Probably resident in montane forests above 1000 m on Santo, and in coastal forest and coconuts on some small islands, otherwise nomadic and may occur anywhere in range. Usually in small flocks of up to 30 birds in canopy of flowering trees and coconuts, most obvious when flying to and from roost at dawn and dusk.
Conservation status Although locally common, absent from many suitable areas. Populations appear to cycle inexplicably through local extinctions and recolonisations. IUCN: Vulnerable.
Range Endemic to Temotu and Vanuatu. Range appears to fluctuate with cycles of extirpations and recolonisations over periods of decades. Recent records from Nendo, Reef Is, Duff Is, Tikopia, Banks Is, Ambae and Santo. Older records from Tinakula and Vanikoro, and across Vanuatu from the Banks Is to Aneityum, except Torres Is.

RED-CHINNED LORIKEET *Charmosyna rubrigularis* Plate 40

(Lori à menton rouge)

Description 17 cm. Small grass-green lorikeet. At close range, shows orange-red bill and legs, small red throat-patch, yellow tail-tip and slightly darker upperparts. In flight, shows yellow underwing-bar and yellow undertail, with obscure red at base of undertail. Immature has less red on throat and shorter tail.
Similar species Sometimes forms flocks with similar Red-flanked Lorikeet from which it differs by little red in plumage, slimmer with longer tail, and calls. From Coconut Lorikeet by much smaller slimmer size and green head and breast. From pygmy parrots and hanging parrot by long tail.
Voice Very high-pitched *weezt-weeezt-* in flight. Incessant quiet high-pitched twittering when feeding, louder and more strident in flight. Quieter and less harsh than Coconut Lorikeet, higher-pitched and less buzzing than pygmy parrots.
Habits Common in montane forest from c.1000–1800 m, uncommon and localised in lowlands including coastal forest but not coconuts. Highly gregarious, usually in flocks of 10–50 in flowering trees, and flying low over forest after dawn and especially before dusk.
Conservation status Usually common, often abundant on New Britain, although rare and local in lowlands. Not threatened.
Range Endemic to New Ireland and New Britain, and also Karkar just west of Melanesia, where occasionally split as separate subspecies *C. r. krakari*, and possibly Lavongai.

MEEK'S LORIKEET *Charmosyna meeki* Plate 40

(Lori de Meek)

Description 16 cm. Small grass-green lorikeet. At close range shows orange-red bill and legs and slightly darker upperparts with bronze wash on upper mantle and slight grey wash on crown. In flight, shows yellow underwing-bar and yellow tips to undertail. Immature has shorter tail and browner bill.
Similar species Differs from Red-flanked Lorikeet, overlapping only in Bougainville lowlands, by plain green head, no red on underwing, and calls. From Coconut and Duchess Lorikeets by green head and breast, smaller size, slimmer body and calls. From pygmy parrots and hanging parrot by longer tail, habits and calls.
Voice Calls incessantly. Single or series of thin high-pitched screeching *tseek-* notes. Clear notes in flight, harsher and louder when alarmed, and quieter continuous buzzing rattle when feeding *zi-zi-zhe-zhe-zhe...* Similar to Yellow-vented Myzomela, higher-pitched, quieter and less harsh than Coconut Lorikeet, and higher-pitched and less buzzing than pygmy parrots.
Habits Resident in montane forests above 1000 m but nomadic and wanders to lowland forests and coastal coconuts. Usually in small flocks of up to 30 birds in canopy of flowering trees. Often mixes with other lorikeets, especially in lowland flowering trees. Flocks fly low over montane forest ridges at dawn and dusk, some descending to lowlands during day.
Conservation status Usually fairly common above 1000 m on Bougainville, Kolombangara and Guadalcanal, but rarer and local in lowlands and on lower islands. IUCN: Near Threatened.
Range Endemic to Solomons, on Bougainville, Isabel, Kolombangara, New Georgia, Guadalcanal and Malaita, with one report from Makira. May be nomadic across the mountainous islands of the New Georgia group including Vangunu and Rendova but no recent records here or on Malaita.

RED-FLANKED LORIKEET *Charmosyna placentis* Plate 40

(Lori coquet)

Description 17 cm. Small grass-green lorikeet with red and blue patches on males. Orange-red bill and legs and red-tipped yellow undertail. Male is green except for red flanks and throat, blue ear-coverts and, in flight, red axillaries and underwing-coverts and yellow underwing-bar. Female is green with yellow-streaked cheeks and, in flight, shows yellow underwing-bar. Immature as female but has less extensive yellow on ear-coverts. Immature male may have small red patch on face and yellow on forehead.
Similar species Sometimes in mixed flocks with Red-chinned Lorikeet. Differs from Red-chinned and Meek's Lorikeets by male's flank and face colours and female's yellow face. From Coconut and Duchess Lorikeets by green head and breast, smaller size, slimmer body and calls. From pygmy parrots and hanging parrot by longer tail, call and habits.
Voice Distinctive hoarse lisping *kssk, kssk* or *tsh-tsh-tsh-* flight call. Thin high-pitched twittering contact calls when foraging, as other *Charmosyna* lorikeets.
Habits Lowland forest, especially degraded forest with flowering trees or coconuts, less common in primary forest and in hills. Mostly in lowlands, but uncommon above 300 m to at least 1000 m on New Britain. Forages in canopy of flowering trees, including scattered trees in open habitats, coconuts and epiphytic flowers within forest understorey. Usually in pairs or small flocks of up to 10.

Conservation status Usually common in lowlands. Not threatened.
Range *C. p. pallidior*, almost endemic to New Ireland, New Britain and Bougainville including all small islands as far as Nuguria and Nissan and unconfirmed records from Lou and Pak off Manus, differs from other subspecies by paler upperparts, paler blue ear-coverts and green rump; elsewhere occurs on Woodlark I. off east New Guinea, and other subspecies occur in Indonesia and New Guinea.

NEW CALEDONIAN LORIKEET *Charmosyna diadema* Plate 40

(Diademed Lorikeet; Lori à diadème)

Description 19 cm. Small grass-green lorikeet with deep blue crown. Orange-red bill and legs, yellow cheeks and throat, yellower underparts, blue wash on thighs and red on vent. Yellow undertail has black and red bases to outer tail feathers. In flight, has narrow yellow underwing-bar and tail-tip. Male and immature unknown.
Similar species Differs from Coconut Lorikeet, Horned and New Caledonian Parakeets by green face and breast, smaller size and slimmer body.
Voice Unknown but presumed to have similar very high-pitched screeching and twittering as other small lorikeets.
Habits Unknown but presumed to be similar to other small lorikeets. Reports from forest, savanna and scrub, including flowering *Erythrina* trees. Probably most likely to survive as nomadic montane forest species.
Conservation status Known only from two specimens collected before 1860 and unconfirmed reports up to 1970s. IUCN: Critically Endangered.
Range Endemic to New Caledonia, where the only known location is Mt Ignambi.

DUCHESS LORIKEET *Charmosyna margarethae* Plate 39

(Lori de Margaret)

Description 20 cm. Medium-small red and green lorikeet with yellow breast-band and long tail. Bright red body and tail, green wings and mantle, and yellow breast-band bordered with black extending narrowly over back. Sides of rump are red in male, yellow in female. Immature has more obscure yellow band without upper black border, dark scaling on body and duller bare parts.
Similar species Yellow bib and red and green plumage are shared only by Yellow-bibbed Lory on Malaita, Guadalcanal and Makira, from which it differs by smaller size with much longer pointed tail and red forehead, thighs and underwing-coverts. From Cardinal and Coconut Lorikeets by smaller size and plumage pattern. From Meek's Lorikeet by larger size and red in plumage.
Voice Distinctive squeaky quality, recalling Moustached Treeswift. Repeated short disyllabic or multisyllabic shrieks, second note lower-pitched e.g. *whee-wow*, *chu-whee* or *ke-leek*. Chattering song like Song Parrot but squeakier and interspersed with flight-calls. Shrieks and high-pitched chatters like other lorikeets.
Habits Commonest in flowering trees in primary hill forests. Less common in coastal lowland forests, locally including coconuts, and montane forest to 1350 m. Usually in small flocks, often mixed with other lorikeets and lories. Nomadic and often found in specific species of flowering trees.
Conservation status Generally local and uncommon. Status clouded by nomadic habits. IUCN: Near Threatened.
Range Endemic to the mountainous Solomons, on Bougainville, Isabel, Kolombangara, Nggatokae, Guadalcanal, Malaita, Makira, Santa Ana and Santa Catalina.

HORNED PARAKEET *Eunymphicus cornutus* Plate 39

(Perruche cornue)

Description 32 cm. Medium-sized long-tailed green parrot with black mask and yellow neck. Black bill and mask, red forehead and two wispy black crest feathers with red tips which project behind or curl above crown. Rest of head and nape yellow, becoming grass-green on underparts and rump, and darker green on upperparts with violet-blue fringes to outer wing and uppertail. Immature is greener, especially on head, with less distinct head markings and horn-coloured bill.
Similar species Differs from New Caledonian Parakeet by head pattern, bluer, longer and more rounded tail, and larger stouter size. From Coconut Lorikeet by lack of dark purple head and red breast, slower flight and different habits. From Ouvéa Parakeet by range and head pattern.
Voice Noisy, often located by call, but does not scold observer like Coconut Lorikeet. Repeated nasal trumpeting *khoo* or *kho-khoot*, similar to New Caledonian Crow but lower-pitched and more trumpeting, and more varied than New Caledonian Parakeet. Softer chattering and range of shrieks and chuckles.

Habits Commonest in humid forest valleys in low mountains, especially on limestone soils, but also in scrubby forest up to 1500 m. Usually in pairs or small flocks of about six birds feeding high in canopy, especially in Araucariacae and *Pinus* trees.
Conservation status Localised and uncommon or rare; may be threatened by rats predating nests which are sometimes on ground, and population estimated to be a few thousand birds. IUCN: Vulnerable.
Range Endemic to New Caledonia, where it occurs in scattered forests across Grand Terre.

OUVÉA PARAKEET *Eunymphicus uvaeensis* Plate 39

(Also treated as a subspecies of Horned Parakeet *E. cornutus*; Perruche d'Ouvéa)

Description 32 cm. Medium-sized long-tailed green parrot with darker green mask and long fine crest. Black bill, small red central forehead-patch and upcurled crest of about six fine dark green feathers. Yellowish-green necksides and underparts, with darker green upperparts and violet-blue fringes to outer wing and uppertail. Immature duller, with less red on crown, horn-coloured bill and paler eye.
Similar species Differs from Coconut Lorikeet by lack of dark purple head and red breast, slower flight and different habits. Differs from Horned Parakeet of Grande Terre by head and crest pattern.
Voice Noisy, often located by call. Loud nasal trumpeting *khoot*, often repeated. Screeching alarm call when flushed is lower-pitched and less strident than Coconut Lorikeet. Also a range of other shrieks and chuckles.
Habits Restricted to native forest but also forages in adjacent gardens. Usually in pairs or sometimes small flocks feeding in forest canopy or in fruit trees and bushes.
Conservation status Localised and uncommon. After declining through forest loss and trapping now increasing through an active conservation programme, with a population of *c.*2000 birds in 2009. IUCN: Endangered.
Range Endemic to Ouvéa, where it is widespread in north and rare but increasing in south.

NEW CALEDONIAN PARAKEET *Cyanoramphus saisseti* Plate 39

(Also treated as a subspecies of Red-fronted Parakeet *Cyanoramphus novaezelandiae*; Perruche calédonienne)

Description 26 cm. Medium-sized long-tailed green parrot with red on head. Mostly grass-green, paler on underparts, with red forehead and eye-stripe, blue outer wing and obscure small red spot on rear flanks. Immature has less red.
Similar species Smaller and slimmer than adult Horned Parakeet with different head pattern and greener, shorter and more pointed tail. From Coconut Lorikeet by lack of dark purple head and red breast, slower flight and different habits.
Voice Nondescript quiet nasal chattering *preep-pruup-*, faster and more nasal than New Caledonian Crow and more monotonous than Horned Parakeet.
Habits Forest, including *niaouli* savanna, *maquis* scrub, *Casuarina* forest and humid forest, to 1500 m, with most records from mosaics of *niaouli* and humid forest between 400–800 m. Usually in pairs or small flocks of 5–10. Feeds at all levels from forest canopy to scrub and on ground.
Conservation status Poorly known, but localised and uncommon or rare. IUCN: Vulnerable.
Range Endemic to New Caledonia, where it occurs in scattered forests across Grand Terre.

SONG PARROT *Geoffroyus heteroclitus* Plate 39

(Singing Parrot; Perruche hétéroclite)

Description 24 cm. Medium-large grass-green parrot with medium-short tail. Male has dull lemon-yellow head and bill and grey collar. Female has brownish-grey wash on head and bill. Both have whitish eye, dark grey underwing with blue underwing-coverts, and dull yellow on undertail. Immature as female but greener head, pale bill and dark eye.
Similar species Distinctive head pattern, flight silhouette, size and calls. Differs from male Eclectus Parrot by smaller size and no red. In flight, differs from Eclectus Parrot by shorter, more pointed wings, longer tail and faster wing-beats. From Purple-bellied, Yellow-bibbed and White-naped Lories by slower wing-beats and longer tail.
Voice Very vocal and sings from perch or in flight, sometimes at night. Melodious warbling of ringing notes slowly oscillating in pitch e.g. *clo-clo-cle-cleo-clo-clo-* or *see-ah-ha, see-ah-hoo*. Single or double note calls e.g. *clee*, *kiap-kiap*, often more screeching than song but less harsh than Eclectus Parrot.
Habits All forest habitats, less common in secondary forest and dry forest, but wanders widely. Commonest in hills, more localised in lowlands and rarely in mountains above 900 m, exceptionally up to 1760 m. Unobtrusive unless calling. Usually in pairs or threes, sometimes in small flocks, in forest canopy. Flies fast, banking low over forest canopy, usually calling.

Conservation status Fairly common but locally uncommon or rare. Not threatened.
Range Endemic to Bismarcks and Solomons.
G. h. heteroclitus is endemic to Lavongai, New Ireland, Djaul, Tabar, Lihir, Umboi, New Britain, Lolobau, Duke of York, and across Solomons from Buka to Malaita and Makira, including most of New Georgia island group, Russell Is, Florida Is and Ulawa but not islands off Makira.
G. h. hyacinthus, endemic to Rennell, has more blue on primary coverts, male has broader grey collar from upper breast to upper mantle, and female has more extensive deeper grey on head.

ECLECTUS PARROT *Eclectus roratus* — Plate 39

(Grand Éclectus)

Description 31 cm. Large parrot, with bright green male and bright red and blue female. Male is grass-green with orange-red bill, red underwing-coverts extending onto flanks, blue primaries and narrow yellow terminal tail-band. In flight, has head stretched out, long rounded wings held low and downcurved, and very short tail. Female is bright red, darker on mantle and wings, with purple-blue lower breast and belly, upper mantle and primaries, and black bill. Immature has brownish bill.
Similar species Distinctive size, plumage, short tail and habits. In flight, differs from Song Parrot, Purple-bellied, Yellow-bibbed and White-naped Lories by plumage, larger size, longer wings, shorter tail and slower wing-beats.
Voice Commonest call, especially in flight, is loud harsh screech *graa-ah*. Louder harsh screech when alarmed but still softer than cockatoos. Harsh *krah*. Ringing *cling-cling* similar to swinging rusty gate. Quiet mewing *kaa*. Rail-like clucking *duk-duk-*...
Habits All forest habitats, commonest in secondary and broken forest with some big trees, but wanders widely. Usually in lowlands but rarely in mountains up to at least 1150 m. Forages in canopy and often raids gardens. Noisy and conspicuous, often perching on exposed branches or flying very high. Often in pairs or small flocks but larger flocks fly to and from roosts. Distinctive flight action of rapid shallow beats with wings not raised above body, interspersed with glides on down-swept wings. Males often seen more than females.
Conservation status Fairly common and tolerant of degraded habitats. Not threatened.
Range *E. r. solomonensis*, endemic to the Admiralties, Bismarcks and Solomons, from Manus to Makira, except St Matthias group, Nissan, Rennell and tiny isolated islands, differs from other subspecies by its smaller size and bill, and brighter paler red and green plumage. Elsewhere, other subspecies occur in Indonesia, New Guinea and far north Australia.

CUCKOOS Cuculidae

Medium to large, long-winged and long-tailed birds. Most are nest parasites, laying eggs in nests of various host species, which rear the chick and which often mob the adults. Generally unobtrusive, often perched motionless for long periods, but call loudly and conspicuously. Fast direct flight with rapid shallow beats of long pointed wings. Coucals *Centropus* are very large, fly poorly on short wings but jump along branches like squirrels, and rear their own chicks. Koel *Eudynamys* and Long-tailed Cuckoo *Urodynamis* are large, black or barred brown, rarely seen but with very loud calls. Channel-billed Cuckoo *Scythrops* is very large, conspicuous by call and shape when flying high overhead. Bronze Cuckoo *Chrysococcyx* is small and short-tailed with glossy green, brown and white plumage. Typical cuckoos *Cuculus* and *Cacomantis* are often hawk-like with brown and grey plumage and yellow bare parts.

BUFF-HEADED COUCAL *Centropus milo* — Plate 42

(Coucal à tête fauve)

Description 64 cm. Huge black and yellow coucal. Pale buffy-yellow head and body with black wings, mantle and tail, and stout decurved black bill. Juvenile is rufous-brown with narrow blackish bars on upperparts, darker head and neck with warm brown streaks and irregular blackish bars on rufous-brown underparts.
Similar species Adult plumage and habits distinctive. Juvenile differs from koels and hawks by relatively plain head pattern, large blackish bill, irregularly marked underparts, broader tail and habits.
Voice Noisy. Regular series of very deep booms, often paired notes like a saw, usually increasing in pitch and increasing then decreasing in volume. Series of deep *wup* notes like imperial pigeon, slowly decreasing in pitch and volume. Single or series of explosive *TCHow* sneezes. Higher-pitched *SChow* like spitting cat. Juvenile screams like small pig.
Habits Forest, especially forest thickets, secondary forest and scrub. Lowlands to *c.*1500 m on Guadalcanal and 1300 m on Kolombangara. Pairs or family parties creep and jump on ground, in thickets and tangles, sometimes high within canopy. Slow and clumsy. Flies weakly, usually gliding down at steep angle.

Conservation status Fairly common. Not threatened.
Range Endemic to central Solomons.
C. m. albidiventris, endemic to Vella Lavella, Bagga, Ranongga, Simbo, Gizo, Kolombangara, Kohinggo, New Georgia, Rendova, Tetepare, Vangunu and Nggatokae, has buffy-yellow extending onto belly.
C. m. milo, endemic to Guadalcanal and Florida Is, has black lower breast and belly.

WHITE-NECKED COUCAL *Centropus ateralbus* Plate 42

(Pied Coucal; Coucal atralbin)

Description 46 cm. Usually pied but polymorphic. Typical morph is glossy black with white head, neck and breast, with buff wash on head and nape, and small white patch on wing-coverts. Head is all white or has black mask or black cap. All-black morph, perhaps subadult plumage, usually has white wing-covert patch. All morphs may have scattered white feathers on wing-coverts, belly and occasionally mantle and wings. Rare leucistic morph is entirely creamy-white. Juvenile is dark sooty-brown, with fine buffy streaks on dark brown head, neck and breast, and soon develops white feathers on breast.
Similar species Pied adult is distinctive. Black adult differs from Violaceous Coucal by usually having small white patches, no pale face-patch, and smaller size. Juvenile differs from Violaceous Coucal by browner plumage and smaller size.
Voice Deep booming *dhu*, usually a duet of paired notes, one higher-pitched than the other, repeated in a series for many seconds, accelerating and increasing in pitch, not as deep as Violaceous Coucal. Gecko-like sucking *tchuk* repeated up to four times.
Habits Lowland forest, especially forest edge, secondary forest, overgrown gardens and scrub with some large trees, less common in mountains to 1400 m. Usually in pairs or small family groups in understorey but forage from ground to lower canopy, jumping between branches and gliding between trees.
Conservation status Fairly common. Not threatened.
Range Endemic to Bismarcks, including New Ireland, Djaul, Umboi, New Britain and Lolobau.

VIOLACEOUS COUCAL *Centropus violaceus* Plate 42

(Coucal violet)

Description 67 cm. Huge glossy black coucal. All black with violet gloss, patch of blue-white skin around dark red eye and whitish legs. Juvenile is duller, with duller eye-patch.
Similar species Adult differs from male Pacific Koel by pale skin around eye, short wings and habits.
Voice Deep disyllabic *wu-wuuu* with longer louder second note, similar to large sheet of metal being flexed, repeated at variable intervals. Sometimes interspersed with rapid deep gulps. Very deep hoarse rasping roar *wrah!-wrah!*
Habits Forest, usually primary or old-growth forest, to c.800 m, rarely to 1370 m. Pairs and singles jump about in dense thickets and vines, often climbing high up trees and gliding down to next tree. Shy.
Conservation status Widespread in small numbers but uncommon on New Ireland. Possibly threatened as restricted to old-growth forest. IUCN: Near Threatened.
Range Endemic to New Ireland and New Britain.

PACIFIC KOEL *Eudynamys orientalis* Plate 42

(Australian Koel; *Eudynamys cyanocephala*; also treated as a subspecies of Common Koel *E. scolopacea*; Coucou bleuté)

Description 41 cm. Rarely seen but commonly heard large cuckoo with long rounded tail. Male is entirely glossy black with greenish-white bill and dull red eye. Female has dark rufous-brown upperparts with darker head, except for fine whitish moustachial stripe, darker barring on wings and tail, and fine black bars on paler brown underparts. Juvenile as female but has paler buffy upperparts, broad black eye-stripe, whitish moustachial stripe and broad black submoustachial stripe.
Similar species Adult male differs from other black birds by pale bill and long tail. Female and immature differ from Long-tailed Cuckoo by darker plumage and dark throat, barred underparts, and no supercilium. From juvenile Buff-bellied Coucal by smaller size, smaller pale bill, more finely barred underparts, and habits.
Voice Noisy, loud and frantic, often calling repeatedly at dusk and dawn, sometimes through night but rarely in day. Series of *ko-el* or *coo-ee* calls, either constant or accelerating and climbing in pitch. Series of similar notes, e.g. repeated *wurroo* or *weir* or *kwoh, kwoh, kwah-kwa-kwakwa…* Female has hawk-like yelping *keek, keek, keek, keek*.

Habits Forest, especially degraded forest, and large trees in open country. Lowlands, especially dry coastal forest, less common in hills to 800 m. Singles and pairs are very secretive forest-canopy fruit-eaters. Melanesian host species are unknown but parasitises nests of medium-sized honeyeaters and cuckooshrikes in Australia.
Conservation status Usually widespread in small numbers but sometimes rare. Not threatened.
Range Bismarcks and Solomons.
E. o. hybrida, endemic to Crown, Long, Tolokiwa and Credner; female has richer orange-buff underparts, a feature of *E. s. rufiventer* of New Guinea.
E. o. salvadorii, endemic to New Ireland and New Britain, including Umboi, Sakar, Lolobau, Watom and Duke of York; male has greenish gloss and female has orange spots on sooty-brown upperparts and dark brown bars on creamy-buff underparts.
E. o. alberti, endemic to Solomons from Buka and Bougainville to Makira and Three Sisters, including many small isolated islands but excluding Rennell; male has bluish gloss, and female is blackish and bright orange-rufous.
[*E. o. cyanocephala* and *E. o. subcyanocephala*, not recorded from Melanesia but may occur as rare migrants; female has black throat or broad submoustachial stripe, paler buff underparts with few markings, and white spots on mid-brown upperparts; breed in Australia and migrate north to New Guinea in March–April, returning September–October.]
Elsewhere, other subspecies breed in Indonesia and New Guinea.

LONG-TAILED CUCKOO *Urodynamis taitensis* — Plate 41

(Long-tailed Koel; *Eudynamys taitensis*; Coucou de Nouvelle-Zélande)

Description 41 cm. Large cuckoo with boldly barred tail slightly longer than body. Head striped with creamy supercilium and moustachial stripe and dark submoustachial stripe, warm brown upperparts with blackish barring, white spots on wing-coverts and tail-tips, buffy-white underparts with heavy brown streaking. Juvenile has warm buffy supercilium and underparts, and white spots across mantle and wings.
Similar species Differs from Pacific Koel by streaked pale underparts, white supercilium and pale throat. From hawks by longer tail, bill shape and head pattern.
Voice Usually silent in Melanesia. Loud shrill upslurred grating whistle *whizz-z-z-z-z-t*, also given after dark and in flight. Rapid hawk-like chatter *zip-zip-zip-*, also given in flight.
Habits Forest and scrub, especially on small outlying islands, to at least 750 m. Usually singles in canopy. Unobtrusive and often shy. Flies with rapid shallow beats of pointed wings.
Conservation status Uncommon to rare migrant to Melanesia, but easily overlooked. Declining but not threatened in New Zealand.
Range Migrant across Melanesia, especially the east. Recorded from Ninigo Is, New Britain, Watom, Duke of York, Nissan, many islands in the Solomons and Temotu, Ambrym, Efate, Aniwa and Grande Terre, New Caledonia. Breeds in New Zealand and migrates to Polynesia and Micronesia, in March–April, returning in September–October.

CHANNEL-BILLED CUCKOO *Scythrops novaehollandiae* — Plate 42

(Coucou présageur)

Description 63 cm. Huge cuckoo with massive decurved bill. Pale grey head and neck, paler breast to vent, and obscure black barring on dark greyish mantle and wings. Long tail has black subterminal uppertail-band and white tips. In flight, shows long head, long pointed wings with black trailing edge, and long tail. Male has grey-black bill with cream tip for 20–30% of length and faint barring on thighs and vent. Female bill is cream on terminal 30–50% and barring extends across flanks and belly. Juvenile has pale buff head, neck and underparts, buff spots on mantle and wing, smaller pinkish bill and dull facial skin.
Similar species Distinctive bill, tail pattern and cross-shape in flight. Differs from Blyth's Hornbill by grey plumage and mostly dark tail.
Voice Harsh screaming cockatoo-like *kree-kree-kree-*, or disyllabic *ee-awk, ee-awk*, often accelerating and increasing in tone. Very loud accelerating series of about eight loud bugling *kwa-oh* notes. Often calls in flight and at night.
Habits Lowland forest, especially degraded coastal forest; seen flying over open habitats. Singles or small flocks. Shy, rarely seen in canopy of large trees, especially figs, but conspicuous in high flight with stiff wing-beats, often calling. Probably parasitises nests of Bismarck Crow.
Conservation status Uncommon in Melanesia. Breeding probable but unconfirmed. Not threatened.
Range Bismarcks, rare vagrant elsewhere. Regular migrant, probably breeding, on Lavongai, New Ireland, Djaul, Long, Umboi, New Britain and Duke of York, sometimes split as *S. n. schoddei* with larger bill and stronger scaling on upperparts, and rare migrant elsewhere in Melanesia, where recorded from Manus, Mussau, small islands off New

Britain and New Ireland, Simbo, Tetepare, Savo and Rennell and Grande Terre, New Caledonia. Breeds in Indonesia and Australia and many migrate north to New Guinea in March–April, returning in October–November.

SHINING BRONZE CUCKOO *Chrysococcyx lucidus* Plate 41

(*Chalcites lucidus*; Coucou éclatant)

Description 17 cm. Very small cuckoo with greenish upperparts and barred underparts. Dark brown crown and upperparts with strong green gloss, especially on mantle and wing-coverts. White face and underparts with black bars, finer or absent on face and throat. Undertail has four white bars on outer feathers. In flight, shows relatively long pointed wings with pale underwing-bar. Juvenile duller above and plain below with obscure dark mottling on face, throat and upper breast, and some bars on flanks.
Similar species Distinctive bronze-green upperparts. Dull immatures differ from other cuckoos by small size and short tail.
Voice Slurred whistles. Descending or level series of 4–12, and sometimes many more, upslurred whistles *feee*. Downslurred, often quavering *tsee-oow*, sometimes preceded by stutter. Dry rattling *tr-tr-trr*. Migrants may give shorter songs or single notes.
Habits Forest, especially open forest and adjacent scrub, often in *Casuarina* trees, to at least 1100 m. Singles forage unobtrusively in canopy. Sometimes in small groups, when often chasing. Slightly undulating flight. Parasitises nests of Fan-tailed Gerygone.
Conservation status Usually uncommon but common on Rennell and New Caledonia, and fairly common on Vanuatu where may disappear from and recolonise some islands. Usually mirrors local abundance of Fan-tailed Gerygone. Migrants usually uncommon. Not threatened.
Range Migrant to Admiralties, Bismarcks and Solomons, and resident on Rennell, Vanuatu and New Caledonia.
C. l. harterti, endemic to Rennell and Bellona; male has copper crown, nape and mantle, and female has more purple crown, bronze nape and mantle, and light brown wash on throat and breast.
C. l. layardi, endemic to Vanuatu and New Caledonia, recorded from many islands from Vanua Lava to Tanna, and from Grande Terre, Ouvéa, Maré and Lifou, has grey wash on forehead becoming slightly maroon on lores, ear-coverts, nape and mantle, very little white above eye, unmarked white throat and limited barring on breast and flanks; Vanuatu birds, sometimes split as *C. l. aeneus*, have more bronze and rufous on neck-sides.
C. l. lucidus, a non-breeding migrant across Admiralties, Bismarcks and Solomons, much rarer in southern Melanesia, where only one definite record from New Caledonia and one of unknown subspecies on Utupua, breeds in New Zealand and migrates north to New Guinea and Indonesia, departing January–April and returning August–November, has entirely green upperparts, extensive white on face, and broad, often greenish bars on underparts.
C. l. plagosus, probably a non-breeding migrant across Admiralties, Bismarcks and perhaps the Solomons, breeds in Australia and migrates north to New Guinea and Indonesia, departing January–April and returning August–November, has green upperparts with bronze on crown and nape, and narrow, often coppery-brown bars on underparts.

FAN-TAILED CUCKOO *Cacomantis flabelliformis* Plate 41

(*C. pyrrhophanus*; Coucou à éventail)

Description 25 cm. Medium-sized cuckoo with long rounded tail. Sooty-grey upperparts and head, with a few white bars and white tips on black uppertail. Uniform rich orange-rufous underparts with bold white bars on black undertail and sometimes a grey throat. In flight, shows pale underwing-bar. Female has paler underparts, often with fine grey barring on breast and vent. Juvenile has blackish-brown upperparts with fine rufous fringes, heavy brown barring on white underparts and larger buff bars on undertail.
Similar species Adult differs from very similar Brush Cuckoo by uniform deeper rufous underparts, darker upperparts, less white on tail and larger size. Juvenile differs from Brush Cuckoo by fine rufous fringes on otherwise plain upperparts, unmarked primaries, and obscure bars on underparts. Juvenile from Oriental Cuckoo by smaller size, lack of clear barring on underparts, and unmarked belly and vent.
Voice Noisy, sometimes calling before dawn and at night. Several different calls which are probably similar across its range, but poorly known. Slow series of disyllabic or multisyllabic quavering *torwee* or *tttttthhheeee* notes, each identical or slowly accelerating and rising in pitch. Series of c.6–8 downslurred mournful quavering trills *peeer*, each trill either identical or becoming longer and lower-pitched, similar to Brush Cuckoo but shorter and sharper. Single whistles. Strident short scream.
Habits Forest including degraded forest in lowlands and hills. Singles perch and flit about in canopy and subcanopy, often picking up insects from ground. Slightly undulating flight. Recorded parasitising nests of Scarlet Robin, fantails, Melanesian Flycatcher and trillers in Vanuatu, and myzomelas, whistlers and trillers in New Caledonia.

Conservation status Fairly common in New Caledonia but uncommon or rare in Vanuatu, where it may be extinct on many islands. *C. f. schistaceigularis* may be threatened, but species not globally threatened.
Range Vanuatu and New Caledonia, and rare migrant or possibly resident in Solomons.
C. f. pyrrhophanus, endemic to Grande Terre, Ouvéa, Maré and Lifou, where possibly a breeding migrant, with records from Isabel, Kolombangara, Guadalcanal and Bellona in May to July probably migrants of this subspecies but may be resident (has been split as *C. f. meeki*), has glossy blackish upperparts and uniform deep rufous underparts.
C. f. schistaceigularis, endemic to Vanuatu where recorded from most islands from Ureparapara to Tanna and Futuna, but recent records only from Aneityum in 2006, has grey throat and upper breast.
[*C. f. flabelliformis* of Australia, with greyer upperparts and cinnamon-buff underparts, may also occur as non-breeding vagrant.]
Elsewhere, other subspecies breed in Australia, New Guinea and Fiji.

BRUSH CUCKOO *Cacomantis variolosus* — Plate 41

(Coucou des buissons)

Description 22 cm. Grey-brown upperparts, head and upper breast, shading into warm buff lower breast and belly. Long tail has small white tips and spots along outer edges of uppertail and bold white bars on undertail. In flight, long pointed wings show pale underwing-bar. Juvenile is warm brown with narrow dark brown and white bars across underparts, bold rufous bars and notches on upperparts and buff bars on tail. Subadults may retain barring on throat and upper belly.
Similar species Adult differs from Fan-tailed Cuckoo by paler underparts, browner matt upperparts, more white on tail and smaller size. Immature differs by conspicuous rufous markings across upperparts, including fringes of primaries and uppertail, and clear solid barring on underparts. Immature from Oriental and Himalayan Cuckoos by irregular markings above and smaller size. From koels by plain head pattern and smaller size.
Voice Noisy. Often sings monotonously for long periods, including before dawn and after dusk. Series of *c.*4–6 downslurred trilled or rolled whistles *fear-fear-fear-* or *peeoo-peeoo-peeoo-*, about one note per second, gradually descending in pitch, sometimes accelerating. Series of accelerating and rising whistles *1,2,3,(4,5)* or *where's-the-tea?*. Rarely, just a single note of either series. See Fan-tailed Cuckoo.
Habits Forest, forest edge and adjacent scrub. Common in hills and lower mountains, but uncommon in coastal lowlands and mountains to at least 1600 m. Singles perch upright, often sitting still for long periods, and glean unobtrusively in canopy. Small groups chase in fast flight. Slightly undulating flight. Parasitises nests of various small birds, including Chestnut-bellied Monarch.
Conservation status Common. Not threatened.
Range Admiralties, Bismarcks and Solomons.
The subspecies are poorly defined and in need of revision.
C. v. blandus, endemic to Ninigo Is, Manus, Rambutyo and Tong, has grey throat and variably pale cinnamon-rufous underparts.
C. v. infaustus, on Long and Umboi, sometimes separated as *C. v. fortior*, has grey breast and rufous-grey belly, elsewhere occurring in Indonesia and New Guinea.
C. v. websteri, endemic to Lavongai, has dark grey underparts except rufous on undertail-coverts and rarely some rufous on breast.
C. v. macrocercus, endemic to New Ireland and New Britain including Djaul, Tabar, Tanga, Lihir, Lolobau and Duke of York, has pale grey upper breast, mixed with orange-rufous on lower breast and orange-rufous belly or sometimes all-grey underparts, but Tabar birds have larger bills and are sometimes split as *C. v. tabarensis*.
C. v. addendus, endemic to Buka, Bougainville, Isabel, Kolombangara and New Georgia group, Guadalcanal, Malaita, Ulawa, Makira and Ugi but not Rennell, has dirty pale grey throat, orange-buff breast becoming brighter orange towards vent, and dark blue-black upperparts.
[*C. v. variolosus*, a possible migrant across Melanesia, with pale grey throat and light buff underparts, breeds in south-east Australia and migrates north, some to New Guinea, from March–October.]
Elsewhere, other subspecies breed in Indonesia, New Guinea and Australia.

[HIMALAYAN CUCKOO *Cuculus saturatus*] — (not illustrated)

(Also combined with Oriental Cuckoo *C. optatus*)

Description 30 cm. Differs from Oriental Cuckoo only by smaller size and song. Flattened wing length is 172–192 mm.
Voice Usually silent in Melanesia. Song is a quick high *huk* note followed by 3–4 identical lower booming notes *huk, hoop-hoop-hoop*.

Range Probably a rare migrant to Bismarcks and perhaps Solomons but rarely separated from Oriental Cuckoo. Breeds in Himalayas to Taiwan and migrates to South-East Asia and possibly New Guinea and Australia.

ORIENTAL CUCKOO *Cuculus optatus* — Plate 41

(Horsfield's Cuckoo; *Cuculus horsfieldi*; also treated as a subspecies of *C. saturatus*; Coucou oriental)

Description 31 cm. Large cuckoo with barred underparts. Most have blue-grey head, upper breast and upperparts with fine black bars on white lower breast to creamy vent; long graduated tail blackish with white spots along outer margins and tip; yellow eye-ring and legs and black-tipped yellow bill. Female has small patch of buffy-rufous on upper breast. Rare hepatic phase of female has rich rufous-brown upperparts, head and upper breast, and white lower breast and belly, all with black barring. Immature has dark brown-grey upperparts with white fringes, and white bars on head, throat and upper breast. Both sexes have hepatic juveniles. Flattened wing length is 186–212 mm.
Similar species From very similar Himalayan Cuckoo only by smaller size and territorial call. Hepatic adult and immature differ from immature Brush and Fan-tailed Cuckoos by larger size and regular chestnut and black bars on upperparts. From koels by plain head pattern, strong bars across whole body and smaller size. From immature Buff-bellied Coucal by smaller size, long pointed wings and habits.
Voice Usually silent in Melanesia. Song is a deep booming pair of equal notes.
Habits Lowland forest and forest edges, and sometimes in mountains to 1100 m. Solitary and unobtrusive. Perches rather horizontally and gleans in canopy.
Range Uncommon migrant or vagrant to Bismarcks and Solomons with records of this species or Himalayan Cuckoo from Manus, New Britain, Nukumanu, Buka, Bougainville, Choiseul, New Georgia, Guadalcanal, Malaita and Ugi in November–April. Breeds across Russia to Japan and migrates to South-East Asia, New Guinea and Australia.

BARN OWLS Tytonidae

Large nocturnal birds with large black eyes within a facial disc, large head and strong feet and talons. Warm buffy-brown upperparts and white or pale buff underparts. Roost during day hidden in dense foliage, tree hollows or caves and occasionally mobbed by smaller birds. Rarely call.

MANUS MASKED OWL *Tyto manusi* — Plate 43

(Also treated as a subspecies of Masked Owl *T. novaehollandiae*; local name at Malai Bay was 'djahn' and at Drabui 'yell'; Effraie de Manus)

Description 33 cm. Large buff and blackish owl with black eyes in pale buff round facial disc. Underparts and rest of head rich buffy-brown with scattered small sooty spots. Crown and upperparts largely blackish with rich buff spots and mottling on mantle and wing-coverts and narrow sooty-and-buff bars on wings and tail.
Similar species Differs from Manus Boobook by prominent facial disc, black eyes, buffy-brown underparts and large size. From Eastern Barn Owl, not known on Manus, by heavy spots on buffy-brown underparts and largely blackish upperparts.
Voice Reported to be duller and harsher than Golden Masked Owl.
Habits Poorly known. All records are from forest at 200–250 m, including one specimen taken when roosting in a cave.
Conservation status Known only from two historic specimens and reported by local people to be very rare. Possibly threatened by forest loss. IUCN: Vulnerable.
Range Endemic to Manus. Specimens taken at Petayia and Metawari, and heard at Drabui. Subfossil bones of masked owls from Mussau and New Ireland suggest that this or closely related species may occur more widely and either are now extinct or overlooked.

GOLDEN MASKED OWL *Tyto aurantia* — Plate 43

(Bismarck Masked Owl; Golden Owl; Effraie dorée)

Description 30 cm. Large golden-buff owl with black eyes and dark line around pale buff facial disc. Underparts and rest of head golden-buff with scattered small sooty spots. Mantle and wing-coverts darker, heavily mottled sooty, wings and tail with narrow sooty bars.
Similar species Differs from New Britain Boobook by prominent facial disc, golden-buff plumage and large size. From Eastern Barn Owl, rare on New Britain, by golden-buff blackish upperparts and heavy black spots on underparts.

[May have variable plumage like Australian Masked Owl *T. novaehollandiae*, in which case palest birds differ from Eastern Barn Owl only by heavy feet and legs, and fully feathered legs.]
Voice Reportedly a long ascending whistle and slightly ascending series of *ka-ka* notes repeated six times per second. Probably has other calls such as screams, screeches and whistles.
Habits Poorly known. All records are from forest and forest edge from lowlands to 900 m, perhaps 1600 m. One was found roosting in a limestone sink-hole.
Conservation status Known from only two field sightings and very few specimens. Probably threatened by logging of lowland forest. IUCN: Vulnerable.
Range Endemic to New Britain, with recent records close to Hoskins. Subfossil bones of a masked owl from Mussau and New Ireland suggest that this or closely related species may occur more widely and are either now extinct or overlooked.

EASTERN BARN OWL *Tyto javanica* — Plate 43

(Pacific Barn Owl; also treated as a subspecies of Barn Owl *Tyto alba*; Effraie des clochers)

Description 33 cm. Large white, cream and buff owl. Prominent black eyes in white heart-shaped facial disc, white underparts. Grey-buff upperparts and rest of head have fine grey, black and white spots and mottling, and white or creamy underparts have scattered sooty speckles. In flight, shows fairly long broad wings with indistinct barring on wings and tail.
Similar species Differs from most night-birds by white and buff plumage and heart-shaped facial disc with black eyes. From Manus and Golden Masked Owls by whiter facial disc, small indistinct blackish spots below, and paler upperparts lacking blackish mottling. See Eastern Grass Owl on New Caledonia.
Voice Thin wavering screech *skee-air*. Rasping *scherr*. Chuckles, snores and hisses; clicks bill.
Habits Open habitats, especially grasslands, farmland, plantations and patchy forest in lowlands. Also in closed forest, especially dry forest on small islands. Roosts and nests in caves, holes in trees and buildings. Singles hunt after dark, rarely during day, from exposed perches such as fence-posts or by slowly flapping, gliding and hovering low over open habitats.
Conservation status Usually rare, but locally fairly common, especially on smaller islands. *T. a. crassirostris* is poorly known and may be threatened. Not globally threatened.
Range Breeds across Melanesia but not on Admiralties and unconfirmed on New Ireland and New Britain.
T. j. delicatula, breeding on Long, a handful of recent records from New Ireland and New Britain, Nissan, Buka, Bougainville, Isabel, Vella Lavella, Kolombangara, New Georgia, Rendova, Guadalcanal, Rennell, Bellona, Malaita, Makira, Ugi, Three Sisters, Santa Ana, Erromango, Tanna, Aneityum, Ouvéa, Lifou, Maré, Grande Terre and Walpole, has few spots on breast. Vanuatu and New Caledonia birds are sometimes separated as *T. a. lifuensis*, and Bellona and probably Rennell birds have been separated as *T. a. bellonae*. Elsewhere, *T. a. delicatula* breeds in Indonesia, Australia and west Polynesia.
T. j. crassirostris, endemic to Tanga, has darker upperparts, broad dark bars on wings and tail, relatively bold spotting above and below, and a deeper bill; could be treated as a separate species.
T. j. interposita, endemic to Temotu and north Vanuatu where recorded from Reef Is, Nendo, Vanikoro and most islands from Banks Is to Efate, is washed light buff to rich tawny on underparts.
Elsewhere, other subspecies breed patchily from South-East Asia to New Guinea.

EASTERN GRASS OWL *Tyto longimembris* — Plate 43

(Australasian Grass Owl; also treated as a subspecies of Grass Owl *T. capensis*; Effraie de prairie)

Description 35 cm. Large open-country owl with black eyes in pale round facial disc. Upperparts and rest of head are golden-buff, barred and mottled dark brown, with small black and white spots. White or pale buff underparts have dark speckles. In flight, upperwings are largely dark with paler buff patch at base of primaries and a few narrow black bars on wings and tail, and underwings are white with dark narrow bars, primary coverts and wing-tips.
Similar species Differs from Eastern Barn Owl by darker browner upperparts, longer legs which project well beyond tail, longer broader wings, dark wing-tips and primary coverts with buff base of upper primaries, more distinctly barred tail, often buff on mask or breast, and habit of perching only on ground.
Voice Loud hissing scream *skairr*, louder than Eastern Barn Owl.
Habits Open habitats, especially grassland and marshes. Flaps slowly, gliding low over ground, hovering and diving head-first onto prey, legs often dangling, and usually perches only on ground. Nocturnal but often appears before dusk or flushed from roost or nest on ground. Regular roost sites are marked by trampled grass, pellets and feathers.
Conservation status Known only from one old specimen which may have been an irruptive vagrant. Status in Melanesia unknown.

Range *T. l. longimembris* has been recorded once from Grande Terre, New Caledonia. Elsewhere, breeds patchily from India to Australia, and perhaps Fiji, and other subspecies breed in east Asia and New Guinea.

OWLS Strigidae

Medium to large nocturnal birds with large eyes, strong feet and cryptic brown plumage. Boobooks lack the facial disc characteristic of most other owls. Roost by day hidden in thick foliage but are occasionally discovered and mobbed by smaller birds. Active at night, usually calling soon after dusk and less often before dawn.

MANUS BOOBOOK *Ninox meeki* Plate 44

(Manus Boobook; Ninoxe de l'Amirauté)

Description 30 cm. Medium-sized owl with heavily streaked underparts. Unmarked rich brown face with yellow eyes. Upperparts and rest of head rufous-brown with irregular white barring, stronger white barring on wing-coverts, and buffy-brown bars on wings and tail. Rufous throat and creamy-white underparts have thick rufous-brown streaks. Juvenile has fewer, less distinct streaks on underparts and heavier white barring on upperparts.
Similar species Differs from Manus Masked Owl, the only other night bird on Manus, by brown plumage, yellow eyes and smaller size.
Voice Series of 4–10 gruff sawing or coughing notes, *grro, grro, grro-groo-groogroogroogroogroogroo*, initially accelerating and becoming louder, and often duetting. Calls regularly at dusk, rarely through night and during day.
Habits Forest, especially large trees in secondary forest and forest edge, at all altitudes. Singles call and hunt from subcanopy.
Conservation status Fairly common. Not threatened.
Range Endemic to Manus and Los Negros.

NEW IRELAND BOOBOOK *Ninox variegata* Plate 44

(Bismarck Boobook/Boobook; *Ninox solomonis*; Ninoxe bariolée)

Description 27 cm. Medium-sized rufous-brown owl with finely barred underparts. Plain warm rufous brown face has yellow eyes. Upperparts and rest of head greyer, with small white spots and bars on mantle and especially wing-coverts, and pale bars on dark wings and tail. Narrow dark brown bars on rufous-brown throat and upper breast-sides and white underparts, becoming further apart on belly. May have cold grey-brown and rufous-brown morphs. Juvenile unknown.
Similar species Differs from Eastern Barn Owl by barred brown underparts, brown face and yellow eyes. From Large-tailed Nightjar by short wings and tail, yellow eyes and habits.
Voice Long series of reverberating frog-like paired notes, *vru-vru* or *kra-kra*, sometimes single notes, with variable tone, often duetting. Similar to Large-tailed Nightjar but deeper, more reverberating and rasping. Calls regularly at dusk and often at dawn but rarely through night.
Habits Forest, often in forest edge or patchy forest, to 1760 m. Singles roost in thickets or holes in trees during day. Calls and hunts at night from forest understorey and subcanopy.
Conservation status Fairly common. Not threatened.
Range Endemic to New Ireland and Lavongai.
N. v. variegata is endemic to New Ireland.
N. v. superior, endemic to Lavongai, is slightly larger and paler.

NEW BRITAIN BOOBOOK *Ninox odiosa* Plate 44

(Russet Boobook, New Britain Boobook; Ninoxe odieuse)

Description 25 cm. Small warm brown owl with broad brown breast-band. Face has narrow white eyebrows, orange eyes and broad white throat-bar often split into two lateral throat-patches. Warm brown head and upperparts with small white spots on head and neck, larger spots on wing-coverts and broken white bars on wings and tail. Upper breast is brown with small white spots, becoming larger spots on lower breast until only a few brown crescents or streaks on white belly. Juvenile greyer with indistinct face markings, dull yellow eyes and more brown on underparts.
Similar species Differs from Eastern Barn Owl and Golden Masked Owl by rich brown plumage including face, and orange eyes. From Large-tailed Nightjar by short wings and tail, yellow eyes and habits.
Voice Series of gruff *wrha* notes continued for several minutes, but often shorter, very slowly accelerating in speed to

about four notes per second, and generally increasing in pitch, but sometimes briefly dropping in pitch. Notes sound as rather flat *poop* recalling fruit dove at distance. Calls regularly at dusk but irregularly through night and at dawn.
Habits Forest, often in forest edge or patchy forest to at least 1250 m. Singles roost in thickets or holes in trees during day and emerge at night to call and hunt from understorey and subcanopy.
Conservation status Widespread in small numbers but threatened by logging of lowland forest. IUCN: Vulnerable.
Range Endemic to New Britain, including Watom.

WEST SOLOMONS BOOBOOK *Ninox jacquinoti* — Plate 44

(Also combined with next three species as Solomons Boobook *N. jacquinoti*; Ninoxe de Jacquinot)

Description 26 cm. Small warm brown owl with plain creamy underparts. Face has narrow white eyebrows, broad white throat-bar and orange-yellow eyes. Warm brown head and upperparts with many buffy speckles and narrow buffy-white bars on wings and tail. Brown upper breast with fine buff bars and creamy lower breast and belly with a few dark bars on lower breast and fine streaks on belly. Juvenile is uniformly sooty with irregular buffy bars on wings and tail, with white soon appearing on throat and belly.
Similar species Differs from Fearful Owl by smaller size, plain creamy underparts and white throat. From Eastern Barn Owl by rich brown upperparts and upper breast, ill-defined brown facial disc and yellow eyes. From Solomons Nightjar and Solomons Frogmouth by short wings and tail, face pattern and large yellow eyes, plain creamy underparts and habits.
Voice Series of reverberating *chong* notes, often accelerating. Sometimes duets, and notes may develop into high-pitched *poop* duet. Calls regularly at dusk, less often at dawn and infrequently through night.
Habits Forest, especially forest edge including large trees in gardens, to at least 2000 m. Singles and pairs roost in thickets during day, and at night call and hunt from understorey and subcanopy of forest.
Conservation status Fairly common but status of *N. j. mono* and *N. j. floridae* unknown. Not threatened.
Range Endemic to west Solomons from Bougainville to Florida Is.
N. j. eichhorni is endemic to Buka, Bougainville, Choiseul and perhaps Shortland.
N. j. mono, endemic to Mono and probably Shortland, has a clear-cut dark brown breast-band.
N. j. jacquinoti, endemic to Isabel, is similar to but slightly larger than *N. j. eichhorni*.
N. j. floridae, endemic to Florida Is, has a creamy face and is larger.
There are also unconfirmed local reports of small brown owls from Kolombangara, New Georgia and Vonavona.

GUADALCANAL BOOBOOK *Ninox granti* — Plate 44

(Also treated as a subspecies of Solomons Boobook *N. jacquinoti*)

Description 24 cm. Small warm brown owl with heavily barred underparts. Face has white eyebrows and throat-bar, and eye usually yellow but may be brownish-yellow. Warm brown head and upperparts have white spots on crown and wing-coverts and irregular buffy-white bars on wings and tail. White underparts have broad warm brown bars, almost solid brown on breast-sides. Juvenile is plain dark brown with white bars on wings and tail and faint white barring on underparts.
Similar species Differs from Eastern Barn Owl by rich brown plumage, brown on breast, ill-defined brown facial disc and yellowish eyes.
Voice Monotonous series of *poop* notes for several minutes, with occasional switch in interval and pitch. Pairs duet with alternating tones, *who-ha, who-ha*… Calls regularly at dusk.
Habits Forest, often forest edge or patchy forest, to 1500 m. Singles roost in thickets during day and at night call and hunt from understorey and subcanopy.
Conservation status Fairly common. Not threatened.
Range Endemic to Guadalcanal.

MALAITA BOOBOOK *Ninox malaitae* — Plate 44

(Also treated as a subspecies of Solomons Boobook *N. jacquinoti*)

Description 22 cm. Small dark rufous-brown owl with finely barred underparts. Brown head has white eyebrows, broad white throat-bar and blackish eyes. Dark brown upperparts have rufous-buff spots and bars which are paler buffy on wing-coverts, and larger white spots or bars on wings. Dark brown underparts have fine off-white bars, especially on the paler rustier belly and flanks. Juvenile is unknown.
Similar species Differs from Eastern Barn Owl by uniformly rich brown plumage.
Voice Probably a monotonous series of deep *poop* notes for several minutes.
Habits Forest. Specimens taken at 900–1200 m.

Conservation status Uncommon or rare and known only from two specimens. May be threatened by loss of lowland forests, and may prove to be Vulnerable.
Range Endemic to Malaita.

MAKIRA BOOBOOK *Ninox roseoaxillaris* Plate 44

(Also treated as a subspecies of Solomons Boobook *N. jacquinoti*)

Description 21 cm. Small warm brown owl with solid brown underparts. Brown head has indistinct buffy eyebrows, broad white throat-bar and blackish eyes. Cinnamon-rufous upperparts have indistinct small white spots on head and wing-coverts, and plain wings. Warm orange-cinnamon underparts have faint buffy bars especially on belly. Juvenile is unknown.
Similar species Differs from Eastern Barn Owl by uniformly rich brown plumage.
Voice Monotonous series of deep *poop* notes for several minutes, about one note per second but varying in interval and pitch, similar to a pre-dawn call of Makira Honeyeater. Reported also to have trisyllabic call *ko-he-go*.
Habits Forest. Recorded in lowlands to at least 600 m. Singles roost in thickets during day, and occasionally active in understorey.
Conservation status Uncommon or rare, and known only from three specimens and a handful of sightings. May be threatened by loss of lowland forests, and may prove to be Vulnerable.
Range Endemic to Makira, probably including Ugi and Santa Catalina.

FEARFUL OWL *Nesasio solomonensis* Plate 44

(Hibou redoubtable)

Description 37 cm. Very large brown owl. Prominent facial pattern with orange-yellow eyes surrounded by black mask and bordered by white on eyebrows and under eyes. Rich orange-rufous plumage with heavy dark brown streaking on underparts, neck and mantle, and broad dark brown barring on wings and tail.
Similar species Differs from West Solomons Boobook by larger size and orange-rufous underparts with heavy dark streaks. From Eastern Barn Owl by streaked orange-buff underparts, patterned face and yellow eyes. From Solomons Nightjar and Solomons Frogmouth by short tail, orange-rufous plumage, large yellow eyes, facial pattern and habits.
Voice Mournful, rather human moaning hoot, *hooooooah*, 1–3 seconds long, evenly pitched until louder rapid terminal upslur, repeated at irregular intervals of at least ten seconds. Calls irregularly through night.
Habits Old-growth forest and forest edge, to at least 2000 m. Nests and roosts by day in epiphytic tangles, especially in large fig trees. Reported to hunt cuscus and other large mammals and birds.
Conservation status Uncommon and threatened by habitat loss. Possibly also declining through loss of prey which is also hunted by humans. IUCN: Vulnerable.
Range Endemic to Bougainville, Choiseul and Isabel, with possible reports from Buka.

FROGMOUTHS Podargidae

Large nightbirds with a large head, heavy bill, wide mouth, short weak legs and long tail.

SOLOMONS FROGMOUTH *Rigidipenna inexpectata* Plate 43

(Cinnamon Frogmouth; also treated as a subspecies of Marbled Frogmouth *Podargus ocellatus*; Podarge ocellé)

Description 37 cm. Large long-tailed night-bird with clear white spots on body and wings. Rufous-brown or grey-brown morphs. Brownish-yellow eye, pale eyebrows, large white spots or bars on wing-coverts and smaller white spots on throat and breast, often combining into white stripe down throat and belly. Darker wings and tail have broad pale bars. Male has darker head and rump and is less rufous than female.
Similar species Differs from Solomons Nightjar by habits, large head and bill, white spots on wing-coverts and underparts but no white on shorter rounded wings. From owls by long tail, broad bill and very small feet.
Voice Poorly known and probably varied. Clear loud quavering whistles, about one second duration and either upslurred or downslurred: *kooww* or *koow-eeeeh*. Often repeated as series of 3–5 whistles, rapidly dropping in volume. Calls irregularly through night.
Habits Forest, including logged forest, to at least 700 m. Singles and pairs are unobtrusive and rarely seen in forest understorey and subcanopy. Probably perch hidden in tangles of leaves during day and on exposed understorey branches at night.

Conservation status Uncommon but likely to be overlooked. Probably Near Threatened.
Range Endemic to Bougainville, Choiseul and Isabel, and possibly Buka.

NIGHTJARS Caprimulgidae

Medium-sized nightbirds with small bill, wide gape short weak legs, and long wings and tail. Nest and roost on ground. Hunt for insects at night in erratic buoyant flight, gliding on raised wings, interspersed with slow stiff wing-beats, or sally from exposed perches, on which they rest horizontally.

[WHITE-THROATED NIGHTJAR *Eurostopodus mystacalis*] (not illustrated)

(Engoulevent moustac)

Description 33 cm. Sooty-brown nightjar with inconspicuous white on throat and near wing-tips. Dark brown with grey mottling especially on crown, mantle, wing-coverts and tail, orange spots especially on wing-coverts, and broad white throat-bar, usually brown in centre. In flight, upperwing is blackish with pale grey panel on inner wing-coverts and small white subterminal spot on each of outer three or four primaries. Immature has rufous tips on upperparts and rufous on inner wing-coverts.
Similar species Differs from Solomons Nightjar by white spots on several wing feathers, orange subterminal spots on all other primaries, narrower dark bars on tail, larger size and call.
Voice Usually silent on non-breeding grounds. In Australia, call is series of deep *kook* notes, rising and accelerating into staccato laughing.
Habits Forest edge, clearings, scrub and open grasslands.
Range One unconfirmed report from Rennell. Breeds in Australia, some migrating north to New Guinea in April–September.

SOLOMONS NIGHTJAR *Eurostopodus nigripennis* Plate 43

(Also treated as a subspecies of White-throated Nightjar *E. mystacalis*; Engoulevent moustac)

Description 27 cm. Brown nightjar with white on throat and near wing-tips. Dark brown with grey mottling especially on crown, mantle and tail, orange spots especially on wing-coverts and indistinct orange-rufous nape. Narrow white throat-bar, broken by brown central throat, and white subterminal spots on 2–4 outer wing feathers. Female and immature have buff instead of white on some wing-spots, duller buffy-orange markings on body and smaller throat-patch.
Similar species Differs from Solomons Frogmouth by white on throat and wings but no clear white spots elsewhere, long pointed wings and habits. From White-throated Nightjar, a potential vagrant, by white restricted to two to four wing feathers, broader dark bars on tail, smaller size and call.
Voice Series of 13–25 staccato notes evenly spaced at about five notes per second, initially rising in pitch, low-pitched with reverberating quality like distant engine or axe hitting wood.
Habits Poorly known but often roosts and nests above tideline on sandy beaches, but not lagoon beaches, and beside mature rainforest; occasionally found inland in open or logged lowland forest. Reported to be commoner on small islands.
Conservation status Rare and localised. Appears to have declined, with very few recent records. Probably Endangered.
Range Endemic to Solomons, where recorded from Bougainville, Shortland Is, Isabel, Vella Lavella, Kolombangara, Gizo, Vonavona, New Georgia, Vangunu, Nggatokae, Rendova and Tetepare.

NEW CALEDONIAN NIGHTJAR *Eurostopodus exul* Plate 43

(Also treated as a subspecies of White-throated Nightjar *E. mystacalis*; Engoulevent moustac; local name at Tao was 'kapa-ru-itchen')

Description 26 cm. Pale greyish-white nightjar with darker streaks and spots. Dark brown wings with orange spots and narrow white subterminal spots on three outer wing feathers. Pale grey upperparts with sooty crown, sooty streaks on mantle, white, grey, rufous and sooty mottling on wing-coverts and indistinct dark bars on tail. Grey-brown underparts, darker on belly, with small white throat-bar.
Similar species Differs from New Caledonian Owlet-nightjar by pale grey-washed plumage, long pointed wings and habits.
Voice Unknown.
Habits Only known specimen was taken in coastal *niaouli* savanna when species was reported from *niaouli* on hillsides. Other closely related species inhabit forest.

Conservation status Only record is single specimen from 1939. Probably Extinct.
Range Endemic to New Caledonia where known from Tao, on the coast near Mt Panié.

LARGE-TAILED NIGHTJAR *Caprimulgus macrurus* Plate 43

(Engoulevent de Horsfield)

Description 27 cm. Brown nightjar with white patches on wings and tail. Dark brown plumage, mottled grey and buff, with black on mantle and scapulars and buffy tips on wing-coverts. Large white corners to tail, large white subterminal bar across wing-tip and narrow white throat-bar. Female has buff wash on slightly smaller white patches on wing-tip and tail.
Similar species Differs from owls, the only other night-birds on the Bismarcks, by long wings and tail with white patches.
Voice Series of 3–10, sometimes many more, loud monotonous *tok, tok...* notes regularly repeated at just less than one second interval, resonating like axe hitting wood. Similar to a pre-dawn call of New Britain Friarbird. Quiet rasping or growling *wrah-wrah-wrah-*, sounding like a frog, higher-pitched, softer and flatter than New Ireland Boobook.
Habits Forest clearings, secondary growth and open habitats close to forest, to at least 900 m. Rarely flushed from ground at very close range during day. Singles and pairs emerge at dusk to fly low over open habitats, or sally from exposed branches often sitting on roads. Usually calls from low branch, with puffed-out white throat, at dusk and less often at dawn.
Conservation status Locally fairly common but often absent. Not threatened.
Range *C. m. schlegelii* breeds across Bismarcks, including Lavongai, New Ireland, Tabar, Lihir, Long, Tolokiwa, Umboi, New Britain, Lolobau and Watom, and elsewhere in Indonesia, New Guinea and north Australia, and other subspecies breed from India to Indonesia.

OWLET-NIGHTJARS Aegothelidae

Nightbirds which appear intermediate between owls and nightjars.

NEW CALEDONIAN OWLET-NIGHTJAR *Aegotheles savesi* Plate 43

(Égothèle calédonien)

Description 29 cm. Long-tailed blackish night-bird. Uniform blackish-brown with very fine greyish bars and vermiculations, strongest on wings and tail. Yellow eyes, fairly long brown legs and tiny bill.
Similar species Differs from New Caledonian Nightjar by short rounded wings and blackish plumage.
Voice Unknown. Other owlet-nightjars have very varied short sharp calls including screams, churrs and whistles.
Habits Rainforest and *niaouli* savanna to at least 1000 m. Solitary. Probably roosts by day in tree-hole or thick tangle and forages at night from perches within forest and perhaps on wing and on ground.
Conservation status Two old specimens, two historical reports and one recent report but none heard in extensive recent surveys across suitable habitat. Possibly exterminated by introduced rats and cats. IUCN: Critically Endangered.
Range Endemic to Grande Terre, New Caledonia, where known historically from near Nouméa and reported from Tchamba valley, Païta and Ni-Kouakoue.

TREESWIFTS Hemiprocnidae

Medium-sized aerial feeders with very long wings and forked tail. Perch upright on exposed branches and sally or hawk after insects.

MOUSTACHED TREESWIFT *Hemiprocne mystacea* Plate 45

(Hémiprocné à moustaches)

Description 29 cm. Very long wings, crossed when perched, and very long forked tail with streamers, often held closed. Grey with darker wings and tail, two long white plumes across face, white on tertials and paler lower belly. In flight, shows long pale underwing-bar. Male has chestnut patch on ear-coverts and longer tail-streamers. Juvenile has shorter wings and tail with orange-buff fringes and spots on upperparts, buff on ill-defined facial stripes and tertial spots, and orange-buff underparts with dark mottling and barring on throat and breast and white barring on belly.

Similar species Distinctive shape, long forked tail and head pattern. Differs from Fork-tailed Swift by deeper fork in longer tail, head pattern, lack of white on throat and rump, and flight action.
Voice Loud downslurred, almost disyllabic, raptor-like squeaking *kiiee* or *hya*. Upslurred nasal *owi*, often repeated four times. High-pitched sharp *kik-kik-* similar to a tern. Harsh chatter *cha-cha-cha-*.
Habits Forest, especially beside edges, gaps, rivers and wetlands, sometimes closed forest or open country with remnant large trees, in lowlands to 900 m. Pairs perch high, swooping down on fast wing-beats to catch flying insect and returning leisurely to same perch. Also hawks above forest, especially at dawn and dusk when sometimes in small vocal flocks.
Conservation status Fairly common. Not threatened.
Range Admiralties, St Matthias Is, Bismarcks and Solomons.
H. m. aeroplanes is endemic to Bismarcks including St Matthias, Lavongai, New Ireland, Djaul, Tabar, Lihir, Tanga, Long, Umboi, New Britain, Watom and Duke of York.
H. m. macrura, endemic to Manus, Rambutyo and Lou, has longer tail and paler upperparts.
H. m. woodfordiana, endemic to Solomons including all but the smallest islands from Buka to Malaita, including Feni and Rennell, is darker with very little pale grey on belly.
H. m. carbonaria, endemic to Makira, Santa Ana and Santa Catalina, is even darker .
Elsewhere, other subspecies breed in east Indonesia and New Guinea.

SWIFTS Apodidae

Aerial insectivores characterised by fast flight with rapid stiff beats of long pointed wings. Legs are very small and weak, bill very small and hardly visible, and plumage grey-brown or black, often with white patches. Stop flying only to roost and nest on walls and roofs of caves, cliffs, inside buildings and large hollow trees. Swiftlets *Collocalia* and *Aerodramus* are small with short, shallow-forked tails. Needletails *Hirundapus* are large with short square tail. Typical swifts *Apus* are medium-large with forked tails.

GLOSSY SWIFTLET *Collocalia esculenta* — Plate 45

(White-bellied Swiftlet; *Aerodramus esculenta*; Salangane soyeuse)

Description 9 cm. Smallest Melanesian swift, with relatively short rounded wings. Glossy blue upperparts with variable white or dark rump, and dark throat and upper breast sharply demarcated from pure white lower breast and belly. Often has narrow white underwing-bar and shows white spots on fanned undertail. Juvenile has pale fringes on wings and greener gloss.
Similar species Differs from other swiftlets by glossy upperparts, sharply demarcated white on underparts, white tail-spots, smaller size, more rounded wings, and flight action. Differs from White-rumped Swiftlet on the Admiralties by narrower white rump. From White-rumped Swiftlet on Vanuatu and New Caledonia by broader white rump. Differs from small bats by shape, flight action and white on plumage.
Voice Usually silent. Occasional very high-pitched chatter. Quiet harsh *chrrr* from flocks.
Habits All habitats, especially forest gaps and clearings, sometimes within forest, at all altitudes. Singles and small loose flocks fly slowly and erratically low over ground and in small gaps in forest, with fluttering wing-beats and gliding on down-swept wings.
Conservation status Common. Not threatened.
Range Breeds across Melanesia but not St Matthias or some Temotu islands.
C. e. stresemanni, endemic to Manus, Rambutyo, Los Negros, Nauna, Tench and Nusa off north New Ireland, has narrow white rump with variable black mottling, large white tail-spots, sharply defined white underparts and white scaling on undertail-coverts.
C. e. nitens, on Crown, Long and Tolokiwa, has plain dark rump and variable tail-spots; elsewhere it breeds across lowland New Guinea.
C. e. kalili, endemic to New Ireland including Lavongai and Djaul, has plain dark rump, small or absent tail-spots and grey upper breast, flanks and undertail-coverts with white scaling.
C. e. spilogaster, endemic to Lihir and Tabar, like *C. e. kalili* but duller greener upperparts and very fine streaks on lower breast and belly.
C. e. hypogrammica, endemic to Nissan, like *C. e. spilogaster* but duller bluer upperparts and very little grey on flanks. Birds on Tanga and Feni and perhaps also Tabar are probably this subspecies.
C. e. tametamele, endemic to New Britain and Bougainville, including Witu, Lolobau, Watom, Buka and Shortland Is, has white on sides of rump, large white tail-spots, and grey upper breast, flanks and undertail-coverts with white scaling.

C. e. becki, endemic to Solomons including many small islets but excluding Bougainville, Rennell and Makira, has plain dark upperparts, small white tail-spots and variable grey, sometimes scaly, belly.
C. e. makirensis, endemic to Makira including Ugi, Three Sisters and Santa Ana, has duller upperparts than *C. e. becki* and white lower breast and belly with a little grey on flanks.
C. e. desiderata, endemic to Rennell and Bellona, like *C. e. makirensis* but has white on sides of rump, and darker throat and upper breast.
C. e. uropygialis, endemic to Utupua, Vanikoro and throughout Vanuatu, has slightly glossy black upperparts with clear narrow white rump, small or absent tail-spots, and plain dark throat and lower breast sharply demarcated from white lower breast and belly.
C. e. albidior, endemic to New Caledonia, on Grande Terre, Ouvéa, Lifou, Maré and Ile des Pins, like *C. e. uropygialis* but has large tail-spots and white fringes on paler throat and upper breast.
Elsewhere, other subspecies breed from South-East Asia to New Guinea.

WHITE-RUMPED SWIFTLET *Aerodramus spodiopygius* — Plate 45

(*Collocalia spodiopygius*; Salangane à croupion blanc)

Description 10 cm. Plumage, size, wing shape and flight actions are intermediate between Glossy Swiftlet and Uniform Swiftlet. Sooty-brown upperparts with clear white or pale grey rump-band; pale grey lower breast and belly usually merge into darker throat and contrast with darker cap, but sometimes throat is paler. Juvenile has pale fringes on wings.
Similar species Differs from Glossy Swiftlet by pale rump-band, hardly any gloss on upperparts, ill-defined paler lower breast and belly, no white on underwing, no white tail-spots, and shape and flight action. Also differs from Glossy Swiftlet with white rumps on Admiralties by broader white rump, and on Vanuatu and New Caledonia by narrower white rump. From Uniform Swiftlet by broad white rump, blacker upperparts, paler lower breast and belly, and shape and flight action. From Whitehead's Swiftlet by flight action, smaller size, clearer whiter rump-band, often paler lower breast and belly, and deeper-forked tail.
Voice Echolocates with clicks. Occasional rattling chatter or trill, usually 3–10 notes.
Habits Over forest and open habitats, especially forest clearings, at all altitudes. Commoner in open habitats, including towns, in New Caledonia. Usually in medium-sized flocks fairly low over vegetation but single birds and small flocks sometimes mix with other swiftlets.
Conservation status Locally common but often absent, especially on mountainous islands. Not threatened.
Range Widespread across Melanesia but patchy and fluctuates in range, with historic extirpations but recent recolonisations on several islands in Vanuatu, and recent range expansions in the Solomons.
A. s. delichon, endemic to Manus, Lou, Pak, Los Negros, Rambutyo and Horno, has sooty-black upperparts with slight gloss, very broad white rump, pale grey underparts and sooty undertail-coverts.
A. s. eichhorni, endemic to Mussau and Emirau, as *A. s. delichon* but paler upperparts, narrower, slightly grey rump and darker underparts.
A. s. noonaedanae, almost endemic to New Ireland and New Britain, including Lavongai, Tabar, Lihir, Long and Watom, as *A. s. eichhorni* but darker above with narrower greyer rump and paler throat; elsewhere occurs on Manam off north New Guinea.
A. s. reichenowi, endemic to the Solomons including Buka, Bougainville, Choiseul, Isabel, Kolombangara, Guadalcanal, Malaita, Makira, Ugi and Three Sisters, like *A. s. noonaedanae* but underparts darker, more uniform and rump darker.
A. s. desolatus, endemic to Temotu including Nendo, Reef Is, Duff Is and Tikopia, like *A. s. reichenowi* but paler grey rump and darker underparts with darker throat.
A. s. epiensis, endemic to north Vanuatu including Ureparapara, Santo, Malo, Malekula, Ambrym and Epi, like *A. s. desolatus* but paler rump and darker underparts, especially throat.
A. s. ingens, endemic to south Vanuatu including Emae, Efate, Erromango, Tanna and Aneityum, has black upperparts with slight gloss and medium-broad white rump, dark throat and pale grey underparts.
A. s. leucopygius, endemic to New Caledonia, on Grande Terre, Ouvéa, Lifou, Maré and Ile des Pins, like *A. s. ingens* but underparts and sides of face almost white.
Elsewhere, other subspecies breed in Fiji, Tonga and Samoa.

MAYR'S SWIFTLET *Aerodramus orientalis* — Plate 45

(*Collocalia orientalis*; Salangane de Mayr)

Description 14 cm. Large dark swiftlet with variable narrow grey rump-band. Upperparts dark sooty-brown, sometimes blackish and glossed bluish, with pale grey frosting over eye and sides of forehead. Underparts uniform sooty-brown, with variably paler throat.

Similar species Differs from Uniform Swiftlet by variable greyish rump-band, variable blue-glossed black upperparts, silvery frosting on head, larger size and shorter tail with shallower fork. Differs from White-rumped Swiftlet by flight action, larger size, more obscure greyer rump-band, uniform underparts, and less forked tail.
Voice Unknown but probably like Uniform Swiftlet.
Habits Unknown but probably flies over forest in mountains in singles and small numbers, often mixed with Uniform Swiftlets.
Conservation status Known only from single specimens from each island, recorded at 900 m and 1200 m, and some unconfirmed sight records, but is probably overlooked. Possibly threatened. IUCN: Data Deficient.
Range Endemic to New Ireland, Bougainville and Guadalcanal but may also occur on other islands.
A. o. leletensis, endemic to Lelet plateau on New Ireland, has very dark upperparts glossed blue and an indistinct grey rump-band.
An undescribed subspecies on Bougainville has browner upperparts with a slightly paler rump-band and darker underparts.
A. o. orientalis, endemic to Guadalcanal, has broader, paler grey rump-band, less obvious blue-glossed blackish upperparts and slightly paler throat.

UNIFORM SWIFTLET *Aerodramus vanikorensis* Plate 45

(Salangane de Vanikoro)

Description 13 cm. Large plain brown swiftlet with long pointed wings and fairly long tail. Grey-brown upperparts, often with darker cap and upperwings, and narrow pale rump-band in some subspecies. Dark cap contrasts with pale grey-brown throat, which shades into dusky underparts.
Similar species Differs from Glossy and White-rumped Swiftlets by larger size, browner, more uniform plumage without white rump-band, longer wings and different flight action. From Mayr's Swiftlet by smaller size, hardly paler rump, dull brown upperparts, lack of frosting on head, and longer tail with deeper fork.
Voice Echolocates around nest sites, and occasionally when foraging, with series of rapid dry clicks. Occasional high-pitched squeaking chatter.
Habits Over any habitat, but commoner over open habitats and in lowlands than other swiftlets. Often in large flocks, flying high, but flies low in rain, and large flocks often fly ahead of rain fronts. More powerful flight with more gliding than small swiftlets.
Conservation status Common but nomadic. Not threatened.
Range Across Melanesia except New Caledonia.
A. v. coultasi, endemic to Manus, Rambutyo, Los Negros and St Matthias, has blackish crown, brown mantle, paler greyer rump and contrastingly pale throat.
A. v. pallens, endemic to New Ireland, New Britain and all associated islands except those listed below, has slightly paler hindneck and rump and contrastingly pale throat.
A. v. lihirensis, endemic to Tabar, Lihir, Tanga, Feni and Nuguria, has crown and tail slightly darker than mantle and rump, dark underparts with paler vent and slightly paler throat.
A. v. lugubris, endemic to Solomons where widespread from Buka to Rennell and Makira but not Tetepare, has uniform dark upperparts with very slightly darker cap, paler rump and uniform dark grey-brown underparts.
A. v. vanikorensis, endemic to Temotu where known from Nendo, Reef Is, Duff Is and Vanikoro, and Vanuatu where widespread, is slightly paler and smaller than *A. v. lugubris*.
Elsewhere, other subspecies breed from Philippines and Indonesia to New Guinea.

WHITE-THROATED NEEDLETAIL *Hirundapus caudacutus* Plate 45

(Martinet épineux)

Description 20 cm. Large thickset swift with long body and short tail and relatively broad wings. Dark brown underparts with white throat and white on vent and extending onto flanks. Darker glossy upperparts with paler mantle and white spots on forehead and tertials. Juvenile has dark fringes on vent-patch.
Similar species Differs from Fork-tailed Swift and Moustached Tree-swift by flight action, short square tail, white on vent, and dark rump.
Voice Usually silent. Rapid high-pitched chatter *trp-trp-trp-*.
Habits Over any habitat but usually forest. Singles or small flocks fly very fast and direct on swept-back wings, or circle more slowly with fluttering wing-beats and glides, or soar with fanned tail.

Range Records from Umboi, Lihir and New Caledonia, but probably rare migrant anywhere in Melanesia, October–April. *H. c. caudacutus* breeds in north-east Asia, migrating south to New Guinea and Australia, and *H. c. nudipes* breeds in Himalayas.

FORK-TAILED SWIFT *Apus pacificus* — Plate 45

(Pacific Swift; Martinet de Sibérie)

Description 18 cm. Large swift with long wings and long, deeply forked tail often held closed. Uniformly sooty with broad white rump, less contrasting white throat-patch and obscure white scaling on paler underbody. Juvenile has narrow white tips to primaries and secondaries.
Similar species Differs from White-throated Needletail by deeply forked tail, white rump, dark vent and slower flight. From White-rumped Swiftlet by larger size, underbody pattern, longer, more pointed wings, and longer, more forked tail. From Moustached Treeswift by shorter forked tail, white rump and throat, no white stripes on head and flight action.
Voice Usually silent. High-pitched screaming *scree*.
Habits High over open lowland habitats. Singles and flocks fly fast and erratically, sometimes mixed with other aerial species.
Range One record from New Georgia but may occur as vagrant anywhere in Melanesia, October–April. *A. p. pacificus* breeds in north-east Asia and disperses south to Australia, and other subspecies breed in Asia.

ROLLERS Coraciidae

Bulky long-winged short-tailed colourful birds which sally from exposed perches or hawk high in sky.

DOLLARBIRD *Eurystomus orientalis* — Plate 49

(Oriental Dollarbird; Rolle oriental)

Description 27 cm. Stocky blue-green bird with short tail and stout orange-red bill. Dusky-brown head and turquoise body, with purple wash on throat, wings and tail. In flight, shows long broad wings with conspicuous silvery patch on outer wing. Juvenile duller, dusky-brown on body and wing-coverts, and has dusky bill, sometimes with yellow.
Similar species Distinctive shape and flight action.
Voice Rasping grating *tek* or *yap*, also given as an accelerating series of c.12 notes. Often given in flight.
Habits Forest edge, especially gardens and clearings in lowlands and hills to 900 m, but also over closed forest and open habitats. Singles and pairs perch upright on exposed branches and sally or hawk after flying insects. Flight is slow and easy with very deep wing-beats or fast and agile when chasing prey or another Dollarbird. Largely crepuscular, sitting through day but hawking actively in evening.
Conservation status Widespread in small numbers. Not threatened.
Range Admiralties, Bismarcks and Solomons.
E. o. crassirostris, endemic to the Admiralties and Bismarcks including most satellite islands but not outlying islands, Feni or Nissan, and rare or absent on Mussau.
E. o. solomonensis, endemic to Feni and the Solomons from Buka east to Makira, including most small islands but not outlying islands or Rennell, has longer tail.
E. o. pacificus, a non-breeding migrant from April to October to New Britain, Manus and probably overlooked amongst other subspecies elsewhere, breeding in Australia and east Indonesia and migrating north to New Guinea, is paler, duller and greyer.
Elsewhere, other subspecies breed from India and Japan to New Guinea.

KINGFISHERS Alcedinidae

Kingfishers are brilliantly coloured blue, orange and white, with very long straight bills, tiny legs and short tails. Singles and pairs sit and wait, swooping down on prey from high perch. 'Forest' species *Actenoides*, *Tanysiptera* and *Todiramphus* are not associated with water and usually take prey from ground or within forest foliage. 'River' kingfishers *Ceyx* and *Alcedo* are smaller and catch fish and other animals from water or forest understorey. Forest species usually have loud advertising calls, and river kingfishers have short shrill flight and alarm calls. Kingfishers usually occur in singles or pairs and nest in holes in banks, dead trees or termite nests.

MOUSTACHED KINGFISHER *Actenoides bougainvillei* Plate 48

(Martin-chasseur à moustaches)

Description 32 cm. Very large orange and blue forest kingfisher. Long red bill. Rich orange head, neck and underparts with two purple-blue stripes on head, eye-stripe from behind eye to nape, and moustachial stripe. Wings and tail dark purple-blue, with paler blue rump. Male has purple-blue mantle and scapulars, olive-green in female and very dark olive-green in immature male. Known from very few specimens, including just one immature and no males of one subspecies.
Similar species Differs from Sacred Kingfisher and Variable Dwarf Kingfisher by larger size, red bill and orange crown.
Voice Calls frequently just before dawn and after dusk. Loud clear ringing laugh *cow, cow—cow-cow-cow-* for c.7–10 notes, trailing off in volume after first few notes.
Habits Old-growth forest. On Bougainville, one recent record from above 800 m, but on Guadalcanal occurs in montane forest at 900–1550 m, occasionally down to 550 m. Reports from Bougainville lowlands are probably erroneous. On Guadalcanal, restricted to patches of old forest, absent from bamboo and secondary scrub for instance on land-slides. Extremely unobtrusive, probably crepuscular and perhaps nocturnal. One bird was seen perched two metres above ground, motionless or slowly pumping its tail, and occasionally moving perch with slightly noisy flight.
Conservation status Very poorly known. One recent record on Bougainville and uncommon at one site on Guadalcanal, but most mountains have not been surveyed. May be threatened by logging on Bougainville and nest-predation by introduced mammals on Guadalcanal. IUCN: Vulnerable.
Range Endemic to Bougainville and Guadalcanal.
A. b. bougainvillei, endemic to Bougainville; female has orange upper back, and is reported to breed in arboreal termite nests.
A. b. excelsus, endemic to Guadalcanal; male is unknown, female has green back and pale orange underparts, and is reported to breed in holes in ground; could be treated as a separate species.

BLACK-CAPPED PARADISE KINGFISHER *Tanysiptera nigriceps* Plate 47

(Black-headed Paradise Kingfisher; also treated as a subspecies of Buff-breasted/Australian/White-tailed Paradise Kingfisher *T. sylvia*; Martin-chasseur sylvain)

Description About 23 cm plus 7–18 cm tail-streamers. Medium-sized forest kingfisher with red bill and extremely long white and blue tail. Black head, nape and scapulars, glossy blue wings and outer tail feathers, white mantle, rump and central tail, and orange-buff underparts. Central tail feathers usually all white, with some blue on outer tail, but some, probably females and immatures, have blue on tail-streamers. Juvenile has more black and blue on shorter tail, brown bill, blue tips on nape, rufous tips on wing-coverts, buff mantle and black fringes on underparts.
Similar species White tail-streamers are distinctive. Also differs from other medium and large kingfishers by red bill, and from Variable Dwarf Kingfisher by white on back and tail.
Voice Cocks tail when calling. Calls often in early morning, fairly often in late afternoon, but rarely during middle of day. On New Britain, rising series of 5–7 short mournful chirps at regular rate over 2–3 seconds. On Umboi, series accelerates to trill, rising then falling in pitch, and lasts 5–7 seconds.
Habits Lowland and hill forest, especially forest edge and secondary forest with dense mid-storey. Commonest in lowlands, but recorded up to 1640 m. Vocal but rather shy, often seen flying away with long white tail trailing conspicuously. Perches in understorey, often cocking or slowly pumping tail.
Conservation status Fairly common. Not threatened.
Range Endemic to New Britain.
T. n. nigriceps, endemic to New Britain including Lolobau and Duke of York, has variable amounts of blue on outer tail.
T. n. leucura, endemic to Umboi, has longer pure white tail.

FOREST KINGFISHER *Todiramphus macleayii* Plate 47

(*Halcyon macleayii*; Martin-chasseur forestier)

Description 20 cm. Medium-sized open-country kingfisher with white wing-patch conspicuous in flight. Dark blue upperparts, brighter on rump and greener on back. White loral spot, collar and underparts, sometimes with clear buff flanks. Female has dark blue hindneck and more often buffy flanks. Juvenile duller, with buff on lores, breast and belly, and buff fringes on crown and wing-coverts.
Similar species White wing-patch, rarely visible when perched, is distinctive, as is purple-blue crown and large round loral spot. Also differs from Collared and Sacred Kingfishers by lacking buff away from flank, unless juvenile, and

black mask not extending onto nape. Also differs from Collared Kingfisher by smaller size and shorter finer bill. From White-mantled and Ultramarine Kingfishers by blue mantle and rump, buff flanks and pale base to lower mandible.
Voice Migrants are usually silent. In Australia, gives series of very rapidly repeated high-pitched notes, and harsh strident chattering *scissor-weeya, scissor-weeya*.
Habits Open habitats, usually on exposed perches over grass. Often gregarious.
Conservation status Rare non-breeding migrant to Melanesia. Not threatened.
Range Rare migrant to Bismarcks and Solomons, mostly March–October. *T. m. incinctus* breeds in north-east and east Australia, with some birds migrating in non-breeding season to south New Guinea, and vagrants recorded from New Ireland, New Britain, Nissan and Kolombangara; has turquoise-green mantle, scapulars and tertials. Elsewhere, other subspecies breeding in east New Guinea and north-west Australia, some migrating to east Indonesia, have non-contrasting blue backs.

WHITE-MANTLED KINGFISHER *Todiramphus albonotatus* Plate 47

(New Britain Kingfisher; *Halcyon albonotata*; Martin-chasseur à dos blanc)

Description 17 cm. Medium-small forest kingfisher with white mantle. Bright pale blue crown, black mask from bill to nape, and bright blue wings and tail. White loral spot, collar, mantle and underparts. Lower back and rump white in male, bright blue in female. Juvenile duller, with white areas washed buff and buff fringes on wing-coverts.
Similar species White mantle distinctive. Also differs from Collared, Sacred and Forest Kingfishers by smaller size, finer all-black bill and no buff wash on adults.
Voice Repeated rapid series of four descending notes, *kee-ku-ko-ko*. Series of *c*.9–12 *kiu* notes, higher-pitched, faster, shorter and more slurred than Collared Kingfisher. Much faster series of similar notes is probably an alarm call.
Habits Lowland forest including forest edge and logged forest to at least 850 m. Unobtrusive and often overlooked in canopy, where may perch on exposed branches.
Conservation status Uncommon but perhaps overlooked. Possibly threatened by clearance and degradation of lowland forest. IUCN: Near Threatened.
Range Endemic to New Britain.

ULTRAMARINE KINGFISHER *Todiramphus leucopygius* Plate 48

(*Halcyon leucopygia*; Martin-chasseur outremer)

Description 21 cm. Medium-sized purple-blue and white forest kingfisher. Purple-blue crown, mantle, wings and tail. Wholly black bill and black mask to nape. Pure white collar and underparts. Inconspicuous pale purple lower rump and chestnut-purple undertail-coverts. Male has white back and upper rump, deep blue in female. Juvenile has buffy underparts and fine black barring on breast and collar.
Similar species Differs from Collared, Sacred and Forest Kingfishers by no buff on collar or underparts, no loral spot, all-black bill, deep-blue crown, and purple on rump and undertail-coverts.
Voice High-pitched bouncing *katch-eeow* or *vree-ow-deedee*, first note loud, abrupt and rising in pitch, second note falling, slurring into one or two level notes, repeated several times. Distantly, sounds like *tchee-ow*; less whistled than Pacific Baza, and quieter, slower and more nasal than Collared Kingfisher.
Habits Lowland secondary forest, from sea-level to at least 700 m. Perches at all levels, especially middle and lower storeys in secondary forest including forest edge, secondary regrowth and gardens, but rare in primary forest.
Conservation status Fairly common to uncommon. Not threatened.
Range Endemic to west Solomons, on Buka, Bougainville, Shortland Is, Choiseul, Isabel, Florida Is and Guadalcanal.

VANUATU KINGFISHER *Todiramphus farquhari* Plate 48

(Chestnut-bellied Kingfisher; *Halcyon farquhari*; Martin-chasseur à ventre roux)

Description 19 cm. Medium-sized forest kingfisher with rich chestnut breast, belly and undertail-coverts. Iridescent purple-blue-black crown, mantle, wings and tail, with paler blue rump, black bill and mask, and white loral spot, throat and collar. Female has white lower belly. Juvenile is duller, the whites washed rufous, with shorter white-tipped bill.
Similar species Differs from Collared Kingfisher by extensive rich chestnut on underparts, darker more purple upperparts and no pale supercilium.
Voice Long accelerating series of *teek* chirps, repeated up to 20 times or for more than a minute. Harsh *cach-cach* alarm call.

Habits Shaded forest in lowlands and hills from 0–700 m, commoner in hills. Usually rare in open secondary habitats, where replaced by Collared Kingfisher, but occurs in dense secondary regrowth. Perches motionless or slowly pumping tail in understorey or canopy, often hidden in foliage, jerking head and tail when alarmed.
Conservation status Fairly common in suitable habitat on Santo. Threatened by logging, clearance for pasture, and perhaps habitat degradation by feral ungulates. IUCN: Near Threatened.
Range Endemic to Vanuatu, on Santo, Aore, Malo and Malekula.

COLLARED KINGFISHER *Todiramphus chloris* Plates 47–48

(White-collared/Mangrove Kingfisher; *Halcyon chloris*; Martin-chasseur à collier blanc)

Description 23 cm. The common medium-large open-country kingfisher. Wide variation between subspecies. Greenish-blue upperparts with brighter blue rump, often a buff loral spot or supercilium and darker mask from bill-base to nape. White or buff collar and underparts. Heavy black bill with pale base to lower mandible. Female often has less buff on supercilium, collar and flanks. Juvenile often has buffy fringes on wing-coverts, and buff wash and dusky fringes on underparts.
Similar species Differs from very similar Sacred Kingfisher by larger size, stockier build, and longer and heavier bill with more angular underside; some subspecies differ by plumage, especially in lacking buff on underparts, bluer upperparts and sometimes white or rufous above black band on nape. Also see Forest, White-mantled, Ultramarine, Vanuatu and Beach Kingfishers.
Voice Calls often. Short series of 2–6 short loud yelping calls, e.g. *ki* or *kiu*. Series of disyllabic yelps, second note either lower, *kee-ku*, or higher *krer-eek*. Longer phrases, e.g. *ki-ki-ki-ku-ku-keeku-keeku-kee-ku*. Loud explosive chatter. Harsh rasping *krrrah*.
Habits Wide range of lowland habitats, usually in degraded forest or perched on tall trees or wires in open-country habitats, including mangroves, rivers, freshwater marshes and suburbs. Uncommon in primary forest, especially around tree-falls and other habitat disturbances. Less common in hills, to 1500 m on New Britain. Occupies wider habitat range in absence of other medium-sized kingfishers, including reefs and mud-flats in Vanuatu, and primary forest on New Ireland and Temotu. Perches conspicuously, often on exposed branches on tallest trees, often chasing or in displaying pairs, one bird pointing upwards with drooped part-opened wings.
Conservation status Generally common. Not threatened.
Range Across Melanesia except for New Caledonia.
Basic characters are given for all recognised subspecies but there is considerable variation within many populations, the taxonomy is not well determined, and some may be treated as separate species.
An undetermined subspecies, similar to *T. c. nusae*, occurs on Wuvulu.
T. c. matthiae, endemic to Mussau and Emirau, has variable green, white or buff crown, usually creamy with black spots, black mask, dark greenish-blue wings, mantle and tail, and white collar and underparts.
T. c. nusae, endemic to New Ireland including Lavongai, Tabar, Lihir, Tanga and Feni, has white loral spot, blackish crown, buffy collar and flanks.
T. c. novaehiberniae, endemic to south-west New Ireland and possibly this subspecies on Djaul, has white collar, underparts and loral spot.
T. c. bennetti, endemic to Nissan, has sooty-green head, mantle and wings.
T. c. stresemanni, endemic to Crown, Long, Tolokiwa, Umboi, Malai, Bali and Witu, has deep blue upperparts, variable white on crown, and white loral spot, collar and underparts except pale buff belly.
T. c. tristrami, endemic to New Britain, including Lolobau and Watom, has buff loral spot, sometimes extending into supercilium, greener upperparts, buff or white underparts and collar except white chin and central belly.
T. c. alberti, endemic to Solomons from Bougainville through New Georgia group to Florida Is and Guadalcanal including most small islands, has buff loral spot, collar, flanks and underparts, paler on throat and belly, and female is duller with paler underparts.
Undetermined subspecies, similar to *T. c. alberti*, occur on Ontong Java, Ndai and Sikaiana.
T. c. pavuvu, endemic to Russell Is, has larger loral spot than *T. c. alberti*.
T. c. mala, endemic to Malaita, has bluer upperparts and paler underparts than *T. c. alberti*.
T. c. solomonis, endemic to Makira including Ugi, has broad rufous supercilium from loral spot towards nape, male with buff and female with white underparts.
T. c. sororum, endemic to the Three Sisters, has longer supercilium joining on nape, and male has paler underparts.
T. c. amoenus, endemic to Rennell and Bellona, is small and greenish-blue with variable supercilium, rufous on male and pale buff on female, and pale buff collar, throat and breast.
T. c. ornatus, endemic to Nendo and Tinakula, has very narrow supercilium, male with deep buff underparts, female with white or pale buff underparts.

T. c. brachyurus, endemic to Reef Is, is like *T. c. ornata* but paler from chin to central belly.
T. c. vicina, endemic to Duff Is, is larger and longer-tailed than *T. c. brachyura*.
T. c. utupuae, endemic to Utupua, has large rufous loral spot and supercilium and white or pale buff underparts.
T. c. melanoderus, endemic to Vanikoro, has distinctive black fringes on breast, small orange-buff loral spot and no supercilium.
Undetermined subspecies, similar to *T. c. utupuae*, occur on Tikopia and Anuta.
T. c. torresianus, endemic to Torres Is, has small buffy loral spot and supercilium, and white underparts.
T. c. santoensis, endemic to Banks Is and Santo, has long rufous supercilium joining at nape, greener upperparts and white underparts.
T. c. juliae, endemic to Maewo, Ambae and Malekula through to Efate, has long rufous supercilium, deeper blue upperparts and often buffy underparts.
T. c. erromangae, endemic to Erromango and Aneityum, has broader rufous supercilium and pale buff flanks and belly.
T. c. tannensis, endemic to Tanna, has broad rufous supercilium and rich buff underparts.
Elsewhere, *c.*26 other subspecies occur from the Red Sea to Polynesia.

BEACH KINGFISHER *Todiramphus saurophagus* Plates 47–48

(White-headed Kingfisher; *Halcyon saurophaga*; Martin-chasseur à tête blanche)

Description 30 cm. Large white-headed coastal kingfisher. Head and underparts are all white except for black eye-stripe and occasionally greenish blur on crown. Mantle, wings and tail are bright deep blue. Underwing is contrastingly black and white. Long heavy black bill has pale base. Juvenile is duller, with buff crown and underparts, and some grey fringes on breast.
Similar species Differs from Collared Kingfisher by white head, larger size, longer bill, longer tail, often bluer upperparts and habitat.
Voice Short series of *c.*3–5 rapid yelping *kill* or *tchu* notes. Occasionally changes pitch, e.g. *tchee-tchu, tchee-tchu,...* Louder, faster and shorter than Collared Kingfisher. Often calls when flying.
Habits Restricted to coasts, usually beach forest, rocky shorelines, reefs and islets, but also mangroves and rarely along sandy beaches. May occur a short distance inland, and often flies over sea. Perches on exposed branches, driftwood or rocks, and may fly and hover up to 100 m offshore.
Conservation status Widespread in small numbers, commoner on small islands and where Collared Kingfisher is absent. Not threatened.
Range Admiralties, St Matthias Is, Bismarcks and Solomons including outlying islands.
T. s. anchoreta, endemic to Wuvulu, Hermit, Ninigo and Kaniet, has crown either all white or all blue-green, but always blue-green on Kaniet which may be separate subspecies or sometimes included within *T. s. admiralitatis*.
T. s. admiralitatis, endemic to Admiralties, where recorded from Manus, Rambutyo, San Miguel and Nauna, has broad eye-stripe and about 40% have some blue-green on crown.
T. s. saurophagus, Bismarcks and Solomons from St Matthias, Tench, Nuguria and Umboi to Makira, including most small islands but not Rennell, rarely has some green on crown on Long, Tolokiwa and Umboi; elsewhere occurs in east Indonesia and around New Guinea.

SACRED KINGFISHER *Todiramphus sanctus* Plates 47–48

(*Halcyon sancta*; Martin-chasseur sacré)

Description 21 cm. Medium-small kingfisher. Greenish-blue crown and mantle, bluer wings, rump and tail, pale buff loral stripe, collar and underparts, darker on flanks and belly. Deeper buff underparts, sometimes with fine black fringes, in fresh plumage. Female is duller and greener, especially on wings and rump. Juvenile has fine black scaling on underparts and buff fringes on wing-coverts.
Similar species Differs from Collared Kingfisher by smaller size, finer build, shorter finer bill with less angular underside, always with buff on underparts, greenish-blue upperparts, no white above black nape-band and is usually silent. Also see Forest, White-mantled, Ultramarine, Vanuatu and Beach Kingfishers.
Voice Migrants are usually silent. Resident birds on New Caledonia are noisy. Short series of 3–5, sometimes 2–12, *kiu* yelps, repeated after a few seconds. Repeated nasal *vrray* or *tu-cree*.
Habits Open lowland habitats including coasts, mangroves, wetlands, suburbia, savanna, gardens and forest clearings but also in closed-canopy forest and mountains to at least 900 m. Hunts from exposed perches, often in loose association with other Sacred or Collared Kingfishers, but rarely in canopy.
Conservation status Localised but sometimes common. Not threatened.

Range Non-breeding migrant across north Melanesia, and resident in New Caledonia. Arrives from March and leaves by September, with occasional birds all year, and breeding reported on Kolombangara, Guadalcanal and Three Sisters. May also occur as migrant elsewhere in Melanesia.
T. s. sanctus is a migrant to the Admiralties, St Matthias Is, Bismarcks and Solomons to Makira including outlying islands such as Ninigo Is and Nuguria but not Rennell or Temotu; elsewhere, breeds in Australia and migrates north to east Indonesia and New Guinea.
T. s. macmillani, endemic to Ouvéa, Maré and Lifou, has deeper buff underparts.
T. s. canacorum, endemic to Grande Terre, New Caledonia and Ile des Pins, is smaller.
Elsewhere, other subspecies are resident on islands south to New Zealand and, possibly a separate species, on Samoa and Fiji.

VARIABLE DWARF KINGFISHER *Ceyx lepidus* — Plate 46

(Variable Kingfisher; *Alcedo lepida*; Martin-pêcheur gracieux)

Description 14 cm. Very small forest kingfisher. Bright purple-blue upperparts, spotted on crown and wing-coverts, and slightly brighter on back and rump. Orange-buff loral spot and underparts except for white throat and white ear-covert patch, and except on Makira where all blue and white. Black or red bill and orange legs. Juvenile duller with blacker bill.
Similar species Differs from Common, Bismarck and Little Kingfishers by size and habitat, and on most islands by more purple upperparts and deeper orange underparts. On Bougainville, Choiseul and Isabel differs from Common and Little Kingfishers by more greenish upperparts and pale buff underparts. On Makira, differs from Common Kingfisher by pure white underparts.
Voice Calls often, especially in flight. Very shrill high-pitched *tzzeep*. Pairs duet, a shorter quieter series of paired notes, *see-see, see-see,...* Longer, clearer and more regular notes than pygmy parrots.
Habits Shaded old-growth forest and dense secondary growth from sea-level to 1400 m. Often beside small streams and pools or wet ground. Perches low in understorey, where unobtrusive unless calling.
Conservation status Fairly common but uncommon on Manus. Not threatened.
Range Manus, Bismarcks and Solomons.
C. l. dispar, endemic to Manus, has red bill, bright blue upperparts and orange underparts, male with dark purple-blue head, female with orange head and small blue stripe on hindcrown.
C. l. mulcatus, endemic to New Ireland including Lavongai, Djaul, Tabar and Lihir, has black bill and pale yellow throat.
C. l. sacerdotis, endemic to New Britain including Umboi, Lolobau and Watom, has blackish-red upper mandible, red lower mandible, and pale orange underparts.
C. l. meeki, endemic to Buka, Bougainville, where sometimes separated as *C. l. pallidus*, Choiseul and Isabel, has black bill, darker, more greenish-blue upperparts, and pale buff underparts and ear-covert patch.
C. l. collectoris, endemic to New Georgia group, including Vella Lavella, Rendova and Tetepare, has orange-red bill, purple-blue upperparts and deep rufous-orange underparts.
C. l. nigromaxilla, endemic to Guadalcanal, like *C. l. collectoris* but with most of upper mandible and some of lower mandible black.
C. l. malaitae, endemic to Malaita, like *C. l. nigromaxilla* but white loral spot and paler upperparts and underparts.
C. l. gentianus, endemic to Makira, has black bill, deep blue upperparts and pure white loral spot and underparts.
Elsewhere, different subspecies, perhaps species, breed in Philippines, east Indonesia and New Guinea.

BISMARCK KINGFISHER *Alcedo websteri* — Plate 46

(Martin-pêcheur des Bismarck)

Description 22 cm. Medium-small river kingfisher. Greenish-blue upperparts, extending as half-collar onto breast-sides. White ear-covert patch, very small loral spot and throat, underparts otherwise creamy-buff. Black legs and heavy bill, often with white tip. Male has creamy underparts and dark scales across breast between half-collar or complete narrow breast-band. Female has buffy-orange underparts and often less blue on breast-sides.
Similar species Differs from Common, Variable Dwarf and Little Kingfishers by partial collar, larger size, creamy underparts, black legs and heavy pale-tipped bill. From Common Kingfisher also by plainer crown and less contrasting rump and back.
Voice Louder, stronger and less sibilant than Common Kingfisher.

Habits Along small, fairly slow-flowing rivers in lowland forest, sometimes in patchy degraded forest and logged forest, and one record from large forest-fringed lake. From sea-level to low hills. Probably replaced by Common Kingfisher on large slow rivers, mangroves and most lakes, and replaced by Variable Dwarf Kingfisher along small streams.
Conservation status Generally uncommon or rare, although may be fairly common on small islands. Threatened by forest loss and impact on water quality. IUCN: Vulnerable.
Range Endemic to Bismarcks, including Lavongai, New Ireland, Lihir, Umboi, New Britain and possibly Feni.

LITTLE KINGFISHER *Ceyx pusillus* Plate 46

(*Alcedo pusilla*; Martin-pêcheur poucet)

Description 11 cm. Tiny bright blue and white coastal kingfisher. Bright purple-blue upperparts and variable breast-band. Pure white underparts, loral spot and ear-covert patch. Black bill and legs. Juvenile has duller greener upperparts and buff wash on white patches, with fine black fringes on breast.
Similar species Differs from Variable Dwarf, Common and Bismarck Kingfishers by white underparts, partial or full breast-band and smaller size.
Voice Short quiet shrill *tseep*.
Habits Beside forested brackish coastal water, especially mangroves and estuaries. Perches on low branches over water and usually seen flying down channels.
Conservation status Locally fairly common but often rare through lack of habitat. Species not threatened but some subspecies may be at risk.
Range Bismarcks and Solomons.
C. p. masauji, endemic to New Ireland and New Britain including Lavongai, Djaul, Tabar and Umboi, has complete blue breast-band.
C. p. bougainvillei, endemic to Buka, Bougainville, Shortland, Choiseul, Isabel and Florida, has partial blue breast-band.
C. p. richardsi, endemic to Vella Lavella, Kolombangara, New Georgia, Vangunu, nearby small islands, Gizo, Rendova and Tetepare, has complete blue breast-band and blue undertail-coverts.
C. p. aolae, endemic to Guadalcanal, like *C. p. bougainvillei* but undertail-coverts white with blue tips.
Birds of unknown subspecies occur on Russell Is and Malaita.
Elsewhere, other subspecies occur in east Indonesia, New Guinea and north Australia.

COMMON KINGFISHER *Alcedo atthis* Plate 46

(River Kingfisher; Martin-pêcheur d'Europe)

Description 16 cm. Small river kingfisher. Upperparts blue with slight green wash, except for vivid blue back and rump, and indistinct paler bars on crown and spots on wing-coverts. White throat and rear ear-covert patch. Rich orange underparts and very small orange spot on lores and behind eye. Black bill and dull orange legs. Female has dark red base to lower mandible. Juvenile is duller with dusky fringes on underparts and dusky legs.
Similar species Differs from Bismarck Kingfisher by darker underparts, no part-collar, patterned crown and wing-coverts, brighter rump and back, orange legs and finer all-black bill. From Variable Dwarf Kingfisher by larger size, black bill, no purple tones to upperparts, darker orange underparts, more barred crown, and habitat.
Voice Sharp shrill *schree*, repeated several times or sometimes repeated rapidly as trill, lower-pitched than Variable Dwarf Kingfisher.
Habits Beside slow-moving rivers and lakes in forest and open habitats, and sheltered coasts, especially estuaries, mangroves and nearby reefs. May occur far inland alongside large slow rivers. Also on smaller streams in the Solomons, especially along coasts and even in towns.
Conservation status Uncommon. Not threatened.
Range Manus, St Matthias, Bismarcks and Solomons.
A. a. hispidoides, on Manus, Mussau, Emirau and across the Bismarcks from Long to Nissan, except far outlying islands, occurs elsewhere in east Indonesia, New Guinea satellite islands and east New Guinea
A. a. salomonensis, endemic to Solomons, from Buka and Bougainville to Makira including many smaller islands but not outlying islands, Russell Is, Florida Is or Rennell, is less green above and has even less orange behind eye.
Elsewhere, other subspecies occur across Europe and Asia.

BEE-EATERS Meropidae

Brilliantly coloured birds with distinctive hawking and sallying flight. Long wings, tail and decurved black bill. Hawk, often high in the sky, or sally from perches and swoop after flying insects.

BLUE-TAILED BEE-EATER *Merops philippinus* Plate 49

(Guêpier à queue d'azur)

Description 23 cm plus up to 9 cm tail-streamers. Greenish bee-eater with blue rump, tail and long central tail-streamers. Narrow black mask through eye, pale stripe under mask and orange-rufous throat. In flight, shows plain green upperwing, blue rump and uppertail and plain rufous underwing. Juvenile is duller with pale chestnut wash on throat and short or no tail-streamers.
Similar species Adult differs from Rainbow Bee-eater by lack of black throat-bar, larger size, more orange on throat, bluer uppertail and broader tail-streamers. Juvenile differs by larger size, more rufous on throat and breast, greener upperparts and sometimes bluer uppertail.
Voice Deep liquid trill, lower-pitched than Rainbow Bee-eater.
Habits Dry open lowland habitats, especially in savanna and grasslands. Breeds in sand-banks. Often small groups perched on trees and wires.
Conservation status Rare and local in Melanesia. Not threatened.
Range New Britain, where localised with records only from Cape Gloucester and Rabaul on New Britain and Long, Umboi and Sakar. Elsewhere, it breeds from India and China to Philippines, Indonesia and New Guinea.

RAINBOW BEE-EATER *Merops ornatus* Plate 49

(Guêpier arc-en-ciel)

Description 20 cm plus up to 6 cm tail-streamers. Greenish bee-eater with blue rump, black tail and narrow central tail-streamers with slightly broader tips. Narrow black mask through eye, black bar on lower throat and orange-yellow throat. Rufous flight feathers on upperwing, green wing-coverts, blue-grey mantle and rump, black uppertail, and plain rufous underwing. Juvenile is duller and lacks throat-band and tail-streamers.
Similar species See Blue-tailed Bee-eater, found only on New Britain.
Voice Liquid melodious *drrrrt*, often repeated, usually given in flight.
Habits Usually in forest edge including degraded forest, clearings, gardens but also open habitats with trees and over closed-canopy forest. Gregarious, sometimes in large flocks especially at roost or on migration but often singles where rare.
Conservation status Local and uncommon non-breeding migrant in Melanesia. Not threatened.
Range Admiralties, St Matthias and Bismarcks, including many outlying Bismarck islands east to Nissan, May–August, rarely March–September, breeding in Australia and migrating to New Guinea and east Indonesia.

HORNBILLS Bucerotidae

Huge noisy fruit-eating birds with long broad wings, long tail and long stout decurved bill.

BLYTH'S HORNBILL *Aceros plicatus* Plate 49

(Papuan Hornbill; Kokomo; *Rhyticeros plicatus*; Calao papou)

Description 75 cm. Huge black forest bird with long white tail and long creamy bill. Distinctive shape of long stout decurved bill, long broad wings and long tail. Pale blue naked skin around eye and on throat. Head and neck pale orange in male, black in female. Juvenile plumage as male but lacks ridges on top of bill. Immatures and adults slowly grow more ridges with age.
Similar species Unmistakable. Largest forest bird, larger than Channel-billed Cuckoo.
Voice Calls often. Loud deep honks and grunts, repeated as regular series, or laughing series rising then falling in pitch. Wings produce distinctive slow 'whooshing' sound in flight, reminiscent of steam engine.
Habits Old-growth forest with large trees to 1100 m, rarely to 1500 m. Singles, pairs and small flocks forage in forest canopy, especially in fruiting figs. Larger flocks gather at communal roosts. Often flies high over land and sea.
Conservation status Fairly common although rare where hunted. Not threatened.
Range Bismarcks and Solomons, including Lavongai, New Ireland and New Britain where sometimes separated

as *A. p. dampieri*, Buka, Bougainville and Shortland Is where sometimes separated as *A. p. harterti*, Choiseul, Isabel, throughout the New Georgia group, Russell Is, Malaita and Guadalcanal where sometimes separated as *A. p. mendanae*. Elsewhere, other subspecies breed in east Indonesia and New Guinea.

PITTAS Pittidae

Brilliantly coloured dumpy birds with very short wings and tail. Hop along forest floor on long legs but shy and often only seen when flushed and fly away, flashing bright blue wing-coverts. Feed on insects in leaf-litter and snails, often breaking their shells on a favoured rock. Loud territorial calls are given from branches or occasionally from ground.

RED-BELLIED PITTA *Pitta erythrogaster* — Plate 49

(Blue-breasted Pitta; Brève à ventre rouge)

Description 17 cm. Multicoloured pitta with blue and red underparts. Shining sky-blue upper breast and orange-red lower breast to undertail-coverts. Brownish head and throat with orange-rufous cap and hindneck, shining green mantle and shining dark blue wing-coverts. In flight shows small white central spot on dark brown primaries and blue rump and uppertail. Female is slightly duller. Juvenile buffy-brown with paler underparts, creamy lower throat, dull blue on rump and tail, orange-red on bill, and soon showing some green, blue and red.
Similar species Only pitta in range, except on Tolokiwa where also Hooded Pitta. Adult is distinctive. Juvenile differs from juvenile Hooded Pitta by buffy-brown head, patterned throat, paler plumage and soon with blue on upperparts.
Voice Territorial call is a low tremulous double whistle, first note rising, then a short stutter and descending second note, *croooo-ee, croo-oow*, taking 2–3 seconds and repeated at 8–30-second intervals for variably long periods. Sometimes a third note similar to second or just second note alone. Alarm call a hoarse *we-ah*.
Habits Forest, usually forest edge and especially secondary growth, to at least 1200 m. Shy and unobtrusive when foraging on ground but more confiding when calling from high perches. Calls, especially in early morning, from branches in subcanopy and sometimes from ground or logs.
Conservation status Uncommon or locally fairly common but seemingly absent from many areas. Species not threatened, but *P. e. splendida* has small population which may be threatened by forest loss.
Range Bismarcks.
P. e. gazellae, endemic to New Britain, including Tolokiwa, Umboi, Lolobau, Watom and probably Duke of York, has a few blue feathers in crown, bright orange-rufous hindcrown and nape, grey-brown throat and variably narrow black band between blue and red on breast.
P. e. novaehibernicae, endemic to New Ireland, has more uniform rufous crown, brownish-red throat and no black breast-band. Birds recorded from Djaul are either this or an undescribed subspecies.
P. e. extima, endemic to Lavongai, is similar to *P. e. novaehibernicae* but has more blue on crown, paler, more orange nape, and bluer mantle.
P. e. splendida, endemic to Tabar, has blackish head with red and occasionally sonic blue on central crown, orange-red nape, narrow black hind-collar, deep blue upperparts, black throat and deep blue and red on underparts.
Elsewhere, other subspecies breed in Philippines, Indonesia, New Guinea and far north Australia.

HOODED PITTA *Pitta sordida* — Plate 49

(Brève à capuchin)

Description 17 cm. Grass-green pitta with black head and neck, silvery-blue wing-covert patch and red central belly to undertail-coverts. Inconspicuous shining necklace under black throat, bluish flanks and black on central mid-belly. In flight, adult shows bright blue wing-coverts and small white central spot on dark primaries. Female slightly duller. Juvenile dull grey-brown with black head, buffy throat, pale reddish undertail-coverts, green-washed wings, orange tip to bill and no white on wing. Immature similar to adult but lacks blue on wing-coverts and has buffy-brown throat and brown spots on underparts.
Similar species Adult plumage distinctive. Juvenile differs from juvenile Red-bellied Pitta by black head, plain throat, darker plumage and soon with green on upperparts.
Voice Sometimes calls at night. Territorial call a loud double whistle, *kuhwee-kuwee?*, second note often slightly higher-pitched, repeated at three second intervals for variably long periods. Alarm call a nasal *kiaow!* Also short rasping notes.

Habits Lowland forest and secondary regrowth. Shy and unobtrusive when foraging, hopping along ground. Calls from ground, logs or very low perches.
Conservation status Status in Melanesia poorly known. Not threatened.
Range *P. s. novaeguineae* breeds on Crown, Long and Tolokiwa off New Britain. New Guinea birds are dispersive and may occasionally reach other islands in Melanesia. Elsewhere, *P. s. novaeguineae* breeds across New Guinea and other subspecies breed from east Himalayas and Philippines to Indonesia.

SUPERB PITTA *Pitta superba* — Plate 49

(Black-headed Pitta; Brève superbe)

Description 21 cm. Large black, blue and red pitta. Glossy black with extensive shining sky-blue patch on wing-coverts and bright red central belly and undertail-coverts. Dark green on tertials and secondaries, heavy black bill and pale pinkish-brown legs. Female slightly duller and smaller. Immature duller with no gloss on black plumage, little gloss on wing-coverts, duller pinker belly and undertail-coverts, and orange tip to bill.
Similar species No other Manus species has black, blue and red plumage. Metallic Starling may flush from ground but lacks blue on wing-coverts.
Voice Territorial call is a loud quavering double whistle, *hwoow-whoow*, similar to Hooded Pitta, repeated regularly for variably long periods. Notes are almost identical, unlike *ku-koo* call of MacKinlay's Cuckoo-Dove which has lower-pitched second note. Harsh chicken-like *gwark* alarm call.
Habits Inhabits secondary regrowth with patches of tall forest within primary forest, with recent records from 100 m. Shy and unobtrusive when foraging, hopping along ground in forest. Calls from low branches or subcanopy to 20 m up in large trees. Wings are thrust closer to body and forward with each note of territorial call.
Conservation status Inexplicably rare and localised. Possibly threatened by introduced predators. IUCN: Vulnerable.
Range Endemic to Manus where historically widespread, but few recent records.

BLACK-FACED PITTA *Pitta anerythra* — Plate 49

(Solomons Pitta; Brève masquée)

Description 16 cm. Typical pitta with blackish-brown head, green mantle and wings, shining sky-blue wing-coverts and buff underparts. Black bill and pale pinkish-grey legs. In flight, appears rather plain with a bright pale blue wing-covert patch, small white patch on primaries, and sometimes blue on uppertail-coverts. Female as male. Juvenile unknown.
Similar species Only pitta in the Solomons but Noisy Pitta *P. versicolor*, not yet recorded from Melanesia but some Australian birds migrate to south New Guinea, and Hooded Pitta may possibly occur as rare vagrants. Differs from Hooded and Noisy Pittas by lacking red and black on belly and vent.
Voice Territorial call is a double whistle, *tooi, tooiii*, second note longer and rising. At close range has tremulous quality of Red-bellied Pitta or an uncoiling spring, but at long range sounds like Hooded Pitta. Repeated at 5–20-second intervals. Sometimes just second note alone.
Habits Recent records from primary forest and patchworks of forest and secondary growth, at 400–600 m. Historical records also from forest on coastal and alluvial plains. Shy and unobtrusive at all times. Calls from low branches, or sometimes subcanopy, especially at dawn and dusk.
Conservation status Recent records only from near Tirotonga village on Isabel where fairly common. Possibly overlooked elsewhere, but call and appearance are distinctive and absent from other surveyed areas. May be threatened by introduced cats and rats. IUCN: Vulnerable.
Range Endemic to Solomons, on Bougainville, Choiseul and Isabel.
P. a. pallida, endemic to Bougainville, is large, with paler underparts almost white on flanks, belly and undertail-coverts, black head sometimes with chestnut band on upper nape and black throat, and some blue on uppertail-coverts.
P. a. nigrifrons, endemic to Choiseul, has black head with rich chestnut-brown hindcrown, becoming paler on nape, and deep buff underparts.
P. a. anerythra, endemic to Isabel, has entire crown rich chestnut-brown, slightly paler on nape, broad black mask from bill to nape, and deep buff underparts.

HONEYEATERS Meliphagidae

Diverse Australasian family with long decurved bills, mostly feeding on nectar, but some are insectivores. Most are boldly patterned in drab colours but many male myzomelas have bright red patches. Often active and pugnacious, sometimes gregarious especially at flowering trees. Noisy, with loud and varied calls. *Myzomela* species are tiny and compact like sunbirds, plumage usually with black or red. Medium-sized species *Stresemannia, Lichmera, Guadalcanaria, Melidectes* and *Glycifohia* are often rather plain but mostly with bold facial patterns. Crow Honeyeater *Gymnomyza* is black, friarbirds *Philemon* have naked faces, and both are large and lanky with rather floppy flight.

GUADALCANAL HONEYEATER *Guadalcanaria inexpectata* Plate 62

(*Meliphaga inexpectata*; **Méliphage de Guadalcanal**)

Description 20 cm. Medium-large elongate honeyeater with yellow stripe on ear-coverts. Slate-grey upperparts with bright olive wing-panel and bright yellow stripe between ear-coverts and neck. Fairly long decurved black bill, dark moustachial and malar stripes, white throat, pale grey underparts with heavy dark streaks on lower throat and breast, and sometimes plain white flanks. Immature has paler yellow neck-stripe and less defined streaking on underparts.
Similar species Distinctive plumage and size.
Voice Usually quiet. Nasal *chow* like a squeaky toy. Bubbling *kee-kee-kee-*.
Habits Montane forest above 1250 m, perhaps down to 950 m. Singles and pairs forage unobtrusively in forest canopy, usually in flowering and fruiting trees.
Conservation status Fairly common in the one montane area which has been explored but status elsewhere is unknown. Not threatened.
Range Endemic to Guadalcanal.

CROW HONEYEATER *Gymnomyza aubryana* Plate 84

(**Méliphage toulou**)

Description 39 cm. Very large black honeyeater with orange-red wattle. Plumage all glossy black, with long rounded tail and fairly long black decurved bill. Orange-red patch around eye, double wattle behind eye, yellow on bill-base and pinkish-yellow legs. Naked facial skin may be yellow. Immature lacks naked facial skin but has yellow patch on ear-coverts.
Similar species Differs from New Caledonian Crow and South Melanesian Cuckooshrike by habits and flight action, wattles, long tail and long decurved bill.
Voice Sings from an hour before dawn. Song is a loud, repeated series of slightly varied phrases, typically a loud nasal note, e.g. *chong*, followed by a descending series, e.g. *tchku-tchku-*... Harsh scolding *tcharr* or *wa-wa* similar to parrot or crow.
Habits Humid forest, including small isolated forest patches, usually on ultrabasic soils, 100–850 m, historically to 1000 m. Occurs in *maquis* scrub up to two km from forest. Singles and pairs are unobtrusive and shy in forest canopy and mid-storey. Loose floppy flight, with long rounded wings, long tail and fairly long neck.
Conservation status Rare and very localised. Estimated to have a population of less than 250 birds. IUCN: Critically Endangered.
Range Endemic to Grande Terre, New Caledonia, where scattered in a few forests in south, including Rivière Bleue area, Kouakoué, Pourina and Ouiné valleys, Rivière Blanche and Mont Pouédihi, and possibly extinct on Mt Panié in north.

[NOISY MINER *Manorina melanocephala*] (not illustrated)

(**Méliphage bruyant**)

Description 25 cm. Grey medium-sized gregarious honeyeater. Grey with white forehead, black crown and cheeks, darker wings with olive wing-panel, dark tail with pale tip, and pale whitish lower breast and belly. Yellow medium-short bill, eye-patch and legs, similar to Common Myna.
Similar species Distinctive on Three Sisters. Differs from medium-sized honeyeaters, e.g. Makira Honeyeater, by black crown and cheeks.
Voice Repeated loud strident notes, e.g. *pwee*, often sounding like bird of prey.
Habits Coconut plantations and open habitats. Small flocks forage at all levels, often hopping on ground, and aggressively chasing and mobbing other birds.
Range Previously on Three Sisters, Solomons, where introduced in 1950s but probably soon died out. Endemic resident in Australia.

NEW BRITAIN FRIARBIRD *Philemon cockerelli* Plate 52

(Polochion de Nouvelle-Bretagne)

Description 34 cm. Large lanky friarbird with dark head and upperparts. Fairly long stout blackish bill and dark brown head separated from dull dark brown upperparts by pale grizzled grey hindneck; pale grey-buff throat and upper breast with slight mottling, sometimes a slight brown breast-band, and becoming warmer buffy-grey-brown on belly; narrow pale terminal tail-bar. Juvenile has paler grey hindneck, olive wash to wings and tail, and yellow wash to breast.
Similar species Differs from New Britain Honeyeater by contrasting dark skin on head, paler underparts, larger size and stouter bill.
Voice Noisy, strident and conspicuous, starting long before dawn. Resonant nasal *thoo* similar to Large-tailed Nightjar, often given as endless series before dawn. Variable single calls, e.g. resonant *thoo* and *klonk*. Variable series of 2–6 disyllabic notes, repeated several times, e.g. *thoo-wit*, *show-ka* and *tee-o-woh*. Hoarse *caw* similar to crow.
Habits Forest, degraded forest and forest edge including gardens and coconuts with tall trees, commonly to 1200 m and uncommonly to 1600 m. Singles, pairs and small groups are noisy and pugnacious but rather shy, foraging in canopy, sometimes in mixed large-species flocks.
Conservation status Common. Not threatened.
Range Endemic to New Britain.
P. c. cockerelli is endemic to New Britain and Duke of York.
P. c. umboi, endemic to Umboi where it occurs to *c*.760 m, is slightly larger with a heavier bill.

NEW IRELAND FRIARBIRD *Philemon eichhorni* Plate 52

(Polochion de Nouvelle-Irlande)

Description 32 cm. Large lanky friarbird with white spotted underparts. Fairly long stout blackish bill and dark brown head, grey-brown mantle, wings and tail with broad white terminal tail-bar. White throat and hindneck with dark mottling, pale brown neck and breast with white spots or scales and plain buff lower belly. Juvenile has some white fringes on upperparts and yellow wash to throat.
Similar species Distinctive spotted underparts, shape and calls.
Voice Varied but less noisy than other friarbirds. Typical song is a three-note rising whistle, *pu-du-leet*. Scolding *schraah*.
Habits Montane forest from at least 750–2200 m. Singles are rather shy in canopy, sometimes loosely with mixed-species flocks.
Conservation status Fairly common. Not threatened.
Range Endemic to New Ireland where known from mountains in far south but possibly also on the Lelet plateau.

MANUS FRIARBIRD *Philemon albitorques* Plate 52

(White-naped Friarbird; Polochion à nuque blanche)

Description 35 cm. Large lanky friarbird with creamy-white neck and underparts. Fairly long stout blackish bill, rich dark brown naked head, rich dark brown mantle, wings and tail with narrow white terminal tail-band, downy white collar and creamy-white underparts.
Similar species Distinctive shape, calls, and white underparts and neck.
Voice Loud, noisy and conspicuous, often duets or calls in group, starting before dawn. Explosive series of usually 2–5 *ko*, *chow*, *chow-ka* and *chow-ka-po* notes. Harsh screech similar to Eclectus Parrot but lower-pitched and less harsh. Loud cackles.
Habits Forest edge, isolated trees and villages, less common in secondary forest and mangrove, and uncommon in closed-canopy forest. Pairs and sometimes small groups conspicuous but shy in canopy and flowering trees. Flies with heavy flaps interspersed with glides, on long broad wings and long neck and tail.
Conservation status Common. Not threatened.
Range Endemic to Manus and probably Los Negros.

NEW CALEDONIAN FRIARBIRD *Philemon diemenensis* Plate 84

(Polochion moine)

Description 28 cm. Large lanky honeyeater with striped face and blue-grey wing-panel. Dark brown head with long stout blackish bill, pale stripe on ear-coverts, dark moustachial stripe and pale throat. Silvery-grey hindneck, dark brown mantle, pale blue-grey fringes on blackish wings and tail, and brighter blue panel on wing-coverts, but blue-

grey can be dull and narrow on worn birds. Long pointed silvery feathers create streaky silvery breast, some streaks extending over buffy-brown belly. Juvenile lacks or has short white streaks on underparts, with plainer head.
Similar species Differs from Dark Brown and Barred Honeyeaters by larger size, stouter bill, and wing and breast pattern.
Voice Calls often and loudly. Varied notes, often sharp but melodious, and usually repeated. Long series of *chow-chow-* notes, accelerating then fading away. Long series of paired *tee-tok* notes, slightly accelerating. Fruity *chong* often repeated 2–3 times. Multisyllabic calls, e.g. *hee-haw* and *popinJAY*. Harsh scolding *tchar*.
Habits Forest and most open habitats with some tall trees including *maquis*. Singles and pairs are conspicuous, active and pugnacious in canopy. Often on open canopy perches.
Conservation status Fairly common. Not threatened.
Range Endemic to New Caledonia, including Grande Terre, Ile des Pins, Lifou and Maré.

NEW BRITAIN HONEYEATER *Melidectes whitemanensis* Plate 52

(Gilliard's Honeyeater; New Britain Melidectes; Bismarck Melidectes; *Vosea whitemanensis*; Méliphage de Whiteman)

Description 22 cm. Plain olive-brown honeyeater with small eye-patch. Whole bird uniformly olive-brown with brighter yellow-green fringes on wings and tail, faint pale streaking on head and neck. Has small yellow-grey naked patch below and behind eye, and long decurved black bill. Female very slightly duller.
Similar species Differs from New Britain Friarbird by smaller size, yellowish wing-panel, less contrasting underparts and finer bill. From Ashy Myzomela by larger size, yellowish wing-panel, eye-patch and stouter bill.
Voice Pairs of soft mellow whistles, second lower-pitched and slightly trilled and downslurred, repeated 3–8 times at 0.7-second intervals.
Habits Montane forest from 1200 m to at least 1750 m, occasionally down to 850 m. Singles are active in mid- and upper storeys of montane forest, often feeding at epiphytic flowers, probing and gleaning, and sometimes in small groups on flowering trees. In flight, has large round broad wings and long tail.
Conservation status Usually uncommon but common on Mt Talawe. Its small population may be threatened by logging extending into lower mountains. IUCN: Near Threatened.
Range Endemic to New Britain but no records from Bainings Mountains.

MAKIRA HONEYEATER *Meliarchus sclateri* Plate 73

(San Cristobal/Makira Melidectes; Graceless Honeyeater; *Melidectes sclateri*; Méliphage de San Cristobal)

Description 25 cm. Large, rather scrawny brown honeyeater with long pale bill. Long creamy bill and broad creamy eye-ring drooping onto rear ear-coverts, sometimes yellowish-green to blue-grey. Olive-brown upperparts with pale yellowish streaks on crown, olive-green fringes on wings and warm russet-brown tail. Long broad dark moustachial stripe. Very pale olive-brown underparts with short narrow dark brown stripes on breast and belly. Juvenile has darker bill, less contrasting head pattern and less distinct streaks on yellower underparts.
Similar species Distinctive proportions and plumage, closest to Pacific Koel from which it differs by its long bill and unbarred tail.
Voice Varied loud, clear, harsh and nasal notes, e.g. repeated *powh*, *koyee*, *quee-arh*. Shrill mewing, e.g. *cheok*, *duit*. Long monotonous series of whistles *whit, whit, whit*… Loud chatters.
Habits Commonest in forest edge but also closed forest, gardens, coconuts and scrub up to 900 m, especially in hills. Noisy and quarrelsome, usually in pairs or mixed-species flocks, foraging in thickets, dense vegetation and large flowers high in forest. Long head, neck, wings and tail are especially prominent in the ungainly and erratic bounding flight.
Conservation status Common. Not threatened.
Range Endemic to Makira.

BOUGAINVILLE HONEYEATER *Stresemannia bougainvillei* Plate 62

(*Meliphaga/Melilestes bougainvillea*; Méliphage de Bougainville)

Description 17 cm. Plain large dark brown honeyeater with long decurved black bill. Olive-grey upperparts with slightly brighter olive fringes on wings and tail, paler greyer underparts, slightly buffier flanks and blue-grey legs. Male is more olive on underparts, where female is greyer. Juvenile greyer with dark grey bill.
Similar species Differs from female Red-capped Myzomela by much larger size and darker, more uniform plumage.

Voice Short series of 4–5 mellow whistles, first note rising then falling, subsequent notes alternately rise or fall. Dry rasping *chht, chht*.
Habits Montane forest from 700 m to at least 1950 m. Singles and pairs are unobtrusive in canopy and subcanopy, sometimes small groups in flowering trees.
Conservation status Uncommon. Not threatened.
Range Endemic to Bougainville.

BARRED HONEYEATER *Glycifohia undulata* — Plate 84

(*Phylidonyris undulata*; Méliphage barré)

Description 19 cm. Medium-sized honeyeater with barred underparts. Dark brown crown and nape has bold white scales, darker ear-coverts, silvery malar stripe, dark upper throat and long fine decurved black bill. Dark brown upperparts, with pale bars on mantle, pale fringes on wings and indistinct green wing-panel, pale grey underparts with black barring but fainter on throat, central belly and vent. Juvenile duller and slightly paler overall, with only faint barring.
Similar species Differs from Grey-eared Honeyeater by barred pale underparts, white speckled head and neck, larger size and longer finer bill. From New Caledonian Friarbird by smaller size, finer bill, and plumage.
Voice Loud fruity notes. Song is a slow series of repeated notes, mostly rich fruity whistles, e.g. *fweeoo*, and some rapid series of shorter clucks, e.g. *chuuk*. Often gives slow series of single calls.
Habits Forest and *maquis*, including dry forest, savanna and gardens, at all altitudes but commoner in mountains and around flowering trees. Singles and pairs are rather unobtrusive, foraging and probing for insects and in flowers, in mid-storey and canopy. Small flocks aggregate and chase around flowering trees. May call from prominent canopy perch.
Conservation status Fairly common. Not threatened.
Range Endemic to Grande Terre, New Caledonia.

VANUATU HONEYEATER *Glycifohia notabilis* — Plate 78

(New Hebrides Honeyeater; White-bellied Honeyeater; *Phylidonyris notabilis*; Méliphage des Nouvelles-Hébrides)

Description 19 cm. Medium-sized honeyeater with streaked white underparts and long decurved bill. Black crown, face and ear-coverts speckled white, especially supercilium, rufous-brown upperparts, and white underparts with dark brown streaks on breast-sides and flanks. Juvenile has plain underparts or faint streaks, and pale streaks and fringes on upperparts.
Similar species Differs from Grey-eared Honeyeater by streaked white underparts and black hood.
Voice Starts calling before dawn. Loud and varied, usually repeated ringing fruity or chirping notes, e.g. *tyau*, *toowyt* and *teewee*. Song is a series of melodious notes and whistles, e.g. *teewee-twytwytwy*. Harsh *schr* or *scherr*. Rapid piping scold.
Habits Forest including tall secondary forest on larger islands but also open degraded habitats on some smaller islands such as Vanua Lava. From sea-level on Vanua Lava but localised in lowlands on Santo and rarely or never recorded in lowlands on other islands. Singles, pairs and small groups are active in canopy and undergrowth of forest, especially around flowers.
Conservation status Common. Not threatened.
Range Endemic to northern Vanuatu.
G. n. notabilis, endemic to Ureparapara, Vanua Lava, Santo and Ambae, has broken spotted white supercilium.
G. n. superciliaris, endemic to Maewo, Pentecost, Malekula, Ambrym, Paama and Epi, has more prominent continuous supercilium, more white on malar stripe and lower ear-coverts, better defined black eye-stripe and less whitish speckling on crown.

GREY-EARED HONEYEATER *Lichmera incana* — Plates 78 & 84

(Dark-brown Honeyeater; Silver-eared Honeyeater; Méliphage à oreillons gris)

Description 16 cm. Medium-small plain grey-brown honeyeater with decurved bill. Dark grey head with dark bare skin around eye, silver wash on ear-coverts and sometimes a slight pale moustachial stripe, olive-brown upperparts with brighter green wing-panel, and paler olive-grey underparts. Occasional yellow-washed birds on Efate. Juvenile is paler and lacks silver on ear-coverts.

Similar species Differs from female Cardinal and New Caledonian Myzomelas by larger size, more elongate shape, plainer plumage and green wing-panel. From Vanuatu and Barred Honeyeaters by darker underparts and plainer plumage.
Voice Loud and noisy, often the dominant bird sound. Calls vigorously from before dawn. Varied loud song of repeated short phrases of various fruity notes and sparrow-like chirps, less melodious than Melanesian and Rufous Whistlers and lacking whiplashes. Tooting *poo-poo-poo-*. Chirping *churrup*, slightly longer and more disyllabic than House Sparrow. Harsh chur.
Habits Open forest, scrub, *maquis*, *niaouli* savanna, coconuts, mangroves, open habitats and urban areas in lowlands and low hills. Noisy and often chasing other birds. Singles and pairs forage restlessly around flowers at all heights, or congregations of up to 30 birds in flowering trees.
Conservation status Common. Not threatened.
Range Endemic to central and south Vanuatu and New Caledonia.
L. i. griseoviridis, endemic to central Vanuatu, including Malo, Malekula, Ambrym, Epi, Efate and all small islands between these, is paler than *L. i. flavocincta* and larger than *L. i. mareensis*.
L. i. flavotincta, endemic to Erromango, is darker grey-brown on chin to breast and has darker, more olive upperparts.
L. i. poliotis, endemic to Ouvéa and Lifou, has paler underparts.
L. i. mareensis, endemic to Maré, has darker grey underparts with more yellow wash than *L. i. poliotis*.
L. i. incana, endemic to Grande Terre and Ile des Pins, is slightly smaller with less grey on throat and brown on neck and breast.

ASHY MYZOMELA *Myzomela cineracea* — Plate 53

(Ashy Honeyeater; also treated as a subspecies of Red-throated Myzomela *M. eques*; Myzomèle cendré)

Description 15 cm. Large long-billed and relatively long-tailed dull grey myzomela. Uniformly dark dull grey plumage, slightly darker on head and throat, paler on belly and sometimes greenish fringes on wings. In flight, shows white underwing. Male has minute or absent pink-red chin-patch. Female has very small pink-red chin-patch and darker throat.
Similar species Differs from other myzomelas by lacking any obvious red in plumage, longer bill, long tail and larger size. From Bismarck Honeyeater by smaller size, plain greyish plumage, fine bill and no eye-ring.
Voice Calls are infrequent, quiet and unobtrusive. Regular series of single or double notes often at dawn *chip-chip-chip* or *chip-chop, chip-chop...* Rapid harsh chattering *chee-chee-chee-*, rising and falling in pitch, quieter and less shrill than hawk. Thin whistled *hoet, hoet...*
Habits Forest, but commoner in degraded forest and scrub, and locally in coconuts, to at least 1200 m. Singles, sometimes pairs, are unobtrusive in all storeys of forest, but most often in understorey, often feeding at epiphytic flowers, sometimes loosely with mixed-species flocks.
Conservation status Common. Not threatened.
Range Endemic to New Britain and Umboi. Umboi birds may be larger and have been treated as *M. c. rooki*.

RED MYZOMELA *Myzomela cruentata* — Plate 53

(Red-tinted Myzomela/Honeyeater; Myzomèle vermillon)

Description 11 cm. Slim myzomela with pink-red male and pink-red or grey-brown female. Male is entirely dull pink-red, darker on head and darker and browner on wings and tail. Female on New Britain is grey-brown with red on forehead, chin and tail. Female of other subspecies as male, but duller paler brownish-red. Juvenile is browner than adults, especially on underparts.
Similar species Pink-red plumage distinctive. Female and juvenile differ from Ashy Myzomela on New Britain by smaller size, redder plumage and red on forehead and tail. From New Britain and New Ireland Myzomelas by redder plumage, red on tail and limited red on head. From Sclater's Myzomela on small islands off New Britain by red on tail and forehead and limited red on throat.
Voice Rapid, almost stuttering trill *tsip-tsip-tsip-*. High-pitched *tsip* or *tseep* notes, more lisping, lower-pitched and longer than sunbirds, often repeated at about two second intervals.
Habits Forest including degraded forest and overgrown coconuts, usually at all altitudes. Singles and pairs forage unobtrusively in canopy especially at flowers where sometimes mixed with other honeyeaters.
Conservation status Fairly uncommon. Not threatened.
Range Bismarcks.
M. c. coccinea, endemic to New Britain and Duke of York, where usually above 800 m; female and juvenile are grey-brown with red on forehead, chin and tail.

M. c. erythrina, endemic to New Ireland where rarely above 1000 m; male is duller, darker and more vinaceous with darker crown, female as male but duller and slightly paler, juvenile dull rosy, browner on breast and belly.
M. c. lavongai, endemic to Lavongai, like *M. c. erythrina* but male slightly brighter, juvenile with buffy-grey underparts.
M. c. vinacea, endemic to Djaul, like *M. c. erythrina* but juvenile dull dark plum-red with slightly paler underparts and slightly darker throat.
M. c. cantans, endemic to Tabar, like *M. c. erythrina* but slightly darker, female greyer on breast and belly, and juvenile much darker with contrasting red throat and red-washed grey-brown underparts.
Elsewhere, *M. c. cruentata*, with brighter male and browner female, breeds across New Guinea. The New Britain and New Guinea subspecies are distinct from the other subspecies and could be treated as separate species.

NEW IRELAND MYZOMELA *Myzomela pulchella* — Plate 53

(New Ireland Honeyeater; Olive-yellow Myzomela; Myzomèle de Nouvelle-Irlande)

Description 11 cm. Red-headed brownish myzomela, fairly fat, appearing pot-bellied in flight. Bright red head and throat, black lores, grey-brown or olive-brown nape and upperparts, dark mottling on breast and pale yellowish-buff underparts. Juvenile has dull olive-green upperparts, throat and breast, and dull yellow-olive underparts, with scattered red feathers on face and throat..
Similar species Differs from Red Myzomela by lack of red wash across upperparts and most of underparts. Juvenile differs from female Olive-backed Sunbird by duller underparts, plain tail and head pattern and may have red feathers. Juvenile from female Black Sunbird by lack of contrasting grey crown and white throat, and may have red feathers.
Voice Buzzing downslurred *pezzzz* or *bzzr*. Nasal *tchu* softer than Bismarck White-eye.
Habits Hill and montane forest above 350 m, occasionally down to 150 m on steep mountains, but commoner at higher altitudes. Singles and small groups forage in canopy and congregate in flowering trees.
Conservation status Fairly common. Not threatened.
Range Endemic to New Ireland, where known from the south and Lelet Plateau and to be expected elsewhere.

NEW CALEDONIAN MYZOMELA *Myzomela caledonica* — Plate 82

(New Caledonian Honeyeater; also treated as a subspecies of Scarlet Myzomela *M. sanguinolenta*; Myzomèle calédonien)

Description 11 cm. Red and black or grey-brown myzomela. Male has scarlet hood, back, rump and upper breast, with black lores, wings and tail, and white flanks and belly. Red breast merges into white lower breast with some streaking and darker mottling. Female is mousy grey-brown, with darker wings and tail, paler underparts with variable, usually indistinct, red wash on forehead and slight red on throat and rump. Juvenile has warmer brown upperparts and broader pale fringes on wings
Similar species Male distinctive. Female differs from Grey-eared Honeyeater by red wash, smaller size, dumpy shape and paler underparts. From Fan-tailed Gerygone by decurved bill, no eye-stripe and no white on tail.
Voice Song is a series of short hurried phrases, usually 2–10 notes per phrase, e.g. short dry rattle of identical notes, double notes *tchu-tchu—tchu-tchu— tchu-tchu-* and piping *tchu-tche*. Very short sharp high-pitched single *tsip* contact calls.
Habits Forest, degraded forest habitats, *niaouli* savanna and *maquis*, and scrub with some large trees. Singles and pairs are active in canopy. Male often calls from prominent canopy perch.
Conservation status Fairly common. Not threatened.
Range Endemic to New Caledonia, on Grande Terre and Ile des Pins.

CARDINAL MYZOMELA *Myzomela cardinalis* — Plates 70, 75, 77, 78 & 82

(Cardinal Honeyeater; Myzomèle cardinal)

Description 12 cm. Fairly large dumpy red and black or olive-brown myzomela. Male has crimson head and body, black wings and tail, and variable amount of black on underparts and back. Female is olive-brown, with paler underparts and variable extent of dull red or red wash on face, throat and rump. Juvenile has duller red wash. Some birds in Vanuatu and Loyalties may lack any red.
Similar species Male distinctive. Female's fine decurved bill and red rump distinctive. On Makira, differs from slimmer Sooty Myzomela and Olive-backed Sunbird by brown plumage. On Rennell, Vanuatu and Loyalties, from Fan-tailed Gerygone by lack of yellow on underparts, plain head pattern and lack of white on tail-tips. On Vanuatu and

Loyalties, from Grey-eared Honeyeater by size, dumpy short-tailed shape, head pattern and lack of olive on wings. On Lifou, from Large Lifou White-eye by longer finer bill, black bill and legs, and uniform upperparts.
Voice Various harsh, often repeated notes. Fruity upslurred *chew-cheewi* or *oh-chewi* or *chewi*. Rapid chattering long series *ch-ch-ch-ch-* oscillating in pitch. Buzzing *brree-oee* or shorter *tee-oh*. Various short hard upslurred notes, e.g. *whit*, some nasal, e.g. *schew*. Typical song is a series of varied jingling phrases of 2–8 mixed melodious and contact calls, e.g. *tzeewyt-tzeewyt—tweet-weet-tweet*. Some variation in calls between islands, including a melodious white-eye-like dawn song only on Rennell.
Habits Forest, scrub and coconuts at all altitudes. Excluded from some habitats by other honeyeaters, e.g. by Sooty Myzomela from forest on Makira, and by Grey-eared Honeyeater from coconuts and scrub on Loyalties. Singles and small flocks are active and pugnacious at all levels but especially canopy. Males are often in small groups, but females and immatures are less common and usually single but sometimes in mixed-species flocks. Flies between close islands and occurs transiently on tiny islets.
Conservation status Common. Used to be caught and plucked for red feather money in Temotu. Not threatened.
Range Makira, Rennell, Temotu, Vanuatu and Loyalties.
M. c. pulcherrima, endemic to Makira, Ugi and Three Sisters, only occurring close to coastal coconuts on Makira; male has black vent and central belly, female has red head, mantle and rump, and red-washed olive-brown underparts, and immature is olive-brown with variable amounts of red.
M. c. sanfordi, endemic to Rennell; male like *M. c. pulcherrima* but more red on belly and vent, and duller crown and throat, immature male has red on rump and red wash on face, underparts and sometimes mantle, female is olive-brown with red head, throat, upper breast and rump, and red wash over some of mantle and lower breast.
M. c. sanctaecrucis, endemic to Temotu, including Nendo, Reef Is, Duff Is, Utupua and Vanikoro, and Torres Is; male like *M. c. pulcherrima* but brighter red, immature male like adult but patchy red on upperparts and neck, female has red rump and red wash on mantle and breast.
M. c. tucopiae, endemic to Tikopia; male has black on lower breast and belly, other plumages unknown.
M. c. tenuis, endemic to northern Vanuatu, including all islands between Banks Is and Efate, like *M. c. cardinalis* but smaller and female has brighter, greener upperparts.
M. c. cardinalis, endemic to Erromango, Tanna and Aneityum; male has black on vent and belly, immature male has red on head, throat, mantle and sometimes neck and rump, and female has dull red on chin and forecrown, sometimes nape, mantle and rump.
M. c. lifuensis, endemic to Ouvéa, Lifou and Maré, where restricted to forest; male has black breast and belly.
Elsewhere, *M. c. nigriventris* breeds in Samoa.

SCLATER'S MYZOMELA *Myzomela sclateri* — Plate 53

(Scarlet-bibbed Myzomela/Honeyeater; Myzomèle de Sclater)

Description 11 cm. Small-island myzomela. Male has bright red throat, sooty head and upper mantle, dark brown upperparts with olive fringes on wings, dusky-brown upper breast fading to pale yellow belly with faint streaks. In flight, shows white on underwing. Female has small, faint or no red throat, dark brown upperparts and pale grey-yellow underparts with darker streaks, paler on central belly.
Similar species Male has distinctive red bib. Female differs from Olive-backed Sunbird by duller, slightly streaked underparts and no supercilium. From female Black Sunbird by brownish head, dusky throat and streaks on underparts. Also see Bismarck Black Myzomela, Ashy Myzomela on Umboi, and Black-bellied Myzomela on New Britain.
Voice Wheezy *tseow-cheeu*, first note upslurred, second lower and downslurred. Nasal *psst* and *tseer*.
Habits Forest, especially in flowering trees and nearby coconuts, at all altitudes. Singles and small groups forage actively at all levels and all altitudes, flocking especially at flowering trees.
Conservation status Common, but rare on large islands such as Umboi. Not threatened.
Range Endemic to small islands off New Britain, including Crown, Long, Tolokiwa, Umboi, Bali, Witu, small islets off north coast of New Britain to Watom and Credner, and elsewhere occurs in mountains on Karkar.

BISMARCK BLACK MYZOMELA *Myzomela pammelaena* — Plate 53

(Ebony Myzomela; Bismarck Black Honeyeater; Myzomèle ébène)

Description 12 cm. All-black myzomela, but grey or whitish underwing. Male is shiny but not iridescent. Female duller. Juvenile dusky, browner on underparts.
Similar species Differs from male Black Sunbird on larger islands by whitish underwings, lack of iridescence on throat and upperparts, shorter bill and longer tail. See Sclater's Myzomela.

Voice Variable and perhaps mimetic. Song is a short series of simple notes, e.g. *shwee, shwee—-suit*. Repeated loud *tchuk* often given at dawn on Mussau. Thin *ssep*. Thin upslurred whistle, *tseeup*, and *tsu*. Harsh scold.
Habits Forest and especially secondary growth, at all altitudes. Noisy and pugnacious, usually in loose small groups of up to 30 birds in all forest levels, congregating in coconuts and flowering trees.
Conservation status Common. Not threatened.
Range Endemic to small islands in Admiralties and Bismarcks.
M. p. ernstmayri, endemic to Ninigo, Hermit and Kaniet Is, and probably this subspecies on Wuvulu, has pale greyish underwings.
M. p. pammelaena, endemic to Admiralties, including small islets off north Manus, Lou, San Miguel, Rambutyo, Tong, Nauna and rare on Manus itself, has greyish-white underwings but is smaller.
M. p. hades, endemic to St Matthias, including Mussau, Eloaua, Emirau and Tench, has whitish underwings and is smaller than *M. p. ramsayi*.
M. p. ramsayi, endemic to Tingwon and small islands off Lavongai and north New Ireland, has whitish underwings and is small.
M. p. nigerrima, endemic to small islands west of New Britain, including Crown, Long, Tolokiwa, Midi, Hein and Siassi, and probably this species recorded once in Kimbe Bay, is large and glossy and has dull grey underwings.

RED-CAPPED MYZOMELA *Myzomela lafargei* — Plate 62

(Scarlet-naped/Red-crowned Myzomela/Honeyeater; Myzomèle à nuque rouge)

Description 12 cm. Greyish-green myzomela, male with black head and scarlet nape. Male has black hood and upperparts with red central crown-patch, green fringes on wings and greenish-yellow breast and belly. Individual variation in extent of red on crown, and some birds have red wash on rump. Female and juvenile have dull olive upperparts without red crown, yellower on breast and belly, and some with red wash on face. Immature male like male but duller olive-brown upperparts, red wash on face and throat, and olive underparts, paler on belly. Immature female is duller, browner above and more olive below.
Similar species Differs from Olive-backed Sunbird by lacking supercilium, male darker above and female duller below, with darker throat and more elongate shape. From Bougainville Honeyeater by much smaller size and yellower underparts.
Voice Rapid twittering song. Short thin metallic *zip* repeated at two second intervals.
Habits Forest including degraded forest to at least 2000 m, and sometimes in coconuts, gardens and villages. Singles, pairs or small flocks forage actively in all storeys. Sometimes in mixed-species flocks and congregates at flowering trees.
Conservation status Fairly common on Bougainville, uncommon on Choiseul and rare on Isabel. Not threatened.
Range Endemic to Bougainville, Choiseul and Isabel, including Buka, Shortland, Fauro and small islands between Choiseul and Isabel.

CRIMSON-RUMPED MYZOMELA *Myzomela eichhorni* — Plate 62

(Yellow-vented Myzomela/Honeyeater; Myzomèle à ventre jaune)

Description 12 cm. Dark greenish or blackish myzomela with red throat and rump. Male is dark olive-brown with darker head, scarlet throat and rump, and paler yellower breast and belly. Pale underwing in flight. Female is duller and more olive, with rusty wash to rump and smaller duller red throat-patch. Immature male like female but has red throat-patch and red wash on forehead. Immature female like adult female but warmer wash especially on rump. Some subspecies are much darker, almost blackish.
Similar species Differs from Olive-backed Sunbird by duller underparts, red on throat and no supercilium.
Voice Rapid high-pitched trilling song, faster than Rufous Fantail and not descending scale. Various loud sharp high-pitched calls, e.g. *bzeet*, some with terminal fading downslur, e.g. *bzeeeee*.
Habits In forest and scrub, sometimes in coconuts, gardens and villages, at all altitudes but commoner in mountains. Usually unobtrusive singles or pairs, but gregarious and vocal in favoured flowering trees, or with mixed-species flocks, in canopy but descends to flowers, particularly ant-plants.
Conservation status Fairly common. Not threatened.
Range Endemic to New Georgia group.
M. e. eichhorni is endemic to Gizo, Kolombangara, Kohinggo, Vonavona, New Georgia, Rendova, Tetepare, Vangunu and Nggatokae.
M. e. ganongae, endemic to Ranongga, has slightly darker upperparts and throat, and female lacks red tones on rump.

M. e. atrata, endemic to Vella Lavella and Bagga, is much darker, male with black upperparts and hood merging into dark yellow-olive belly, and red rump and throat, occasionally with some red on nape, female similar but dark olive, almost black, on head.

RED-VESTED MYZOMELA *Myzomela malaitae* Plate 62

(Red-bellied/Malaita Myzomela/Honeyeater; Myzomèle de Malaita)

Description 13 m. Male is red and black, female brown. Male has crimson throat, breast, flanks and rump, blackish upperparts and neck-sides with green gloss and olive fringes on wings, and dark grey central belly and vent. Female has grey-brown upperparts, olive fringes on wings, tawny-olive underparts often washed red on throat. Juvenile male like female with red forehead and central throat, and often reddish on rump.
Similar species Female differs from Olive-backed Sunbird by tawny underparts and darker, sometimes red-washed throat.
Voice A rather unobtrusive single or double *tsup-tsup*.
Habits Forest and forest edge, commoner in primary forest above 1000 m. Singles are unobtrusive in canopy, descending with mixed-species flocks or to feed on ant-plants. Sometimes perch on prominent canopy branches.
Conservation status Uncommon. Probably declining as most forest is slowly being cleared for gardens. IUCN: Near Threatened.
Range Endemic to Malaita.

BLACK-HEADED MYZOMELA *Myzomela melanocephala* Plate 62

(Black-headed Honeyeater; Myzomèle à tête noire)

Description 12 cm. Olive myzomela with black hood. Olive-green with glossy black forehead, face and throat, darker tail and wings, and paler flanks and belly. In flight, shows pale underwing. Female duller with less black on head and throat. Juvenile rufous-brown with indistinctly darker head. Immature like female but duller and browner with less definite hood.
Similar species Differs from Olive-backed Sunbird by dull olive underparts, darker head and throat, and no supercilium.
Voice Repeated high thin *zhip* or *tzwhit*, sometimes a series of piped notes, softer than congeners.
Habits Forest but more often forest edge and sometimes in gardens, to 1550 m. Singles and sometimes small groups are active but unobtrusive in forest canopy, subcanopy, flowering trees and ant-plants.
Conservation status Fairly common. Not threatened.
Range Endemic to Guadalcanal, including Savo and Florida Is.

SOOTY MYZOMELA *Myzomela tristrami* Plate 62

(Tristram's Myzomela/Honeyeater; Myzomèle de Tristram)

Description 12 cm. Uniformly dull black myzomela, with slight gloss, especially in male. In flight, shows some white on underwing at base of primaries. Juvenile has sooty-black upperparts, grey-olive underparts and black-tipped orange-yellow bill. Immature has scruffy black-and-grey mottling on underparts.
Similar species Differs from Cardinal Myzomela by black or grey plumage and slimmer shape. From Chestnut-bellied Monarch on Ugi by smaller size, dumpy shape and long decurved black bill.
Voice Song is a short nasal whistle, then a fast then slow twitter, e.g. *oowae-oo, chit-it-it-it, chit, chit, chit*. Short harsh *tchuk*. Series of softer churrs, twitters and chatters.
Habits Forest and scrub, sometimes in coconuts. Commoner along coast where overlaps with Cardinal Myzomela. Active and pugnacious in pairs and small groups, often in understorey.
Conservation status Common on Makira but rare on Ugi. Not threatened.
Range Endemic to Makira, including Santa Ana, Santa Catalina and Ugi.

BLACK-BELLIED MYZOMELA *Myzomela erythromelas* Plate 53

(New Britain Red-headed Myzomela/Honeyeater; Myzomèle à ventre noir)

Description 10 cm. Tiny short-tailed red-headed myzomela. Male is glossy black with bright red head and throat. Female is olive-brown, paler on belly, has smaller, duller, more orange-red head and throat, faint pale streaks on underparts and olive fringes on wings. Juvenile male similar to female but has more extensive brighter red on head.

Similar species Male is distinctive but note all-black Black Sunbird. Female differs from Red Myzomela by more extensive red on head, no red on rump or tail, and smaller size. From immature Sclater's Myzomela on offshore islands by red extending above eye and paler brown upperparts.
Voice Repeated double high-pitched notes, second lower than first: *tze-tzu, tze-tzu…* Trill of 4–5 very high-pitched notes *tsi-tsi-tsi-tsi*. Single high-pitched notes. Calls are thinner and quieter than Black Sunbird, without trills, slurs and varied notes.
Habits Forest, especially secondary forest and forest edge but rarely away from large trees, to 1000 m; generally replaced at higher altitudes by Red Myzomela. Singles and sometimes small groups are active in canopy, often in flowering trees where sometimes mixed with other honeyeaters.
Conservation status Fairly common. Not threatened.
Range Endemic to New Britain.

AUSTRALASIAN WARBLERS Acanthizidae

Small insectivorous birds with drab plumage and short pointed bills.

FAN-TAILED GERYGONE *Gerygone flavolateralis* — Plates 75, 78 & 82

(Fan-tailed Warbler; Gérygone mélanésienne)

Description 10 cm. Tiny warbler with white spots near tip of outer tail feathers. Greyish head with a narrow white supercilium and eyelids, olive upperparts, white throat and upper breast, and yellow lower breast and belly. Female is paler. Juvenile has browner upperparts, uniformly yellow underparts and no supercilium.
Similar species Distinctive head pattern and white tail-tips. Differs from white-eyes by grey head, white throat, paler plumage and slimmer shape. From female myzomelas by short bill.
Voice Long rushed series of light clear simple notes, composed of repeated identical series of 2–7 notes, e.g. *teww-wee-heet* or *hee-weetaweet*, generally rising and falling in pitch.
Habits Forest, especially secondary forest and regrowth, at all altitudes and sometimes commoner in mountains. Restless and vocal, in pairs, small chasing groups or mixed-species flocks, in all forest storeys. Host species of Shining Bronze Cuckoo.
Conservation status Common. Not threatened.
Range Endemic to Rennell, Vanuatu and New Caledonia.
G. f. citrina, endemic to Rennell, has brighter yellow extending to lower breast, greener upperparts, white eye and white spot on outer three pairs of tail feathers; could be treated as separate species.
G. f. correiae, endemic to Vanuatu, where it has a fluctuating range with recent records from Vanua Lava, Gaua, Santo, Maewo, Ambae, Malekula, Ambrym, Epi and Emae, and historical records from Pentecost, Malo and Lopevi, is brighter than *G. f. flavolateralis* with smaller white spots on outer four tail feathers.
G. f. lifuensis, endemic to Lifou and Ouvéa, where sometimes separated as *G. f. rouxi*, has smaller white tail spots than *G. f. flavolateralis*.
G. f. flavolateralis, endemic to Grande Terre and Maré, has white spots on all except the central pair of tail feathers.

BUTCHERBIRDS Cracticidae

Medium to large pied birds with heavy bills and loud fluty calls.

[AUSTRALASIAN MAGPIE *Gymnorhina tibicen*] — (not illustrated)

(*Cracticus tibicen*; Cassican flûteur)

Description 41 cm. Large pied crow-like bird. Black, with large white nape-patch, wing-patch, rump, undertail-coverts and tail-base, large grey-blue bill and long dark legs. Male is glossy black. Female is duller with greyish nape and rump. Juvenile is dull with brown wash, mottling and barring.
Similar species Distinctive large size and pied pattern.
Voice Loud melodious organ-like yodels and whistles.
Habits Grassland, parkland and open habitats. Singles or small groups forage on ground, flying up to trees.
Conservation status Introduced to Melanesia. Not threatened.
Range Previously on Guadalcanal, where *G. t. tibicen* was introduced to Honiara between at least 1944 and 1953, but no longer occurs. Native in Australia and far south New Guinea, and introduced to Fiji and New Zealand.

WOODSWALLOWS Artamidae

Medium-fat pied birds which sally from exposed perches or hawk in graceful gliding and soaring flight. Short square tail and long triangular wings, broader than swallows, with heavier, more gliding flight. Gregarious, often perching close to each other on a dead branch.

WHITE-BREASTED WOODSWALLOW *Artamus leucorynchus* Plates 81 & 85

(Langrayen à ventre blanc)

Description 18 cm. Dark slate-grey woodswallow with white rump and breast to undertail-coverts. Stout blue-grey bill. Juvenile has pale tips on wings and tail, buffy fringes on head, mantle and wing-coverts, and brownish bill.
Similar species Distinctive shape and habits. Differs from swallows by white rump, dark throat and unmarked square tail. From trillers by black throat and plain wing.
Voice Rolling *chirrp*. Nasal chatter. Scolds. Quiet mimetic song.
Habits Open habitats with scattered trees, including gaps in closed forest, forest edge, parks and savanna to at least 900 m. Perches conspicuously on dead branch or wires, often rotating or pumping tail. Forages in graceful gliding flight. Mobs predators such as birds of prey.
Conservation status Fairly common, often common in suitable habitat. Not threatened.
Range Vanuatu and New Caledonia.
A. l. tenuis, endemic to Vanuatu, where recorded from Vanua Lava, Gaua, most islands between Maewo and Santo south to Efate and historical but not recent records from Erromango, Tanna and Aneityum, has black crown and throat.
A. l. melaleucus, endemic to New Caledonia, on Grande Terre, Ile des Pins, Lifou and Maré, is larger.
Elsewhere, other subspecies across South-East Asia to Palau, New Guinea and Australia.

WHITE-BACKED WOODSWALLOW *Artamus insignis* Plate 59

(Bismarck Woodswallow; Langrayen des Bismarck)

Description 19 cm. White woodswallow with sooty-black head, throat, wings and tail. Stout blue-grey bill, and pale blue-grey eye-ring. Juvenile has brown wash on head and hindneck, and white tips on wings and tail.
Similar species Distinctive plumage, shape and habits. Differs from swallows by white back, dark throat and unmarked square tail.
Voice Loud metallic *zwink!* or *zwink!-zwink!*, often repeated. Quiet fantail-like scratchy warble.
Habits Edge of closed forest, including clearings, and also forest interior to at least 900 m. Pairs or groups up to ten perch on exposed branches, flap up and glide in circles over forest, returning to same perch. Pumps tail and waves it in circles.
Conservation status Generally rare but locally fairly common. Not threatened.
Range Endemic to New Britain and New Ireland, and a vagrant to Watom.

DUSKY WOODSWALLOW *Artamus cyanopterus* (not illustrated)

(Langrayen sordide)

Description 18 cm. Grey-brown woodswallow with black and white tail. Plain dark smoky-brown with darker mask, stout blue-grey bill, white streak on grey-blue wings and white terminal band on black tail. In flight, shows white underwings and tail-corners. Juvenile is paler brown with many buffy streaks on head and body.
Similar species Distinctive woodswallow shape and habits.
Voice Rapid series of harsh *vut, vut...* scolds. Rolling nasal chirps and chatter. Quiet mimetic song.
Habits Open forest, savanna and forest edge. Often associates with mixed species flocks. Habits as other woodswallows.
Range One recent record from Grande Terre, New Caledonia. Breeds in Australia, with some local migration.

CUCKOOSHRIKES AND TRILLERS Campephagidae

Cuckooshrikes and trillers are elongate long-winged long-tailed forest birds, occasionally feeding on ground. They often forage in mixed-species flocks with other medium-sized birds. All fly with slightly undulating flight, often including short glides, sometimes on down-swept wings. Cuckooshrikes are medium to large birds, with similar black, blue-grey and white plumage to cuckoos, but stout bills reminiscent of shrikes; habitually flick their wings, especially on landing. Trillers are smaller and dumpier, with pied male and grey-brown and whitish female.

BLACK-FACED CUCKOOSHRIKE *Coracina novaehollandiae* Plates 51, 61, 74 & 84

(Échenilleur à masque noir)

Description 33 cm. Large pale grey cuckooshrike with black face and white belly. Pale grey upperparts, blacker on wings and tail, whitish tail-tips, black forehead, face and throat sometimes shading into grey breast, and white belly to undertail-coverts. Female has less black on forehead. Immature has pale grey forehead and throat, with black only on ear-coverts, and fine barring on throat and breast.
Similar species Differs from most other cuckooshrikes by clearly defined black face-patch, larger size, similar to North and South Melanesian Cuckooshrikes, and open habitats. Immature differs from White-bellied Cuckooshrike by larger size, black extending behind eye onto ear-coverts, and greyer underparts.
Voice Plaintive *plee-urk*. Repeated rolling *shri-lunk* often given in flight. Loud purring or churring.
Habits Open habitats with trees, including savanna, coasts, suburbs, plantations, forest edge and edges of fields and airstrips. Often forages in small flocks, flying between trees with undulating flight.
Range Scarce migrant to north Melanesia and New Caledonia, with records of *C. n. melanops* from New Ireland, Nissan, Umboi, New Britain, Witu, Duke of York, Bougainville, Gizo, Rennell and New Caledonia. Elsewhere, *C. n. melanops* breeds in Australia and migrates north to New Guinea, and three other subspecies breed elsewhere in Australia, some migrating to Indonesia and New Guinea.

SOUTH MELANESIAN CUCKOOSHRIKE *Coracina caledonica* Plate 80 & 84

(Also combined with next species as Melanesian Cuckooshrike *Coracina caledonica*; Échenilleur calédonien)

Description 35 cm. Very large dark grey cuckooshrike with pale yellow eye. Uniformly slaty-grey, blacker around lores and eye, and short heavy black bill. Female is slightly paler with dusky lores. Juvenile has pale grey fringes, broad buffy fringes on wings and dull eye.
Similar species Differs from New Caledonian Cuckooshrike by larger size, darker blackish plumage, yellow eye and lack of any chestnut. From rare vagrant Black-faced Cuckooshrike by much darker plumage and yellow eye. From New Caledonian Crow by elongate shape, longer tail and yellow eye. From starlings by larger size, no iridescence, and long, slightly rounded tail.
Voice Loud starling-like whistle *zweee* or *tseeoo* usually upslurred and often repeated. Song is a series of chattering guttural *kwa-kwawa-kwawa* or *kwawa-wa—seee—kwawa-wa—seee* phrases. Loud harsh contact and aggression calls and chatters.
Habits In forest and forest edge, including savanna, parks and suburbs. Less common in mountains, to at least 1200 m. Forages slowly, usually in pairs or groups up to five, in canopy of forest, especially the tallest emergent trees. Often calls from exposed perches in tree-tops.
Conservation status Fairly common. Not threatened.
Range Endemic to Vanuatu and New Caledonia.
C. c. thilenii, endemic to Santo, Malo and Malekula, is grey, male with indistinct black mask, female paler with smaller mask.
C. c. seiuncta, endemic to Erromango, is paler grey.
C. c. lifuensis, endemic to Lifou, is darker.
C. c. caledonica, endemic to Grande Terre including Ile des Pins, is smaller and paler.

NORTH MELANESIAN CUCKOOSHRIKE *Coracina welchmani* Plate 61

(Also combined with previous species as Melanesian Cuckooshrike *Coracina caledonica*; Échenilleur calédonien)

Description 32 cm. Very large grey-black cuckooshrike. Uniformly dark slaty-grey with slightly paler grey underparts, and short heavy black bill. Male has glossy black face and throat. Female has small area of black on ear-coverts. Immature has indistinct black face-patch and faint pale grey fringes.
Similar species Differs from other cuckooshrikes by larger size (but same as Black-faced Cuckooshrike), little contrast in dark grey and black plumage, although other grey cuckooshrikes may appear blackish in poor light, and no paler fringes on wings or spots on tail. From starlings by larger size, lacking iridescence, and long slightly rounded tail. From crows by elongate shape, longer tail and smaller dark bill.
Voice Long descending whistle reminiscent of falling bomb. Shrill creaking *chi*, often repeated. Loud harsh contact and aggression calls and chatters.
Habits Restricted to montane forests, except in the New Georgia group where commoner in mangroves and coastal forest, often degraded forest. Forages slowly, usually in pairs, in canopy of forest, especially the tallest emergent trees.

Conservation status The three montane subspecies are rare and very poorly known but their habitat is not under threat. The Kolombangara subspecies is uncommon and appears to be tolerant of degraded habitat. Not threatened.
Range Endemic to Solomons.
C. c. bougainvillei, endemic to Bougainville, usually found in high mountains but sometimes in lowlands, is dark grey, male with black head, neck and upper breast, female with blackish mask.
C. c. welchmani, endemic to Isabel where restricted to mountains, is slightly darker with less defined black mask and throat.
C. c. kulambangrae, endemic to Kolombangara, New Georgia and Vangunu, to at least 940 m but commoner by coast; male has grey breast.
C. c. amadonis, endemic to Guadalcanal where recorded between 1050–1300 m, is darker, male with black head, neck and upper breast, female dark grey with blacker face, throat and breast.

BARRED CUCKOOSHRIKE *Coracina lineata* Plates 51, 61, 73 & 74

(Yellow-eyed Cuckooshrike; Échenilleur linéolé)

Description 23 cm. Medium-sized blue-grey cuckooshrike with lemon-yellow eye. Blue-grey upperparts with darker wings and tail. Male is plain blue-grey except for black mask on lores and darker wings and end of tail. Female has fine black-and-white barring on lower breast to undertail-coverts. Juvenile has creamy scaling on upperparts, especially head and wing-coverts, and barred underparts. Immature has pale fringes on wings and variable barring on underparts.
Similar species Distinctive yellow eye and barring. Differs from other cuckooshrikes by bluer plumage, slightly dumpier shape and rounder wings. From Oriental Cuckoo by habits and yellow eye not eye-ring.
Voice Loud nasal downslurred whistle *chee-ow* or *gwaa*, often given in flight. Quiet nasal chattering.
Habits Forest, especially forest edge, degraded forest and large isolated trees, from sea-level to 900 m, rarely to 1200 m. Usually in small groups, foraging in canopy and mid-storey. Also eats fruit, sometimes feeding in fig trees. Unobtrusive unless flying between trees.
Conservation status Fairly common. Not threatened.
Range Bismarcks and Solomons.
C. l. sublineata, endemic to New Ireland, New Britain and Lolobau, male with variable slight barring on belly and undertail-coverts.
C. l. pusilla including *C. l. nigrifrons*, endemic to Buka, Bougainville, Shortland, Choiseul, Isabel and Guadalcanal, is slightly smaller, male with no barring.
C. l. ombriosa, endemic to Vella Lavella, New Georgia, Gizo, Rendova and Tetepare, is slightly darker, female with more obvious black mask and wider black bars on underparts.
C. l. malaitae, endemic to Malaita, is slightly paler, male with slight white bars on belly, female with narrower black bars.
C. l. makirae, endemic to Makira; male is plain blue-grey with black lores, darker wings and tail, and indistinct white bars on breast becoming clear black-and-white bars lower on belly and undertail-coverts.
C. l. gracilis, endemic to Rennell and Bellona; both sexes have barred underparts.
Elsewhere, other subspecies breed in New Guinea and east Australia.

WHITE-BELLIED CUCKOOSHRIKE *Coracina papuensis* Plates 51 & 61

(Échenilleur choucari)

Description 25 cm. Very pale cuckooshrike with prominent black mask. Pale grey head with black bill and mask through eyes. Mid-grey upperparts with pale fringes on wing and tail, and greyish-white underparts. Juvenile has buffy fringes on upperparts, breast and wing-coverts, and less distinct black mask.
Similar species Slimmer and longer-winged than other cuckooshrikes with very pale underparts and black mask. From immature Black-faced Cuckooshrike by smaller size, black mask not beyond eye, and whiter underparts.
Voice Surprised disyllabic squeal *chew-ee* or *whee-chu*. Sharp *tzik*. Harsh scolding *trr-trr-trr-*.
Habits Forest edge and trees in open habitats, parks, towns, coasts, mangroves and locally in closed forest, including lower montane forest on New Britain. Sea-level to 900 m, occasionally to 1400 m. Pairs or small groups forage in canopy and mid-storey of large trees, often on bare branches and other exposed perches such as wires, rarely on ground.
Conservation status Common. Not threatened.
Range Admiralties, Bismarcks and Solomons.

C. p. ingens, endemic to Manus and Los Negros, is largest subspecies, with largest bill, and has been treated as a separate species.
C. p. sclateri, endemic to New Ireland and New Britain, including Lavongai, Umboi, Lolobau, Watom and Duke of York, is large and dark, with obvious grey on breast.
C. p. perpallida, endemic to Buka, Bougainville, Shortland, Choiseul, Isabel and Florida Is, is smaller and much paler.
C. p. elegans, endemic to New Georgia group including Gizo, Rendova and Tetepare, Russell Is and Guadalcanal, is slightly darker.
C. p. eyerdami, endemic to Malaita, has darker grey upperparts and breast.
Elsewhere, other subspecies occur in east Indonesia, New Guinea and Australia.

NEW CALEDONIAN CUCKOOSHRIKE *Coracina analis* — Plate 84

(Échenilleur de montagne)

Description 28 cm. Plain dark grey cuckooshrike with orange-rufous vent and undertail-coverts. Slightly browner tail and especially wings, and rufous underwing-coverts often visible at shoulder. Heavy black bill, dark eye and relatively long tail. Juvenile is paler with buff fringes on wings, and buff wash and black mottling on head and underparts.
Similar species Distinctive deep rufous vent. Also differs from South Melanesian Cuckooshrike by dark eye and shorter wings. From Striated Starling by paler plumage, longer tail and dark eye.
Voice Loud explosive sneezes, e.g. *klnngGG* or *klngg-klngg*. Slurred whistles e.g. *tcheeow-tcheeeee*. Rasping squeals.
Habits Forest, including nearby scrub, in hills and mountains, usually above 600 m but sometimes down to 200 m. Pairs forage in canopy and mid-storey. Regularly jerks wings and flicks tail, and often perches with raised tail or raised head and tail. Jerky flight.
Conservation status Fairly common. IUCN: Near Threatened.
Range Endemic to New Caledonia, on Grande Terre and Ile des Pins.

COMMON CICADABIRD *Coracina tenuirostris* — Plates 51 & 61

(Slender-billed Cicadabird; Échenilleur cigale)

Description 25 cm. Dark grey, or brown and orange cuckooshrike. Male is dark blue-grey with indistinct blackish face-mask, pale fringes on black wings often forming silvery panel on secondaries, and black tail with mid-grey central feathers and tips. Female has blue-grey crown, rufous-brown upperparts, slight pale supercilium, dark eye-stripe, black centres and rufous fringes on wings, olive-brown tail with rufous corners, and buff to rufous underparts, often with fine black barring. Juvenile like female with brown cap, buffy fringes above and black spots below; subadult male is blotched grey.
Similar species Male differs from Barred Cuckooshrike by dark eye, more black on face, slimmer shape and darker greyer plumage. Male from Solomons Cuckooshrike by darker grey plumage and blackish on face. Female is distinctive, but see Varied Triller and Shining Bronze Cuckoo which have blackish bars on off-white underparts.
Voice Variable between subspecies. Song is a loud ringing series of 10–70 repeated downslurred, almost disyllabic *kweee-kweee-* notes, often slowing at end of series, faster than similar song of Steel-blue Flycatcher. Faster, higher-pitched and slightly accelerating *kweer, kweer, kweer-kweer-*. Harsh upslurred *schree-er?* or *tchu-wit?*, sometimes repeated, when slower than similar song of Steel-blue Flycatcher. Harsh rattling chatter.
Habits Forest, including secondary forest and forest edge, from sea-level to 1400 m. Singles and pairs are rather unobtrusive in canopy and mid-storey. Flicks wings less than other cuckooshrikes.
Conservation status Fairly common. Not threatened.
Range Admiralties, St Matthias Is, Bismarcks and Solomons.
C. t. admiralitatis, endemic to Manus, male with dark slate-grey, female with blue-grey crown, rufous-brown upperparts and orange-rufous underparts with bars from throat to belly.
C. t. matthiae, endemic to Mussau and Emirau, is larger than *C. t. admiralitatis*, female paler with light orange-buff underparts.
C. t. remota, endemic to New Ireland, Lavongai, Djaul and Feni; male is paler mid-grey, and female has deep rufous unbarred underparts, but Feni female is sometimes barred and may represent a separate subspecies.
C. t. ultima, endemic to Tabar, Lihir and Tanga, like *C. t. remota* but female has darker greyer upperparts and paler underparts.
C. t. muelleri breeds on Long and Sakar, male has paler grey fringes on wings, and female has paler buff underparts; elsewhere breeds on New Guinea.
C. t. rooki, endemic to Umboi, is like *C. t. admiralitatis* but smaller and darker.
C. t. heinrothi, endemic to New Britain and Lolobau, is larger than *C. t. rooki* and female has variably pale or deep orange-buff underparts and variable barring.

C. t. saturatior, endemic to Solomons from Buka and Bougainville through Choiseul and Isabel to most islands in the New Georgia group; female is unbarred and has rufous-brown back and rufous-orange tail.
C. t. erythropygia, endemic to Guadalcanal and Malaita including Florida Is, Savo and Ulawa, is paler, female unbarred and less rufous.
C. t. nisoria, endemic to the Russell Is; female is barred from chin to belly and has darker upperparts.
Elsewhere, other subspecies or species occur in east Indonesia, north Australia and Micronesia. Some of these subspecies could be treated as separate species.

MAKIRA CICADABIRD *Coracina salomonis* — Plate 73

(Also treated as a subspecies of Common Cicadabird *C. tenuirostris*; Échenilleur cigale)

Description 23 cm. Grey cuckooshrike, female with deep orange underparts. Male is plain mid-grey with black loral stripe, black tail and black centres to wing feathers. Female like male except uniform deep rufous-orange underparts and pale orange on outer tail. Juvenile like female but has whitish tips and black subterminal bars on upperparts and whitish tips and indistinct blackish mottling on paler underparts; immature like female; subadult has blotched underparts.
Similar species Male differs from Barred Cuckooshrike by dark eye, paler grey plumage and slimmer shape. Female differs from Chestnut-bellied Monarch by uniform underparts.
Voice Song is a slightly decelerating series of 7–14 nasal whistled *tu-sweeo*, each note with a short sharp upslur and longer downslur, latter becoming longer through the series. Loud disyllabic calls *chi-beet* or *pity-you* and chatters, often repeated as a rapid series.
Habits Forest and secondary forest but uncommon in secondary scrub, to at least 900 m. Pairs or threes forage in dense foliage, sometimes with mixed flocks especially Spangled Drongos.
Conservation status Fairly common. Not threatened.
Range Endemic to Makira.

SOLOMONS CUCKOOSHRIKE *Coracina holopolia* — Plate 61

(Black-bellied Cicadabird; Solomons Black-bellied Cuckooshrike; Échenilleur des Salomon)

Description 21 cm. Small pale grey cuckooshrike, male with glossy black underparts. Male has pale grey crown, mantle, wings and rump, paler on wing-coverts and secondaries, blackish tail, black tertial centres and primaries, and glossy black underparts and face. Female is uniformly pale grey with less black on wings and tail than male and sometimes with fine dark eye-stripe. Juvenile has brown and creamy fringes on upperparts and black and pale grey bars on underparts. Immature is barred black and pale grey on throat, breast and undertail-coverts, less distinct on flanks and belly.
Similar species Contrasting black and pale grey of male distinctive. Female differs from Common Cicadabird and Barred Cuckooshrike by paler grey plumage, uniform grey face and dark eye. Barring of immature differs from Barred Cuckooshrike by extending onto throat and breast.
Voice Rasping or quavering upslurred *vrhee*, *vvrreeeoo* or *toe-hee*, often repeated up to ten times. *C. h. pygmaea* notes are often downslurred, decelerating and dropping in pitch. Harsh chattering *chur-chur-ur-ur*.
Habits Forest, including forest edge and secondary forest. Sea-level to 1200 m but commoner in lowlands on Guadalcanal and hills on Kolombangara and Malaita. Singles, pairs and threes glean in canopy, and also hover and sally.
Conservation status Fairly common but easily overlooked, especially on Bougainville, Guadalcanal and Malaita, to uncommon, especially on Choiseul and Isabel. IUCN: Near Threatened.
Range Endemic to the Solomons from Bougainville to Malaita.
C. h. holopolia is endemic to Buka, Bougainville, Choiseul, Isabel and Guadalcanal.
C. h. pygmaea, endemic to Kolombangara, New Georgia, Vangunu and Nggatokae, where less common in lowlands, is smaller and has slightly darker upperparts.
C. h. tricolor, endemic to Malaita, where not recorded from lowlands, is paler grey on wings, male with black forehead and hindcollar.

VARIED TRILLER *Lalage leucomela* — Plate 50

(Échenilleur varié)

Description 18 cm. Medium-sized black, grey and white triller. Male has glossy black upperparts with white broad supercilium, two wing-bars, fringes on secondaries and tertials, bars on rump and tail corners. White underparts with fine black barring and unmarked orange-buff vent. Female has dark grey, not black, on upperparts, and more barred greyer underparts. Juvenile has fine pale scaling and barring on upperparts, and short dusky streaks, becoming broken bars, on underparts.

Similar species Distinctive. Differs from pied monarchs by head markings and bars and buff on underparts.
Voice Varied nasal or mewing calls, often repeated or combined in various combinations. Short *tchow* or *vrrah*, or longer *krEE-er*. Series of slurred *kwEEerr* notes, slower than Common Cicadabird. Whistled *pee-u*. Cat-call *whEE-whEEo* or *whit-whit-whEEo*.
Habits Forest edge, secondary forest and dry coastal forest, less common in closed forest and mountains to 1400 m. Pairs or small flocks forage in canopy. Flicks wings less often than cuckooshrikes. Flies with short glides.
Conservation status Fairly common. Not threatened.
Range Bismarcks.
L. l. falsa, endemic to New Britain including Umboi, Sakar, Lolobau, Watom and Duke of York; male has underparts barred except on white belly and orange-buff vent and undertail-coverts, with buff extending to flanks and lower breast, female with blackish bars on pale grey underparts.
L. l. karu, endemic to New Ireland, has greyer underparts and orange-buff only on lower belly to undertail-coverts.
L. l. albidior, endemic to Lavongai, is like *L. l. karu* but male has fewer bars, female whiter underparts.
L. l. sumumae, endemic to Djaul, has no orange-buff, male with very little barring on flanks, female barred from chin to belly.
L. l. tabarensis, endemic to Tabar, male has unbarred white underparts with pale buff undertail-coverts, and more white on wings, female with dark grey upperparts, variable faint barring on breast and flanks, and cream or grey wash on underparts.
L. l. ottomeyeri, endemic to Lihir, is like *L. l. tabarensis* but has plain white underparts, male with greyer rump and perhaps faint barring, female barred on breast and flanks.
Elsewhere, other subspecies occur in New Guinea and north Australia.

MUSSAU TRILLER *Lalage conjuncta* — Plate 50

(Also treated as a subspecies of Varied Triller *L. leucomela*; Échenilleur varié)

Description 16 cm. Dumpy black, white and rufous triller. Black upperparts with green gloss, large white patches on wing-coverts and rump, white fringes on tertials and secondaries, and white tips on outer tail. White face, throat and upper breast clearly marked from orange-chestnut lower breast to vent. Female unknown, perhaps with duller upperparts. Juvenile unknown.
Similar species Distinctive.
Voice Short nasal calls, e.g. *tchu*, often repeated in short phrases, e.g. *tchow-tchow-de-weet*.
Habits Poorly known. Forest, possibly only in closed forest in hills. Singles, pairs and threes chase around in canopy.
Conservation status Only known from one specimen and two sets of field observations. Locally common but poorly known. Threat status unknown.
Range Endemic to Mussau.

POLYNESIAN TRILLER *Lalage maculosa* — Plates 76 & 80

(Échenilleur de Polynésie)

Description 15 cm. Pied triller with conspicuous white supercilium. Male has dull black upperparts with white supercilium, some fine white barring, broad white fringes on wings and tail-tips, and some grey on rump. White face and underparts with black eye-stripe and faint barring on neck and flanks. In flight, shows white underwing-bar. Female has dark brown upperparts and more bars on underparts. Juvenile is browner with creamy tips on upperparts, buff fringes to wings and buff washed underparts, sometimes barred.
Similar species Differs from Long-tailed Triller on Vanuatu by long prominent supercilium, shorter tail and dumpier shape, and, if present, bars on underparts, pale lower mandible and white on crown. From Buff-bellied Monarch by underparts pattern, eye-stripe and habits.
Voice Various combinations of short, sharp and nasal notes, e.g. *schrr*, *TCHup*, *TCHup-teeeu*. Trilled series of *tchee* or *scheer* notes, often accelerating. Squealing *wheest!* Rolling whistle *vrreee*. Short melodious whistling song *zee-tzee-tzee*.
Habits Forest, including forest edge, secondary growth, parks and gardens to at least 1400 m. Rare in closed forest in Temotu but restricted to montane forest on Santo. Groups of up to four forage unobtrusively in canopy, occasionally dropping to ground in open habitats, or chase each other vocally and aggressively. Calls from prominent perches.
Conservation status Fairly common in Temotu, but uncommon or rare in most of Vanuatu. Not threatened.
Range Temotu and Vanuatu south to Efate.

L. m. melanopygia, endemic to Utupua and Nendo, has little barring or spotting on breast-sides, but birds on Nendo are larger, have paler rumps and may represent an undescribed subspecies.
L. m. vanikorensis, endemic to Vanikoro; male has small white spots and bars on crown and back, and more grey on rump.
L. m. modesta, endemic to Santo, Malo, Malekula, Paama, Epi, Tongoa and Emae; male has more extensive grey on rump and pale grey, sometimes buff, wash on breast and flanks.
L. m. ultima, endemic to Efate including Nguna and Emau, is like *L. m. modesta* but has more white mottling on crown and back, more grey on rump and usually unmarked underparts.
Elsewhere, other subspecies occur in Fiji, Tonga and Samoa.

LONG-TAILED TRILLER *Lalage leucopyga* — Plates 71, 80 & 84

(Échenilleur pie)

Description 17 cm. Pied triller with white or buff wing-patch, rump and underparts. Male has glossy brown-black upperparts with large white wing-covert patch, grey-white rump, fine white fringes on tertials and outer tail and sometimes a small white line across lores. Plain white, sometimes pale buff, underparts. Female has browner upperparts and buffier white patches. Juvenile is browner and buffier, with pale tips to upperparts, some dark mottling on breast and pale bill-base.
Similar species Differs from Polynesian Triller on Vanuatu between Santo and Efate by small or no supercilium, longer tail and more elongate shape, unmarked underparts, plain black crown and all-black bill. From Buff-bellied Monarch on Vanuatu by habits and plain white underparts. From White-collared Monarch on Makira by habits, white throat and face and black nape.
Voice Variable calls. Repeated whistle, perhaps a song *tche-tchu*, first note ascending and second descending in pitch; sometimes more slurred *br-r-reet* or *tyoor-r-rt*. Series of c.6–10 ringing *kwee* notes. Nasal *dhu* or *prrp*.
Habits Usually in forest edge or scrub, including secondary regrowth, gardens, villages and savanna, but also primary forest. Singles or groups of up to five forage in canopy or lower down in open habitats.
Conservation status Fairly common. Not threatened.
Range Endemic to Makira, Vanuatu and New Caledonia.
L. l. affinis, endemic to Makira including Ugi, has no white on supercilium and pure white rump.
L. l. deficiens, endemic to Banks Is and Torres Is, has greyish rump, more white on tail and less white on wing-coverts.
L. l. albiloris, endemic to Vanuatu on all islands from Santo to Efate, has fine white supercilium to above eye, more white on tail and greyish rump.
L. l. simillima, endemic to Tanna, Erromango, Aneityum and Ouvéa, Lifou and Maré, has buff wash on male breast and most of female underparts, small or broken supercilium, and whiter rump.
L. l. montrosieri, endemic to Grande Terre on New Caledonia, has faint buff across all underparts, more white on wing-coverts, and grey-white rump.
Elsewhere, *L. l. leucopyga* is extinct on Norfolk I., south of New Caledonia.

WHISTLERS Pachycephalidae

Thickset with heavy bill and head, gleaning in undergrowth rather more slowly and deliberately than monarchs and other forest passerines. Male is usually brightly coloured, female is duller and juvenile often has a distinct plumage. Vocally varied and loud, sometimes creating an overwhelming dawn chorus.

BISMARCK WHISTLER *Pachycephala citreogaster* — Plate 54

(Also treated as a subspecies of Common Golden Whistler *P. pectoralis*; Siffleur doré)

Description 16 cm. Typical golden whistler. Male has black hood, white throat and yellow underparts; female is olive and buffy. Male has glossy black head and broad breast-band with large white throat-patch, bright yellow underparts extending onto nape as collar, and olive upperparts with black centres to larger wing feathers and tail. Female has olive-brown upperparts with darker tail, mottled greyish-white throat, and buffy breast becoming dull yellow on belly and yellower on vent. Juvenile like female but has pale bill and extensive rufous on wings. Plumage may be all rufous when just fledged. Immature variable, often with distinct first-year male plumages.
Similar species Very like Mangrove Golden Whistler, from which it differs by occurring on larger islands, darker legs, slighter bill, ill-defined dull greenish fringes on wings and tail, male with duller greener mantle and lesser wing-coverts, female with indistinct rufous breast-band or plain breast and dark brown uppertail. Male on New Ireland and nearby

islands is like Golden Monarch but differs by white throat, black crown and greenish upperparts. Female differs from Golden Monarch by paler throat, darker breast and no eye-spot.

Voice Male has varied loud and often explosive calls, usually repeated short phrases of 2–5 notes, often ending in whiplash or ringing fruity note, e.g. *chow-chow* or *wo-didy, wo-didy* or *whit-whit—chong*. Louder, faster, more varied, whistled and whiplashed but less scolding than Golden Monarch. Quieter on Mussau, New Ireland and New Britain, where usually only sings loudly at dawn. Female and juvenile usually give quiet clucking *chup...chup...* like domestic chick or louder *tck* or *tchuk* notes or monotone whistles.

Habits Forest but rarely in heavily degraded or drier forest except on Mussau where common in regrowth forest. Common at all altitudes but uncommon in lowlands of New Britain. Often unobtrusive but can be noisy. Male often forages alone in canopy and mid-storey, female, often with a juvenile, in mid-storey and undergrowth, or sometimes with mixed-species flocks.

Conservation status Common. Not threatened.

Range Manus, Mussau and Bismarcks.

P. c. goodsoni, endemic to Manus; male has olive-green upperparts, female a narrow cinnamon breast-band.

P. c. sexuvaria, endemic to Mussau, is like *P. c. goodsoni* but male has brownish wash on upperparts, female a less distinct breast-band.

P. c. citreogaster, endemic to New Britain and New Ireland, including Lavongai, Djaul, Feni, Tolokiwa and Umboi, is like *P. c. goodsoni* but male has lemon-yellow underparts, female a greener mantle and more contrasting darker breast-band.

P. c. tabarensis, endemic to Tabar; male has orange-yellow underparts, female an off-white throat, pale cinnamon breast-band and deep yellow breast and belly.

P. c. ottomeyeri, endemic to Lihir, like *P. c. tabarensis* but female has browner crown and duller breast and belly.

Currently, these subspecies are combined with *P. c. collaris* and *P. c. rosseliana* of the Louisiade Is off south-east New Guinea to form the Bismarck Whistler but the taxonomy of the Golden Whistler group is unsettled and likely to change.

ORIOLE WHISTLER *Pachycephala orioloides* — Plates 63 & 72

(Also treated as a subspecies of Common Golden Whistler *P. pectoralis*; Siffleur doré)

Description 17 cm. Variable golden whistler. Male has black and olive upperparts and yellow underparts with a black breast-band, and female has olive upperparts and yellow or buffy underparts. Many varied subspecies, some possibly separate species. Male has glossy black head and broad breast-band (except on Malaita) with large yellow throat-patch, bright yellow underparts, extending onto nape as collar in many subspecies, and olive upperparts with black centres to larger wing feathers and tail, and more extensive black in some subspecies. Female has dull olive upperparts, often with slightly greyer cap, and dull yellow or buff underparts, faintly streaked in some subspecies, indistinct grey, rufous or olive breast-band, often yellow on vent and sometimes rufous on wings. Juvenile is usually similar to female but has pale bill and extensive rufous on wings. Plumage may be all rufous when just fledged. Variable immature plumages, some birds only attaining adult male plumage after three moults.

Similar species Only whistler on most islands. Very like Mangrove Golden Whistler on small islands around Bougainville, from which it differs by occurring on larger islands, male with yellow throat, and female and juvenile with green or brown fringes on tail and secondaries and no greyish breast-band. From Bougainville and Guadalcanal Mountain Whistlers, male has yellow throat and female has olive-brown crown and yellowish throat.

Voice Varies between subspecies. Usually has loud explosive song of melodious fruity whistles, often interspersed with or ending in whiplash. Often loud and continuous song at dawn, with shorter phrases through day. Quiet thin contact notes often given by female and juvenile, e.g. *chup...chup...* Monotone whistles. Quiet very harsh scold *sch-hree*.

Habits Forest, often in tangles of vines, but rarely in heavily degraded forest. Usually common at all altitudes but some subspecies uncommon in lowlands. Often unobtrusive but can be noisy, especially when several pairs join to display and chase. Male often forages alone in canopy and female, often with a juvenile, in mid-storey or undergrowth.

Conservation status Common to uncommon. Not threatened. However *P. o. melanonota*, *P. o. melanoptera* and *P. o. littayei* are uncommon and may be threatened, and there may be no recent records of *P. o. pavuvu*.

Range Across Solomons except smallest islands.

P. o. bougainvillei, endemic to Buka, Shortland Is and Bougainville, where rare below 600 m and replaced above 1200–1500 m by Bougainville Mountain Whistler; male has yellow throat, female dull brownish-olive upperparts, rufous wings, and grey-washed yellow or pale grey underparts.

P. o. orioloides, endemic to Choiseul, Isabel and Florida Is; male has yellow throat, female has dull brownish-olive upperparts, rufous wings, and yellow underparts, paler on throat and sometimes washed olive or rufous.

P. o. pavuvu, endemic to Russell Is, is like *P. o. orioloides* but male has paler olive upperparts and more olive on uppertail-coverts, and female has yellow bill and is paler overall without cinnamon below.

P. o. centralis, endemic to Kolombangara, Kohinggo, New Georgia, Vangunu and Nggatokae, where less common in lowlands; male like *P. o. orioloides* but narrow or absent yellow collar, female has whitish throat, pale yellow underparts with olive on breast and flanks, darker upperparts, with browner head, greenish-olive mantle, and juvenile is streaked on breast and flanks.
P. o. melanonota, endemic to Vella Lavella, Bagga and Ranongga; male has entire upperparts and broad breast-band black, and yellow throat and belly, and female is variable, with rufous cap, dark olive mantle and tail with cinnamon wings and uppertail-coverts, pale yellow underparts with paler throat, sometimes with olive breast-band or rufous wash; some females have patchy black on upperparts and breast-band, and on Ranongga male sometimes has olive fringes on wings, and female and immature lack rufous cap.
P. o. melanoptera, endemic to Rendova and Tetepare; male like *P. o. orioloides* but has black wing with some olive or grey fringes and no yellow collar, and female is cinnamon-rufous, washed olive on mantle and uppertail and washed yellow on belly.
P. o. cinnamomea, endemic to Guadalcanal, where replaced above *c.*1100–1400 m by Guadalcanal Mountain Whistler; male like *P. o. orioloides*, and female has dull rufous-brown upperparts, rufous wings, cinnamon underparts, darker on breast, sometimes faintly streaked or yellowish, and pale yellow vent.
P. o. sanfordi, endemic to Malaita, where uncommon below 800 m; male lacks black breast-band and yellow collar, and female has dull rufous-olive upperparts, browner head, distinct dark streaks on dull buffy underparts, and plain yellow vent.
P. o. christophori, endemic to Makira and Santa Ana, where commoner in lowlands, is smaller and has the most distinct plumages of any subspecies in this group, the male with yellow, olive or black crown and ear-coverts, yellow on neck-sides but no full collar, and female with olive upperparts with browner head but no rufous in wings, yellowish underparts with greenish breast-band.
Currently, these subspecies are separated from other Golden Whistlers to form Oriole Whistler but the taxonomy of the Golden Whistler group is unsettled and likely to change, with more subspecies being treated as full species.

MELANESIAN WHISTLER *Pachycephala caledonica* Plates 77, 79 & 83

(New Caledonian Whistler; also treated as a subspecies of Common Golden Whistler *P. pectoralis*; Siffleur calédonien)

Description 17 cm. Typical golden whistler with white throat, male with black breast-band and yellow underparts. Male has black or dark grey hood and breast-band, olive upperparts with black on wing-coverts and sometimes tail, white throat, and yellow or orange-yellow underparts. Female has olive or brown upperparts, dirty white throat, and indistinct olive, grey or brown breast-band, buffy or yellow on belly and yellow on vent. Juvenile like female but has rufous fringes on wings and yellower underparts.
Similar species Only whistler on Vanikoro, Vanuatu and Loyalty Is. On Vanuatu, differs from Buff-bellied Monarch by dark cap extending below eye and lack of white on wings and tail. Male on Grande Terre differs from Rufous Whistler by olive mantle and wings, and orange-yellow underparts. Female differs from Rufous Whistler by olive upperparts and unstreaked yellow underparts. Female on Grande Terre from Yellow-bellied Robin by habits, no grey breast and no bright yellow on belly.
Voice Song is a repeated series of variable short loud phrases, each usually repeated a few times before the next. Phrases are usually a series of 3–7 fluid notes, or ringing *chong* notes, sometimes ending in whiplash. More melodious than Grey-eared Honeyeater, with whiplashes. Female gives quiet harsh *chup...chup...* contact calls.
Habits Wet forest, often commoner in degraded forest, forest edge and gardens and locally in dry forest, at all altitudes but less common in mountains. Singles and pairs glean unobtrusively in lower storeys and on ground, male often solitary and higher in mid-storey. Sometimes with mixed-species flocks.
Conservation status Common. Not threatened.
Range Endemic to Vanikoro, Vanuatu and New Caledonia.
P. c. vanikorensis, endemic to Vanikoro; male has white throat, medium-broad black breast-band, bright yellow underparts, black upperparts except for olive mantle and broad fringes on wings, female has grey cap grading into brown-olive mantle and olive rump and tail, mottled off-white throat, brownish breast-band and yellow lower breast to vent, and juvenile has more rufous head and sometimes yellow on throat.
P. c. intacta, endemic to Vanuatu on all larger islands from the Bank Is to Efate but sometimes split into further subspecies; male has white throat, narrow black breast-band and narrow yellow collar, yellow underparts and yellow-olive mantle, wings and tail, female has brownish head, becoming more olive on rump, narrow brown breast-band, very pale yellow belly and brighter yellow vent.
P. c. chlorura, endemic to Erromango; male like *P. c. intacta* but mantle more olive, female has greyer head, olive mantle and pale yellow lower breast and belly, and juvenile has very little yellow below.

P. c. cucullata, endemic to Aneityum; male like *P. c. intacta* but some olive fringes on crown and nape, and brownish wash to upperparts, and female has browner upperparts.
P. c. littayei, endemic to Lifou and Ouvéa, is larger and heavy-billed, female with narrow olive-buff breast-band, grey crown, olive mantle, browner wings and tail.
P. c. caledonica, endemic to Grande Terre and Ile des Pins, New Caledonia; male has dark grey hood and very narrow breast-band, and yellow-orange underparts.
Currently, the subspecies from Vanikoro south are separated from other Golden Whistlers to form the Melanesian Whistler but the taxonomy of the Golden Whistler group is unsettled and likely to change, with more subspecies being treated as full species.

WHITE-THROATED WHISTLER *Pachycephala vitiensis* Plate 77

(Fiji Whistler; also treated as a subspecies of Common Golden Whistler *P. pectoralis*; Siffleur doré)

Description 15 cm. Typical golden whistler, male with black hood and breast-band, white throat and yellow underparts. Male has black upperparts and breast-band, with variable olive fringes on mantle and wings, white throat, and yellow lower breast to vent. Female has olive-brown upperparts, dirty white throat, slight brownish breast-band and dull yellow underparts. Juvenile like female but has rufous fringes on wings and buffier underparts.
Similar species Only whistler in these islands. From female Santa Cruz Shrikebill by yellow on underparts and relatively short black bill.
Voice Male song is a series of short melodious phrases of fruity notes and whiplashes, e.g. *chu-chu-chu-choWEE*. Single whiplash notes. Thin monotone whistle. Female gives slow series of quiet *chup, chup...* notes.
Habits Forest, including degraded forest and drier forest on small islands. Male is often solitary, in all forest storeys, and female, often with a juvenile, in lower storeys and on ground.
Conservation status Common. Not threatened.
Range Temotu.
P. v. ornata, endemic to Nendo, Reef Is and Duff Is; male has white throat, narrow black breast-band, bright yellow underparts tending to orange on vent, upperparts black except for olive fringes on wings, female has grey-brown upperparts, pale chin, and cinnamon breast becoming yellower on belly and vent; mantle more olive on Reef Is and Duff Is.
P. v. utupuae, endemic to Utupua; male like *P. v. ornata* but has olive mantle and fringes to wings, and uniform yellow underparts.
Currently, these subspecies are combined with golden whistler subspecies in Fiji to form the White-throated Whistler, but the taxonomy of the Golden Whistler group is unsettled and likely to change.

MANGROVE GOLDEN WHISTLER *Pachycephala melanura* Plates 54 & 63

(Black-tailed Whistler; Siffleur à queue noire)

Description 16 cm. Typical golden whistler. Male has black head and breast-band, white throat, bright yellow underparts and collar, green mantle and wing-covert fringes, and black wings and uppertail, with pale grey wing-panel on secondaries and primaries. Female has faint grey streaks on white throat and grey-buff upper breast, yellow underparts, olive-grey upperparts, greener on mantle and black uppertail. Juvenile is rufous when first fledged, then like female but rufous on wings and pale bill.
Similar species Very like Bismarck and Oriole Whistlers which only overlap on Tolokiwa and perhaps coastal New Britain and Bougainville. Male differs by white throat, grey fringes to primaries and secondaries (but immature has rufous fringes), black uppertail sometimes with fine greenish fringes, brighter green mantle and wing-coverts, and paler grey-brown legs. Female differs by black uppertail with some olive-brown fringes, especially at base, grey fringes on primaries and secondaries, greyish breast-band, and paler grey-brown legs. Juvenile like female. Differs from Golden Monarch on larger islands in New Ireland group by plumage pattern.
Voice Song is typically a few melodious notes, then a whiplash; shorter, more melodious and with fewer whiplashes than Bismarck and Oriole Whistlers. Long *whooee* call.
Habits Coastal vegetation and degraded forest, including scrub and coconuts. Singles and pairs glean actively in understorey.
Conservation status Common. Not threatened. However there are few recent records of *P. m. whitneyi*.
Range Small islands around Bismarcks and Bougainville and may occur rarely on coasts of New Britain and Bougainville.
P. m. dahli is endemic to islets between New Ireland and Lavongai, small Lihir islands, Tanga, Nissan, Crown, Long, Tolokiwa, small islets around Umboi and New Britain, Witu and Duke of York.
P. m. whitneyi, endemic to small islands off Bougainville and Buka, is variable and probably a hybrid with Golden

Whistler; male has variable yellow in throat, more olive edges on secondaries and darker olive mantle, and female has duller browner upperparts, browner fringes on wings, more olive on basal and central tail, and broader buffy breast-band.

RENNELL WHISTLER *Pachycephala feminina* Plate 75

(Also treated as a subspecies of Common Golden Whistler *P. pectoralis* or Oriole Whistler *P. orioloides*; Siffleur doré)

Description 15 cm. Sexes similar, with olive-rufous upperparts and dull yellow underparts. Dull rufous head, wings and tail, more olive on mantle, and dull yellow throat, vent and undertail-coverts, more buff on breast and flanks. Prominent black eye with pale buff eye-ring, sometimes a short rufous supercilium over eye, a fairly large horn or dull pink bill and dark grey legs. Female duller. Juvenile duller than female and often rustier on crown and underparts.
Similar species Distinctive on Rennell.
Voice Loud song with repeated phrases of melodious notes such as *chuk-chuk-trutrutretretretre...*, often with terminal flourish but no whiplash notes. Harsh loud alarm *tchara-tchara-tchara*. Long series of deep *choop... choop...* notes.
Habits Forest, especially dense understorey of primary forest and dense regrowth. Singles are unobtrusive, usually perched close to or on ground, sometimes on edge of mixed flocks.
Conservation status Fairly common. Not threatened.
Range Endemic to Rennell.

GUADALCANAL HOODED WHISTLER *Pachycephala implicata* Plate 63

(Also combined with Bougainville Hooded Whistler *P. richardsi* as a single species: Hooded/Mountain Whistler *P. implicata*; Siffleur des Salomon)

Description 16 cm. Dark grey, olive and yellow montane whistler. Male has dark grey head and throat, dull brownish-olive body, slightly paler underparts and darker wings and tail. Female has mid-grey cap, dull olive upperparts, white throat, narrow buffy breast-band and dull yellow lower breast and belly. Young juvenile has dull olive and rufous upperparts and dull orange-rufous underparts.
Similar species Male differs from Oriole Whistler, which overlaps between c.1100–1400 m, by all-black throat. From similarly coloured Black-headed Myzomela by habits, size and bill. Female differs from Oriole Whistler by grey head, white throat and no brown or rufous tones in plumage. Young juvenile from Guadalcanal Thicketbird by shorter tail and plainer head.
Voice Song, usually given at dawn, is simpler, quieter and less melodious than Oriole Whistler: simple fruity notes and whiplashes, e.g. *toy-whit* and *choy-whit-whit*. Quiet *chup...chup...* Harsh *chik*. Short thin monotone whistle.
Habits Forest above 1100 m, commoner in upper montane forest above 1400 m. Singles and pairs glean unobtrusively in all storeys of forest. Female often forages on mossy tree-trunks.
Conservation status Common. Not threatened.
Range Endemic to Guadalcanal.

BOUGAINVILLE HOODED WHISTLER *Pachycephala richardsi* Plate 63

(Also treated as a subspecies of Hooded/Mountain Whistler *P. implicata*; Siffleur des Salomon)

Description 16 cm. Black or grey, olive and yellow montane whistler. Male has glossy black hood and upper breast, bright golden-olive upperparts, black on wings and tail, and dull yellow underparts. Female has mid-grey cap, bright olive upperparts, white throat, broad clear grey breast-band and greenish-yellow lower breast and belly. Young juvenile has rufous upperparts with olive fringes to wings, tail and crown, and tawny underparts. Juvenile like female but slightly duller.
Similar species Male differs from Oriole Whistler, which overlaps at c.1200–1500 m, by all-black throat. Female differs from Oriole Whistler by grey head, white throat and no brown or rufous tones in plumage. Young juvenile from Bougainville Thicketbird by shorter tail and plainer head.
Voice Song, usually given at dawn, is shorter and less melodious than Oriole Whistler. Short series of 1–6 simple fruity and whiplash notes, e.g. *whee-wu-wu-chee chee whit* and *whit chu whit chu*. Simple contact call *wheu, wheu...* Harsh *chik*.
Habits Singles and pairs glean unobtrusively in lower storeys of montane forest from 1200 m to at least 1750 m.
Conservation status Fairly common. Not threatened.
Range Endemic to Bougainville.

RUFOUS WHISTLER *Pachycephala rufiventris* — Plate 83

(Siffleur itchong)

Description 15 cm. Grey whistler with orange or buffy underparts. Male has mid-grey upperparts, white throat with narrow black border creating eye-stripe and black breast-band, and pale buffy-orange underparts. Female has brown-grey upperparts, no black around indistinct white throat, and fine black streaks over throat and especially orange-buff breast and belly. Juvenile like female but with rufous fringes on wings and more olive on upperparts.
Similar species Differs from Melanesian Whistler by grey upperparts and pale rufous or buffy underparts, female with fine dark streaks.
Voice Song is a series of phrases of repeated ringing melodious notes and trills, shorter and simpler than Melanesian Whistler, with fewer rich melodious notes and more whiplashes, often just an upslurred whistle followed by downslurred whiplash.
Habits Open and degraded forest, dry forest, savanna and scrub at all altitudes. Singles and pairs forage unobtrusively in all storeys including on ground.
Conservation status Common. Not threatened.
Range *P. r. xanthetraea* is endemic to Grande Terre on New Caledonia; male has narrower eye-stripe than other subspecies which breed from Indonesia to Australia.

ORIOLES Oriolidae

Medium-large forest canopy birds with fairly long stout bills and rich melodious calls. Species outside Melanesia are often brightly coloured.

OLIVE-BACKED ORIOLE *Oriolus sagittatus* — Plate 59

(Loriot sagittal)

Description 26 cm. Medium-sized bird with heavy black streaks on white underparts. Greyish-green head and upperparts with fine dark streaks, grey-brown wings and tail with white spots on tail-corners and fringes on wings. Male has pink-red bill and eye, and green wash on throat. Female has duller pink bill and duller upperparts. Immature has dark grey-brown bill and eye, grey-brown upperparts with little or no green, and buff wash on wings and underparts.
Similar species Distinctive streaked underparts, shared only by juvenile Metallic and Singing Starlings, from which it differs by larger, often pink bill and patterned upperparts.
Voice Song is a series of short melodious phrases of 2–4 rolling mellow notes, e.g. *orry-orry-ole*. Harsh scolding.
Habits Forest, especially degraded forest and scattered trees. Singles, pairs or small groups feed in forest canopy.
Conservation status Vagrant to Melanesia. Not threatened.
Range One record from New Britain. Probably *O. s. sagittatus*, which breeds in east Australia and migrates north in April–September, and two other subspecies breed in north Australia and far south New Guinea.

DRONGOS Dicruridae

Medium-sized glossy black birds with long, usually forked tails and red eye. Often in mixed-species flocks, perching upright in forest mid-storeys and swooping after insects. Noisy and aggressive, often mobbing other species.

SPANGLED DRONGO *Dicrurus bracteatus* — Plates 59, 69 & 73

(Drongo pailleté)

Description 30 cm. Glossy black bird with 'fish-tail'. Tail is forked, splayed outwards and tips are usually twisted upwards. Uniformly black with purple-blue gloss, especially on wings, electric blue spots on crown, neck and breast, and red eye. Juvenile is dull sooty-black with dark brown eye.
Similar species Distinctive tail shape and habits. Moulting and immature birds differ from Metallic Starling by forked or square tail, clear blue spots on adult and dull eye of immature.
Voice Varied calls, usually repeated simple harsh metallic notes or chattering, piping and whistling. Noisy on New Britain, where calls include a screeching *darrr-EE* or *schrEEE*. Metallic trill *dzu-ur-ur-ur* or *dzop-dzop-tzeeu*, harsher than Long-tailed Myna. Flatter *dhu*. Ascending series of scratchy notes followed by whistle. On Guadalcanal, calls

less and more quietly, including phrases of about four simple harsh notes, e.g. *shee-zurr-shee*. Slightly more vocal on Makira, including trilling chatters of 3–8 notes. Rapid trilled mechanical *whee-whee-whee, whee-whee-whee...* Long series of ringing *ki-ki-* like hawk or *pee-pee-* like Collared Kingfisher. Upslurred *scheeEE* or *chu-ee-EE*. Explosive *whit!* Loud, thin swelling whistle.
Habits Closed forest, forest edge and dense secondary forest to 1600 m on New Britain, to at least 700 m on Guadalcanal and all altitudes on Makira. Singles, pairs or groups of up to seven perch upright within forest, flick tail and sally after insects, often in mixed-species flocks. Usually in mid-storey and lower canopy, often in thickets. Obtrusive and very active on New Britain, often chasing each other and mobbing other species. Unobtrusive and often shy in Solomons. Tail is often fanned and flicked.
Conservation status Common on New Britain, uncommon on Guadalcanal and fairly common on Makira. Not threatened.
Range New Britain, Guadalcanal and Makira.
D. b. laemostictus, endemic to New Britain, including Umboi and Lolobau, has deep tail-fork and long iridescent neck-hackles.
D. b. meeki, endemic to Guadalcanal, has flat tail, shallow tail-fork, shorter neck-hackles and different habits and calls; and could be treated as a separate species.
D. b. longirostris, endemic to Makira, has a much longer, more curved bill, very shallowly forked flat straight tail and different habits and calls; and could be treated as a separate species.
Other subspecies occur from Indonesia to Australia and New Guinea.

PARADISE DRONGO *Dicrurus megarhynchus* — Plate 59

(Ribbon-tailed or New Ireland Drongo; Drongo de Nouvelle-Irlande)

Description 40–63 cm including tail-streamers. Glossy black bird with long forked tail and very long twisted outer tail feathers. Tail-streamers are often broken or absent. Uniformly black with blue gloss, especially crown, wings and tail, and small bright blue spots on neck and breast, and red eye. Female is smaller with shorter tail-streamers.
Similar species Distinctive long tail. Short-tailed birds differ from Metallic Starling by forked or square tail and clear blue spots on breast and habits.
Voice Noisy, with variable loud calls. Loud shrieking rasp *schrEER, EEER*. Harsh melodious *sch-sch-brip*. Series of melodious, simple, slurred and disyllabic whistles. High-pitched fluty notes. Rattling *ch-ch-ch*.
Habits Closed forest including secondary and montane formations from sea-level to 1800 m. Fairly shy, but loud and active, often chasing each other, in mid-storey and lower canopy. Usually in pairs.
Conservation status Fairly common. Not threatened.
Range Endemic to New Ireland.

FANTAILS Rhipiduridae

Small long-tailed birds characterised by fanning, cocking and waving tail and often drooping wings when foraging, perhaps to flush out insects. Always in singles or pairs, often in mixed-species flocks in lower forest storeys. Confiding and inquisitive, often investigating and scolding an observer. Melanesian birds are divided into pied species which are less active, brown species which have white facial patterns, and rufous species which have bright contrasting patterns and are hyperactive.

WILLIE WAGTAIL *Rhipidura leucophrys* — Plates 54, 64 & 71

(Rhipidure hochequeue)

Description 20 cm. Large pied fantail of open habitats. Black head, throat and upperparts with white lower breast to vent, indistinct white supercilium, small white tips to primary coverts and some white mottling on throat and malar. Juvenile is duller with broader dull eyebrow and buffy tips to wing-coverts.
Similar species Distinctive in open habitats. Differs from Cockerell's Fantail, Northern Fantail and pied monarchs by habitat, habits, larger size and no white on throat, wings and tail.
Voice Sings at night and calls often. Slow accelerating series of c.4–7 fruity notes, often to tune of '*sweet pretty creature*'. Harsh *tchak*. Nasal *tseep*.
Habits Open habitat including coasts, small islets, mangroves, rivers, grasslands, urban areas and sometimes forest clearings, to 800 m. Conspicuous and pugnacious. Runs on ground and sallies from low perches, drooping wings and waving, but rarely fanning, tail.

Conservation status Common. Not threatened.
Range Bismarcks, St Matthias Is and Solomons.
R. l. melaleuca breeds across Bismarcks including Mussau, Eloaua, Emirau, Lavongai, New Ireland, Djaul, Tabar, Lihir, Crown, Long, Tolokiwa, Umboi, New Britain, Bali, Witu, Lolobau, Watom, Duke of York, and all Solomons east to Makira (but excluding Russell Is, Rennell and some small isolated islands). Elsewhere, it breeds from Indonesia to New Guinea, and two other subspecies breed in Australia.

NORTHERN FANTAIL *Rhipidura rufiventris* Plate 54

(Rhipidure à ventre chamois)

Description 17 cm. Large dark grey fantail with dark grey breast-band. Dark grey with white throat, creamy belly and vent, and variable white fringes on tertials and tips to outer tail feathers. Indistinct white fleck above eye and sometimes white streaks on breast. Juvenile has browner upperparts and breast-band with buffy tips on wing-coverts. Young juvenile has broad white supercilium and wing-covert panel, and heavy white mottling on breast, crown and mantle.
Similar species Differs from Willie Wagtail by habits and habitat, dark throat, grey plumage, white on wings and tail. From juvenile pied monarchs and female Satin Flycatcher by long tail, grey breast-band and no orange on underparts.
Voice Short song of 5–7 sweet whistled notes, usually low-pitched first note, second higher, then others descending. Longer trill of tinkling notes alternating in pitch and often with jumbled end. On Manus and Mussau at least, 2–3 quavering whistles, second higher-pitched. *Pink* contact call, sometimes repeated as trill.
Habits All forest habitats, especially open and degraded forest, at all altitudes. Less active than typical fantails, perching rather upright on exposed perches and sally-gleaning, sometimes wagging or cocking tail but never fanning tail or drooping wings. Often in mixed-species flocks.
Conservation status Common. Not threatened.
Range Admiralties, St Matthias Is and Bismarcks.
R. r. niveiventris, endemic to Manus and Rambutyo, has white belly and dark grey mantle and breast-band.
R. r. mussai, endemic to Mussau, has buff belly and darker grey mantle.
R. r. setosa, endemic to New Ireland, Lavongai and Djaul, has white belly, paler grey upperparts and breast-band, and broader white wing fringes.
R. r. gigantea, endemic to Tabar and Lihir, has white belly, broad fringes on tertials and secondaries, dark grey upperparts and breast-band.
R. r. tangensis, endemic to Tanga, has very pale buff belly, pale grey upperparts and narrow fringes on wings.
R. r. finschii, endemic to New Britain, Lolobau, Watom and Duke of York, has buff belly, light grey mantle and broad white fringes to secondaries and tertials.

COCKERELL'S FANTAIL *Rhipidura cockerelli* Plate 64

(White-winged Fantail; Rhipidure de Cockerell)

Description 17 cm. Black fantail with white on underparts and wings. Glossy black upperparts with indistinct fine white supercilium, faded browner wings and variable white on tertials. Black throat and breast with variable white spots on breast and white belly to vent.
Similar species Differs from Willie Wagtail by habits, habitat and white on wings and throat. From pied monarchs by habits and lack of white on face and tail. From male Steel-blue Flycatcher by black breast, and white on wings, throat and breast.
Voice Song is a hurried jumbled series of musical whistled *chup* and *chip* calls and whistles, usually starting with 2–3 slower notes, then a rushed series rising and falling in pitch. Fruity *chup* calls, sometimes repeated.
Habits Primary and closed secondary forest and forest edge to 1150 m. Less active than most fantails, behaving more like flycatcher. Perches upright, waves but rarely fans tail, and sallies from exposed perches in mid-storey and canopy of forest, often in mixed-species flocks.
Conservation status Fairly uncommon and intolerant of degraded forest. IUCN: Near Threatened.
Range Endemic to Solomons, but not Makira or Rennell.
R. c. septentrionalis, endemic to Bougainville, including Buka and Shortland, has large white spots on breast and extensive white on tertials.
R. c. interposita, endemic to Choiseul and Isabel, has slightly more white on tertials than *R. c. septentrionalis*.
R. c. lavellae, endemic to Vella Lavella and Ranongga, has small white spots on lower breast, narrow white fringes to tertials, dark grey mantle and sometimes a tiny white spot on tail corners.

R. c. albina, endemic to Kolombangara, Kohinggo, New Georgia, Vangunu, Rendova and Tetepare, has very small or no white streaks on breast, narrow white fringes to tertials, very small white tip to outer tail feathers and a slightly paler mantle.
R. c. floridana, endemic to Florida Is, has less white on tertials than *R. c. septentrionalis*.
R. c. cockerelli, endemic to Guadalcanal, has medium-sized spots on breast and broad white fringes to tertials.
R. c. coultasi, endemic to Malaita, has plain white throat, large white spots on black breast, very fine white fringes on tertials, greyer mantle and browner wings and is larger; could be treated as a separate species.

GREY FANTAIL *Rhipidura albiscapa* Plates 71, 79 & 83

(Also combined with New Zealand Fantail *R. fuliginosa*; Rhipidure à collier)

Description 15 cm. Small greyish-brown fantail with narrow black breast-band. Grey-brown upperparts, darker on tail which has buffy-white tips and fringes. Short white supercilium, ear-covert streak, double wing-bar and tertial fringes. White throat, narrow black upper breast-band and pale buff underparts. Juvenile is duller with buff wash to white markings on upperparts and buff fringes to wing-coverts.
Similar species Differs from Streaked Fantail by black breast-band, unspotted underparts, grey mantle, smaller, slighter and longer-tailed. From Makira Fantail on Makira by underparts pattern, greyer upperparts and ill-defined pale tail-tips.
Voice Song is a simple ascending series of c.5–10 pure notes, with slight terminal flourish, higher-pitched than Streaked Fantail but lower than Rufous Fantail. Sharp nasal *tut* or *tseu* calls, often repeated.
Habits In forest including edge and gaps on Makira, more restricted to edge and degraded habitats including scrub and isolated trees in Vanuatu, and in all forest, scrub and savanna habitats on New Caledonia. All altitudes but only above 500 m on Makira. Active and restless. Usually flycatches from perch but also gleans actively in all storeys of forest, often with drooped wings and fanned tail.
Conservation status Common but uncommon on Makira. Not threatened.
Range Makira, Vanuatu and New Caledonia.
R. a. brenchleyi is endemic to Makira and across Vanuatu but no recent records from Torres Is, Maewo and Pentecost.
R. a. bulgeri, endemic to New Caledonia, on Grande Terre and Ile des Pins and possibly vagrant to Lifou, has paler underparts.
Elsewhere, other subspecies occur on Norfolk Is and in Australia.

BROWN FANTAIL *Rhipidura drownei* Plate 64

(Rhipidure brun)

Description 16 cm. Plain brown montane fantail. Grey-brown upperparts with greyer head, browner wings and paler brown tail with pale buff tips and outer fringes. Very fine short white supercilium and sometimes ear-covert streak. Pale throat and buffy-grey underparts with indistinct white streaks. Juvenile duller, often lacking head markings, with dull throat and broader wing-bars.
Similar species Differs from Rufous Fantail by dull colours, plain tail and lack of black breast-band.
Voice Stuttering series of high-pitched tinkling notes or c.12 clear melodious notes, fluctuating in pitch. Harsh *chk*. Harsh *schrr*. Sharp *chee* often repeated.
Habits Montane forest above 700 m, usually higher. Actively gleans and sallies, often with fanned tail, in all storeys.
Conservation status Common. Not threatened.
Range Endemic to Bougainville and Guadalcanal.
R. d. drownei, endemic to Bougainville above 900 m, occasionally down to 700 m, has indistinct pale grey head-stripes, two buffy wing-bars, mottled throat and ochre wash on undertail-coverts and tail.
R. d. ocularis, endemic to Guadalcanal above 1300 m, occasionally down to 1150 m, has clear white head-stripes and plain white throat and undertail-coverts; could be treated as a separate species.

MAKIRA FANTAIL *Rhipidura tenebrosa* Plate 71

(Dusky Fantail; Rhipidure ombré)

Description 17 cm. Plain dark brown fantail with white tail-tips. Dark brown, slightly greyer on tail and paler and greyer on underparts. Narrow white throat-bar, sometimes dark in centre, two golden wing-bars and conspicuous white tips to tail. Hardly visible white supercilium and ear-covert streak. Juvenile has buff fringes on wings and some on underparts.

Similar species Differs from Grey Fantail by dark underparts below small throat-patch, darker browner upperparts and clear white tail-tips.
Voice Often quiet. Short harsh, usually upslurred notes, e.g. *chit*, *cheet*, *chleet-it*, *chitoo-weet*, sometimes strung together as twittering song. Clear resonant *teenk*, deeper than other fantails on Makira. Nasal *tchikee*.
Habits Closed forest. Commonest in hills, from sea-level to 700 m. Often inactive for extended periods. Gleans with drooped wings and half-fanned tail in understorey, often in pairs in mixed-species flocks.
Conservation status Usually uncommon and restricted to closed-canopy forest. IUCN: Near Threatened.
Range Endemic to Makira.

RENNELL FANTAIL *Rhipidura rennelliana* — Plate 75

(Rhipidure de Rennell)

Description 16 cm. Plain dark grey-brown fantail, with white on outer tail feathers. Tiny white supercilium, buff double wing-bar and fringes to wings, paler throat and paler belly becoming off-white on undertail-coverts. Juvenile is deeper cinnamon below and has rusty fringes on wing-coverts.
Similar species None on Rennell.
Voice Sings before dawn. Song is 8–15 clear high-pitched *chip* and more nasal *chee* notes with fluctuating pitch and rhythm. Short squeaky call.
Habits Forest and forest edge. Active, often in pairs in mixed-species flocks. Gleans with drooped wings and cocked half-fanned tail in lower storeys.
Conservation status Common. Not threatened.
Range Endemic to Rennell.

STREAKED FANTAIL *Rhipidura verreauxi* — Plates 79 & 83

(Spotted Fantail; *Rhipidura spilodera*; Rhipidure tacheté)

Description 17 cm. Stout dark brown fantail with spots or streaks on breast. Dark brown upperparts, greyer on head and tail and rustier on mantle. Short white supercilium and ear-covert stripe and pale whitish fringes to wing-coverts and tertials, and fringes and tips to tail. White throat, pale grey lower breast and belly with heavy black spots or short streaks on breast, sometimes to belly, and buffy flanks. Juvenile duller with buff fringes to wings.
Similar species Differs from Grey Fantail by lack of breast-band, heavily spotted underparts, rusty-brown mantle, pale on lower mandible, larger, stouter size and shorter tail.
Voice Song is a rapid stutter of clear tinkling notes, rising and falling in pitch, lower-pitched than Grey Fantail, and sometimes interspersed with *chup* notes. Nasal *chup*, sometimes extended into long regular series, deeper than Grey Fantail. White-eye-like *chap*.
Habits Usually in closed forest, less common in degraded forest, montane forest and dry forest, to 1500 m. Less active than Grey Fantail. Singles and pairs sally and actively glean, with drooped wings and waved, cocked and fanned tail, often in mixed-species flocks.
Conservation status Common. Not threatened.
Range Vanuatu and New Caledonia.
R. v. spilodera is endemic to Vanuatu, on all except the smallest islands from Vanua Lava to Efate.
R. v. verreauxi, endemic to New Caledonia, on Grande Terre, Lifou, Maré and Ile des Pins, has heavier spotting on breast, more white on wing-coverts and rustier mantle.
Elsewhere, three other subspecies occur in Fiji.

BISMARCK FANTAIL *Rhipidura dahli* — Plate 54

(Bismarck Rufous Fantail; Rhipidure des Bismarck)

Description 14 cm. Dull rufous fantail with short white supercilium and moustachial stripe. Dull grey head merges into dull orange-rufous upperparts with darker centres to wing feathers, especially lesser coverts, and broad dark subterminal tail-band. Dull grey breast and rich buff underparts. Female has paler crown, ear-coverts and throat. Juvenile has paler, less defined head pattern with buff supercilium and creamy moustachial stripe.
Similar species Distinctive colour.
Voice Nasal buzzing *vee-ee* or *vhee* like squeaky toy. Series of shorter, less nasal *vee-vee-vee-* calls. Short jumbled song based on this note rising and falling in pitch.
Habits Undergrowth and thickets in forest at *c.*800–1800 m and locally in lowlands to sea-level. Singles or pairs, often in mixed-species flocks, actively glean and flutter, often fanning and cocking tail.

Conservation status Fairly common. Not threatened.
Range Endemic to Bismarcks.
R. d. antonii, endemic to New Ireland, has narrower paler tail-band restricted to inner tail feathers.
R. d. dahli, endemic to New Britain and Umboi, has broad black subterminal tail-band and is paler on lores and ear-coverts.

MUSSAU FANTAIL *Rhipidura matthiae* — Plate 54

(Matthias [Rufous] Fantail; Rhipidure des Saint-Matthias)

Description 15 cm. Striking black, white and rufous fantail. Glossy black head and breast with white blaze on forecrown and broad moustachial stripe. Rufous-orange upperparts, brighter on tail and darker on wings, silver belly, and buff flanks and vent. Juvenile is duller, with dark brown nape and breast, and less clear markings.
Similar species Distinctive plumage. Mussau Triller has similar colours but white face, throat and breast.
Voice Loud explosive song of about ten fruity warbled notes, *pwit-pwit-chiddley-diddley...* Series of sucking *tchu-tchu-tchu-* notes. Soft *pink* flight call. Loud ringing *hwit*.
Habits Forest, especially forest edge and tree-fall gaps, including secondary regrowth and scrub. Active in undergrowth, often in mixed-species flocks, gleaning and chasing, often fanning and cocking tail.
Conservation status Common but may be threatened by logging and forest loss. IUCN: Near Threatened.
Range Endemic to Mussau.

MALAITA FANTAIL *Rhipidura malaitae* — Plate 64

(Rhipidure de Malaita)

Description 16 cm. Plain dull orange fantail with prominent dark eye. Dull rusty-orange with darker wings, slightly darker crown and paler buffier underparts, palest on throat. Juvenile has identical plumage.
Similar species Differs from Rufous Fantail by plain tail and underparts.
Voice Thin quiet *seep* and *see-seep* calls. Song is unknown.
Habits Montane forest above 600 m, usually above 1000 m. Singles or pairs are active, drooping wings, cocking and fanning tail, often in mixed-species flocks.
Conservation status Very little known. Fairly common in 1930s, when 37 specimens where collected, but only three records in recent years. IUCN: Vulnerable.
Range Endemic to Malaita, where range is poorly known and seen in recent years only on Mt Ire and Arullange village.

MANUS FANTAIL *Rhipidura semirubra* — Plate 54

(Manus Rufous Fantail; Rhipidure de l'Amirauté)

Description 14 cm. Rufous fantail with bright rufous upperparts. Bright rufous crown, mantle and rump, darker browner wings and dark brown tail with bold white tips. White throat, narrow white eye-ring, black face and broad upper breast-band, black spots on lower breast, white belly, buffy flanks and rufous undertail-coverts.
Similar species Distinctive rufous colour.
Voice Song is a series of scratchy whistles, usually starting with a few slow full notes then a rushed series descending in pitch. Single thin whistles.
Habits Forest, scrub and coconut plantation undergrowth. Very active, often fanning and cocking tail and drooping wings, in all storeys from ground to subcanopy.
Conservation status Locally common. It appears to have become extinct for unknown reasons from Manus, where common and widespread until 1934. IUCN: Vulnerable.
Range Endemic to Admiralties, where currently found on Rambutyo, Tong, San Miguel, Anobat, Pak and Sivisa, and likely to occur on other small islands, but extinct on Manus.

RUFOUS FANTAIL *Rhipidura rufifrons* — Plates 64, 71 & 76

(Rhipidure roux)

Description 15 cm. Bright rufous, black and white fantail. Brown head, mantle and wings, bright orange-rufous rump, tail-base and forehead, and remainder of tail black with broad white tips. White throat in most subspecies, black breast-band breaking into black spots on lower breast, and buffy underparts. Juvenile is duller, slightly browner on tail and underparts.

Similar species Differs from other fantails by bright orange-rufous on upperparts, contrasting black and white tail and clear black breast-band.
Voice Song is a few short evenly spaced high-pitched notes, then a rapid descending tinkling trill. Single thin sibilant whistles *peep*. Sharp *tsu*.
Habits Forest, especially degraded forest and clearings, including mangroves, often commoner in hills, from 0–1200 m. Usually in understorey but also on ground in clearings. Hyperactive, invariably with drooped wings and waving fanned tail.
Conservation status Common. Not threatened but some subspecies have extremely small ranges.
Range Solomons and Temotu.
R. r. commoda, endemic to Buka, Bougainville, Shortland, Choiseul and Isabel, has nearly half the central tail feathers rufous.
R. r. granti, endemic to Vella Lavella, Ranongga, Bagga, Gizo, Kolombangara, New Georgia, Rendova, Tetepare, Vangunu and Nggatokae, like *R. r. commoda* but has black ear-coverts.
R. r. rufofronta, endemic to Guadalcanal, has only the base of tail feathers rufous, and blackish-brown ear-coverts.
R. r. brunnea, endemic to Malaita, where only above 400 m, like *R. r. rufofronta* but darker upperparts and blacker ear-coverts.
R. r. russata, endemic to Makira, has entire mantle rufous and a narrow black breast-band.
R. r. kuperi, endemic to Santa Ana and probably this subspecies on Santa Catalina, like *R. r. russata* but darker neck merges into rufous mantle, and more rufous on forehead.
R. r. ugiensis, endemic to Ugi, like *R. r. kuperi* but no or very small white patch on throat, paler rufous on upperparts and darker flanks.
R. r. agilis, endemic to Nendo, has white band across chin and malar stripe, black throat, and duller brown forehead, mantle, rump and small area of tail-base.
R. r. utupuae, endemic to Utupua, has white forehead and supercilium, black chin and throat but broad white malar stripe, dull rusty-brown crown, neck and mantle.
R. r. melanolaema, endemic to Vanikoro, like *R. r. utupuae* but olive-grey upperparts lack rusty tone, less white on supercilium, less extensive black on upper breast, and flesh-coloured lower mandible.
Elsewhere, other subspecies from Indonesia to Micronesia, New Guinea and Australia.

MONARCHS Monarchidae

Medium-sized passerines, similar to flycatchers. Usually common and familiar members of mixed-species foraging flocks in forest. Rather aggressive, often scolding or mobbing other birds or observer, and respond strongly to imitation of harsh contact calls and whistles. *Mayrornis* and *Neolalage* are small atypical monarchs, often with cocked tails. Shrikebills *Clytorhynchus* are large lanky monarchs with long heavy hooked bills, often foraging noisily in tangles of epiphytes and dead wood. Typical monarchs are divided into pied monarchs *Symposiachrus*, often with distinct juvenile plumages, chestnut-bellied monarchs *Monarcha*, and the sexually dimorphic Golden Monarch *Carterornis*. Monarch flycatchers *Myiagra* are large-headed, sexually dimorphic and sally after insects.

VANIKORO MONARCH *Mayrornis schistaceus* — Plate 76

(Monarque schistacé)

Description 14 cm. Small slate-grey monarch with cocked tail. Slaty-grey body with darker wings, black tail and broad white tips to outer three tail feathers. Slightly paler underparts and almost white undertail-coverts. Juvenile has less contrasting tail-tips and an orange-pink base to bill.
Similar species Distinctive plumage and shape.
Voice Noisy. Trisyllabic quavering whistle *whee-hee-oow*. Scolding *scha-scha*. Chattering *schschschsch-*. Juvenile call a continuous *ch-ch-ch-*, harsher than Cardinal Myzomela.
Habits Forest, forest edge and regrowth adjacent to forest, to at least 450 m. Singles and pairs glean actively in canopy and subcanopy, often with mixed-species flocks or Rufous Fantail. Tail nearly always cocked, occasionally fanned or flicked up and down.
Conservation status Common. Probably declining as it does not occur in open secondary forest and would be susceptible to logging and forest loss. IUCN: Near Threatened.
Range Endemic to Vanikoro.

BUFF-BELLIED MONARCH *Neolalage banksiana* Plate 79

(Vanuatu Monarch/Flycatcher; Monarque des Banks)

Description 15 cm. Small black, white and golden monarch. Black crown, mantle, breast-band and much of wings and tail. White face, including throat and neck, and outer tail which looks all white from below. Variable tone of cream to orange-buff on wing-coverts, tertials, rump and especially lower breast and belly. Female is duller with smaller pale wing-patch. Juvenile has brownish-black upperparts, with dark mottling on white patches on face and wings, and yellowish bill.
Similar species Differs from trillers by habits, golden colour and black breast-band. From male Melanesian Whistler by pale patches on wing and tail, and white extending over eye.
Voice Thin quavering whistle, about one second long. Harsh scolding *tzuk*, often repeated. Rapid series of chattering notes *tzu-tzu-tzu...* or buzzing notes *chrr, chrr*.
Habits Forest, degraded forest and adjacent scrub, at all altitudes. Pairs and threes are slow stolid gleaners in understorey and subcanopy, often with half-cocked tail.
Conservation status Common. Not threatened.
Range Endemic to Vanuatu, where recorded from Vanua Lava, Santo, Malo, Maewo, Ambae, Pentecost, Malekula, Ambrym, Epi and Efate.

SOUTHERN SHRIKEBILL *Clytorhynchus pachycephaloides* Plate 79 & 83

(Monarque brun)

Description 19 cm. Large plain brown monarch with heavy blue-grey bill. Fairly plain plumage, with dark warm brown upperparts and lighter, greyer underparts. Darker tail, especially undertail, contrasting with broad white tips to outer tail feathers. Juvenile has dark brown bill.
Similar species Distinctive heavy bill and tail pattern. Differs from Melanesian Whistler by white on tail and lack of yellow on underparts. Differs from Grey and Streaked Fantails by plainer plumage, heavy bill and clearer white tail-tips.
Voice Long clear, slightly quavering whistle, usually strongly upslurred or downslurred. Churring scold, often about five notes rolled into each other, e.g. *tree-tchrr-tchrrtchrrtchrr*, often preceding a whistle.
Habits Closed-canopy wet forest to 1100 m, not in lowlands of Efate and Erromango. Singles and pairs forage in shady tangles and thickets in lower storeys and subcanopy of forest, often crunching and tossing dead leaves and bark. Noisy but unobtrusive, commonly with mixed-species flocks, and sometimes cocks tail.
Conservation status Fairly common but rare or absent in lowlands of Efate and Erromango. Not threatened.
Range Endemic to Vanuatu and New Caledonia.
C. p. grisescens is endemic to Vanuatu, where recorded from Torres Is to Emae, Efate and Erromango.
C. p. pachycephaloides, endemic to Grande Terre, New Caledonia, has more rufous upperparts and more buff on underparts.

SANTA CRUZ SHRIKEBILL *Clytorhynchus sanctaecrucis* Plate 76

(Also treated as a subspecies of Black-throated Shrikebill *C. nigrogularis*; Monarque à gorge noire)

Description 19 cm. Pied male and plain brown female have stout, fairly long blue-grey bill. Male has glossy black hood with clear white ear-covert patch, sooty upperparts and white underparts from lower breast to vent, white tips to a variable number of tail feathers and sometimes a fine white supercilium. Female is uniform rufous-brown, slightly paler around face and underparts. Juvenile probably like female, with immature male developing grey, then black around face, and pale buff underparts. Male may take two years to attain adult plumage.
Similar species Female differs from White-throated Whistler by uniform brown plumage without any yellow, and longer bluer bill. From Sanford's White-eye by heavy grey bill, grey legs and lack of silver eye-ring.
Voice Male gives a long clear rich swelling whistle, often with 2–4 slurred pulses, usually upslurred and becoming quieter at end, and usually repeated as short series. Various deep harsh scolding notes, often repeated.
Habits Poorly known but only recorded from primary forest at 80 m and 550 m. Pairs forage alone or in mixed-species flocks in understorey of shady mature forest. Sometimes forages on ground, tossing leaves. Male often cocks tail and shivers drooped wings when calling.
Conservation status Poorly known but appears to be rare, known from two specimens and one sighting of two pairs, and restricted to old-growth forest. Susceptible to any increase in logging. IUCN: Endangered.
Range Endemic to Nendo.

RENNELL SHRIKEBILL *Clytorhynchus hamlini* — Plate 74

(Monarque de Rennell)

Description 19 cm. Orange-brown shrikebill with black mask. Warm orange-brown, darker on wings and tail, paler on underparts, and often shows white under wing. Very long blue-grey bill and glossy black mask and upper throat. Female duller. Juvenile duller than female, especially the mask.
Similar species Distinctive.
Voice Sings before dawn and through day. Varied fluting whistling song, often three notes repeated every three seconds at variable pitches, e.g. *kwy-oh-wee* or *ku-ku-kurrah* or bouncing *toy-oy-oyh*. Churring *t-t-t-t-* or *etch-etch-etch-*, often interspersed within song. Harsh *trrk* scold.
Habits All forest and secondary regrowth habitats on Rennell. Singles and pairs forage in understorey, often with mixed-species flocks.
Conservation status Fairly common. Not threatened.
Range Endemic to Rennell.

MANUS MONARCH *Symposiachrus infelix* — Plate 55

(*Monarcha infelix*; Monarque triste)

Description 15 cm. Pied monarch with white ear-covert patch. Glossy black upperparts, throat and upper breast with large white ear-covert patch, variable white wing-covert patch and variable black and white on tail. Juvenile has pale grey or grey-buff upperparts, variable white wing-covert patch, pale grey throat and upper breast, and creamy lower breast to vent.
Similar species Distinctive pied plumage. Differs from Northern Fantail by shiny black plumage and black throat.
Voice Harsh scolding calls, with faster shorter notes than Shining Flycatcher. Long quavering whistle, usually upslurred at end, or sometimes ending with two fluid *twit-twit* notes.
Habits Closed-canopy forest, but rare in secondary, mangrove and submontane forest. Pairs and singles actively glean, sometimes fluttering, in undergrowth to subcanopy of forest.
Conservation status Rather uncommon and rare in secondary forest. IUCN: Near Threatened.
Range Endemic to Admiralties.
S. i. infelix, endemic to Manus, has white outer tail feathers.
S. i. coultasi, endemic to Rambutyo, Tong and possibly other islands, has white rump and tail except black tips of inner tail feathers, more white on ear-coverts, and variably more white on wing.

MUSSAU MONARCH *Symposiachrus menckei* — Plate 55

(White-breasted Monarch; Matthias Monarch; *Monarcha menckei*; Monarque des Saint-Matthias)

Description 15 cm. Mostly white monarch with variable irregular black patches on face, wings and tail. Black forehead, face and throat sometimes extending as large spot on ear-coverts and may have small spots on crown, mantle, breast and belly. Black wings with white tertials and variable extent of white on wing-coverts. Black central tail feathers and increasing extent of white tips out to largely all-white outer tail feathers. May become whiter with age. Juvenile has black mask, black or grey crown and upperparts, less white on tail and, briefly, buffy-pink wash on underparts.
Similar species Distinctive pied plumage. From Northern Fantail by white on upperparts and lack of breast-band. From Mussau Triller by white on upperparts and all-white or pale pink underparts.
Voice Loud harsh scolding *trukk-trukk*. Infrequently gives long quavering whistle, similar to Manus Monarch.
Habits Common in forest and fairly common in secondary regrowth habitats. Singles and pairs, rarely in mixed flocks, glean sluggishly in lower storeys and often flick their wings.
Conservation status Common. May be at risk from extensive logging. IUCN: Near Threatened.
Range Endemic to Mussau.

BLACK-TAILED MONARCH *Symposiachrus verticalis* — Plate 55

(Bismarck Pied Monarch; *Monarcha verticalis*; also treated as two species including Djaul Monarch *S. ateralbus*; Monarque des Bismarck)

Description 16 cm. Pied monarch with black bib and tail. Glossy black bib, forehead, crown and upperparts with white face, neck-sides, underparts, wing-covert patch and rump. Variable amount of white on wing-coverts, occasionally has white hindcollar or small white tips to outer tail feathers. Female averages less white. Juvenile has grey crown, nape and mantle, brown wings, soon developing buff or white patch on wing-coverts, and dirty white rump. Juvenile face and underparts are washed orange-pink, darkest on upper breast and fading across belly.

Similar species Adult is distinctive but differs from Varied Triller by black throat. Juvenile differs from Island Monarch by pale throat and pale on wing-coverts and tail. Juvenile from female Satin Flycatcher by pale on face, wing-coverts and rump. Juvenile from female Lesser Shining Flycatcher by pale patches, greyer upperparts and more orange underparts.
Voice Long thin quavering whistle, often 2–3 pulses repeated, quieter and higher-pitched with less distinct pulses than Shining Flycatcher. Buzzy churring alarm calls.
Habits Fairly common in closed-canopy forest, less common in secondary and montane forest, and absent from above 1400 m and semi-deciduous forest. Singles and pairs, often in mixed flocks. Flicks wings and tail and also flutters and hovers, especially on Lavongai and Djaul. Usually in canopy, sometimes in undergrowth.
Conservation status Fairly common. Not threatened.
Range Endemic to Bismarcks.
S. v. verticalis is endemic to Lavongai, New Ireland, Umboi, New Britain and Duke of York.
S. v. ateralbus (Djaul Monarch), endemic to Djaul, has white tips to outer three pairs of tail feathers, more white on rump, and slightly larger size, juvenile with more extensive orange on face.

SOLOMONS MONARCH *Symposiachrus barbatus* Plate 65

(Solomons Pied Monarch; Black-and-white Monarch; *Monarcha barbatus*; Monarque pie)

Description 15 cm. Pied monarch with white patches on face and wing-coverts. Glossy black head, throat and upperparts with white lower ear-covert patch, usually connected to white underparts, large white wing-covert patch and white tips to outer tail feathers. Juvenile has grey head, darker ear-coverts, browner upperparts, orange-buff lores and throat fading paler to vent, and variably sized buffy to off-white wing-covert patch.
Similar species Adult differs from Cockerell's Fantail by white ear-covert patch, bold white wing-covert patch and different habits. Juvenile differs from female Steel-blue Flycatcher by orange-washed underparts and pale on wing-coverts and tail. Juvenile from Island Monarch by pale throat and pale on wing-coverts and tail.
Voice Thin pulsing whistle, usually upslurred, lower-pitched and less distinctly syllabic than Chestnut-bellied Monarch. Various scolding notes, harsher than Chestnut-bellied Monarch.
Habits Closed-canopy forest to at least 1200 m but rare in flat lowland forest and heavily degraded forest. Singles and pairs glean and flutter in mixed-species flocks in understorey and subcanopy.
Conservation status Rather uncommon. IUCN: Near Threatened.
Range Endemic to Solomons.
S. b. barbatus, endemic to Buka, Bougainville, Shortland, Choiseul, Isabel, Florida and Guadalcanal, has black bib separate from black wings, and white only on outer tail feathers.
S. b. malaitae, endemic to Malaita, has extensive white on tail, large black bib connecting to black wings, and some white scaling on lower border of bib; could be treated as a separate species.

KOLOMBANGARA MONARCH *Symposiachrus browni* Plate 65

(Brown's Monarch; *Monarcha browni*; Monarque de Brown)

Description 15 cm. Typical pied monarch with black breast and white face-patch. Black head and large bib, with white lower breast to vent and large white patches on ear-coverts, wing-coverts and tail-tips. Juvenile has dark grey ear-coverts, grey crown and mantle, grey-rufous wing-coverts soon developing orange to white wing-covert patch, orange-buff underparts from chin to belly and white vent and undertail-coverts.
Similar species Differs from Cockerell's Fantail by white ear-covert patch, bold white wing-covert patch and different habits. Juvenile differs from female Steel-blue Flycatcher by orange-washed underparts and pale on wing-coverts and tail.
Voice Thin pulsing whistle, usually upslurred, lower-pitched, weaker and less distinctly syllabic than White-capped Monarch. Harsh *scheer-scheer* scold, harsher than White-capped Monarch.
Habits Fairly uncommon and shy in primary forest to 600 m. Actively gleans, fans tail and sometimes flutters in understorey to subcanopy.
Conservation status Rather uncommon. May be threatened by logging and forest loss. IUCN: Near Threatened.
Range Endemic to New Georgia island group.
S. b. browni is endemic to Kolombangara, Vonavona, Kohinggo, New Georgia and Vangunu.
S. b. meeki, endemic to Rendova and Tetepare, is very similar but has slightly less white on outer tail feathers.
S. b. ganongae, endemic to Ranongga, has small black bib not connecting to wings, more white on tail and slightly less white on wing-coverts.
S. b. nigrotectus, endemic to Vella Lavella and Bagga, has small black bib not connecting to wings, no white on wing-coverts and slightly more white on tail than *S. b. browni*; could be treated as a separate species.

WHITE-COLLARED MONARCH *Symposiachrus vidua* Plate 72

(*Monarcha viduus*; Monarque à col blanc)

Description 15 cm. Pied monarch with white collar. Plain black head and throat, separated by broad white collar from black mantle, wings and tail, with white rump, tail-tips and scaly wing-patch of variable extent. Juvenile slightly browner with dark bill.
Similar species Differs from Long-tailed Triller by black throat, white collar, tail pattern and habits.
Voice Thin pulsing whistle, lower-pitched and less distinctly syllabic than Chestnut-bellied Monarch. Whistle is often prefixed with one or two whipped or fluid notes. Scolding calls similar to Chestnut-bellied Monarch.
Habits Usually in closed forest, less common in secondary forest, forest edge and mountains to at least 800 m. Gleans and flutters, usually in pairs, often in mixed-species flocks in lower and mid-storeys of forest.
Conservation status Fairly common. Not threatened.
Range Endemic to Makira.
S. v. vidua is endemic to Makira and Santa Ana.
S. v. squamulatus, endemic to Ugi, has different calls, scales on breast below more extensive black throat, and less white on collar and wing-coverts, but great variation in the amount of white; could be treated as a separate species.

ISLAND MONARCH *Monarcha cinerascens* Plates 55 & 65

(Monarque des îles)

Description 18 cm. Large plain dull orange and grey monarch. Dull ash-grey upperparts, throat and upper breast, sharply demarcated from dull orange-buff lower breast and belly. Prominent black eye on plain face and heavy steel-blue bill. Juvenile has duller browner plumage and pale pink base to blacker bill.
Similar species Differs from Bougainville and Chestnut-bellied Monarchs by grey not black upperparts. From very similar juvenile White-capped Monarch by paler, more sharply demarcated underparts not extending onto mid-breast, completely plain head and larger paler bill. From juvenile pied monarchs by no pale patterning on wings or tail, and uniform colour and tone both above and below.
Voice Song is a repeated downslurred disyllabic whistle, rarely mixed with a few musical notes. A variety of short scolding notes, less harsh than other monarchs.
Habits Open secondary forest, scrub, beach forest and coconuts but also closed-canopy forest on smaller islands. Gleans and occasionally flycatches but more sluggish than other monarchs. Usually pairs and singles in undergrowth.
Conservation status Locally common. Not threatened.
Range Admiralties, St Matthias Is, Bismarcks and north Solomons, where only on small islands and, rarely, along coast of larger islands.
M. c. fulviventris, on small islands in Wuvulu, Ninigo, Hermit, Kaniet and Admiralty Is (including San Miguel, Tong, Nauna but not Manus), is rather washed-out orange below, but all subspecies are rather variable between islands.
M. c. perpallidus, on small islands off St Matthias and New Ireland (including Mussau, Tench, Lavongai, Djaul, Tabar, Lihir, Tanga and unconfirmed from inland New Ireland), is slightly brighter and darker below.
M. c. impediens, on small islands off New Britain (including islands west of New Britain, Witu, Watom and very locally along coasts of New Britain), northern atolls (including Feni, Nissan and atolls across to Ontong Java, Ndai and Sikaiana) and small islands off Bougainville, Shortland, Choiseul and Isabel (including Ramos and Borokua), is deeper, more rufous, below and darker grey above; also occurs on Karkar and perhaps mainland New Guinea, and other subspecies occur in Indonesia and New Guinea.

BOUGAINVILLE MONARCH *Monarcha erythrostictus* Plate 65

(Also treated as a subspecies of Chestnut-bellied Monarch *M. castaneiventris*; Monarque de Bougainville)

Description 17 cm. Large black and chestnut monarch. Glossy black head, upperparts and breast, deep chestnut lower breast and belly, and pale blue-grey bill. Male has pale yellow crescent in front of eye. Female has rufous spot in front of eye. Juvenile has browner wings and tail.
Similar species Differs from Island Monarch, which only occurs on small islets, by black upperparts and eye-spots.
Voice Long pulsed descending whistle, repeated after a few seconds. Whistles may also ascend, remain on constant pitch, accelerate and reach crescendo. Scolding rasps. Rasps are softer and whistles lower-pitched and more syllabic than Solomons Pied Monarch, but very like Chestnut-bellied Monarch.
Habits Primary forest, less often secondary forest, to 1300 m. A rather slow and stolid gleaner in all forest storeys. Usually in pairs, often in mixed-species flocks.
Conservation status Fairly common. Not threatened.
Range Endemic to Buka, Bougainville, Shortland and Fauro.

CHESTNUT-BELLIED MONARCH *Monarcha castaneiventris* Plates 65 & 72

(Monarque à ventre marron)

Description 17 cm. Large black and chestnut monarch. Glossy black head, upperparts and breast, deep chestnut lower breast and belly, and pale blue-grey bill. Female has less gloss on upperparts. Juvenile is duller with browner wings and darker bill.
Similar species Differs from juvenile Solomons Monarch by plain black upperparts and throat and rich uniform chestnut underparts. From Island Monarch, which rarely overlaps on small islands off Isabel, by darker chestnut underparts extending further onto mid-breast, and slightly smaller darker bill.
Voice Strong whistle, about one second long, often with one or two pulses or quavers, falling in volume and often given before dawn. Calls are variable and include lower-pitched, non-quavering, upslurred and downslurred whistles. A chattering series of *cha-cha-cha-* notes. A range of scolding rasps. On Makira, a quavering, strongly downslurred or upslurred whistle of half-second duration. Whistles are louder, lower-pitched and more distinctly syllabic than pied monarchs, and rasps are softer.
Habits Primary and secondary forest, less often regrowth and scrub, to 1100 m, rarely to 1450 m. *M. c. ugiensis* is common in scrubby regrowth, beach forest and forest edge, but less common in closed-canopy rainforest. A relatively slow and stolid sally-gleaner in undergrowth and mid-storeys. Commonly in mixed-species flocks where noisy and obtrusive.
Conservation status Common. Not threatened.
Range Endemic to Solomons, excluding Bougainville and New Georgia group.
M. c. castaneiventris is endemic to Choiseul, Isabel, Guadalcanal, Savo, Florida Is and Malaita.
M. c. obscurior, endemic to Russell Is, is darker, and black extends further down breast and flanks.
M. c. megarhynchus, endemic to Makira, is larger with a distinctly larger bill and longer tail.
M. c. ugiensis, endemic to Ugi, Three Sisters, Santa Ana and Santa Catalina, is entirely glossy blue-black but wings are often faded brown, and juvenile may have some tawny fringes on lower belly; could be treated as a separate species.

WHITE-CAPPED MONARCH *Monarcha richardsii* Plate 65

(Richard's Monarch; Monarque à nuque blanche)

Description 17 cm. Large black, white and rufous monarch. Glossy blue-black head, upperparts and breast, deep chestnut lower breast and belly, variable extent of white on crown and hindneck, and pale blue-grey bill. Distinct juvenile plumage has mid-grey upperparts, head and upper breast with less defined border with dull chestnut underparts. White on head is initially restricted to eyelids, then eyebrow, then many intermediate and mottled patterns in subadults.
Similar species Juvenile differs from juvenile Kolombangara Monarch in lack of pale patterning on wings or tail, and uniform colour and tone both above and below. Juvenile from Island Monarch, unrecorded in the New Georgia group, by darker chestnut underparts extending further onto mid-breast, where less clearly defined from grey throat, usually some white on head and smaller darker bill.
Voice Quavered whistle, often disyllabic *quee-hee*, stronger and lower-pitched than Kolombangara Monarch. Various scolding calls, less harsh than Kolombangara Monarch, include long quavering or piping series.
Habits Common in forest and scrub, less common in mountains to 1100 m. Stolid gleaner often in small flocks or mixed-species flocks, at all levels in forest and foraging more than other monarchs in creepers and tangles.
Conservation status Common. Not threatened.
Range Endemic to New Georgia island group, including Vella Lavella, Ranongga, Gizo, Kolombangara–New Georgia–Vangunu–Nggatokae group, Rendova and Tetepare.

GOLDEN MONARCH *Carterornis chrysomela* Plate 55

(*Monarcha chrysomela*; Monarque doré)

Description 13 cm. Male is patchy bright orange-yellow and black, female plain greenish-yellow. Male has bright golden-yellow head, underparts, wing-panel and rump, and glossy black face and throat, mantle, wings and tail. Female has yellow-olive upperparts, darker on wings and tail, and dull yellow underparts with pale spot before eye. Juvenile like female but has darker bill and may lack eye-spot.
Similar species Male differs from Bismarck Whistler and Mangrove Golden Whistler by black throat, yellow cap and yellow on wing. Female eye-spot distinctive; differs from female whistlers by lacking pale throat.
Voice Varied. Song is a jumble of varied melodious warbles, short whistles and short harsh notes. Series of short whistles often followed by one or two melodious notes, e.g. *whit-whit...whit-whit...chou-cho*. Explosive *chow-chit*. Single and chattering series of *cha* or *chacha* notes. Scolding *schra*. Similar to Bismarck Whistler but quieter and slower, whistles less whipped.

Habits Primary and degraded forest to 1400 m, especially forest edges and gaps. Active gleaner in mid- and upper storeys, often in small groups or mixed-species flocks, with habits intermediate between monarchs and whistlers.
Conservation status Common. Not threatened.
Range New Ireland and nearby islands.
C. c. chrysomela is endemic to New Ireland and Lavongai, with one vagrant record from New Britain.
C. c. whitneyorum, endemic to Lihir; male has more yellow in wing and less orange on crown, and female is greener.
C. c. tabarensis, endemic to Tabar; male lacks orange on cap and female has greener upperparts.
C. c. pulcherrimus, endemic to Djaul; male has yellow mantle and female has more yellow on forehead, face and rump, and tawny-olive crown and mantle.
Elsewhere, other subspecies occur in New Guinea and satellite islands.

LEADEN FLYCATCHER *Myiagra rubecula* (not illustrated)

(Monarque rougegorge)

Description 15 cm. Flycatcher with plain grey upperparts and grey or orange throat and breast. Male has glossy blue-grey upperparts, head, throat and upper breast, and white breast to vent, with slightly darker face and throat. Female has dull grey upperparts, pale orange-buff throat and breast, but breast sometimes darker, and white lower breast to vent.
Similar species Male differs from other *Myiagra* flycatchers by paler blue-grey upperparts and slightly darker face and throat. Also from Satin Flycatcher by grey extending onto breast in bulging, slightly convex line, perpendicular to edge of wing. Female from very similar Satin Flycatcher by lack of gloss on crown, slightly paler upperparts and sometimes paler throat. Female from Melanesian Flycatcher by paler throat and breast, less distinct eye-ring, paler greyer upperparts and indistinct white on outer tail.
Voice Harsh deep *zhirrp*, often repeated. Song is a strident series of paired whistles *see-here, see-here, see-kew, see-kew* or *lip-rik, lip-rik*.
Habits Open forest and forest edge in lowlands. Actively flycatches from high in trees. Quivers tail rapidly up and down, and raises crown feathers when calling.
Range Two old specimens from New Britain and probably New Ireland. *M. r. rubecula* breeds in Australia, some migrating to south New Guinea in March–November, and other subspecies breed in Australia and south New Guinea.

STEEL-BLUE FLYCATCHER *Myiagra ferrocyanea* Plate 64

(Solomons [Satin] Broadbill/Flycatcher; Monarque acier)

Description 14 cm. Male is glossy black and white, female variably pale grey, buffy-orange and white. Male is plain glossy purple-black except for white lower breast and belly. Female has ash-grey crown, sometimes ash-grey mantle, brown upperparts with broad rufous fringes on wings and tail, and white underparts, washed pale cream. Juvenile like female but more defined rufous fringes to wings. Immature male has black spots or band on breast.
Similar species Distinctive plumage, shape and habits.
Voice Variable calls. Series of c.5–15 upslurred rasping whistles *kwee?-kwee?-kwee?-*, varying in speed but slower and more disyllabic than Common Cicadabird. Faster flatter rattle *do-do-do-*. Scolding *scheep*, *wheesh* or *whee-itch*, often repeated, higher-pitched and softer than monarchs. Ringing *hooow-wit?*
Habits Forest, degraded forest and scattered large trees to at least 1500 m. Actively sallies and flycatches in canopy, often in pairs, small flocks or mixed-species flocks. Distinctive tail shivering, and often raises crown feathers, producing square-shaped head.
Conservation status Common. Not threatened.
Range Endemic to Solomons, excluding Makira and Rennell.
M. f. cinerea, endemic to Buka, Bougainville and Shortland; female has grey head, rufous mantle, wings and tail, grey wash on throat and buffy belly, flanks and undertail-coverts.
M. f. ferrocyanea, endemic to Choiseul, Isabel, Florida Is and Guadalcanal; female as *M. f. cinerea* but has white underparts.
M. f. feminina, endemic to all islands in New Georgia group, except Simbo; female has grey head, mantle and scapulars, and dull grey-brown wings and tail.
M. f. malaitae, endemic to Malaita; female has darker grey head and mantle, and dull brown wings and tail except for narrow rusty fringes to secondaries.

MAKIRA FLYCATCHER *Myiagra cervinicauda* Plate 72

(Ochre-tailed Flycatcher; Ochre-headed Flycatcher; Monarque de San Cristobal)

Description 14 cm. Male is glossy black and white, female pale rufous with grey head. Male is black with green-blue gloss, greyer on mantle, with white lower breast and belly. Female has ash-grey head and pale grey eye-ring, orange-brown mantle and darker wings, paler rufous fringes to wing and tail, pale orange-buff outer tail feathers, deep orange throat and breast and buff belly.
Similar species Distinctive plumage, shape and habits.
Voice Fluid rattle *toi-toi-toi*. Repeated paired notes *kwo-kee* or *kwo-chip*, sometimes almost monosyllabic *tooi*. Long downslurred tinny *scheer*.
Habits Forest to 700 m, less common in logged and degraded forest and mountains. Quietly flycatches, hovers and gleans in forest canopy, often in pairs and mixed-species flocks. Wags or shakes tail and often raises crown feathers, producing square-shaped head.
Conservation status Fairly common. Possibly threatened by logging and forest loss. IUCN: Near Threatened.
Range Endemic to Makira, including Ugi and Santa Ana.

MELANESIAN FLYCATCHER *Myiagra caledonica* Plates 75, 76, 79 & 83

(New Caledonian Flycatcher/Broadbill/Broad-billed Flycatcher; Monarque mélanésien)

Description 14 cm. Male is glossy black and white, and female has orange and white underparts. Male is glossy green-black except greyer mantle and white lower breast and belly. Female has mid-grey head and neck, silvery eye-ring, dull brown upperparts, darker tail with white on outer feathers, dull buffy-orange throat and breast, and white belly. Juvenile like female but duller with buff fringes on upperparts and pale bill.
Similar species Distinctive plumage, shape and habits.
Voice Less vocal than other flycatchers. Loud ringing notes repeated 2–7 times at about three notes per second, e.g. *quee?-quee?-* and rattled *dhu-dhu-dhu-*. Single or series of scolding notes, e.g. *scherp*, *sch-schrr* and *schee-aah*.
Habits Forest, especially open forest and secondary growth, including mangroves and isolated trees, less common in mountains to at least 1200 m. Singles or pairs, often in mixed-species flocks, flycatch from exposed perches, often slowly pump tail and sometimes raise crown feathers.
Conservation status Fairly common, but uncommon on Rennell. Not threatened.
Range Endemic to Rennell, Vanuatu and New Caledonia.
M. c. occidentalis, endemic to Rennell, has fine white fringes on outer tail feathers, male with greyer mantle and rump, female with mid-grey mantle.
M. c. marinae, endemic to northern Vanuatu, from Torres Is to Efate including many small islands, has slightly more olive upperparts and lacks white on tail.
M. c. melanura, endemic to Erromango, Tanna, Aneityum and Maré, is slightly larger.
M. c. viridinitens, endemic to Ouvéa and Lifou, has fine white fringes on two pairs of outer tail feathers.
M. c. caledonica, endemic to Grande Terre and Ile des Pins, has more extensive white on outer tail feathers.

VANIKORO FLYCATCHER *Myiagra vanikorensis* Plate 76

(Vanikoro Broadbill; Monarque de Vanikoro)

Description 13 cm. Male is glossy blue-black and orange, female blue-grey and orange. Male is glossy blue-black with dull orange lower breast and belly, fading to vent. Female has blue-grey head and mantle, browner wings with narrow buffy fringes, brown tail with buffy outer fringes, and buffy-orange underparts, paler on throat, belly and vent. Juvenile has whiter fringes on wings, more white on tail-tips and paler underparts.
Similar species Distinctive plumage, shape and habits.
Voice Ringing series of *kwee-kwee-kwee-* notes. Series of paired notes *tee-too, tee-too...* Rasping scold *scheer-scheer.*
Habits Forest and especially forest edge at all altitudes. Pairs, often in mixed-species flocks, are quiet and unobtrusive in forest canopy, sometimes shivering tail.
Conservation status Fairly common. Not threatened.
Range *M. v. vanikorensis* is endemic to Vanikoro.
Elsewhere, other subspecies occur on Fiji.

SATIN FLYCATCHER *Myiagra cyanoleuca* Plate 56

(Monarque satiné)

Description 16 cm. Male is glossy blue-black and white, female blue-grey, orange and white. Male is uniformly glossy blue-black, with white lower breast and belly, and white extending further onto central breast than on sides. Female has blue-grey upperparts, browner wings and tail, sometimes with paler fringes, very narrow white eye-ring, rich orange throat and breast, and white belly. Juvenile like female but buff fringes to wing-coverts.
Similar species Only recorded from Bismarcks, where plumage and habits distinctive, but see Leaden Flycatcher. Male differs from very similar resident *Myiagra* species of Solomons to New Caledonia by larger size, bluer gloss and never any white fringes to tail. Female differs from these resident *Myiagra* species by plainer grey upperparts and narrow white eye-ring.
Voice Song is a series of strident notes alternating in pitch, e.g. *wu-chee, wu-chee*… Rasping *bzzurt* or *zhurp*, often repeated.
Habits Open forested habitats, isolated trees and scrub. Single birds flycatch actively in canopy, often shivering tail, sometimes fanning tail and erecting crown feathers.
Conservation status Rare migrant. Not threatened.
Range Migrant to Bismarcks, where recorded from Umboi, New Britain and Lihir and may occur on other islands including Solomons, mostly May–August but some records throughout year. Breeds in Australia and some migrate to New Guinea.

SHINING FLYCATCHER *Myiagra alecto* Plate 56

(*Piezorhynchus alecto*; Monarque luisant)

Description 17 cm. A distinctly large, lanky flycatcher with angular crown. Male is uniformly glossy blue-black with very glossy flat cap and blue-grey bill. Female has blue-black head, rich rufous upperparts and tail, and white throat and underparts. Juvenile like female but breast and belly washed rufous.
Similar species Female plumage distinctive. Male differs from very similar Lesser Shining Flycatcher, not on Admiralties or small islands, by habitat, stretched display posture, larger size, longer tail, longer bill, orange-red mouth and flatter shinier cap.
Voice Calls often. Variable. Trill of c.8–16 clear whistles, slightly accelerating and increasing in volume, longer with more distinct notes than Manus and Black-tailed Monarchs. Rapid trill of about ten clear whistled whiplash notes. Distinctive loud grating *schreer*, sometimes drawn out into two syllables, much longer than scold of Manus and Black-tailed Monarchs. Single or series of rich liquid *klok*, *klokt* or *kloo-up* notes.
Habits Forest and scrub understorey and thickets, especially beside water, even in reed-beds, and coasts, including mangroves and overgrown coconuts, to at least 700 m. Rarely in closed-canopy forest except on islands where Lesser Shining Flycatcher absent. Often in pairs, shy but vocal and often mobs observer, close to or on ground. Actively gleans and flycatches, raises crown feathers, fans tail, male often calling with extended neck, wagging fanned tail and exposing orange-red mouth; several males often chase and posture. Flies with slow deep wing-beats.
Conservation status Common. Not threatened.
Range Admiralties and Bismarcks, where *M. a. chalybeocephala* breeds on Manus, Ponam, Lou, Pal, Rambutyo, Lavongai, New Ireland, Djaul, Tabar, Tanga, Feni, Umboi, New Britain, Duke of York and small islands off New Britain; elsewhere in New Guinea, and other subspecies in Indonesia, New Guinea and Australia.

MUSSAU FLYCATCHER *Myiagra hebetior* Plate 56

(Also treated as conspecific with Velvet Flycatcher *M. eichhorni*; Monarque terne)

Description 15 cm. Male is uniformly glossy green-blue-black, with rounded crown and less gloss on face. Female has dull blue-black head, rich rufous upperparts, darker tail and creamy underparts, shading to buff on belly. Juvenile like female but has dark brown crown, rufous-washed breast and pale base to bill.
Similar species Female is distinctive, but similar to Shining Flycatcher which is not on Mussau. Male differs from Ebony Myzomela by bill shape and habits, and is very like Velvet Flycatcher which is not on Mussau.
Voice Varied. Series of 5–6 loud ringing whistles, each increasing in volume, and series increasing in pitch, sometimes preceded by short warble. Fast series of 8–11 *see-see-* notes, series descending in pitch. A couple of short metallic notes followed by whiplashes or upslurred notes, e.g. *tzu-tzu-whit-whit-whit*, *tsip-tsip-toweee*. Loud buzzing scold *tzzzr* and quieter softer *schrr*, sometimes repeated as series.
Habits Singles and pairs glean and flycatch in shady understorey of forest and adjacent secondary growth. Flicks tail up, often fanned, when calling.

Conservation status Fairly common. May be vulnerable to forest degradation.
Range Endemic to Mussau.

VELVET FLYCATCHER *Myiagra eichhorni* Plate 56

(Lesser Shining Flycatcher; Dull Flycatcher; also treated as conspecific with Mussau Flycatcher *M. hebetio*; Monarque terne)

Description 16 cm. Male is all glossy blue-black and female is rich rufous and grey. Male is uniformly glossy blue-black with fairly rounded crown and less gloss on face. Female has grey head and underparts, varying in tone and sometimes with buff on flanks and vent and rich rufous upperparts, darker on wings and tail. Juvenile has rufous wash on underparts.
Similar species Male differs from very similar Shining Flycatcher by habitat, habits, smaller size, shorter tail, shorter bill, orange gape and more rounded matt crown cap. Female differs from Shining Flycatcher by grey head.
Voice Varied calls overlap with those of Shining Flycatcher. Long wobbling whistle increasing in tone, sometimes upslurred. Thin whistle of 12–18 downslurred notes descending scale similar to Black-tailed Monarch. Series of 4–7 ringing fluid whistles *fwit-fwit-fwit-fwit-*. Laughing ringing *schee-hee-hee-hee*. Repeated ringing lisped *scherrr?*. Long scold *schr-schr-schr-*. Loud scolding *trrr*. Quiet harsh *trrr*. Scolds sometimes repeated as series.
Habits Closed-canopy wet forest, commoner in mid-montane forest to at least 1300 m, especially thickets, less often in secondary forest or mangroves. Singles and pairs, often associating with mixed-species flocks or with other understorey species, glean and flycatch in understorey. Fairly shy but vocal and inquisitive. Tail often cocked but never wagged, fanned or shivered.
Conservation status Rather uncommon. Not threatened.
Range Endemic to Bismarcks.
M. e. eichhorni, endemic to Lavongai, New Ireland, New Britain and Watom; female has darker grey head and underparts.
M. e. cervinicolor, endemic to Djaul; female has paler grey head, almost white lores and eye-ring, wings and tail similar rufous to rest of upperparts, and very pale grey or white underparts and buff wash on belly and vent.

CROWS Corvidae

Large heavy all-black birds with stout, slightly downcurved bills and strong legs. Loud harsh 'cawing' calls. Melanesian species typically occur in pairs in forest canopy.

NEW CALEDONIAN CROW *Corvus moneduloides* Plate 85

(Corbeau calédonien)

Description 41 cm. Glossy black crow with medium-length, slightly upturned pointed bill. Blackish eye, bill and legs. Relatively bulky, with broad wings and medium-length tail in flight.
Similar species Differs from South Melanesian Cuckooshrike by glossy black plumage, medium-length tail, dumpy shape and dark eye. From Crow Honeyeater by lack of red facial skin, relatively short tail and shallow wing-beats.
Voice Fairly fast series of nasal barks *wha-wha-wha*, similar to Horned Parakeet but higher-pitched and less trumpeting. A deep throaty *kra-ah*. Quieter, more nasal chatters.
Habits Forest including degraded forest, dry forest and savanna. Pairs or small groups of up to five forage in subcanopy. Flicks wings when perching, like cuckooshrike. Sometimes carries stick in bill as tool to extract food from holes.
Conservation status Fairly common. Not threatened.
Range Endemic to New Caledonia, on Grande Terre and introduced to Maré, and previously introduced to Lifou where now no longer occurs.

WHITE-BILLED CROW *Corvus woodfordi* Plate 66

(Guadalcanal Crow; Corneille à bec blanc)

Description 41 cm. Bulky black crow with massive white bill. Bill is slightly downcurved with black tip and sometimes pink or blue wash. Plumage all black, with green gloss, blue-grey eye and blackish legs. Fairly short square tail and appears very front-heavy in flight.
Similar species Distinctive white bill, size and shape.
Voice Loud rolling *kraah* or *AO*, often repeated in short series. Softer *rowk* in flight.

Habits Closed forest and forest edge, and may forage in nearby coconut plantations, from sea-level but commoner in hills, to 1000 m, occasionally 1250 m. Singles, pairs and threes forage by hopping about in canopy or perching above canopy. Flicks or shuffles wings when perched. Fluttering flight with shallow wing-beats.
Conservation status Fairly common. Not threatened.
Range Endemic to Choiseul, Isabel and Guadalcanal. Birds on Choiseul and Isabel are sometimes split as *C. w. vegetus* on basis of larger bills.

BOUGAINVILLE CROW *Corvus meeki* — Plate 66

(Corneille de Meek)

Description 41 cm. Bulky black crow with massive, slightly downcurved black bill. Plumage is all glossy black, with blackish eye and legs. Fairly short square tail and appears very front-heavy in flight. Immature has pale blue-grey eye.
Similar species Distinctive size and shape.
Voice Loud nasal *kow!* or *wha!*, often repeated in short series. Slightly longer *whaa!-haa!-haa!* in flight.
Habits Closed forest and forest edge, and may forage in adjacent open habitats including gardens and coconut plantations, from sea-level to low mountains, occasionally to 1600 m. Singles, or groups of up to five, forage by hopping about in canopy or descending to fruit bushes and ground. Flicks wings when perched. Fluttering flight with shallow wing-beats.
Conservation status Fairly common. Not threatened.
Range Endemic to Bougainville, including Buka and Shortland Is.

BISMARCK CROW *Corvus insularis* — Plate 59

(Also treated as a subspecies of Torresian Crow *C. orru*; Corbeau de Torres)

Description 41 cm. Glossy all-black crow with heavy black bill and pale blue eye. Juvenile is duller and has pale blue eye but immature may have brown eye.
Similar species Distinctive size, shape and habits.
Voice Noisy. Short nasal calls often repeated a few times, e.g. *khah, kor.* Higher-pitched, more nasal and faster than similar calls of Red-knobbed Imperial Pigeon. Much deeper repeated *ank*. Occasionally, a popping call, and slurred *khe-aarh*.
Habits Open habitats, especially coconut and oil palm plantations, also forest edge and towns but uncommon in closed forest in lowlands and hills, rarely mountains up to 1575 m on New Britain and at least 720 m on New Ireland. Usually singles and pairs forage on ground during day but flocks gather at communal roosts, flying high overhead at dusk and dawn. Flies with deep wing-beats and short glides with wings held below body.
Conservation status Fairly common. Not threatened.
Range Endemic to Bismarcks, including Lavongai, New Ireland, Djaul, Umboi, Sakar, Witu, New Britain, Lolobau, Watom and Duke of York.

AUSTRALASIAN ROBINS Petroicidae

Melanesian species are small birds with very small bills, watching from exposed perches and dropping onto or sallying after insects. Usually in pairs but sometimes join mixed-species flocks.

TORRENT FLYROBIN *Monarchella muelleriana* — Plate 56

(Torrent Flycatcher; River Flycatcher; Miro des torrents)

Description 14 cm. Medium-sized flycatcher found on fast rivers. Sooty-black cap with white forehead-spots, black wings and tail, pale grey mantle and rump, white throat and pale grey underparts. Juvenile probably lacks forehead-spots, has creamy flecks on crown, pale grey tips on wing-coverts and tail, faint brown mottling on upper breast and pale bill and legs.
Similar species Distinctive plumage and habitat.
Voice Dry rattle of several identical notes. On New Guinea, *M. m. muelleriana* has high-pitched monotone whistle, given singly or repeated about ten times as accelerating but fading trill similar to Common Sandpiper.
Habits Fast-flowing rocky rivers from at least 300 to 750 m. Pairs flycatch and drop to ground from conspicuous perches on boulders, bare landslides and bare branches alongside rivers. Undulating flight along riverbed on long wings, calling, and sometimes wags and bobs tail.
Conservation status Rare, but species is not threatened on New Guinea.

Range New Britain.
M. m. coultasi is endemic to New Britain where only recorded from four rivers in east. Plumage differs considerably from *M. m. muelleriana* of New Guinea; could be treated as a separate species.

YELLOW-BELLIED FLYROBIN *Microeca flaviventris* Plate 85

(Yellow-bellied Robin; *Eopsaltria flaviventris*; Miro à ventre citron)

Description 15 cm. Dumpy robin with yellow belly. Olive-grey upperparts, grey face, neck and breast, white throat and bright yellow lower breast and belly below indistinct dark breast-band. Juvenile is plain dark brown with pale buff tips and streaks on upperparts, and paler underparts; soon develops some yellow on underparts.
Similar species Differs from Melanesian Whistler by habits and dumpy shape. From Fan-tailed Gerygone by habits, dumpy shape and grey breast-band.
Voice Varied. Loud warble of repeated varied short phrases, including many liquid notes and rapid short piping notes, richer than Melanesian Whistler and lacking whiplashes. Phrases may be connected with monotonous high-pitched insect-like *tsip-tsip...* notes. Harsh buzzing alarm call. Flat regular series of *chip-chip-chip-* similar to female Melanesian Whistler.
Habits Shady wet forest, also locally in lowland dry forests and open forest, to 1500 m. Pairs are confiding but unobtrusive in undergrowth, dropping onto ground. Often perches on side of tree-trunk.
Conservation status Common. Not threatened.
Range Endemic to New Caledonia, on Grande Terre and Ile des Pins.

BISMARCK FLYROBIN *Microeca* sp. Plate 56

Description About 12cm. Small dumpy flycatcher with rounded head. Dark eye is prominent in plain face with faintly dusky cap, pale supercilium and dark eye-stripe. Dark olive-brown upperparts with darker wings and pale buffy-grey underparts with darker breast and slight yellow wash on flanks. Short dark bill has pale lower mandible, and short dark legs.
Similar species Distinctive small size, dumpy shape, short bill, flycatching habits and colour. Differs from other New Guinea *Microeca* species by dark legs, plain brownish upperparts, uniform underparts and song.
Voice Rapid series of about seven sweet clear whistled phrases of one upslurred melodious note followed by 1–4 shorter sharper notes: *swit-tee* or *sweet-toi-toi-*.
Habits Forest and forest clearings, less often recorded from closed forest where probably overlooked. Pairs flycatch, sometimes flicking or lowering wings and tail, from exposed branches of tall trees in forest clearings. Recorded from lowlands on New Britain and 700–1400 m on New Ireland.
Conservation status Rare. Known only from a few sightings but no specimens, so it has not been named or even confirmed as a new species. Possibly threatened.
Range Endemic to New Ireland and New Britain, with several records from Mt Agil in southern New Ireland, Limbin in central New Ireland, and single records from Kilu Ridge, Lavege and Gigipuna in central north New Britain.

PACIFIC ROBIN *Petroica multicolor* Plates 67, 70 & 79

(Also treated together with Australian *P. boodang* as Scarlet Robin; Miro écarlate)

Description 10 cm. Small dumpy robin, usually with some red on breast. Typical male has black hood and upperparts with white forehead-spot, large white wing-patch and white outer tail-fringes, and scarlet breast and belly with white flanks and vent. Male of some subspecies has brown head or entire plumage like female. Typical female is similar but has brown upperparts, reduced white patches and pale scarlet wash on grey-brown underparts. Immature like female but has buffy-white markings and little or no red. Juvenile is uniformly brown with buff streaks and mottling.
Similar species Distinctive white on wings, red on underparts, and habits. Red on underparts shared only by Cardinal Myzomela, from which it differs by lacking red on head and mantle, and Midget Flowerpecker, from which it differs by white on black or brown upperparts and no dark stripe on lower breast.
Voice Often sings at dawn. Variable between subspecies. On Bougainville, a high-pitched tinkling song. On Guadalcanal, song is a repeated stuttering *titty-titty-too*. On Vanuatu, a wheezy scratchy song and a cadence of sweet whistles *twee-weeweeweet*. Most subspecies have a call of 3–5 electronic tinkling *tip-tip-* notes at half-second intervals, repeated incessantly. Harsh *schrrr* scold. On Vanuatu, a thin *tseep*, intermediate between similar calls of Island Thrush and Blue-faced Parrotfinch.
Habits Usually restricted to forest and adjacent forest edge, in mountains in Solomons. Usually in pairs, perching in mid-storey and canopy, flicking wings and tail, flitting and dropping onto ground. Unobtrusive but confiding.
Conservation status Fairly common. Not threatened.

Range Vanuatu and mountainous Solomons, on Bougainville, Kolombangara, Guadalcanal and Makira.
P. m. septentrionalis, endemic to Bougainville above 1200 m; male is typical, female has warm olive upperparts with no white on forehead, very little white on wing, grey-buff throat and vent, and pale scarlet lower throat to belly.
P. m. kulambangrae, endemic to Kolombangara above 1000 m, like *P. m. septentrionalis* but female has warmer upperparts and brighter scarlet underparts.
P. m. dennisi, endemic to Guadalcanal above 1400 m, occasionally down to 1150 m; male has black head with white forehead, female like dull brown-headed male, with paler scarlet underparts and white or brown chin.
P. m. polymorpha, endemic to Makira above 800 m, like *P. m. dennisi* but some males have rusty-brown head with pale brown forehead-spot, female has paler upperparts and browner crown.
P. m. soror, endemic to Vanua Lava; male has dark brown upperparts, scarlet reaches high on throat, small buffy wing-patch and very little buff on outer tail fringes, female like male but ill-defined buffy forehead-patch and less scarlet on underparts.
P. m. ambrynensis, endemic to Gaua, Mere Lava, Santo, Malo, Malekula, Maewo, Ambae, Ambrym, Paama, Lopevi, Epi, Tongoa and Tongariki; male has very little white on secondaries or primaries, female has orange-red lower throat to lower belly, grey upper throat, pale buff forehead and small wing-patch like male.
P. m. feminina, endemic to Emae, Efate, Nguna and Emau; male has brown upperparts with red wash on crown, white upper throat, small buffy wing-patch and very small pale patch on outer tail, female like male but warmer paler upperparts, indistinct buffy forehead-patch and less scarlet on underparts.
P. m. cognata, endemic to Erromango, like *P. m. feminina* but male has less scarlet on upper throat, more white on outer tail and greyer upperparts with very little red wash, female similar but exact differences unknown.
P. m. similis, endemic to Tanna and Aneityum; male like *P. m. ambrynensis* but has duller browner upperparts, grey-brown throat and more white on wing, female probably with greyer upperparts, white throat and orange-red restricted to breast and upper belly.
Elsewhere, other subspecies breed in Norfolk I., Fiji and Samoa.

BULBULS Pycnonotidae

Medium-sized African and Asian birds with rather short wings and medium-long tails and slender bills.

RED-VENTED BULBUL *Pycnonotus cafer* — Plate 84

(Bulbul à ventre rouge)

Description 22 cm. Stocky thrush-like blackish bird with spotted white belly. Black head and upper breast with short shaggy crest and dusky-brown upperparts with pale buffy scales and fringes. Blackish lower breast has pale fringes merging into dusky spots on lower breast, unmarked white belly, and an inconspicuous deep red vent. In flight, shows conspicuous white rump and narrow white tail-tip. Juvenile is browner with more orange vent.
Similar species None.
Voice Melodious, fruity chirping notes, e.g. *pee-plo, pee pee-plo*, chattering *peep-peep-* or *pwit-wit-*. Song is a cheerful repetitive series of these notes.
Habits Bushes, especially in towns and gardens, also agricultural fields and open forest. Pairs or small flocks feed on fruit in trees and bushes, sometimes sallying for flying insects. Rather obtrusive and aggressive. Often on exposed perches.
Conservation status Uncommon non-native. Not threatened.
Range Introduced to New Caledonia in 1980s, where currently spreading out from Nouméa, from at least Tontouta to Plum, probably *P. c. bengalensis*. Elsewhere, native to Indian subcontinent and introduced to Polynesia including Fiji.

SWALLOWS Hirundinidae

Swallows and martins are small aerial insectivores with long pointed wings and forked tails often with streamers. Swoop and flit over open habitats and often perch on wires and bare branches. Gregarious, nesting under overhangs on buildings, cliffs or dead trees. Similar to swifts but have shorter, more angled wings, and to woodswallows but are slimmer and longer-winged.

[SAND MARTIN *Riparia riparia*] — Plate 50

(Common Sand Martin; Bank Swallow; Hirondelle de rivage)

Description 12 cm. Small dumpy brown and white swallow. Dull chocolate-brown upperparts, underwings and shallowly forked tail, and white underparts with distinct clear-cut brown breast-band.

Similar species Distinctive white underparts with breast-band. From Red-rumped Swallow and Tree Martin by plain upperparts.
Voice Harsh rasp *tschrrr*.
Habits Over open habitats usually by fresh water. Gregarious, often mixed with other swallows.
Range One unconfirmed record from New Britain. Elsewhere, five subspecies breed in temperate America and Eurasia, migrating south to tropics in September–April, and very rarely reaching Philippines and New Guinea.

BARN SWALLOW *Hirundo rustica* Plate 50

(Hirondelle rustique)

Description 18 cm (including tail-streamers). Slender swallow with pale underparts below dark breast-band. Glossy blue-black upperparts, chestnut forehead and throat, separated from white underparts and underwing-coverts by dark breast-band. Deeply forked tail has row of white spots near tip and long streamers on outer feathers, longer in male. Wing-tip is shorter than tail-tip when perched. Immature is duller, with buff on forehead and throat, breast-band often incomplete and no tail-streamers.
Similar species Differs from Pacific and Welcome Swallows by whiter underparts, dark breast-band, long tail-streamers of adult and from Pacific Swallow by white spots on tail. From Red-rumped Swallow and Tree Martin by plain upperparts, breast-band, chestnut throat and white vent.
Voice Thin *tswit*, often repeated as a twitter.
Habits Open habitats especially by fresh water. Gregarious, often mixed with other swallows.
Range One record from Horno Is near Manus, probably *H. r. gutturalis*. Breeds across temperate northern hemisphere and migrates to tropics, including small numbers in New Guinea in September–March.

PACIFIC SWALLOW *Hirundo tahitica* Plates 50, 66, 71, 76, 81 & 86

(Hirondelle de Tahiti)

Description 13 cm. Only swallow in most of Melanesia. Glossy blue-black upperparts, pale rufous forehead, throat and upper breast, and pale brownish-grey underparts and underwing-coverts. Forked tail has pointed corners but no streamers and only on New Britain has a subterminal row of small white spots. Wing-tip and tail-tip are about equal when perched. Immature duller, with paler buffy-orange throat and fine pale fringes on wings.
Similar species Differs from Barn and Welcome Swallow by dusky underparts, lack of dark breast-band, no tail-streamers or white spots on tail, except on New Britain, and dark undertail-coverts with pale fringes. From Red-rumped Swallow and Tree Martin by plain upperparts, rufous throat and white vent. From swiftlets by wing shape, forked tail, rufous throat and flight action.
Voice Thin rushed *tswee* or rolling *prr-up*, often repeated as a twitter.
Habits Open habitats, especially beaches, ports, timber-yards and towns. Pairs, small flocks and occasionally large flocks swoop low over ground. Often nests in buildings and dead trees along coast. Occurs inland only around towns, villages and large rivers.
Conservation status Localised but common in small areas of suitable habitat. Not threatened.
Range Across Melanesia but only a rare migrant to New Caledonia.
H. t. ambiens, endemic to New Britain, including Witu, Watom and Duke of York, has paler underparts, often has white spots on tail and may have dark breast-band.
Birds on Crown, Long, Tolokiwa, Umboi, Malai and Sakar are intermediate with *H. t. frontalis*, endemic to New Guinea, with larger white tail-spots, whiter underparts and smaller size. Intermediates may occur on other islands west of New Britain.
H. r. subfusca, widespread across the Admiralties and Bismarcks (except New Britain, St Matthias and far outlying islands), Solomons (including small islands such as Ugi and Ulawa but not Rennell or far outlying islands), Temotu, Vanuatu and New Caledonia (where breeds on Ouvéa but only rare migrant on Grande Terre, Lifou and Maré), never has white on tail and has duskier underparts. Birds on New Ireland show some intermediate features of *H. t. ambiens*. Elsewhere, *H. t. subfusca* breeds in Fiji and Tonga and other subspecies breed from south India and Japan to Tahiti.

WELCOME SWALLOW *Hirundo neoxena* Plate 86

(Hirondelle messagère)

Description 15 cm. Glossy blue-black upperparts, chestnut-orange forehead, throat and upper breast, and dusky to creamy-white underparts and underwing-coverts. Deeply forked tail has small white subterminal spots and long streamers on outer feathers. Tail-tip is longer than wing-tip when perched. Immature is duller with short tail-streamers.

Similar species Differs from Pacific Swallow by longer tail-streamers, white spots on tail and paler grey underparts. From Barn Swallow by dusky underparts and underwing-coverts, lack of breast-band, shorter tail-streamers and dark brown spots on undertail-coverts.
Voice Thin *seep*, often repeated as a twitter.
Habits Open habitats especially grassland and fresh water. Gregarious, often mixing with other swallows.
Range Regular migrant in small numbers to New Caledonia, mostly Grande Terre but also Ouvéa, Lifou and Maré, recorded throughout year but most April–October. Three subspecies breed in Australia and New Zealand with rare vagrants reaching New Guinea.

RED-RUMPED SWALLOW *Cecropis daurica* Plate 50

(*Hirundo daurica*; Hirondelle rousseline)

Description 19 cm. Large swallow with orange-chestnut rump. Glossy blue-black crown, back, wings and tail, orange-chestnut rump and behind eye, and white face, neck-sides and underparts with fine black streaks. Black tail and tail-coverts with long streamers on outer feathers. Immature duller with paler rump and face, shorter tail-streamers and pale fringes to wing-coverts and tertials.
Similar species Differs from other swallows by pale rump, black undertail-coverts, pale throat, longer tail-streamers and larger size. From Tree Martin by tail-streamers and streaked underparts.
Voice Short harsh call *djuit*. Alarm note *krr*. Short twittering song.
Habits Open habitats, mostly grasslands and towns, often close to water. Gregarious, often mixed with other swallows. Flight is slower, heavier and with more soaring than other swallows.
Conservation status Rare migrant. Not threatened.
Range *C. d. japonica* is an irregular migrant to New Britain and New Ireland and a rare vagrant to Bougainville in December–January. It breeds in north Asia and migrates to South-East Asia, with a few reaching Australia and New Guinea from September–April. Elsewhere, other subspecies breed in Europe, Africa and Asia.

TREE MARTIN *Petrochelidon nigricans* Plates 50, 66 & 86

(*Hirundo nigricans*; Hirondelle des arbres)

Description 13 cm. Small swallow with pale rump and short notched tail. Blue-black upperparts with buffy-white or greyish-white rump and indistinct dull rufous-buff forehead. Buffy-white underparts with fine black streaks on throat and breast. Immature duller with pale rufous fringes on wings.
Similar species Differs from most swallows by pale rump and throat. From Red-rumped Swallow by lack of tail-streamers. From White-rumped Swiftlet and woodswallows by wing shape and flight action.
Voice Sweet twittering based on *tsweet* notes.
Habits Open habitats, especially forest edge, grasslands, wetlands and towns. Gregarious and mixes with other swallows and swiftlets. Flight more erratic and fluttering than other swallows, with flicked shallow wing-beats and glides.
Range *P. n. nigricans* is a rare migrant to New Ireland, Lihir, Nissan, New Britain, Witu, Buka, Bougainville, Guadalcanal, Malaita and New Caledonia from April to October. It breeds in Australia and many migrate north, some to New Guinea. Other subspecies breed in Australia and Timor.

BUSH WARBLERS Cettiidae

Small insectivorous understorey forest birds with dull brown plumage and loud whistling songs.

SHADE BUSH WARBLER *Cettia parens* Plate 71

(Shade Warbler; *Vitia parens*; Bouscarle de San Cristobal)

Description 12 cm. Small brown forest warbler with fairly long tail and long legs. Plain rufous-brown upperparts, slightly brighter on crown and especially forehead, with paler orange-rufous supercilium and dark eye-stripe. Paler orange-brown underparts with paler yellowish throat. Juvenile is darker olive-brown with bright olive-yellow throat and no supercilium.
Similar species Differs from Cardinal Myzomela and Mottled Flowerpecker, the only other small plain brown birds on Makira, by supercilium and eye-stripe, and habits.
Voice Song is a long loud pure whistle, slowly increasing in pitch, sometimes disyllabic, then about three variable

quick short notes *oooOOO*, *ee-u-ee*, *hoooOOO-de-de de* or *doOOdoOO—tchu-tchee-tchu-tchu*. Second half of song is sometimes overlaid by nasal chirps, probably from duetting female. Harsh churring *tchr*, sometimes a rapid series *tr-tr-tr-*.
Habits Forest, mostly primary forest with dense undergrowth, especially thickets along streams and abandoned gardens, above 500 m. Pairs forage in undergrowth, moss on tree-trunks, and canopy of stunted montane forest. Tail often half-cocked. Unobtrusive and fairly shy.
Conservation status Fairly common. Not threatened.
Range Endemic to Makira.

BOUGAINVILLE BUSH WARBLER *Cettia haddeni* Plate 67

(Odedi is an alternative English name based on the Nasioi language name; Kopipi in Rotokas language; Bouscarle de Bougainville)

Description 13 cm. Small dark dumpy warbler with rufous head and grey underparts. Dull dark rufous-brown upperparts, brighter and more orange on head, especially forehead and face, and brighter fringes to warm brown wings. Off-white throat and dark grey underparts with off-white spots and mottles, especially on midline. Indistinct head pattern with prominent black eye, slight dark eye-stripe, and indistinct orange supercilium. Fairly short narrow tail and fairly long orange-brown legs.
Similar species Differs from Bougainville Thicketbird by lacking blackish crown and eye-stripe, dark greyish underparts with off-white spots, and shorter tail.
Voice Song is a beautiful series of loud high-pitched pure whistles, a total of c.15 notes in rising phrases of two or three notes at intervals of a few seconds.
Habits Montane forest at 700–1500 m. Reported to forage mostly on ground, sometimes in association with Island Thrush, and to be shy.
Conservation status Fairly common. May be at risk from introduced species. IUCN: Near Threatened.
Range Endemic to Bougainville, where recorded from Mt Balbi to the Crown Prince Range.

LEAF WARBLERS Phylloscopidae

Very small active greenish birds, usually in forest canopy.

ARCTIC WARBLER *Phylloscopus borealis* Plate 57

(Pouillot boreal)

Description 12 cm. Small stout warbler with prominent long supercilium and wing-bar. Olive-green upperparts with long yellow-white supercilium from bill to hindneck and fine white bar on greater wing-coverts and sometimes a second bar on median wing-coverts. Greyish or yellowish-white underparts. Pale yellowish-brown legs.
Similar species Differs from Island Leaf Warbler by call, stouter, larger size, greenish head same colour as upperparts and longer broader supercilium.
Voice Loud sharp *dzip* or *dzrt*.
Habits Forest, especially mangroves and secondary forest. Forages in canopy, less active than Island Leaf Warbler.
Range Rare vagrant, with one record from Kaniet, probably *A. b. kennicotti* which breeds in Alaska and migrates to the Philippines. Elsewhere, other subspecies breed across north Eurasia and migrate to tropical Asia including Indonesia in September–May.

ISLAND LEAF WARBLER *Phylloscopus poliocephalus* Plates 57, 67 & 71

(Also treated as two species including Makira/San Cristobal Leaf Warbler *P. makirensis*; Pouillot des îles)

Description 10 cm. Very small green warbler with prominent silvery supercilium. Dull olive-green upperparts with brighter green fringes to wing feathers, fine yellowish greater wing-covert bar, whitish throat, dull yellow breast and belly and greener flanks. Darker greyer head has long fine silvery supercilium and dark eye-stripe. A few birds have indistinct paler central crown-stripe. Juvenile duller.
Similar species Differs from all other small greenish birds by pale supercilium. From white-eyes in silhouette by dumpier shape and shorter tail. See Arctic Warbler and Kolombangara Leaf Warbler.
Voice Sings often when foraging: a weak high-pitched rapid warble of 3–10 notes, rising as one or two series, repeated up to six times. Quiet nasal *pwit* or *dzip* call.

Habits Canopy of montane forest, especially mossy forest, but also lowland primary and degraded scrubby forest on Mussau. Groups of up to four birds, often with mixed-species flocks, especially white-eyes, glean actively in small branches, sometimes flicking wings.
Conservation status Fairly common and not threatened but no recent records from Isabel and Malaita.
Range High mountain islands of Bismarcks and Solomons, plus Mussau.
P. p. matthiae, endemic to Mussau where occurs at all altitudes, has yellow breast and belly, paler grey crown and head with indistinct paler central crown-stripe, and white tail-corners.
P. p. leletensis, endemic to New Ireland above 840 m, is larger than *P. p. matthiae* with darker crown and pure white throat.
P. p. moorhousei, endemic to New Britain including Umboi, occurring above 1100 m, but not yet recorded from East New Britain, has brownish-olive crown and mantle, and duller yellow underparts including throat.
P. t. bougainvillei, endemic to Bougainville above 700 m, has dirty greyish-yellow underparts, and crown slightly darker than dull brownish-green upperparts.
P. p. becki, endemic to Isabel, Guadalcanal and Malaita above 800 m, has brighter yellow underparts, dirty white throat and greener crown.
P. p. pallescens, endemic to Kolombangara above 940 m, has greyish-white underparts, sometimes with slight yellow or green wash, darker on flanks, and darker crown.
P. p. makirensis (Makira Leaf Warbler), endemic to Makira above 500 m, has dirty white throat and lemon-yellow underparts, and has often been treated as a separate species.
Elsewhere, other subspecies breed in east Indonesia and New Guinea, but some could be treated as separate species.

KOLOMBANGARA LEAF WARBLER *Phylloscopus amoenus* Plate 67

(Sombre Leaf Warbler; Pouillot de Kulambangra)

Description 11 cm. Very small, stout, dull green warbler. Dark olive or olive-brown upperparts, darker on head, becoming almost black on forehead, and indistinct paler greater covert bar. Head has long indistinct supercilium, indistinct eye-stripe, dark mottled ear-coverts, and relatively heavy dull brownish-pink bill. Dull, fairly dark yellow-olive underparts with indistinct streaking, and variably coloured pinkish-brown legs. Short-tailed and dumpy.
Similar species Differs from Island Leaf Warbler by darker plumage, blackish forehead, no pale grey on head, and stockier build with thick neck and sturdy paler legs. See possible vagrant Arctic Warbler.
Voice Quiet warbling song of 3–12 notes, e.g. *teed-did-lee, deed, deed*, descending and becoming louder; shorter and sharper than Island Leaf Warbler. Sharp metallic *zik* or *tzik* call.
Habits Moss forest above 1200 m, usually above 1400 m. Singles and pairs forage by hopping low, often on ground and mossy tree-trunks, but also in small branches and occasionally up to subcanopy. Often in mixed-species foraging flock, sometimes in close proximity to Island Leaf Warblers.
Conservation status Uncommon in its extremely small range of *c*.21 km^2. Although no specific threats are identified, it is possibly threatened by predation by introduced mammals and catastrophic habitat damage. IUCN: Vulnerable.
Range Endemic to Kolombangara.

REED WARBLERS Acrocephalidae

Medium-sized brown birds of wetlands, usually beds of reeds *Phragmites*, with a loud repetitive song.

[ORIENTAL REED WARBLER *Acrocephalus orientalis*] Plate 58

(Rousserolle d'Orient)

Description 19 cm. Medium-large brown warbler of wetlands. Warm olive-brown upperparts with prominent whitish supercilium and dark eye-stripe, and whitish underparts with warm buff flanks and vent. Most have indistinct greyish streaking on lower throat and upper breast.
Similar species Differs from Australian Reed Warbler by indistinct greyish streaks on upper breast if present, fresh plumage in October–December, stouter longer bill, stronger supercilium extending further behind eye, often larger pale tips to outer tail feathers, quicker, lower-pitched calls and song. Also see Gray's Grasshopper Warbler.
Voice Loud *chack*. Soft churring. Unlikely to sing in Melanesia but song less explosive, harsher and more grating, faster, lower, softer and with less variation between phrases than Australian Reed Warbler.
Habits Tall grasses and scrub beside water, especially reeds. Migrants may occur in any coastal habitats.
Range Rare vagrant, with one probable record from Kaniet. Breeds in Siberia and north China to Japan and migrates south to India to Indonesia, rarely to Australia, in September–May.

AUSTRALIAN REED WARBLER *Acrocephalus australis* Plates 58 & 67

(Also treated as a subspecies of Clamorous Reed Warbler *A. stentoreus*; Rousserolle d'Australie)

Description 16 cm. Medium-large warm brown warbler of reed-beds. Plain warm olive-brown upperparts with distinct short whitish supercilium and dark eye-stripe, and pale buff underparts, whiter on throat and central belly. Fairly long fine bill is brownish-grey above and pink below. Orange-yellow mouth, visible when singing.
Similar species Distinctive waterside habitat. See Australian Reed Warbler and Gray's Grasshopper Warbler.
Voice Song is a series of phrases, each phrase a different ringing or liquid note repeated 2–5 times, e.g. *katchee-katchee-katchee, chutch-chutch, dzee-dzee-dzee*... Short nasal *chee*. Harsh *chak* and churring.
Habits Reed-beds and other tall wetland grass and sometimes bushes, along rivers, lakes and swamps, but not dry *kunai* grassland. Singles and pairs cling to reed-stems.
Conservation status Locally common. Not threatened.
Range *A. a. toxopei* breeds on New Ireland, Long, Umboi, New Britain, Buka, Bougainville, Isabel and Guadalcanal; elsewhere breeds in New Guinea with other subspecies in Australia.

GRASSBIRDS Megaluridae

Medium-sized brown birds of grassland or forest thickets, with a long tail and loud song.

PAPUAN GRASSBIRD *Megalurus macrurus* Plate 58

(Also treated as a subspecies of Tawny Grassbird *M. timoriensis*; Mégalure fauve)

Description 20 cm. Large long-tailed streaky warbler of open grasslands. Warm buffy-brown upperparts with rufous cap above pale supercilium, and heavy black streaks on back, wings and long ragged tail. Buffy-white underparts, darker on breast-sides, with some fine black streaks on breast or flanks, especially in juvenile. Juvenile has brownish cap and yellowish wash on underparts.
Similar species Distinctive shape, habitat, and rufous cap. Differs from Golden-headed Cisticola by larger size and longer tail. From Australian Reed Warbler and vagrant Oriental Reed Warbler and Gray's Grasshopper Warbler by streaked upperparts and longer ragged tail. From Bismarck and Rusty Thicketbirds by habitat and streaked upperparts.
Voice Unknown in Melanesia. In New Guinea, calls often. Sharp *tzick*. Upslurred whistle *whist*. Downslurred whistle *cheyup!*, repeated at 4–10-second intervals. Repeated clucking *buk-buk-*.
Habits Tall dense grassland and grassy scrub, including swamps, in lowlands. Singles and pairs forage secretively within grass and on ground, occasionally calling from slightly raised perch or in song-flight. Flushes with low flight, trailing its long tail.
Conservation status Rare. Not threatened.
Range *M. m. interscapularis* is endemic to Lavongai, New Ireland, New Britain and Watom, with probably this subspecies on Tolokiwa, and is paler with greyer underparts than other subspecies elsewhere in New Guinea. Taxonomy of this species and Tawny Grassbird *M. timoriensis* is poorly known and Melanesian birds may prove to belong to either species.

NEW CALEDONIAN THICKETBIRD *Megalurulus mariei* Plate 83

(New Caledonian Grassbird; Mégalure calédonienne)

Description 18 cm. Long-tailed ground warbler with conspicuous broad white supercilium. Prominent white supercilium, dark mask and white throat. Warm dark brown upperparts, darker on crown and brighter on rump and tail. Warm buff breast-sides and duller flanks, fading to off-white central belly and vent. Medium-long slightly decurved black bill and long pale pink legs.
Similar species Distinctive long tail, head pattern and habits. Differs from fantails by long supercilium, long bill and plain tail and wings.
Voice Song is a slow series of harsh *tchak* notes mixed with whistles and trills, similar to a reed warbler. Harsh explosive *pwit*. Quiet trilled churring.
Habits Scrubby habitats, typically a mixture of shrubs, ferns and herbs, often on metal-rich soils used for mining (*maquis minier*). Also occurs in tall grass savanna, secondary bush, *Lantana* thickets and clearings within forest. Commoner above 400 m, to at least 1000 m. Singles and pairs creep secretively on or close to ground. Occasionally appears on top of vegetation to investigate observer, or may fly short distance over low vegetation. Sometimes cocks tail.
Conservation status Locally common in suitable habitat but secretive and often overlooked.
Range Endemic to New Caledonia, where scattered across Grande Terre.

NEW BRITAIN THICKETBIRD *Megalurulus grosvenori* Plate 58

(Bismarck Thicketbird/Thicket-Warbler; *Cichlornis grosvenori*; also lumped with Bougainville, Guadalcanal and Santo Thicketbirds as Melanesian Thicketbird *M. whitneyi*; Mégalure de Gilliard)

Description 18 cm. Long-tailed ground-warbler with black mask. Dark rusty-brown upperparts, crown and long graduated tail with pointed tips. Broad rufous-buff supercilium over broad sooty mask from bill to ear-coverts. Paler rufous-buff underparts, richer orange on breast, flanks and undertail-coverts.
Similar species Differs from Rusty Thicketbird, in lowlands up to at least 1400 m, by black face-mask, clearly defined supercilium, rufous-orange underparts and pointed tail feathers.
Voice Poorly known. Occasional single notes.
Habits Undergrowth with bamboo in montane forest on karst limestone at or above 1580 m. Known to hop on ground, low stems and up to one metre in bushes.
Conservation status Known only from two specimens and one seen in 1959, but no-one else has searched at these altitudes. IUCN: Vulnerable.
Range Endemic to New Britain, where known only from the Whiteman Mountains.

BOUGAINVILLE THICKETBIRD *Megalurulus llaneae* Plate 67

(Bougainville Thicket-Warbler; *Cichlornis llanae*; also lumped with New Britain, Guadalcanal and Santo Thicketbirds as Melanesian Thicketbird *M. whitneyi*; Mégalure de Bougainville)

Description 17 cm. Long-tailed ground-warbler with orange-rufous supercilium. Dark sooty-olive upperparts, crown and fairly long graduated tail with pointed tips. Black eye-stripe from bill to just behind eye. Broad orange-rufous supercilium and underparts, browner on flanks and belly. Juvenile has plain dark brown upperparts, with no head markings, and rich cinnamon-chestnut breast with blackish streaks becoming finer on flanks and belly.
Similar species Differs from Bougainville Bush Warbler by blackish eye-stripe and crown, and rich orange-rufous underparts.
Voice Clear melodious whistle of one or two notes, followed by final note of higher pitch but similar length.
Habits Montane forest, perhaps favouring bamboo thickets, above 1200 m. Hops and scuttles on or close to ground, sometimes with slightly cocked tail. Secretive but inquisitive.
Conservation status Poorly known but probably uncommon and local and may be at risk from introduced cats and rats. IUCN: Near Threatened.
Range Endemic to Bougainville, where recorded only from Crown Prince Range.

GUADALCANAL THICKETBIRD *Megalurulus turipavae* Plate 67

(Guadalcanal Thicket-Warbler; *Cichlornis turipavae*; also lumped with Santo Thicketbird as Guadalcanal Thicketbird *M. whitneyi* or with New Britain, Bougainville and Santo Thicketbirds as Melanesian Thicketbird *M. whitneyi*; Mégalure de Guadalcanal)

Description 18 cm. Long-tailed ground-warbler with rufous supercilium. Dark olive-brown upperparts, darker on crown, and long graduated blackish tail with pointed tips. Broad black eye-stripe from bill. Rich buff-brown supercilium and underparts.
Similar species No similar species in Guadalcanal mountains.
Voice Unknown, probably clear whistles like other thicketbirds.
Habits Upper montane forest, recorded at 1200–1550 m in forest with both dense bamboo undergrowth and sparse undergrowth. Singles seen hopping on ground, often with slightly cocked and spread tail, flying short distances low over ground.
Conservation status Known only from three records. May be at risk from introduced cats and rats. IUCN: Near Threatened.
Range Endemic to Guadalcanal, where known only from Turipava above Honiara, but likely to be more widespread.

SANTO THICKETBIRD *Megalurulus whitneyi* Plate 78

(Santo Thicket-Warbler; *Cichlornis whitneyi*; also lumped with Guadalcanal Thicketbird *M. turipavae* as Guadalcanal Thicketbird *M. whitneyi* or with New Britain, Bougainville and Guadalcanal Thicketbirds as Melanesian Thicketbird *M. whitneyi*; Mégalure de Whitney)

Description 17 cm. Long-tailed dumpy ground-warbler with rufous supercilium. Dark rufous-brown upperparts, with darker crown, broad eye-stripe or mask and long graduated tail with pointed tips. Rich rufous supercilium and underparts with slightly darker flanks. Female is paler.

Similar species No similar species in Santo mountains.
Voice Song is a short explosive series of usually two or three pure crystal-clear notes, sometimes followed by a short sweet warble. Explosive alarm call is a repeated rapid series of piercing churrs *tzwee-zweeweeweewee*, level in pitch or slightly descending.
Habits Montane forest with dense undergrowth at 500–1550 m, rarely down to 160 m in wet forest. Pairs, also singles and family groups, hop and scurry on ground, often with tail slightly fanned and cocked, or forage up to two metres in undergrowth and fly short distances very low over ground. Secretive.
Conservation status Fairly common. May be at risk from introduced cats and rats. IUCN: Near Threatened.
Range Endemic to Santo, where probably widespread.

RUSTY THICKETBIRD *Megalurulus rubiginosus* Plate 58

(Rufous-faced Thicketbird; *Ortygocichla rubiginosa*; Mégalure rubigineuse)

Description 19 cm. Long-tailed ground-warbler with rufous face and underparts. Dark rufous-brown upperparts, crown and long graduated tail with rounded tips. Bright muddy-orange underparts, darker on ear-coverts, and very short dark brown supercilium behind eye. Juvenile is darker, especially face and underparts.
Similar species Differs from New Britain Thicketbird, known from one record at 1580 m, by orange lores, muddy-orange underparts and rounded tail feathers.
Voice Song is a series of 3–6 pure crystal-clear notes, first note often longer or slurred, second note lower-pitched and last notes slurred together, repeated 3–5 times at 10-second intervals. Differs from a similar Northern Fantail song by pure tone of notes. Alarm call a wet churring *brrrr*, repeated up to ten times.
Habits Lowland and hill forest with dense ground vegetation, especially in thickets along streams, roads and landslides, including dense overgrown gardens, also in secondary forest and more open forest at higher altitude, but not in dry forest and much rarer in coastal lowlands; 50–1400 m. Singles, pairs and small family groups hop and scurry on ground, fallen logs or very low in ground vegetation, sometimes flying low for very short distances. Tail often cocked and fanned, jerks and flicks wings and tail when nervous. Very secretive and shy but inquisitive.
Conservation status Uncommon. Not threatened.
Range Endemic to New Britain, where widespread.

GRAY'S GRASSHOPPER WARBLER *Locustella fasciolata* Plate 58

(Gray's Warbler; Locustelle fasciée)

Description 18 cm. Medium-large brown warbler with long rounded tail. Rufous-brown to olive-brown upperparts with prominent long silvery supercilium and dark eye-stripe. Off-white throat, greyer on breast, buff flanks and undertail-coverts and pinkish legs. Immature has yellowish wash on underparts.
Similar species Differs from Oriental and Australian Reed Warblers by grey or yellow-washed underparts, pinkish legs, longer silvery supercilium, more rounded tail, strongly curved margin to shorter wing, and long buff undertail-coverts reaching over half-way along tail.
Voice Loud *tek*, *tek-tek* and *tchuk*.
Habits Dense undergrowth, especially secondary growth, dense grassland and swamps. Extremely skulking and reluctant to fly. Forages close to ground, often walking on ground.
Range One record from New Ireland in April. Breeds in Siberia, wintering south to Philippines, Indonesia and west New Guinea.

CISTICOLAS Cisticolidae

Very small grassland warblers, usually buffy-brown with dark streaks and loud calls.

GOLDEN-HEADED CISTICOLA *Cisticola exilis* Plate 58

(Bright-headed Cisticola; Cisticole à couronne dorée)

Description 10 cm. Tiny grassland bird with heavy black streaks on buffy-brown upperparts. Warm buffy-brown plumage, warmer on rump, with heavy black streaks on back and wings, buff-tipped blackish tail and white on central underparts. Long orangey legs. Male has plain yellow-rufous crown and short tail. Female has black streaks on crown, paler underparts and slightly longer tail. Juvenile has heavy black streaks on crown, browner upperparts and yellower underparts.

Similar species Differs from other warblers by tiny size and blackish streaks.
Voice Buzzy mewing or sneezing *tzzzuuu*. Song is a buzz followed by one or two short disyllabic chirps *tzzzuuu-teeu*, repeated, sometimes with several initial buzz notes. Churring. Ticking *t-t-t-*.
Habits Open grassland and savanna to at least 1000 m. Pairs and small groups are usually inconspicuous within dense grass. Climbs up grasses to inspect observer, often perching with wide-splayed legs. During rains, male sings from exposed perch, including bushes and wires, or in song-flight where male flies vertically up, sings from high bouncing circling flight and dives back to ground.
Conservation status Locally common. Not threatened.
Range *C. e. polionota* is endemic to Bismarcks, including Lavongai, New Ireland, Tabar, Lihir, Long, Umboi, Sakar, New Britain, Watom and Duke of York, and differs from other subspecies in lacking an eclipse non-breeding plumage. Elsewhere, other subspecies breed from India to New Guinea and Australia.

WHITE-EYES Zosteropidae

Small warbler-like birds of forest canopy and low scrub. Usually insectivorous but some, especially the larger species, are partly frugivorous. Widespread and often common in Melanesia. *Zosterops* are typically green above and yellow and white below with a broad white eye-ring, but many species lack a noticeable eye-ring; *Woodfordia* are large with a white supercilium and darker mask. Usually gregarious and often core species in mixed-species flocks. Most species call continuously. Some sing strongly at dawn, and some again in the afternoon. Juvenile similar to adult but often has duller plumage and less contrasting eye-rings.

BISMARCK WHITE-EYE *Zosterops hypoxanthus* — Plate 57

(Black-headed White-eye; Zostérops des Bismarck)

Description 11 cm. White eye-ring contrasts with dusky hood. Blackish lores and forehead, dark brown hood of variable extent and tone, shading onto dull olive upperparts. Dirty yellow underparts, often brighter yellow on central throat, and medium-short blue-grey bill and legs.
Similar species Only white-eye in its range. Differs from Olive-backed Sunbird by dark head and white eye-ring.
Voice Chick-like *cheep* contact call. Nasal *dhzu* contact call. Longer upslurred nasal note *zoyeee*. Short 'springing' series of notes *zhe-he-he*. Rarely sings, a sweet warble of simple melodious notes, e.g. *tso-wop-tso-ee-tso-*.
Habits Forest, especially forest edge, secondary forest and scrub. From sea-level but rare below 500–800 m on New Ireland, Umboi and New Britain, where common in montane forest to at least 1800 m. Pairs and small flocks forage actively in canopy, often in mixed-species flocks, conspicuous by their constant calling.
Conservation status Fairly common. Not threatened.
Range Endemic to Manus and Bismarcks.
Z. h. admiralitatis, endemic to Manus, has browner hood sometimes extending as far as upper breast, and narrow white eye-ring.
Z. h. ultimus, endemic to Lavongai and New Ireland, has smaller hood hardly extending onto nape, brighter upperparts and underparts, and broader eye-ring.
Z. h. hypoxanthus, endemic to Umboi, New Britain and Watom, has small blacker hood and clearly marked yellow throat.

LOUISIADE WHITE-EYE *Zosterops griseotinctus* — Plate 57

(Zostérops de la Louisiade)

Description 12 cm. Fairly plain olive white-eye with prominent white eye-ring, dull orange-yellow bill and dark brown legs. Dull olive plumage is slightly paler and yellower on underparts, especially throat, belly and vent.
Similar species White eye-ring is distinctive within range.
Voice Sings often, c.15 simple melodious notes in fairly rushed series, often accelerating at end, and repeated after short pause. Typical contact calls include *tchu*, *tchu-tchu* and *tch-tch-tch*. Springing *tRrRrRr*.
Habits Forest of all types, gardens and coconut plantations. Small flocks forage in canopy, often eating small fruits and in association with monarchs and other small birds.
Conservation status Common, at least on Long and Nissan. Not threatened.
Range *Z. g. eichhorni* is endemic to Nauna, Nissan, Crown, Long and Tolokiwa. Birds on Nauna are sometimes separated as *Z. g. ottomeyeri*, being slightly smaller with yellower lores and throat, and those on Long and probably Crown and Tolokiwa have yellower underparts and yellower legs. Elsewhere, other subspecies, which could treated as a separate species, occur in the Louisiade Is off south-east New Guinea.

YELLOW-THROATED WHITE-EYE *Zosterops metcalfii* Plate 68

(Zostérops à gorge jaune)

Description 11 cm. Bright white-eye with yellow and silvery underparts. Dull olive upperparts, dark around lores, usually a narrow white eye-ring, lemon-yellow throat, upper breast, vent and undertail-coverts contrasting with a silvery lower breast and belly. Dark grey bill and legs.
Similar species Differs from Grey-throated White-eye, above 900 m on Bougainville, by yellow throat and dumpier, typical white-eye shape and jizz.
Voice Sings strongly at dawn, a variable series of *c*.6–9 melodious notes often ascending then descending a scale. Strong loud *chu* or *tchup* contact call. Springy *tse-se-se-se* call.
Habits Forest, especially secondary forest and gardens, to 900 m, occasionally to 1200 m. Pairs or small flocks of up to 30 birds forage actively in canopy and mid-storey, often in mixed-species flocks.
Conservation status Common. Not threatened.
Range Endemic to Bougainville, Choiseul, Isabel and Florida Is.
Z. m. exiguus, endemic to Buka, Bougainville, Shortland Is and Choiseul, has yellowish-horn lower mandible.
Z. m. metcalfii, endemic to Isabel, has black bill except for yellow on extreme base.
Z. m. floridanus, endemic to Florida Is, has black bill but no white eye-ring.

RENNELL WHITE-EYE *Zosterops rennellianus* Plate 75

(Bare-ringed White-eye; Rennell name is Suusuubagu; Zostérops de Rennell)

Description 12 cm. Plain olive white-eye with dull orange bill and legs but no white eye-ring. Narrow blue-grey eye-ring looks like small dark eye-patch. Plain dull olive plumage, slightly darker above, and slight yellow wash on throat and vent; creamy axillaries are often exposed under wing.
Similar species Plain olive plumage and yellow bill are distinctive on Rennell.
Voice Chattering series of weak contact notes *chu, chu, chu...* Springy *zhe-hee-hee*. Sings rarely, a fast trill or warble of repeated notes 7–11 seconds long, e.g. *trhu-trhu-trhu-trhu-trhu-trhu*, *chwit-chwit-chwit*, *kril-kril-kril*, *chrrr-chrrr-chrrr*, slightly longer and faster than Bare-eyed White-eye.
Habits Forest, especially forest edge, less common in regrowth and scrub. Usually forages quietly in pairs and small flocks, often on edge of mixed-species flocks, mostly in lower levels. Often creeps along trunks and branches.
Conservation status Fairly common, but less common than other Rennell endemics. Not threatened.
Range Endemic to Rennell.

VELLA LAVELLA WHITE-EYE *Zosterops vellalavella* Plate 68

(Banded/Belted White-eye; Zostérops de Vella Lavella)

Description 12 cm. Yellow-billed white-eye with greenish breast-band. Dull olive upperparts, with blackish lores, broad white eye-ring and dull orange-yellow bill and legs. Yellow throat, broad dull olive breast-band, pale grey lower breast and belly, and greenish-yellow vent and undertail-coverts.
Similar species Differs from female Olive-backed Sunbird by eye-ring and greenish breast-band.
Voice Sings strongly in early morning. Slow series of about ten downslurred notes with irregular short pauses. Strong *tse* contact call. Springy *tse-tse-se-se* call.
Habits Forest, usually forest edge but also primary forest and regrowth including coconut plantations with some undergrowth and scattered old trees. Pairs or small numbers are rather unobtrusive in canopy, sometimes with mixed-species flocks.
Conservation status Fairly common and appears to be tolerant of degraded forest. May be threatened as it is likely to be declining from extensive logging on Vella Lavella. IUCN: Near Threatened.
Range Endemic to Vella Lavella and Bagga.

GIZO WHITE-EYE *Zosterops luteirostris* Plate 68

(Yellow-billed White-eye; Splendid White-eye; Zostérops de Gizo)

Description 12 cm. Bright olive and yellow white-eye with orange-yellow bill and legs. Dull olive upperparts, with blackish lores and forehead, medium-narrow white eye-ring and fairly long stout bright orange-yellow bill. Lemon-yellow underparts with faint green wash on upper breast and flanks, and dull orange-yellow legs.
Similar species Differs from female Olive-backed Sunbird by eye-ring and short, almost straight bill.

Voice Sings strongly in early morning. Song is stronger, longer and more melodious than other white-eyes, a slow series of loud sweet notes, with some harsh inserts like a reed warbler or Collared Kingfisher. Loud *tcheep* call, similar to Metallic Starling. Strong springy call *tse-tse-se-se*. Soft *pee-u* contact call.
Habits Forest edge, regrowth and mature plantations especially close to remnants of mature secondary forest. Singles and small groups forage actively in bushes and treetops, often mixed with other insectivorous species.
Conservation status Locally common close to remnant forests but the very little remaining forest on Gizo is being slowly degraded. IUCN: Endangered.
Range Endemic to Gizo.

RANONGGA WHITE-EYE *Zosterops splendidus* — Plate 68

(Splendid White-eye; Zostérops de Ganongga)

Description 12 cm. Olive and yellow white-eye with black bill and bright orange-yellow legs. Dull olive upperparts with blackish around lores and broad white eye-ring. Plain lemon-yellow underparts, sharply separated from green neck-sides along throat, but greenish wash on breast-sides and fading out along flanks.
Similar species Differs from female Olive-backed Sunbird by eye-ring and short, almost straight bill.
Voice Sings often, especially at dawn, a short simple series of 3–10 staccato notes. Contact call *cheu* is slightly louder and more disyllabic than other white-eyes.
Habits Forest, usually forest edge but also old-growth forest and regrowth and thickets with scattered old trees. Sometimes feeds in flowers of coconuts. Pairs or small groups forage quietly.
Conservation status Fairly common. It may be reliant on large old trees in its small range. IUCN: Vulnerable.
Range Endemic to Ranongga.

SOLOMONS WHITE-EYE *Zosterops kulambangrae* — Plate 68

(New Georgia White-eye; *Zosterops rendovae*; Zostérops des Salomon)

Description 12 cm. Olive white-eye with fairly long fine black bill, yellowish legs and sometimes a very narrow white eye-ring or white belly. Dull olive upperparts with blackish lores, and slightly brighter underparts which are slightly yellowish, especially on throat and central belly to vent. Juvenile has pale throat and belly and greener breast and flanks.
Similar species From Kolombangara White-eye (above 450 m on Kolombangara) by very narrow white eye-ring, some yellow in plumage and yellowish legs.
Voice Sings mostly at dawn, a loud, fairly long descending series of simple melodious notes, e.g. *twoy-twoy-twoy-tuu-tuu...* Song of *Z. t. paradoxus* is higher-pitched; that of *Z. t. tetiparius* is faster with narrow pitch range, mostly hoarse notes, similar to Song Parrot. Chick-like *cheep* contact call. Louder *dhu* contact call is slightly shorter than Kolombangara White-eye. Springy *wh-hehehe* call.
Habits Forest, especially forest edge but also primary forest and gardens. Lowlands and hills, less common above 400 m on Kolombangara to at least 1350 m. Pairs or small flocks forage in canopy, often with mixed-species flocks.
Conservation status Fairly common. Not threatened.
Range Endemic to the New Georgia island group.
Z. k. kulambangrae, endemic to Kolombangara, Vonavona, Kohinggo, New Georgia, Vangunu and Nggatokae, has narrow white eye-ring and plain olive underparts.
Rendova White-eye *Z. k. paradoxus* (=*Z. k. rendovae*), endemic to Rendova, has small area of dark skin around eye but no white eye-ring, yellow from belly to undertail-coverts, except flanks are dull olive as breast and upperparts; could be treated as a separate species.
Tetepare White-eye *Z. k. tetiparius*, endemic to Tetepare, has small area of dark skin around eye but no white eye-ring, dirty white belly and grey flanks, rarely very pale yellow, pale yellow vent and undertail-coverts, and throat and breast slightly paler than *Z. k. paradoxus*; could be treated as a separate species perhaps combined with *Z. k. paradoxus*.

KOLOMBANGARA WHITE-EYE *Zosterops murphyi* — Plate 68

(Kolombangara Mountain White-eye; Hermit White-eye; Zostérops de Murphy)

Description 12 cm. Plain olive white-eye with very broad white eye-ring. Uniformly dull olive, duller and greyer than other white-eyes, only slightly paler on underparts, with slight yellow wash on throat and central belly. Rather dumpy with dark legs and fairly long black bill with yellow base to lower mandible.
Similar species Differs from Solomons White-eye, leaf-warblers and myzomela by huge white eye-ring.

Voice Sings occasionally, warbling phrases of up to five seconds of sweet notes, less broken into syllables and more mumbling than Solomons White-eye. Flocks call continuously, including a nasal *dhu*, chattering *pee-o* and shriller nasal *byeet*, sounding like distant Metallic Starling colony.
Habits Montane forest above 400 m, rarely 350 m. Less common in mid-mountain forest and stunted upper montane forest. Pairs or flock, sometimes over 100 birds, especially at higher altitudes where commonest bird. Flocks are noisy, passing rapidly through canopy, often jumping ahead several trees, followed by other species.
Conservation status Locally abundant around 1000 m, but uncommon at lower altitudes. Not threatened but it has extremely small geographical range.
Range Endemic to Kolombangara.

GREY-THROATED WHITE-EYE *Zosterops ugiensis* — Plates 68 & 70

(*Zosterops rendovae* but does not occur on Rendova; Zostérops à gorge grise)

Description 12 cm. Slender warbler-like white-eye with olive upperparts and pale grey underparts. Dull olive upperparts with slightly brighter greener wings, silvery-grey underparts, slightly darker on upper breast and often yellow undertail-coverts. Medium-length black bill, dark blue-grey legs, and sometimes a narrow white eye-ring. Juvenile lacks brownish forehead of Bougainville and Makira adults.
Similar species Differs from Island Leaf Warbler by stockier shape, yellow undertail-coverts on Bougainville and Guadalcanal, and no supercilium or darker greyer head. Differs from Yellow-throated White-eye, up to 1200 m on Bougainville, by greenish throat.
Voice Sings at dawn, a series of rolling mellow *zuuu-hrr* notes sometimes interrupted by occasional *ch-ch-ch* rattles. Soft *she-she-* contact call. Chick-like *cheep*. Calls and song are more mellow than other white-eyes.
Habits Forest, especially forest edge and secondary forest but rarely in low bushes. Mostly in hills and mountains, less common in stunted upper montane forest, and rare or nomadic in lowlands. Small flocks and pairs are active in mid-storey and canopy, often mixed with warblers and other small insectivores.
Conservation status Fairly common to abundant, especially at higher altitudes. Not threatened.
Range Endemic to Bougainville, Guadalcanal and Makira.
Z. u. hamlini, endemic to Bougainville, where rare below 900 m, possibly down to 750 m, has narrow white eye-ring, dark brown forehead, green throat, darker grey breast and yellow undertail-coverts.
Z. u. oblitus, endemic to Guadalcanal, where common above 500 m and rare down to 300 m, has narrow dark grey eye-ring, silvery-grey underparts with darker breast and pale yellow undertail-coverts, and no brown on forehead.
Z. u. ugiensis, endemic to Makira, where common above 500 m but occasionally down to 50 m, has silvery undertail-coverts, sooty-brown forehead, and sometimes a very narrow white eye-ring.

MALAITA WHITE-EYE *Zosterops stresemanni* — Plate 68

(Zostérops de Malaita)

Description 13 cm. Fairly large stout plain olive white-eye. Dull olive with brighter fringes to darker wings, and more yellowish on rump and underparts especially throat, belly and vent. Indistinct dark grey bare skin around eye, stout yellowish-horn bill and greenish-grey legs.
Similar species Differs from female Midget Flowerpecker and Red-vested Myzomela by greenish plumage including underparts, and stout pale bill. From Oriole Whistler by smaller size, lack of buff or rufous tones, and stout pale bill.
Voice Song is a thrush-like series of melodious notes, e.g. *chu-chu-chee-peu-*, heard mostly at dawn but occasionally through day. Typical white-eye *peu* contact call. Springy *chu-chu-chu-chu*.
Habits Forest edge, bushes and gardens, commoner in secondary regrowth and especially in hill and montane forest to at least 1250 m. Rare in old-growth forest and on coastal plain. Forages in small flocks at all levels but mostly in canopy, sometimes mixed with other species, feeding mostly on small fruits.
Conservation status Fairly common to uncommon. Not threatened.
Range Endemic to Malaita.

SANTA CRUZ WHITE-EYE *Zosterops sanctaecrucis* — Plate 77

(Nendo White-eye; Zostérops de Santa Cruz)

Description 12 cm. Olive white-eye with short dark grey bill, lores and eye-ring creating slight mask. Dull olive upperparts, slightly darker wings and tail with slightly brighter fringes, slightly paler underparts, especially chin, central belly, vent and undertail-coverts, and dark blue-grey legs. Dumpy, with short rounded wings in flight.

Similar species Differs from female Cardinal Myzomela by uniform greenish plumage and short straight bill.
Voice Sings especially at dawn, a rich melodious warble of fruity notes. Subsong is a stuttering series of short notes, e.g. *zhay-zhay-zhe-*. Nasal *zhay* contact call. Harsh nasal scolding note. Bubbling trill *brrrrrrp*.
Habits Forest, including secondary forest and gardens close to forest. Pairs or small flocks, usually 4–7 birds, are active in canopy and fruiting trees.
Conservation status Fairly common. Not threatened.
Range Endemic to Nendo (Santa Cruz).

VANIKORO WHITE-EYE *Zosterops gibbsi* — Plate 77

(Zostérops de Vanikoro)

Description 12 cm. Olive white-eye with a relatively long, slightly decurved black bill and pale orange legs. Narrow pale grey eye-ring. Slightly darker wings and tail and slightly paler olive underparts with yellowish throat. Juvenile has duller plumage and legs, and dull brownish bill.
Similar species Differs from female Cardinal Myzomela by uniform greenish plumage and orange legs.
Voice Sings through day, varied phrases of usually 6–20 melodious notes, slower, shorter and less melodious than Santa Cruz White-eye. Subsong of about five notes similar to contact calls but longer. Quiet buzzing *vruh-vruh* contact call. Flight call similar but higher-pitched. Loud harsh nasal scold similar to Cardinal Myzomela.
Habits Forest, mostly secondary forest and forest edge in lowlands but common in primary forest at higher altitudes (above 600 m). Pairs forage quietly in canopy. Also forages underneath branches, among dead leaves, and on tree-trunks.
Conservation status Locally common. Has very small range but is not threatened.
Range Endemic to Vanikoro.

VANUATU WHITE-EYE *Zosterops flavifrons* — Plate 78

(Yellow-fronted White-eye; Zostérops à front jaune)

Description 12 cm. Small yellowish-green white-eye with broad white eye-ring. Yellowish-olive upperparts with darker wings and tail, conspicuous white eye-ring, fine dark bill and darker lores, yellow forehead and underparts, and dark grey legs.
Similar species Differs from Silvereye by uniform upperparts and underparts without any grey, slimmer shape and yellow forehead. From other birds by white eye-ring.
Voice Sings especially at dawn, a melodious warble of c.10–15 soft fruity notes, similar to Silvereye but slower, more melodious and with fewer harsh notes. Contact call *chip* or *tzeep* given continuously, slightly higher-pitched and shorter than Silvereye. High-pitched staccato chattering scold.
Habits Forest including all types of degraded forest, scrub, gardens and bushes in open habitats, at all altitudes. Usually in large flocks but also in pairs and small groups, foraging actively at all heights.
Conservation status Very common. Not threatened.
Range Endemic to Vanuatu.
Z. f. gauensis, endemic to Gaua, has typical yellow forehead but yellower upperparts and browner bill.
Z. f. perplexa, endemic to Vanua Lava, Mere Lava, Maewo, Ambae, Pentecost, Ambrym, Paama, Lopevi, Epi and Tongoa, has greener underparts and small faint yellow forehead-patch.
Z. f. brevicauda, endemic to Malo and Santo, has shorter tail and fairly dull breast and throat.
Z. f. macgillivrayi, endemic to Malekula, lacks yellow on forehead and dark lores and is duller yellow below, contrasting less with flanks.
Z. f. efatensis, endemic to Efate and Erromango, has distinct yellow forehead, and underparts are yellower.
Z. f. flavifrons, endemic to Tanna and Aniwa, has darker upperparts and darker greener underparts.
Z. f. majuscula, endemic to Aneityum, is larger, has darker upperparts, slightly greener underparts, slightly paler forehead and largely black bill.

SMALL LIFOU WHITE-EYE *Zosterops minutus* — Plate 82

(Zostérops minute)

Description 10 cm. Small white-eye with green upperparts, yellow underparts and broad white eye-ring. Fairly bright olive-green upperparts with yellowish forehead, dark lores and broad white eye-ring. Yellow underparts with contrasting silvery-white flanks, becoming pale grey on belly. Dark grey legs and short bill with paler lower mandible.

Similar species Differs from Silvereye by uniform green upperparts, yellow breast, yellowish forehead, less contrasting white eye-ring and smaller size. From Large Lifou White-eye by white eye-ring, yellow underparts, smaller size and slender shape.
Voice Typical *dhu* and *zhe* contact call. Ringing alarm call. Song unknown.
Habits Forest, especially forest edge, secondary forest and gardens, but not coconut plantations or tidy villages. Forages in flocks of up to 25 birds, or pairs, often mixed with Silvereyes and other species, usually in canopy.
Conservation status Very common. Not threatened but has very small range.
Range Endemic to Lifou.

GREEN-BACKED WHITE-EYE *Zosterops xanthochroa* Plate 82

(Zostérops à dos vert)

Description 11 cm. Typical white-eye with broad white eye-ring and pale grey flanks. Dull olive upperparts with broad white eye-ring, greenish-yellow throat, often extending as narrow midline stripe on breast, with grey or buffy-grey flanks, often a bright white stripe along closed wing, and yellowish vent. Short dark bill and blue-grey legs.
Similar species Differs from Silvereye by greenish underparts, green mantle, paler greener lores and smaller size. From other small birds by broad white eye-ring.
Voice Song is a rapid jumbled warble of short notes and whistles. Plaintive nasal *tseep* contact call. Springy *tsee-tsee-tsssEee* call.
Habits Wet and dry forest, including forest edge, but less common than Silvereye in scrub, gardens and parks, at all altitudes but less common above 1000 m. Pairs and small flocks move rapidly through canopy.
Conservation status Very common. Not threatened.
Range Endemic to New Caledonia, where widespread on Grand Terre, Maré and Ile des Pins.

SILVEREYE *Zosterops lateralis* Plates 78 & 82

(Grey-backed White-eye; Zostérops à dos gris)

Description 12 cm. Fairly large white-eye with broad white eye-ring, grey mantle and paler grey breast. Olive head, blackish around lores and forehead, with contrasting white eye-ring, dark grey mantle and scapulars, contrasting with olive-green wings, rump and tail. Yellowish-green throat, pale grey breast, paler silvery on belly. Stout horn-coloured bill and dark grey legs.
Similar species Differs from Vanuatu White-eye on Vanuatu, Small Lifou White-eye on Lifou and Green-backed White-eye on New Caledonia and Maré by grey back, pale grey breast and silvery belly, darker face and stouter shape.
Voice Sings occasionally, a short chattering warble of c.6–15 melodious notes and more nasal *wheo* notes, similar to contact calls. Contact call, given continuously when foraging, is a deeper longer *whEE* than small white-eyes.
Habits Secondary forest, bushes and gardens, but usually absent from closed-canopy forest. Pairs and small flocks forage at all heights, including on ground, less active than smaller white-eyes, often feeding on small fruits.
Conservation status Fairly common. Not threatened.
Range Vanuatu and New Caledonia.

Z. l. valuensis, endemic to Mota Lava, has almost uniformly green upperparts, slightly buff underparts, and yellower throat and vent.

Z. l. tropicus, endemic to north Vanuatu, from Torres Is and Banks Is through Santo to Malo and probably on Ambae, Maewo and Pentecost, has grey mantle.

Z. l. vatensis, endemic to south Vanuatu, from Malekula to Aniwa, is large, with grey on back, black below eye, with blacker forehead and crown on southern islands, where sometimes split as *Z. l. macmillani* on Tanna and Aniwa, is larger with darker grey on upperparts and blacker face.

Z. l. melanops, endemic to Lifou, is even darker grey on upperparts with more black around face and darker grey underparts.

Z. l. nigrescens, endemic to Maré and Ouvéa, is paler grey with less extensive black on face.

Z. l. griseonota, endemic to Grand Terre and Ile des Pins, has black restricted to lores, paler grey mantle and greyer breast.

LARGE LIFOU WHITE-EYE *Zosterops inornatus* Plate 82

(Zostérops de Lifu)

Description 14 cm. Large grey and olive white-eye, lacking any eye-ring. Dull olive hood, grey mantle, brighter olive wings and tail, paler olive throat, buffy-grey flanks and pale grey underparts. Long stout pale pink legs and fairly long heavy dark bill with dull pink lower mandible. Appears dumpy and front-heavy.

Similar species Differs from Silvereye and Small Lifou White-eye by lack of eye-ring, pale legs and stocky shape, and from Small Lifou White-eye by no yellow on underparts and larger size. From female Cardinal Myzomela and Grey-eared Honeyeater by uniform greenish plumage, shorter tail and shorter, stouter bill.
Voice Sings through day, a rushed rich warble of 6–15 notes, richer and more melodious than other white-eyes on Lifou. Flight-call richer, more melodious and slightly higher-pitched than Silvereye. Unlike other white-eyes, does not habitually give contact call.
Habits Forest, especially forest edge, secondary forest and gardens, but usually in or around large trees. Singles or pairs, sometimes groups of up to five birds, forage slowly and unobtrusively, often in fruiting trees and bushes, sometimes in flowers.
Conservation status Fairly common. Not threatened but has very small range.
Range Endemic to Lifou.

BARE-EYED WHITE-EYE *Woodfordia superciliosa* Plate 75

(Rennell name is Ghagha; Zostérops de Woodford)

Description 14 cm. Unusual grey-brown white-eye with fairly long bill and silvery margin around dark eye-mask. Relatively long stout slightly decurved horn-coloured bill, dark grey lores and eye-mask, surrounded by silvery supercilium extending around and under mask and merging into pale grey throat. Dull greyish-brown upperparts, browner on cap, with paler greyish-buff underparts and grey legs. A dumpy, front-heavy and short-tailed bird, broad-winged in fluttering flight. Juvenile has paler bill.
Similar species Much larger and stockier than Fan-tailed Gerygone.
Voice Occasionally sings pre-dawn, a brief rapid warble, slightly shorter and slower than Rennell White-eye. Chattering contact notes, e.g. *chocho-cho-cho-* or mumbled *whee-whee-whee* or harsher *tch-tch-tch-...* Short single contact notes, e.g. soft whistled *tyoo* or *chuchee* or rolling *drick*. Loud piping alarm call *wika-wika-wika-*.
Habits Forest, especially forest edge, gardens and degraded habitats. Small groups, usually 3–8 birds, move fairly slowly through all levels of vegetation, often mixed with other species, gleaning insects and often feeding on small fruits.
Conservation status Abundant. Not threatened.
Range Endemic to Rennell.

SANFORD'S WHITE-EYE *Woodfordia lacertosa* Plate 77

(*Sanfordia lacertosa*; Zostérops de Sanford)

Description 15 cm. Unusual dark brown white-eye with fairly long decurved bill and silvery eye-ring. Rufous-buff upperparts including crown, paler rufous-buff underparts including face. Broad ill-defined silvery eye-ring, pale lores and ear-coverts, relatively long dull buff-yellow or yellow bill and dull yellow-horn legs, both sometimes with slight pink wash. Broad rounded wings and fairly short-tailed in flight.
Similar species Distinctive long pale bill and rufous-buff colour.
Voice Quiet creaking *kwee-kwee-kwee-*. Harsh nasal *tcha-tchaa-tchaa* or *kreh!*, louder and harsher than Santa Cruz White-eye. Song is unknown.
Habits Poorly known. Forest, including secondary forest with some remaining large trees. Pairs forage rather slowly in canopy and mid-storeys, sometimes feeding on fruits.
Conservation status Appears to be fairly common but very poorly known. May be threatened if it proves to be dependent on old-growth forest. IUCN: Near Threatened.
Range Endemic to Nendo (Santa Cruz).

STARLINGS Sturnidae

Mostly medium-sized black birds, but some are brown or with white patches. Vocal frugivores, foraging in trees in pairs or flocks. Glossy Starlings *Aplonis* are glossy black or dull brown and juvenile is often dull and streaked. Mynas *Mino* and *Acridotheres* are stocky and short-tailed, with bold white wing-patches.

METALLIC STARLING *Aplonis metallica* Plates 59, 69 & 73

(Shining/Colonial Starling; Stourne luisant)

Description 24 cm. Long-tailed glossy starling with conspicuous red eye. All black with green and purple gloss and fairly long pointed feathers on neck. Tail varies in length but is long and pointed in adults with central two feathers projecting about 2 cm. Juvenile has shorter rounded tail, dark brown upperparts with slight green gloss, and creamy-white underparts with heavy blackish streaks. Eye starts dark brown then olive, then greenish-yellow, then orange-red. Immature has glossy black upperparts like adult and streaked underparts like juvenile, but sometimes almost plain underparts with few streaks.

Similar species Adult tail shape is distinctive. Also differs from Singing Starling by slighter bill and greener glossier plumage. From White-eyed Starling on Bougainville to Guadalcanal and Atoll Starling on Nissan and Kilinailau Is by red eye, tail shape and smaller bill. From Spangled Drongo on New Britain, Guadalcanal and Makira by uniform gloss without clear spots, and red eye. Juvenile streaks are shared only by Singing Starling, from which it differs by tail shape, often darker upperparts and more regular streaks on creamier underparts.

Voice Variable loud, simple harsh notes. Continuous chattering of foraging flocks and at nests. Buzzing contact calls *scheep*, *tzu* and upslurred *tze-up*. Metallic *kleee*. Harsher *chak*. Quiet short high-pitched repetitive song of repeated trills, tinkles and warbles.

Habits Forest edge, secondary forest, scattered trees and gardens close to forest, but uncommon in closed forest. Lowlands and hills to *c.*600 m on most islands, rare in mountains to maximum 1400 m on New Ireland. Usually feeds in canopy but also low fruiting bushes, often with other frugivorous species. Highly gregarious, often in dense fast-flying flocks with loud whoosh of wing-beats. Breeds in noisy colonies of tens or hundreds of bulky nests hanging from prominent tree.

Conservation status Common, abundant on some islands. Not threatened.

Range Admiralties, St Matthias Is, Bismarcks and Solomons.

A. m. nitida, endemic to the Admiralties, Bismarcks and Solomons, including Rambutyo, Tong and outer Admiralty Is, St Matthias Is. and Kilinailau Is (but not other tiny outlying islands or Rennell).

A. m. purpureiceps, endemic to Manus and Los Negros, has shorter tail and less glossy head.

Elsewhere, other subspecies occur in east Indonesia and north Australia.

SINGING STARLING *Aplonis cantoroides* — Plates 59, 69, 73 & 74

(Stourne chanteur)

Description 19 cm. Short-tailed glossy starling with conspicuous red eye. All black with blue-green gloss, fairly long pointed feathers on neck and medium-short square tail. Juvenile has grey-brown upperparts with slight green gloss, sometimes paler brown on crown and mantle, and off-white underparts with heavy dusky streaks. Eye starts dark brown, then yellowish, then orange-red. Immature has glossy black upperparts like adult and streaked underparts like juvenile, but sometimes almost plain underparts with few streaks.

Similar species Adult and immature differ from Metallic and White-eyed Starling by short square tail. Also differs from Metallic Starling by heavier bill, and less and bluer gloss. From White-eyed Starling on Bougainville to Guadalcanal by red eye. From Atoll Starling on Ninigo and Rennell Starling on Rennell by red eye, slimmer shape and medium-length tail. From Spangled Drongo on New Britain, Guadalcanal and Makira by uniform gloss without clear spots, and red eye. Streaked juvenile is similar only to Metallic Starling, from which it differs by tail shape, often paler upperparts and fewer, less distinct, streaks on whiter underparts.

Voice Loud clear notes, often downslurred or upslurred *klee*, *tseeup*, *toyee*. Quiet short scratchy but melodious warbling song. Most calls are similar to Metallic Starling but also a softer, more melodious downslurred *tu-leep*.

Habits Trees and bushes in open habitats including forest edge, plantations, gardens, villages, towns and along rivers and coasts, but rare in forest. On some islands, restricted to coastal towns. Lowlands with occasional records to 900 m on New Britain and 750 m on Bougainville. Usually feeds in canopy but also low fruiting bushes, often perching on buildings, wires and dead branches. Adults are usually in pairs or small flocks, but juveniles in larger flocks, sometimes mixed with Metallic Starlings. Breeds in small colonies in holes in dead trees, buildings or rock faces.

Conservation status Locally common, but rare on some islands such as Nissan, Makira and Rennell. Not threatened.

Range Admiralties, St Matthias Is, Bismarcks and Solomons, including all main islands and Wuvulu, Hermit Is and Rennell but not other tiny outlying islands. Elsewhere, occurs across New Guinea and satellite islands.

ATOLL STARLING *Aplonis feadensis* — Plates 59 & 69

(Stourne des Fead)

Description 20 cm. Dumpy yellow-eyed starling of tiny islands. All black with green and some blue gloss, lemon-yellow eye and broad round wings and short square tail. Juvenile is dull sooty-brown with variable pale buff scales on underparts, more striped on vent, and eye is first blue, then green, then yellow.

Similar species Differs from Singing and Metallic Starlings on Hermit Is, Nissan and Kilinailau Is by yellow eye, more rounded wing and shorter tail.
Voice Varied squeaky high-pitched calls. Thin monotone whistle. Upslurred *tseeup* or *weee-eee*. Repeated ringing *te-dowlee*, rising, falling then rising in pitch. Song is a short rapid jumble of notes, reminiscent of Song Parrot.
Habits Forest, forest edge, gardens and coconuts. Pairs or small flocks forage at all levels and often perch in dead treetop. Solitary nests in holes in dead trees or coconut stumps.
Conservation status Common, but only on tiny islands. Potentially at risk from cyclones and other disasters on its tiny land area. IUCN: Near Threatened.
Range Endemic to small atolls north of Bismarcks and Solomons.
A. f. heureka is endemic to Ninigo Is and Hermit Is, and probably this subspecies on Tench and Wuvulu.
A. f. feadensis, endemic to Nissan, Nuguria, Kilinailau Is and Ontong Java, has shorter tail, longer more pointed neck-hackles, and heavier bill.

RENNELL STARLING *Aplonis insularis* — Plate 74

(Stourne de Rennell)

Description 17 cm. Fat short-tailed yellow-eyed starling. All black with green and blue gloss and slightly elongated neck feathers. In flight, has broad round wings and bulging belly. Juvenile is dull grey-brown with pale buff scales on underparts, more striped on vent, and blue, then green, then lemon-yellow or orange-yellow eye. Immature like adult but dark brownish-grey.
Similar species Differs from adult Singing Starling by yellow eye, shorter tail, rounder wings, shorter neck feathers and bluer gloss. Juvenile differs from juvenile Island Thrush by black bill and legs, short tail and habits.
Voice Explosive sharp *tzik* flight call. Thin high-pitched *tss* contact call. Song is a quiet, rushed jumble of about five high-pitched creaky notes.
Habits Forest edge, also open forest and gardens. Pairs, sometimes singles or threes, forage in canopy, often in isolated trees, and in bushes, sometimes on ground, and call from dead tree-tops. Usually feeds on fruit but also snails, breaking shells against rocks. Solitary nests in holes in tree or coconut stump.
Conservation status Fairly uncommon. Not threatened.
Range Endemic to Rennell.

WHITE-EYED STARLING *Aplonis brunneicapillus* — Plate 69

(Stourne aux yeux blancs)

Description 21 cm and up to 12 cm tail-streamers. White-eyed glossy starling with elongate central tail feathers. All black with green gloss, bluer on wings and tail, duller browner crown, lower breast and belly, fairly elongate neck feathers, conspicuous white eye and very heavy black bill. Fairly long rounded tail, with very long central pair of feathers often broken or missing. Female has less gloss and shorter tail-streamers. Juvenile has purple gloss on crown, browner underparts with some fine white streaks from throat to mid-belly, grey-brown or olive eye, no tail-streamers and paler, finer bill.
Similar species Distinctive white eye and long tail-streamers, if present. Also differs from Metallic and Singing Starlings by heavier bill and tail shape. Juvenile also differs from Metallic and Singing Starlings by streaks on browner underparts, heavier bill and bulkier build.
Voice Harsh *kwaitch*. Whistled *kwee-kwee-chee-er*, last note harsher. Harsh chatter *chk-chk-chk-*. Song is a mixture of these whistles and harsh notes.
Habits Forest, especially forest edge in hills and lowlands including swamp forest, trees in clearings and nearby secondary growth from sea-level to at least 800 m. Forages in canopy and bushes, often perched on exposed branches. Gregarious, foraging in small flocks, sometimes mixed with Metallic and Singing Starlings. Nests in small colonies, each nest tunnelled into epiphytes in an isolated large tree in a forest clearing.
Conservation status Rare. Probably threatened by habitat loss and, at least historically, by human predation on nesting colonies. IUCN: Endangered.
Range Endemic to Solomons with records from Bougainville, Choiseul, Rendova and Guadalcanal.

BROWN-WINGED STARLING *Aplonis grandis* — Plate 69

(Stourne des Salomon)

Description 25 cm. Large bulky black starling with pale brown primaries. All black with purple and green gloss and

dark brown primaries and secondaries, fading pale brown. Long feathers on neck, throat and upper breast often appear streaky grey. Eye red-brown, sometimes red or dark grey-brown. In flight, fairly round wings and square medium-long tail. Juvenile is duller, with short neck feathers, darker primaries and orange-red eye.
Similar species Distinctive contrasting pale brown wings.
Voice Quieter than other starlings. High-pitched whistles, usually slightly upslurred, similar to Midget Flowerpecker but not multisyllabic. Clicks and pops, often combined as *erikk-pop*, and often throws back head when calling. Short harsh *chik* in flight. Song is a long chattering series of warbles, squeaks, chatters and clicks. Noisy whirring flight.
Habits Forest edge, including closed forest, secondary forest, gardens, villages and sometimes scattered trees in open habitats, in lowlands and hills, to c.1000 m on Kolombangara, 750 m on Bougainville, 1200 m on Guadalcanal and 800 m on Malaita. Usually in pairs, rarely small flocks, feeding mostly on fruit in canopy and often on exposed canopy perches. Nests are single, large bulky domes of sticks high in an exposed fork of prominent tree.
Conservation status Fairly common. Not threatened.
Range Endemic to Solomons, from Bougainville to Guadalcanal.
A. g. grandis is endemic to Bougainville including Buka and Shortland Is, Choiseul, Isabel, throughout the New Georgia group and Florida Is.
A. g. macrura, endemic to Guadalcanal, has shorter broader throat-hackles.
A. g. malaitae, endemic to Malaita, has white eye, slimmer shape and no *erikk-pop* call; could be treated as a separate species.

MAKIRA STARLING *Aplonis dichroa* — Plate 73

(San Cristobal Starling; Stourne de San Cristobal)

Description 20 cm. Glossy black starling with brown wings and darker brown medium-short tail. Black head, body and wing-coverts have a slight purple-green gloss, fairly elongated neck and throat feathers, tawny-brown primaries, secondaries and tertials, which fade paler, and chestnut-red, orange or tawny eye. Juvenile is duller, has shorter neck feathers and pale yellow-brown eye.
Similar species Differs from other starlings and cuckooshrikes by black plumage contrasting with brown wings and tail.
Voice Varied whistles, squeaks, croaks, clucks, pops and soft chattering. Song is a repeated series of slurred notes. Thin high-pitched *tseep*, similar to Finsch's Pygmy Parrot but lower-pitched, longer and never quavering.
Habits Forest edge and secondary forest, less common in closed forest, commonest in hills to at least 800 m. Singles, pairs, small flocks, or mixed with other species, foraging in canopy. Solitary nest is a compact ball of sticks in dense subcanopy.
Conservation status Common. Not threatened.
Range Endemic to Makira.

RUSTY-WINGED STARLING *Aplonis zelandica* — Plates 77 & 80

(Rufous-winged Starling; Stourne mélanésien)

Description 19 cm. Dumpy brown starling with rusty-orange wing-patch. Dull grey-brown upperparts with darker streaked cap and blackish loral mask, blackish on wing-coverts and scapulars, rufous-chestnut patch across flight feathers, and brighter tawny-rufous rump. Paler underparts, mottled with paler fringes and tawny-chestnut flanks and undertail-coverts. Juvenile may have whitish eye.
Similar species Differs from Mountain Starling, only on Santo, by greyer plumage, clearer rusty wing-patch, paler buffier underparts and dark eye.
Voice Quiet, inconspicuous calls. Short thin metallic whistles, e.g. *twee*, *zee-twee* or upslurred *zoooee*, *tsee-tsu-sseeee*. Sharper *tswee* flight call. Harsh upslurred whistle *kerrahh*. Harsh throaty series of clicks. Song is short irregular phrases of clicks and metallic whistles.
Habits Forest, including forest edge, secondary growth and gardens, from sea-level to over 1000 m, but usually commoner in hills, especially on Santo. Pairs, sometimes small groups up to five, forage in subcanopy, sometimes on exposed perches in canopy and forest edge or gardens.
Conservation status Uncommon, often rare. IUCN: Near Threatened.
Range Endemic to north Vanuatu, Nendo and Vanikoro.
A. z. maxwellii, endemic to Nendo (Santa Cruz), has browner underparts and chestnut-orange vent.
A. z. zelandica, endemic to Vanikoro, has slightly paler underparts.
A. z. rufipennis, endemic to Vanuatu, including Ureparapara, Vanua Lava, Gaua, Mere Lava, Santo, Ambae, Malo, Pentecost, Malekula, Ambrym, Paama and Lopevi, is warmer brown with brighter buffy-brown underparts and orange vent.

STRIATED STARLING *Aplonis striata* — Plate 85

(Stourne calédonien)

Description 18 cm. Medium-small glossy black or pale grey starling with red-orange eye and heavy black bill. Male is all black with greenish gloss and dull dark brown wings and tail. Eye varies from red to orange-yellow. In flight, appears fairly round-winged and short-tailed. Female is pale grey, darker on lores, wings and tail, slightly streaked on throat and paler on lower breast to undertail-coverts. Juvenile is similar to female but has browner eye.
Similar species Differs from South Melanesian Cuckooshrike and New Caledonian Cuckooshrike by orange or red eye, short tail and uniform glossy black or grey plumage. Male differs from Island Thrush by blackish legs and bill.
Voice Noisy. Loud clear thin whistles, e.g. *zhe* or *clee*, often sharper and more metallic in flight. Clear *chew-wee*. Rushed warbling song with clear clicks, squeaks and fluid warbles.
Habits Forest, savanna and gardens, also nearby coconuts and villages. Pairs and flocks of up to 25 birds forage in at all levels in forest, occasionally on ground where it breaks snails against rocks, flying fast through canopy, and perching on exposed tree-tops.
Conservation status Common. Not threatened.
Range Endemic to New Caledonia.
A. s. striata is endemic to Grande Terre and Ile des Pins.
A. s. atronitens, endemic to Ouvéa, Lifou and Maré, has larger bill, male has more green gloss on head and female is darker, sometimes much darker grey with greenish gloss.

MOUNTAIN STARLING *Aplonis santovestris* — Plate 80

(Santo Mountain Starling; Vanuatu Starling; local name is Mataweli; Stourne d'Espiritu Santo)

Description 17 cm. Dumpy, rather uniform rufous-brown starling with white eye. Rufous-brown with slightly darker crown, wings and tail, brighter rufous edges on wings, brighter rufous lower back and rump, paler underparts and white eye. Female duller. Juvenile unknown.
Similar species Differs from Rusty-winged Starling by more uniform rufous-brown plumage, especially underparts, plainer wings and white eye.
Voice Short thin monotone whistle repeated several times *tzee—tzee—tzee-* or slurred *tzeetzeetzee*, lower-pitched and fuller than Palm Lorikeet. Loud twittering song. Soft disyllabic clicks. Song is a series of dissimilar thrush-like whistles given about every four seconds, with each phrase comprising *c.*2–5 slurred whistles and trills over less than a second.
Habits Montane forest, especially on the highest mountain-tops, recorded from 1200–1700 m but has also been reported from lowlands. Singles and pairs forage unobtrusively in forest understorey, especially in thick moss and epiphytes, sometimes in stunted canopy.
Conservation status Can be locally common, but often rare and very few observers have reached the species's altitude. IUCN: Vulnerable.
Range Endemic to Santo, where recorded only from Mt Watiamasan, Mt Tabwemasana and Peak Santo.

POLYNESIAN STARLING *Aplonis tabuensis* — Plate 77

(Stourne de Polynésie)

Description 19 cm. Dumpy brown starling with paler underparts and pale wing-patch. Plain grey-brown upperparts with darker cap, dull yellow-brown eye and pale buff wing-panel on secondaries. Dark buff underparts with scattered pale buff streaks on breast, paler belly and unstreaked yellow-buff undertail-coverts. In flight, shows long rounded wings and medium-short tail. Juvenile has dull rufous-brown eye.
Similar species Distinctive.
Voice Thin whistles, often upslurred *tsee*, *tsee-up*. Clicks. Short song is variable, often whistles, e.g. *see-oh-see-too*.
Habits All habitats on the tiny islands that it inhabits. Pairs or small flocks forage most commonly in subcanopy.
Conservation status Common. Not threatened.
Range Temotu, on Tinakula, Reef Is and Tikopia.
A. t. pachyrampha, endemic to Tinakula and Reef Is, including Lomlom, Nepani and Matema, has a slightly green-glossed dark cap.
A. t. tucopiae, endemic to Tikopia, has less streaking on darker underparts and slight purple gloss on only slightly darker cap.
Elsewhere, other subspecies breed across Fiji, Tonga and Samoa.

LONG-TAILED MYNA *Mino kreffti* — Plates 59 & 69

(Also treated as a subspecies of Yellow-faced Myna *M. dumontii*; Mino de Dumont)

Description 28 cm. Large black bird with yellow-orange eye-patch and bill. Glossy black with bright yellow-orange bill, legs and large comma-shaped eye-patch, yellow lower belly, and white wing-patch, upper and undertail-coverts. In flight, looks black with short white bar across primaries. Juvenile has paler eye-patch and yellow belly.
Similar species Distinctive large orange eye-patch. Also differs from Common Myna on Guadalcanal and Russell Is by glossy black plumage, white uppertail-coverts and habits.
Voice Noisy and loud. Varied whistles and clear liquid ringing notes, including upslurred whistles *tsseoo?* Up- then downslurred whistles, *whee-oow*. Some whistles end in fluid notes, e.g. *tssee-och* and *tsee-tswock*. Clear liquid notes *plllonk*, *klow-kit* and *tloo-tee-oow*. Creaking *whee-ow*. Grating *grree-oow*. Cat-like *me-ow*. Noisy whirring wing-beats.
Habits Forest, especially forest edge, secondary forest, isolated trees in gardens and clearings, and locally in coconuts. Commonest in lowlands and hills to *c.*600 m, occasionally up to 1000 m on New Britain and 1100 m on Bougainville. Usually in pairs, sometimes in small flocks with other starlings and pigeons, especially in figs. Spends much time calling from bare tree-top perches.
Conservation status Common. Not threatened.
Range Endemic to Bismarcks and Solomons, including Lavongai, New Ireland, Tanga, Umboi, New Britain, Lolobau, Duke of York and from Buka and Bougainville to Malaita and Ulawa, with shorter-tailed birds on New Britain and Umboi sometimes separated as *M. k. giliau* and smaller birds on Guadalcanal, Malaita and Ulawa sometimes separated as *M. k. sanfordi*.

COMMON MYNA *Acridotheres tristis* — Plates 69, 80 & 85

(Indian Myna; Martin triste)

Description 25 cm. Large starling-like bird which walks on open grassland. Glossy black head and neck with orange-yellow bill and bare skin around eye, dark brown body with white central belly to undertail-coverts, dark brown wings with large white patch on primaries, blackish tail with white tip and long yellow legs. In flight, shows conspicuous white on primaries, underwing-coverts and tail. Juvenile is paler and duller with browner head and bare parts.
Similar species Differs from Long-tailed Myna on Guadalcanal and Russell Is by smaller yellow eye-patch, largely brown plumage, dark uppertail with white tip, and habits.
Voice Noisy. Combinations of short whistles, harsh screeches and squawks, melodious notes and mimicry of other birds. Song is a series of varied notes each repeated two or three times. Raucous chattering at roosts.
Habits Short grassland and towns, especially cattle pasture and air-strips, less common in coconut plantations and villages. Wider habitat range away from people on Tanna and New Caledonia. Lowlands and hills in suitable habitat, to at least 350 m. Pairs and small flocks forage on ground, with bouncing walk and long hops, and often perch on buildings and cattle. Roosts communally, usually in towns.
Conservation status Locally common, abundant in towns and New Caledonia. Introduced. Not threatened.
Range *A. t. tristis* occurs on Solomons, Vanuatu and New Caledonia, including the north coast of Guadalcanal, Russell Is, Three Sisters, Santo, Malo, Paama, Epi, Efate, Tanna, Futuna and Grande Terre, and used to occur on Bougainville where now extirpated. Elsewhere, it is native to south and South-East Asia and introduced to Polynesia, New Zealand and Australia.

COMMON STARLING *Sturnus vulgaris* — (not illustrated)

(European Starling; Étourneau sansonnet)

Description 21 cm. Dumpy glossy black bird with short tail and medium-long fine pointed bill. All black with purple and green gloss, variable creamy or white spotting and pale fringes on wing and tail. Breeding adult has almost no spots and pale yellow bill, with blue base in male and pinkish base in female. Non-breeding adult has white spots across underparts, buff spots across upperparts and blackish bill. Juvenile is plain grey-brown with black bill.
Similar species Differs from Striated Starling and other starlings by white spots, dark eye and fine bill.
Voice Varied, including whistles, wheezes and sharp calls. Song is a series of whistles and warbles, often mimicking other species. Rolling *prrrp* on taking flight.
Habits Short grassland and towns. Flocks forage on ground, with quick jerky gait and probing into grass like a wader, and feed in fruiting bushes and trees. Fast flight, with rapid changes of direction. Roosts communally, often in towns or wetlands.
Conservation status Rare vagrant. Introduced. Not threatened.
Range One record from Ouvéa in 2004 and a possible record from Vanuatu. Elsewhere, it is native to Europe and introduced to many countries including Tonga, New Zealand and Australia.

THRUSHES Turdidae

Thrushes are medium-sized, rather elongate birds, usually foraging singly on the forest floor. Secretive and shy, they are often seen when flushed from the ground. Their plumage is dark brown or black, often with bold white markings, medium-length straight bills and medium-long stout legs.

RUSSET-TAILED THRUSH *Zoothera heinei* — Plates 57 & 66

(Also treated as a subspecies of Bassian Thrush *Z. lunulata* or Scaly Thrush *Z. dauma*; Grive de Heine)

Description 20 cm. Brown thrush with black scaly crescents. Warm buff-brown upperparts have small black crescents, two indistinct pale wing-bars, blotchy primary bases and pale tertial tips. Off-white underparts with buffy upper breast have scattered larger crescents. Heavy black bill and long pinkish legs. In flight, shows white corners to tail and black and white underwing-bars.
Similar species Distinctive scaly brown plumage. In flight, differs from Bronze Ground Dove by slower whirring flight without glides, and longer tail.
Voice Very thin sibilant *tssep* call, louder than Bismarck Myzomela. Loud alarm call *chack*. Rushed series of *chuk* or *tak* notes similar to Island Thrush. Song unknown but Australian *Z. h. heinei* has two long whistles *peeeeer, pooee*, slowly falling and repeated at intervals of a few seconds.
Habits On Mussau, thick understorey of lowland forest, especially overgrown gardens and secondary growth. Singles or pairs feed on ground and fly up to low perches. Skulking but not very shy. The only specimen known from Choiseul was in montane forest.
Conservation status Locally fairly common but poorly known. *Z. h. eichhorni* is not threatened but *Z. h. choiseuli* is Data Deficient and possibly Endangered, known only from one record in 1904.
Range Mussau and Choiseul.
Z. h. eichhorni, endemic to Mussau, is smaller, has white wing-covert spots and primary flashes, and fewer black crescents than *Z. h. heinei* and *Z. h. papuensis*, and could be treated as a separate species.
Z. h. choiseuli, endemic to Choiseul, has warmer orange-buff spots on wing-coverts and primary fringes, heavier black scaling on upperparts and breast, and richer buff wash on underparts than *Z. h. eichhorni*.
Elsewhere, *Z. h. papuensis* is a rare and local resident scattered in New Guinea and *Z. h. heinei* breeds in north-east Australia.

NEW BRITAIN THRUSH *Zoothera talaseae* — Plate 57

(Also combined with Bougainville Thrush *Z. atrigena* as North Melanesian Ground Thrush or Black-backed Thrush; Grive de Nouvelle-Bretagne)

Description 23 cm. Sooty-grey thrush with white underparts and wing-bars. Dark slate-grey upperparts with black fringes, two broken white wing-bars and white spots on face. White underparts with black scales on sides of breast and flanks, and pale pinkish-brown legs. In flight, shows broad white tips to outer tail feathers and black underwing with white stripe. Juvenile is unknown.
Similar species Differs from other black and white birds, e.g. trillers, fantails and monarchs, by habits and larger size. When flushed, differs from Island Thrush by white corners to tail, greyer upperparts and white underparts.
Voice Unknown but presumably has a thin high-pitched call like other *Zoothera* thrushes.
Habits Poorly known. Montane forest, with records from 1300 m at Mt Birik on Umboi, and at 1540 m on Mt Talawe, 600 m at Talasea, 950–1050 m on Mt Otu and 940–1485 m on Mt Roma on New Britain. Singles recorded on ground, flushing off with low fast whirring flight.
Conservation status Appears to be rare and localised but probably overlooked. IUCN: Near Threatened.
Range Endemic to Umboi and New Britain, where probably widespread in mountains.

BOUGAINVILLE THRUSH *Zoothera atrigena* — Plate 66

(Also combined with New Britain Thrush *Z. talaseae* as North Melanesian Ground Thrush or Black-backed Thrush; Grive de Nouvelle-Bretagne)

Description 20 cm. Blackish thrush with white underparts and wing-spots. Slaty-black upperparts and tail with a few large white spots on wing-coverts forming two broken wing-bars. White underparts with black scales on flanks. Black bill and legs. In flight, shows black underwing with white stripe. Juvenile is unknown.
Similar species Differs from other black and white birds, e.g. fantails and monarchs, by habits and larger size. When flushed, differs from Island Thrush by white underparts and wing-spots.

Voice A thin high-pitched call as in other *Zoothera* thrushes.
Habits Poorly known. Montane forest around 1500 m and reported to feed in gardens of taro (Araceae crops) within montane forest. Singles recorded on ground, flushing off with low fast whirring flight.
Conservation status Rare and very localised but probably overlooked. IUCN: Near Threatened.
Range Endemic to Bougainville where known from one region in the Crown Prince Range.

MAKIRA THRUSH *Zoothera margaretae* Plate 73

(San Cristobal Thrush; also combined with Guadalcanal Thrush *Z. turipavae* as White-bellied Thrush and also with New Britain Thrush *Z. talaseae* as North Melanesian Ground Thrush; Grive de San Cristobal)

Description 23 cm. Brown thrush with scaly underparts. Plain dark olive-brown upperparts with two irregular wing-bars of white spots, and buffy mottling on head. Creamy-white underparts, throat mottled brown, breast and flanks with large dark brown scales, and central belly to undertail-coverts plainer white. Dark bill and long pink legs. In flight, shows dark underwing with white stripe. Juvenile has more obvious dark scales on upperparts and pale spots on crown.
Similar species When flushed, differs from Bronze Ground Dove by slower whirring flight without glides.
Voice Song is a simple series of tuneless clicks, grates and whistles, often with long gaps between notes. Call a very thin, high-pitched *tseeeep* becoming quieter but varying in length and lacking quaver of Variable Dwarf Kingfisher, and higher-pitched and less ringing than White-collared Monarch. Soft *chook*. Sharp *chik*. Wings whirr in flight.
Habits Forest in hills and lower mountains, including overgrown gardens, 200–700 m. Distinct preference for upper reaches of steep gullies. Singles and pairs forage on ground but usually sing from understorey thickets. May emerge onto paths to feed at dawn. Skulking and shy.
Conservation status Locally fairly common in surveyed areas. IUCN: Near Threatened.
Range Endemic to Makira.

GUADALCANAL THRUSH *Zoothera turipavae* Plate 66

(Also combined with San Cristobal Thrush *Z. margaretae* as White-bellied Thrush and also with New Britain Thrush *Z. talaseae* as North Melanesian Ground Thrush; Grive de Guadalcanal)

Description 20 cm. Brown thrush with scaly underparts. Plain dark grey-brown upperparts with indistinct buffy eye-ring. Creamy-buff underparts with large dusky-brown scales, most prominent on flanks, and whiter on central belly and vent. Black bill and long dark legs. In flight, shows dark underwing with white stripe. Juvenile has two broken wing-bars of orange-buff spots.
Similar species Differs from Island Thrush by browner plumage, scaly underparts and black bill and legs.
Voice Loud melodious song, a series of slurred whistles, short trills and repeated modulated whistles, with occasional call notes. Sings regularly at dawn, moving song-post every few minutes, but rarely in day. Very thin high-pitched *tssss*, occasionally lengthened into a hiss.
Habits Poorly known. Montane forest at 1400–1500 m. Singles recorded on or very close to ground. Skulking but not shy of a stationary observer.
Conservation status Known only from one specimen and two sightings at one site but probably overlooked. IUCN: Vulnerable.
Range Endemic to Guadalcanal where known only from Turipava above Honiara.

ISLAND THRUSH *Turdus poliocephalus* Plates 57, 66, 74, 77, 80 & 85

(Merle des Îles)

Description 20 cm. Blackish-brown thrush with bright orange-yellow bill, legs and eye-ring. Plumage varies greatly between subspecies but is usually dark brownish-black, often with rufous, grey or white on underparts. Female is often paler or with paler markings. Juvenile is sometimes plain, sometimes brown with paler spots and streaks on upperparts and/or black spots and bars on underparts. Some subspecies also have a distinct subadult plumage.
Similar species Differs from *Zoothera* thrushes by uniform plumage, yellow bare parts and plain dark underwing. Differs from other plain dark birds such as starlings, large honeyeaters and thicketbirds by habits and yellow bare parts.
Voice Calls often. Variable throaty calls such as *cha*, *chhok* or *tchik*, often repeated slowly, or rapidly as a chattering alarm call given in flight or when perched. Thin weak *tseeet* whistle. Some subspecies have a quiet melodious fluting song. These calls are similar to Common Blackbird *T. merula*.
Habits Forest floor. Montane on most large islands but down to sea-level on some islands. Singles or small family groups feed in leaf-litter, sometimes in low fruiting bushes, of primary and secondary forest and secondary regrowth.

Confiding on some islands but shy on others.
Conservation status Locally common but uncommon and declining or even extinct on some islands in Vanuatu and New Caledonia. Species not at risk but several subspecies threatened or believed extinct.
Range Scattered across Melanesia, missing from many islands in Admiralties and Solomons.
T. p. heinrothi, endemic to Mussau, is brown-black with slightly paler underparts; fairly common at all altitudes.
T. p. tolokiwae, endemic to Tolokiwa, is dark grey-brown with slight paler fringes on belly, female paler with broad rufous fringes on belly, juvenile with rufous spots on head and wing-coverts, and pale streaks on underparts; fairly common above 750 m.
T. p. beehleri, endemic to south New Ireland, has blackish upperparts with grey-brown face and throat, female browner with paler brown fringes on belly; common above 1500 m.
An undetermined subspecies, endemic to the Nakanais of New Britain, is uniform brownish-black, slightly paler on underparts, the presumed female being slightly paler; locally fairly common at 1400–1650 m.
T. p. bougainvillei, endemic to Bougainville, is uniform brown-black, female with greyer back and brown fringes on belly, and juvenile with more pale fringes on underparts; fairly common above 1200 m.
T. p. kulambangrae, endemic to Kolombangara, is brown-black, female and juvenile with some orange fringes on underparts; fairly common above 1040 m.
T. p. sladeni, endemic to Guadalcanal, is brown-black and slightly paler on underparts; fairly common above 1200 m.
T. p. rennellianus, endemic to Rennell, is sooty-brown with rufous or sometimes white fringes on flanks to undertail-coverts, female paler and browner, juvenile even paler and browner; common at all altitudes.
T. p. vanikorensis, endemic to Utupua, Vanikoro, Santo and Malo, is brown-black with slightly greyer underparts, female with paler underparts and white tips to undertail-coverts, subadult with buff fringes on underparts, juvenile browner with orange and brown spots and bars on underparts; fairly common at all altitudes on Santo but has not been recorded recently on Utupua or Vanikoro.
T. p. placens, endemic to Ureparapara and Vanua Lava, has dull brown upperparts, greyer throat and breast, rufous belly especially in female, subadult with broad whitish streaks on undertail-coverts, juvenile with pale orange tips to wing-coverts; common from at least 0–500 m on Vanua Lava.
T. p. whitneyi, endemic to Gaua and this or another subspecies on Mere Lava, is sooty-black with slightly browner face to breast, female with browner upperparts, chestnut fringes to flanks and belly, and whitish streaks on undertail-coverts, subadult with broader fringes and streaks, juvenile with orange-buff underparts with sooty spots on breast and flanks, and smaller spots on belly and vent; fairly common from at least 100–500 m.
T. p. malekulae, endemic to Pentecost, Malekula and Ambrym, and this or another subspecies on Maewo and Ambae, has brown-black upperparts, slightly greyer underparts, orange-rufous on flanks and belly and white vent, female with upperparts washed olive and a buff breast, subadult more uniform sooty with white undertail-coverts, juvenile with pale-streaked brown upperparts and dark brown spots on pale buff breast and flanks; common on Malekula in dry lowland forest and wet hill forest.
T. p. becki, endemic to Paama, Lopevi, Epi and Emae, is brown-black with paler grey face and underparts, and white central belly and white streaks on undertail-coverts, female with more rufous on flanks, subadult with orange wash on flanks and belly, juvenile paler, spotted dark brown with some pale wing-covert tips, pale buff breast-sides and white central belly; one recent series of records from 300 m on Epi.
T. p. efatensis, endemic to Efate and Nguna, is sooty-brown with white streaks on vent and undertail-coverts, female and subadult slightly browner with rufous-brown breast and flanks, juvenile with pale spots on head and wing-coverts, buff throat and buff-brown underparts with darker spots; at least one recent record at *c.*150 m.
T. p. albifrons, endemic to Erromango, is brown-black, with white head, throat and breast, sometimes with white or rufous fringes on belly in male and greyish-buff in female, rufous central breast and some white on undertail-coverts, juvenile dull brown with yellow-buff spots and streaks on upperparts, buff throat, and rufous-brown underparts with darker spots and bars and white lower belly and vent; one recent record above 300 m.
T. p. pritzbueri, endemic to Tanna, and Lifou and this or another subspecies on Futuna, has head and breast creamy-white or very pale grey in male, duller brownish-grey in female with dark rufous lower breast and belly, juvenile entirely rufous-brown with paler spots and streaks, and white lower belly and vent; uncommon in hills above *c.*400 m on Tanna but probably extinct at all altitudes on Lifou.
T. p. mareensis, endemic to Maré, male with black upperparts and brownish-black underparts with white streaks on undertail-coverts and faint white tips on flanks and belly, female browner, more rufous on underparts, sometimes with grey belly, juvenile entirely dull brown with orange-buff spots and streaks and white vent and undertail-coverts; probably extinct.
T. p. xanthopus, endemic to New Caledonia and adjacent small islands, and possibly extinct except for the very small islet of Yandé, is plain rufous-brown, mottled paler on underparts and white around vent.
Elsewhere, another 35 subspecies occur from Sumatra and Taiwan to Fiji and Samoa. Many subspecies are very distinct and could be treated as separate species.

SONG THRUSH *Turdus philomelos* (not illustrated)

Description 22 cm. Brown thrush with prominent small black spots on underparts. Plain olive-brown, upperparts with mottled ear-coverts, and creamy underparts with small round black spots. Dark bill with yellowish base and dull pink legs. Immature has pale shaft-streaks on mantle and wing-coverts.
Similar species Differs from Island Thrush by black spots on underparts and dull bare parts.
Voice Short sharp *tsip* often given in flight. Alarm call a series of *chook* or *kup* notes becoming louder and faster. Song is a series of loud ringing melodious simple phrases each repeated 2–4 times.
Habits Forest, scrub and nearby short grassland, especially parks and suburbia. Runs and hops on ground, forages for fruit in bushes, and sings from high perches.
Range One record from Vanuatu. Recorded in the 1930s, presumably from the introduced population in New Zealand. Elsewhere, occurs in Europe to central Russia, with introduced populations in and around New Zealand including Norfolk Island and Lord Howe Island.

CHATS AND FLYCATCHERS Muscicapidae

The only Melanesian species of this large family is a small thrush-like flycatcher.

PIED BUSH CHAT *Saxicola caprata* Plate 58

(Pied Chat; Tarier pie)

Description 14 cm. Small dumpy bird which perches conspicuously in open habitats. Male is glossy black with white wing-streak, rump and vent. Female is dark grey-brown with indistinct streaking, slightly paler underparts, white rump and vent and blackish tail. Juvenile male like female but has pale buff spots on head, breast and upperparts, and white wing-streak and rump. Juvenile female similar but has buffy rump and lacks white wing-streak.
Similar species Male is distinctive. Female differs from Varied Triller by white rump, indistinct white on wing and faint streaking but lacks barring on underparts.
Voice Song is a weak high-pitched warble of repeated phrases of 4–8 irregular notes, changing phrase after several repetitions. Song sometimes given in flight with slow wing-beats between two high perches, and at night. Harsh *tsak-tsak* call, often mixed with plaintive *hweet* call.
Habits Open habitats, especially grasslands with low scrub but also in gardens, generally in lowlands but also in hills to at least 1200 m. Perches conspicuously on branches, posts, wires, rocks and tall grass, and drops to ground to pick up insects. Flicks wings.
Conservation status Rare and local in Melanesia. Not threatened.
Range *S. c. aethiops* breeds locally on New Ireland, Long, Watom and New Britain but no records from west New Britain, and elsewhere breeds in lowland north New Guinea, and other subspecies occur across central and south Asia and New Guinea.

FLOWERPECKERS Dicaeidae

Very small dumpy birds with short stout bills and short tails. Feed on small fruit and insects in the canopy, calling frequently as they fly fast between treetops.

RED-BANDED FLOWERPECKER *Dicaeum eximium* Plate 52

(Dicée des Bismarck)

Description 8 cm. Tiny dumpy bird, mostly brown with red rump and white on underparts. Plain brown upperparts except for red rump and black tail, grey-brown sides of neck extending onto upper breast-sides, otherwise underparts white with buffy-olive flanks. Male has red central breast-spot continuing as dark midline stripe on lower breast and belly, and bronze gloss on upperparts. Female has white stripe down underparts midline and short white supercilium. Juvenile like female but has ill-defined underparts pattern and soon develops red rump.
Similar species Distinctive stubby shape, short bill and underparts pattern.
Voice Single notes and series of notes but no trills. Hard sucking *tik* or *tck*, lower-pitched than sunbirds. High-pitched *psst* or *tsee*.
Habits Forest, including degraded forest and forest edge but rarely coastal or montane forest, to 1000 m, rarely to 1500 m. Singles or pairs forage in canopy of forest.

Conservation status Fairly common. Not threatened.
Range Endemic to Bismarcks.
D. e. layardorum, endemic to New Britain, including Lolobau and Watom, has greyer head and green gloss on upperparts.
D. e. eximium, endemic to Lavongai and New Ireland, is browner especially on head, neck and breast-sides.
D. e. phaeopygium, endemic to Djaul, has much duller or no red on rump.

MIDGET FLOWERPECKER *Dicaeum aeneum* Plate 62

(Solomons Flowerpecker; Dicée des Salomon)

Description 8 cm. Tiny dumpy bird with blue-green upperparts and buff flanks. Dark grey upperparts with blue or green gloss, grey face and breast-sides, white throat, buffy-olive flanks and creamy belly and vent. Male has red central breast and dark grey lower breast. Female lacks red, but has creamy-white stripe from chin to belly, duller upperparts, white eyelids and sometimes a short white loral stripe or supercilium. Juvenile has darker buffier underparts and pale bill.
Similar species Distinctive stubby shape, short bill, male with red central breast, female with white stripe on underparts.
Voice Song is a series of *tik* notes, then high-pitched notes. Repeated metallic high-pitched *tik*, more metallic and constant than Olive-backed Sunbird. Repeated very high thin sibilant *tssssp* or *tssee-tseep*, similar to Finsch's Pygmy Parrot but longer gaps between notes. Two or three note *tzu-de* or *tzu-de-du*.
Habits Forest, including secondary scrub with isolated trees, and montane forest to highest altitudes.
Singles and pairs are active in canopy, less often understorey.
Conservation status Common. Not threatened.
Range Endemic to the Solomons.
D. a. aeneum, endemic to Buka, Bougainville, Shortland, Choiseul, Isabel and Florida Is, has upperparts glossed blue.
D. a. malaitae, endemic to Malaita, has upperparts with faint blue gloss, paler underparts and longer thinner bill.
D. a. becki, endemic to Guadalcanal, has upperparts glossed green, flanks darker olive, and throat-patch more scarlet.

MOTTLED FLOWERPECKER *Dicaeum tristrami* Plate 70

(Dicée de San Cristobal)

Description 9 cm. Tiny dumpy dark brown and white bird with tiny bill. Chocolate-brown crown and upperparts, black chin and variable bib, variable whitish supercilium extending down behind ear-coverts, white scaling on crown, face and bib, and pale brownish-white underparts. Male has blackish bib from chin and lower ear-coverts onto upper breast. Female has smaller brown bib and more white around eye and ear-coverts. Large individual variation in extent of white on face, amount of scaling and size of bib. Juvenile has plainer head, bib and breast.
Similar species Distinctive tiny size, dumpy shape and brown plumage.
Voice Short harsh calls, often repeated, when perched and in flight, varying in harshness, e.g. *tzip* or *zeet*, *tch* and *tsu*. Quiet guttural warbling song.
Habits Forest but commonest in degraded forest and forest edge, sometimes in coconuts. All altitudes but commonest in hills and mountains. Singles and pairs are active and pugnacious in forest, especially canopy, often feeding in fruiting trees and ant-plants, and hovering.
Conservation status Common. Not threatened.
Range Endemic to Makira.

SUNBIRDS Nectariniidae

Small nectivorous and insectivorous birds with long decurved bills. Active and brightly coloured, similar to *Myzomela* honeyeaters but lack red in plumage and with slightly longer bills.

BLACK SUNBIRD *Leptocoma sericea* Plate 52

(*Nectarinia aspasia*; Souimanga satiné)

Description 11 cm. Small dumpy bird with long decurved bill. Male is entirely glossy black with an iridescent green crown, green-blue wing-coverts and mantle, blue throat and purple tail. Female has mid-grey head, olive upperparts with browner wings, black tail with white corners, pale grey throat and dull yellow underparts. Juvenile has yellower throat and greyer underparts than female. Immature male initially has black malar stripe.

Similar species Male differs from Bismarck Black Myzomela on small islets by iridescent patches, dark underwings and slightly longer bill. Female differs from female Olive-backed Sunbird and myzomelas by grey head and white throat.
Voice Song is a rapid tinkling cadence for up to four seconds. High-pitched sibilant single and slurred notes, eg *zi*, *pit*, *swee*, sometimes alternating in pitch, sometimes repeated as a series or trill. Chattering scold. Notes are louder and more varied than Black-bellied Myzomela.
Habits Forest edge, scrub and coconuts, less common in closed forest; in lowlands, less common in hills to 1400 m. Singles and pairs are active around canopy and flowers, often mixed with other small birds and sometimes hovering.
Conservation status Common. Not threatened.
Range Bismarcks.
L. a. corinna, endemic to New Ireland, including Lavongai, Djaul, Tabar, Lihir and Duke of York, male with blue throat.
L. a. eichhorni, endemic to Feni, male with bluish-purple throat, greyer crown and bluer wing-coverts.
L. a. caeruleogula, endemic to New Britain, including Umboi, Sakar, Bali and Watom, is smaller than *L. a. corinna*. Elsewhere, other subspecies breed in east Indonesia and New Guinea.

OLIVE-BACKED SUNBIRD *Cinnyris jugularis* — Plates 52, 62 & 70

(Yellow-bellied Sunbird; *Nectarinia jugularis*; Souimanga à dos vert)

Description 11 cm. Small sunbird with bright yellow underparts and narrow supercilium, and long decurved bill. Dull olive upperparts and dark tail with white corners. Male has metallic purple-blue throat and upper breast. Female has uniformly yellow underparts. Juvenile like female but has duller underparts. Immature male initially has broad blue stripe on central throat and upper breast.
Similar species Male is distinctive. Female differs from Black Sunbird and myzomelas by uniform bright yellow underparts. Female from Black Sunbird by no grey head.
Voice Song is a fast twittering trill of short thin whistles. Repeated sharp high-pitched *zit*, softer and slower than flowerpeckers. Rather nasal upslurred *toy?*, sometimes disyllabic.
Habits Open forest habitats, including towns, scrub, mangroves and coconuts but rarely in closed forest. Commonest along coast but occasionally inland to 800 m. Singles and pairs are active and aggressive, often hovering around flowers.
Conservation status Common. Not threatened.
Range *C. j. flavigaster*, endemic to the Admiralties, St Matthias Is, Bismarcks and Solomons, including Ninigo Is, Hermit Is, Admiralties, St Matthias, New Ireland, New Britain and all but the smallest islands in the Bismarcks, and throughout the Solomons including Ulawa, Ugi and Three Sisters but excluding Makira, Rennell and the most far-flung atolls, has deeper yellow underparts than other subspecies. Elsewhere, other subspecies breed from South-East Asia to Australia.

SPARROWS Passeridae

Small heavy-billed seed-eating birds with short wings and rather long tails, similar to finches and waxbills. Sparrows are brown with a slightly forked tail and usually found close to buildings.

HOUSE SPARROW *Passer domesticus* — Plates 81 & 86

(Moineau domestique)

Description 15 cm. Rather stocky, often scruffy grey-brown sparrow with heavy bill. Adult male has pale grey cap, cheeks and underparts with black bill and throat, rufous-brown upperparts with buff and black striping, white wing-bar and grey rump. Non-breeding male has grey wash to nape and throat, and yellow-horn bill. Adult female has grey-brown underparts and buffy-brown upperparts with broad buffy supercilium, black and buff mottling and striping on mantle and wings, white wing-bar and yellowish bill. Juvenile like female but often paler, more distinct supercilium and paler bill.
Similar species Often the only species in town centre habitats. Female differs from Common Waxbill and mannikins by larger size, blackish mottling on mantle and wings, and long, slightly forked tail. Male differs from Eurasian Tree Sparrow, a potential vagrant, by unmarked pale cheeks, grey cap and extensive black bib.
Voice Repeated monotonous *chirp* or *chirrup*. Harsher *chissik*. Soft *swee*. Song is a series of *chirp* notes varying in pitch.

Habits Towns, feeding in all habitats especially buildings, bare areas, short grassland and scattered trees. Sometimes in nearby farms and agricultural fields. Gregarious, hops on ground and scratches in dust.
Conservation status Introduced to just two islands in Melanesia where now common. Not globally threatened.
Range *P. d. domesticus* is an introduced resident on Efate and New Caledonia. Currently restricted to Port Vila on Efate but widespread across Grande Terre on New Caledonia, except for the east coast, and may spread to other towns. Elsewhere, various subspecies are native to Eurasia, with introduced populations in Australia and New Zealand.

EURASIAN TREE SPARROW *Passer montanus* (not illustrated)

(Moineau friquet)

Description 13 cm. Thickset brown sparrow with chestnut cap and black spot on white cheeks. White cheeks and nape with chestnut cap, black ear-covert spot and chin, rusty-brown mantle and wings with black and buff streaks and white wing-bar and plain buffy underparts. Juvenile is similar but has dusky cheeks and paler bill.
Similar species See House Sparrow above. Differs from Common Waxbill and mannikins by larger size, blackish mottling on mantle and wings, and shorter slightly forked tail.
Voice Repeated chattering *chirp* or *chirrup*. Disyllabic *tsuWITT*. Dry *tett-ett-* flight-call. Song is a rapid series of varied *tsvit*-like notes.
Habits Towns, feeding in all habitats especially buildings, bare areas, short grassland and weeds. Gregarious, hops on ground, scratches in dust.
Range A new colony in Kimbe, New Britain, and single records from Honiara and Auki, Solomons. May occur anywhere, especially towns with ships arriving from Asia. Elsewhere, native across Europe and Asia, and introduced to south-east Australia.

WAXBILLS Estrildidae

Very small heavy-billed seed-eating birds flying fast on short whirring wings, similar to the introduced finches and sparrows. Waxbills *Estrilda* are gregarious grassland finches with silvery barred plumage. Parrotfinches *Erythrura* are secretive, uncommon and unobtrusive forest species with bright green plumage with red and blue patches. Munias or mannikins *Lonchura* are gregarious grassland species, with black, brown and white plumage and a blue-grey bill. Many species are kept in captivity and escaped individuals have been reported from Melanesia.

COMMON WAXBILL *Estrilda astrild* Plates 81 & 86

(Astrild ondulé)

Description 12 cm. Very small finch with red bill and mask, and relatively long pointed tail. Bright waxy-red bill and broad mask through eye, grey-brown upperparts, off-white cheeks, paler grey-brown underparts, black undertail-coverts and indistinct red belly-patch, with fine dark barring everywhere except face and throat. Juvenile has black bill, smaller duller red eye-mask and less distinct dark barring.
Similar species Differs from juvenile Chestnut-breasted Mannikin and Chestnut Munia by paler greyer plumage, red eye-mask and bill, and longer tail. From sparrows by smaller size, red eye-mask and bill, finely barred mantle and wings, and longer pointed tail.
Voice Short sharp *pit* or *tchik*. Quiet nasal *cher* flight call. Song is a short series of notes e.g *cher, pee, dit, chewi*.
Habits Tall grassland, especially wet grassland, and adjacent short grassland, cultivation and gardens. Gregarious. Perches on grass stems and feeds, often acrobatically, on seed-heads, hops on ground with raised tail, and flies in dense flocks with short whirring wings, often landing on fences or bushes.
Conservation status Introduced, locally common and probably still increasing. Not globally threatened.
Range *E. a. astrild* is a non-native resident on Efate and New Caledonia, on Grande Terre and Ile des Pins, where now widespread in suitable habitat, but extirpated from Santo. Elsewhere, various subspecies are native to sub-Saharan Africa, and introduced populations elsewhere, including Tahiti and Hawaii.

BLUE-FACED PARROTFINCH *Erythrura trichroa* Plates 60, 67, 81 & 86

(Diamant de Kittlitz)

Description 12 cm. Bright green finch with blue face and red tail. Plain bright grass-green with deep blue on face and forehead onto crown, darker green wings and rusty-red rump and uppertail. Female is slightly duller with less blue. Juvenile is duller with yellower underparts, pale bill and no blue on face.

Similar species Distinctive size, green plumage and red tail. Adult differs from Royal Parrotfinch on Vanuatu by blue face and green neck. Juvenile differs from Royal Parrotfinch by lack of blue tint on neck, smaller bill and no red on crown.

Voice Quiet very thin *tsit* notes, including a rapid descending series of 2–5 notes. In flight, regularly repeated *zz* notes, about one per second. Lower-pitched and better-defined notes than pygmy parrots.

Habits Forest and secondary forest, especially with thickets, bamboo and *Casuarina* trees, at all altitudes but commoner in mountains on high islands. Singles, pairs or small loose flocks forage unobtrusively at all levels of forest, occasionally with mixed-species flocks. In Vanuatu, also occurs in open habitats including forest clearings, gardens and short grass lawns.

Conservation status Local, usually uncommon or rare but easily overlooked. Not globally threatened.

Range Scattered across Melanesia.

E. t. sigillifera breeds on New Ireland and New Britain, including Crown, Long, Tolokiwa, Umboi and Feni; elsewhere, breeds on New Guinea and north Australia.

E. t. eichhorni, endemic to Mussau and Emirau where fairly common, has more blue on forehead and more orange rump.

E. t woodfordi, endemic to Guadalcanal and probably this subspecies on Bougainville and Kolombangara, where rare and usually montane, has smaller, more violet-blue face-patch and more orange rump and tail.

E. t. cyanofrons, endemic to Lifou, Maré and Vanuatu, including Gaua, Ambae, Ambrym, Lopevi, Efate, Nguna, Emau, Erromango, Tanna and Aneityum, has violet-blue face extending further on crown.

Elsewhere, other subspecies occur in Indonesia to Australia and Micronesia.

RED-THROATED PARROTFINCH *Erythrura psittacea* — Plate 86

(Diamant psittaculaire)

Description 12 cm. Bright green finch with red face, throat and tail. Plain grass-green except for red forehead, face, throat and upper breast, and rump and uppertail. Long pointed tail. Female is slightly duller with less red on throat. Juvenile is duller with yellower underparts, with no red on face and pale bill with dark tip; young juvenile has pale wash on face.

Similar species Distinctive size, green plumage and red tail.

Voice Very thin high-pitched single or series of *pst* notes. Song is probably a trill based on this note.

Habits Forest edge, scrub and grassy habitats, including fields, savanna, tracks within forest and edge of *maquis* scrub, but uncommon within closed forest. Singles, pairs and small flocks usually feed on ground but also in bushes and forest canopy, including *Casuarina* trees.

Conservation status Common. Not globally threatened.

Range Endemic to New Caledonia where widespread on Grande Terre and Ile des Pins.

ROYAL PARROTFINCH *Erythrura regia* — Plate 81

(Also combined with Samoan Parrotfinch *E. cyaneovirens* as Royal Parrotfinch *E. cyaneovirens*, or with Samoan and Red-headed Parrotfinch *E. pealii* as Red-headed Parrotfinch *E. cyaneovirens*; Diamant des Nouvelles-Hébrides)

Description 12 cm. Bright red, blue and green forest finch. Bright red crown and face, rump and uppertail, bright blue nape, mantle, neck-sides and underparts from chin to flanks, and blue-green wings, belly and vent. Female has greener mantle, wings, breast and flanks. Juvenile is duller, largely green with paler underparts, pale bill with dark tip and grey-blue face.

Similar species Distinctive size, colours and red tail. Adult differs from Blue-faced Parrotfinch by blue plumage with red head. Juvenile differs from Blue-faced Parrotfinch by blue tint on neck, heavier bill and usually some red on crown.

Voice High thin *seep* notes, repeated more frequently in flight, similar to other parrotfinches. Single thin drawn-out *treeeeee* alarm call. Song is a series of high trills.

Habits Old-growth forest and forest edge and, on smaller islands, degraded and open habitats with large fig trees. Commoner in hills and mountains especially on larger islands. Singles, pairs and rarely small flocks feed in canopy of fig trees. Usually shy.

Conservation status Uncommon or rare on most islands but fairly common on Epi, Tongoa and Emae. IUCN: Vulnerable.

Range Endemic to Vanuatu, where recent records from Gaua, Santo, Epi, Tongoa, Emae and Efate, and older records from Ambae, Pentecost, Malekula, Ambrym, Paama, Lopevi and Aneityum. Efate birds are sometimes split as *E. r. efatensis* and Aneityum birds, with greener back and belly, sometimes as *E. r. serena*.

STREAK-HEADED MANNIKIN *Lonchura tristissima* Plate 60

(Streak-headed Munia; Capucin à tête rayée)

Description 10 cm. Fairly uniform blackish-brown mannikin with buffy-yellow rump. Heavy blue-grey bill, dark rufous-brown upperparts with variable, often indistinct, pale markings, sooty-brown underparts, bright buffy-yellow rump and black tail. Head and nape have paler buffy streaks, upper mantle has pale grey spots, lower mantle has fine rufous bars, and wing has some creamy-white tips and wing-bars. Female has less streaking on upperparts and face, less yellow on rump and indistinct scaling on underparts. Juvenile has dull orangey rump and less distinct streaks on head.
Similar species Differs from juvenile Hooded Mannikin by much darker underparts and pale streaks, spots and bars on upperparts.
Voice Buzzing *zhu* or *tseed*, softer and lower-pitched than Hooded Mannikin. Short explosive *tzip!* Song is a rapid jumbled 7–8-second series of nasal, squeaky and simple notes. (Call descriptions from New Guinea.)
Habits Forest edge, clearings, cultivation and grassland, always close to forest, in lowlands. Pairs and small flocks feed on grasses, weeds and bushes.
Conservation status Rare and localised on Umboi, where first seen in 1998. Not globally threatened.
Range Probably breeds on Umboi. Most similar to *L. t. calaminoros* on Karkar but there are no specimens and it may represent an endemic subspecies. Elsewhere, *L. t. calaminoros* breeds across central north New Guinea and Karkar, and other subspecies breed in south and west New Guinea.

CHESTNUT MUNIA *Lonchura atricapilla* Plate 81

(Chestnut Mannikin; also treated as a subspecies of Black-headed Munia/Mannikin *L. malacca*; Capucin à dos marron)

Description 11 cm. Chestnut-brown mannikin with black hood. Heavy blue-grey bill, black head, neck and upper breast, chestnut-brown body and wings but wings may fade paler, yellowish-orange rump and uppertail, and darker central belly to vent. Often appears plain dark brown. Female has duller hood, paler upperparts and less dark on belly. Juvenile is uniform and pale, with buffy-brown upperparts and tawny-buff underparts, soon becoming darker on head.
Similar species Adult is distinctive, Juvenile differs from House Sparrow by plain plumage, small size and short tail. From juvenile Chestnut-breasted Mannikin by uniform underparts and unmarked or dark head.
Voice Quiet nasal *dhu*, softer and lower-pitched than Vanuatu White-eye. Song is a long series of bill-snapping and very quiet whistling.
Habits Grassland, especially long grass in wet fields, also grassy patches around towns, roadsides, wetlands and mangroves, in lowlands, but not dry grasslands in hills. Dense flocks feed on grasses and fly up to fences and low bushes.
Conservation status Introduced. Locally common. Not threatened.
Range Introduced to Santo, where now widespread including Aore and Malo, and Malekula since the 1990s. Elsewhere, it is native in India to China.

HOODED MANNIKIN *Lonchura spectabilis* Plate 60

(New Britain Mannikin; Hooded Mannikin; Capucin à capuchon)

Description 10 cm. Clean-cut mannikin with glossy black hood, brown upperparts and creamy-white underparts. Heavy blue-grey bill, yellow-orange rump and tail, black central belly to undertail-coverts and sometimes faint brown barring on breast and flanks. Juvenile is paler buffy-brown, faintly streaked black on face and throat, with paler buff on underparts and brighter rufous rump. Immature soon develops darker head.
Similar species Adult's clear-cut creamy-white underparts are distinctive. Individuals with dark markings on underparts differ from Buff-bellied Mannikin by otherwise white breast and belly, smaller bill and paler mantle. In flight, differs from Buff-bellied Mannikin by paler mantle, contrasting strongly with black head, and yellower rump and uppertail. Juvenile differs from very similar juvenile Buff bellied Mannikin by smaller bill, but note that juvenile has smaller bill than adult. From Streak-headed Mannikin on Umboi by much paler underparts and unmarked upperparts.
Voice Soft nasal *peep*. Staccato *tch-tch-tch-*. Higher-pitched, more metallic and less buzzing than Buff-bellied Mannikin. Song is a series of *wee* notes, clicking and long whistles. (Song description from New Guinea.)
Habits Grassland, commonest in extensive drier grasslands in lowlands, also grassy cultivation. Gregarious, often in large flocks, feeding low in grass and flying up to perch on grass-tops or low branches or fences.
Conservation status Locally common. Not globally threatened.

Range *L. s. spectabilis* is endemic to New Britain, where local with most records from north coast, and Long, Tolokiwa, Umboi and Watom. Elsewhere, other subspecies breed across north and central New Guinea.

FORBES'S MANNIKIN *Lonchura forbesi* — Plate 60

(New Ireland Mannikin/Munia; Capucin de Nouvelle-Irlande)

Description 11 cm. Black-headed mannikin with orange-brown underparts. Massive blue-grey bill, glossy black head and neck, warm orange-chestnut mantle and wings, brighter orange-buff rump and uppertail, and rich orange-brown underparts with sooty central belly to undertail-coverts. Sometimes has silvery speckling on breast, or blackish speckling on flanks and belly. Juvenile is paler buffy-brown, streaked dark on crown and faintly streaked black on face and throat, paler buff on underparts and brighter rufous rump-patch; head soon becomes darker.
Similar species Juvenile differs from Hunstein's Mannikin on north New Ireland by paler plumage, pale throat and breast, lack of streaking on lower breast, and streaked crown.
Voice Nasal *dhu* flight call. Song is unknown.
Habits Grassland, including small grassy and weedy areas in forest clearings, in lowlands and hills to 1000 m. Small flocks or pairs.
Conservation status Poorly known with few recent records of small numbers of birds, but widespread and habitat not threatened.
Range Endemic to New Ireland, where known from a few scattered sites across the whole island.

HUNSTEIN'S MANNIKIN *Lonchura hunsteini* — Plate 60

(Mottled Mannikin/Munia; also treated as two species including New Hanover Mannikin *L. nigerrima*; Capucin de Hunstein)

Description 10 cm. Sooty-black mannikin with frosty silvery spots on head, bright orange-chestnut rump and uppertail, and heavy blue-grey bill. Some variation in extent of silvery spots but usually cover crown, nape and sides of neck, sometimes including face, upper breast and scattered on lower breast, but no spots on Lavongai birds. Female is greyer, with brighter uppertail-coverts and more often has white spots on flanks. Juvenile has dull brown upperparts with warm brown rump and uppertail, darker head and throat with streaks on breast, and pale tawny lower breast and belly. Immature soon develops pale speckling.
Similar species May overlap with Forbes's Mannikin. Silver-spotted black adults are distinctive. Juvenile differs from juvenile Forbes's Mannikin by darker plumage, dark throat and upper breast, streaking on lower breast and plain or spotted crown.
Voice Quiet tinkling *ti-ti-ti-*. Nasal *dzu* flight call. Song is unknown.
Habits Grassland, especially when extensive, also small grassy and weedy areas in forest clearings and grassy cultivation, in lowlands and hills. Gregarious.
Conservation status Locally common. Habitat not threatened but appears to have a very small range and small population.
Range Endemic to Lavongai and New Ireland, where only recorded from Kavieng south for c.120 km.
L. h. hunsteini is endemic to New Ireland.
L. h. nigerrima (New Hanover Mannikin), endemic to Lavongai, lacks any silvery spots and has paler orange rump and uppertail-coverts; sometimes treated as a separate species.
Elsewhere, introduced to Pohnpei north of New Guinea, where sometimes considered to be a separate subspecies *L. i. minor.*

CHESTNUT-BREASTED MANNIKIN *Lonchura castaneothorax* — Plates 81 & 86

(Chestnut-breasted Munia; Capucin donacole)

Description 11 cm. Variegated mannikin. Heavy blue-grey bill, blackish face and throat, speckled grey crown and nape, rich rufous-chestnut mantle and wings, bright golden rump and uppertail, orange breast, narrow black lower breast-band, white lower breast and belly with short thick black bars along flanks, and black undertail-coverts. Juvenile is plain pale grey-brown, with grey head, fine pale buff streaks on face and pale buff underparts with deeper buffy-orange on breast.
Similar species Adult is distinctive. Juvenile differs from House Sparrow by plain plumage, small size and short tail. Differs from Common Waxbill by short tail, dumpy shape and lack of red bill and eye-stripe.
Voice Nasal *dhu* flight call. Song is a long series of high-pitched notes, e.g. *weee, tuee cheeeouk, ching.*

Habits Flocks feed in grassland, cultivation and savanna, especially damp grassland, in lowlands and hills.
Conservation status Introduced. Fairly common and probably still increasing in numbers and range on New Caledonia but rare or localised on Santo where no recent records.
Range Introduced to Grande Terre, New Caledonia, where now widespread, and Santo, Vanuatu, where rare and local, probably *L. c. castaneothorax*. Elsewhere, six subspecies breed in Australia and New Guinea, and introduced to French Polynesia.

BUFF-BELLIED MANNIKIN *Lonchura melaena* Plates 60 & 67

(Bismarck/Thick-billed Mannikin/Munia; Capucin de Nouvelle-Bretagne)

Description 11 cm. Heavy-billed mannikin with black spots on orange-buff belly. Massive blue-grey bill, black head to lower breast, dark rufous-brown mantle and wings, fiery-orange rump and uppertail, orange-buff belly with black spots or bars on flanks, and black central belly and vent. Juvenile is pale buffy-brown, faintly streaked darker on face and throat, paler buff on underparts, and brighter rufous rump-patch. Immature soon develops darker head and throat.
Similar species Distinctive orange-buff belly with heavy black spots. On New Britain, differs from rare Hooded Mannikins with dark spots on underparts by black breast, orange-buff belly, heavier bill and darker mantle. In flight, differs from Hooded Mannikin by darker mantle, contrasting poorly with black head, and darker rump and uppertail. Juvenile differs from very similar juvenile Hooded Mannikin by heavier bill, but note that juvenile has smaller bill than adults, and richer buff underparts. On New Ireland, differs from Forbes's Mannikin by blackish breast and mantle.
Voice Nasal upslurred *peep*, lower-pitched, less metallic and more buzzing than Hooded Mannikin. Song is unknown.
Habits Grasslands, commonest in extensive wet lowland grasslands, but also grassy cultivation and grassy forest clearings to 1200 m. Usually in small flocks.
Conservation status Locally common on New Britain but absent from large areas. Although only known from a few locations, it probably occurs more widely. There are no apparent threats, but *L. m. bukaensis* has not been seen on Buka in recent years, was only known from a very small population, and may be extinct. However, recent discovery of species on New Ireland may indicate range expansion or that *L. m. bukaensis* survives in this island.
Range Endemic to Bismarcks and Buka.
L. m. melaena endemic to New Britain, where recorded only in north-east from Hoskins to Rabaul and no records from south, has brown crown and more black on flanks, sometimes solid black but often hidden under wings, and fiery-orange to rufous rump and uppertail.
L. m. bukaensis, endemic to Buka, where known only from around airstrip but reportedly more widespread, and perhaps this subspecies on New Ireland, where recorded from Kavieng to Limbin, has black crown, darker upperparts, less black on flanks, and darker rufous or chestnut rump and uppertail.

WAGTAILS Motacillidae

Small ground birds with very long tails which are habitually pumped up and down, not wagged from side to side. Walk or run on short grassland or along rivers. Two other migrant species, Citrine Wagtail *M. citreola* and White Wagtail *M. alba* are rare vagrants to Australia and may occur in Melanesia. (Note that Willie Wagtail is an unrelated fantail which habitually wags its long tail.)

EASTERN YELLOW WAGTAIL *Motacilla tschutschensis* Plate 50

(Also combined with Western Yellow Wagtail as Yellow Wagtail *M. flava*, or split into additional species including Green-headed Wagtail *M. taivana;* Bergeronnette printanière)

Description 17 cm. Elongate ground bird with relatively long dark legs and long black tail with white outer feathers. Non-breeding adult has olive-green or olive-brown upperparts with yellow or white supercilium, dark ear-coverts, white fringes on blackish wing-coverts and tertials, and pale yellow or white underparts. Breeding adult has yellow-green upperparts and bright yellow underparts. Male is brighter with bold, often blue-grey head patterns. Immature like non-breeding adult but upperparts browner and underparts buffy-white, often with dark necklace or breast-band.
Similar species Distinctive long tail and actions. Differs from Grey Wagtail by non-contrasting olive rump, greener upperparts, bolder wing-covert fringes, black legs, shorter tail and often no yellow on vent.
Voice Thin wheezing *szweep*, often given in flight, more explosive than Pacific Swallow.
Habits Short grasslands, swamps, mud and edges of lakes, occasionally along rivers or coasts. Singles or small groups walk and run on ground, pumping tail, sometimes perching in low bushes and following cattle.

Range Rare vagrant to Bismarcks and Bougainville. Breeds in east Asia and migrates south to tropical Asia, rarely to New Guinea, usually October–April.
M. f. simillima, recorded once from New Britain and Bougainville; adult male has grey head, white supercilium, yellow or white chin and often grey on breast.
M. f. taivana, recorded once from New Ireland; adult male has greenish head and back, dark green ear-coverts and yellow supercilium and chin.
Other subspecies or species, which may also occur as rare vagrants, breed from Europe to Alaska and migrate south to tropical Africa and Asia.

GREY WAGTAIL *Motacilla cinerea* Plate 50

(Bergeronnette des ruisseaux)

Description 18 cm. Elongate ground bird with relatively long pink-brown legs and long black tail with white outer feathers. Grey upperparts with white supercilium, blackish wings, buffy-white underparts with some yellow, and bright yellow vent, rump and tail-coverts. In flight, shows white wing-bar and white outer tail feathers. Breeding male has underparts all yellow except black throat. Immature has browner upperparts, indistinct supercilium and often dark breast-sides.
Similar species Distinctive long tail and actions. Differs from Eastern Yellow Wagtail by contrasting yellow rump, greyer upperparts, plainer wings, pinkish legs, longer tail and always yellow on vent.
Voice Loud metallic disyllabic *chitik* or *tzit-tzit*, often given in flight.
Habits Usually alongside fast-moving rivers and streams, also gravel roads and paths and air-strips. Singles walk and run, pumping tail, on banks of rivers and stones within rivers. Perches low in open bushes and trees.
Range Rare vagrant to Bismarcks, recorded once on Wuvulu and New Ireland, probably *M. c. robusta*. Elsewhere, six subspecies breed across Eurasia, migrating south to tropical Africa and Asia east to New Guinea, mostly from September to April.

FINCHES Fringillidae

Small heavy-billed seed-eating birds with short wings and rather long tails, similar to sparrows and waxbills. Finches are only known from one vagrant record.

COMMON REDPOLL *Carduelis flammea* (not illustrated)

(*Acanthis flammea*; also treated as Lesser Redpoll *C./A. cabaret*; Sizerin flammé)

Description 12 cm. Small streaky brown bird with very short stout bill and forked tail. Dark brown upperparts with dark streaks, two pale wing-bars, red forehead, black chin, and buffy-white underparts with heavy dark brown streaks. Breeding male has pink-red on face and breast. Female and immature have less red on forehead and little or no red on breast.
Similar species Differs from House Sparrow by streaking on underparts and red patches. From Common Waxbill by red on forehead, not through eye, and streaking.
Voice Repeated sharp metallic *cha-cha-* call, sometimes mixed with buzzing *bzzzz*, often given in flight. Thin upslurred *tsooet?* Song is a trill based on call notes, often given in song-flight.
Habits Forest and scrub edge and grasslands with scattered trees. Small groups feed on seeds on ground or in canopy.
Range Two records of single vagrants to Vanuatu, on Aneityum in 1961 and Tanna in 2008, presumably from the introduced population of *C. f. cabaret* in New Zealand. Elsewhere this subspecies occurs in northern Europe and other subspecies across northern Eurasia and America.

GAZETTEER

Island name	old / alternative name	Island group*	Archipelago	Nation
Alokan		Gu	Solomons	Solomon Islands
Ambae	Aoba	Vu	Vanuatu	Vanuatu
Ambrym		Vu	Vanuatu	Vanuatu
Aneityum	Anatom	Vu	Vanuatu	Vanuatu
Aniwa		Vu	Vanuatu	Vanuatu
Anuta	Cherry	Te	Temotu	Solomon Islands
Aore		Vu	Vanuatu	Vanuatu
Bagga	Mbava	NG	Solomons	Solomon Islands
Baluan		Mn	Admiralties	Papua New Guinea
Banks Is		Vu	Vanuatu	Vanuatu
Bellona		Rl	Solomons	Solomon Islands
Big Tabar		NI	Bismarcks	Papua New Guinea
Boang		NI	Bismarcks	Papua New Guinea
Bougainville		Bv	Solomons	Papua New Guinea
Buka		Bv	Solomons	Papua New Guinea
Chesterfield Reefs		GT	New Caledonia	New Caledonia (France)
Choiseul		Bv	Solomons	Solomon Islands
Crown		NB	Bismarcks	Papua New Guinea
Djaul		NI	Bismarcks	Papua New Guinea
Duff Is		Te	Temotu	Solomon Islands
Duke of York		NB	Bismarcks	Papua New Guinea
Efate		Vu	Vanuatu	Vanuatu
Emae		Vu	Vanuatu	Vanuatu
Emirau		Mu	St Matthias Is	Papua New Guinea
Epi		Vu	Vanuatu	Vanuatu
Erromango		Vu	Vanuatu	Vanuatu
Fauro		Bv	Solomons	Solomon Islands
Feni Is		NI	Bismarcks	Papua New Guinea
Fenualoa		Te	Temotu	Solomon Islands
Florida Is	Nggela Is	Gu	Solomons	Solomon Islands
Futuna		Vu	Vanuatu	Vanuatu

Island name	old / alternative name	Island group*	Archipelago	Nation
Gaua	Santa Maria	Vu	Vanuatu	Vanuatu
Ghaghe		Bv	Solomons	Solomon Islands
Gizo	Ghizo	NG	Solomons	Solomon Islands
Grande Terre	New Caledonia	GT	New Caledonia	New Caledonia (France)
Green Is		NI	Bismarcks	Papua New Guinea
Guadacanal		Gu	Solomons	Solomon Islands
Hermit Is		Mn	Admiralties	Papua New Guinea
Hunter I		GT	New Caledonia	New Caledonia (France)
Ile des Pins		GT	New Caledonia	New Caledonia (France)
Iles Belep		GT	New Caledonia	New Caledonia (France)
Isabel	Santa Isabel	Bv	Solomons	Solomon Islands
Kaniet Is	Anchorite Is	Mn	Admiralties	Papua New Guinea
Kilinailau	Carteret Is	Bv	Solomons	Papua New Guinea
Kohinggo		NG	Solomons	Solomon Islands
Kolombangara	Kulambangara	NG	Solomons	Solomon Islands
Lavongai	New Hanover	NI	Bismarcks	Papua New Guinea
Lifou	Lifu	Lo	New Caledonia	New Caledonia (France)
Lihir Is		NI	Bismarcks	Papua New Guinea
Lolobau		NB	Bismarcks	Papua New Guinea
Lomlom		Te	Temotu	Solomon Islands
Long		NB	Bismarcks	Papua New Guinea
Lopevi		Vu	Vanuatu	Vanuatu
Los Negros		Mn	Admiralties	Papua New Guinea
Lou		Mn	Admiralties	Papua New Guinea
Maewo	Aurora	Vu	Vanuatu	Vanuatu
Mahur		NI	Bismarcks	Papua New Guinea
Makalom		Te	Temotu	Solomon Islands
Makira	San Cristobal	Mk	Solomons	Solomon Islands
Malaita		Ml	Solomons	Solomon Islands
Malekula		Vu	Vanuatu	Vanuatu
Malendok		NI	Bismarcks	Papua New Guinea
Malo		Vu	Vanuatu	Vanuatu
Manus		Mn	Admiralties	Papua New Guinea

Island name	old / alternative name	Island group*	Archipelago	Nation
Maré		Lo	New Caledonia	New Caledonia (France)
Masahet		NI	Bismarcks	Papua New Guinea
Matthew I		GT	New Caledonia	New Caledonia (France)
Mbanika		Gu	Solomons	Solomon Islands
Mborokua		Gu	Solomons	Solomon Islands
Mere Lava		Vu	Vanuatu	Vanuatu
Mono		Bv	Solomons	Solomon Islands
Mota Lava		Vu	Vanuatu	Vanuatu
Mussau		Mu	St Matthias Is	Papua New Guinea
Nauna		Mn	Admiralties	Papua New Guinea
Ndai	Dai; Gower	MI	Solomons	Solomon Islands
Nendo	Ndeni; Santa Cruz	Te	Temotu	Solomon Islands
New Britain		NB	Bismarcks	Papua New Guinea
New Georgia		NG	Solomons	Solomon Islands
New Ireland		NI	Bismarcks	Papua New Guinea
Nggatokae	Gatukai	NG	Solomons	Solomon Islands
Nggela Sule		Gu	Solomons	Solomon Islands
Nifiloli		Te	Temotu	Solomon Islands
Ninigo Is		Mn	Admiralties	Papua New Guinea
Nissan	Green	NI	Bismarcks	Papua New Guinea
Nuguria Is	Fead Is	NI	Bismarcks	Papua New Guinea
Nukapu		Te	Temotu	Solomon Islands
Nukumanu		Bv	Solomons	Papua New Guinea
Nupani		Te	Temotu	Solomon Islands
Ontong Java		Bv	Solomons	Solomon Islands
Ouvéa	Uvea	Lo	New Caledonia	New Caledonia (France)
Paama		Vu	Vanuatu	Vanuatu
Pak		Mn	Admiralties	Papua New Guinea
Pavuvu		Gu	Solomons	Solomon Islands
Pentecost		Vu	Vanuatu	Vanuatu
Pileni		Te	Temotu	Solomon Islands
Rambutyo		Mn	Admiralties	Papua New Guinea
Ramos		Bv	Solomons	Solomon Islands

Island name	old / alternative name	Island group*	Archipelago	Nation
Ranongga	Ganonga	NG	Solomons	Solomon Islands
Reef Is	Swallow Is	Te	Temotu	Solomon Islands
Rendova		NG	Solomons	Solomon Islands
Rennell		Rl	Solomons	Solomon Islands
Russell Is		Gu	Solomons	Solomon Islands
Sakar		NB	Bismarcks	Papua New Guinea
San Jorge		Bv	Solomons	Solomon Islands
Santa Ana	Owaraha	Mk	Solomons	Solomon Islands
Santa Catalina	Owariki	Mk	Solomons	Solomon Islands
Santa Isabel	Ysabel	Bv	Solomons	Solomon Islands
Santo	Espiriru Santo	Vu	Vanuatu	Vanuatu
Savo		Gu	Solomons	Solomon Islands
Shortland		Bv	Solomons	Solomon Islands
Sikaiana	Stewart Is	Ml	Solomons	Solomon Islands
Simberi		Nl	Bismarcks	Papua New Guinea
Simbo		NG	Solomons	Solomon Islands
Surprise I		GT	New Caledonia	New Caledonia (France)
Tabar Is		Nl	Bismarcks	Papua New Guinea
Takuu (Tauu)	Mortlock Is	Bv	Solomons	Papua New Guinea
Tanga Is		Nl	Bismarcks	Papua New Guinea
Tanna		Vu	Vanuatu	Vanuatu
Tatau		Nl	Bismarcks	Papua New Guinea
Taumako		Te	Temotu	Solomon Islands
Tench		Mu	St Matthias Is	Papua New Guinea
Tetepare	Tetepari	NG	Solomons	Solomon Islands
Three Sisters		Mk	Solomons	Solomon Islands
Tiga		Lo	New Caledonia	New Caledonia (France)
Tikopia		Te	Temotu	Solomon Islands
Tinakula		Te	Temotu	Solomon Islands
Tingwon		Nl	Bismarcks	Papua New Guinea
Tolokiwa		NB	Bismarcks	Papua New Guinea
Tong		Mn	Admiralties	Papua New Guinea
Tongoa		Vu	Vanuatu	Vanuatu

Island name	old / alternative name	Island group*	Archipelago	Nation
Torres Is		Vu	Vanuatu	Vanuatu
Ugi	Uki Ni Masi	Mk	Solomons	Solomon Islands
Ulawa		Ml	Solomons	Solomon Islands
Umboi	Rook	NB	Bismarcks	Papua New Guinea
Unea		NB	Bismarcks	Papua New Guinea
Ureparapara		Vu	Vanuatu	Vanuatu
Utupua		Te	Temotu	Solomon Islands
Vangunu		NG	Solomons	Solomon Islands
Vanikoro	Vanikolo	Te	Temotu	Solomon Islands
Vanua Lava		Vu	Vanuatu	Vanuatu
Vella Lavella		NG	Solomons	Solomon Islands
Vonavona	Wana Wana	NG	Solomons	Solomon Islands
Wagina		Bv	Solomons	Solomon Islands
Walpole I		GT	New Caledonia	New Caledonia (France)
Watom		NB	Bismarcks	Papua New Guinea
Witu Is		NB	Bismarcks	Papua New Guinea
Wuvulu		Mn	Admiralties	Papua New Guinea

* as used in distribution bars and checklist (see page 37)

INDEX

Numbers in **bold** type refer to plate numbers
Numbers in plain type refer to species accounts

A

B

D

E

M

N

Q

R

U

V

W

X

Z